THE GLOBAL ECONOMY IN TRANSITION
Second Edition

BRIAN J. L. BERRY

EDGAR C. CONKLING

D. MICHAEL RAY

Prentice-Hall International, Inc.

Acquisition editor: Dan Kaveney
Editorial/production supervision and
    formatting/composition: Aksen Associates
Copy editor: Peter Zurita
Cover design: Bruce Kenselaar
Manufacturing manager: Trudy Pisciotti
Editorial assistant: Betsy Williams

Portions of this volume previously appeared in *The Global Economy: Resource Use,
    Locational Choice, and International Trade*
Previous edition published under the title of *The Global Economy*

Printed in the United States of America
10 9 8 7 6 5 4 3 2 1

ISBN 0-13-273293-9

Prentice-Hall International (UK) Limited, *London*
Prentice-Hall of Australia Pty. Limited, *Sydney*
Prentice-Hall Canada Inc., *Toronto*
Prentice-Hall Hispanoamericana, S.A., *Mexico*
Prentice-Hall of India Private Limited, *New Delhi*
Prentice-Hall of Japan, Inc., *Tokyo*
Simon & Schuster Asia Pte. Ltd., *Singapore*
Editora Prentice-Hall do Brasil, Ltda., *Rio de Janeiro*
Prentice-Hall, *Upper Saddle River, New Jersey*

Contents

5 ENERGY, MINERALS, AND THE ENVIRONMENT   117

6 PRICE AND OTHER MECHANISMS FOR REGULATING EXCHANGE   161

7 RENT GRADIENTS, LAND USE, AND THE STRUCTURE OF GLOBAL SYSTEMS   194

8   COMPARATIVE COSTS AND THE GEOMETRY OF INDUSTRIAL LOCATION   219

9   SCALE, EXTERNALITIES, AND AGGLOMERATION: THE EVOLVING STRUCTURE OF GLOBAL INDUSTRY   241

10   TECHNOLOGY TRANSITIONS AND PATTERNS OF GROWTH   293

11   PATTERNS AND DYNAMICS OF GLOBAL ECONOMIC TRANSACTIONS   331

12 TRADE REGIMES AND GLOBAL DEVELOPMENT   394

Preface

We find that we are shooting at a moving target. When we wrote *The Geography of Economic Systems,* published in 1976, the main concerns were with the crisis-ridden nature of the times. An energy crisis had been added to famine, war, and pestilence. The division between First and Second Worlds was widening amidst an accelerating nuclear arms race. Raw-material producers had gained new market power and were using their cartels to raise prices and redistribute wealth, simultaneously threatening the prosperity of the First World, the bases of international trade, and forcing the poorest countries into a Fourth World that was beyond help and hope. We felt that resource politics, the limits to growth, and the goals and methods of economic planning by sovereign nation-states had to be addressed as central concerns. A book was offered with 12 systematically organized chapters that examined global patterns and interdependencies, 12 regionally organized chapters that explored the distinctiveness of nation-states, and a final chapter that proposed that simultaneous interdependence and difference could be comprehended in a general system theory framework.

Whereas the systematic part of the book was well-received, the regional chapters were not. Instructors and critics thought that economic geography should be taught systematically, focusing on the core of location and trade theory. More should be said about the history and changing philosophies of the field, about the economic fundamentals necessary to an understanding of location and trade, about resource problems, and the limits to growth. The number and scale of the chapters should be attuned to the requirements of a single-semester course. We listened to these criticisms and suggestions as we prepared *Economic Geography,* published in 1987. Enduring elements of theory were taken from the 1976 text and enhanced. The regional chapters hit the cutting room floor. As we addressed issues of population and resources, more attention was given to the "limits-to-growth" debate. We also recognized that the world economy was in the throes of rapid change. The inflationary spiral of the late 1970s peaked in 1980–1981, and collapsed. Prices were tumbling, old industries were collapsing, and new technologies were appearing. We introduced Nikolai Kondratiev's long-wave theory and Gerhard Mensch's "metamorphosis model" to try to make sense of the changes in a macrohistorical perspective.

The new text was well-received, except by those who considered the long-wave idea to be discredited nonsense and those who considered the enhanced economics fundamentals too difficult or too advanced for a beginning economic geography text. We were, however, confounded by the rapidity of change. Communism collapsed, markets expanded, old resource problems waned, the demographic transition accelerated, world transactions increased as multinationals proliferated, and new foundations for competitive advantage emerged. Globalization appeared as a potent force, but so did countervailing claims for cultural distinctiveness and integrity. Change had been sufficiently dramatic that the revision became *The Global Economy. Resource Use, Locational Choice, and International Trade,* published in 1993. We dropped materials on local trade and urban hierarchies, on the older heartland–hinterland development paradigm, on First–Second–Third–Fourth World differences, and on resource limitations, and added materials on the emergent processes shaping economic development, on the reinforcement of cultural differences, on the nature and role of multinationals, and on the fifth-wave thoughtware economy.

Our evaluators and critics approved of the changes, but thought they did not go far enough. If this was a book about the global economy, why bore the students with a history of changing approaches to the study of economic geography, and why defer the discussion of multinationals to Chapters 10 and 13? Deal more forthrightly with the nature of globalization, they said, catch up with the nature and consequences of the extraordinary technological changes and economic restructurings that have occurred since 1980–81 and, while you are doing it, cut back from 14 chapters to 11 or 12 to permit chapter-per-week student assignments.

In *The Global Economy in Transition,* we have tried to respond to these suggestions, retaining only 50 percent of the materials in *The Global Economy,* and reshaping the new materials into a 12-chapter structure organized around the theme of globalization:

- Chapter 1 explores the role of political and technological changes in the worldwide triumph of markets, the role of multinational enterprise in the process of globalization, and the emergent bases of competitive advantage.
- Chapter 2 examines the declining role of the nation-state and the continuing reinforcement of cultural differences at both civilizational and regional scales.
- Chapters 3 to 5 focus on the declining role of population and resources, the original factors of production, in global development. Since 1980, the demographic transition has accelerated, global food shortages have been pushed off the list of the world's most pressing crises, brainpower has replaced muscle power, transmaterialization has changed the nature of resources and dematerialization the nature of products.
- Chapters 6 to 10 present the resulting shifts in locational choice and regional specialization. Elementary price theory leads to a discussion of rents, to the decline of Thünenization in the face of plummeting transportation costs, and to the ascendance of Ricardian Development in a world of created resources. Elementary comparative cost theory leads to a discussion of scale and externalities and to the role of increasing returns in the new geography of concentration. Elementary long-wave theory leads to a discussion of the role of the new information technologies in corporate downsizing, to the emergence of decentralized networks of interdependent specialists, and to the appearance of the world of telework.
- Chapters 11 and 12 complete the book by considering the nature and consequences of increasing specialization and interdependence in light of the new forms of global transactions that are replacing the older geography of world trade. Input factors and components move intrafirm, final goods are fabricated close to the point of consumption, and national boundaries count for little as larger economic communities evolve. For most items, a theory of multinational enterprise and of foreign direct investment must be substituted for a theory of international trade.

We doubt that *The Global Economy in Transition* will be our last attempt to codify these trends. As we said, we are shooting at a moving target as the global economy evolves. Theories of sustainable development, created resources, increasing returns, network organization, and global transactions are still being crafted. We expect to write *The New Economic Geography* in time for the third millennium. Your suggestions as to what this new book should and should not contain will be welcomed.

Acknowledgments

Many individuals in universities, business, and government have helped in supplying materials and ideas for this new edition. They include Professors Gordon Mulligan, University of Arizona; Günter Krumme, University of Washington; Edward J. Malecki, University of Florida; Jill Boberg, University of Maryland; Ian MacLachhan, University of Lethbridge; Michael Chisholm, University of Cambridge; Peter Dicken, University of Manchester; Shue Tuck Wong, Simon Fraser University; Alan MacPherson, State University of Buffalo; Roland Allison, retired from the College of St. Mark and St. John, Plymouth; Harley Johansen, University of Idaho; and Jeffrey Osleeb, Hunter College, CUNY. Officials from the Government of Canada helped with special tabulations. We thank particularly John McVey and Dr. John Baldwin. Many companies supplied detailed information, particularly the Confederation of British Industry, P. And O. Ferries, and John Buxton of Lloyd's of London. At the University of Texas at Dallas, Dr. Heja Kim performed noble duty in managing the preparation of the text materials in electronic form; Stephanie Martin worked extremely hard to develop the new glossary; several cohorts of students provided criticisms, suggestions, and requests that helped shape this new edition; and both creative feedback and collateral support were provided by Royce Hanson, Edward J. Harpham, Euel Elliott, and Paul Waddell. To all we are grateful.

Brian J. L. Berry
Edgar C. Conkling
D. Michael Ray

About the Authors

Brian J. L. Berry

Brian J. L. Berry is the Lloyd Viel Berkner Regental Professor and Professor of Political Economy at the University of Texas at Dallas. He received his B.Sc. (Economics) degree from the University of London in 1955, and his M.A. and Ph.D. degrees in geography from the University of Washington in 1956 and 1958. He has held academic and administrative positions at the University of Chicago, Harvard University, and Carnegie-Mellon University, and is a former President of the Association of American Geographers. He is a member of the National Academy of Sciences and the British Academy, and holds the Victoria Medal of the Royal Geographical Society and the Anderson Medal in Applied Geography. He is the author of several hundred books, articles, and other professional publications. Throughout his career, he has been concerned with bridging theory and practice, and has been heavily involved in urban and regional development planning and policy making in both advanced and developing countries.

Edgar C. Conkling

Edgar C. Conkling is Professor Emeritus at the State University of New York at Buffalo, where he is on the faculty of the International Trade concentration, a graduate program that prepares students for careers in international business. He also served as chairman of the Geography Department at SUNY/ Buffalo and as editor of the *Professional Geographer* and coeditor of *The Annals of the Association of American Geographers*. Educated at the University of Chicago and Northwestern University, he was for several years manager of the home office of a multinational corporation headquartered in Chicago. His research has been concerned principally with regional economic integration in Western Europe and Latin America. In addition to his works in international trade, he has published on the subjects of rural land use theory and regional development. Since retiring from active teaching in 1989, he has continued writing on the changing spatial patterns of world trade and on the regional variations in cultures that are encountered by businesses operating abroad.

D. Michael Ray

D. Michael Ray is Professor of Geography at Carleton University, Ottawa. He received his B.A. at the University of Manchester in 1956, an M.A. at the University of Ottawa and a Ph.D. at the University of Chicago. He has held academic posts at the Universities of Ottawa, Waterloo and the State University of New York at Buffalo as well as working in business and government. His principal research interests are in quantitative analysis and regional policy, and his publications include assessments of the impact on regional development and employment of investment by multinational corporations undertaken for the Government of Canada and for the International Labor Office, employment generation by small firms and statistical techniques for defining homogeneous regions for Statistics Canada, as well as the analysis of problems of regional disparities and urban growth. His previous books include *Market Potential and Economic Shadow, Dimensions of Canadian Regionalism,* and *Canadian Urban Trends.*

1

The Forces
Promoting Globalization

OVERVIEW

The world's economies are being transformed by a combination of technological and political changes.

Technological changes—improvements in transportation and communications—are reducing barriers to international interchange, leading to greater globalization of economic systems.

The collapse of communism and worldwide relaxation of governmental intervention into economic life have facilitated globalization via the removal of institutional barriers to trade and development, producing a worldwide triumph of markets.

The principal instruments of globalization are multinational corporations that, by their activities, are producing increasing efficiency in the use of the world's resources.

A new competitive advantage paradigm that grows out of increased globalization helps clarify emergent economic differences. Regions pass from an early factor-driven stage of development to one that is investment-driven, from that to an innovation-driven stage, and finally to a stage that is wealth-driven. Different factors determine competitiveness at each of these stages.

OBJECTIVES

- to describe the technological and political factors contributing to globalization of economic activity
- to analyze the nature of multinational corporations and their role in promoting globalization
- to outline the factors that determine competitive advantage
- to offer a new model of stages of economic development

1

THE TRIUMPH OF MARKETS

Following the global economic crisis of 1980–1981, and culminating with the opening of the Berlin Wall in November 1989, an extraordinary sequence of events began to unfold that is transforming the world's economies. Economist Paul Krugman, who we encounter in Chapters 11 and 12, says that the result is a "new economic geography" requiring new theories of location and trade. The changes have been both technological and political. The pace of technological change, the collapse of communism, and the worldwide triumph of markets have, together, shattered the global economic and political order that had existed since the end of World War II. Pulling in one direction have been forces promoting globalization, whereas the cultural factors discussed in Chapter 2 have pulled in the other.

Among the technological factors promoting globalization two stand out according to Cable (1995): *transport costs* are falling with improved physical communications, and *advances in computing power and telecommunications*—digital systems, fiber optics, and satellite technology—are transforming the ease, speed, quantity, and quality of information flows. Because transactions and communications costs and times are falling rapidly, many goods and services that were provided locally (e.g., perishable and seasonal items; components of integrated production processes; "back office" accounts—routine office work not requiring customer contact; and design work) are becoming tradable internationally, and therefore exposed to new types of competition. Global communication systems now make it possible for companies to coordinate their production planning and financial operations across a wide range of countries, and to run truly global operations. Information itself has become tradable: management consultancy; films, records, and compact discs; television news; telecommunications services; and software systems, design, and programming. Computerization and advanced telecommunications that provide near-instantaneous linkage also have transformed international finance. Capital has become highly mobile and there now are global markets for currency transactions and all forms of marketable securities. This was speeded by financial deregulation: the removal of capital controls and controls over interest rates, and the lifting of barriers to entry into banking and other financial services. The globalization of finance made possible by new technology and liberalization policies have reinforced each other. Around the world, countries have abandoned inward-looking "statist" models of development in favor of private enterprise, lowered barriers to trade, and a secondary role for the state.

As these technological changes were unfolding, *major political upheavals* also occurred. First, communist governments were ousted throughout Eastern Europe. The process of political change in Eastern Europe typically followed a two-step pattern, according to Gregory and Stuart (1995). First, unpopular totalitarian communist regimes were replaced by reform-minded communists who formed coalition governments with noncommunists. In this phase, the communist party's monopoly on political power was broken. In the second stage, a noncommunist coalition government was elected on a platform of closer alliance with the West and the establishment of a market economy. With the opening of the Berlin Wall, the pace of such changes accelerated. The two Germanies became one and the Cold War ended. In 1990 former Soviet President Gorbachev's drive to restructure the Soviet economy took on a new urgency as the Soviet empire vanished. Many Soviet republics asserted their right to self-determination and declared their independence. By the end of 1991, Gorbachev and the Soviet Union had been replaced by states attempting to develop markets, while fighting alliances of communists and ethnic nationalists for political control.

Underlying these political shifts was a simple economic truth. Centrally directed socialist systems do not work and cannot compete. They produce only sporadic growth (see Box 1.1). Although they assure some degree of equality to their citizens, it is often violated by party members' claims of special privilege. Quite demonstrably, these systems have been far more destructive of the environment than political and economic systems of any other kind. The nuclear disaster at Chernobyl rendered vast areas of Belarus uninhabitable. Former East Germany's nuclear plants are equally dangerous. The Aral Sea is vanishing. Even once-pristine Lake Baikal is being polluted by pulp mill effluent.

What Mikhail Gorbachev did not fully appreciate when he called for *perestroika* was that the rules determining the economic geography of a major section of the globe were going to have to change if growth is to produce rising levels of welfare. The communist system of central direction and party control would have to be replaced by individual initiative and the discipline of markets in the economic arena, and by individual freedoms and democratic institutions in the sphere of politics. Private enterprise would have to replace state monopoly; competition would have to replace the "dictatorship of the proletariat." Because communist economies were so flawed, it took only his first tentative initiatives for the world order crafted by Lenin and Stalin to disintegrate. It took only the first stages of disintegration for Russian traditionalists to demand a return to that country's deeply embedded authoritarian traditions, setting in motion a continuing political debate about that country's future. The failure of an attempted coup brought Boris Yeltsin to power, and by late 1991, he had embarked upon broad-ranging economic reforms including liberalization of prices, removal of restrictions on trade, and the privatization of factories. By early 1995, more than 3,000 state-run enterprises had been sold, and close to 90 percent of Russia's industrial work force was employed in privatized

---

BOX 1.1 The Benefits of Democratic Market Institutions to the Developing Nations

In his 1991 doctoral dissertation at The University of Texas at Dallas entitled 'The Impact of Government Size on Economic Growth,' James S. Guseh discovered not only that greater governmental size takes a toll on economic growth, but also that the type of economic and political freedoms present in a country affects the magnitude of this toll. Using the annual growth rates of real per capita gross national product of 59 middle-income developing countries for the period 1960–1985 as his measure of economic growth, and controlling for other variables that affect the growth rate, he discovered that if the share of gross national product consumed by government increases by 10 percent, different types of economic and political freedoms take the following tolls of growth relative to democratic market economies:

		Political freedoms		
		Democratic Institutions	*Partially Democratic*	*Nondemocratic*
Economic freedoms	*Market Economy*	Base Case	0.07% slower	1.2% slower
	Mixed Economy	No Difference	0.03% slower	0.8% slower
	Socialist Economy	1% slower	1.7% slower	2.2% slower

For the 59 middle-income developing countries he studied, the price of a 10 percent increase in government size in a socialist economy was a 1 percent reduction in the annual growth rate, compared with the base case of a market economy. The price of nondemocratic political institutions was a 1.2 percent per year comparative reduction in the growth rate. By combining the two, nondemocratic socialist systems had annual growth rates that were 2.2 percent slower than democratic market systems. Little wonder, then, that democratic market systems are triumphing across the globe!

---

enterprises. Yeltsin's popularity was short-lived, however. The pain of conversion to a market economy has been substantial, and both former communists and ethnic nationalists continue to campaign for a return to authoritarianism and a state-run economy.

A different path was taken in China, where communist leaders sought to learn from the Soviet experience. Mass protests in Beijing that called for liberalization were brutally suppressed. Rather than simply closing down or selling off loss-making state enterprises, the Chinese leadership decided to let the dynamism of the private sector gradually reduce the state's share of the economy. The role of the communist party would be to guarantee public order and stability. In important ways this strategy seems to be working, although at continuing human cost. In 1978, state-owned enterprises accounted for 78 percent of China's industrial output; by the end of 1994 that figure had fallen to 43 percent.

The relaxation of government intervention into economic life was global. Although change was less dramatic in the West, the 1980s witnessed voter repudiation of the more extreme forms of social democracy. The 1980s were dominated by Reaganism in the United States and by Thatcherism in England—both movements designed, at least in theory, to replace the ills of "big government" with the benefits of the market. In Germany, the conservative Christian Democratic Party strengthened its hold over German politics at the expense of the Social Democratic and Environmentalist (Green) parties. Western conservatism put into motion policies designed to reduce the role of government in the economy and to shift existing government functions from federal to state and local levels. Tax reductions were used to improve incentives, welfare programs were cut, and privatization was encouraged in Great Britain and Germany. Even Sweden, long a symbol of welfare statism, experienced a voter backlash against excessive social expenditures and high tax rates. In France, however, privatization has been vigorously opposed by an alliance of bureaucrats and trade unionists, the principal beneficiaries of the country's "statist" (i.e., state-run) economy, and the nation's telecommunication, airline, utilities, defense, and financial services remain government-run.

The conservative economic policies that characterized the industrialized West spread into Latin America and Asia in the 1980s, often at the behest of the World Bank and the International Monetary Fund, key sources of development aid and assistance. In Latin America, programs were initiated to reestablish private enterprise, and experiments with planned socialism were largely aborted. The first to benefit was Chile, which experienced an extraordinary economic renaissance. In Asia, the remarkable rise of the "Four Tigers" (Singapore, South Korea, Taiwan, and Hong Kong) demonstrated that poor countries could industrialize rapidly and compete in world manufacturing markets by employing laissez-faire economic policies, and thus make rapid progress up the ladder of economic development. The examples of what could be achieved stimulated reforms in Thailand, Malaysia, and Indonesia that have led to these countries' growth to accelerate in the 1990s. The strong economic performance of the Four Tigers contrasted sharply with the stagnation of India, Pakistan, and other low-income countries that continued to pursue economic policies of state interventionism and protection, however, imposing excessive bureaucratic burdens and sapping efficiency and growth. Entering the scene belatedly, even India saw a growth spurt once policy makers decided that they, too, had no choice but to liberalize (Chapter 2, Box 2.4), but elsewhere—particularly in Africa—ilnefficient state-run enterprises continue to dominate national economies and retard progress.

THE NATURE AND ROLE OF MULTINATIONAL ENTERPRISE

Despite the influence of international organizations like the World Bank, the principal change agents reshaping the global economy are, however, the growing numbers of multinational enterprises (MNEs), sometimes called transnational corporations (TNCs). MNEs account for a rising volume of *foreign direct investment* (FDI) and a large and increasing proportion of international trade.

The MNE is a company that is headquartered in one country but controls productive facilities and sales outlets in other countries. Its operations involve flows of capital, goods, services, and managerial and technical personnel among its subsidiaries. Ultimately, this leads the enterprise to assume a global outlook and strategy.

The world's 14 richest nations were headquarters to 7,000 MNEs in 1969, and 24,000 in 1994. By 1995, there were some 37,000 MNEs in the world, controlling about a third of all private-sector assets, and accounting for a quarter of the goods produced in the world's market economies. The International Labor Office estimates the direct employment in MNEs to be at least 65 million. The proportion is 3 percent of the world total, rising to 10 percent in the developed world. For individual countries, the proportions have reached very high levels, including Canada, where more of the mining, petroleum, and manufacturing sectors are owned or controlled by foreign MNEs than by domestic firms. Foreign MNEs also play a dominant role in other developed countries such as Belgium, France, and Italy.

The largest MNEs have sales exceeding $100 billion annually. If MNEs and countries are ranked on the basis of sales or GNP, then half of the top hundred are nation-states and the other half are MNEs. The sheer scale of MNE production gives MNEs a dominant share of international trade, largely via transfers of components, investments, profits, and services among their plants and offices in various countries. The global economy is now one in which the value of production financed by foreign direct investment (i.e., of the output of foreign branches of MNEs) exceeds that of traditional foreign trade. Complicating matters, upward of one half of all international trade now is *intrafirm*—shipments of parts, components, subassemblies, and so on, during the manufacturing process, rather than of finished goods and services.

The growing prominence of the multinational enterprise lends a new perspective to trade theory, which we discuss in Chapters 11 and 12. The traditional theory of international trade considers countries to be the principal actors in world commerce, exchanging finished goods and services. Today, however, individual enterprises are the primary agents in transnational transfers, largely between different parts of their organizations, and what is shipped is seldom the finished product, which tends to be assembled locally. A theory of international economic interaction must take into account the ability of multinational concerns to modify countries' endowments of natural resources by moving human and physical capital from one part of the world to another, creating new assets and enabling production to occur in locations where it might, earlier, have not occurred. The MNE is able to produce in that country where the costs of materials, labor, capital, and transportation are minimized and to use "transfer pricing" to shift its profits to the country with the lowest tax rates (although this practice is frowned upon by many countries, including the United States and Canada). MNEs play a major role in the international transfer of technology, whether it is "hard" technology, such as new types of machines, or "soft" technology, such as Japan's just-in-time inventory organization. MNEs are now more likely to seek profits from the foreign use of their own technologies by operating these technologies in foreign-based plants that they own or control than by producing in their home nation and exporting the finished output. Hence, the MNE has a unique potential for making the most efficient allocation of the world's resources.

How is the MNE able to modify the international economic environment so effectively? One advantage is the information-gathering ability afforded by its many branches and representatives throughout the world, linked by modern means of communication. This "scanning capability" gives the firm an immediate awareness of opportunities, problems, and new developments in the many places where it conducts business. A second advantage is the enormous store of capital, technology, and managerial skills that an MNE can draw upon.

Corporations such as General Motors or Exxon can generate greater worldwide sales in a year than the gross national products of all but 25 or so sovereign nations. This inspires both awe and apprehension. Host countries for overseas affiliates suspect them of holding allegiance to the firm's home government. The firm's true devotion is to its own fortunes and those of its stockholders, however. Nevertheless, MNEs are under increased scrutiny from both their home and host governments, and they must contend with repeated attempts to impose restrictions on their operations. (Appendix 1.1 discusses the public-policy issues raised by the activities of multinationals. Read it so that you understand the complexities of MNE/host country relationships.)

Historical Roots

This attention focused on multinationals is fairly new, reflecting their recent rise to prominence. Yet their roots go deep into the eighteenth and nineteenth centuries, to the colonial operations of British, Dutch, and French trading companies that exploited the resources of their governments' overseas possessions, and often led their home countries into colonial adventures. This tradition has been continued into the present century by the overseas activities of giant oil, mineral, and fruit companies. Manufacturing firms were slower to develop foreign operations, partly because of the lack of good transport and communications and, especially in the case of U.S. companies, a preoccupation with growing home markets. Nevertheless, a few pioneering industrial firms, such as Singer, Westinghouse, Kodak, and Western Electric, went abroad with their new products and manufacturing technologies, and their number gradually increased until the Great Depression brought world trade to a near-standstill.

It was following World War II that multinational enterprises burst upon the world commercial scene. One surge came in the 1960s, when U.S. multinationals moved abroad in numbers, aided by developments in transport and communications, industrial technology, and by new forms of corporate organization. At the same time, international trade was expanding rapidly, aided by tariff reductions. Investment follows trade. American MNEs were quick to take advantage of the enlarged market afforded by the newly created European Economic Community (now the European Union, EU), and by opportunities elsewhere in the world, to develop new sources of oil, minerals, and other commodities. Foreign direct investment surged.

The pace of expansion by U.S. MNEs slackened following the economic crisis of the mid-1970s, however, and competitors began to emerge. As recently as 1975, the total value of foreign investments by American MNEs was eight times as large as that of Japanese companies; by the end of the 1980s, U.S. foreign holdings were only three times as large as Japan's. The total value of Japanese foreign corporations is not an accurate measure of their importance, however, because many of these undertakings are joint ventures with local firms. Furthermore, Japanese multinationals have a very different functional and organizational makeup, which involves intercompany linkages that are not reflected in official data. (Read Appendix 1.2 for an outline of the distinctive nature of Japanese and other non-Western MNEs.)

Foreign direct investment by multinational corporations is a comparatively recent development for Japan. Because of an official ceiling on capital outflows imposed to save scarce foreign exchange during the early postwar period, Japanese firms were slow to invest abroad. Until the Ministry of Finance lifted the ban in the late 1960s, Japan was mainly an exporter of domestically produced manufactured goods. Japanese foreign trade was managed by large trading companies, which also sought assured supplies of raw materials for Japan's domestic industries.

Since 1969, the Japanese government has encouraged direct investment abroad, however. Edgington (1993) sees Japanese FDI as then having passed through three stages: (1) a *linear linkup to Japan* during the 1970s in which overseas units were strongly connected to their Japanese headquarters, but lacked any significant links to each other, even within the same host country; (2) a transitional period of *international specialization and mesh* during the 1980s in which corporations began to reorganize and connect their production and supply bases on a global scale; and (3) a final stage of "global localization"—the *tetrapolar strategic division of the world* of the late 1980s and 1990s, designed to provide insurance against international currency fluctuations and the emergence of major trade blocs. These stages are diagrammed in Box 1.2. The latest overseas investment strategy reflects a belief that the global economy in the next decades, will be dominated by a "triad" of highly competitive economic powers (North America, the European Union and a Japan-dominated Asian bloc), relative to which the rest of the global economy will be structured (Ohmae, 1985). It also reflects cost pressures in Japan arising from rapid appreciation of the yen (called *endaka*) and the desire to avoid friction caused by growing balance-of-trade surpluses. Acquisition of foreign firms provided rapid access to overseas markets and supplies, and resulted in a dramatic increase in Japanese foreign direct investment after the mid-1980s. This, in turn, facilitated the development of self-sufficient subsidiary networks in each of the triad regions

Organizational Structure

As other countries' MNEs have increased their involvement in the world economy, they, too, have developed a characteristic organizational form. The parent company usually is headquartered in the country of principal ownership,

---

BOX 1.2 Globalization of Japanese Manufacturing Corporations

Japanese MNEs have moved overseas in three stages, as diagrammed:

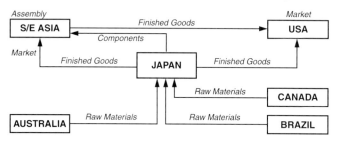

(a) *Linear linkup to Japan.* Overseas units sell Japanese products or ship raw materials to Japanese factories. Only in South and East Asia and in the United States do Japanese-owned plants assemble Japanese components into finished products.

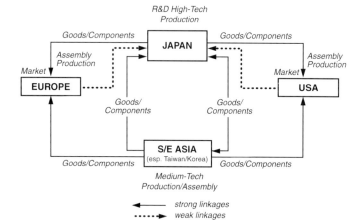

(b) *International specialization and mesh.* "Meshing" of overseas subsidiaries into decentralized networks begins. There is international sourcing of parts and products.

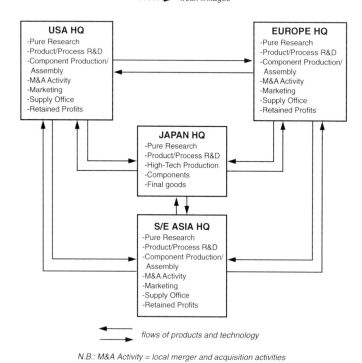

(c) *Tetrapolar strategic division of the world.* Integrated networks are established in each of the triad regions, and there is an emphasis on self-sufficiency of the networks in each of the three regions—a device to provide insurance against international currency fluctuations and the emergence of new trade blocs in Europe and North America.

Source: Adapted from David W. Edgington (1993), *The Globalization of Japanese Manufacturing Firms,* Growth and Change 24: 87–106.

although several exceptions to this exist. Royal Dutch Shell, for instance, is 60 percent Dutch owned and 40 percent British, and it maintains headquarters both in The Hague and in London. The stock in most MNEs is publicly held and is available to individual investors of any nationality, although a number of prominent multinationals are still privately held. During an MNE's early years, its headquarters management and staff are typically natives of the home country, but in time the company brings into its home office talented individuals from its overseas affiliates. The headquarters company is the control center for the firm's worldwide operations, and the decisions made there take on a global perspective. The management group in the home office is responsible for systemwide strategic planning and must decide what goods are to be manufactured, where in the world to make them, where to procure raw materials, and what global markets to target.

The company's foreign affiliates include both producing units and sales outlets. Many companies are following the Japanese example and forming their overseas affiliates into integrated systems, within which the individual branches exchange products, materials, and capital. For example, European affiliates of Ford and General Motors exchange parts, subassemblies, and finished vehicles from one country to another in an elaborate intracompany network. In addition to their wholly or partially owned affiliates abroad, multinationals customarily maintain connections with other foreign enterprises not under corporate control, but through such arrangements as joint ventures, distributorships, and licensing agreements.

The international integration of an MNE can be either "vertical" or "horizontal." In the case of *vertical integration,* a branch in one country sends partially manufactured subassemblies or intermediate products to another affiliate elsewhere for further processing or for final assembly. Finished products then go to all affiliates for sale in their own national markets. In the case of *horizontal integration,* each branch makes a particular line of finished products, the choice depending on its comparative advantage, and shares these with all other units of the enterprise.

Role in Global Redistribution of the Factors of Production

The most significant feature of the MNE, from both a practical and a theoretical standpoint, is its role as an efficient agent for transferring capital, managerial skills, technology, product design, and commodities among countries. Matching the scarcities of one country with the surpluses of another, it helps to achieve a global equalization of factors; and by transferring innovations among nations, it is a major agent of technological change.

The transfer of managerial skills is a distinctive function of the MNE. Relying on the firm's superior informa-

tion-gathering ability, the headquarters company discovers and exploits opportunities that lie beyond the capabilities of domestic concerns. The MNE is also better able than local companies to bear the risk of such ventures because of its great size and financial strength and its experience in similar circumstances elsewhere.

Having decided to invest in a new foreign undertaking, the firm then performs its second key function, the transfer of capital. This can be in the form of real capital (machinery and equipment) or financial capital or a combination of the two. Depending on political and economic circumstances, the company can fund the project with capital generated within its own system—obtained either directly from the parent concern or from the earnings of overseas affiliates—or it can rely on borrowed funds, either in the host country or elsewhere.

The third major function of the MNE is to create technology and transfer it throughout its system. A newly established affiliate generally receives an infusion of technology from the headquarters company. Indeed, at one time all research and development took place in the parent concern, but today many MNEs share this function among their various constituent companies.

Finally, the MNE is a principal generator of international trade, notably the transfers of raw materials, components, and finished products that take place among the company's many branches. The current trend is for an MNE to integrate production and marketing between the parent and its overseas affiliates. Such coordination permits the firm to maximize the gains from international specialization: Each product is manufactured in that combination of locations having the lowest costs and in sufficient quantity to enjoy economies of scale. The company's ultimate aim in integrating its international operations is to serve every national market with a full line of its products and to do so at the lowest unit costs.

Theories of the Multinational Enterprise

The multinational enterprise has attained prominence recently, so that a cohesive theory on the subject has yet to emerge. Because most writers have approached the MNE from the perspectives of their individual academic disciplines, the resulting works lack the generality that is now essential. This accumulating body of literature however, does offer answers to two sets of questions: (1) What causes a firm to go abroad and succeed in a foreign environment against competition from both domestic firms and other multinationals? (2) What happens to the character of the firm during the course of internationalization?

An Outline of Leading Theories. What are the distinguishing characteristics of firms that enter into multinational production? One common trait is the expectation of greater profits from foreign ventures than those received by local competitors in the same areas. It is essential that MNEs receive a higher return because they must overcome problems not borne by domestic firms. Local producers know the language and customs, can expect a greater measure of customer good will and government favor, have a closer awareness of local market conditions, and avoid the extra time and expense that the MNE has to bear because it operates from a distance. The MNE is able to obtain a greater return because it has advantages that no other firms possess. Chief among these are superior knowledge and large size and scope of operations.

Leadership in innovation is the usual form of superior knowledge monopolized by MNEs. Innovativeness is a key element in technology-intensive industries such as pharmaceuticals and electronics. As a group, MNEs expend more on research and development than other firms, and they are able to transfer this technology abroad with little additional cost. Local firms, on the other hand, have to invest heavily to develop a competing technology. Another kind of knowledge monopoly is found in those industries that rely upon high levels of marketing skill—for example, convenience foods and beverages (McDonald's or Coca-Cola) or cosmetics (Estée Lauder). To acquire its superior knowledge, the MNE needs a home environment that offers high levels of technical and managerial skills and has a well-developed, affluent market. This is one reason why only a few countries serve as home bases for multinationals.

A second advantage is superior size and scope of operation. In most industries, foreign direct investment is dominated by only a few large concerns; in other words, these activities are *oligopolistic* in nature. These companies continually jostle with each other for larger shares of the world market. Because of their size and their ability to produce in many countries, they can achieve the most economical scale of operations. If the local market is too small to absorb all of the output, the affiliate can send its surplus to the company's branches in other countries. Domestic producers do not usually have this option. MNEs also may integrate their operations vertically to gain assured sources of supply. In this way, they can avoid dependence on others and, at the same time, are able to deny such supplies to their competitors.

Large size permits the firm to assume a greater range of functions itself. By thus "internalizing" its various international operations (i.e., integrating them within its own operations), it can avoid buying and selling to other companies in foreign areas, or licensing its technology to them. The MNE thereby protects the secrecy of its technology and minimizes the effects of governmental restrictions. It is mainly for this reason that most international transfers of technology and managerial skills take place among units of the same firm and MNEs sell a high proportion of their exports to their own affiliates.

MNEs intently watch their competitors' actions. If one company sets up operations in a new area or if it markets a new product, its competitors immediately take action to prevent any loss of their market shares. Each firm is concerned to maintain its rate of growth relative to its rivals as a way of preserving market share, and it seeks to erect barriers to the entry of new firms into its markets.

MNEs thus are highly interdependent in their decision making. If one firm enters a foreign market, its rivals usually follow it there to minimize the risk to their market shares. These defensive actions create a bandwagon effect, including so-called "reverse investment" in which MNEs compete in each others' home markets. For instance, the U.S. tire company, Goodyear, operates in France, and the French firm, Michelin, makes tires in the United States. Although they turn out comparable goods, these firms are careful to differentiate their products by means of brand names and advertising. Even this kind of product differentiation constitutes a knowledge asset of the firm.

To compete successfully in an alien environment, the multinational enterprise must choose carefully which countries to enter. A number of country characteristics enter into this decision: location, resource endowments, size and nature of market, and political environment. Although the relative influence of these elements changes from one time to another, the strongest attraction for U.S. firms has been proximity—as suggested by the high proportion of investments made in nearby Canada and Mexico. U.S. multinationals have also preferred to invest in countries with familiar cultures—notably English-speaking Canada, Britain, and Australia—and with large markets offering economies of scale. To protect their investments, MNEs favor countries that have stable governments. They may also seek to reduce risk by locating where the legal environment is most favorable. Thus, major accounting firms such as Ernst & Young and Price Waterhouse have moved their British partnerships offshore to Jersey, in the Channel Islands, which offers the auditors limited liability protection for claims made against the firms. Not only do these country traits influence the decision to do business in a country, but they also determine the way in which MNEs enter that market. For operating in those countries with stable governments and large, prosperous markets, multinationals generally prefer foreign direct investment. In dealing with those poorer underdeveloped countries having a high level of political risk, MNEs rely mainly on exporting, together with some licensing of local production, but with only a minimum of direct investing.

Globalization of the Firm.   The other aspect of MNE theory is concerned with the questions of how, when, and why a firm becomes multinational and what happens to its organizational arrangements during this process. As we saw

The Forces Promoting Globalization 9

in the Japanese case, globalization of a company typically occurs in three stages.

1. *Move to exports.* In the first stage, a firm that previously served only its domestic market begins to export some of its output, as well as reaching overseas to control its sources of raw materials. Often, the transition from domestic to foreign sales is unplanned, taking place in response to unsolicited orders received directly from potential customers overseas or indirectly by way of local buying agents for foreign purchasers. At this point, the company has neither the specialized facilities to prepare shipments for export nor personnel skilled in export procedures. It therefore hires outside specialists to perform these functions. If orders from abroad continue to arrive, the firm will find it cheaper and more expedient to establish its own export department or foreign division, consisting of an experienced manager and a few clerks.

As this new foreign business begins to yield economies of scale and enhanced profit margins for the company, it begins to pursue export sales more actively. The firm appoints distributors in key market areas abroad, and in time it develops a network of such distributorships. Meanwhile, the firm may license its technology to local manufacturing firms in some host countries. When foreign operations become sufficiently extensive to warrant it, the company sends traveling representatives to service the network. At this point, the firm may undertake a reorganization of its basic structure. It may form a separate corporate entity in the home country for the purpose of minimizing taxes and providing more efficient service, and it may establish foreign marketing subsidiaries in key countries. Up to this point, the company has served its overseas customers solely with exports from its own production in the home country.

2. *Internationalization of production.* The second phase of globalization arrives when the company decides to manufacture in other countries. The decision to produce abroad usually follows the discovery that exports to a given national market have reached a level sufficient to justify building a factory there. Such a venture is especially attractive if production is market-oriented, that is, it costs less to manufacture at a location close to final consumption. A further incentive may be the sudden imposition of governmental barriers to imports in a key market. In some instances, tax concessions or other special inducements by the foreign government may reinforce the decision. Having determined to set up production in the overseas market, the firm must then decide whether to build a wholly new factory or to acquire an existing firm in the foreign area. After production is under way in several overseas locations, the firm may integrate its foreign subsidiaries in a "mesh," either vertically or horizontally, to gain economies of specialization.

3. *Globalization of outlook and organization.* Foreign operations may generate eventually so large a proportion of the company's total revenue that the headquarters

management comes to think of the firm's business primarily in global terms. Accompanying this change in perspective is the globalization of the headquarters staff through worldwide recruitment of *cosmopolitan* executives who no longer identify with the firm's home country but with the company as a global entity. Cosmopolitans, according to former Harvard Business School dean Rosabeth Kanter, are rich in three assets: *concepts*—the best knowledge and ideas; *competence*—the ability to operate at the highest standards of any place in the world anywhere; and *connectedness*—the best relationships, which provide access to the resources of other people and organizations throughout the world (Kanter, 1995). Bringing those assets to the places they work, they transmit a more universal culture (which, in the eyes of "locals" threatens the identity of groups and localities). Although the head office still makes strategic decisions affecting the system as a whole, leadership by cosmopolitans allows greater autonomy of overseas branches, and decentralized networks may evolve, such as Japanese MNEs' tetrapolar strategic division. In this final phase, the firm has become fully globalized.

GLOBAL COMPETITIVE ADVANTAGE

The combination of technological and political changes that have unfolded since 1980, combined with the rapid rise to dominance of large multinational corporations, means that we should no longer think of a world economy divided by the differences between the First (Western, market), Second (communist, planned), Third (developing), and Fourth ("basket-case") Worlds, as we have since the end of World War II. All now are parts of the global system of markets.

Four broad processes are associated with globalization according Kanter: *mobility* of capital, labor, and ideas, made possible by the revolution in telecommunications; *simultaneity,* by which the time lag between introduction of a product or service in one place and its adoption at other places has declined precipitously; *bypass,* by which an increasing array of technological alternatives enables innovations to go around existing structures; and *pluralism,* by which multiple centers of expertise and influence have emerged. Together, she says, these four processes put more choices in the hands of individual and organizational customers, generating a *globalization cascade*—mutually reinforcing feedback loops that strengthen and accelerate the globalizing forces.

As a result of those globalizing shifts, what also has emerged is the need for a new paradigm to explain competitive advantage: why some regions grow and others do not; why countries differ in the industries in which they specialize; why particular countries become the home of many of the world's leaders in particular industries-—Germany in chemicals; Switzerland in pharmaceuticals; Japan in electronics, cameras, robotics, and facsimile machines; the United States in computers, software, movies, and commercial aircraft. After a 4-year study of 10 important trading nations in which he paid particular attention to the competitive advantage of firms in global industries, Kanter's Harvard colleague Michael Porter (1990) concluded that four broad attributes shape the environment in which firms compete and promote or impede the creation of competitive advantage: factor conditions; demand conditions; the nature of supporting industries; and firm strategy, structure, and rivalry. Taken together, they suggest a new sequence of stages of economic development.

Factor conditions are what economists have conventionally called the "factors of production"—land and other resources, labor, and capital. Much of the conventional theory of international trade rests on these factors. Porter believes that a new grouping of these factors is necessary to understand the ways in which they now impinge on competitive advantage. He distinguishes among the following:

1. *Physical resources.* The abundance, quality, accessibility, and cost of land, water, mineral, and timber deposits, together with other physical traits such as location, time zone, and climate.

2. *Human resources.* The quantity, skills, and cost of personnel, including cultural factors that bear on the work ethic.

3. *Infrastructure.* The type, quality, and user cost of the transportation and communications systems, health care, cultural institutions, and so on.

4. *Knowledge resources.* A nation's supply of scientific and technical knowledge and know-how.

5. *Capital resources.* The amount, type, and cost of capital available to finance industry. Important variables include national savings rates, the structure of capital markets, and governmental policies that affect the money supply and interest rates.

This list includes what Porter calls traditional or *basic factors,* such as resources, climate, location, and numbers of people, and modern or *advanced factors,* such as educated personnel, research-and-development capabilities, and advanced digital communications infrastructure. Figure 1.1, a map of the country-to-country variations in the percentage of gross domestic product derived from agriculture, gives some indication of different countries' dependence on basic factors today. Figure 1.2, which maps the distribution of

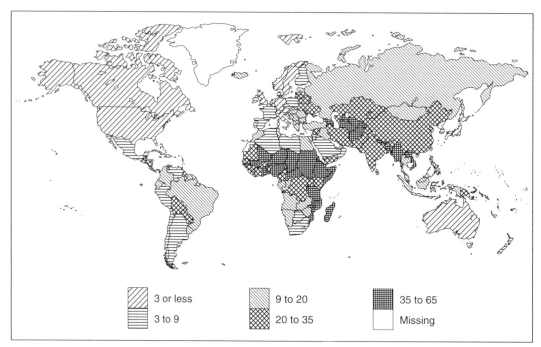

FIGURE 1.1   Percent of GDP in agriculture. GDP (gross domestic product) is the total output for final use of the goods and services produced by an economy by both residents and nonresidents. It differs from GNP (gross national product), which is composed of GDP plus or minus net factor income from abroad—the income residents receive from abroad for factor services minus payments made to nonresidents who contribute to the domestic economy. [*Source:* Data from the *1995 Britannica Book of the Year* (Chicago: Encyclopaedia Britannica, 1995).]

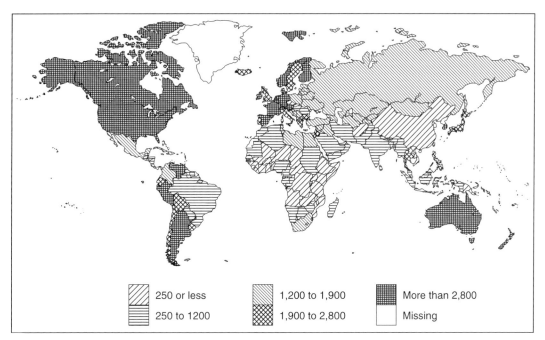

250 or less	1,200 to 1,900	More than 2,800
250 to 1200	1,900 to 2,800	Missing

FIGURE 1.2 Third-level students per 100,000 population. One measure of a country's investment in human capital is the relative number of its people who are provided with higher education. [*Source:* Data from the *1995 Britannica Book of the Year* (Chicago: Encyclopaedia Britannica, 1995).]

third-level students—those enrolled in colleges or technical schools—reveals the countries that are investing in human capital in order to increase their stock of advanced factors.

Basic factors are of diminishing necessity and widened global availability because of changes in product design and improvements in transportation and communications. Advanced factors are now the most significant determinants of competitive advantage, and in contrast to basic factors, which are *endowed,* they can be *created* through education and investment in research. The difference is important. Many basic factors such as natural resources are fixed in availability and may impose upper limits to growth. Advanced factors impose no such limits.

The relevant *demand conditions,* Porter says, are those to be found in domestic markets: the composition of buyer needs; the size and pattern of growth of domestic demand; and the ways in which domestic preferences are transmitted to foreign markets. They influence the ability to achieve economies of scale in production, and the rate and character of improvement and innovation. Sophisticated and demanding domestic buyers force local firms to meet high standards in terms of product features, quality, and service, and thus pressure them to be more innovative, upgrading competitive advantage as they do it. Japanese home market conditions, for example, have led to pressure to innovate and produce products that are *kei-haku-tan-sho* (light, thin, short, small), and the result is a stream of

products that are exceedingly successful internationally. This is an example, Kanter argues, of the fact that in the global economy, power comes from influence over consumption, not as traditional theorists argue, from control over the means of production. As mobility and alternatives give consumers more choices, power shifts from those producing goods and services to those buying them.

Supporting industries are part of the surrounding environment that fosters success by providing "dynamic externalities" (discussed in Chapter 9). Especially important are supplier industries: Sweden's innovative ball-bearing and cutting-tool producers could not have flourished without the country's strength in specialty steels. It was the Swiss dye industry that created conditions leading to a successful move into pharmaceuticals, which in turn has led to world dominance in production of food flavorings. The relationships with home-based suppliers are particularly important in the process of innovation and upgrading. Italy's leather manufacturers work closely with shoe producers, monitoring fashion trends and planning new products. The advantages are those of external economies and market expansion provided by multiple producers and supporting specialists, helping create new products and finding ways to reduce costs.

Firm strategy, structure, and rivalry involve corporate goals and management systems. It is important for competitiveness whether firms are small and production is fragmented or whether there are relatively few firms pro-ducing standardized products on large-scale production lines. It is important whether firms seek to maximize prof-its each quarter or are willing to accept a lower immediate return to ensure long-run market advantages. Where com-panies are owned by investors who seek rapid growth of share prices, pressure is on the company to produce the best quarterly earnings statements, and thus to maximize profits in the short run. Elsewhere, as in Germany and Switzerland, long-term capital gains have been exempt from taxation, and corporate strategy is directed to corporate performance over much longer periods of time. In Sweden, there is great suspicion of wealth, and taxation prevents its accumulation, a powerful disincentive to business initiative-—the very contrast to the United States, where the rate of new business formulation is, accordingly, much higher. Vigorous domes-tic rivalries result from new business formation, encourag-ing competitiveness.

Four Stages of Economic Development

Putting these factors together, Porter says that he now sees four stages to economic development: factor-driven; invest-ment-driven; innovation-driven; and wealth-driven. Economies progress by upgrading their positions in global markets through achieving competitive advantages in exist-ing industries and developing the capability to compete suc-cessfully in higher-productivity industries. Part of this upgrading process involves the simultaneous loss of posi-tion in industries that are more price-sensitive or that

require less sophisticated skills and technology. These become the domain of regions farther down the skills lad-der, a process known as "filtering." Thus, as economic growth occurs, nations and regions are linked on the ladder of success as they compete to supply global markets.

The first, or *factor-driven,* stage is one in which com-petitive advantage derives from the basic factors of produc-tion: rich endowments of natural resources and abundant cheap labor. Firms compete on the basis of price in indus-tries that use simple, widely available technologies imported from other nations, frequently financed by foreign capital. For the resource-dependent, there is extreme sensi-tivity to world economic cycles and to exchange rates, because these affect demand and prices. As Figure 1.3 reveals, many of the world's nations remain at this factor-driven stage in which merchandise exports are dominated by primary commodities. Some of these nations, painfully poor, are pressed to the threshold of subsistence. Others, like Saudi Arabia and the Gulf States, have flourished because of the earnings of their staple exports. Some have progressed beyond physical resource dependence by apply-ing their abundant supplies of inexpensive labor to produce, for example, textiles and clothing; see Figure 1.4.

The second, or *investment-driven,* stage is based on the willingness and ability to invest in modern, efficient facilities representing the best technology available in global markets. This not only involves investment in new technology, but the upgrading of factors of production from the basic to the advanced, development of modern infra-structure, and domestic rivalry that pushes down costs,

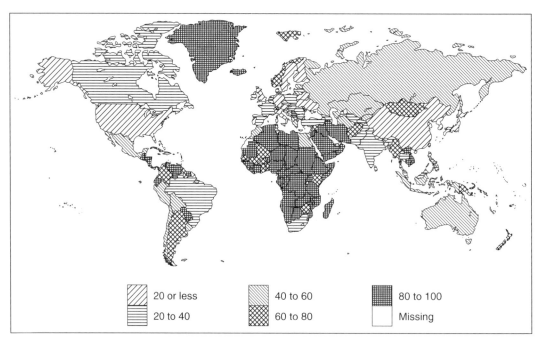

FIGURE 1.3   Percentage share of merchandise exports in primary commodities, including fuels, minerals, and metals.[*Source:* Data from the *1995 Britannica Book of the Year* (Chicago: Encyclopaedia Britannica, 1995).]

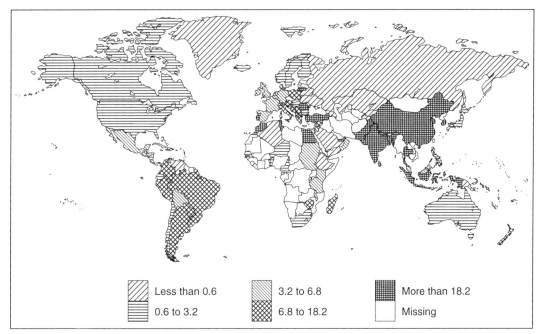

FIGURE 1.4 Percentage share of merchandise exports in textiles and clothing. [*Source:* United Nations, *Yearbook of International Trade Statistics 1993* (New York: United Nations, 1995).]

improves quality, introduces new products, and modernizes processes. Firms still compete in relatively standardized, price-sensitive markets, especially those where domestic demand is large. The focus, however, is on industries with significant scale economies and capital requirements, a large labor cost component, producing standardized products with a readily transferable technology. A typical example is the manufacture of machinery and transport equipment; see Figure 1.5. The significant competitive advantages are low labor costs and modern facilities. During this stage, industrial employment increases rapidly, as do wage and other factor costs, but over time, this erodes competitive advantage. Prime examples of successful investment-driven economies are Japan after World War II and Korea and Taiwan in the last quarter-century. The results have been startlingly different: South Korea's economy is dominated by very large-scale firms and that of Taiwan by large numbers of highly competitive small-scale enterprises.

The third, or *innovation-driven,* stage is different because at this stage firms actively create new technologies, new products, and new markets. The capacity to innovate opens up new industries that compete internationally in narrower market segments. Competitive advantage is no longer based on factor costs, but on productivity derived from high skill levels and advanced technology. Firms became multinational, competing globally with self-contained strategies and their own international marketing organizations, service networks, and brand reputations. They also begin to produce in many nations, fabricating components and sub-

assemblies in some and finished products in others. Two trends unfold simultaneously in this stage. Industry clusters *deepen* as supplier industries expand, compete, and specialize, and *widen* as the range of products expands and new industrial clusters emerge. Within the industry clusters, innovation leads to spinoffs and to a rapid rate of new firm formation. Critically important are highly skilled human resources, high-quality service industries and infrastructure, and the most advanced transportation and communications facilities. The service industries, in particular (discussed in Chapter 10), rise to account for more than 60 percent of the labor force; see Figure 1.6. At this stage, rising skills, education, and incomes breed growing domestic demand for new products and sophisticated services that can become the basis of new international competitiveness. And once again, as nations move to more sophisticated competitive advantage, their less-advanced industries are lost to countries farther down the technology ladder. An accompanying problem may be sharpening regional differences within countries between those areas receiving innovation-led growth and those areas losing factor-driven and investment-driven economic activity.

The final *wealth-driven* stage is reached if a nation achieves levels of affluence that reduce the drive to succeed, especially among the young, undermining innovativeness and investment. As Figure 1.7 reveals, it has not been the former world leaders in the North Atlantic region that have grown most rapidly in the past quarter-century. The problem is that people, business leaders, and politicians can become complacent and self-indulgent. Priorities are based

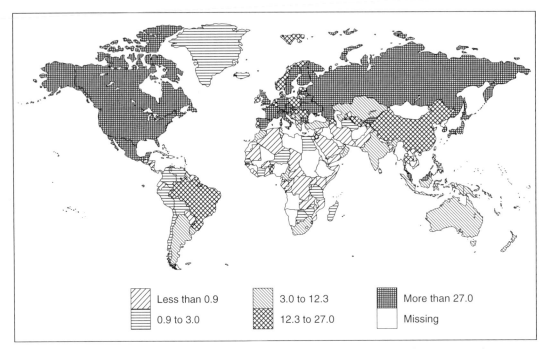

FIGURE 1.5   Percentage share of merchandise exports in machinery and transport equipment. [*Source:* Data from the *1995 Britannica Book of the Year* (Chicago: Encyclopaedia Britannica, 1995).]

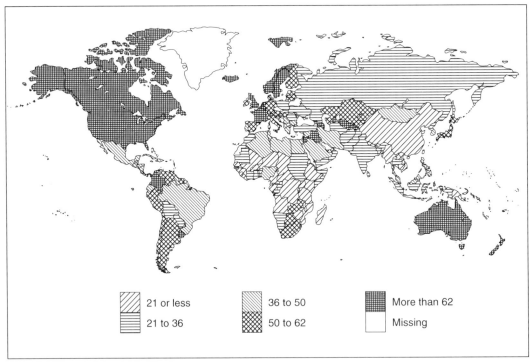

FIGURE 1.6   Percentage of labor force employed in the service industries. [*Source:* Data from United Nations Development Programme (UNDP), *Human Development Report, 1995* (New York: Oxford University Press, 1995), pp. 176, 201.]

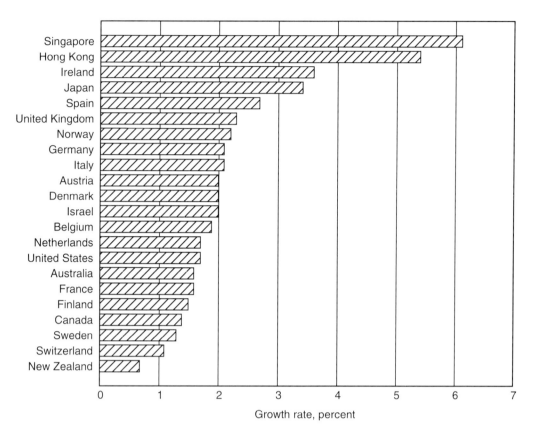

FIGURE 1.7 Average annual growth rates of per capita GNP for the world's high-income non-OPEC economies, 1980–1993. The countries are, in ranked order from highest to lowest growth rates: Singapore, Hong Kong, Ireland, Japan, Spain, United Kingdom, Norway, Germany, Italy, Austria, Denmark, Israel, Belgium, Netherlands, United States, Australia, France, Finland, Canada, Sweden, Switzerland, and New Zealand. [*Sourc*e: Data from the World Bank, *World Bank Development Report 1995* (New York: Oxford University Press, 1995), p. 163.]

on use of already accumulated wealth and come to be dominated by risk-reducing stewardship rather than by risk-taking leadership. Preservation comes to dominate over creativity and change. Competitive rivalry is lost, there are declining motivations to invest, and powerful firms collude with each other and with government to insulate their positions by fixing prices and protecting markets, resulting in a "sclerotic" condition (Box 1.3). There may be less interest in technical education and a switch of priorities to social goals. A wealth-driven nation with apparently successful large-scale companies will come to be affected by sagging growth, rising long-term unemployment, and burdensome taxation. The United Kingdom was a classic case in point after World War II, losing its competitive edge in the final decades of imperial power and experiencing the consequences when domination of imperial markets was ended

by the independence of former colonies. The new "mini-Britain" suddenly had to compete in world markets, but was saddled with old industries and infrastructure, corporate leaders who had forgotten how to be innovative, and labor organizations seeking redistribution of old wealth rather than creation of new enterprise. In three decades, the former world leader sagged as other European nations forged ahead. It took the period of conservative government under Margaret Thatcher, with all its disruptive social consequences, to privatize state-run enterprises and to reintroduce incentives for innovation-led growth. The side effect of such growth, however, is that some benefit far more than others, and some may lose. Social tensions increase, and along with them calls for greater fairness. Unfortunately, efficiency and equity are trade-offs, and achieving balance is an art, not a science—a task for the world of politics, not of economics.

BOX 1.3 Mancur Olsen on the Rise and Decline of Nations

Mancur Olsen argues that in societies that permit free trade and free organization, coalitions form around marketable goods and services. Groups of producers, like those who grow wheat or own oil, organize or protect their assets and, if possible, boost profits by raising prices. Physicians and lawyers do much the same in joining professional societies. Labor unions organize workers to bargain for wages.

In the early stages of this coalition-building process, there are relatively few interest groups, and their memberships are small compared to the society in which they operate. As they develop, they try to impose a variety of specialized rules on the economy that supports them. By law or collusive contract, they make penalties for those who would market the same goods or services outside the group. They also offer selective advantages to those who join and cooperate. Because these groups are small (Olsen says they typically include no more than 1 percent of the people in their state), they have no incentive to boost members welfare. Instead, they concentrate on promoting their own narrow interests, even at the cost of retarding the general economy.

A modest effort at self-aggrandizement may bring great rewards.

In time, tariffs, price supports, monopoly prices, wage guarantees, and business codes grow more numerous. All are intended to channel commerce into areas that benefit the special groups that fought for them. The combined effect is to create obstacles to trade and to prevent innovation. The economy suffers. In the past, nations suffering from this affliction have enjoyed renewed growth after a cataclysm has intervened to wipe out existing trade barriers or when new territory has been opened for development. Sometimes the power of a domestic group is undercut by low-cost imports, if the imports are not blocked. Rarely has any nation abolished special-interest codes voluntarily.

Inflation may be a common symptom of nations in a sclerotic condition, because it offers a brief measure of relief from economic stagnation. Special-interest groups, being run by committee rule, generally maneuver slowly. For this reason, they cannot always adjust their demands upward as rapidly as the nominal value of goods and services increases. This is

particularly true if inflation appears suddenly, without warning. Thus, inflation may be tolerated because it temporarily devalues the cost of products within the control of special interests. In time, this form of relief fails because the special interests soon catch up and raise their demands in pace with inflation.

In the contrary case, during periods of sudden price decline, the advantage held by interest groups is intensified. Those who operate outside the protection of a group may be forced to lower prices or wages. But the interest groups, again moving slowly, haggle over proposals while the storm rages around them. They may not reduce their demands until a recession has already damaged the economy. After a period of negotiation, they may begin to adjust, but by then investment in new projects will have been cut short, worsening the prospects for recovery. Thus, there is a real risk that the inflexibility of special-interest groups can lead in bad times to a vicious downward spiral.

Source: Mancur Olsen, *The Rise and Decline of Nations: Economic Growth, Stagflation, and Social Rigidities* (New Haven: Yale University Press, 1982).

Government Policy and the Multinational Enterprise

Given their size and pervasive influence in international economic affairs, multinational enterprises receive a great deal of attention from government policy-makers. Official positions on MNEs vary widely from country to country, however, largely because of their unique legal status. As yet no international authority exercises jurisdiction over them. Under existing law, therefore, a multinational is merely a group of national companies, each subject to the laws of the land in which it is domiciled. In the absence of any international regulatory mechanism, an MNE exists in an atmosphere of uncertainty, which imposes extra costs because of the widely differing legal requirements under which its various branches function. At the same time, the absence of international constraints provides the firm with opportuni-

ties denied domestic companies. This is the basis for the common view that MNEs manufacture in those lands where costs are lowest and declare their profits where taxes are least. It also explains the frequent accusation that multinationals do not show adequate social responsibility toward the countries in which they operate.

In these circumstances, it is not surprising that both home countries and host countries tend to have love-hate feelings toward multinationals. The intensity of these attitudes varies from country to country, being greatest in some less-developed countries (LDCs). On the positive side, an LDC is likely to hold exaggerated expectations of the benefits it will gain from the arrival of a multinational. Government leaders expect the new company to provide a badly needed solution for their unemployment problems, to supply an infusion of managerial and scientific knowledge that will help close the technology gap, to reduce the drain on their foreign exchange, to contribute tax revenues to the national treasury, and to develop natural resources and thus relieve some of their regional disparities.

It is not until some time after the investment has already been made that negative attitudes begin to surface. Host countries—Canada, for instance—may complain that foreign-owned firms bring the "wrong kind" of employment, that citizens of the country do not receive enough technical and managerial jobs. They charge that MNEs threaten their national sovereignty because company decisions are made in another country. Some LDCs associate multinationals with neocolonialism because foreign-owned concerns seem to continue the pattern of economic exploitation practiced by their former colonial masters. They see the MNE draining the country's resources and begin to ask what will be left after the oil or copper or bauxite gone. Or they may object that the country's balance of payments is suffering because the MNE is repatriating too much in profits to the home company. They complain, too, about the kind of technology that MNEs bring to them: They say that these firms introduce capital-intensive techniques and equipment originally designed to suit company needs in their labor-short, capital-rich homelands but that are not appropriate for poor countries needing jobs for their masses of unemployed labor.

Multinational enterprises thus find themselves immersed in a complex set of relationships that pit against each other the differing perspectives of home country, host country, and the firm itself. Many people contend, for example, that a foreign investment represents a gain for the host country and a loss for the home country. Some regard the profits repatriated by the subsidiary to its parent company as a gain for the home country and a drain on the host country. Among other questions are the possibility of political control of overseas subsidiaries by the home government (the *extraterritoriality* issue), government seizure of foreign-owned companies (the *expropriation* issue), and special performance requirements exacted of MNE subsidiaries by their hosts.

The relationships between host countries and multinationals have both economic and political sides. In balance, does a country gain or lose economically from foreign investment? A number of studies in Australia, Canada, and the United Kingdom confirm that foreign-owned firms operating in developed countries produce a measurable rise in the gross national products of their hosts. Although the evidence for LDCs is more variable, the employment-generating effects of MNEs have proved to be very great in a number of cases. In Mexico and Brazil, for example, foreign-owned firms account for half of all industrial employment. The impact of multinationals has been even more striking in the newly industrializing lands of East Asia, where electronics firms and other export-oriented, labor-intensive industries employ great numbers of workers in assembly operations.

The success of host countries in acquiring new technology from MNEs depends on the absorptive capacity of the local society and economy. Many LDCs lack a sufficient number of educated and trained people to manage and staff industries that are technologically complex. Yet a number of countries, such as India, Mexico, and South Korea, have succeeded in training many of their people for such activities. One element limiting the amount of new technology that host countries can gain from MNEs is the reluctance of such firms to part with proprietary information.

To calculate the actual net economic impact of foreign direct investment on host countries calls for balancing a number of factors. On the plus side are MNE payments for local labor, capital, and land, the taxes paid to local governments, and the gains by domestic firms that benefit from a quickening local economy. On the minus side are the *opportunity costs* to domestic factors of production-—labor, land, and capital-—that might have been used otherwise, and the loss of funds sent out of the country as profits, dividends, interest, royalties, and fees. Most such calculations have shown gains for the host countries. The exceptions are those cases where host governments have made too many tax concessions to attract MNEs in the first place.

That disagreements should arise between MNEs and their hosts seems inevitable, because governments tend to look for unrealistically quick returns, and that MNEs and their hosts usually have different perspectives on costs and benefits. Such disagreements may grow with the passing of time, as the initial inflow of investment tapers off and the firm repatriates profits to the parent concern. At this point, the host government may make new demands, bolstered by its increased bargaining power now that the company has committed its resources and cannot afford to shut down operations. The government and the MNE then may do a great deal of jockeying to arrive at a mutually satisfactory agreement on how to divide the benefits from the investment.

The political issues that arise between a multinational and its host government are often more difficult to resolve. Public debate often involves not only officials and politicians, but also labor leaders, local business interests, the press, and those in academia. Underlying such discussions is the question of whether the economic benefits of foreign investment are sufficient to outweigh the perceived threat to national sovereignty. The usual presumptions are that an MNE exercises a certain power over the local economy, that it is directed in this from a control center elsewhere, and that the government of the home country exerts a sinister influence over the company.

Although this picture may be overdrawn, company interests and host-country interests are not likely to coincide. The multinational seeks to maximize returns to its entire MNE system, whereas the host government looks to its national welfare—economic, social, and military. Local officials resent the ability of an MNE to make decisions that affect the country's welfare independently of their control. They suspect MNEs of avoiding taxes and manipulating prices to the benefit of company interests.

The most contentious issue dividing MNEs and host governments is the perceived threat to national sovereignty by home-country pressures on MNE's overseas operations. Giving some substance to this fear, the U.S. government has openly imposed its will on the overseas affiliates of its MNEs. It has, for example, prohibited Canadian subsidiaries of American companies from trading with Cuba. In addition to the friction caused by such efforts to assert political control over MNE foreign operations, controversy arose in the 1990s as a result of attempts to apply U.S. antibias laws outside the country. U.S. courts were being asked to decide cases involving alleged discrimination by foreign subsidiaries against employees on the basis of race, national origin, religion, or sex.

This "extraterritoriality" issue has severely strained American relations with other governments. Several countries have warned the United States that international law recognizes the rights of nations to regulate conduct within their own borders. These conflicts have created perplexing dilemmas for U.S. multinationals operating in countries whose laws are based on very different cultural practices.

Political considerations may lead host governments to place various restrictions on foreign ownership. Indeed, most countries exclude certain industries from foreign ownership entirely, particularly defense industries. Many governments prohibit foreign ownership of banks, public utilities, communications, and, increasingly, minerals. In the U.S. Midwest, several states even restrict foreign ownership of farmland. Some countries—notably France, Japan, and Mexico—prohibit foreign acquisition of local firms and several countries maintain strict review procedures for all proposed foreign takeovers.

Today, more and more governments are requiring foreign investors to acquire local partners when setting up new affiliates. Such joint ventures are especially popular among LDCs, which perceive them as a way of gaining access to new technology, limiting the outflow of repatriated profits, and minimizing the influence of foreigners over the local economy. Arrangements of this kind have become fairly standard throughout Latin America and Southeast Asia.

Another policy tool favored by host governments is to impose performance requirements on foreign-owned enterprises. For instance, as a way of creating jobs, the MNE may be required to use a specified proportion of local personnel. Some countries provide companies with timetables for employing local persons as managers and technicians. Governments may require that firms set up training programs or establish local laboratories to perform R&D, or they may force MNEs to increase the local content of the products they assemble in the host country, especially automobiles. Some newly industrializing countries with large foreign debts—for example, Mexico and Brazil—have required MNEs to export specified percentages of their output.

The most extreme measure of all is government seizure of foreign-owned companies. In recent years, a rash of such expropriations has occurred in some Third World countries where the political processes have fallen into the hands of economic nationalists, many of whom oppose foreign ownership in any form. International law recognizes the right of governments to expropriate foreign enterprises, considering this merely an exercise of national sovereignty, but this law also specifies that the previous owners of such properties receive prompt, adequate, and effective compensation for the loss. Compensation is a key issue today, for many LDCs are failing in this. When compensation is not forthcoming, home governments may retaliate against offending countries. The United States, for instance, has in some cases cut off foreign aid and credits to delinquent nations.

The opposite side of these questions has to do with the relationships between MNEs and their home governments. The United States has no overall policy toward U.S.-based multinationals, but the government has asserted its authority regarding certain specific issues. Prior to World War II, the United States not only placed no restrictions on foreign operations by its MNEs, but it also stood ready to ensure that other governments did not discriminate against them. In several instances, it intervened militarily in their behalf.

After the war, the government encouraged foreign direct investment by U.S. multinationals as a form of foreign aid, but focused this upon LDCs especially after Europe had fully recovered. The United States entered into treaties with other countries guaranteeing fair treatment of its MNEs. When balance-of-payments problems began to arise in the 1960s, the U.S. government set quotas on foreign direct investment, forcing its multinationals to do their borrowing abroad.

As foreign investment by U.S. firms expanded, domestic criticism of them grew louder. Labor unions claimed that American firms were exporting jobs with their "runaway plants"—factories set up in East Asia, along the Mexican border, and in other low-labor-cost places—to produce goods formerly made at home. Some domestic critics objected to what they saw as the loss of U.S. production through the transfer of technology abroad. Others decried the "unfair" advantages gained by U.S. multinationals in the favorable treatment accorded them under U.S. tariffs and in their ability to avoid restrictive U.S. laws to take advantage of concessions from foreign governments. Empirical studies tend to discount these claims, finding that MNEs as a whole have enjoyed faster growth in output than domestic firms, have higher rates of export growth, and generally have favorable balances in their own trade with the world.

Tax policy is another area of controversy between MNEs and their home governments. How do you prevent these firms from escaping taxation but at the same time avoid taxing them doubly? In the United States, the problem is compounded by the desire of state governments to tax MNEs operating within their jurisdictions. Some states favor taxing all production that takes place within their borders but exempts their foreign production. Other states insist on taxing all production of their MNEs throughout the world. U.S. antitrust laws prevent companies from cooperating with each other in ways that reduce competition. The United States also prohibits U.S. firms from making "questionable" payments abroad. Other countries make no such efforts to prevent bribery, which is an accepted part of doing business in many Third World nations and some industrialized ones as well.

The evidence indicates that under ideal conditions, everyone gains from foreign direct investment. Most of the problems that arise between multinationals and governments can be attributed to the lack of a uniform international policy for such enterprises and the absence of a mechanism for regulating their activities worldwide. Agreement among nations is needed to ensure that multinationals are good corporate citizens of the countries where they operate and to make certain that the world receives full economic benefit from this efficient form of business organization with its potential for allocating the world's resources in the most effective manner.

APPENDIX 1.2

The Non-Western Multinational

Many of the most dynamic multinational enterprises now edging toward the center of the global economic stage come from East Asia. Though some of these non-Western concerns match the leading MNEs of Europe and America in size and power, they exhibit certain traits that differentiate them from those in the West.

The prime MNEs in this group have their homes in Japan. Others are home based in the "Four Tigers"—South Korea, Taiwan, Hong Kong, and Singapore, and yet others are emerging in Thailand, Malaysia, and Indonesia.

Several shared attributes have helped to shape the new breed of multinational emerging on the Pacific rim. These traits arise from the blend of religions and ethical systems, especially Buddhism and Confucianism, that prevail in most East Asian cultures. Centuries ago these beliefs diffused from China to Korea and Japan, where they have intermingled with indigenous religions, notably the Japanese Shinto, and thence throughout Southeast Asia as Chinese merchants and entrepreneurs migrated into new markets.

A fundamental source of motivation and discipline among East Asians is Confucianism, an ethical system that places a high value on education and assigns a special virtue

to hard work, obedience, and the obligations of the individual in a structured society. In Japan, Zen Buddhism has been influential, with its requirement of rigorous individual discipline and self-control, as well as its emphasis on simplicity and taste. East Asian societies are group-centered; the interests of the individual are subordinate to those of the whole, whether in the family, the village, or the place of work.

Japanese Multinationals. Though certain trading companies (*sogo shosha*) could lay claim to being among the earliest multinationals, the great surge of Japanese FDI overseas is a new phenomenon. Despite the recency of their appearance, some of these firms have already seized a major share of world markets. This swift success stems from a number of conditions relating to the organizational makeup of these companies, to the cultural system on which they draw, and the unique economic and political environment from which they spring.

Japanese multinationals are not directly comparable with those of North America and Europe because they are organized differently. Japanese companies are divided into three functional classes: manufacturing, marketing, and financial. Firms of the three types join together to form enterprise groups, called *keiretsu,* which are linked by mutual ownership, interlocking directorships, and operational ties based on mutual understandings. Some of these enterprise groups are descended from family-controlled combines, *zaibatsu,* dating to the earliest period of Japanese industrialization. Commonly, a trading company (*sogo shosha*) and a large bank form the core of such a group, together with a number of manufacturing concerns. Functionally, the member companies are closely integrated, but their relationship is so informal that they are not usually viewed in the same light as an IBM or a General Electric. Yet several *keiretsu* greatly exceed the leading European and American MNEs in total sales. Towering over other Japanese *keiretsu* is mighty Mitsubishi, with total global sales of $175 billion (see the table of Japan's top six *keiretsu* and their principal member companies). In the past two decades, some of the larger Japanese manufacturing firms, such as Sony, have internationalized their production independently of any enterprise group. This action has had a bandwagon effect, drawing other Japanese competitors, as well as hordes of their suppliers, into overseas operations.

The intragroup cooperation that takes place among member companies is consistent with the Japanese cultural heritage, which places group values over those of the individual. Pervading the entire corporate system, this outlook is expressed in a sense of togetherness within a family-type environment, a *ringi seido* (consensus) system of decision making, assignment of tasks to groups, with little differentiation among individual job definitions, and continuous on-the-job training. It is a system that relies on close

Japan's six leading keiretsu

	Core Companies in Group
Mitsubishi	28
Mitsubishi Corporation	
Mitsubishi Bank	
Mitsubishi Heavy Industries	
Dai-ichi Kangin	47
Seibu Department Stores	
Shimizu	
Yokohama Rubber	
Fuyo	29
Marubeni	
Nissan Moror	
Canon	
Mitsui Group	
Toyota Motor	24
Toshiba	
Toray Industries	
Sanwa	44
Teijin	
Ohbayashi	
Kobe Steel	
Sumitomo	20
NEC	
Sumitomo Chemical	
Sumitomo Metal Industries	

Source: *Business Week*, September. 24, 1990, p.100.

face-to-face contacts and the shared understandings of a homogeneous culture. Consequently, non-Japanese managers of overseas affiliates are often at a disadvantage in the decision-making process. This problem is all the greater because Japanese foreign operations tend to be tightly controlled from the home base.

Many factors have contributed to the growing success of Japanese foreign operations, some stemming from Japanese management techniques and others relating to conditions in the home country. Japanese multinationals benefit from a smoothly functioning production technology and a well-developed organizational technology that includes effective methods of quality control and minimizing inventory costs. Most Japanese overseas operations are located close to their local markets, as seen in the case of Japanese auto manufacture in the United States.

Among the many home-base advantages enjoyed by Japanese multinationals is the country's remarkable ability to create not only an abundance of finance capital but also to upgrade human capital by means of an effective system of public education supplemented by corporate on-the-job training. MNEs have gained by high public investment in research and development. An informed public reacts instantly to perceived national crises, as in the concerted national effort to conserve energy. The Japanese consuming public, the world's second largest, also contributes through its insistence on perfection in the products it buys. This creates an intensely competitive home market, which thoroughly prepares Japanese MNEs for competing in the world market with goods they have been forced to refine before taking them abroad.

Korea's Multinationals.   Among the growing number of LDC-based multinational corporations listed annually among the *Fortune* 500 are many based in newly industrialized countries on the Pacific Rim. Unlike those Third World MNEs originating in resource-rich countries (for example, the oil-exporting Middle East) or those coming from countries with large markets (Brazil, Mexico, India), multinationals spawned by the East Asian newly industrialized countries (NICs) draw on a labor-rich home environment as the foundation for their ventures abroad. Cheap labor may be more abundant in other newly developing countries, but East Asia's workers constitute a resource of unusual quality.

South Korea is typical of the East Asian NICs in its devotion to making the best of the human resources it has in order to compensate for the physical resources it lacks. As workers, Koreans are disciplined, hardworking, and well-educated. The population is linguistically and racially homogeneous; and, in the aftermath of a bitter civil war, it is remarkably free of class divisions. Moreover, Korea has made an unusually strong commitment to upgrade this valuable resource by means of a highly developed secondary, university, and technical educational system, supplemented by advanced training abroad for many individuals.

Not only do Koreans look to Japan as a model for their development strategy, they also regard Japan as a competitor to be beaten. Korean companies have been quick to seize opportunities for invading Japanese product lines as structural changes in Japan make some forms of manufacture less economical. In standardized types of mass production, Korean firms are highly competitive on the basis of cost. However, Korea's population of 43 million offers a home market only one-third as large as Japan's, and consumer tastes are not as sophisticated. On the whole, Korea lags several years behind Japan in its level of advancement.

As their economy matured and as domestic wages rose, Korean firms began to enter into foreign ventures. Although the initial moves took place in the late 1960s, it was not until the early 1980s that outward FDI exceeded inward FDI. The first companies to go abroad were construction firms, which had gained their experience as contractors in the construction of U.S. military bases in Korea at the end of the Korean War and later in Vietnam. Korean construction companies were subsequently very active in the Persian Gulf oil states. Other industries that pioneered in foreign undertakings were plywood and textile manufacturers. Once started on this course, Korean firms have been remarkably quick to manufacture in other countries, in lines as diverse as consumer electronics, automobiles, and videotapes.

Very large industry groups, known as *chaebol,* dominate the Korean economy. Many of these giant firms grew out of the large general trading companies that predate them. Unlike Japan's *keiretsu,* which are loosely joined by informal links and interlocking directorships, the *chaebol* are closely held corporations run by strong, aggressive chief executives who usually were the company founders. The families that founded the top 30 *chaebol* still own 60 percent of their combined equity. The *chaebol* enjoy much government favor and support. The leading *chaebol* are Hyundai, Daewoo, Samsung, and LG Group, all multibillion-dollar companies that invest heavily in research and development and compete fiercely both at home and overseas. Together, they employ only 3 percent of the Korean workforce, but they account for 33 percent of the total sales of all South Korean companies and ship 60 percent of total exports.

MNEs Based in Taiwan. The other Tigers—Taiwan, Singapore, and Hong Kong—have produced similarly aggressive multinational enterprises. Unlike Korea, these three small nations are dominated by ethnic Chinese population. Taiwan had been a Japanese colony prior to World War II. An island lying only a few miles off the coast of China, it became a sanctuary for the defeated Kuomintang (Nationalist) Chinese forces following the revolution. The native Taiwanese were overwhelmed by the flood of refugees, who took political control and shortly created a vibrant export-driven economy. By several measures, Taiwan is the most successful of the Tigers. Now the world's twelfth-largest exporter, it has accumulated a cash surplus greater even than Japan's and has achieved the second-highest per capita GNP in East Asia. Virtually all Taiwanese complete elementary school, and 45 percent get at least some higher education.

One of the world's most densely populated countries, Taiwan gained its manufacturing success by reason of an abundance of cheap labor and a robust entrepreneurial spirit. Its industries initially were largely of a low-technology, copycat type, involving only minimal research and development, and conducted in hundreds of small establishments. Government-imposed exchange controls, aided by a strong currency, kept the country's burgeoning supply of money at home. By the mid-1980s, however, pressures had begun to mount: Wages rose rapidly, and Taiwan's traditional manufactures could no longer compete with nearby Malaysia, Thailand, and Indonesia. Industrial output and exports slumped.

The country's response was twofold. One solution was to shift from cheap assembly to higher levels of technology. New semiconductor factories sprang up, and Taiwanese computer companies aggressively doubled their share of the world market. The second reaction was to "go global." In 1986 the government ended the tight exchange controls that had restricted overseas investments, and a huge capital exodus ensued.

For Taiwan's small companies this meant transferring, unaltered, their low-wage, low-tech operations— shoes, garments, handbags, tennis rackets, plastics—to Thailand, Malaysia, the Philippines, Indonesia, and China. They poured billions of dollars into the nearby Chinese coastal province of Fujian, which, with its 29 million population, became a Taiwanese industrial zone. In time, larger companies followed, bringing to Fujian more sophisticated products, such as chemicals, video recorders, and computers.On the whole, however, the favored target for the larger investors was the United States. Taiwan's premier computer maker, Acer Inc., led the way in 1987 with its purchase of a U.S. firm, Counterpoint Computers. Following this came Taiwanese acquisition of the venerable American Bridge Company, eight Texas savings and loan associations, Princeton Publishing Labs, and Wyse Technology—one of Silicon Valley's leading manufacturers of terminals and personal computers—and Wyndham Foods (Girl Scout cookies), among others.

The City-States as Springboards for FDI. The city-states of Hong Kong (population 5.8 million) and Singapore (12.7 million) share similar histories of British colonial control. Singapore gained independence in 1965. Hong Kong, however, returned to Chinese control in 1997. Both are island countries with exceptional locational advantages for trade and foreign investment: Hong Kong is the main point of entry into Kuangtung Province, China's leading industrial region, and Singapore is situated on the main sea and air routes linking East Asia with Europe and the Middle East, and midway between Malaysia and Indonesia. As a legacy of longtime British control, both have English-speaking populations, a positive attraction to foreign investors. Though each has enjoyed rapid growth and rising standards of living, Hong Kong has practiced freewheeling capitalism under a relaxed government policy of nonintervention in economic matters, whereas Singapore has achieved similarly successful results under a government program that closely managed all aspects of the economy.

The same locational characteristics that, under British rule, had made Singapore the principal entrepôt of Southeast Asia, served to attract particular types of foreign investment in the post-independence era: shipbuilding and repair; refining; port and terminal services; airlines; printing; regional corporate headquarters for U.S., Japanese, and European MNEs; and a growing array of financial and business services benefiting from the presence of an English-speaking population.

Singapore was also successful in developing into a manufacturing center for multinationals requiring a low-cost, literate work force within a setting that offers excellent roads, air service, port facilities, and telecommunications. When the labor-cost advantage was lost to neighboring Asian lands, Singapore's policy of upgrading the quality of its work force and infrastructure enabled the country to restructure its economy to capital and skill-intensive, high-value-added activities such as electronics and scientific equipment.

Playing an essential part in this economic restructuring was a rising group of Singapore-based multinationals. As rising wages deprived local industries of their competitive advantage in labor-intensive forms of production, they shifted their manufacturing activities to neighboring countries with abundant supplies of cheap labor. In this undertaking, these firms were able to build on their accumulated production experience and to avail themselves of the well-developed Singapore banking community for the capital needed for these foreign ventures.

The Fourth Tiger, Hong Kong, was the pioneer in this type of outward FDI, and it has led the other NICs in the number of such investments throughout Southeast Asia. Hong Kong interests have established a stake in Communist Chinese enterprises even greater than that of their Taiwanese counterparts. As China's longtime window to the outside world, Hong Kong was uniquely situated for such undertakings. Reinforcing this locational edge were the many family ties and other personal links that Hong Kong entrepreneurs enjoyed within the Canton and Kuangtung areas. Hong Kong's highly developed international finance sector furnished crucial support for these and other foreign undertakings of locally based MNEs. Indeed, some of the financial institutions have themselves gone global, a notable example being the Bank of Hong Kong and Shanghai, which entered the U.S. market through its acquisition of New York–based Marine Midland Bank.

Hong Kong's international role however, has been threatened by the resumption of Chinese political control. Distrusting China's assurances that it will not alter the existing economic framework, Hong Kong's ethnic-Chinese entrepreneurial class began an exodus from the colony during the second half of the 1980s, taking their very substantial supply of capital with them.

VOCABULARY

The following terms and concepts introduced in this chapter are defined in the Glossary at the end of the book. Be sure that you know them. It is important that you build up an appropriate vocabulary. The Glossary also includes terms that are used in this chapter but that appear on vocabulary lists later in the book.

advanced factors of production
back office accounts
balance of payments
basic factors of production
basket-case countries
Buddhism
capital
capital-intensive
capital resources
chaebol
coalition governments
communications costs
competence
competitive advantage
concepts
Confucianism
connectedness
consensus system of decision making
cosmopolitans
demand conditions
dictatorship of the proletariat

distributorship
economic policy instruments
economies of scale
economies of specialization
endaka
exchange rate
expropriation
extractive industries
extraterritoriality
factor conditions
factor-driven development
factors of production
filtering
financial deregulation
firm strategy
First World
foreign direct investment (FDI)
four stages to economic development
Four Tigers
Fourth World
global communications systems

global economic geography
globalization
globalization cascade
government barriers to imports
government intervention
gross domestic product (GDP)
hard technology
horizontal integration
human resources
incentives
industrialization
industry clusters
information gathering
infrastructure
innovation-driven development
internalizing
international economic integration
international finance
international specialization
international trade
internationalization

intrafirm transfers	*perestroika*	state monopoly
investment-driven development	physical resources	statist
kei-haku-tan-sho	private enterprise	supporting industries
keiretsu	privatization	tariff
knowledge-intensive industries	product differentiation	tax concession
knowledge resources	profit margin	technological change
labor-intensive industries	purchasing power of currencies	technology transfer
laissez-faire	quota	tetrapolar strategy
less-developed countries (LDCs)	repatriation	Third World
liberalism	resource dependent	tradable goods and services
liberalization policies	resource endowment	trade barriers
licensing agreement	reverse investment	transactions costs
linear linkup	*ringi seido*	transfer of capital
locals	sclerotic conditions	transfer of skills
market economy	Second World	transfer of technology
meshing	simultaneity	transnational corporations (TNCs)
multinational enterprises (MNEs)	soft technology	vertical integration
neocolonialism	*sogo shosha*	wealth-driven development
newly industrialized country (NIC)	stagnation	world economic cycles
opportunity cost	state interventionism	*zaibatsu*

TOPICS FOR DISCUSSION

1. Briefly describe the changes leading to globalization of the world economy.

2. What MNEs operate in your area? Obtain the annual report of one of them. List the MNE's main products, brand names, and the countries in which it operates. Does the report indicate an international strategy of expansion?

3. What are the essential similarities and differences between U.S. and Japanese multinational corporations? Take two examples, such as Ford Motor Company and Nissan.

4. To what extent do countries formerly classified as members of the "Fourth World" fit into Michael Porter's factor-driven stage of economic development? In what ways are their development potentials limited by their factor dependence?

5. It is said that the former Second World's socialist economies will be unable to make the transition to market systems without first reintroducing private property. Why should this be so?

6. The world's top 500 MNEs are headquartered in only 19 urban regions (North America: New York, Chicago, Los Angeles, San Francisco, Philadelphia–Wilmington, Dallas–Fort Worth, Houston, St. Louis, Detroit, Pittsburgh; Asia: Tokyo, Osaka–Kobe, Seoul; Europe: London, Paris, Ruhrgebiet, Frankfurt, Randstadt, Rome). What do you conclude about the nature of control and strategic planning in the global economy?

7. What steps should a wealth-driven economy take to reestablish innovation-driven growth? What problems are likely to arise if a country makes such a transition?

FURTHER READINGS

Cable, V. (1995). The Diminished Nation-State. *Daedalus.* 124: 23–54.

   A discussion of the impact of globalization upon the role and functions of the nation-state.

Dicken, Peter. (1992). *Global Shift: The Internationalization of Economic Activity, 2nd ed.* London: Paul Chapman.

   The first two sections of the book, Patterns of Global Shift (pp. 11–88) and Process of Global Shift (pp. 91–227), are essential reading.

Doti, James L., and Dwight R. Lee (1991) *The Market Economy: A Reader.* Los Angeles: Roxbury.

   A collection of important essays on the political, economic, and philosophical underpinnings of a market system.

Dow, M. Bradley, and Pradeep Kumar. (1990) *Multinational Enterprises and Employment: The Canadian Experience.* Working Paper No. 61. Geneva: International Labor Office, Multinational Enterprises Program.

One of a valuable, comprehensive set of studies. MNEs have played an exceptionally important role in Canada's economic development.

Gregory, P. R., and R. C. Stuart. (1995). *Comparative Economic Systems.* Boston: Houghton Mifflin.

A thorough discussion of the nature of different economic systems and of the changes that have unfolded since 1980.

Kanter, Rosabeth Moss. (1995) *World Class. Thriving Locally in the Global Economy.* New York: Simon and Schuster.

A literate and provocative view of the forces promoting globalization of the world economy.

Ohmae, Kenichi. (1985) *Triad Power: The Coming Shape of Global Competition.* New York: The Free Press.

A thoughtful discussion of the emergence of a tripolar global economic structure.

Porter, Michael E. (1990) *The Competitive Advantage of Nations.* New York: The Free Press.

Provides a new look at the factors responsible for economic growth and a new classification of the stages of economic development.

2

The Factors Reinforcing Regionalization

OVERVIEW

As globalization runs its course, powerful forces seek to differentiate and divide the world economy in new ways.

The role of nation-states is being weakened, replaced at greater geographical scale by global policy regimes and civilizational differences, and at smaller scale by "region states."

Underlying these drives to reinforce distinctiveness are cultural differences.

Cultural traditions, which reproduce contrasting political ideologies, are transmitted, reinforced, and shaped by the values implanted in children during their childhood socialization. The role of the family is critical: Different family types implant different sets of values.

OBJECTIVES

- to describe the changing role of the nation-state
- to outline the emergence of global policy regimes, civilizational conflict, and the rise of "region states"
- to explore the concept of culture, and to lay out the dimensions of cultural variation
- to explain why different cultural traditions persist and maintain differentiated culture regions

THE END OF HISTORY?

Francis Fukuyama, an American political historian, claimed that the collapse of communism in 1989 heralded "the end of history," at least as he had known it, centering on the twentieth-century conflict between the capitalist First World and the communist Second World. The triumph of markets and the resulting speeding up of globalization seemed unstoppable. What appeared to be becoming near-universal was a world of the type envisioned by Adam Smith in *The Wealth of Nations*—a world in which economic development arises from the self-interested activities of individuals interacting in the marketplace, producing the greatest good for all by seeking to maximize their personal welfares under free-market (*laissez-faire*) conditions. What seemed to be in retreat was a world of the type envisioned by Karl Marx in *Das Kapital,* in which economic development is controlled by social and political institutions, and in which "developmental states" forego markets and organize their resources for nation building in a planned, goal-seeking manner.

Fukuyama clearly overstated his case. There still are major differences in the motivations and preferences of economic actors across the globe. As *The Economist* noted on November 20, 1993, the "big trend in the world economy is toward 'regionalism' and the reassertion of economic geography. Politics has made it possible, but market forces are driving it forward." As globalization runs its course, powerful countervailing forces are pulling for regional reorganization at scales that are both greater and smaller than that of the nation-state, leading to the question of whether nation-states will persist as key actors in global economic organization. Many think that the role of the nation-state is declining, and that cultural differences are emerging as alternative foundations for togetherness and distinctiveness, producing new and different scales of political-economic organization. These countervailing forces are the subject of this chapter.

The concern for *culture* echoes Max Weber's argument in his book *The Protestant Ethic and the Spirit of Capitalism* that individuals are programmed by their cultures to act in ways that are more or less likely to promote development. Weber argued that in Western Europe, the Protestant ethic reinforced the spirit of capitalism, because the new religion made hard work and success a virtue at the time that market systems were replacing the communal worlds of the Middle Ages. Others have pointed to the role of the Confucian ethic in the rapid economic growth of East Asia since World War II. A systematic understanding of the links between culture and development, and the ways in which they impinge upon the viability of nation-states, is essential.

THE DECLINING ROLE OF THE NATION-STATE

The globe is covered by a mosaic of independent nation-states of different sizes and histories. Their number continues to increase, even as their power appears to be eroding. With the collapse of communism many new states were created by dividing the former Soviet Union, Czechoslovakia, and Yugoslavia into units composed of people who, in the words of the nineteenth-century philosopher and economist John Stuart Mill, became "nations" by virtue of their wish to be governed together, a wish arising from common sympathies created by shared language, history, and beliefs.

Nation-states have well-defined roles and responsibilities. Their basic functions are *legislative,* in which the society's primary goals are determined and the general rules are formulated for maintaining (or changing) the existing social order; *administrative,* which deals with the execution of the basic rules and with the organization of the technical activities needed for their efficient execution; *party-political,* which mobilizes support for different measures and for the holders of different political positions; and *juridical,* concerned with testing the validity of the rules and laws by applying them to concrete cases in society. The body of law serves to define the range of acceptable behavior and provides for the imposition of sanctions on those who transgress.

The central governments of nation-states assure their power by maintaining a monopoly over the use and regulation of force within their boundaries, enabling them to impose sanctions and use the police power to implement their societies' main collective goals, to maintain internal order, and to regulate foreign relations. Within nation-states, there is an attempt to socialize men and women to uniform and shared ways of life and to maintain common belief systems that define the essential traits of national character. The founder of modern Germany, Otto von Bismarck, captured this role when he argued that the first years of education are ideal for implanting a code of loyalty to the state in the hearts and minds of young people. He thus concluded that the state should control the educational system. In the same vein, in the United States during the nineteenth century, assurance was sought that the children of successive waves of immigrants would learn to speak a common language and read about American ideals in Horatio Alger stories, to ensure successful assimilation to the mainstream. When assimilation and socialization do not occur, the state is in jeopardy.

As the world's nation-states emerged, diverse groups were merged through unification of economies, provision of common legal systems, and the growth of mass public educational systems. The result was a set of *core identities*— usually those of the dominant groups within society—that imposed themselves as the mainstream paradigms of economic, political, and social life. Each core identity is composed of a system of thought and action that lasts longer than the lifespans of the individuals who belong to a society, because it is transmitted from one generation to the next during childhood socialization and the process of education. It persists as an organized body of custom, consisting of traditions, ideas, values, myths, and symbols. Part consists of the *norms* for, and the standards of, behavior. Another part consists of *ideologies* justifying and rationalizing selected ways of behaving. If society is an organized set of individuals with a given way of life, the core identity is that way of life. A society is an aggregate of social relations, and the core identity is the content of those relations. It is this core identity that we call *culture*. Differences in culture are at the basis of differences in political-economic life.

Nation-states, *"polities,"* have shaped economic performance not only because they have intervened in the attempt to control inflation or the rate of growth or the degree of inequality in society, but also because they have defined and enforced explicit economic rules that reflect the central values of their cultures: antitrust legislation in the United States, to foster competition; state-run monopolies, fixed prices, and quotas in the former Soviet Union, to secure alternative communist goals. Global economic integration is weakening the ability of nation-states to intervene using conventional policy toolkits such as taxes, public spending, interest rates, credit controls, exchange rates, capital controls and income policies, however. The combination of telecommunications development, deregulation, increasing market openness, and removal of exchange controls for example, has replaced regulated, segmented national financial markets by a single *global capital market.* Capital is now so mobile that markets ensure that holders of financial assets receive roughly the same risk-adjusted real return everywhere. Any country that offers significantly lower returns will experience capital outflow and a rapidly depreciating exchange rate. The sheer scale of profit-seeking finance capital that can be mobilized in currency markets far exceeds what any government, or even governments acting in concert, can put against it. Foreign exchange trading in the world's major financial centers—principally New York, London, and Tokyo, linked instantaneously on a 24-hour basis—exceeds a trillion dollars a day, a multiple of more than 50 times of the daily amount of world trade and greater than the total stock of foreign exchange reserves held by all governments.

The effects on nation-states have been complex: Individuals, companies, and governments have more access to cheaper finance, but individual countries are more exposed to internationally transmitted shocks, and national regulators have been obliged to cede control to global markets that are either wholly unregulated (currency markets), lightly self-regulated (bond markets), or imperfectly regulated (e.g., multinational banking). The results have been profound. The October 7, 1995, issue of *The Economist* reported that in Britain, a former chancellor of the exchequer opined that "The plain fact is that the nation state as it has existed for nearly two centuries is being undermined. The ability of national governments to decide their exchange rate, interest rate, trade flows, investment and output has been savagely crippled by market forces." One of Britain's leading political commentators agreed: "[the state's] powers over the price of money tax rates, industrial policy, the rate of unemployment, have been blown away."

The explosive growth of foreign direct investment, largely in the hands of multinational enterprises (MNEs), also has affected the economic sovereignty of nation-states in a variety of ways. The sense of identity associated with "national" companies and the loyalties flowing from that identity are being replaced by a new global cosmopolitanism, as we saw in Chapter 1. Multinationals have their own political agendas. Thus, the White House complains that Bill Gates, founder and chairman of Microsoft, has met more frequently with Jiang Zemin, President of China, than has Bill Clinton. Microsoft has global business interests that transcend U.S. foreign policy. The company is so large that it does not need the State Department to open doors. Microsoft thinks of itself as a company based in the United States that is global. Its software is making it possible for individuals to communicate across international boundaries and to create groups and information pools that are outside all government authority. To take full advantage of that software, societies are becoming more open, deregulated, and interactive. Steve Ballmer, head of Microsoft's worldwide operations, says, "Once you let people on the Internet, the control aspects are reasonably out the window."

The dominance of MNEs in trade flows has changed the meaning of "exports" and "imports." Are U.S. "exports" simply the goods and services that pass across U.S. borders or do they include the production of U.S. subsidiaries in Canada, Mexico, and Europe and/or the sales to Japanese subsidiaries in the United States? In a wholly integrated, globalized world such issues would not be of great concern, but in a world where national governments retain some policy discretion and people care about national economic "success," they must still be addressed. The conventional benchmarks are, however, useless; the United States, for example, runs a large trade "surplus" if the operations of U.S. MNEs abroad are taken into account, but a large "deficit" if only trade flows across U.S. borders are considered.

The mobility of capital and the importance of FDI have subtly changed the nature of national economic policy. Governments have long worried about "national competitiveness," by which they have usually meant the competitiveness of exports and import competing activities. This concern has expressed itself in the idea that exports should be promoted and imports discouraged. Yet "competitiveness" is no longer predominantly a trade issue. Rather, as Michael Porter emphasized, it is about creating the right business conditions—infrastructure, deregulation of markets, skilled and educated labor, financial stability—to attract or retain mobile capital. Nation-states do retain some degrees of freedom to accomplish this task. Governments still spend considerable shares of their nations' gross domestic products (GDPs), varying from 20 percent in Singapore to 33 percent in the United States, 49 percent in Germany, and 68 percent in Sweden. Behind these differences are correspondingly large differences in underlying economic philosophy: in the size of the welfare state, in the extent of income redistribution through taxes, in industrial and labor-market policies, in ownership and/or regulation of natural monopolies. Globalization is making even this task more difficult, however. The factors of production are increasingly mobile: capital wholly so, and professional and skilled labor partly so. Trade and/or migration shifts the relative returns to capital and labor among countries, eroding differences that national economic policies would like to create.

EMERGENCE OF GLOBAL POLICY REGIMES

Globalization is largely private-sector-driven. It represents a shift in the locus of decision making not only from the nation-state to transnational actors, but also from national governments to the private sector. For this reason, economic liberalization and globalization have gone hand in hand. As this has occurred, there has emerged a demand for activities at scales greater than the nation-state that global markets cannot provide, but which reinforce globalization. These include the rule of law and dispute settlement needed for an open system of trade and investment; common standards for weights, measures, and interconnections; management of global communications networks like aviation, telecommunications, and sea-lanes to prevent congestion and disasters; management of environmental concerns like Antarctica, the atmosphere, and oceans, and to stop cross-border pollution as with acid rain and sewage dumping in shared seas like the North Sea; and the assurance of global financial stability.

All of these require institutional development beyond the nation-state. Some of this development has been self-regulating, because the main commercial users have a collective interest in providing for their common good, as is the case with bond markets (International Securities Markets Association) and industrial standards (the International Standards Organization). In some cases, national organizations provide the institutional cement (as when individual nations' central banks collaborate in the Bank of International Settlements). Some involve mixed public/private-sector participation, as in the International Telecommunications Unions. But mostly there is sovereignty pooling by governments through new institutions (the World Trade Organization; the World Meteorological Organization) and treaty obligations (the Antarctic Treaty; the Montreal Protocol). A complex but rich system of governance is growing up to manage those aspects of globalization that neither global markets nor nation-states acting individually can or will provide. As this governance evolves, it provides a variety of sources of supranational authority, and accordingly decreases the power and authority of the nation-state.

CIVILIZATIONAL CONFLICT

Other tendencies seem destined to subdivide the world at a scale greater than that of the nation-state according to Samuel Huntington (1993). The fundamental source of this new scale of global divisiveness, Huntington says, is neither ideological nor economic, but cultural. The principal divisions are between the groups of nations that constitute different civilizations: Increasingly, it is the clash of civilizations that dominates global politics.

Huntington considers a civilization to be a cultural entity. Villages, regions, ethnic groups, nationalities, religious groups, he says, all have distinct cultures at different levels of cultural heterogeneity. The culture of a village in southern Italy may be different from that of a village in northern Italy, but both share in a common Italian culture that distinguishes them from German villages. European communities, in turn, share cultural features that distinguish them from Arab or Chinese communities. Arabs, Chinese, and Westerners are not part of any broader cultural entity, however. They constitute civilizations. *A civilization is the highest cultural grouping of people and the broadest level of cultural identity people have short of that which distinguishes humans from other species.* It is defined both by common objective elements, such as language, history, religion, customs, institutions, and by the subjective self-identification of people, the product of centuries of enrichment and reinforcement.

Civilizational identity, Huntington says, will be increasingly important in the future, and the world will be shaped in large measure by the interactions among seven or eight major civilizations: Western, Confucian, Japanese,

Islamic, Hindu, Slavic-Orthodox, Latin American/Catholic, and possibly African. The most important conflicts of the future will occur along the geographical and cultural "fault lines" separating these civilizations, for example, in the Balkans and the Caucasus.

There is, he says, a chain of cause and effect that links globalization to contemporary expressions of cultural identity. As the world becomes a smaller place, the interactions between peoples of different civilizations are increasing. These increasing interactions intensify *civilizational consciousness*—the awareness of differences between civilizations and commonalities within civilizations. This growth of civilization consciousness is sharpened by the role of the West. The West is at a peak of power. In reaction, a return-to-the-roots phenomenon accompanied by a rejection of Western values is occurring among non-Western civilizations. Groups opposed to the West are trying to rally support among members of their own civilizations—what has been called a "kin-country syndrome."

One consequence is that economic regionalism is increasing along civilizational lines. The European community rests on the shared foundation of European culture and Western Christianity. Common culture is facilitating the rapid expansion of economic relations between the People's Republic of China and Hong Kong, Taiwan, Singapore, and the overseas Chinese communities in other Asian countries. Culture and religion also form the basis of the Economic Cooperation Organization, which brings together 10 non-Arab Muslim countries.

Huntington sees the fault lines between civilizations replacing the political and ideological boundaries of the Cold War as the flash points for crisis and bloodshed. The clash occurs at two levels. At the micro-level, adjacent groups along the fault lines struggle, often violently, over the control of territory and each other, as in the case of Bosnia. At the macro-level, different civilizations compete for relative military and economic power, struggle over the control of international institutions and third parties, and competitively promote their particular political and religious values. The central axis of this political and economic conflict as Huntington sees it, will be between the West and "the Rest," driven largely by the responses of non-Western civilizations, such as Islam, to Western power and the diffusion of Western values.

THE RISE OF "REGION STATES"

Nation-states are also losing their role to smaller regional entities. Rosabeth Kanter, who we encountered in Chapter 1, says that one of the great paradoxes of our time is that the *cosmopolitans* who control MNEs are antilocal, valuing choice over loyalty to particular communities and cultures,

whereas *locals* value loyalties over choices, preferring to preserve distinctions and protect their own groups. Cosmopolitans try to break through barriers and overcome limits by creating powerful, border-spanning networks; locals, threatened by globalization and the spread of universal values, react by trying to preserve and erect new barriers by political means. The paradox is thus that *while economies are globalizing, politics is localizing.* Smaller entities are trying to achieve or restore local sovereignty.

The Japanese-American economist Kenichi Ohmae argues that these smaller units can become viable economic entities: The role of the nation-state is not merely being diminished as globalization increases; nation-states may be dysfunctional units for organizing economic activity in a world with fewer and lower boundaries. On the global economic map, he says, the lines that matter are not national boundaries, but those defining *region states.* The boundaries of the region state need not be imposed by political fiat. They are drawn by the global market for goods and services. The primary linkages of region states tend to be with the global economy and not with their host nations. They are effective points of entry into the global economy because the very characteristics that define them are shaped by the demands of that economy. They tend to have between 5 and 25 million people, centering on a significant metropolitan region. This is small enough for its citizens to share certain economic and consumer interests but of adequate size to justify the infrastructure—communication and transportation links and quality professional services—necessary to participate economically on a global scale. It is at such a scale, he says, that one can best discern the cultural factors that bear on the work ethic, on the nature of demand, on preferences for one kind of organizational structure over another, and on attitudes to risk taking and experimentation.

It is these cultural factors that are leading to increasing distinctiveness as globalization runs its course. Culture—the philosophical ideals, values, ideologies, religious beliefs, and passions that give meaning to people's lives, producing differences in beliefs, goals, planning, and action—is the differentiator that is being sharpened not merely at civilizational but also at region-state scale by increasing interdependence.

Others concur. Joel Garreau argues that North America in fact consists of nine regions with different cultural traditions and economic and political interests. Daniel Delamaide divides Europe into eight "superregions." William Barnes and Larry Lederer, writing for the National League of Cities, argue that the U.S. economy is a common market of local economic regions. Neil Pierce calls these regions "citystates," characterized by alliances between strong companies and strong core communities that link directly to the global economy, their identities sharpened by their awareness of cultural differences.

THE CULTURAL FOUNDATIONS OF TOGETHERNESS AND DISTINCTIVENESS

What do we know about culture and the ways it varies across the globe? To Dutch anthropologist Geert Hofstede (1980) culture is the "collective programming of the mind" that differentiates the motivation and behavior of members of one social group from those of other groups. It is through culture that societies give meaning to their environments, organizing their life around particular symbols and myths. Culture shapes perceptions and behavior by directing that selective attention be paid to some details of reality, permitting some actions and forbidding others.

Central to this programming of the mind is the transmission of *values,* broad preferences for one state of affairs over others. People face moral dilemmas, ambiguous circumstances where several choices of proper behavior are possible. Values are priorities for sorting out and implementing one code of behavior rather than others. The act of prioritizing involves emotional commitment. The commitment arises because values are learned during the process of childhood socialization, when individuals come to accept that a particular form of life is meaningful.

What people are socialized to is a particular *paradigm,* a dominant set of beliefs that organizes the way they and other members of their group perceive and interpret the world around them: A *social paradigm* contains the survival information needed for the maintenance of a culture. It results from generations of learning whereby dysfunctional beliefs and values are discarded in favor of those most suited to collective survival. An individual element of a social paradigm is difficult to dislodge once it becomes firmly entrenched because shared definitions of reality are anchored in it. The values, norms, beliefs, and institutions of paradigms are not only beliefs about what the world is like. They are guides to action, and they serve the function of legitimating and justifying courses of action, that is, they function as ideologies, and ideologies drive politics.

Is each culture idiosyncratic or are there systematic variations? This was the question asked by Geert Hofstede as he worked for a large multinational corporation that was seeking to understand why the same facts and instructions sent from headquarters to corporate officers based in different cultures produced different results. After completing attitudinal surveys in 40 different countries and analyzing the results, Hofstede concluded that differences among cultures were far greater than differences within them, lending strong support to the idea that most nation-states were characterized by a dominant cultural mainstream (social paradigm), although they might also have subgroups with cultures valuing alternative or opposing ideals. He also concluded that cultures varied along four separate dimensions. He called the first three *individualism-collectivism, power-distance,* and *uncertainty avoidance,* and the fourth,

masculinity. A better term for the last would be *sex-role differentiation.* Let us look at each of these and then see how they combine to differentiate the world's cultures.

Individualism versus Collectivism

The first important dimension of variation was between cultures in which the individual is the locus of responsibility and action, and cultures in which it is the collectivity that matters. In individualist cultures Hofstede's respondents said that individuals should look after their own interests and the interests of their immediate family (husband, wife, and children). On the other hand, in collectivist cultures it was said that any person through birth and later events belongs to one or more cohesive collectives ("in-groups"), from which he or she cannot detach himself or herself. The in-group (e.g., the extended family with grandparents and either paternal or maternal uncles, aunts, and cousins—or on a larger scale, the nation and its governmental institutions) should protect the interests of its members but in exchange can expect their permanent loyalty. Study Table 2.1.

Individualist cultures tend to share the following traits:

- Worship of the independent actor
- Protestant (modernist) ethic
- Market economies
- Balanced-power political systems
- Policies and practices that allow for initiative and apply to all (universalism)
- Promotion from both inside and outside organizations, based on market value (cosmopolitanism)

Collectivist cultures, on the other hand, are most typically characterized by the following:

- Stress on identity and roots
- Traditionalist ethic
- Nonmarket economies
- Unbalanced-power political systems
- Policies and practices that are based on loyalty and individual sense of duty and vary according to specific social relations (particularism)
- Promotion from inside, based on family and friendship networks (localism)

Hofstede showed that *the degree of individualism correlates highly with contemporary levels of economic development across the globe, as measured by per capita*

TABLE 2.1

Contrasts between individualist and collectivist cultures

Traits of Highly Individualist Cultures	Traits of Collectivist Cultures
(i) Emphasis on individual initiative, decisions, and achievement	(i) Emphasis on belonging to groups and organizations that make decisions and protect people in exchange for their loyalty
(ii) The belief that in society, everyone is supposed to take care of himself or herself and his or her immediate family	(ii) "We" consciousness and collectivity orientation: identity rooted in the social system
(iii) "I" consciousness and self-orientation: identity based in the individual	(iii) Emotional dependence of the individual on organizations and institutions
(iv) Emotional independence of the individual from organizations or institutions	(iv) The invasion of private life by organizations and clans to which the individual belongs: opinions predetermined
(v) Belief that everyone has a right to a private life and opinion	(v) Expertise, order, duty, security provided by the organization or clan
(vi) The idea that the same value standards should apply to all: universalism	(vi) Value standards that differ for in-groups and out-groups: particularism

gross national product ($R = 0.82$; see Figure 2.1). His "individualism" scores are charted in Figure 2.2.

Power-Distance

Power-distance is the characteristic of a culture that defines the extent to which the less-powerful persons in society accept inequality in power and consider large social distances to be normal. Inequality exists within all cultures, but its extent and the degree of it that is accepted vary from one culture to another. The belief patterns of "high P-D" and "low P-D" cultures are contrasted in Table 2.2. High-inequality cultures have the following typical traits:

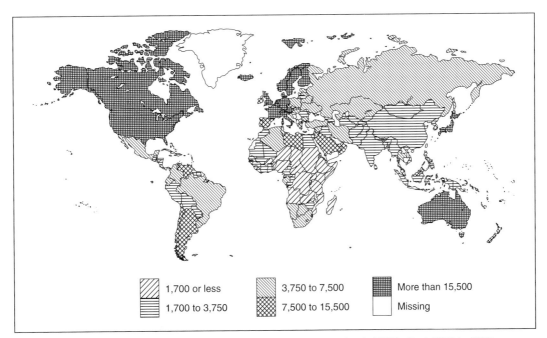

1,700 or less
1,700 to 3,750
3,750 to 7,500
7,500 to 15,500
More than 15,500
Missing

FIGURE 2.1 Real gross domestic product (GDP) per capita, in PPP$. Real GDP is GDP that has been adjusted to account for the fact that official exchange rates to U.S. dollars frequently do not reflect the relative purchasing power of currencies. The United Nations International Comparison Project developed models of real GDP on an internationally comparable scale using purchasing power parities (PPP) instead of exchange rates as conversion factors. It is the resulting "international dollars" that are reflected here. [*Source*: Data from the United Nations Development Programme (UNDP), *Human Development Report, 1995* (New York: Oxford University Press, 1995), pp. 178–208.]

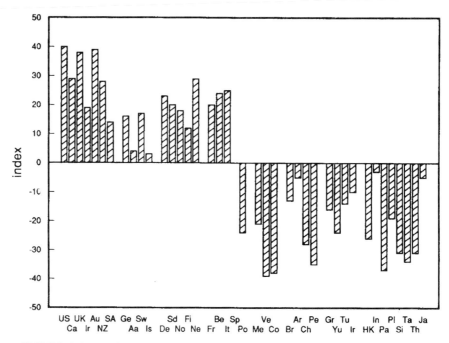

FIGURE 2.2   Hofstede's individualism index scores plotted for groups of countries as deviations from the mean.

- Autocratic or oligarchic governments
- Sudden changes in form of government (revolution and/or instability)
- Polarization between left and right with a weak center if political parties exist
- Tax system protects the wealthy
- Success of religions stressing stratification
- Ideologies of power polarization
- Elitist theories about society

- Greater centralization and tall organization pyramids with a large proportion of supervisory personnel
- Large wage differentials

An analogous list of traits for low-inequality cultures is as follows:

- Pluralist governments based on outcome of majority votes

TABLE 2.2

Contrasts between high P-D and low P-D cultures

Belief Patterns in High P-D Cultures	*Belief Patterns in Low P-D Cultures*
(i) There is and should be an order of inequality in which everyone has his or her rightful place: high and low are of different kinds and are protected by this hierarchical order.	(i) Inequality and hierarchy in society should be minimized: All should be interdependent and should have equal rights.
(ii) A few should be independent: most should be dependent.	(ii) Any power that is used should be legitimate and is subject to the judgement between good and evil.
(iii) Power is a basic fact of society that antedates good or evil: Its legitimacy is irrelevant	(iii) The way to change a social system is by redistributing power.
(iv) The way to change a social system is by dethroning those in power.	(iv) There is an underlying harmony between the powerful and the powerless.
(v) There will always be conflict between the powerful and the powerless.	(v) Cooperation among the powerless can be brought about based on solidarity.
(vi) Cooperation among the powerless is difficult to bring about because of the low faith that people have in each other.	

- No sudden changes in form of government (evolution and stability)
- Political parties that exist tend to be in the center, with relatively weak left and right wings
- Tax system aimed at redistributing wealth
- Success of religions stressing equality
- Ideologies of power equalization
- Pluralist theories about society
- Less centralization and flatter organization pyramids with small proportion of supervisory personnel
- Smaller wage differentials

A useful indicator of power-distance is the degree of income inequality within countries. For a map showing the global variations, see Figure 2.3. Hofstede's P-D scores are charted in Figure 2.4. If countries are cross-classified using their individualism and P-D scores, insights are provided about the principal types of political economies to be found in the world today. Refer to Box.2.1.

Uncertainty Avoidance

The third of Hofstede's axes of cultural variation is that of "uncertainty avoidance"—the characteristic of a culture that defines the extent to which people within the culture are made nervous by situations they consider to be unstructured, unclear, or unpredictable, and the extent to which they try to avoid such situations by adopting strict codes of behavior and a belief in absolute truths. Table 2.3 contrasts the belief patterns of "high U-A" and "low U-A" cultures.

The traits of high uncertainty-avoidance cultures are:

- Greater dependence of citizens on authorities and less tolerance for citizen protest
- More elaborate legal system
- More intolerant activist state religions
- Popularity of ideological thinking
- More structuring of activities
- More written rules
- More ritual behavior

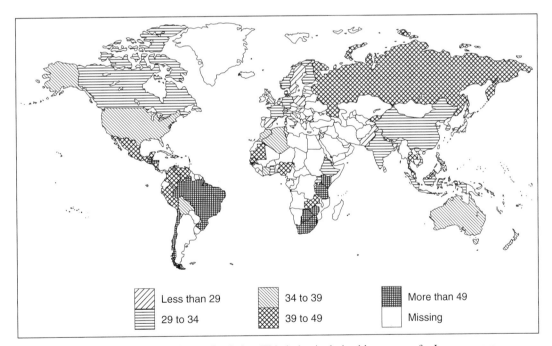

FIGURE 2.3 Income inequality index. This index is derived by means of a Lorenz curve, which measures the difference between a curve that represents the hypothetical ideal case where all socioeconomic classes have an equal share of national income, and a curve derived by plotting the actual income distribution among the socioeconomic classes of a given country. The country with the highest index value, and thus the greatest income inequality, is Brazil; the country with the lowest index is Hungary. In general, the countries of northern Europe have the most nearly equitable income distributions and those of Latin America and southern Africa have the greatest inequalities. [*Source*: Data from the World Bank, *World Development Report 1995* (New York: Oxford University Press, 1995), pp. 220–221.]

BOX 2.1 A Typology of Political Economies

Types of Political Economies in the
Individualism/Power-Distance Space

	High P–D	Mean	Low P–D
High Individualism	Laissez-faire liberalism-		Romantic egalitarianism
		Polyarchy	Welfare state
		Oligarchy	Democratic Socialism
Mean	Caste		
	Feudalism		
Low Individualism	"Traditional society:" Gemeinschaft		Ideal-type Communism

Countries Located in the
Individualism/Power-Distance Space

	High P–D	Mean	Low P–D
High Individualism	Laissez-faire liberalism-		Anglo
		Latin America	
		South Africa	Scandinavia
Mean	India	Japan	
		Middle East	
Low Individualism	East & S.E. Asia		

The two diagrams above show where different types of political economies lie in the two-dimensional individualism/collectivism versus power-distance space, and where individual nation-states are located in this same space.

The top left-hand corner (high individualism, high power-distance) is occupied by *ideal-type laissez-faire liberalism*, the main features of which are the following:

- *View of human nature*. Humans are highly individualistic and competitive, motivated by rational calculation of self-interest.
- *Nature of social system*. Free markets and private property are the foundation of economic and political freedom. The 'invisible hand' of the market is the allocator. Society is the sum of the individuals who make it up: If individuals maximize their

welfare, this will produce the greatest social good.
- *Central values*. Values include individual liberty and private property (laissez-faire) as well as freedom from restraint.
- *Orientation to social change*. Change occurs in an incremental way as a result of individual actions.
- *The ideal system*. Free-market capitalism exists. Production is

On the other hand, the traits of more tolerant cultures are:

- "Looser" societies
- Stronger feelings of citizen competence and more tolerance for citizen protest
- More casuistic approach to legal issues
- De facto religious tolerance
- Popularity of pragmatic thinking
- Less structuring of activities
- Fewer written rules
- Less ritual behavior

Hofstede's U-A scores are charted in Figure 2.5. *One indicator of the extent to which economic uncertainty*

prevails is the inflation rate mapped in Figure 2.6. If countries are cross-classified on the basis of their P-D and U-A scores, fascinating contrasts in social organization are revealed. Refer to Box 2.2.

Sex-Role Differentiation

The final dimension identified by Hofstede arises because cultures use the biological difference between men and women to define vastly different social roles for the sexes. Highly "masculine" cultures expect men to be assertive, ambitious, and competitive, to strive for material success, and to respect whatever is big, strong, and fast. They expect women to nurture, to care for the quality of life, for children, and for the weak. Less-masculine cultures define

increased through individual decisions. Least government is the best government.

- *Concept of community.* The concept is 'Community of Limited Liability'—the marketplace as community.

The bottom right-hand corner (low individualism, low power-distance) is occupied by *ideal-type communism*, the main features of which are these:

- *View of human nature.* Humans have no meaning that is not provided by the community of which they are part; the individual's interest is subjugated to that of the collectivity.
- *Nature of the social order.* Social order is based on equality, to eliminate the class conflict that destabilizes capitalism.
- *Central values.* Equality and community solidarity are important.
- *Orientation to social change.* Change is produced by inherent conflicts and contradictions within the system; it is dialectical.
- *Ideal system.* Worker/community ownership and control of the means of production through democratic decision-making processes exists.

- *Conception of community.* Community is the solidarity of equal power based on the abolition of social classes.

The main diagonal, running from top left to bottom right, is readily recognizable as the axis along which capitalism and socialism are opposed.

Off the diagonal, in the lower-left quadrant, the central values are those of *authoritarian conservatism*, including feudal and other aristocratic systems, as well as caste-stratified and fascist societies. Its main features are these:

- *View of human nature.* Cynical view of humans as inherently aggressive, selfish, competitive and hierarchical, motivated by biological urges.
- *Nature of the social order.* Humans need society to protect themselves from each other. Inequality and hierarchy are natural and necessary.
- *Central values.* These values involve authority, order, and tradition as well as freedom within prescribed bounds.
- *Orientation to social change.* Change is disruptive and should be minimized.
- *Ideal system.* Paternalistic capitalism exists, where there is stability through elite-controlled growth.

- *Conception of community.* "Gemeinschaft," as illustrated in the feudal estate, is ideal.

The top-right quadrant is best typified by the twentieth-century philosophy of the *welfare state*:

- *View of human nature.* This view is the same as liberalism, but not as cynical. Individuals can be motivated by altruism under certain circumstances.
- *Nature of social system.* Social system has tendencies toward instability, concentration of power, and injustice; it requires government fine-tuning to keep it running smoothly. Capitalism with a meritocratic structure is the best form of society.
- *Central values.* Individual civil rights and equal opportunity are important.
- *Orientation to social change.* Humans, through the vehicle of the state, must intervene to make appropriate modifications in the system. Social change is evolutionary.
- *The ideal system.* Welfare-state capitalism exists. Expand and adjust the pie through state-guided development.
- *Concept of community.* "Community without Propinquity": Social networks and associations are not bound by territoriality.

overlapping social roles for the sexes, in which men need not be ambitious or competitive but may put the quality of life over material success and may respect whatever is small, weak, and slow. In both masculine and nonmasculine cultures, the dominant values within political and work organizations are those of men. In masculine cultures, these organizational values stress material success and assertiveness; in nonmasculine cultures, they stress quality of life and welfare for the weak.

The belief patterns of more- and less-masculine cultures are contrasted in Table 2.4. Highly masculine cultures share the following traits:

- The emphasis is on aggressive pursuit of success.

- Men and women follow different types of higher-level education.
- Men are breadwinners, and women are cake-winners.
- Some occupations are considered typically male, others, female.
- There are fewer women in more-qualified and better-paid jobs.
- Fertility is based on male income.

In cultures with less sex-role differentiation, the dominant traits are as follows:

- Emphasis is on caring and sharing.

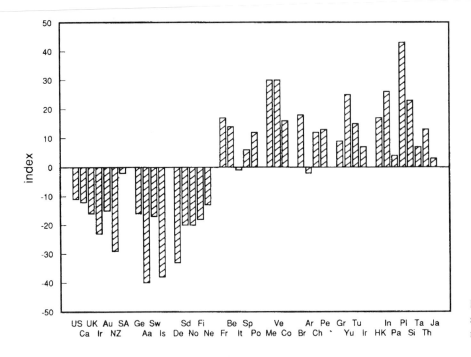

FIGURE 2.4   Hofstede's P-D index scores plotted as deviations from the mean.

- Men and women follow the same types of higher education.
- Men and women can both be breadwinners.
- There is less occupational segregation.
- There are more women in more-qualified and better-paid jobs
- Fertility is controlled by female labor force opportunity

Among the indicators of sex-role differentiation and therefore of degree of masculinity are the total fertility rate, the extent of female labor force participation, and the extent to which women participate in the political process. These are mapped in Figures 2.7, 2.8, and 2.9. Hofstede's "masculinity' scores are charted in Figure 2.10. For the results of cross-classifying countries on their U-A and masculinity scores see Box 2.3.

From Family to Culture Region: An Explanation of Cultural Traditions

Another anthropologist, Emmanuel Todd, has offered a bold hypothesis to explain why distinct cultural traditions

TABLE 2.3

Contrasts between high U-A and low U-A cultures

Belief Patterns in High U-A Cultures	*Belief Patterns in Low U-A Cultures*
(i) High anxiety and stress: There is an inherent uncertainty in life that is a continuous threat.	(i) Ease, lower stress: The uncertainty inherent in life is more easily accepted and each day is taken as it comes.
(ii) Strong superegos and more showing of emotions: Assertive nature of self and others is accepted.	(ii) Weaker superegos and less showing of emotions: Assertive behavior is frowned upon.
(iii) Strong need for consensus: Conflict and competition can unleash aggression and should therefore be avoided.	(iii) More acceptance of dissent: Conflict and competition can be contained on the level of fair play and used constructively.
(iv) Intolerance: Deviant persons and ideas are dangerous.	(iv) Deviance is not felt as threatening; there is greater tolerance.
(v) Concerns with security in life: Conservatism, law, and order are essential.	(v) There is more willingness to take risks in life and less conservatism.
(vi) Achievement is defined in terms of security.	(vi) Achievement is determined in terms of recognition.
(vii) Search for ultimate, absolute truths and values is ongoing.	(vii) Relativism and empiricism exist.
(viii) Written rules and regulations are needed.	(viii) The belief exists that there should be a few rules as possible.
(ix) Belief in experts and their knowledge exists: Ordinary citizens are incompetent versus the authorities.	(ix) There is a belief in generalists and common sense and that the authorities are there to serve the citizens.

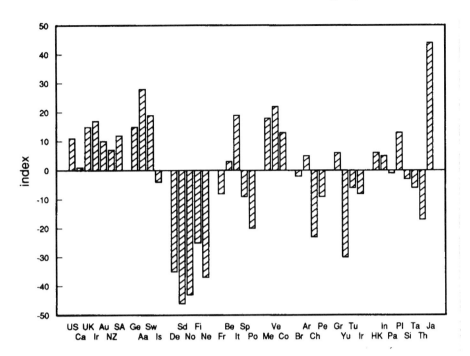

FIGURE 2.5   Hofstede's U-A index scores, plotted as deviations from the mean.

persist and reproduce contrasting political ideologies. *Family relations,* he says, *serve as the model for political systems by defining the relationship between the individual and authority.* The family shapes the worldview of its children, reproducing people who share the same beliefs and values. Each generation absorbs parental values and bases its own child rearing on those values; the system is self-perpetuating. In turn, the values shape the individual's expectations about larger social, economic, and political relationships beyond the family at the level of region, nation-state, and civilization. The resulting political ideologies are no more than family relations writ large.

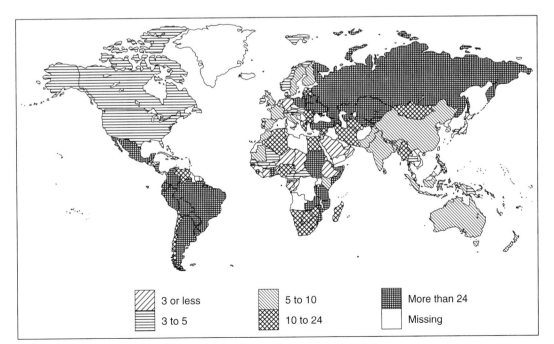

FIGURE 2.6   Average annual inflation rate, 1980–1993 [*Source*: Data from the World Bank, *World Development Report, 1995* (New York: Oxford University Press, 1995), pp. 162–163.]

BOX 2.2 Types of Social Organization

	Small Power-Distance	Large Power-Distance
Weak Uncertainty Avoidance	Countries: Anglo, Scandinavian, Netherlands Organization type: implicitly structured Implicit model of organization: market	Countries: Less-developed Southeast Asian Organization type: personnel bureaucracy Implicit model of organization: family
Strong Uncertainty Avoidance	Countries: German-speaking, Finland, Israel Organization type: workflow bureaucracy Implicit model of organization: well-oiled machine	Countries: Latin, Japan, Near Eastern, Socialist Organization type: full bureaucracy Implicit model of organization; pyramid

If power-distance is cross-classified with uncertainty avoidance, contrasts in social organization are revealed. One sees, for example, the Germanic well-oiled machine (lower-left quadrant) contrasting with Southeast Asia's family-type personnel bureaucracies (upper-right quadrant). The principle diagonal contrasts Anglo-Saxon an Latin Europe.

There are across the globe, he argues, only eight basic family types. These are mapped in Figure 2.11. The first four types are derived by cross-classifying the opposing forces of liberty-authority and equality-inequality (Hofstede's individualism/collectivism versus power-distance) to define the essential features of the four fundamental family types found in Europe:

The first of the family types, the *absolute nuclear family* of the Anglo-Saxon world, socializes children to individualized values: They must strive to succeed to be able to support their own independent nuclear family units.

	Inequality	Equality
Liberty	1. Absolute nuclear family	2. Egalitarian nuclear family
Authori ty	3. Authoritarian family	4. Community family

One result has been a preference for utilitarian concepts of individual rights and liberties: Individuals must be the ones to act to maximize their own welfare; the best society is one

---

TABLE 2.4

Contrasts between more- and less-masculine cultures

Belief Patterns in Highly Masculine Cultures	Belief Patterns in Less-Masculine Cultures
(i) Men should behave assertively and women should care.	(i) Men need not be assertive but can also take caring roles.
(ii) Sex roles in society should be clearly differentiated: father used as a model by boys; mother by girls.	(ii) Sex roles in society should be fluid; both father and mother used as models by boys and girls.
(iii) Men should dominate in all settings: there is a machismo (ostentative manliness) ideal; women can be kept ignorant.	(iii) Differences in sex roles should not mean differences in power; unisex and androgyny ideal; more equal partnership of men and women.
(iv) Weaker position of the mother in the family: male-dominated fertility decisions.	(iv) Stronger position of the female: female decisions in fertility decisions.

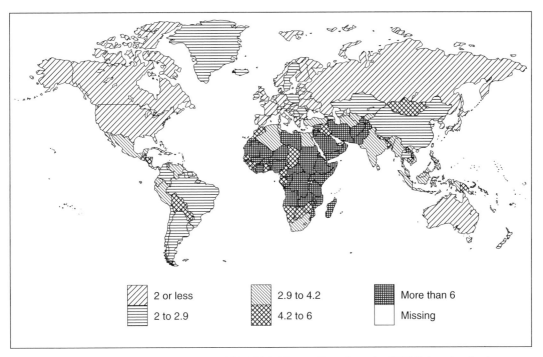

FIGURE 2.7   Total fertility rate, 1991–1994. [*Source*: Data from the *1995 Britannica Book of the Year* (Chicago: Encyclopaedia Britannica, 1995), pp. 786–791.]

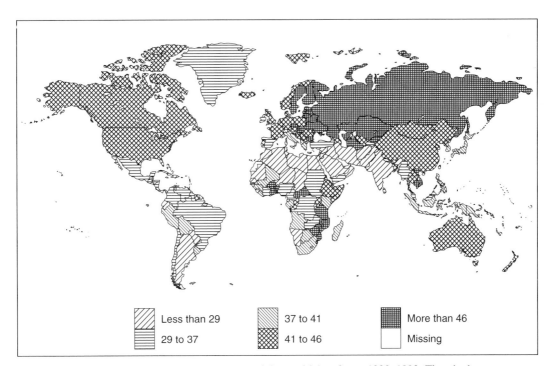

FIGURE 2.8   Women as a percentage of the total labor force, 1990–1992. That the lowest rates are in Islamic countries, followed by many Catholic nations, India, and Japan reveals that religious values are among the strongest factors in establishing and maintaining sex-role differentiation. [*Source*: Data from the *1995 Britannica Book of the Year* (Chicago: Encyclopaedia Britannica, 1995), pp. 798–803.]

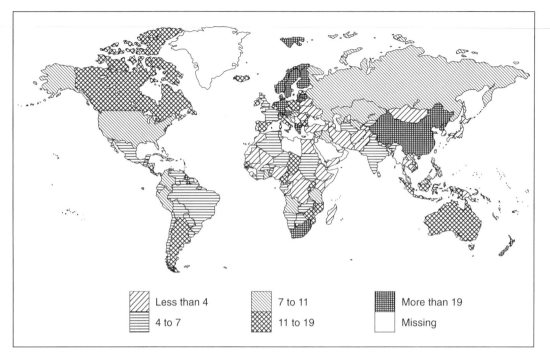

FIGURE 2.9 Females as a percentage of legislators in national parliament, 1994. [*Source*: Data from UNDP, *Human Development Report, 1995* (New York: Oxford University Press, 1995), pp. 60–62.]

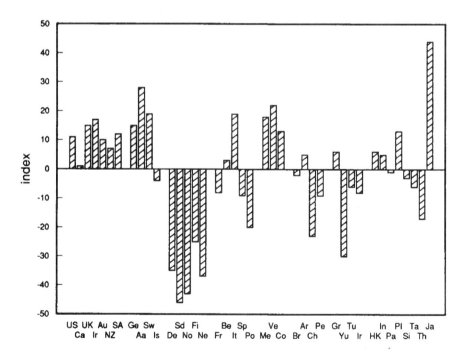

FIGURE 2.10 Hofstede's masculinity scores, plotted as deviations from the mean.

BOX 2.3 Types of Motivation Driving Behavior

	Low Sex-Role Differences	High Sex-Role Differences
Weak Uncertainty Avoidance	Countries: Northern Europe and Netherlands Motivation by success and belonging Success measured partly collectively and partly by the quality of human relationships and the living environment	Countries: United States, Great Britain and former Dominions Motivation by individual achievement Success measured by wealth, recognition, and self-actualization
Strong Uncertainty Avoidance	Countries: Socialist Motivation by security and belonging Success measured by group solidarity and performance rather than by individual wealth	Countries: Japan, German-Latin, Greece Motivation by personal security Success measured by wealth and by hard work within the organization

Cross-classification of countries on the uncertainty-avoidance and masculinity axes provides insights into four different types of motivation that drive behavior. In the diagram, "Anglo" achievement orientation contrasts with the collective-security orientation of the socialist state; likewise, Northern European concepts of individual success combined with belonging contrast with German-Japanese notions of personal security secured by hard work within the organization.

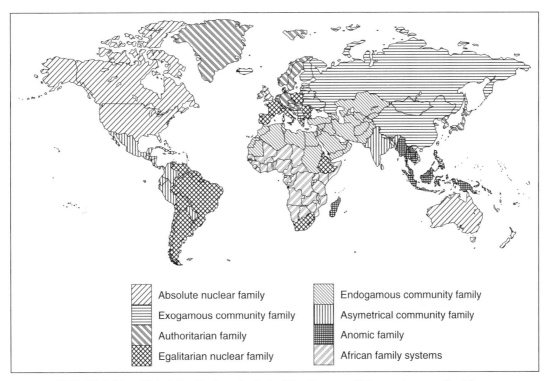

FIGURE 2.11   Global distribution of principal family types. This map is generalized from Todd's illustrations, which show detailed regional variations within nation-states, particularly in Western and Southern Europe. [*Source*: Data from Emmanuel Todd, *The Explanation of Ideology* (Oxford: Basil Blackwell, 1985), p. vi.]

in which each individual has maximized his or her own happiness. The kind of philosophy that comes to characterize such a society is laissez-faire liberalism.

Opposed to the individualist nuclear family is the *exogamous community family,* characterized by equality between brothers and cohabitation of married sons and their parents. The principal regions in which this family form has dominated historically are Russia, Albania, central Italy, China, and Vietnam. In these regions, in Todd's view, modern revolutionary movements have transferred the egalitarian values of the family to the level of the state. Individual rights are crushed by the political system in the same way they were destroyed in the past by the extended family.

The *authoritarian family* involves inequality of brothers laid down by inheritance rules, with transfer of an unbroken patrimony to one of the sons. The traditional regions dominated by this family form were Germany, Austria, Bohemia, peripheral regions of France, northern Spain and Portugal, Japan, and Korea.Primogeniture implies inequality, and with inequality there is a presumption of the dominance of the powerful and the deference of the weak. The result at the societal level is the use of authority to guarantee stability, frequently manifested in the development of elaborate bureaucratic hierarchies and of large-scale organization. Thus, feudal aristocratic systems, fascism, bureaucratic socialism, and Catholicism can and often have coexisted. There is also strong tendency to demand conformity and to persecute that which is alien or different: The notion of cultural "purity" is strong. What results are the mainstream values of authoritarian conservatism.

Dialectically opposed to the authoritarian family type is the *egalitarian nuclear family* of northern France and Italy, central and southern Spain, central Portugal, Greece, Romania, Poland, and Latin America. The defining features are equality of brothers laid down by inheritance rules. The outcome of socialization by his family type is a continual tension between the individualism demanded by the nuclear family and the equality built into the rules of inheritance. The first demands individual effort that can only result in inequality; the second requires rules and regulations to ensure that the goal of equality is met. As a result of this fundamental contradiction, Todd says, one sees a continuing tension at the societal level between liberal democracy on the one hand and bureaucratized central controls on the other, and at its worst, between anarchy and militarism.

To complete his world map, Todd identified four additional family types. One socializes children in the Arab world, Turkey, Afghanistan, Azerbaijan, Turkmenistan, Uzbekistan, and Tadzhikistan. The *endogamous community family* is characterized by equality between brothers established by inheritance rules, cohabitation of married sons with their parents, and frequent marriages among cousins.

This is the anthropological reality, says Todd, that lies beneath the theological appearance of Islam, built of close-knit groups and clans. The extended household remains all-important, but the authoritarian role of the father is replaced as a regulatory mechanism by custom. Relationships tend to be horizontal rather than hierarchical and vertical, and the power of the fraternal bond surpasses the others, a bond that is strengthened by the presumption of equality. Islamic tradition recognizes two fundamental institutions, religion and the family. Accordingly, central administration and the state remain relatively weak, and this weakness of the state results in political fragmentation. Islam rejects both the Western notion of the freely acting individual who escapes both the family and the state and the communist notion of the individual escaping from his family into the body of the state; instead, it recognizes only two levels of social integration, the family and the community of believers (the *Ummah*).

A sixth family type is the *asymmetrical community family* of central and southern India and Sri Lanka, dominated by systems of *caste.* The essential family features are equality between brothers defined by inheritance rules and cohabitation of married sons with their parents. Such families socialize children to a society in which groups within society are separated from each other, obsessed by fear that physical contact is polluting. Endogamous marriage is enforced within the subcaste, the small localized groups corresponding to particular occupations and regions. An overarching ideology is that of racism, of the superiority of certain castes and the inferiority of others, with people born into positions in which they must remain throughout their lives. The only way out is through reincarnation, provided that people behave in ways exemplary of their given status in the present life. The orientation, then, is antithetical to change, demanding obedience, guaranteeing the stability of the caste hierarchies, and promoting structured inequality. Read Appendix 2.1 for a discussion of the difficulties faced by India in its attempt to develop, as a consequence of culture as expressed in caste and religion.

An *anomic family* form is characteristic of Burma, Cambodia, Laos, Thailand, Malaysia, Indonesia, the Philippines, Madagascar, and the South American Indian cultures, Todd says. It is defined by uncertainty about equality between brothers, inheritance rules that are egalitarian in theory but flexible in practice, cohabitation of married children with their parents rejected in theory but accepted in practice, and consanguineous marriage possible, often frequent. A particular type of social and political system characterizes states with this family form, not centralized and hierarchical (which is associated with vertical family systems) but "centrified." The anomic family works in a particular way, unregulated, permissive, not accustoming its members to the principle of discipline, and only weakly integrated by communitarian ideas of neighborhood cooperation. So the centrified state, equally weakly integrated, with the family and the communitarian idea the only basis of cohesion, is likewise equally weakly structured. There are advantages: relative equality of men and women; absence of constraint that permits rapid inroads to be made by new ideas and technologies, and their ready absorption into the structure of the family and society. The disadvantages reside in the absence of traditional power bases for organizing and running a modern state, a task that therefore frequently falls into the lap of the only hierarchically organized, goal-oriented bureaucracy available, the military.

A final category is reserved by Todd for sub-Saharan *African family systems,* characterized by absence of stable interpersonal relationships, except between mother and children, and by polygyny (men have multiple wives and sexual partners). Vertical (patrimonial) power relationships are limited, weakening socialization to the concept of authority, and undermining the idea of discipline. The instability of relationships doomed to failure many of the experiments in democracy that the colonial powers left in place. With weak bases for state formation, the army has become preeminent, the only organized game in town, often acting in support of a charismatic leader. But lack of stability has

meant frequent power shifts that drive a vicious circle: Because there is instability, there is poor economic performance; because economic performance is weak, there is more instability. See Figure 2.12.

Todd's hypotheses are provocative, providing an explanation for the persistence of deep-seated cultural differences that serve as a counterweight to the globalizing force of multinational enterprise. As a management consultant, Hofstede realized the importance of these differences. There are, he said, no universal solutions to organization and management problems, only culturally relative ones. Thus, the Confucian work ethic has provided a particular way of achieving growth in East Asia (Box 2.4). Familial and regional ties are of fundamental importance to the economic practice and business organization of Chinese society. For details, read Appendix 2.2. Civilizations, nation-states, and region-states have different cultural heritages that are largely invisible but have powerful consequences, not only for multinational corporations, but for economic growth and political life viewed more broadly. The invisible part—the *collective unconscious*—consists of the values that are held by a majority of the population and that are transferred from generation to generation through early life experience in family and schools, and through

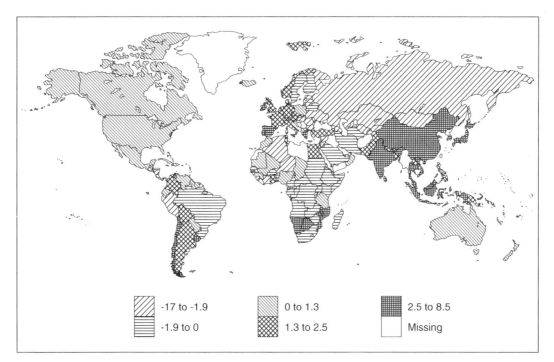

FIGURE 2.12 Annual growth rates of real per capita GNP, 1985–1994. This map reveals the rapid rates of economic growth experienced in recent years by the newly industrializing nations of eastern and southern Asia. It also shows severely negative effects of the collapse of communism on the countries of Eastern Europe and the successor states of the former Soviet Union, which have experienced a sharp decline in national product per capita. Note, too, that many other countries have suffered economic deterioration during this period. [*Source*: Data from the World Bank, *The World Bank Atlas 1996* (New York: Oxford University Press, 1995), pp. 18–19.]

BOX 2.4 Cash Value of the Confucian Work Ethic

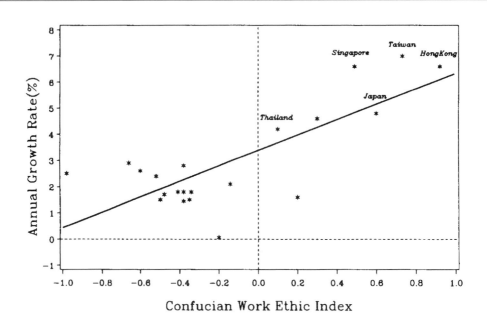

The Confucian work ethic involves a number of ideas: that the government must assume full responsibility for the well-being of its people; that leadership is obligated to provide, to enrich, and to educate the people; and that bureaucrats are not merely functionaries, but leaders, intellectuals, and teachers.hers. Driven by this ethic, Japan and the "Four Tigers"of East Asia have transformed themselves into 'development states' with single-minded attention to wealth and economic power that has centered on the ability of the central government to forge bonds of trust with the business community, the intelligentsia, and the working class. To measure the consequences, Michael H. Bond and Geert Hofstede developed a 'Confucian Work Ethic' index. This index was estimated for a group of 21 countries. Values were compared with the average annual growth rates of per capita GDP from 1965 to 1984, as in the accompanying graph, and it was found that there was a strong relationship between the two ($R = 0.77$). Bond and Hofstede concluded that the Confucian work ethic had a real 'cash value'; that is, that it was the driving force behind "Confucian capitalism,"predicated on harmony and consensus rather than competitive conflict in the market, leading to coordination of actions between government, business, and labor. See Michael H. Bond and Geert Hofstede, 'The Cash Value of Confucian Values,' in Stewart R. Clegg and S. Gordon Redding (eds.), *Capitalism in Contrasting Cultures* (Berlin and New York: Walter de Gruyter, 1990), pp. 383–389.

socialization in organizations and institutions. The stability of cultures over long periods of history is achieved through a system of constant reinforcement, because societal norms lead to particular political, organizational, and intellectual structures and processes, and these in turn lead to self-fulfilling prophecies in peoples' perceptions of reality that reinforce the societal norms. Culture defines the preferred type of political economy, and therefore the ways in which growth and development are achieved. It also shapes reproductive behavior, and therefore relationships between populations and their resources, as we shall see in Chapter 3.

APPENDIX 2.1

The "Indian Problem" and Its Solution

The Economist's *Survey of the Indian Economy,* May 4, 1991, and its articles entitled "An Indian Tiger"and "India's Businesses. Blinking in the Sunlight", April 9, 1994, offer both a view of cultural constraints on development and the role of economic liberalization in promoting growth. Paraphrasing, in 1991 The *Economist* wrote that India's future looked more threatened than for many years. This, it said, was not the fault of wicked colonial masters or wicked Western capitalists or the cruel hand of fate, as Indians maintained. It was largely India's own doing. The Gandhian belief in self-reliance that informed the fight for independence had deteriorated into isolationism; that, combined with a chauvinist pride in the system that the heroes of independence had built, prevented Indians from seeing how badly it had served them. Nowhere else, not even in communist China or the Soviet Union, was the gap between what might have been achieved and what has been achieved as great. The country is rich in the resources that matter most for economic advance—not physical resources (which it also has), but human resources. Indians are capable of punishingly hard work; remarkably for people so poor, they are thrifty; they are entrepreneurial; they are ambitious and materialistic. When Indians have ignored the Hindu injunction never to cross the "black sea" and travel abroad, they have prospered within a generation. It was at home that hundreds of millions were imprisoned in a sink of despair and degradation. The country remained divided by violence over caste and religion. In 1991, economic growth was slowing, and poverty on a scale that defies the imagination seemed beyond all remedy.

The problem was twofold. Since independence in 1947, India had pursued a policy of self-sufficiency, managed by a proliferating bureaucracy that had combined the worst of central-planning ideas borrowed from the Soviet Union with the traditional rigidities of caste. Major industries were nationalized. Licenses and direct controls regulated much of the rest of the economy. Firms were told where to locate and what to charge. Small, labor-intensive firms were favored over bigger, capital-intensive ones; hand-loom weavers were favored over power looms, and so on.

After a fashion, the policy succeeded. A civil servant could show you the view from his window and tell you with pride that almost everything you see in his country—cars, buses, scooters, radios, televisions, you name it—was made in India. True, he would admit, quality is not all it might be. Agreed, the designs are not bang up-to-date. (Only in India was it possible for a car buyer to choose between a brand-new 1950s Austin and a factory-fresh 1950s Hillman.) "But then ours is a poor country, what can you expect?"

In excuses for failure, too, India supplied all it needs. India had two great excuses. The first was sheer weight of people, and the continuing growth of numbers clearly was a heavy burden on the economy. The second excuse was that poverty tends to be self-reinforcing. India started from behind; it was a struggle merely to prevent the gap from growing. The country's educated elite talked complacently of the "Hindu rate of growth": "Never forget that India was crippled by its colonial past, that the rich First World will refuse to let it catch up, that democracy costs India one or two percentage points of growth a year."

The real problem, said *The Economist*, was that of culture and religion, however. Hinduism promotes acceptance and resignation by those of lower caste. The centrally directed state created by the post-independence intellectuals used the moral imperative of Hindu philosophy to blunt the spur of competition, and reproduced in the bureaucracy administrative hierarchies as rigid as those of caste. The ambition and materialism unlocked when Indians move elsewhere was constrained at home by rigidities inherited at birth, reinforced both by childhood socialization and by the directed management of the state.

In 1994, however, *The Economist* could write that although in 1991 India was effectively broke, with only enough foreign currency to pay for about a fortnight's imports, today it is paying back the IMF loan and its reserves are bulging as foreign investors rush in to build factories and snap up shares in Indian companies. The IMF persuaded India to turn its back on the policy of trade protection and import substitution that had been in place since the country became independent. In response to IMF pressure, India set about a bold policy of trade liberalization, moving toward the implementation of market strategies using traditional macroeconomic tools to handle budgetary deficits, inflation, and balance of payments. Import tariffs were slashed and capital controls cut. The government loosened its stranglehold on business by dismantling the license system that governed all economic activity, moving toward deregulation in the private sector and decentralization of decision making in the public sector. As a result, growth picked up, inflation fell, exports rose, private-sector investment expanded, an the stock market soared, with foreigners rushing in to invest. Indians' biggest complaint is that the policy has been implemented in a way that favors foreign multinationals. Foreign companies are not bound by domestic restrictions on raising capital and generally pay fewer taxes; local businessmen complaint of being exposed to foreign competition while they are still unable to fire workers in order to become more efficient. It is illegal in India to close a business without official approval.

One of the positive outcomes is the development of information-age activity clusters, for example, in the city of Bangalore, where companies produce software for the international market. Thanks to a satellite link built by the government, their terminals are hooked to a network that keeps them wired to their customers in the United States and Europe. The workers, all graduates of India's seven institutes of technology, earn about one-eighth of their counterparts' salaries in America. Bangalore is India's Silicon Valley. Foreign multinationals such as IBM, Texas Instruments, Digital Equipment Corporation, Hewlett-Packard, Motorola, and 3M have set up local operations. The city will soon have a $150 million science park.

But problems remain. An unbelievable bindweed of bureaucratic regulations still throttles everyday business.

The "license raj" may have been banished, but the "inspector raj" lives on. An appalling infrastructure produces regular power cuts and turns the 1,500-kilometer (950-mile) road journey from Delhi to Bombay into a 4-day marathon. The government says it wants foreign capital for new power stations and wide highways between the big cities, but progress has so far been painfully slow, and that for power stations stymied by the termination of contracts for one partially completed major foreign investment. Whether or not the pace of change can be maintained depends on the ability to maintain policies of economic liberalization and market openness in the face of a resurgent Hindu nationalism that is campaigning aggressively against foreign direct investment in India.

APPENDIX 2.2

Family and Region in Chinese Business

In Chinese society, family ties are defined broadly to include distant relations and in-laws. Although usually centered on kinship and clan, they may extend outward to include coregional dialect networks and college friends. Thus, when China launched its Strategic Economic Zones to encourage foreign direct investment, they attracted enterprise from three of the most important dialect groups among the overseas Chinese: the Cantonese, who predominate in Hong Kong; the Fujianese or Hokkien, who make up 85 percent of Taiwan's population, and much of Singapore's; and the Teochews from around Shantou. The Teochews include Hong Kong's most respected billionaire, Li Ka-shing, the Ma family which controls the Oriental Press Group there; and most of the Chinese community in Thailand, including the Sophonpanich family, who built up the Bangkok Bank. Also important in mainland development are four other dialect groups: the Shanghainese, the Hainanese, the Hokchia, and the Hakkas. The principal overseas Chinese families, according to *The Economist* are tabulated below..

Family ties form a system of contacts that is elastic and flexible, yet durable over time. The relationships among the extended family members are based on established norms of reciprocity that are understood and generally accepted by those operating within the networked system. Ownership and management of Chinese businesses usually remains in the family. When large-scale operations are extended overseas, a prominent pattern for the spin-off project to be controlled by a son or son-in-law. An important element that helps to cement extended family ties is business trust. In order for the established norms of reciprocity to operate effectively, business people must trust that the other players will uphold certain social norms. In large-scale, international business ventures, where transactions take place across great distances, initial personal trust is often won on the basis of reputation.

Paraphrasing from Mitchell (1995): in the late Ming and Qing dynasties, much of the standardization of currency and institutionalization of credit and acceptable interest rates was implemented by merchant associations (*huiguan*). These associations aided in the organization and disciplining of economic behavior in the marketplace, as well as being involved in money lending. A number of merchant associations are still prominent in Hong Kong, Taiwan, and overseas Chinese communities in Southeast Asia and are involved in money lending in large-scale and long-term transactions.

The pooling of capital resources is also a common method of coordinating investment moneys within the extended family system. Many contemporary Chinese business people rely on mutual aid associations (*hui*) for venture capital. In these groups, trust is an important element in bonding the business transaction. By pooling funds and

Family	Base	Main Company	Business
Cheng Yu-tung	Hong Kong	New World Development	Property, telecoms, infrastructure
Kwok Brothers	Hong Kong	Sung Hung Kai Properties	Property
Lee Shau Kee	Hong Kong	Henderson Land	Property, convention centres
Li Ka-shing	Hong Kong	Cheung Kong	Property, telecoms, ports, energy
Eka Tjipta Widjaja	Indonesia	Sinar Mas	Paper, timber, banking, food, chemicals, property
Liem Sioe Liong	Indonesia	Salim Group	Food, cement, property, consumer goods
Prajogo Pangestu	Indonesia	Barito	Timber, paper, cars
Lim Goh Tong	Malaysia	Genting	Casinos, mining, theme parks, hotels
Robert Kuok	Malaysia	Kerry	Sugar, property, media hotels, drinks, food
Quek/Kwek family	Malaysia/Singapore	Hong Leong	Property, hotels, banking
Lucio Tan	Philippines	Fortune Tobacco	Brewing, tobacco, airlines, hotels, banking
Chang Yung-fa	Taiwan	Evergreen	Shipping, airlines
Tsai family	Taiwan	Cathay Life Insurance	Insurance, property
Yue-Che Wang	Taiwan	Formosa Plastics	PVC, petrochemicals, semiconductors
Sophonpanich family	Thailand	Bangkok Bank	Banking, insurance, stockbroking
Chearavanont family	Thailand	Charoen Pokphand	Agriculture, food, telecoms, aquaculture, property, beer
Lamsam family	Thailand	Thai Farmers Bank	Banking, trading, agribusiness, insurance

obtaining capital through informal channels, the bulk of the principal necessary for a business venture often can be accumulated long before the business venture is initiated. In terms of the repayment of interest on the principal, the amount of time taken to repay is less crucial than the eventual success of the operation, because success adds another nodal point to an expanding business web. Because the obligations of repayment are flexible, the use of the capital by the debtor is also considerably more flexible. The money may or may not be called on to produce more money within a set amount of time, but the rate of interest is set by the consensus of the family or informal group. Chinese businesses that borrow from savings pools, or from within the extended family network, or even from personal connections within the banking system, are thus in an advantageous competitive position in comparison with other businesses whose loans are constrained by the necessity to return the capital plus interest within a specified time period.

In Chinese business practice, the use of information is of crucial importance. In the past, owing partially to the lack of a widely standardized money system, Chinese merchants relied heavily on numerous channels of information regarding transactions in geographically distant regions. In contemporary Chinese business networks, the exchange of information remains an integral part of the financial network and is institutionalized via a mixed system of commodity and "gift" exchange. Gift exchange operates within systems characterized by interlocking personal ties (*guanxi*—"connections"). In the *guanxi* economy, the exchange of gifts functions as a transaction between persons that ordinarily leads to economic profit or gain, but that does not function as a purely economic exchange: *Guanxi* exchange takes place between individuals or groups familiar to each other in a context where mutual obligations are well-known.

The binding of gifts to the persons involved in the exchange is the primary quality *guanxi*: The receiver of the gift is indebted to the donor, has lost stature through the acceptance of the gift, and must reciprocate the gift in order to regain face and remain within the social network. Repayment of the debt is predicated on this understanding of moral obligation. It can take place in a number of ways— all of which are distinctive from both barter and simple commodity exchange.

In China's state-run economy, *guanxi* could include gift capital, symbolic capital, office capital, or political capital. In overseas Chinese networks, it often involves gifts of "information capital." Good information, of course, can be converted into major profits quite easily. Good information, such as insider or early news, can be shared because of the position of those who acquire and disseminate it. Such information enabled Li Ka-shing, initially a plastics tycoon, to take over one of the major British trading houses (*hongs*) in Hong Kong (Hutchinson Wharf) in the 1970s, to use this to accumulate massive amounts of capital on the basis of Hong Kong's successful export industry (much of which went into Hong Kong's speculative property market and stock exchange), and thence into investments elsewhere. Li's move to foreign direct investment in, for example, Vancouver, Canada, was hastened by securities regulators who discouraged further local investment by him because his companies controlled more than 10 percent of the Hong Kong stock exchange, by the insecurity about Hong Kong's future produced by the 1989 Tienamen Square massacre in Beijing, and by banking deregulation in Canada that permitted Li to form a number of joint ventures, including the Canadian Imperial Bank of Commerce and the Bank of British Columbia. Family members head the foreign ventures. To preserve the family's worldwide interests, Li Ka-shing transferred a major share of his assets to the Cayman Islands in 1995, following in the footsteps of the largest British *hong*, Jardines, which moved the base of its operations to Bermuda in 1983.

References

The Economist (1996). The Limits of Family Values, *Survey of Business in Asia.* March 9, pp.10–12.

Mitchell, Katharyne (1995). Flexible Circulation in the Pacific Rim. Capitalisms in Cultural Context. *Economic Geography.* 71: 364–82.

Seagrave, Sterling (1995). *Lords of the Rim.* London: G. P. Putman's Sons.

VOCABULARY

The following terms and concepts introduced in this chapter are defined in the Glossary at the end of the book. Be sure that you know them:

absolute nuclear family	antilocal	balanced power-political systems
administrative functions	asymmetrical community family	bond market
African family systems	authoritarian family	capital outflow
anomic family	autocracy	caste

centrified state	global financial markets	oligarchy
civilization	*guanxi*	particularism
civilization consciousness	*hongs*	party-political functions
civilization identity	*hui*	pluralism
clan	*huiguan*	polities
clash of civilizations	ideologies	polygyny
collective unconscious	import competing	power-distance
collectivism	income inequality	primogeniture
competitiveness	individualism	private sector
core identities	inflation	Protestant ethic
cosmopolitanism	information age	purchasing power parity (PPP)
cultural fault lines	information capital	Qing dynasty
culture	inspector raj	real return
culture region	institutional development	recession
currency market	internationally transmitted shocks	reciprocity
depreciation	isolationism	region states
development state	juridical functions	returns to capital
economic liberalization	kin-country syndrome	returns to labor
economic regionalism	kinship	sex-role differentiation
egalitarian nuclear family	legislative functions	social paradigm
endogamous community family	license raj	stagflation
exogamous	localism	strategic economic zones
exogamous community family	locals	total fertility rate
extended family	Ming dynasty	uncertainty avoidance
finance capital	nation-state	universalism
financial assets	national competitiveness	values
gift exchange	neoclassical economics	vertical family systems
global capital market	norms	wage differential

TOPICS FOR DISCUSSION

1. Michael A. Goldberg and John Mercer offer the following contrasts between the United States and Canadian cultures in their book *The Myth of the North American City* (Vancouver: University of British Columbia Press, 1986):

CANADA	UNITED STATES
Deferential behavior	Assertive behavior
Collective	"Frontier" individualism
Respect for authority	Distrust for authority
Elitist/oligarchic	Egalitarian / democratic
Self-restraint	Self-indulgence
Social liberalism	Economic conservatism
Cautious / evolutionary	Dynamic / Experimental
Peace / order / good government	Pursuit of happiness

What differences in the structure of the Canadian and U.S. economies might be a consequence of these cultural variations?

2. Consider the area in which you live. Can it be considered to be part of a "region-state"? If so, what gives it its identity?

3. Take a world map and locate the "civilizational fault lines" that are the current "flash points" for crisis and bloodshed. Which civilizations are in conflict at each flash point? What are the issues precipitating each of the crises?

4. How do oppositional subcultures define themselves relative to your national mainstream? For example, consider

   Quebec nationalists vs. Canada

   Scottish nationalists vs. Great Britain

   Black separatists vs. the United States

5. How and why does Confucian capitalism differ from Western capitalism?

FURTHER READINGS

Barnes, William R., and Larry C. Ledebur. (1994). *Local Economies: the U.S. Common Market of Local Economic Regions.* Washington, DC: National League of Cities, 1994.

Develops the thesis that the U.S. economy is a common market of local economic regions.

Delamaide, Daniel. (1994). *The New Superregions of Europe.* New York: Dutton.

Argues that instead of nation-states, Europe will increasingly function as a set of eight superregions, such as the Slavic Federation.

Garreau, Joel. (1981). *The Nine Nations of North America.* Boston: Houghton Mifflin.

Suggests that North America in fact consists of nine regions with different cultural traditions and economic and political interests.

Herbig, Paul A., and Fred Palumbo. (1994). The Effect of Culture on the Adoption Process: A Comparison of Japanese and American Behavior. *Technological Forecasting and Social Change.* 46: 71–101.

Links culture to differences in innovativeness.

Hoecklin, Lisa. (1995). *Managing Cultural Differences: Strategies for Comparative Advantage.* Wokingham, UK: Addison-Wesley.

An effective use of cultural analysis to identify the strategies that MNEs should pursue in different world regions.

Hofstede, Geert. (1980). *Culture's Consequences: International Differences in Work-Related Values. Beverly Hills:* Sage.

Presents the most comprehensive empirically based framework for understanding cross-national variations in culture.

Huntington, Samuel P. (1993). The Clash of Civilizations. *Foreign Affairs.* 72: 22–49.

Argues that civilizations are the highest level of cultural differentiation, and that clashes between civilizations will structure the world system in the decades ahead.

Ohmae, Kenichi. (1993). The Rise of the Region State. *Foreign Affairs* 72: 78–88.

Says that the nation-state no longer is the most important economic unit. Rather, urban-centered regions of 5 to 25 millions link directly with the global economy, bypassing nation-states.

Pierce, Neil. (1993). *Citistates. How Urban America Can Prosper in a Competitive World.* Washington, DC: Seven Locks Press.

Argues that combinations of strong companies and strong communities are the viable regional economic units in the world today.

3

Population: The Ultimate Resource

OVERVIEW

Human populations are spread very unevenly over the world: Great numbers of people concentrate within a relatively few regions, leaving vast land areas virtually empty. This pattern has been shaped by the physical needs of human beings for food, comfort, and opportunities for a livelihood, as well as the values embedded within their cultures. The world map shows four great population concentrations and several lesser ones. This spatial irregularity of population distributions extends to subnational levels.

Modern technological developments in the production and distribution of food and other human needs have made it possible to support large numbers of people even as medical advances have increased the survival rate and longevity of human populations. The result has been a remarkable acceleration in the rate of population growth in recent times.

A number of theories have arisen to help find meaning in the phenomenon of population growth and to aid in predicting its future course. One line of study has pursued the relationship between population growth and economic development. This work aims to help in coping with present
and anticipated problems of population growth in factor-driven economies and to provide an understanding of the problems of adjustment that population decline is beginning to raise in some industrialized countries.

As rates of population growth diverge among regions, a very different population map of the future is taking shape. Most developed areas are already at or near zero population growth (ZPG), ensuring that their share of global population will continue to shrink. Though 95 percent of future population growth will occur in less-developed countries, some will grow faster than others. Within a century, Africa will likely hold a quarter of all humanity, and most of the world's largest cities will be in less-developed countries.

Population projections are not at all certain for the world's poorest areas, however, and for some they are mere guesses. Such uncertainties raise crucial questions: Can the world support nearly 12 billion people before the end of the next century? Can human populations reach such concentrations without irretrievable damage to their living space?

OBJECTIVES

- to examine both the existing spatial pattern of human populations and the factors that have caused the pattern to assume such an irregular shape

- to describe the processes by which populations grow or decline and to examine the theories that have been advanced to explain them

- to outline demographic transition theory, relating population growth and economic development

- to observe present demographic trends and show how these vary among countries at different levels of development

- to predict the changes in the population pattern that the twenty-first century will bring if current trends persist

- to consider the implications of these evolving patterns, noting the problems they will likely pose for future generations

PRESENT DISTRIBUTION
OF HUMAN POPULATIONS

The countervailing processes of globalization and regionalization are not unfolding on a blank slate, but on a globe already structured by earlier phases of development. The first of these phases centered on what Michael Porter calls the basic factors of production: population, endowments of natural resources, and their interrelationships. It resulted in close relationships between populations and their immediate resource endowments. With modernization, the scale of development shifted. Populations reached further afield and created distinctive regional patterns of resource use and exploitation, a *demographic transition* occurred that changed the dynamics of population growth, and education transformed people from a basic to an *advanced factor* in the production process. The population variable changed from one composed of mere numbers to what economist Julian Simon calls *the ultimate resource:* brain power and inventiveness. Faced with challenges, this "ultimate resource" has designed solutions to problems of growth and development in a dynamic of change in which the population–resource relationship is continually being transformed. When people were one of the basic factors, economic systems were structured by immediately accessible natural resource endowments. Today, brainpower and inventiveness produce new technologies that create resource endowments and restructure the world in which people live and work.

Numbers of People: International Comparisons

Reflecting earlier phases of resource dependence, the spatial pattern of world population is exceedingly uneven, as Figure 3.1 shows. This map is deliberately gross, because of the nature of population data. The chief sources of these data are official records, especially those compiled by national governments and the United Nations. Some of this information is of doubtful reliability, particularly that relating to less-developed countries; for some states in Africa, Asia, and Latin America, no dependable statistics exist at all. Interpreting data of such uncertain quality requires caution, all the more so when one is making comparisons over time. Studies by the United Nations have disclosed, for instance, that official censuses in parts of Africa have suffered from underenumeration and that the populations of some of these countries are much larger than had been suspected. Only in 1982 did the People's Republic of China, which contains nearly a quarter of all humanity, undertake

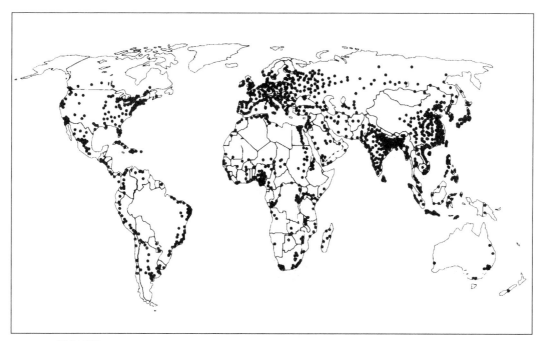

FIGURE 3.1   World population (1 dot = approximately 3 million people). Although this scale of representation can give only a general impression of the world pattern, the four major population nodes stand out clearly. The two largest concentrations are in East Asia, especially Eastern China and the southeastern coast of Japan, and in South Asia, where the main focus is on the deltas of the Ganges and Brahmaputra rivers. Somewhat smaller, the European node reaches its peak in the lower courses of the Rhine and Thames. The smallest of the four nodes is in the northeastern United States and adjacent border areas of Canada. For more precise information on world population, see Figure 3.2 and Tables 3.1, 3.2, and 3.3.

its first real census; only rough estimates had hitherto been possible. Complicating comparisons of data over time are the many boundary changes of recent decades, such as that resulting from the separation of Bangladesh from Pakistan. Furthermore, measures of population characteristics are not standardized internationally.

Comparative analyses thus require judgment and careful qualification. The problem is less acute for developed countries, which have fairly reliable data. To minimize data problems among the developing countries it is often desirable to aggregate information by continental groupings.

Population Size.   From Table 3.1 and Figure 3.2, it is apparent that the continents differ greatly in population size. Asia contains nearly three-fifths of the world's people. The most rapidly growing population is that of Africa, which overtook Europe during the 1980s to become the second largest among the continents. With only 0.5 percent of the world's people, Oceania (Australia, New Zealand, and the islands of the South Pacific) has the smallest population of all the continental groupings.

In Table 3.2 the individual countries with the largest populations are listed in rank order. Altogether, 78.3 percent of the world's people live in these 25 nations. One in every five lives in China, and one in six lives in India. Note that 13 of the countries are Asian. These continental and country totals do not give an accurate impression of population concentration, however. One reason for this is that the

world's populous countries differ so greatly in areal extent (Table 3.2, column 3).

Population Density.   Differences among countries become more obvious if we relate numbers of people to land area, to derive a measure of population density (Table 3.2, column 5). The simplest measure of density is that used in Table 3.2, namely, *arithmetic density,* which is the total number of people divided by the total land area. Some of the greatest densities occur in tiny city-states such as Monaco, with 15,316 persons per square kilometer. This is similarly true of those city-states occupying small islands, as, for example, Hong Kong (5,800 people per square kilometer) and Singapore (2,800 per square kilometer). Excluding such cases, as well as all island nations smaller than 10,000 km^2, we find that the 25 countries listed in Table 3.3 are the most densely populated in the world. Of these, Europe contributes seven. Less-developed countries that have risen in this ranking during the period are Bangladesh, South Korea, India, Sri Lanka, the Philippines, Vietnam, North Korea, and Pakistan—all in East or South Asia—Rwanda and Burundi in Central Africa, and El Salvador, Jamaica, Haiti, and the Dominican Republic in Central America and the Caribbean. Also appearing in Table 3.3 are two small neighbors at the eastern end of the Mediterranean, Lebanon and Israel. Note that 7 of the 25 densest populations belong to island nations: Japan, Sri Lanka, the United Kingdom, Jamaica, Haiti, the Philippines, and the Dominican Republic.

TABLE 3.1

World distribution of population by region, 1995

Region	Population [a] (thousands)	Percent of World Population	Density (population per sq km)	Cropland [b] ha per person	Total Hectares (thousands)
World	5,759,276	100.0	43.3	0.25	1,461,962
Africa	744,009	12.9	24.6	0.27	200,745
Asia (excluding former USSR)	3,407,594	59.2	23.5	0.11	389,247
Europe (excluding former USSR)	516,043	9.0	06.0	0.28	144,556
Latin America [d]	482,476	8.4	23.5	0.31	151,182
North America [c]	291,802	5.1	15.1	0.80	232.200
Oceania	28,790	0.5	3.6	1.62	46,723
Former USSR	288,562	3.6	12.9	0.80	232,244

Sources: United Nations, *World Population Prospects 1992.* Population Series No. 135, Population Division of the Department for Economic and Social Information and Policy Analysis (New York: United Nations. 1993); United Nations Development Programme, *Human Development Report 1994* (New York: Oxford University Press, 1994).

[a] Projected.

[b] Cropland includes arable land and permanent cropland. Data are for 1990.

[c] North America consists of Canada and the United States.

[d] Latin America includes all countries south of the U.S. border: Mexico, Central America, the Caribbean, and South America.

[e] Data for the former USSR are aggregated outside of regional totals.

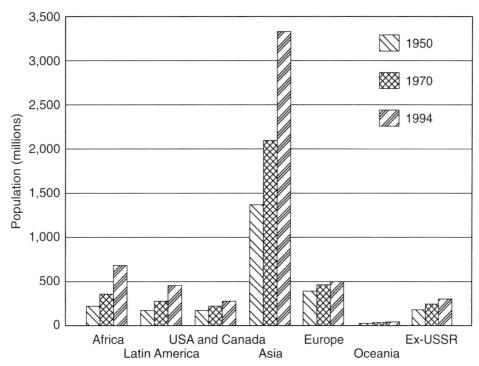

FIGURE 3.2   Regional shifts in world population 1950–1994. The major continental areas differ greatly in the numbers of people they contain, and the disparities among them have widened still further during the past four decades. Asia, which holds two of the world's largest population concentrations, has continued to increase its numbers. Also on the ascendancy is Africa, which in the 1980s passed Europe to take second place among the continents. Latin America, another growth area for Third World populations, is steadily gaining on Europe. Northern America (the United States and Canada) lags slightly behind the fifth-place former USSR. Oceania (Australia and New Zealand, plus the islands of the South Pacific) accounts for only 0.5 percent of the world's people. [*Sources:* Data from *World Population Prospects 1988* (New York: United Nations, 1989), and *1995 Britannia Book of the Year* (Chicago: Encyclopaedia Britannia, 1995).]

The Food and Agriculture Organization (FAO) of the United Nations has estimated the proportion of land available for crops (*arable* land) in each of the major regions. From this information, it is possible to derive a measure of *physiological density,* which relates the size of a population to amount of cropland (arable land and permanent crops) available for its support. Table 3.1 lists this information for each of the continental areas and for the world as a whole. Note that in 1994, the average person in the world could draw on only one-quarter of a hectare (two-thirds of an acre) of cropland (column 5 in Table 3.1); 25 years earlier, the amount available per person had been 0.4 hectare (1 acre). A majority of the world's people live in areas having less than the world average of one-quarter hectare. The number of hectares per person has declined throughout the developing world; in Asia, it is now only 0.11 ha. Although Europe as a whole has a larger ratio of cropland to total land area than any other continent, its population densities are so great that the average European can draw upon only 0.28 ha.

Physiological density is only a rough measure, however, for it does not take into account the variable quality of cropland. Although the per capita supply of cropland in Africa is slightly above the world average, the productivity of the land is generally much below that of North America or Europe. A large part of Latin America's cropland is of poor quality also. Similarly misleading is the large amount of cropland per person shown for Oceania, a sparsely populated region with only 1.4 percent of the world's total cropland.

Limits of Habitation.   Population density figures for entire continents, or even countries, can convey only limited information. As the population map (Figure 3.1) demonstrates, densities are rarely consistent throughout national territories, and many major population concentrations cross national boundaries. Let us explore the reasons why certain areas have become more heavily occupied than others.

TABLE 3.2

Twenty-five countries with largest populations, 1992

| Country (ranked according to size) | Population (millions) | Land Area | | Density (population per sq km) | Percent of World Population |
		Square Kilometers (thousands)	Percent of World Area		
1 China	1,187	9,560	7.3	124.2	21.8
2 India	880	3,290	2.5	267.5	16.2
3 United States	255	9,370	7.1	27.2	4.7
4 Indonesia	191	1,910	1.5	100.1	3.5
5 Brazil	154	8,510	6.5	18.1	2.8
6 Russian Federation	149	17,080	13.0	8.7	2.7
7 Pakistan	125	771	0.6	162.0	2.3
8 Japan	125	378	0.3	329.4	2.3
9 Bangladesh	120	144	0.1	829.9	2.2
10 Nigeria	116	924	0.7	125.4	2.1
11 Mexico	88	1,960	1.5	45.0	1.6
12 German	80	357	0.3	224.6	1.5
13 Vietnam	70	332	0.3	209.3	1.3
14 Philippines	65	300	0.2	217.3	1.2
15 Iran	62	1,650	1.3	37.3	1.1
16 Turkey	58	779	0.6	75.0	1.1
17 Italy	58	301	0.2	192.0	1.1
18 United Kingdom	58	245	0.2	235.5	1.1
19 France	57	552	0.4	103.4	1.0
20 Thailand	56	513	0.4	109.4	1.0
21 Egypt	55	1,000	0.8	54.9	1.0
22 Ethiopia	53	1,220	0.9	43.5	1.0
23 Ukraine	52	604	0.5	86.4	1.0
24 South Korea	44	99	0.0	445.5	0.8
25 Myanmar	44	677	0.5	64.5	0.8
Total	4,202	62,526	47.5	67.2	77.1
World Total	5,449	131,638	100.0	41.4	100.0

Source: United Nations Development Programme, *Human Development Report, 1994* (New York: Oxford University Press, 1994).

For the most part, the pattern of world population we see today took form at a time when human beings gained their livelihood directly from the land. It is not surprising, therefore, that those parts of the earth's land surface with little or no human habitation—about three-fifths of the total— are physically unsuited to agriculture. Figure 3.3 provides a generalized view of those regions that are too dry, too wet, too cold, or too mountainous for the ordinary forms of cultivation. In some cases two or more of these negative conditions coincide in a particular area. Note, however, that few of the major world regions are entirely devoid of human beings. Within some broad nonarable areas are localities that have special conditions permitting the practice of agriculture—desert oases, for example. Some areas that lack farmland contain nonagricultural settlements, located near valuable mineral deposits, biotic resources (such as forest products), recreational facilities, or other special assets.

Excessive aridity virtually excludes farming from large portions of the world. The amount of moisture available to crops varies according to the evaporation rate in an area. At least 10 inches of annual rainfall are usually required in the middle latitudes, but 30 inches or more may be needed in the tropics to replace evaporation losses. Much of the earth's surface is either desert (less than 10 inches of rain per year) or steppe land (between 10 and 20 or 30 inches) and thus mostly unsuited to agriculture. Within such dry lands, exceptional circumstances however, may permit irrigated agriculture in favored localities. For example, "exotic" rivers such as the Nile or the Colorado, with sources in regions of high rainfall, pass through arid lands where their waters may support large agricultural populations. In some desert areas, oases grow around local springs or wells drawing on deep underground veins of water. But vast expanses of the Sahara and other major

TABLE 3.3
Most densely populated countries, 1992

Country (ranked according to density)	Density (population per sq km)	Land Area (thousand sq km)
1 Bangladesh [b]	829.9	144
2 South Korea [b]	445.5	99
3 The Netherlands	410.8	37
4 Japan [b]	329.4	378
5 Belgium	322.6	31
6 Lebanon	290.0	10
7 Rwanda	288.5	26
8 Sri Lanka	268.2	66
9 India [b]	267.5	3,290
10 El Salvador	257.1	21
11 Haiti	242.9	28
12 Israel	242.9	21
13 United Kingdom [b]	235.5	245
14 Jamaica	227.3	11
15 Germany [b]	224.6	357
16 Philippines [b]	217.3	300
17 Vietnam [b]	209.3	332
18 Burundi	207.1	28
19 Italy [b]	192.0	301
20 North Korea	186.8	121
21 Switzerland	165.9	41
22 Pakistan [b]	162.0	771
23 Dominican Republic	153.1	49
24 Nepal	146.1	141
25 Moldova	129.4	34

Source: United Nations Development Programme, *Human Development Report, 1994* (New York: Oxford University Press, 1994).

[a] Includes only those countries with areas greater than 10,000 sq km.

[b] Also appears on list of countries with largest populations.

deserts are either remote from water supplies or lack true soils to permit agriculture on their barren sandy or rocky surfaces. Arid regions with deposits of valuable minerals such as petroleum, nitrates, or metallic ores may attract some human habitation, but such activities normally require only small numbers of workers and rarely affect the general population pattern to an important degree.

On the other hand, some large regions support only small populations because they receive too much rainfall. The great equatorial basins of the Amazon and Congo rivers support a dense rain forest vegetation, leading some people to believe that these lightly populated areas could become productive agricultural lands suitable for resettlement of the world's surplus millions. Scientific evidence does not support this idea. The basic problem is the inherently low quality of tropical rain forest soils. Heavy rains throughout the year leach the soluble mineral plant food elements out of the soil and carry these to depths beyond the reach of ordinary shallow-rooted food plants. The deceptively lush growth of native trees results from the ability of these forest giants to send their taproots deep into underground deposits of nutrients. Most areas with tropical rain forest climates are thus lightly settled; Amazonia, for instance, supports only one person per square kilometer. Important exceptions are to be found in certain areas where local soil conditions permit successful farming despite heavy rainfall and rapid leaching. Thus, the Indonesian island of Java is able to support some of the world's highest rural population densities on its rich soils, which are periodically renewed by volcanic deposition. In some other places, sizable numbers of people obtain a livelihood from the cultivation of tropical tree crops such as rubber, bananas, and cacao.

Possibly the most forbidding of all climatic features is excessive cold. Ice and snow permanently cover great areas near the poles and on the higher mountains. Adjacent to the polar sheets are even greater expanses where low temperatures and short growing seasons prevent ordinary agriculture. Because most food plants require at least 3 months

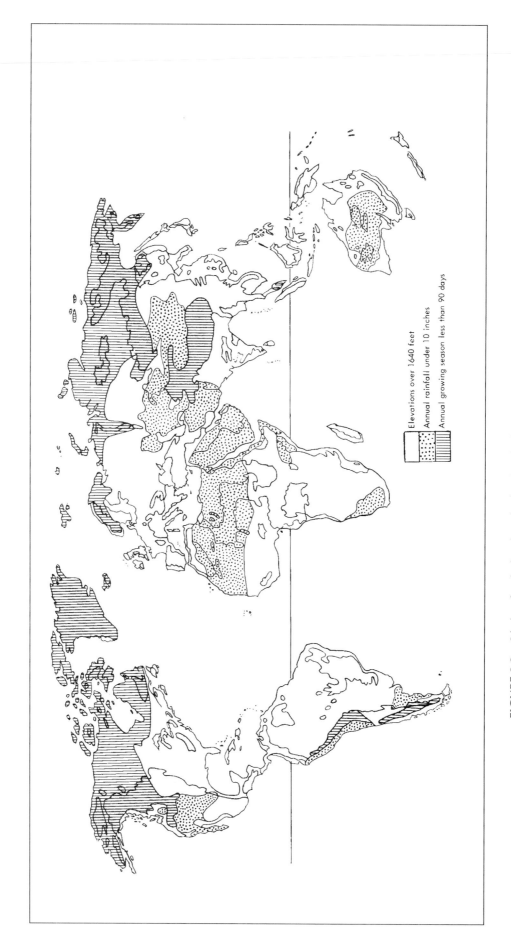

FIGURE 3.3 Limits of agricultural production. Much of the earth's land surface is too mountainous or too dry or has too short a growing season to support the usual forms of agriculture.

Elevations over 1640 feet

Annual rainfall under 10 inches

Annual growing season less than 90 days

without frost to reach maturity, the limit of the 90-day growing season usually represents the poleward boundary of agricultural production (Figure 3.3). The colder climates of course, do, support some human habitation: Exploitation of minerals employs limited numbers, fishing provides a livelihood along the coasts, and forest products support scattered populations along the southern margins where temperatures are high enough for tree growth.

Farming is impossible in those mountainous areas with slopes too steep for soil to cling. The higher mountains are also too cold for ordinary crops because temperatures drop with increasing elevation. In the middle and upper latitudes, forestry is confined to the lower slopes because temperatures at higher elevations are too low for trees to grow. Nearer the equator, on the other hand, the moderate temperatures and gentler slopes of highland basins provide ideal farming conditions; in tropical America these are the preferred places for human habitation (compare Figure 3.1 with Figure 3.3).

Grazing is often possible in areas that are too dry or cold for agriculture. With their sparse natural covering of grasses and herbaceous plants, the steppe lands are used for this purpose, as are the basins and upper slopes of some mountainous regions. Reindeer herding takes place even in the far north of Eurasia and Alaska. Such lands have a meager *carrying capacity* for grazing animals, however, and they therefore support only scattered human populations.

Although such extreme climatic conditions limit the spread of human beings into the more hostile areas, physical capabilities of the land do not bear a perfect relationship to the patterns of population density, however. One important influence is length of settlement. In those parts of Asia and the Middle East where people have lived continuously since the emergence of human life on earth, population densities are particularly high. By contrast, farmlands of superior quality in the more recently settled Americas have far lower densities.

Modern technology has modified the influence of physical factors on settlement patterns. Today, if human beings have a compelling reason to live in an inhospitable area, they create artificial environments. Heating, air conditioning, desalinization of water, and drainage are some of the costly measures that technology offers for residents of otherwise inhospitable surroundings. Perhaps the ultimate artificial environments are those found in great cities. These places develop an economic momentum and a physical environment of their own, attracting and providing for their populations regardless of the inherent physical characteristics of the land on which they are built.

The Empty Areas. Having noted the factors that limit human habitation, we may now examine some of those regions that have few people (Figures 3.1 and 3.3). One almost empty area is the enormous arctic region of North America, which includes northern Alaska, Canada, and Greenland. Also sparsely settled are the dry lands of western North America. Two virtually unpopulated regions in South America are the tropical rain forests of Amazonia and the great deserts of the south: the Atacama of Chile and Peru and the Patagonian region of Argentina. Africa has three prominent empty areas: the vast Sahara Desert in the north, the tropical rain forests of equatorial Africa, and the Kalahari and Namib deserts of the south. Even Eurasia, the most populous of continents, has two unpopulated areas, the great polar fringes of Russia and Scandinavia, and the deserts of central Asia and the adjacent highlands. Of all the inhabited continents, Australia, with its "dead heart," has the largest proportion of unoccupied land. Antarctica, which is covered by a huge ice sheet up to 2 miles thick, has no permanent human habitation at all, save at a couple of scientific research stations.

The Major Population Nodes. Contrasting with these empty areas are four great population nodes that dominate the world population map. The three largest, all in Eurasia, together comprise more than three-fifths of humanity. The *East Asian* node includes Japan, Korea, and eastern China and has a middle-latitude location with generally favorable climatic conditions for agriculture. The inhabitants are concentrated within the large river floodplains and deltas on the Chinese mainland and the densely packed coastal plains and river valleys of mountainous Japan and Korea. This region has an ancient history of habitation, and contributing to the high population densities have been cultural traditions that favor large families. Although intensive agriculture supports high rural densities, a large and efficient industrial economy enables Japan to sustain a population more than half that of the United States and to do so on a group of mountainous islands having a combined area less than that of Montana.

Second in size is the *South Asian* node, which includes most of India, Pakistan, and Bangladesh, in addition to the island of Sri Lanka and parts of Myanmar. Here the greatest population densities are in areas with a heavy monsoon rainfall. The only limit on the growing season is the availability of water, as warm temperatures prevail 12 months of the year. The largest cities and highest rural densities are found in the river deltas and floodplains and along the coastal plains, but even the drier interior of the Indian peninsula bears large numbers of people. Despite the generally poor quality of the soil, agriculture remains the chief life support. High birth rates continually strain food supplies, however.

Europe west of the Ural mountains constitutes the third great population node. This region enjoys one of the most reliable of all agricultural climates, especially in its western portions. With moderate temperatures, a dependable supply of rainfall well distributed throughout the year (except along the Mediterranean), and a long growing season, Europe produces some of the world's best crop yields. Of all the continents, Europe also has the largest proportion of its land area devoted to agriculture. Despite their productivity, Western Europe's farms employ only a small proportion of the labor force, however. Relatively few people are engaged in exploiting Europe's mineral and biotic resources. Most are employed in manufacturing and service activities; hence, there is a high degree of urbanization. Like the population nodes of Eurasia, this is a region of long settlement, dating at least to the end of the last Ice Age.

The population node of *Eastern North America,* large as it is, has only a fraction of the people contained in each of the three major Eurasian concentrations. This region includes the "megalopolis" of the Middle Atlantic seaboard of the United States with its westward extension in the Great Lakes region of the Middle West and southern Ontario and Quebec, together with the associated rural populations of this important farming area. Despite a midlatitude climate, the growing seasons are decidedly shorter here than in most parts of the other three population nodes. Eastern North America also has historically important natural resources, including coal, iron ore, natural gas and oil, and a variety of other raw materials. Unlike the other three population nodes, this region was settled fairly recently and experienced rapid growth mainly through immigration and natural increase during its formative period. As in Western Europe, agriculture in Eastern North America is efficient and productive but occupies only a small percentage of the labor force.

Lesser Population Clusters. In addition to these major concentrations, at least 14 smaller population clusters appear on the world map. One is the *Los Angeles–Central Valley–San Francisco* area of California, until recently the fastest-growing concentration in the United States. The magnificent scenery and benign climate of this area have been prime attractions, but shortages of water and other environmental and economic problems threaten its continued growth. Another small cluster includes the *Vancouver, B.C.,* and *Puget Sound–Fraser River* areas of the Pacific Northwest, likewise a region of pleasant physical surroundings.

Mexico City and adjacent parts of the central plateau offer some of the most attractive climatic conditions in Mexico. Although agriculture is limited, this area contains a large part of the country's population and has become the center of a growing industrial district. The valleys of the *Central American highlands* contain most of the population of the isthmian region. Although widely separated from each other, the *islands of the Caribbean* are among the most densely populated areas of the Western Hemisphere.

The rapidly increasing population of South America is mainly concentrated at various points along the continental margins. Largest of these clusters is the *Central Plateau and Northeast Coast of Brazil,* the leading industrial area of Latin America and one of its principal agricultural districts as well, despite the difficult problems of supporting a swelling population. The *Rio de la Plata* district is the heart of Argentina's and Uruguay's populations; it contains most of the industry and is the focus of commercial agriculture. *Middle Chile,* another area of pleasant climatic conditions and productive agriculture, contains the majority of that country's people. The *Highland Basins of the Northern Andes,* extending from Lal Paz, Bolivia, northward through Peru, Ecuador, Colombia, and Venezuela, provide an attractive environment similar to that of the Central American highlands.

One of the most unusual population concentrations occupies the *Valley of the Lower Nile River* in North Africa. Here some of the highest rural densities in the world are compressed within the narrow confines of the irrigated floodplain and delta of an exotic stream that flows from the humid East African highlands through one of the driest of deserts (less than 1 inch of rainfall per year). The *Gulf of Guinea* coast of West Africa supports large numbers of people, especially in Ghana and Nigeria, where subsistence agriculture is the main occupation. In *East Central Africa,* some of the world's highest fertility rates are producing high levels of population growth despite widespread disease and frequent intertribal conflicts. Another concentration of people in that continent is in the *Republic of South Africa.* The coastal belt of this country has a pleasant Mediterranean-type climate and its interior is rich in valuable minerals, including gold, diamonds, coal, and iron. The final population node includes *Eastern Australia and New Zealand.* Australia's people live mainly along the southeast coastal lowland, which, by contrast with the arid center and west, receives adequate rainfall, has moderate temperatures, and offers most of the country's agricultural potential.

Intracountry Variations

Regional Concentrations. National population figures for most countries obscure large internal variations in density. Even a country as small as Belgium, with an overall density of 324 persons per square kilometer, has its lightly populated Ardennes uplands. Though the United Kingdom as a whole has a high density, several regions, such as central Wales, the Pennine uplands, and the Scottish Highlands, have few people. Even greater differences occur in Brazil, where the large and economically active population of the São Paulo–Rio de Janeiro region and the crowded rural northeast contrast markedly with the virtually empty Amazonian north. Likewise, the densely peopled Toronto–Golden Horseshoe district of Canada is entirely different from the nearly vacant Arctic lands of the Canadian north.

Some of the greatest regional variations are in China. Despite a huge population, China's overall density is only 115 persons per square kilometer. This is lower than the densities of most of its neighbors in eastern and southern Asia and much less than those of Western Europe. China's population is concentrated mainly in the coastal and central provinces, where most of the cultivated land is found. The Chengtu Plain in Szechwan Province supports exceedingly high rural population densities, whereas great areas in the arid west remain nearly unpeopled.

Why does the Chinese population remain so unevenly distributed after more than 40 centuries? One reason is the extreme variation in the physical capabilities of the land. Wide differences in soils, temperatures, and rainfall have profoundly influenced the locational choices of a predominantly agricultural people. At any early date, China developed a "hydraulic civilization" depending on irrigated production of a staple foodstuff, rice. Even where underused agricultural opportunities seem to exist, however, the Chinese historically, have been unusually reluctant to move, owing to the influence of ancestor worship, of traditionally strong ties to family and village, and of regional language differences that hamper communication. Furthermore, extreme poverty has been endemic in China for centuries. Lacking savings, being vulnerable to a variety of natural calamities, and having little assurance of bettering themselves elsewhere, the Chinese have preserved a remarkably stable population pattern. Communist control also prevented significant redistribution of population among provinces, although important shifts occurred locally.

Urbanization.   The ultimate population concentration, of course, is in cities. One of the notable events of recent decades has been the rush of people from farms to cities and from smaller urban places to larger ones. By 1989, 77 percent of the people in the world's most industrialized countries lived in urban places, as opposed to 71 percent in 1965; the percentage now exceeds 80.

Gregariousness among human beings appears to be instinctive: The survival of early peoples depended on their living close to others of their kind. Throughout history, people have established cities for defense as well as for the various social and economic advantages of cooperative efforts. Both commerce and industry enjoy numerous savings by locating within urban areas, as later chapters will show. Among their other important roles, cities also serve as centers for administrative control, education, and culture, and as points of convergence for transportation routes.

Nevertheless, the very large city is a phenomenon of modern times; indeed, the word "civilization" is derived from the Latin term for city. Primitive human activities provided an insufficient surplus of food to support a large nonfood-producing population. Subsistence gathering, hunting and fishing, herding, and agriculture supply barely enough food for the members of family, clan, or tribe, and are very extensive in their use of land; migratory peoples may require 5 square kilometers or more to feed each individual. Although the well-organized Romans were able to mobilize production to support sizable urban populations, this capacity was lost in Europe when the Roman legions vanished. As Marco Polo discovered, however, the Chinese were able to maintain large cities throughout the period when medieval Europe's urban centers remained small.

Modern urban growth resulted from three essential developments. The first was the *Agricultural Revolution* of the late eighteenth century, which, for the first time, allowed European farms to feed a large nonagricultural population. Farm yields increased because of improved cultivation methods, new crops, scientific breeding of both plants and animals, consolidation of land holdings, and better communications and transportation. Transmitted across the Atlantic, the agricultural revolution brought similar results to the United States where agricultural employment steadily declined as a percentage of the total labor force. In 1820, farm labor represented 72 percent of the gainfully employed, but by 1900, this figure had dropped to 37 percent; in 1990, less than 2 percent of the labor force worked on farms, where they grew enough food not only to support the other 98 percent of the population but also great quantities for export overseas. Beginning about the same time, the *Industrial Revolution* brought the factory system, which hastened the growth of large concentrations of people. Simultaneously, the *Transportation Revolution* permitted cheap, fast, and dependable distribution of food, industrial raw materials, and other goods required by expanding urban populations.

The ultimate result of the agricultural, industrial, and transportation revolutions has been the creation of great metropolises, for which population estimates vary depending on how they are defined. The population of metropolitan London increased eightfold during the most recent century and a half, reaching 10.6 million people in 1990. During that same period, New York's metropolitan area attained a population of 15.7 million. Eclipsing New York's population today are Tokyo (25.8 million in 1992) and São Paulo (19.2 million). Close behind are Mexico City (15.3 million), Shanghai (14.1 million), and Bombay (13.3 million).

The degree of urbanization in a country usually corresponds to its level of economic development: In general, the most urbanized countries also have the highest per capita gross national products (see Figures 3.4 and 3.5). Studies have shown that those countries ranking highest in urbanization also tend to rank highest on indices of transportation, communications, energy production and consumption, national and per capita incomes, and foreign trade. In developed countries, urban pursuits—manufacturing and the services—employ most workers, including a majority of those actually residing in rural areas.

As Figure 3.4 shows, however, several developed countries are exceptions to this general relationship. Thus, among the industrialized countries, a few are less urbanized than their per capita GNPs would suggest. Switzerland, for example, is only 60 percent urbanized and Italy is only 67 percent urbanized. On the other hand, not counting such city-states as Singapore and Hong Kong, one of the most urbanized of all is Australia, with an urban population of 85 percent—hardly the picture of a nation of sheep growers and wheat farmers.

Within countries, the degree of urbanization varies from one region to another. Urban development in the United States has produced dense concentrations of cities along each coast and on the shores of the Great Lakes. In the lightly settled, largely rural plains, and Rocky Mountain states, urban centers tend to be smaller and more scattered. The most rapid growth is now taking place in the south and the west, as the population moves from "snowbelt" to "sunbelt."

The typically lower levels of urbanization in less-developed countries stem mainly from their greater dependence on agricultural employment. Some of the lowest percentages are in Asia, especially such remote, mountainous countries as Bhutan and Nepal, which have only 5 percent and 10 percent urbanization, respectively. Even in a country as large as Bangladesh, only 16 percent of the people live in cities. More striking yet is China, where 26 percent of a total population of 1.1 billion live in urban places. In India, 26 percent of the nation's 880 million people are urban. Levels of urbanization are likewise exceedingly low in sub-Saharan Africa; for example, Rwanda (5 percent), Burundi (6 percent), Mozambique (13 percent), and Tanzania (33 percent). On the other hand, in the semi-industrialized Republic of South Africa 60 percent of the population is urban.

Urbanization has proceeded much further in Latin America than in Africa or in South and East Asia. Several of the more prosperous countries of South America have now attained higher levels of urbanization than found in North America or most of Europe. Venezuela, Uruguay, Argentina, and Chile all have well over 80 percent of their

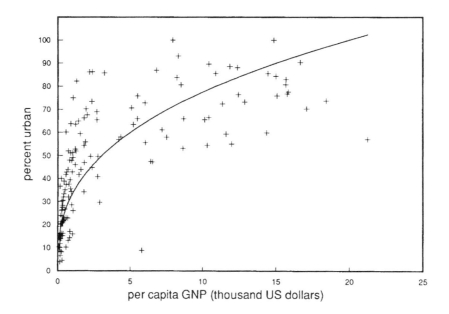

FIGURE 3.4 Relationship between urbanization and per capita gross national product ($R^2 =$ 0.614). Although the correlation is fairly close for nations at the lower end of the developmental scale, it is less strong for the more-advanced economies, which differ considerably in their degree of urbanization. A number of European states are not as urbanized as their per capita GNPs would suggest, notably the Alpine lands of Switzerland and Austria and the southern countries of Italy, Portugal, and Greece. Also falling below the regression line are the former USSR and most of Eastern Europe. By contrast, the United Kingdom and the Netherlands are well above the line. Unusually high levels of urbanization are likewise found in Australia, New Zealand, and the southern-cone countries of South America. Predictably, the city-states of Singapore and Hong Kong appear at the very top of the diagram. [*Source:* Data from the *1990 Britannica Book of the Year* (Chicago: Encyclopaedia Britannica, 1990).]

people in urban places, and Mexico and Brazil are two-thirds urban. Much lower levels prevail, however, in some Andean countries, in most of the Caribbean, and in parts of Central America.

Another Third World area that is substantially urbanized is the Middle East (Figure 3.5). Contrary to the usual image of the Islamic world, the Middle East is a region of large cities. Moreover, the exceptionally high rates of natural increase prevalent among urban-dwelling Middle Easterners are further swelling the populations of those centers.

Indeed, despite the mainly rural character of most lower-income countries, some of the world's great cities are in less-developed lands. Only the most backward societies lack cities altogether. Typically, a less-developed country has only one truly large city and this dwarfs all other urban places in the land. For instance, Managua, capital of Nicaragua, is 7 times the size of Leon; and the capital of Ethiopia, Addis Ababa, is 13 times Dire Dawa.

In addition to the usual commercial functions of a large urban place, the primacy of the preeminent city of a less-developed country is reinforced by domination of the economically active parts of the country and service as the focus of national political, social, and cultural life. As befits a position at the lower end of the developmental scale, however, the city's economic functions tend to be limited in scope. Manufacturing, transportation, and communications are usually poorly developed, except insofar as they link demands of the developed world to the resources of the developing country's hinterlands.

POPULATION GROWTH

How and why did this pattern of population develop, and how is it changing? Anthropologists believe that human existence on earth extends back at least 600,000 years and possibly more than 2 million years prior to that. Quantitative information before A.D. 1650 must be estimated from circumstantial evidence based on our knowledge of how early human beings gained their livelihood and of the capacity of the land to support primitive economies. We know, for example, that subsistence gathering and hunting and fishing, as practiced by a few remaining primitive

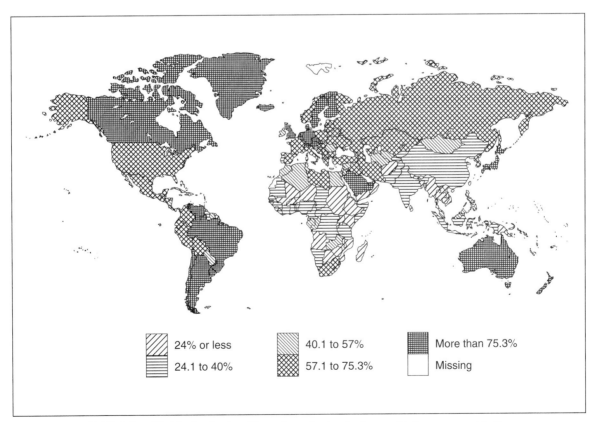

24% or less
24.1 to 40%
40.1 to 57%
57.1 to 75.3%
More than 75.3%
Missing

FIGURE 3.5   World urbanization. Throughout the developing world, the movement to the cities is accelerating, especially in Latin America and the Middle East. Exceptions to this trend are found in sub-Saharan Africa and parts of Southern Asia, particularly the Himalayan kingdoms, where urbanization levels continue to be very low. [*Source:* Based on data from the *1995 Britannia Book of the Year* (Chicago: Encyclopaedia Britannia, 1995).]

peoples in the world's remotest peripheries today, require as much as 2 square miles per person. Even the most rudimentary agriculture, on the other hand, can normally support much denser populations. Supplementing such estimates as these are the scattered records of early communities, particularly those of the Roman Empire, together with other archaeological and historical evidence.

Accelerating Growth.   The estimates of early populations, together with data accumulated from modern censuses and projections of current growth trends, provide enough information for us to construct curves of world population growth like that shown in Figure 3.6. The main impressions given by this curve are its persistent upward trend and its accelerating rise in recent times. Until the modern era, world population increased slowly, with periods of actual decline. Only within the past 300 years—a tiny fraction of human tenure on earth—has world population grown at consistently high rates.

During the preagricultural era, before 8000 B.C.,when only rudimentary tools and weapons were in use, not more than 5 million people inhabited the earth. Numbers increased to between 200 million and 250 million by the beginning of the Christian era and possibly as many as 257 million by the end of the first millennium. Within the next 300 years, the population of Europe began to rise, and the world total may have reached as much as 384 million by A.D. 1300.

The following century brought a series of plagues that reduced Europe's population so drastically that the popula-

tion of the world as a whole declined. From 1400 to 1650, however, European civilization enjoyed a rebirth, and European peoples began an energetic conquest of new lands. Although Europe's population likely rose at more than twice the world rate during this period, the indigenous population of the Americas probably declined sharply as a result of the impact of European invasion. Population estimates undertaken for 1650 indicated a world total of about 500 million. Within the next two centuries, the total rose even more rapidly, doubling to approximately 1 billion people by 1850. By 1930, the population had reached 2 billion, and by 1970, 3.6 billion. The amount of land per person has diminished since, as world population has continued its climb, reaching 5 billion in 1986.

The Growth Curve.   Accelerating growth has caused a continual steepening of the population curve. In A.D. 1300, the annual rate of growth for the world was perhaps 0.11 or 0.12 percent. By the 1930s, the annual rate had reached 1.0 percent, and by the 1960s, it had risen to 2.1 percent. Another way of looking at this is to note the number of years it takes for the world's population to double. Between 8000 B.C. and A.D. 1650 this doubling required 1500 years; but the next doubling, between 1650 and 1850, took only 200 years. Eighty years later, by 1930, population had doubled again, and it had once again doubled by 1975, a mere 45 years.

If instead of plotting world population on an arithmetic scale as in Figure 3.6 we use a double-logarithmic scale (Figure 3.7), which emphasizes rates of change, we discover a number of details obscured in the previous diagram. We find that three main surges of population have occurred during human history rather than only one, and that each surge was apparently associated with a major technological breakthrough that increased the capacity of the world economy to support more people. The developments that fostered these bursts of population were the toolmaking, agricultural, and industrial revolutions. Figure 3.7 also suggests a fourth technological revolution in the making, a result of advances in the use of computers, robotics, and knowledge use in an "information society," which also promise quantum increases in productivity.

The Growth Mechanism

Two dynamic processes are responsible for the growth of populations and for regional variations in numbers of people: These processes are *natural increase* and *migration:* The basic demographic equation states that population change equals births minus deaths (national increase) plus immigration minus emigration (net migration). In what follows we focus, on national increase.

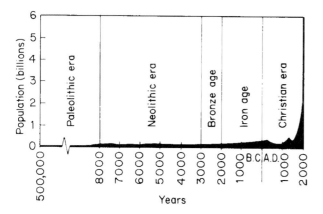

FIGURE 3.6 Growth of world population. Note that, after having gained but little during the thousands of years of early human life, population began a slow rise during Roman times, slipped backward during the Dark Ages, and began to rise again by the fourteenth century, when the bubonic plague brought a sharp but temporary decline. Since then, population growth has accelerated rapidly. [*Source: After Population Bulletin*, 18(1).]

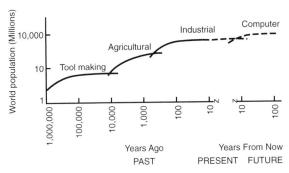

FIGURE 3.7 Technological revolutions and world population growth. Population growth for the past million years plotted on a log–log scale shows a series of surges, each associated with a technological revolution that has increased the earth's capacity to support human life. Some technological optimists have also suggested that widespread adoption of computers may lift productivity sufficiently to support a new surge of population growth in coming decades. [*Source:* Adapted with modifications from Edward S. Deevey Jr., "The Human Population." Copyright © 1960 by Scientific American, Inc. All rights reserved.]

Birth Rates, Death Rates, and Rates of Natural Increase.   Birth rates are commonly expressed in terms of yearly births per thousand people. For example, at the beginning of 1993, the population of the United States was 256,516,000 people, and the number of births in that year was 4,039,000. Dividing the number of live births by the midyear population in year *x* and multiplying by 1,000 gives a birth rate of 15.7 for the year. Similarly, we obtain the 1993 crude death rate for the United States by dividing the total number of deaths, 2,268,000 by the average total population in that year and multiplying by 1,000, which gives a crude death rate of 8.8. The rate of natural increase is the difference between the birth and death rates, or 6.9 per 1,000. The rate of natural increase is often also expressed as a percentage, that is, so many people per 100 per year, which in this case would be 0.69 percent. This rate for the United States is typical of industrialized countries, but it is well below the rate of 1.7 percent for the world as a whole.

Although these are the most commonly used forms of birth and death rates, meaningful population analyses and predictions require more refined measures. The *crude birth rate* described before is not as revealing as the *fertility rate,* which is the number of births in a given year per thousand women of childbearing age (15 to 49). Fertility rates are more useful for comparing anticipated changes in a young population having a large number of females with those of a more mature population. They are also generally higher in rural than in urban areas, among lower classes than upper classes, and among blue-collar workers than professionals,

although these differentials have diminished in more advanced countries as educational levels and the quality of mass communications have risen.

Likewise, the *crude death rate* does not give as much information as the *age-specific death rate,* defined as the number of deaths per thousand in a particular age group. One widely used age-specific death rate is the *infant mortality rate,* or the number of deaths in the first year of life per thousand live births. This is one of the more valuable indices of socioeconomic well-being. Another measure that performs a similar function is *life expectancy,* that is, the average age at death of the inhabitants of a given area.

Events Affecting Population Increase.   Until the eighteenth century, birth rates approaching 50 per thousand were typical throughout the world, but they were generally balanced by similarly high death rates, and rates of natural increase remained low. The death rate was the more volatile of the two measures. The most dramatic causes of fluctuations in death rates were disease, famine, and war. The bubonic plague A.D. 1348 to 1350) quickly reduced Europe's population by at least one-fourth, and the London plague of 1665 eliminated one-third to one-half of that city's population. Endemic diseases, such as malaria, have been almost as destructive to certain populations, even in more recent years.

Many of the deaths attributed to disease in some parts of the world are the indirect effects of hunger and malnutrition; indeed, the correlation among disease, hunger, and death rates is very high. Periodic famine, caused by floods, droughts, insect plagues, and war, was one of the earliest population controls. China had an estimated 1828 famines between 108 B.C. and A.D. 1911, an average of about one per year. Nine to 13 million Chinese died between 1869 and 1876 alone. Nor are famines unknown to this present century. The USSR suffered 5 to 10 million deaths attributable to famine between 1918 and 1922 and between 1932 and 1934. India lost from 2 to 4 million in 1943. Starvation also accompanies warfare. Among some primitive peoples, as in the Indonesian province of West Irian, intertribal wars have been a major and customary cause of death. The two world wars in this century reduced populations throughout Europe.

Famines, epidemics, and war also affect birth rates, by reducing the ability to conceive and by disrupting normal family life; however, voluntary means of reducing births have had the most pervasive and prolonged effects on population growth. Although birth control has been the most effective means of population control in modern times, early societies limited population growth by such means as infanticide, sexual taboos, killing the sick and aged, and restrictions on marriage. Abortion is of growing significance. The extent to which birth control is practiced, as well as the choice of methods, is influenced by cost and the availability of information, within a framework of religions, customs, attitudes, technological development, and degree of urbanization.

Population Theory

The steeply rising curve of world population shows clearly that the historic balance between births and deaths has been seriously disturbed in the last three centuries. Fear that pressure of population on resources would result has given rise to a number of population theories, the most familiar being that of Rev. Thomas Malthus, written in 1798. The eighteenth century had been a period of optimism concerning the perfectibility of humankind, combined with the view that a large population is a source of national strength. By the end of that century, however, a reaction had taken place. The Industrial Revolution in Britain had brought with it a rapid increase in population, and the appearance of bad times soon caused the growth in numbers to seem excessive. A period of poor harvests, high food prices, and much misery provided the setting for Malthus's pessimistic statement.

Malthus.   Thomas R. Malthus was an English clergyman, historian, and economist, born in 1766 to the English landed gentry and educated at Cambridge. In his famous *Essay on the Principle of Population,* he expressed the view that it is not desirable for a population to expand indefinitely without the assurance that the means for supporting that population can keep pace. Malthus concluded that population has a natural tendency to increase rapidly as long as food, or "subsistence," is available. If unchecked, population will go on doubling itself every 25 years, that is, it will increase at a "geometric ratio" (2, 4, 8, 16, 32, etc.). At the same time, even under the most favorable circumstances, he believed that the food supply cannot increase faster than at an "arithmetic ratio" (3, 6, 9, 12, 15, etc.). The number of people to be fed thus would quickly overtake and exceed the food supply.

Malthus believed that the *ultimate check* to population growth is exhaustion of the food supply. This ultimate check of course, would, cause death from starvation, but more usually either of two kinds of immediate checks intervenes. One is the *preventative check,* resulting from the ability of human beings to recognize the consequences of their behavior. This preventative check Malthus called "moral restraint," by which he, being a good churchman, meant postponement of marriage, "accompanied by strictly moral behavior"—the purpose being to avoid having children before the parents are able to support them. The second intervening influence is the *positive check,* "all of those causes which tend in any way prematurely to shorten the duration of human life." These include "vice"—those mis-

fortunes we bring upon ourselves, such as war and the various consequences of immoral behavior—and "misery"—unavoidable products of the laws of nature, especially plagues and famines. The positive checks act to limit population growth by raising death rates, whereas the preventative checks accomplish this same result by reducing birth rates.

According to Malthus, the lowest stratum of society is most affected by positive checks. In mature societies, these forces cause the population to rise and fall in a cyclical fashion. In times of prosperity, young people can support a family at an earlier age, there are thus more children, and the population increases. This in turn causes the price of labor (wages) to fall when the children seek work. The ensuing hard times bring the Malthusian checks into play. The age at which young people marry increases, and less children are born, which relieves the problem of labor oversupply when they reach working age. Prosperity then returns, bringing with it new opportunities for earlier marriage and a repetition of the population growth cycle.

Malthus was enormously influential. His basic ideas had a pervasive effect not only on philosophical, economic, social, and political thought, but also on the physical sciences, legislation, and popular education. Out of his work grew a school of population study that, with modifications, persists today. Many believe that *spaceship earth* has finite resources and a fragile environment, and that the world is rapidly approaching limits to growth that will be signaled by major conflicts and crises. Others disagree. Marxists claim that the problem is not resource limitation, but maldistribution caused by exploitation of the poor and powerless by the rich and powerful. Modern theorists such as Julian Simon claim that it is people who are the "ultimate resource," capable of using their brainpower to overcome any temporary restrictions by inventing new activities and improved life-styles. We will have more to say about the debate between Malthusian prophets of doom and *technological optimists* such as Simon in Chapters 4 and 5.

Demographic Transition

The rapid growth of Europe's population confirmed Malthus's predictions, but the remarkable increase in European prosperity did not. He did not anticipate the effects that development might have on the forces determining population size. The close interrelationship between the processes of development or "modernization" and those of population growth lend support to the views of anti-Malthusians, such as Simon.

The European Experience.   The demographic history of modern Europe illustrates some of these relationships. Prior to the Industrial Revolution, when death rates and birth rates were very high, Europe's population was fairly stable. Urban death rates were especially high, and city growth was made possible only by heavy immigration. The unwholesome urban conditions responsible for high mortality rates resemble those of many cities in less-developed countries today: unemployment and poverty, uncertain food supply, contaminated water, inadequate housing, lack of sewage disposal, and poor medical service.

The Industrial Revolution that began in Britain during the second half of the eighteenth century had profound effects on both death and birth rates. The application of inanimate energy to mining and manufacturing greatly increased total and per capita output of goods. The rising incomes that resulted from greater production made possible the purchase of food in larger quantities and of higher quality. Incomes also provided financial support for better sanitary practices and for medical research. Although these improvements in food supply and public health evolved gradually, their cumulative effect was to substantially reduce death rates, especially infant mortality rates, and to make cities capable of sustaining their populations. Much of the total rise in population during the succeeding two centuries since the Industrial Revolution can be attributed to improved conditions in the cities.

Related to these urban and industrial developments, and essential to them, was the accompanying revolution in agriculture. Previously, British agriculture had consisted mainly of subsistence farms producing very little surplus for cash sale. Even the richest agricultural regions were unable to grow sufficient food to support more than 15 to 20 percent of their populations in urban activities, such as manufacturing, commerce, and government. Near the end of the eighteenth century, however, in response to growing urban demands, farmers began to breed higher-quality livestock, introduce new high-yielding crops, and develop farm techniques that increased the output of traditional commodities. Through the "enclosure movement," medieval open fields and common lands were reallocated into compact and individually owned farmsteads, and the many landless laborers who were displaced made their way to the growing cities. Thus, as the Industrial Revolution made larger urban concentrations necessary, new developments in agriculture supplied the additional food required to support a growing nonfarm population, and reorganization of the agricultural landscape (which took the form of waves radiating from the new cities) forced surplus farm workers into the growing urban labor force.

Important innovations in transportation took place at the same time as these industrial and agricultural developments. The construction of roads, canals, and railways, and the invention of new types of vehicles, greatly expanded the range of distribution and collection. No longer was it necessary for communities, or even countries, to be self-sufficient in raw materials and foodstuffs. Local crop failures thus became far less likely to cause hunger and famine. Not only goods but also people and ideas circulated freely over greater distances, thereby accelerating the rate of scientific discoveries, including those related to health.

As these events combined to bring about a steady decline in death rates, birth rates also were dropping, although at a slower rate. The Industrial Revolution influenced birth rates in ways not anticipated by Malthus. It did this first of all by concentrating people into towns and cities, where they no longer had the need for large families that they once had on the farm. At the same time, the decline in infant mortality removed an important incentive for large numbers of births. And as ideas of the French Enlightenment spread over Europe, more time was devoted to women's education, and age at marriage rose. With effective changes in attitude toward family size, the practice of contraception spread. Beginning among upper-income groups in urbanized areas, contraception diffused to lower levels of society and into rural areas. Malthus could not have foreseen this, and he would not have approved of it if he had.

The development of contraception did not exert its full force until this present century. Most of the nineteenth-century reductions in birth rates came from increased age of marriage. Europe was only able to escape what might have been excessive population pressures because its surplus peoples migrated in large numbers. These migrants brought rich virgin lands into cultivation and shipped grain and other commodities back to their former homelands. In this century, the population of Western Europe has stabilized as death rates and birth rates have come into balance at new low levels. As the same demographic trends diffused to other industrializing nations, the advanced countries have eluded the Malthusian trap. The immediate worry today is for the less-developed countries, where rapidly growing populations threaten to fulfill Malthus's gloomy prophesy.

Population Growth in the Less-Developed World.
Some of the densely settled lands of eastern and southern Asia, especially China and India, likely reached their optimum population densities as agriculturally based peasant societies centuries ago. The Chinese population apparently fluctuated at a high level over an extended period, rising in good times and falling in bad times, high birth rates offset by war, plague, and famine. This pattern was disturbed by the coming of European colonial control, which brought a new burst of population growth in such lands as Indonesia and India. Colonial administrations reduced internecine fighting among native populations and introduced economic improvements, causing death rates to fall below persistently high birth rates.

Since World War II, much of the less-developed world has experienced a population crisis as improved public health delivery and better food distribution caused further declines in mortality rates. Unlike the gradual reduction of death rates in today's developed countries, which had to await a whole series of medical advances over a period of two centuries, today's less-developed countries have imported low-cost, highly effective, death-reduction measures that were ready-made. Areas otherwise untouched by modernization have benefited from sophisticated medical technology. So successful have these programs been that crude death rates in the less-developed world fell from 24.3 in 1950 to only 9.9 per thousand by the 1990, hardly different from the rate of 9.8 for developed countries. Death rates for several developing countries have actually dropped below those of the developed world. Thus, left with an unusually young population after years of runaway population growth, Costa Rica had a death rate of only 3.8 by 1987.

Meanwhile, birth rates remain high throughout most of the developing world. As Figure 3.8 shows, crude birth rates exceeding 40 per thousand are typical of countries at the lower levels of development. Some African countries—Niger and Uganda, for example—have crude birth rates of 50 per thousand or more. In 1990, Eastern Africa as a whole

had a rate of natural increase of more than 3.0 per annum, and Western Africa was increasing at a rate of 3.26. In the Middle East, rates of natural increase are high and still rising, especially around the Persian Gulf. For instance, by the mid-1990s Iraq's population was increasing by 3.7 percent per annum, Saudi Arabia's by 3.8 percent, and Syria's by 3.5 percent. This *population explosion* in the developing world will have added another billion people to the world total by end of the final decade of the present century.

Unlike the European colonial powers of the previous century, the less-developed countries of today cannot ship their surplus populations to new lands, although some, such as Indonesia and Brazil, are attempting to send people from their overcrowded "heartlands" into lightly populated outlying regions. Consequently, rates of growth for the developing countries remain high. At the same time, rates of population growth continue to diminish among advanced countries, falling to only 0.53 percent for the group in 1990. This represents a decline of about one-third within one decade. Population growth has essentially halted in Western Europe, where several countries—notably Hungary,

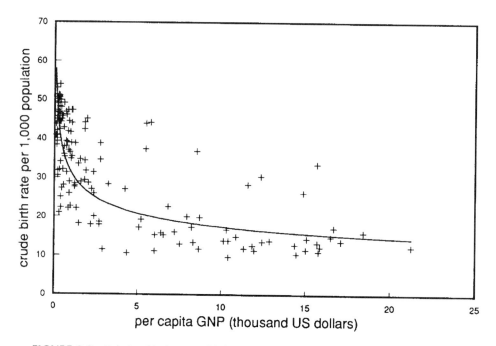

FIGURE 3.8   Relationship between birth rates and per capita GNP, 1987. Countries at the lowest levels of development tend to have the highest birth rates. Tightly clustered at the upper left of the diagram are nearly 50 low-income African and Middle Eastern nations. At higher levels of per capita GNP, the extreme positive anomalies (those countries lying above the regression line in this diagram) are Middle Eastern oil exporters. This suggests that, although the relationship between income and birth rates is strong ($R^2 = 0.615$), cultural factors play an important part, too. The role of culture is likewise apparent in the clustering of low-income East Asian countries at the lower left of the diagram. European countries, and Japan, constitute most of the cases below the line at higher-income levels. The United States lies very close to the line, suggesting a birth rate corresponding closely to what might be expected of a country with its per capita GNP. [*Source:* Based on data from the *1990 Britannica Book of the Year* (Chicago: Encyclopaedia Britannica, 1990).]

Denmark, Austria, and Germany—are actually seeing their populations shrink. Even in their periods of most rapid growth, the more-developed countries of today never attained rates of population increase approaching present rates in the developing world.

The already crowded lands of Asia and Africa have felt the most immediate and obvious impacts of this growth, but the less densely populated Latin American countries are also affected. One important consequence of high growth rates is a youthful age distribution. Figure 3.9 compares the age structure of a rapidly growing population, Malawi, with that of a mature population, Switzerland. In Malawi 48 percent of the population is below the age of 15, as opposed to only 13.5 percent in Switzerland. Africa as a whole has more than 45 percent of its population in this dependent age group. The Islamic lands of Southwest Asia have similarly high percentages of the young, as do some Central American countries.

Transition Theory. This international comparison of demographic characteristics suggests that countries undergo a *demographic transition* as they ascend the ladder of development. The study of this process has given birth to *transition theory,* which serves as a tool for predicting future population changes of developing countries and offers a means for anticipating the problems that accompany these changes. According to this theory, a country passes through three demographic phases as it develops (see Figure 3.10).

In the first phase, the population remains fairly stable. It is kept in equilibrium by the combination of a high birth rate and a similarly high, but fluctuating, death rate. This

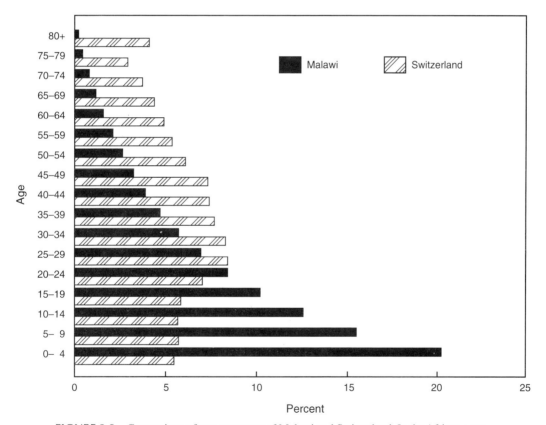

FIGURE 3.9 Comparison of age structures of Malawi and Switzerland. In the African country of Malawi, nearly half (48.3 percent) of the population is under the age of 15. Such a young population is typical of less-developed countries with high birth rates and declining death rates. By contrast, only 13.5 percent of Switzerland's population is in the under-15 group, which is common for developed countries with birth rates and death rates that are both low. Note also that in the case of Switzerland, the 5-year age groups below 20 years become progressively smaller, indicating that the birth rate is still falling. In the upper age groups, the proportions of the two populations are reversed: Nearly 1 out of every 8 Swiss is 65 years or older; only 1 out of every 40 Malawians reaches that age. [*Source:* Based on data from the *United Nations Demographic Yearbook* (New York: United Nations 1995).]

describes the demography of societies as diverse as preindustrial Europe, premodern China, and small population groups living in the rain forests of the Amazon and Congo basins.

When the development process commences, the country enters the second phase. As diets and health improve, the death rate drops; but the birth rate remains high throughout the earlier stages of the development process before it, too, begins to decline. During Phase II, therefore, the two curves diverge, producing a *demographic gap*. This is the period of rapid population growth, or "population explosion." Much of Latin America and the Middle East and parts of Africa and southern and eastern Asia are at this point. Subsequent maturing of the economy brings urbanization, higher per capita incomes, and various social changes, especially better-educated women, all of which favor smaller families. The accompanying changes in social attitudes therefore act to reduce the birth rate during the latter part of Phase II.

When at last the birth rate has fallen to a level approximating that of the already low death rate, Phase III has been reached. In this final phase, it is the birth rate that fluctuates about some mean, a response mainly to fluctuations in the business cycle. When times are good, more women enter the labor force, and child rearing is deferred. It is when times are bad that women are more likely to stay home and choose instead to raise a child. The countries of Western Europe, Anglo-America, and Oceania, as well as Japan, have attained this new low-level equilibrium.

Transition theory actually represents a generalization of the Western European experience. Recent events have shown that the history of today's industrialized nations offers a less-than-perfect model for predicting demographic change in today's less-developed countries, however. Fertility rates in less-developed countries are much higher than they were in premodern Europe, a result of religious beliefs, marriage customs, land tenure arrangements, and other cultural factors. People will eagerly accept innovations that improve their health and increase their longevity, but they do not easily relinquish traditional attitudes toward marriage and the home.

Illustrating this problem, Figure 3.11 contrasts the demographic changes now taking place in Sri Lanka with those experienced previously by Sweden. After a century and a half of declining birth and death rates, Sweden has now reached the point of "zero population growth," where it will likely remain for the foreseeable future. Although Sri Lanka's demographic transition began only a few decades ago, it is progressing far more rapidly than Sweden's. Note that at the start of this process, Sri Lanka's birth and death rates were both much higher than Sweden's had been and that the death rate has dropped more steeply, actually falling below that of Sweden because of Sri Lanka's very young population. The resulting population bulge will continue well into the next century.

Adding to the difficulties of applying transition theory to contemporary conditions is that countries such as India and China are more densely populated than was preindustrial Europe.

Despite these problems, the central features of the transition theory remain valid. First, the death rate always begins its decline before that of the birth rate. Second, changes in the death rate are the main determinant of variations in the rate of population growth in less-developed lands, but fluctuations of the birth rate are the principal determinant in advanced societies.

A Demographic Classification of Countries. Most population forecasts and regional analyses now make use of transition theory in some manner. The Population Division of the United Nations has devised a classification system that subdivides the second phase of demographic transition into three parts. It is important to know whether a country is just entering this critical period of rapid population expansion and thus has the major part of its population growth ahead of it, is in the middle or most explosive part of the phase, or is about to emerge from this part of the cycle.

Figure 3.12 illustrates this application of transition theory, and Figure 3.13 shows how the countries of the world fit into the scheme. The shaded portion of Figure 3.12, which indicates the dimensions of the demographic

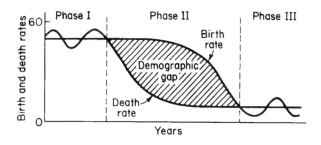

FIGURE 3.10 Transition theory. At the beginning of a country's development, the death rate tends to drop quickly, whereas the birth rate remains high for an extended period before it, too, begins to decline. The divergence of these two rates creates a demographic gap, or "population explosion," which continues until equilibrium is finally reestablished during the later stages of development.

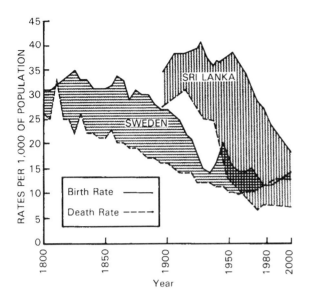

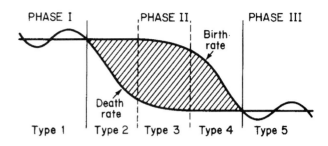

FIGURE 3.12 United Nations classification of countries according to population growth types. Phases I, II, and III correspond to the major stages of demographic transition, whereas Types 1 through 5 refer to classes of countries according to their demographic characteristics.

FIGURE 3.11 Contrast between demographic transitions in Sri Lanka and Sweden. Sweden's transition extended over nearly two centuries and has now concluded with birth and death rates at a low equilibrium. Sri Lanka's transition began a century later and is proceeding rapidly. Note that Sri Lanka's death rate has declined steeply and is now actually lower than Sweden's because of Sri Lanka's much younger population. Sri Lanka's birth rate is still far higher than its death rate, resulting in continued rapid population growth. [*Source:* From Halfdan Mahler, "People," *Scientific American*, 243(3) (September 1980): 66–77. Copyright © 1980 by Scientific American, Inc. All rights reserved.]

gap, has been subdivided into three subcategories designated with Arabic numerals. Five population growth types result. Type 1 countries have high birth rates and high, fluctuating death rates, producing stable populations with growth rates generally under 1 percent. This combination is now rare: Most former Type 1 countries now have at least begun their demographic transitions.

The transition process commences with the Type 2 countries, which have high birth rates and high but declining death rates. The two curves are beginning to diverge, indicating the start of the expansionary Phase II of the demographic transition. Population growth is well over 1 percent and climbing. A few African lands remain at this stage, as well as a handful of southern and southeastern Asian nations. Most Type 2 countries of a decade ago, however, have now proceeded to the next level of growth.

By the end of the 1980s, the majority of African nations could be classified as Type 3 countries, having entered the most explosive part of Phase II. This combina-

tion of high birth rates and low death rates results in very rapid population growth. Sharing this critical stage are most of the already crowded lands of the Middle East and South Asia, notably India with its 880 million people. Mexico, Central America, and a few South America countries are also in this part of the demographic transition.

The distinguishing features of Type 4 countries are a declining birth rate and low death rates. The effect of this is shrinking growth rates as these nations move closer to low-level equilibrium. A major part of Latin America has progressed to this point, as well as Turkey and Sri Lanka —populous countries that are gaining in the struggle to bring birth rates under control.

With their low but fluctuating birth rates and low death rates, Type 5 countries have attained the final phase of the demographic transition. Growth rates rarely exceed 1 percent, and in many cases, they are much less. All the world's older industrialized nations are at this state, and several European countries are at or below zero population growth.

Consequences of Population Growth and Decline

The relationship between population growth and food supply was Malthus's chief concern, and this subject continues to preoccupy most writers on population today. Vital as the question of feeding an expanding world population may be, however, this is by no means the only problem resulting from population increase. As most Third World countries have discovered, rapid population growth creates other economic, social, political, and environmental problems that complicate the developmental process. Meanwhile, some

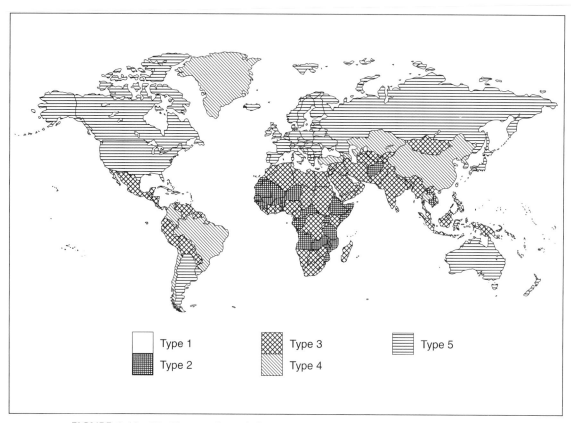

FIGURE 3.13   World map of population growth types. The 1980s saw important demographic changes throughout the world, and these trends continued into the mid-1990s. During this period, most of Africa shifted from the ominous UN Type 2 category into the explosive Type 3 stage of the demographic transition. In this it has been joined by the Middle East and densely populated South Asia, together with Mexico, Central America, and parts of Andean South America. Nevertheless, birth rates are declining in several Latin American countries, and semi-industrialized Argentina and Uruguay have now joined the ranks of demographically mature Type 5 countries. Encouraging progress toward population stability has also been made in East Asia, especially by China, with its billion-plus population (now Type 4), and Japan, Korea, Taiwan, and Hong Kong (Type 5 countries). The older industrialized lands have long ago completed their demographic transitions, and some European populations are beginning to shrink, as are those of some successor states to the former Soviet Union. [*Source:* Based on data from the *1995 Britannica Book of the Year* (Chicago: Encyclopaedia Britannica, 1990).]

mature industrial societies are having to adjust to another kind of demographic change—zero population growth, or even decline.

Problems of a Growing Population.   All too frequently a less-developed country finds its developmental gains wiped out by overly rapid population growth. Arriving at the end of the year with increased output, it discovers that these additional goods must be divided among a still larger number of people. The problem of diminishing per capita food supplies is one of the most worrisome effects of excessive population growth, not only because of humanitarian concerns but also because of its political and economic consequences.

Figure 3.14 shows that many of the less-developed countries are finding it difficult to supply the daily nutritional needs of their people. The diagram suggests a fairly close relationship between daily per capita food energy (calories) and level of development (measured by per capita *gross national product,* GNP). Even so, the average developing-world family spends a larger proportion of its income on food than does the typical family in advanced societies. Referred to as *Engel's law,* this relationship is illustrated by the case of Ghana, where half of family income goes for food, or Honduras, where a family spends more than two-fifths of its income in this manner. By contrast, a Danish family spends less than one-fourth of its income on food, and a Canadian family spends about one-fifth.

Not only do most people in the developing world consume less food per day, but they are also more likely to suffer from dietary deficiencies. The poorer the population, the more dependent the people are on starchy foods, such as grains and root crops. The essential "protective" foods, which are most costly, are generally lacking in the diets of the poorest peoples, as shown by the relationship between GNP and consumption of proteins (Figure 3.15), and especially animal proteins (Figure 3.16). These associations between diet and development imply that a rise in per capita income should bring a drop in the percentage of income spent on food, an increase in the total amount consumed (until some optimal level is reached), and a shift from cheaper starches to more expensive and nutritious foods, especially animal products ("indirect calories").

Despite the difficulties of feeding their growing populations, most underdeveloped countries employ a majority of their labor forces in agriculture (Figure 3.17). Much of this agriculture is of an unproductive sort. Consider the plight of Asian or African peasants on their plots of exhausted land, which are so tiny that they must be devoted almost entirely to grains and other foods for direct human consumption. In their poverty, these peasant farmers are caught up in a vicious circle. Unable to afford machinery, fertilizer, or improved seeds, they can only apply increased quantities of human labor in their efforts to raise levels of output. This provides a motivation to have large families, which in turn means more mouths to feed. High rates of population growth in less-developed countries therefore tend both to reduce the quantity and quality of per capita food consumption and to affect adversely the conditions for producing that food.

In addition to its impact on food supply, rapid population growth causes economic stress. As the most accessible and highest-quality resources are used up, it becomes necessary to turn to less-productive farmlands, grazing

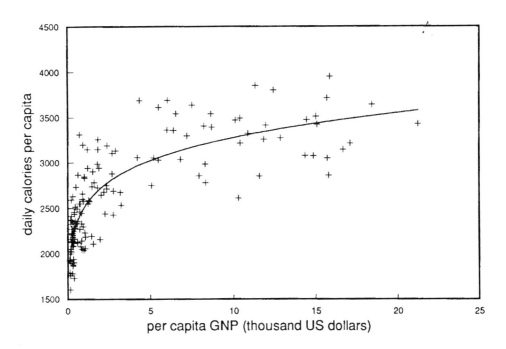

FIGURE 3.14 Relationship between per capita calorie consumption and level of development ($R^2 = 0.704$). This diagram lends support to Engel's Law, which says that poor families allocate larger proportions of their incomes to food than do richer ones. Note that the regression line climbs steeply at first but quickly tapers off at higher levels of per capita GNP. Clustered in the lower-left corner of the diagram are 43 impoverished countries with daily calorie consumptions averaging below the 2,240 considered essential to support normal human health and activity. Twenty-five of these countries are in sub-Saharan Africa, 11 are in Asia, and most of the remainder in Latin America. The more affluent nations vary considerably in the amounts of food they consume, mainly as a result of cultural differences in dietary patterns. Thus, Japan and the newly industrialized countries of East Asia are well below the regression line, as is most of Scandinavia. The lands of central and southern Europe are generally well above the line. What these country averages do not disclose, however, are the large numbers of poorly fed people within some of the wealthiest nations. [*Source:* Based on data from the *1990 Britannica Book of the Year* (Chicago: Encyclopaedia Britannica, 1990).]

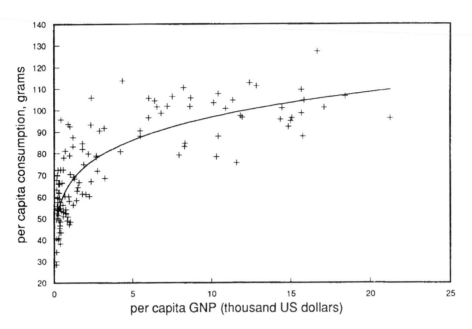

FIGURE 3.15   Relationship between per capita protein consumption and level of development ($R^2 = 0.654$). In addition to the issue of providing a sufficient quantity of food for the
world's people (see Figure 3.14) is the question of ensuring its nutritional quality, measured
here by the amount of protein in the average daily diet. At the lower end of this scale are 63
countries whose populations consume less than 75 grams per person; none of the 63 has an
annual per capita GNP exceeding $1,800. The majority of these are African or Asian, includ-
ing such populous nations as India and Pakistan, but a few are Latin American. Among the
higher-income nations are a number that consume unusually large quantities of protein. These
are mainly economies with large animal industries (Argentina and New Zealand) or fisheries
(Iceland). Several Mediterranean lands, especially Greece, are big consumers of protein and
thus appear well above the regression line in the diagram. Prominent among those better-off
countries consuming less-than-expected quantities of protein are Japan and the newly industrialized nations of East Asia, all with ancient traditions of rice culture. [*Source:* Data from
the *FAO Production Yearbook 1987* (Rome: Food and Agriculture Organization of the United
Nations, 1988), and the *1990 Britannica Book of the Year* (Chicago: Encyclopaedia
Britannica, 1990).]

lands, fisheries, and forests, and to mineral deposits that are
more remote and of poorer quality. Overexploitation of
these resources brings environmental deterioration. The
resulting decline in output for each additional new unit of
input—referred to as the *law of diminishing returns*—produces upward pressure on global commodity prices.
Scarcity provides opportunities for the creation of cartels,
such as the Organization of Petroleum Exporting Countries
(OPEC), which are able to set artificially high prices for the
commodities over which they share oligopolistic control.
The problem is only solved by technological innovation, as
we shall see in Chapters 4 and 5.

Population growth underlies the worsening global
problem of unemployment. In the industrialized lands,
when young people born during the "baby-boom" era of the
1950s and 1960s reached an employable age, they entered
the labor force more rapidly than jobs could be created for
them; consequently, these age groups have since experi-

enced high unemployment rates. The problem is far worse
in the less-developed countries, where high birth rates are
flooding labor markets with millions of new workers. In
these nations, available farmland quickly becomes overcrowded, and fledgling industries cannot generate manufacturing employment rapidly enough to absorb the overspill
from the countryside. The result is high unemployment,
which would be even greater if they included all the *under-
employed,* the surplus workers who remain on the family
farms even though their labor is not really needed there.
India, already burdened with massive unemployment and
underemployment, has little hope of finding sufficient work
for the more than 5 million young people entering the labor
force each year. In neighboring Bangladesh, at least one-
third of the work force is unemployed.

Other related economic and social ills result from
overly rapid population growth. With millions of job-
seekers pouring into their cities each year, many developing

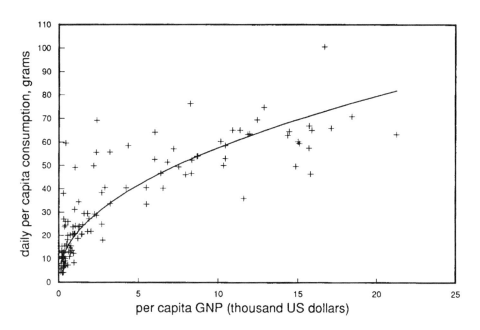

FIGURE 3.16 Relationship between per capita animal protein consumption and level of development. Consumption of animal proteins offers a better measure of nutritional quality than does the total amount of protein in the diet (see Figure 3.15), and it is highly correlated with per capita GNP ($R^2 = 0.768$). Looking at the availability of the higher-quality proteins found in meat, fish, and milk products gives a different view of nutrition in several major world areas than does access to total protein alone. Some of the world's poorest populations derive most of their protein from vegetable sources of inadequate nutritional value. This is true of the impoverished countries of Africa and South Asia shown tightly clustered in the lower left-hand corner of the diagram. Many Latin Americans also rely on vegetable sources for much of their protein (beef-producing Argentina and Uruguay are exceptions). Most Western Europeans consume ample quantities of animal proteins, especially in those countries with large animal industries, such as Ireland. Australia and New Zealand also rank high for this same reason. The world's leading consumer of animal proteins, however, is Iceland, where fishing is the leading industry and supplies a principal item of diet. [*Source:* Data from the *FAO Production Yearbook 1987* (Rome: Food and Agriculture Organization of the United Nations, 1988), and the *1990 Britannica Book of the Year* (Chicago: Encyclopaedia Britannica, 1990).]

countries are wrestling with a host of severe urban problems: overcrowding, inadequate housing, and lack of sanitation and health services, in addition to severe unemployment.

A further burden for developing countries with high birth rates is the large number of people in the dependent ages. With one-third to one-half of their people under the age of 15, these countries find it exceedingly difficult to provide needed services, especially education. So many children are reaching school age each year that schools cannot be built or staffed fast enough to accommodate them. Compulsory education laws are thus of little practical significance, and literacy rates are in some cases actually falling, which diminishes the quality of the labor force.

Thus, plagued by excessive population growth, many less-developed countries are trapped in a vicious circle of poverty, malnutrition, and disease. Despite improvements in

public health delivery that have reduced death rates and therefore fueled the very population expansion that retards their development efforts, the developing countries still lag behind the industrialized nations in quality of health care. Indeed, such indicators of health as life expectancy are strongly correlated with level of development, which is measured by per capita GNP (see Figure 3.18). A direct link exists between birth rates and the health of women and children: After repeated pregnancies, mothers become debilitated and vulnerable to death in childbirth, and the mortality rates of their infants rise.

Finally, rapid population growth may have adverse political consequences. The many economic and social problems of rapidly growing populations are major sources of internal political instability in many developing countries. Declining domestic farm output, for instance, can undermine the stability of governments, as shortages and

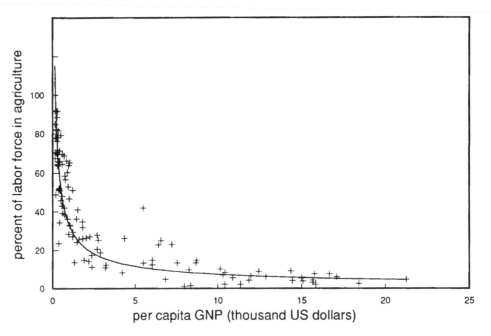

FIGURE 3.17   Relationship between level of development and percent of labor force in agriculture. This association is very strong ($R^2 = 0.805$). In the poorest countries of sub-Saharan Africa and southern Asia, agriculture engages virtually all the working population. Among the extreme cases are Nepal (92.1), Burundi (91.7), and Rwanda (91.8). This percentage drops steeply with increasing levels of per capita GNP, however, tapering off gradually thereafter. Among the higher-income countries, the primary occupations employ relatively small numbers of workers, even in such major exporters of agricultural commodities as Canada, the United States, Australia, and Argentina. Most of Western Europe is below the regression line. Prominent among those middle- and upper-income countries rising above the line are several oil-rich states in the Middle East, together with the USSR and East European countries, whose agricultural sectors use labor inefficiently. [*Source:* Data from the *FAO Production Yearbook 1987* (Rome: Food and Agriculture Organization of the United Nations, 1988), and the *1990 Britannica Book of the Year* (Chicago: Encyclopaedia Britannica. 1990).]

rising prices bring popular unrest. Food riots in Egypt during the 1970s and later in Poland underscored the political dangers of an inadequate food supply. Many countries are forced to divert scarce foreign exchange from development to pay for food imports. At the same time, differential rates of population growth among countries often produce international political strains. If, for example, the population of one country is increasing faster than the populations of its neighbors, this may arouse fears that the overcrowded country may attempt to seize adjacent lands to relieve internal population pressures. The suspicious attitude toward Iran held by other Persian Gulf countries, whose populations are much smaller, stems partly from this source; Indochina has endured centuries of warfare between overpopulated neighbors contending for the rice-basket areas of the Mekong delta. History offers innumerable examples of wars of conquest prompted by the desire on the part of one country for relief from overcrowding.

Problems of Declining Populations.   In the industrialized countries of Western Europe and North America, uneasiness is arising over an opposite demographic trend—population decrease. Despite some disagreement about the precise consequences of population decline, it is generally conceded that these consequences are pervasive. The demographic effects are the most obvious. Population growth depends not only on birth rates but also on the number of women reaching childbearing age. Hence, until recently, the arrival of postwar babies into this age group has ensured a substantial growth in population, despite a continuing decline in birth rates. Even though family size in the United States now has dropped to a two-child average, which is below the replacement level, births will exceed deaths for the rest of the century. Meanwhile, the age structure of the United States population has begun to change, affecting the mix of goods and services demanded. Smaller numbers of children are entering the schools, whereas the proportion of

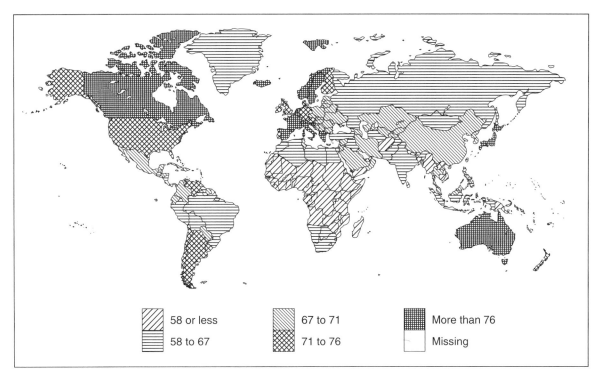

FIGURE 3.18 Life expectancy at birth. A measure of the general level of health in a population, life expectancy ranges from less than 45 years in some of the poorest countries to nearly 80 years in richer ones. The lowest life expectancies are concentrated in sub-Saharan Africa and parts of South Asia, which are also areas of poor nutrition (see Figures 3.16 and 3.17). Life expectancy continues to rise in the industrialized countries. Japan and Hong Kong are the current leaders, but life expectancies exceeding 75 years are common throughout Western Europe. Longevity is rising steadily in the newly industrializing countries of East Asia and in such South Asian countries as Sri Lanka, complicating the problem of containing population growth in those crowded lands. Life expectancy has declined in some former Soviet Bloc countries following the collapse of communism and the disorganization of society that ensured. [*Source:* Data from the *World Bank Atlas 1996* (Washington, DC: The World Bank, 1996).]

the population aged 65 and above is growing. In these trends, the United States is following on the heels of the European countries. Most of these have arrived at the point of zero population growth, and some are beginning to see their populations shrink.

A declining population is an aging population. As life expectancy increases and people live to more-advanced ages at a time when birth rates are declining, the proportion of a country's citizens in the retirement ages rises. A nation in which this process is occurring with remarkable rapidity is Japan (Figure 3.19). With what is now the world's highest life expectancy, the Japanese population is being transformed from one that has been relatively young into one that is quickly aging.

The changing nature of the dependency problem is evident from Figure 3.20, which illustrates the diverse conditions that exist today in major world regions, together

with the situation that the United Nations expects to prevail in A.D. 2025. The developed regions, with their mature, stable populations contrast sharply with the less-developed regions, whose populations are still very young. If we compare the child-dependency ratios (the child population under 15 expressed as a relationship to the number in the productive years from 15 through 64) with the elderly-dependency ratios (the number 65 or older as a proportion of those in the intermediate years), it is apparent that a comparatively small number of Africans and Latin Americans in the economically active age group must support very large numbers of children but few elderly persons. In Canada and the United States, and in Europe, a mainly middle-aged work force must provide for a great many retirees. The UN projections for A.D. 2025 suggest that the heavy burden of child dependency will diminish somewhat for the LDCs as population growth begins to come under control, especially in East Asia. For the developed regions, however, caring for a growing elderly population will become increasingly onerous.

The aging of its population confronts a society with new kinds of problems. Prominent among these is the heavy cost of providing adequate national pension programs, as shown by the strains that have emerged in the U.S. social security system. A response to the longer-term problem of declining numbers of active workers has been to reverse a trend toward earlier retirement; in the United States, the customary age of retirement has shifted from 65 as mandatory retirement rules have been eliminated altogether.

A second cost burden imposed by an aging population stems from rising medical bills for treating diseases of the elderly. In the United States, there is a continuing crisis over the soaring expenditures for health care, exacerbated by a rapidly developing medical technology that prolongs life at an ever-rising cost.

Helping to compensate for higher outlays for pensions and health care in a mature population, a falling birth rate may serve to hold education expenditures in check. But the educational level of the labor force is a major determinant of economic growth, especially in an era when new knowledge-intensive information age industries have begun to replace older industries that employ unskilled workers in assembly-line production. The need for adult education and retraining for older employees displaced from declining industries is growing as fewer young workers, many of whom have above-average education levels, enter the labor force, and as a surplus work force of displaced workers in their fifties grows.

The product mix of consumer demand changes as the population shifts from the "Pepsi generation" to the "Geritol generation" and as needs shift from high chairs to wheelchairs. Adjusting production levels to changes in the demand mix is more difficult if the labor force is aging and the proportion of new, more mobile, workers is falling, although this may hasten the adoption of new computerized technologies: robots on the assembly line and computer terminals that enable information rather than people to be moved. Certainly, most current innovations in industry are substituting information software and capital for labor in

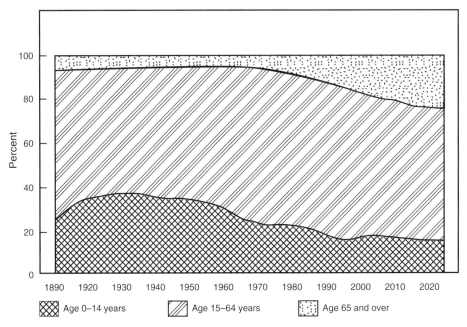

FIGURE 3.19 Japan's aging population. Although Japan's industrialization began in the latter part of the nineteenth century, its population structure resembled that of a Third World country until after World War II. The birth rate was high and life expectancy was low, forcing those Japanese in their economically active years to support large numbers of dependent children, but relatively few elderly persons. This diagram illustrates the extraordinary speed with which postwar Japan brought its birth rate under control and extended the life-span of its citizens. Today, the Japanese have the world's highest life-expectancy rate (along with the Icelanders), posing a wholly new set of dependency problems. [*Source:* For 1890–1985, Japan, Bureau of Statistics, Population Censuses; for 1990–2025, Institute of Population Problems, Ministry of Health and Welfare, Population Projections for Japan, 1985–2085 (Tokyo, 1987).]

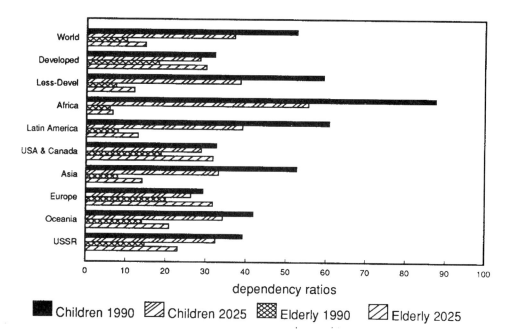

FIGURE 3.20   Age-dependency ratios for the world and major regions, 1990 and 2025 (UN medium-variant projections). The child-dependency ratio represents the ratio of the population 0–14 years of age, to the economically active group aged 15–64, per 100. The elderly-dependency ratio is the ratio of the population aged 65 years and older to the population of intermediate age, per 100. This measure indicates the relative number of persons in each dependency category that must be supported by the economically active population. In the least-developed areas, the working age population must support relatively large numbers of dependent children; in the more-developed areas, workers must provide for large numbers of retirees. By the year 2025, the more-developed regions can anticipate having to support more elderly people than children. For the less-developed areas, the huge burden of child dependency will likely diminish somewhat. [*Source:* Data from *World Population Prospects 1988* (New York: United Nations, 1989.]

the production process, as we shall see in Chapters 8, 9, and 10, calling on smaller numbers of better-trained, higher-quality workers.

Finally, a decline in population can have an impact on public opinion and policy making. An older population generally holds more conservative views on public questions. Furthermore, as we discovered during the 1930s, when birth rates dropped steeply in North America and Europe in response to the Great Depression, many people reacted with feelings of extreme anxiety, fearing an adverse effect on national prosperity and security. Although population decline does indeed pose problems of adjustment, these merely signal the need for creative public policy rather than calling for programs to encourage higher birth rates. Students of such problems generally believe that the average person will be substantially better off economically if population growth follows a two-child family pattern rather than a three-child family, or more.

FUTURE POPULATIONS

Predictions

Because of the differential progress of the demographic transition, the spatial pattern of the human population is undergoing changes that will make tomorrow's world population map look very different from today's. The kinds of demographic change now occurring create innumerable problems for the present and threaten even graver ones for the future. If we are to devise strategies to cope with such problems, we must have forecasts of future population growth that are sufficiently reliable to pinpoint the trouble spots and to quantify the potential danger. In the past, population forecasting was notoriously poor; most earlier projections greatly underestimated the rates at which growth was to occur. Thus, in 1949, Colin Clark forecast a world population of 3.5 billion by 1990, a figure that was exceeded before 1970. The main reason for such errors was the failure of demographers to anticipate the important declines in mortality and increases in life expectancy that advances in medical technology and the provision of public health care would bring. Today's forecasts have become more reliable, as demographers sharpen their analytical tools and receive better information. The 1980–1981 series of censuses around the world tended to confirm the improved quality of United Nations projections. These projections benefited from much improved data on fertility and mortality, especially from larger countries, such as China, India, Bangladesh, and Indonesia. Caution is always necessary, however. Trends can change, sometimes quickly. And no forecast can allow for the unexpected: catastrophes such as global wars, massive famines, or the spread of AIDS, or unanticipated developments in technology or social organization that reduce birth rates, or medical breakthroughs that increase longevity.

The World in the Twenty-First Century

The United Nations Population Division now concludes that the 1990s mark a turning point in population history. The steep rise in growth rates for the world as a whole during the 1950s resulted from a sharp drop in mortality, accompanied by only a slight retreat in the birth rate. World population reached a peak growth rate of 2.06 percent at the end of 1960s, then receded during the 1970s to a plateau of about 1.73 percent in the 1980s. On the basis of these trends, the United Nations predicted in 1990 that the world rate would begin another modest decline in the 1990s that would continue into the new century (Figure 3.21). The effects that these growth-rate changes have had on the numbers of people in the world are apparent from Figure 3.22. Having risen from only 2.3 billion people in 1940, global population reached 5.3 billion by 1990 and was expected to arrive at the 6 billion mark in 1998, a year in which annual additions to world numbers will peak at slightly less than 100 million people.

Note that this peak year for increases to total world population, 1998, follows by almost exactly three decades the period during which the world growth rate had peaked. This illustrates the principle of *population momentum,* which refers to the propensity of a previously increasing population to continue expanding for a generation or more after growth rates have fallen. This is a natural consequence of the youthfulness of a rapidly growing population.

The numbers anticipated for the year A.D. 2025 in the 1990 forecasts (Figure 3.22) are higher than those projected by the United Nations during the mid-1980s. The optimism underlying the earlier projections had been based on an apparent easing of population growth rates everywhere except Africa and parts of South Asia. Most of all, forecasters were lulled by a decline occurring in China's growth rate at that time owing to a government policy that severely restricted family size. Obviously, any event affecting China's population—more than one-fifth of the world's people—is of great importance to demographers. The forecasts were eased upwards in 1990 because of an unforeseen rise in the Chinese birth rate after 1985, and because of unexpected increases in South Asia. Fertility rates, which had earlier shown promise of lessening, did not do so. Death rates, on the other hand, dropped even faster than anticipated. Changes in the 1990s have forced the forecasters to revise their estimates once again, however. Between 1990 and 1994, the world population growth rate was calculated by UN demographers to have fallen much more rapidly than expected, from the 1.73 percent of the 1980s plateau to 1.57 percent, confirming the optimism of the early 1980s. This was due to faster-than-anticipated fertility declines in parts of Africa and South Central Asia, and "baby busts" in Eastern Europe and the former Soviet Union. The expectation now is for world population to reach 6230 million by the year 2000. The newly projected total for A.D. 2025 is 8,472 million.

The steeply rising curve in Figure 3.22 during the first decades following World War II appeared to confirm Malthus's prediction of exponential population growth, precipitating a plethora of books on limits to growth. The 1990s transition suggests that the growth curve is assuming the characteristic S-shape of logistic growth as the growth rate slows down, however, something Malthus did not foresee. S-shaped growth curves have upper limits. Projecting the trends still further, UN demographers expect the world as a whole to attain zero population growth (ZPG) toward the end of the twenty-first century. In 1984, the United Nations confidently projected an eventual total of 10.2 billion by that time; in 1994, it revised that estimate to 11.19 billion. This is the U.N. "medium," or "most likely," figure.

Even though the world as a whole will reach ZPG by the end of the twenty-first century, the various world regions will attain that level at different times (Figure 3.21). Since 1950, the rate of population growth in the more-developed regions has fallen from 1.3 percent to only 0.5 percent and is expected to reach zero soon after A.D. 2025. By contrast, the growth rate of less-developed populations, after achieving a high of 2.5 percent at the end of the 1960s, is giving ground only grudgingly. As a result of these diverging trends, the share of world population accounted for by each of the two major categories of countries is changing (Figure 3.22). The more-developed regions contained one-third of the total in 1950 but only a quarter by 1990, and this proportion is expected to fall to one-fifth by A.D. 2025.

The United Nations bases its projections on a number of demographic trends, reflected in the contrasting age–sex

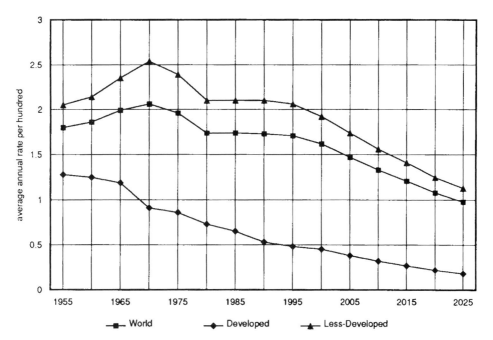

FIGURE 3.21 Population growth rates, 1950–1985 projected to A.D. 2025, for the world and developed and less-developed regions (5-year averages). The growth rate for the world as a whole rose steeply during the 1950s and early 1960s, owing mainly to declining death rates. At the end of the 1960s, the world rate peaked at an annual rate of 2.06 percent, then fell sharply for a time, misleading population forecasters concerning true underlying trends. The United Nations expects the world rate to resume its decline in the 1990s. The most significant influences on these world trends come from the Third World, where growth rates have yielded only reluctantly to downward pressures. Population growth rates for the more-developed regions, already low by the 1950s, have maintained a consistent downward trend. UN experts expect a rate of only 0.18 percent for this group by A.D. 2025, a level consistent with a shrinking population. [*Source:* Data from United Nations, *World Population Prospects 1988* (New York: United Nations, 1989).]

structures of populations in more-developed and less-developed countries. Sweden and Kenya exemplify these two groups. With only 17 percent of its people below the age of 15 and more than 18 percent 65 years and older, Sweden has the typical old-age distribution of a mature population (Figure 3.23a). Kenya, on the other hand, has much higher levels of fertility and mortality and hence a very young population (Figure 3.23b). Nearly half of its inhabitants are under 15 and only 3 percent are 65 or older.

Reinforcing the growth effects of a youthful population, the inhabitants of less-developed countries are living much longer than they did a few years ago (Figure 3.24). In 1950, the life expectancy at birth of people in less-developed regions was only 41 years; by 1985, it had risen to 57.6 years, and by A.D. 2025, it is expected to reach 70.4 years. The corresponding figures for people in developed regions are 65.7 years in 1950, 72.3 in 1985, and 78.7 in 2025. Thus, the gap between the two regions is quickly closing, from a difference of 24.7 years in 1950 to a mere 8.3 years in 2025.

It is apparent, therefore, that most of the population growth of the next 100 years will be in less-developed areas. Growth has already diminished in Europe, North America, and Russia, and it has begun to slow in East Asia (Figure 3.25). Latin American growth is easing somewhat also. The region that is contributing the largest absolute numbers to world population is Southern and Southwestern Asia. Africa is the area with the most rapid growth rates.

Another way of viewing the effects of different growth rates on future population distributions is to compare doubling times—the number of years it will take for populations to grow to twice their present sizes. Note from the map (Figure 3.26) that if current growth rates continue, many countries in Africa and the Muslim Middle East will have doubled their populations within 25 years or less. Most of the other lands in these two regions, along with nearly all of South Asia, will have accomplished this within 25 to 36 years. Contrast these with Western Europe, where most populations will require as much as 700 years to double; indeed, some have already begun to shrink. Next, let us

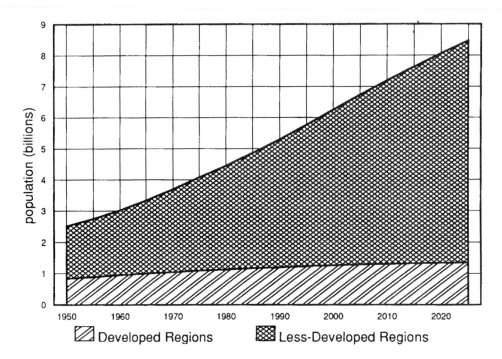

FIGURE 3.22 Population of the world and developed and less-developed regions, 1950–1985, projected to A.D. 2025. The slope of the curve for total world population continued to rise more steeply until the 1990s. Thereafter, based on the growth rate trends shown in Figure 3.21, it is expected to slow its ascent. According to optimistic UN projections, total world population should level off during the latter part of the twenty-first century. Note that by far the greater share of the additions to total world population come from the less-developed regions. Populations in the more-developed regions are scarcely growing at this time and will likely begin to shrink in the coming century. [*Source:* Data from United Nations, *World Population Prospects 1988* (New York: United Nations, 1989).]

examine more closely the growth trends and their effects in major world areas.

The More-Developed Regions

With low birth rates closely balanced by low death rates, the more-developed regions are classified as Type 5 countries according to the UN system. Fertility rates have declined steadily in these regions since 1950 and are now below replacement levels. This trend is a consequence of circumstances that discourage having children: high incomes, urbanization, high levels of female education, large numbers of women in the work force, postponement of marriage, widespread use of contraception and abortion, delayed age of giving birth to the first child, and rising divorce rates. Life expectancy is rising at a reduced rate because most illnesses are largely under control except for those related to old age, which tend to be more intractable.

Population stability has thus become general throughout the industrialized regions, and the projected size of future populations in those areas is likely to increase only slowly and at a diminishing rate. The more-developed peoples now total a little more than 1.2 billion, and they will probably rise to no more than 1.4 billion before leveling off during the first half of the next century. They will therefore become an ever-smaller proportion of global population (Figure 3.27). Nevertheless, population growth rates vary somewhat among developed countries because of differences in their circumstances and in the timing of their demographic change.

Europe, the first region to experience a demographic transition, has the most mature population of all. Fertility is so low that some European countries have already begun to decline in numbers (see Figure 3.26). As recently as 1950, Europe had 15.6 percent of the world's people; today, it has only 9 percent, and by A.D. 2025, it is expected to have only 6 percent. Though growth rates are diminishing fastest in Northern and Western Europe, they are declining in all parts of the continent. Italy, for example, recorded the world's lowest fertility rate in 1989.

In Northern America (Canada and the United States), societal changes have brought fertility levels to historic

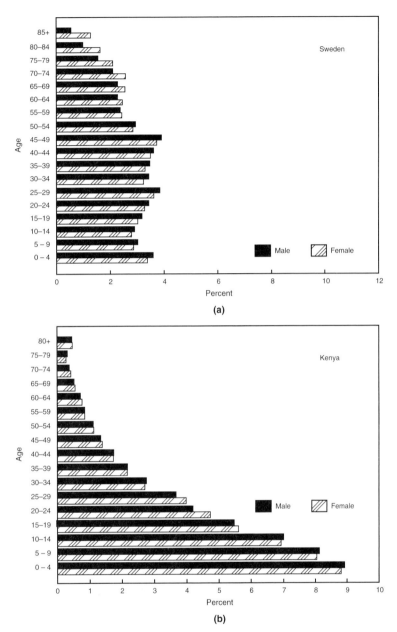

FIGURE 3.23 Contrasting age–sex structures of a more-developed and a less-developed country, Sweden and Kenya, respectively. Sweden's mature population, with a fairly even distribution of people in all age groups, forms the tubular-shaped structure typical of older industrialized countries. The diagram for Kenya forms the broad-based triangle of a rapidly growing population common among countries at lower levels of development. Nearly half of Kenya's population is under 15 years of age, and each new cohort of children is larger than the one preceding it. Because few Kenyans live to old age, the cohorts at higher age levels are severely diminished in size. Note also the differences between the two populations in their sex ratios (the proportion of males to females) at increasing age levels. As is usual for all human beings, males in both countries outnumber females during the early years, but the higher mortality of males causes the ratio to fall in later years. In Sweden's case, however, the excess of males over females continues until their late fifties, owing to superior medical care. After that, the proportion of females steadily increases until, beyond age 80, it is double that of the male share. The decline in Kenya's sex ratio begins at age 20, but the shift is gradual thereafter. [*Source:* Data from *United Nations Demographic Yearbook* (New York: United Nations, 1995).]

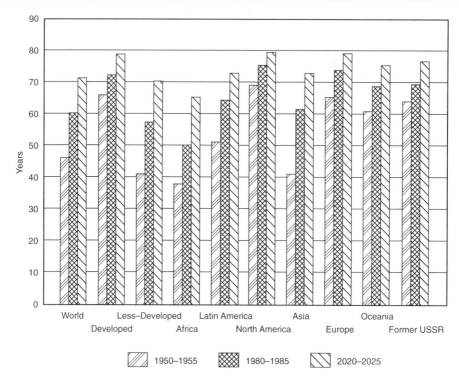

FIGURE 3.24 Life expectancy at birth, both sexes, for the world and for developed and less-developed regions, A.D. 1950 to 2025. The life expectancy of populations in less-developed countries was only 41 years in 1950, but it has continued to rise in the years since and is anticipated to reach 70 years by 2025. Life expectancy has likewise risen in the more-developed populations, but the rate of increase has been slower, partly because it was higher to begin with (65.7 in 1950) and partly because mortality rates are harder to reduce at the ages now attained by most people in those countries. Life expectancy in the latter group is projected to rise to 78.7 by 2025. The United Nations therefore predicts that the gap between the life expectancies of developed and less-developed populations will have shrunk from 24.7 years in 1950 to only 8.3 years in 2025. If this trend continues, the difference between the two populations would be eliminated before the end of the twenty-first century. The implications of this for the growth of future populations are profound. [*Source:* Data from United Nations, *Population Prospects 1988* (New York: United Nations, 1989).]

lows. Despite the large number of women from the postwar baby boom generation who reached childbearing age during the 1970s and 1980s, birth rates did not rise proportionally. Northern America's population is therefore projected to increase at an annual rate of only 0.6 percent in the 1990s. Having fallen from 6.6 percent of world population in 1950 to its current 5.2 percent, Northern America is expected to comprise only 3.9 percent of the total by A.D. 2025 (Figure 3.27).

An interesting case is that of Japan, which had an exceedingly high birth rate until the end of World War II. At that time, official policy changed abruptly, as the Japanese saw the difficulties of accommodating a rapidly expanding population within a small island nation no larger than California. Thus, they quickly brought population growth under control by using such means as contraception and abortion. Small families are now the rule in Japan, and the

growth rate and age structure are similar to those of the United States.

Russia has also entered the ranks of UN Type 5 countries. There is, however, considerable variability among other former Soviet republics (which are generally drawn up along ethnic lines). Births have fallen below replacement levels among the ethnic Russians. But in the Central Asian republics, fertility remains high—nearly double that of Russia and comparable to rates found in less-developed lands. The cause is the firmly embedded cultural bias among Muslim minorities that favors very large families.

The Less-Developed Countries (LDCs)

As the populations of the more-developed regions stabilize, those of the less-developed areas continue to soar. The United Nations expects the poorer countries to account for

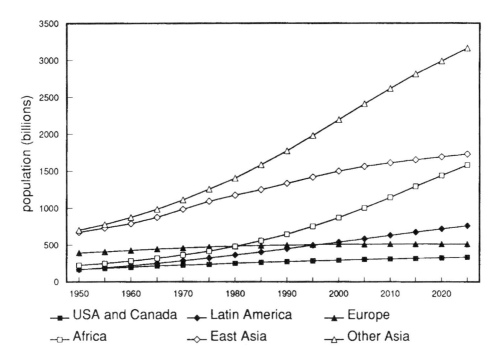

FIGURE 3.25   Estimates and projections of world population by major world regions, A.D. 1950 to 2025. As the populations of the more-developed regions mature, they will begin to level off and decline early in the next century, according to UN projections. The rate of population growth in East Asia (Japan, North and South Korea, China, Taiwan, Hong Kong, and Mongolia) is also easing somewhat, as is that of Latin America. Elsewhere in the Third World, the rate of growth continues little abated. Other Asia (the remainder of the continent after East Asia is subtracted) will be contributing the greatest absolute numbers to future populations, but the region whose population is climbing at the most alarming rate is Africa. Thus, future additions to world population are to come predominantly from two major problem areas in the less-developed world. (The former USSR is not shown here because its growth curve would have been obscured by that of the United States and Canada, to which it closely corresponds). [*Source:* Data from United Nations, *Population Prospects* 1988 (New York: United Nations, 1989).]

95 percent of world population growth between now and the middle of the next century. Although birth rates are beginning to decline in some important areas, they generally remain very high elsewhere. Meanwhile, throughout much of the less-developed world, mortality rates are falling and people are living longer.

Although continued population growth is the dominant trend among less-developed countries, each region seems to be taking its own path. Some of these paths are easier to predict than others, mainly because fertility rates vary greatly from region to region. Several less-developed countries have achieved low levels of fertility, whereas others have fertility rates as high as ever. Fertility is a complex matter: Although high fertility is closely linked to poverty, it has deep cultural roots, reinforcing the differentiating trends discussed in Chapter 2. Thus, we cannot be certain when it will start to fall in those areas where it is currently high, nor can we be sure how fast its decline will be.

Figure 3.28 shows the widely differing expectations for future total fertility rates. Demographers at the United Nations predict that fertility will continue to decline rapidly in eastern Asia, that it will decrease more rapidly in southern Asia than in Latin America, and that it will lag far behind the others in Africa. For the remainder of this century, Asia will remain a serious problem area, not just because of its high rate of growth, but because of the enormous population to which those rates apply. Once again, the situation differs from one country to another, however. Some countries have begun to make substantial progress and may attain zero population growth early in the next century; others remain slow. Both types are present in southern Asia. Fertility rates are dropping rapidly in the industrialized city-state of Singapore, where total fertility is now well below the replacement level of two children per family, especially for the ethnic Chinese. On the other hand, several other low-income countries—Cambodia, Afghanistan, and

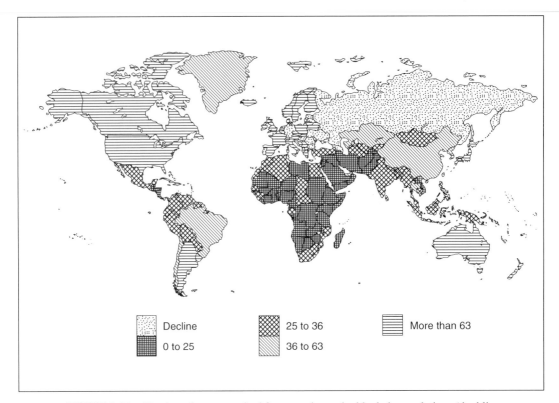

FIGURE 3.26   Number of years required for countries to double their populations (doubling times), assuming the continuation of 1990–1995 growth rates. If current trends continue, much of Africa, the Middle East, and the tropical Americas will have twice as many people within another generation as they do now. Little future growth is expected, however, in Northern America, Europe, or Japan and the newly industrialized lands of East Asia. Indeed, several European countries are already seeing their populations shrink. Most of the East European countries newly released from communism have declining populations, as do many of the independent republics remaining from the breakup of the former USSR. [*Source:* Based on data from the *1995 Britannica Book of the Year (Chicago: Encyclopaedia Britannica, 1995).*] A note on method: According to H. S. Shryock, J. Siegel, et al., *The Methods and Materials of Demography* (New York: Academic Press, 1976), doubling time may be calculated most easily by dividing the number 69.3 (the natural logarithm of 2 multiplied by 100) by the growth rate in percent per year. Thus, a population growing at 2 percent per year would take 69.3/2, or just under 35 years, to double.

Pakistan—still have very high fertility and mortality rates. The same is true of the Muslim countries of Southwest Asia—both those that are rich in oil and those that are not. A notable exception among Islamic nations is semi-industrialized Turkey, which maintains a strict separation between religion and the state and is beginning to get its population under control. The other countries of southern Asia, nearly a billion people in all, are making only slow progress.

In eastern Asia, even though China's most recent census has forced an upward revision in the estimated total population, a dramatic reduction in population growth is taking place. This is occurring not only in the middle-income industrialized countries—Taiwan, South Korea, and the city-state of Hong Kong—but most notably in China itself. Prior to the 1949 revolution, China was a UN Type 1 country. The new government effected a remarkable reduction in the death rate by improving food distribution, raising literacy levels, and introducing health-care facilities in virtually every rural community. The result was explosive population growth, adding 400 million people—almost as many as in all of Europe—to an already overpopulated agricultural country.

Influenced by Mao Zedong's philosophy, China's rulers at first did nothing to stem this growth, believing that the more people the better. Subsequently, a more pragmatic leadership awoke to the fact that 30 percent of national income was being drained off to support the additions to the population. The government therefore established a new policy, setting a target of zero population growth by A.D.

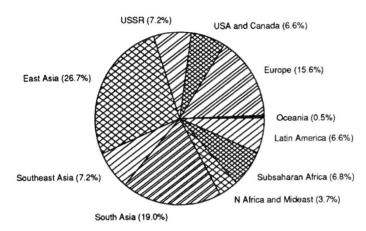

1950

USSR (7.2%)   USA and Canada (6.6%)

Europe (15.6%)

East Asia (26.7%)

Oceania (0.5%)

Latin America (6.6%)

Southeast Asia (7.2%)   Subsaharan Africa (6.8%)

N Africa and Mideast (3.7%)

South Asia (19.0%)

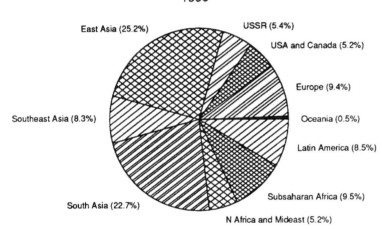

1990

East Asia (25.2%)   USSR (5.4%)

USA and Canada (5.2%)

Europe (9.4%)

Southeast Asia (8.3%)   Oceania (0.5%)

Latin America (8.5%)

Subsaharan Africa (9.5%)

South Asia (22.7%)

N Africa and Mideast (5.2%)

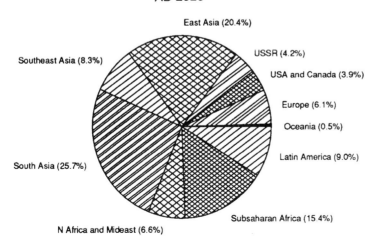

AD 2025

East Asia (20.4%)

Southeast Asia (8.3%)   USSR (4.2%)

USA and Canada (3.9%)

Europe (6.1%)

Oceania (0.5%)

Latin America (9.0%)

South Asia (25.7%)

Subsaharan Africa (15.4%)

N Africa and Mideast (6.6%)

FIGURE 3.27 Regional shares of world population, A.D. 1950, and projected for 1990 and 2025. The population growth trends indicated previously in Figure 3.10 would produce major changes in regional shares, as revealed sequentially in these diagrams. Here we see each of the more-developed regions gradually shrinking in relative size, especially Europe. During this same period, most of the less-developed regions experience explosive growth, notably South Asia, subSaharan Africa, Latin America, and the Islamic lands of North Africa and the Middle East. According to this United Nations scenario, however, East Asia's share of world population declines as China and other populous lands in that crucial area reach the final stages of the demographic transition. [*Source:* See Figure 3.25.]

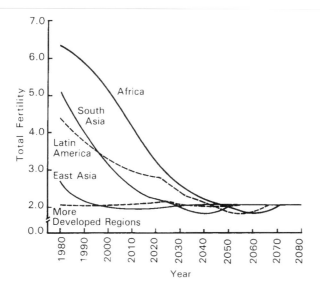

FIGURE 3.28   Projected total fertility rates by world regions—UN medium variant, A.D. 1980 to 2080 as assessed in 1980. The United Nations anticipates wide variation among regions in the timing of the decline in their total fertility (average number of births per couple during their lifetime). Rates will likely remain very high in Africa well into the twenty-first century. [*Source:* After U.N. Population Division, Population Bulletin No. 14, 1983.]

2000, with a standard of one child per family, backed by a combination of rewards and penalties. This policy quickly reduced fertility, cutting the former birth rate of 40 per thousand to only 18 per thousand in 1984 and 1985.

Enforcement of such a radical change in traditional practices has, however, been exceedingly difficult in a country as large and diverse as China and especially in the countryside. During the second half of the 1980s, therefore, birth rates began creeping up, forcing the government to raise its estimates for the period to 23.3 per thousand. The rise came as a result of the arrival to childbearing ages of the baby-boom generation of the 1960s, as well as a relaxation of the official one-child-per-couple policy. Small as the increase in birth rate may appear, when applied to a population of more than a billion people, it translates into a truly significant addition to the world total. Nevertheless, China's progress in population control has been impressive; the country is compressing its demographic transition into an uncommonly short time span.

This dramatic reversal of China's tradition of large families compares with similar changes achieved earlier by ethnic Chinese populations living in Taiwan, Hong Kong, Singapore, and elsewhere in Asia. This prompted demographers to speculate that the Chinese culture is particularly receptive to the idea of lower fertility. The abruptness of the shift in mainland China is clear from the current age structure of that country, as shown in Figure 3.29. Note that although the diagram assumes the broad-based form typical of less-developed countries with young populations, it contracts sharply in the lowest age groups owing to the recent decline in birth rate. Trends such as these underscore UN predictions that East Asia's population, now 25 percent of the world total, will drop to only 20 percent by A.D. 2025, yielding its first-place position in Figure 3.27 to South Asia.

Africa is the only continent where population growth rates have actually risen during the past two decades, as more countries become Type II. All of Africa is a demographic problem area, but the most serious problem is in sub-Saharan Africa. Two-thirds of the world's poorest nations are in this region, confirming the much-noted poverty–population link. Recent data indicate that fertility rates are still rising in some countries, but declining in others, for example, Madagascar, Tanzania, Zambia, Zimbabwe, and Gambia. In 1950, Africa south of the Sahara held only 6.8 percent of the world's people, roughly equivalent to Northern America's population at the time; today, this proportion has risen to 9.5 percent, and by A.D. 2025, it is projected to reach 15.4 percent (Figure 3.27).

Despite fertility declines, population growth rates are still high. The nature of the worsening population crisis is illustrated by the widening demographic gap in one troubled area, East Africa (Figure 3.30). The overall birth rate is little diminished since 1950, but the death rate is dropping. Tropical Africa has some of the highest total fertility rates ever recorded—for example, 8.5 children per woman in Rwanda. Some demographers conclude that the populations of this region have a greater cultural propensity to high fertility than other peoples at similar levels of development. Populations are exceedingly young, as Kenya's age structure illustrates (Figure 3.23b). Although changes are occurring, one thing is sure: The twenty-first century will see continued population growth, posing grave problems in a region where many people are already pressing the resources of the land. If Malthus has any continuing validity, it is here.

A strong cultural bias toward large populations also characterizes the male-dominated Islamic lands of North Africa and the Middle East. Fertility rates are high,

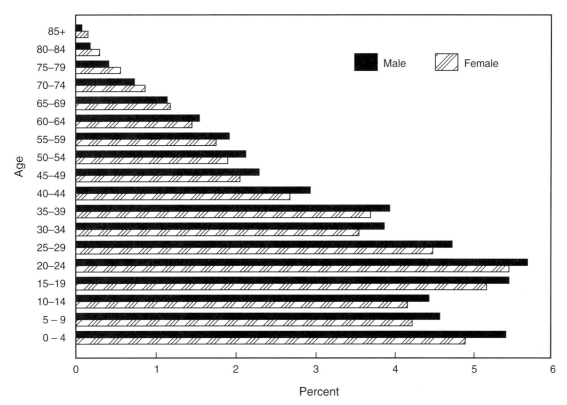

FIGURE 3.29 Age–sex structure of China's population, 1990. The shape of this diagram is typical of less-developed countries except for the unusual constriction in the sizes of the youngest age groups, evidence of the effectiveness of the Chinese government's strict population policy. The increase in the proportion of under-5-year-olds results from the coming of China's baby-boom generation to childbearing age and also by difficulties in enforcing the country's one-child-per-couple policy. Another unique feature of China's population structure is the substantial excess of males over females, a result of traditional cultural practices limiting the number of girl babies. Note also the reduced size of those groups born during the social upheavals of the "Great Leap Forward" and the "Cultural Revolution." [*Source:* Data from *United Nations Demographic Yearbook* (New York: United Nations, 1995).]

especially in those countries with the most-conservative religious traditions, such as Libya (7.12 children per woman) and Saudi Arabia (7.28). Yet as urbanization and development proceed in parts of the area, some signs of diminishing growth rates have appeared. Turkey and Egypt, two of the more advanced countries in the group, are leading the way with moderate decreases in fertility, especially in the larger cities. Tunisia is following closely behind, suggesting that some other countries of the region will eventually take the same path. Yet the ultimate outcome in this region is not at all certain, given the recent upsurge of Muslim fundamentalism.

Latin America's population began to soar in the early post–World War II period, the result of successful programs to reduce death rates. Birth rates remained high, however, and most Latin American nations have exceedingly young populations. Latin America has all the conditions conducive to high fertility: widespread poverty, female illiteracy, and a cultural bias toward large families, reinforced by the Catholic church's strictures against birth control. As life expectancy continues to rise, this region comprises an expanding share of total world population.

But Latin America also is very diverse, and some parts fit this description better than others, A number of low-income countries—notably Honduras, Haiti, and several smaller island nations of the Caribbean—have persistently high levels of fertility and galloping population growth. Certain other high-fertility countries, somewhat less impoverished, have very low death rates and exploding populations. Prominent in this group are Bolivia, Ecuador, Paraguay, and parts of Central America. On the other hand, a number of countries have achieved some reduction in

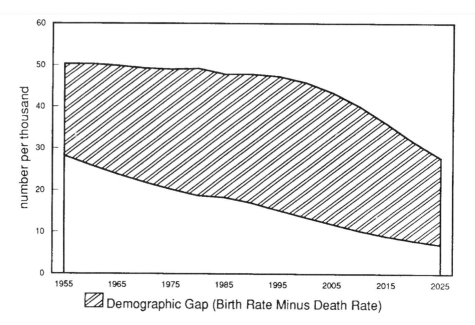

FIGURE 3.30 Birth and death rates in East Africa, A.D. 1955–1990 and projected to 2025. The widening demographic gap in East Africa is typical of all sub-Saharan Africa, where a population explosion is now in progress. Death rates are steadily declining, but birth rates remain stubbornly high. The decline in birth rates projected by the United Nations to begin around the turn of the century is no more than a hope; no evidence for it now exists. Indeed, current fertility rates for these countries are the highest ever recorded anywhere. [*Source:* Data from United Nations, *World Population Prospects 1988* (New York: United Nations, 1989).]

fertility and thus moderated their rates of population growth. Among these are Brazil, Venezuela, Colombia, Peru, Mexico, Costa Rica, Panama, and Cuba. Finally, in southernmost Latin America, semi-industrialized Argentina, Uruguay, and Chile have already attained low levels of fertility and mortality and should be reaching zero population growth early in the next century.

Despite this evidence of demographic change, Latin America's population is destined to rise from 8.5 percent of the world total now to 9 percent by A.D. 2025. At the end of World War II, Latin America had fewer people than Northern America: In another hundred years, it will have more than three times as many. As yet only a few countries in Latin America are actually overcrowded, notably El Salvador and several Caribbean islands. Although densities are otherwise well below those common in Asia and West Africa, present trends will doubtless change this.

With 95 percent of the world's future population growth taking place in the less-developed regions, it is to be expected that several of the LDCs will assume top rank among the most populous nations, leapfrogging a number of industrialized countries along the way. In Figure 3.31, the 16 hundred-million-plus countries of A.D. 2025, as projected by the United Nations, are arrayed in order of their anticipated population sizes in that year. Note that only three industrialized countries remain in this top group—the former USSR (awaiting the UN's recognition of its collapse, and the need for separate forecasts for the countries that have replaced it), the United States, and Japan. With their static populations, all European countries have been crowded off the list. This would seem to suggest that less-developed nations will necessarily exert an increasing influence in global affairs, if only because of their overwhelming size.

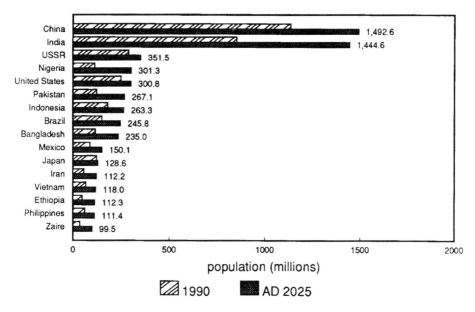

FIGURE 3.31 Projected largest countries in A.D. 2025, UN medium variant. As an outcome of the divergent growth trends of developed and less-developed regions, the most populous countries of the future will be mainly in the Third World. China, already by far the largest, is projected to have a population of nearly 1.5 billion by the end of the first quarter of the new century. Even more striking is the projected population of India, which is expected ultimately to exceed that of China. Note that by the year 2025, Nigeria will have replaced the United States as the fourth largest nation, and Bangladesh and Mexico will have passed Japan. [*Source:* Data from United Nations, *World Population Prospects 1988* [New York: United Nations, 1989).]

VOCABULARY

Here are vocabulary items that appear for the first time in this chapter. Be sure you learn them. They are defined in the Glossary:

accelerating growth	crude birth rate	immigration
age distribution	crude death rate	indirect calories
age–sex structure	demographic gap	Industrial Revolution
age-specific death rate	demographic transition	infant mortality rate
agricultural revolution	dependency ratio	information society
arable land	doubling time	labor force
aridity	elderly-dependency ratios	law of diminishing returns
arithmetic density	empty area	life expectancy
baby-boom era	enclosure movement	limits of habitation
biotic resource	endemic disease	literacy rates
birth rates	Engel's law	logistic curve
business cycles	fertility rate	Malthus
carrying capacity	gross national product (GNP)	Malthusian trap
child-dependency ratios	growth curve	megalopolis
crisis area	hydraulic civilization	metropolis
cropland per person	immediate check to population growth	migration

modernization

mortality rate

natural increase

neo-Malthusian

Organization of Petroleum Exporting Countries(OPEC)

patrimony

physiological density

population clusters

population curve

population decrease

population density

population distributions

population explosion

population growth rates

population node

population projection

population–resource ratio

positive check to population growth

preventative check to population growth

primate city

principle of population momentum

protective foods

regional population concentrations

stable population

stationary population

subsistence

technological optimists

transition theory

transportation revolution

Type 1 countries

Type 2 countries

Type 3 countries

Type 4 countries

Type 5 countries

ultimate check to population growth

"ultimate resource"

underemployment

unemployment

urbanization

zero population growth (ZPG)

TOPICS FOR DISCUSSION

1. Why did world population grow so slowly prior to the seventeenth century, and why has its growth accelerated since? What gave rise to the three surges of population growth that occurred in the past? Describe the new developments that promise a quantum change in the world's productive capacity and explain why these developments are less likely to produce a renewed surge in world population growth.

2. What did Malthus perceive as the "ultimate" check to population growth? Describe his "preventative" and "positive" checks. What solution to the problem of excessive population growth did he advocate? Why might we regard Malthus as a pioneer in the movement for women's liberation? Explain why Malthus's predictions for Western Europe failed to materialize. Where in the world today are his predictions apparently being borne out to some degree? Why?

3. The dark band across Africa in the map above and to the right has been called the "Crisis Area." What do you think is meant by this? List the probable criteria for this designation. What other areas of the world could be given this name for similar reasons?

4. The diagram to the right appeared in a textbook on population. What does it purport to show, and what is wrong with it?

5. What phenomenon does the graph on page 91 reveal? Why did the upswings and downswings occur?

6. Describe and explain the differences in age composition of populations in advanced countries and those in less-developed ones. How do the occupational structures of these two categories of countries differ and why? What

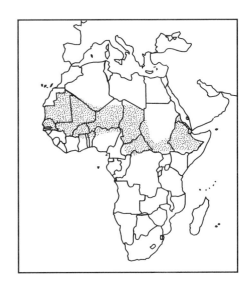

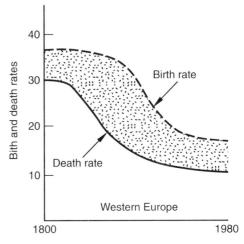

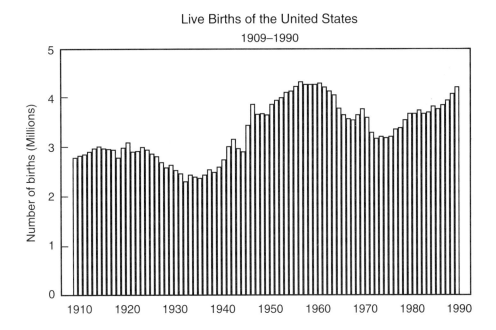

Live Births of the United States
1909–1990

economic and social problems do these population characteristics create in each case?

7. The demographic transition has diffused along the pathways of globalization." Discuss. Is there evidence that Michael Porter's fourfold classification of types of economies might be correlated with a typology of demographic development?

8. How is a world population map for the year 2050 likely to differ from a map of today's population? Explain the wide variations in population growth projected for different Third World areas. Which world regions are of greatest concern to students of population? Explain.

FURTHER READINGS

Brown, L. R., et al. (1995).*The State of the World 1995.* New York: Norton,

A classic Malthusian assessment, updated annually.

Horiuchi, Shiro. (1992) Stagnation in the Decline of the World Population Growth Rate During the 1980s. *Science* 257:761–5.

The author argues that the world population growth rate after World War II passed through three phases: the rise in the 1950s and 1960s, the fall (though still at a positive level) in the 1970s, and a plateau in the 1980s. The rise was produced by the global decline in death rates, the fall was mainly due to the reduction of fertility in a number of developing countries, and the stagnation of growth rate decline was attributable to three major factors. First, substantial fertility declines started around 1970 and stalled around 1980 in both China and India. Second, the age structure of population changed in favor of higher birth rates. Third, although fertility started to decline significantly around 1970 mainly in East Asia, Southeast Asia, and Latin America, few countries have begun fertility declines since then. Many countries in sub-Saharan Africa and South Asia have not started substantial fertility reductions, deepening the gap between developing countries that are moving to lower fertility levels and those that are left behind.

Kates, Robert W. (1983). *The Human Environment: Penultimate Problems of Survival.* Natural Hazards Research and Applications Center, Special Publication No. 6. Worcester, MA. Clark University, The Center for Technology, Environment, and Development,

Considers three related sets of issues: population growth and resource use; income disparities and their potential for widespread unrest and conflict; and environmental problems resulting from technological change.

Kelley, Allen C. (1988). Economic Consequences of Population Change in the Third World. *Journal of Economic Literature,* 26:1685–1728.

An outstanding survey that concludes that economic growth in the LDCs would have been more rapid if population growth had been slower, particularly where usable land and water are scarce and costly, where property rights to land and resources are poorly defined, and where government policies are biased against labor. Population's positive impact was greatest where resources were abundant, where possibilities for scale economies were greater, and where markets were most efficient.

Mahler, Halfdan. (1980) People. *Scientific American.* 243: 66–77.

Comparing demographic trends in developed and less-developed countries, the Director General of the World Health Organization describes the adverse effects that rapid population growth has on the general level of health in a society and examines the implications for development.

Simon, Julian L. (1981). *The Ultimate Resource.* Princeton: Princeton University Press.

The "ultimate resource" is humankind. This book presents the possibility of evolution in social organizations, because people innovate, both solving problems and creating new technologies.

United Nations. (1993). *World Population Prospects 1992.* Population Series No. 135. Population Division of the Department for Economic and Social Information and Policy Analysis. New York: United Nations,

The basic source of population information.

Van De Walle, Etienne, and John Knodel. (1980). Europe's Fertility Transition: New Evidence and Lessons for Today's Developing World. *Population Bulletin.* 34 (6). Washington, DC: Population Reference Bureau,

Analyzes changes in marital fertility among European populations since the eighteenth century. The wide differences among countries in the timing of fertility decline suggests the influence of cultural factors.

4

Food Supplies: A Limit to Growth

OVERVIEW

Continuing population growth brings into question the earth's capacity to provide the necessary food, energy, and industrial raw materials during the coming century. The developing countries will exert most of the new pressures on resources. Thanks to new technology, the global food supply will be probably adequate to feed a global population of 11 to 12 billion.

Economists and environmentalists continue to differ on questions of resource availability in the long run. Environmentalists believe in the fixity of supply of nonrenewable resources, and therefore of limits to growth. Economists believe that a continuing search for substitutes removes resource constraints on development.

The best hope for increasing food supply appears to be by raising the productivity of existing farmland. The "green revolution" has had notable success in this effort in the developing countries, following the major surge in U.S. agricultural productivity produced by "chemical agriculture." The hope for the future resides in biotechnology's ability to engineer new varieties.

Current patterns of malnutrition and hunger are unrelated to food availability, reflecting breakdowns of local production, transportation, or distribution caused by war or natural catastrophe.

OBJECTIVES

- to understand the nature and availability of the earth's resources
- to learn about conflicting "environmentalist" and "economist" views of the future supply of critical resources
- to appreciate the difficulties of ensuring an adequate supply and equitable distribution of food for future populations

CAN THE WORLD SUPPORT
ITS FUTURE POPULATIONS?

Growing Pressures

Does the earth have enough natural resources to provide for the 11 to 12 billion people expected eventually to live here? The answer depends on what happens to the two parts of the population–resource ratio. In Chapter 3, we examined those elements influencing the numerator of this fraction—numbers of people. In this chapter and the one to follow, we consider the many complex issues affecting the denominator: the problem of how much food, energy, and raw materials the earth can be made to yield and whether the physical environment can remain habitable with intensifying human use.

The shape of future world populations is now beginning to emerge. Demographers now feel that we are approaching that turning point when the population growth curve will start to moderate its rate of climb and will assume the characteristic S-shape of the logistic curve. Although the world's population as a whole is expected to reach steady state some time in the latter part of the next century, however, the timing will vary greatly from one part of the world to another. Stability will arrive last in the poorest countries, where growth still remains high. Hence, it is safe to predict that the future drain on resources will come increasingly from parts of the Third World.

While population is assuming a new global pattern, the denominator of the ratio is likewise changing. Two things are happening to the resource part of the fraction: Per capita resource use is growing as development proceeds and incomes rise, and new kinds of resource needs are arising. When Malthus first posed the overpopulation problem in 1798, food supply was the factor limiting population growth. By the middle of the next century, the supply of mechanical energy had joined food as a necessary requirement for a society that was industrializing and advancing technologically. A century later, pollution was added to the list of limits to growth in recognition that industrialization and urbanization were beginning to harm the environment. Then, in the 1970s, growing scarcities produced skyrocketing prices of raw materials and energy, and raised new questions about the adequacy of world reserves (Meadows et al., 1972).

There is evidence, however, of a long-run waxing and waning of environmental concerns. Periods of prosperity cause consumption to rise, straining available supplies of physical resources, intensifying environmental pressures, and forcing up prices. This heightens the general awareness of resource limitations, prompts greater research on such problems, and leads to official measures to minimize the impacts of shortages and rising prices. Succeeding epochs of depression reduce demand, causing prices to fall and bringing relief from the scarcities that had earlier prevailed. Officialdom and the general public lose sight of resource problems, and long-term research and development suffer. Transitions from global prosperity to hard times, marked by stagflation crises, have occurred at intervals of roughly 50 years ever since the Industrial Revolution in the eighteenth century, as we shall see in Chapter 10. Half way between these crises, deep depressions have marked the troughs separating hard times from the resumption of growth. The latest of these "long waves" crested in the 1980–1981 stagflation crisis, after enhancing the bargaining power of raw material and energy-exporting nations and providing the conditions for the commodity price shocks and other global economic crises of the late 1970s. After the crest, prices for the commodities formerly in short supply fell as resource-hungry industries collapsed, setting in motion a period of rapid technological change that always follows such long-wave peaks. Changing technologies altered the structure of demand for raw materials, reducing pressures on some while shifting demand to others. The history of resource use is a history of such transitions from boom and shortage to "bust" and replacement.

The Nature of Resources

Alternating periods of scarcity and abundance affect attitudes toward the relative importance of resources. Likewise, technological change alters perceptions of what actually constitutes a resource. Even at a particular level of technology, conflicting views on this subject may be held by those with differing professional perspectives.

Changing Conceptions. In a real sense, the term *resource* refers to the supply of anything that may be regarded as useful or necessary to human beings, including other human beings—a store on which we can draw as we need it. *Natural resources* are those that humans obtain from the biological and physical environment. Such resources are neither absolute nor constant; material objects do not actually become resources until human beings conceive them as such. Thus, what we class as resources changes as our perceptions of them change, or as new technology or rising prices make their exploitation feasible. Oil bubbling from the ground in ancient Persia was a nuisance, but it is a vital source of energy and export earnings to modern Iranians. Uranium was a waste product of Canada's radium mining operations during the 1930s, but since then the old mine tailings have been reworked to recover the newly valuable uranium ore remaining in them. The abundant but low-grade Lake Superior taconite ores became a commercially exploitable resource only when the rich Mesabi iron deposits gave out.

There are different types of resources (Figure 4.1). At a given state of technology, the absolute supply of certain

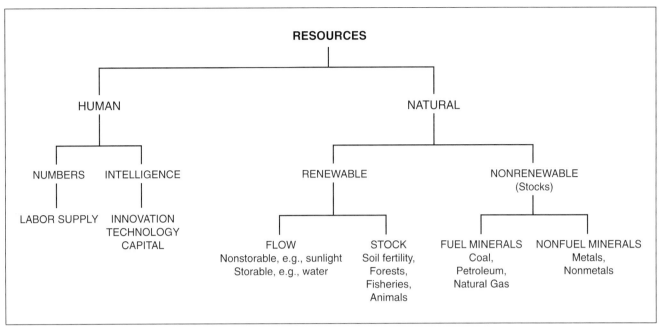

FIGURE 4.1   A typology of resources.

natural resources can be sustained at a given level or even increased. These are the *renewable resources*—those capable of replenishing themselves or being replenished by human beings. Stocks of biotic resources, such as forests, animal populations, and fish, are of this type. Even soils can be made to recover from excessive use; many of the soils of Western Europe and southeastern Asia have been made and remade by human beings. *Flow resources*—such as running water, winds, ocean tides, and solar rays—represent another type of renewable resource, available to produce energy. Ordinarily, they must be used as they appear or they are lost, although water can be stored in reservoirs.

Resources that cannot regenerate are referred to as *nonrenewable resources.* Most minerals fall into this category. The concentration of mineral ores in economically exploitable quantities relies on physical processes that normally require millions of years. Once a given deposit has been mined out, that resource for all practical purposes ceases to exist. Both increasing prices and advancing technology spur the search for new deposits to replace the old; both factors enable more remote and lower quality deposits to be exploited. The total known world reserves of a particular mineral therefore tend to rise and fall as new deposits are identified and older ones are exhausted. Cyclicality is evident due to rising and falling prices; dramatic shifts accompany technological change.

Conflicting Views of Nonrenewable Resources.
Determining future resource prospects is complicated by both measurement and conceptual problems. The definitions of population and food supplies are straightforward;

the definition of nonrenewable resources is complex. Experts disagree not only on what constitutes a resource but also on how to measure the quantity of it that exists. One group holds an "environmentalist" view, another an "economist" view.

The environmentalist view of nonrenewable resources is that the world has a fixed upper *carrying capacity* of population that it can support and of resources that it can supply. Technology can raise current levels toward, but not beyond, the full potential of the world's productive capacity. The environmentalist focus is long-term. His or her concern is with the results of the next doubling of the world's population and the impact of that doubling on environmental pollution and on demand, leading to a belief that growth must be limited to rates that are *sustainable* in the long run.

The alternative view offered by many economists is that resources are not fixed in amount but created, in response to needs, through market mechanisms. If a resource becomes scarce, its price rises and the quantity consumed drops. The price increase stimulates both an increase in supply and a search for substitutes. Human ingenuity and innovativeness, they point out, have led to information-age demand not for rare or scarce materials, but for products made from raw materials that are both widely available and inexpensive—silicon in particular.

Both environmentalists and economists offer persuasive arguments for their viewpoints. The environmentalist view appeals to common sense. The metaphor of "spaceship earth" comes naturally to mind. There must be a fixed, finite supply of oil on this, our spaceship. Every barrel we use is one less barrel that remains. But how much actually remains and how long will it last? Information is scanty at best, particularly in the less-developed parts of the world. Estimates of ultimately recoverable reserves of crude oil from conventional sources rose sharply from 600 billion barrels in 1942 to 2,480 billion in 1965 as new discoveries were made. Since then, estimates have fluctuated at or above the 2,000-billion-barrel mark. Proven reserves, a more reliable measure commonly used in the oil industry, are much lower, but the industry only "proves" its reserves for 10 to 20 years into the future, leading those who subscribe to the economist view to place little value on such figures, preferring a much more flexible approach (Figure 4.2).

The differences dividing these two schools of thought became evident during the intense debate that followed Meadows et al. (1972), which reported on an elaborate analysis of the resource question as viewed from an environmentalist perspective. See Box 4.1 for a summary of this study and the controversy it provoked.

Political Problems. In addition to the conceptual and measurement questions surrounding this issue, another unpredictable aspect concerns the *politics of resources*. This problem arises because deposits of many essential resources are concentrated in certain parts of the world and under the control of particular sovereign nation-states, whereas demand is concentrated in other regions. In part, the wars of the twentieth century have been resource wars—the

attempts by resource-deficient countries to reach out for "lebensraum" (living space), and for the materials needed to maintain modern industry, particularly oil. The Gulf War was an attempt by Iraq to control a greater share of the world's known oil reserves that was defeated by the West, seeking to ensure its oil supplies.

FOOD SUPPLY

Food as a Limit to Growth

With these caveats in mind, let us now look at the problems of providing food for future populations. The principal sources of food are diagrammed in Figure 4.3. The possibility that population growth might outstrip the earth's capacity to supply enough food is of as much concern today as it was in Malthus's time, although the immediacy of this problem is much debated. Two contrary trends are partly responsible for the uncertainty. On the one hand, soil erosion, urban encroachment on farmland, and other human and natural processes are acting to diminish the supply of agricultural land; on the other hand, technological developments are raising the efficiency of food production by increasing output per unit of physical resources. The answer to the problem also depends on the level of dietary quality deemed acceptable. To raise the global average of food consumption to levels now prevalent in the richer countries would be a major task, considering the high proportion of animal proteins and fresh green vegetables entering into such diets.

The problem of maintaining the world food supply does not appear to be critical in the short run. The world now produces plenty of food. That some people starve is a matter of inadequate means of distribution and of dislocations caused by civil unrest and war, not of shortfalls in production. Global food production has more than doubled since World War II, and the current total is more than sufficient to feed everyone on earth. Even by the end of this century, the total supply seems likely to be adequate, assuming that productivity continues to increase at current rates. Predictions for the new century depend not only on dietary standards, however. Environmentalists point to the possibilities for unfavorable climatic changes, and continuing loss of productive capacity through such factors as soil erosion. Economists and other technological optimists see continuing breakthroughs in food production technology. Smil (1994) believes that the right price signals and better education will significantly increase food output. Diffusion of existing improved field efficiencies and reduction of waste could boost global food production by 50 percent from 1990 levels. New crop-boosting innovations, particularly the fruits of biotechnology, could feed even more. Smil writes (p. 283):

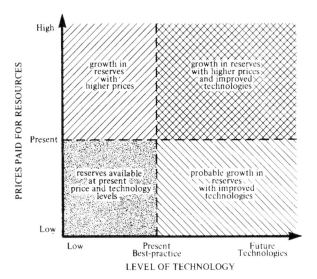

FIGURE 4.2 The economist's view of world resources. This figure is suggested by a diagram in G. Alexanderson and B. I. Klevebring, *World Resources: Energy, Metals and Minerals* (New York: Walter de Gruyter, 1978), p. 6. It implies that the quantity of resources available responds to prices and technology. Resource prices rise in the face of scarcity, but supplies do not run out.

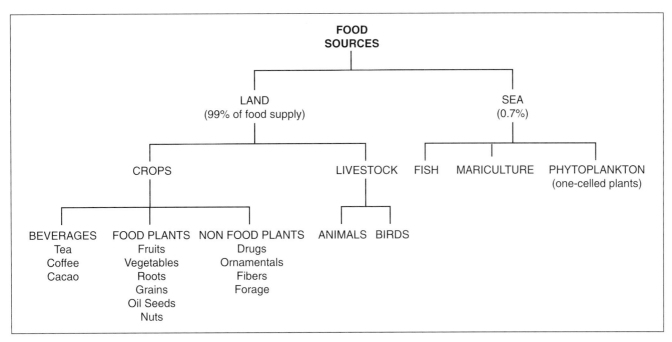

FIGURE 4.3 Sources of food.

There is no compelling reason to believe that the three generations between 1990 and 2050 will see fewer practical advances in food production than were experienced in the 60 years before 1990. In 1930 synthetic ammonia was still a rare and expensive commodity, tractors did not even have low-pressure rubber tires, there was neither hybrid corn nor short-stalked, high-yielding wheat and rice varieties, soybeans were an insignificant crop outside China, and there were no synthetic herbicides or effective insecticides and fungicides.

Even if a brilliant forecaster had identified both the existence and the extent of these inputs and commodities by 1990, would he have situated these advances amid 5.3 billion people, GATT negotiations, collapsing Communism, and microcomputers? And yet in combination these realities shape the current performance of global farming no less decisively than new agronomic techniques

Even though total output will probably prove sufficient, the thorny problem remains of ensuring that all the world's inhabitants receive an equitable share of these supplies. Regional differences in production and consumption are enormous: Food is just not reaching everyone who needs it, and the disparities are widening. North America and Europe have been overproducing at a time when their populations are stabilizing, whereas food output has lagged behind population growth in many less-developed countries (see Figure 4.4).

Countries deficient in food output are of two main kinds. One group includes the oil-exporting countries of the Middle East and the newly industrializing countries of the Pacific rim, which are able to make up for inadequate food production by selling abroad their petroleum and manufactured goods to finance imports of needed foodstuffs.

The other group of food-deficit countries consists of those less-developed countries that are too poor to buy needed food supplies abroad, especially those where civil war is dislocating populations, production, and distribution. They include Ethiopia, Somalia, the Sudan, Chad, and other countries of Africa south of the Sahara, further afflicted by periodic drought.

Even more common than famine is chronic malnutrition. Hunger is a significant world problem, affecting possibly a billion people. Note from Figure 4.5 how widespread are low dietary levels throughout Africa and southern Asia and parts of Latin America.

Hunger and malnutrition contribute to stunted physical growth, a lower resistance to disease, higher childhood death rates, and arrested mental development. Studies in Latin America have identified malnutrition as either the main or a contributing cause of 57 percent of all deaths between the ages of one to four. In Brazil, children in this age group accounted for four-fifths of all deaths. In the less-developed world as a whole, according to estimates of the United Nations Food and Agriculture Organization (FAO), more than two-thirds of the present group of children will develop illnesses related to malnutrition. Upon reaching adulthood, many of the survivors will remain mentally or

BOX 4.1 Are There Limits to Growth?

The environmentalist vision of a growing population pressing against fixed upper limits of nonrenewable resources gained worldwide attention with the publication in 1972 of *The Limits to Growth*, the first report for the Club of Rome's Project on The Predicament of Mankind. The Club of Rome was formed in 1968 by prominent industrialists and scientists from around the developed world who were convinced that the major problems facing humanity are so complexly interrelated that traditional institutions and policies cannot cope with them. They felt that "systems dynamics" models were needed to make wiser decisions. These mathematical tools can be made to account for the fact that population growth, for instance, depends on trends in food production, pollution, and industrial output, and each of these in turn depends on the others.

Limits to Growth projects world population, food supplies, industrial output, and pollution over a long duration, to the year 2010, with dramatic results. World population is projected to continue its exponential growth until it overshoots the world's carrying capacity, and the world's economic system collapses. This unstable pattern of overshoot and collapse is projected to occur even if the constraints on population growth are successively reduced. Doubling natural resource reserves, cutting pollution to one-fourth of its present level, increasing agricultural productivity, and introducing birth control were each added as assumptions in the model simulations, but the general results remained the same. The precise sequence of events that triggers the catastrophic fall of population numbers differs according to the specific

assumptions, but the basic pattern is always the same: overshoot and collapse, as illustrated by Figure 4a. The key policy conclusion of the study, therefore, is that an immediate slow-down in economic growth must be initiated so as to create an equilibrium between population and resources.

Limits to Growth was subjected to intensive scrutiny by scientists in

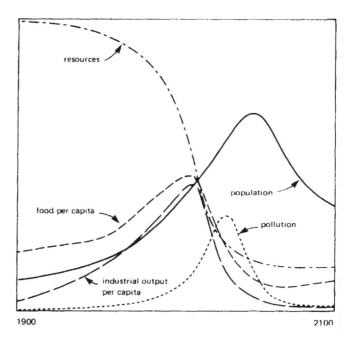

FIGURE 4a Limits to growth: a simulation of world collapse. Dennis Meadows and his colleagues projected overshoot and collapse of the world's population unless world economic and population growth slowed immediately. In this model, collapse occurs because of the depletion of nonrenewable resources, shown by the dramatic drop in the resources curve. This collapse triggers declines in food per capita and industrial output per capita. [Source: D. H. Meadows, D. L. Meadows, J. Randers, and W. W. Behrens, The Limits to Growth (New York: Universe Books, 1972), p.97.]

physically handicapped to the extent that they will either be dependent on society for their support or will be able to contribute little to it because of their reduced productivity. Hunger and malnutrition are clearly a serious drag on the economic development of impoverished nations.

The main cause of hunger in the world today is simply poverty. As comparison of Figures 2.1 and 4.5 shows, the correspondence between low per capita food intake and low per capita income is very close. In addition, wide

variations in food consumption occur within countries, especially those less-developed nations with great income disparities, and even in some of the richer industrialized countries, such as the United States, where a surprising number of people go to bed hungry every night.

Regional disparities threaten to widen still further in the years to come. Although food requirements will change little among developed countries, demand in the less-developed nations will rise steeply through the remainder of the

every discipline dealing with population and resources. As a result, every facet of the work has been attacked by one critic or another, and some telling points have been made. Nevertheless, most subsequent scenarios of the future have made at least some reference to the concerns it raised. Interest was reawakened in the work of an earlier prophet of doom, the Rev. Thomas R. Malthus, whose *Essay on the Principle of Population* in the late eighteenth century similarly attracted widespread debate on physical limits to growth and on the policy consequences that followed. Indeed, one critic labeled Meadows 'Malthus with a computer.'

The criticisms were of four kinds and related to (1) the relationships between population and the supply of resources, (2) the use of world averages rather than specific regional data, (3) the growth of the system components and the nature of growth itself, and (4) the stability of such models under differing assumptions.

The fourth and perhaps most serious flaw in *Limits to Growth* is that quite different results are obtained if new assumptions reflecting a technological-optimist view are incorporated into the model. Robert Boyd, a zoologist, assumes, for example, that an additional key variable is needed in the model developed by Meadows and colleagues, namely technology. He further assumes that investment in technology would accelerate if there were a decline in quality of life and that this increase investment would, in turn, increase the growth of technology. He then assumes that a growth in technology would increase food output, decrease the consumption of natural resources, and decrease pollution. He also assumes that birth rates would fall with an increase in food supplies once these were above

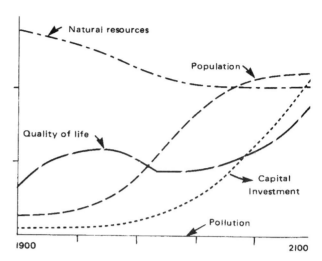

FIGURE 4b The greening of the globe: a technological-optimist view of the future. Robert Boyd makes changes in the Meadows model by allowing changes in technology to produce optimistic results for food production, pollution levels, and quality of life. The result is a "new age" with a stable population level and improving quality of life. [*Source:* Robert Boyd, "World Dynamics: A Note," *Science* 177 (August 1972):516–519.]

some minimal level. The results of incorporating these assumptions into the Meadows model are that population grows to a steady-state level by the year 2000 and that, as population growth slows, the quality of life increases (see Figure 4b).

Limits to Growth demonstrates that systems modeling is limited by the assumptions used. It cannot resolve underlying theoretical conflicts. Meadows and his colleagues argue that the basic behavior of the world models appears to be so fundamental and general that they do not expect their broad conclusions to be substantially altered by further revisions. That is, world population overshoot and collapse appear inevitable if world population and economic growth continue their present course. In fact, Meadows and his associates are incorrect. Boyd demonstrates that computer simulations simply feed back the assumptions fed in. Start off with a Malthusian framework and the models make Malthusian predictions. Begin with optimistic assumptions and an optimist future unfolds; in "computerese": garbage in, garbage out (GIGO). The computer models fail to resolve the crucial difference between the two viewpoints; they merely project the consequences of the investigators' initial assumptions onto a time scale.

twentieth century. Income growth will add some of the new demand, but the greater part of it will come from population growth. World food output therefore will have to increase. Physical limitations will make it difficult for some countries to produce the additional food they will require, so food will be a growing element of world trade, and continuing food aid will be a part of the international agenda. Beyond A.D. 2000, food needs will continue to rise. Let us now consider the opportunities for meeting these future food needs from

conventional sources, and examine the possibilities offered by new food production technologies.

Conventional Sources of Food Supply

All types of food trace their origins to solar energy that has been captured by green plants through the process of photosynthesis. The plants are then consumed by herbivo-

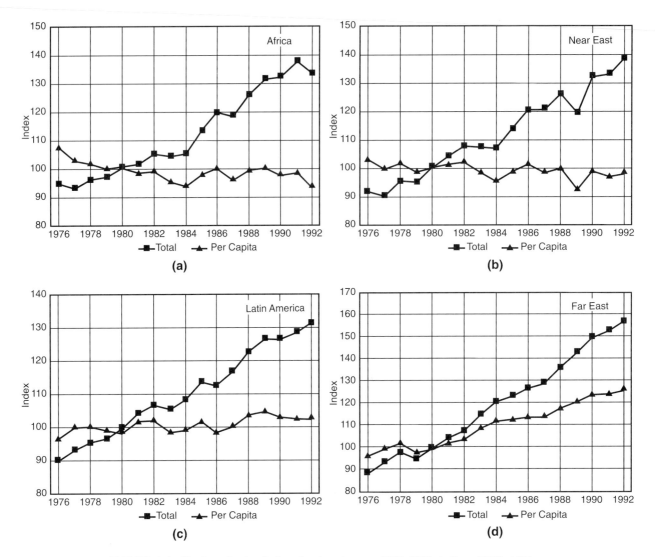

FIGURE 4.4   Food production in less-developed areas, 1976–1992, indices (1979–1981 = 100). Aided by the green revolution, total food production has generally risen in all four areas, with the greatest increase occurring in the Far East; but per capita output has lagged, especially in Africa and the Near East. Recurring droughts magnify the wide fluctuations in African harvests. [*Source:* Data from the *FAO Production Yearbook 1993* (Rome: Food and Agriculture Organization of the United Nations, 1995).]

rous animals, which may be eaten by carnivorous animals. In the sea, the food chain commences with the phytoplankton, tiny one-celled plants that are eaten by certain fish, which are themselves eaten by larger ones. More than 99 percent of the world's food supply currently comes from agriculture, and a mere 0.7 percent derives from the sea.

Agriculture and Grazing.   Only 37 percent of the world's land area is used for the production of food. Two-thirds of this is devoted to permanent pasture, leaving only 11 percent for field and tree crops. Major portions of total

cropland are in Asia, North America, Africa, and the former USSR (Figures 4.6 and 4.7). The figures can be misleading, however, because these lands vary greatly in their productive capacity and in the numbers of people they must support. A more revealing measure, therefore, is the amount of cropland per person (Figure 4.8): Asia, with nearly a third of the world's cropland, has only 0.14 hectare per person; North America has nearly two-thirds of a hectare per person. Because of the large quantity and high quality of its usable land, North America has been a major surplus food supply area from the time of the first European settlement. Despite its small overall size, Europe has the largest pro-

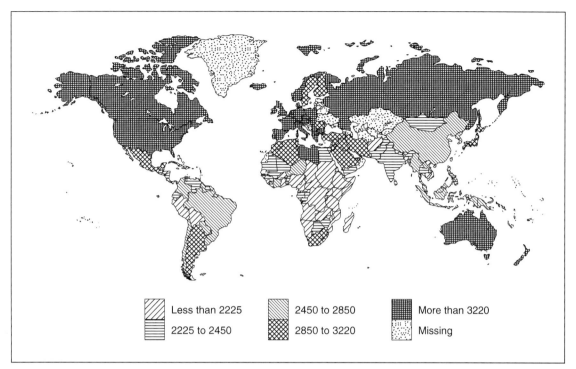

FIGURE 4.5   Daily per capita energy supply in calories. Food supplies in 29 mainland African countries are currently below the 2,334 calories per person cited by the United Nations Food and Agriculture Organization (FAO) as the minimum requirement for that region; in 12 of these, per capita daily food supplies are less than 2,000 calories. Similar food-supply deficiencies also exist in five Asian and five Latin American countries. The most poorly fed nation of the Western Hemisphere is Haiti, whose daily average food consumption is only 2,005 calories. [*Source:* Based on data from the *Britannica Book of the Year 1995* (Chicago: Encyclopaedia Britannica, 1995).]

portion of its land area in crops of any region (almost 29 percent); through intensive use, this acreage contributes more than enough to feed that continent's very large population. Though Oceania would appear to be an important source area as measured by persons per hectare, we must keep in mind that this lightly populated region accounts for only 3.6 percent of the world's cropland (Figure 4.5).

Despite the great variety of food crops grown throughout the world, a surprisingly few of these crops carry the main burden of feeding the human and animal populations. The overwhelming leaders are the grains, especially wheat, corn, and rice—in that order (Figures 4.9, 4.10, and 4.11). Being exceedingly transportable and having a multitude of uses, these commodities are staples of world diets even though they are relatively low in protein. (The millets and sorghums, another large family of grains, are locally important sources of animal and human foods in much of the world but do not figure as importantly in the world grain trade.) The world grain supply is therefore a dependable barometer of the global food situation. The total output of grain has increased steadily since the end of World War II. Per capita production has risen only slowly, however, because population growth has consumed much of the gain.

The patterns of world grain production and trade have shifted in recent years (Figure 4.12). Although both South America and Asia were net exporters of grain prior to World War II, both have since become net importers. Africa, never important as a source of world grain, has been a net importer since 1950. The former USSR and Eastern Europe barely produce enough grain for their own needs, and in bad years, they have had to import huge quantities. Western Europe has long had a substantial output of grain, mainly wheat, but generally did not produce enough to satisfy all of its needs. In recent years, however, the European Union's Common Agricultural Policy, with its generous subsidies to farmers, induced such an increase in output that Western Europe now faces an oversupply. Oceania (principally Australia) has relatively large grain surpluses, but these represent less than 1 percent of total world cereal output.

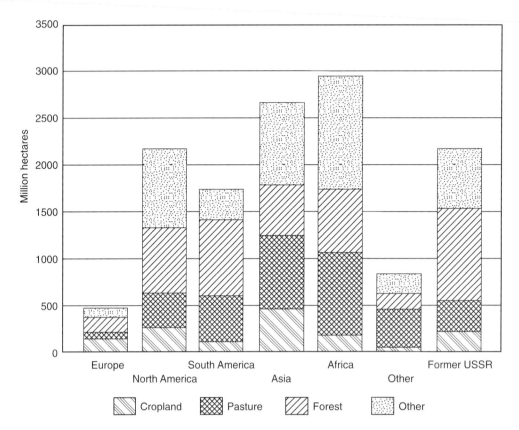

FIGURE 4.6   Land use of major world regions, million hectares. The regions vary greatly in their shares of the world's total land area and also in the ways in which this land is allocated to competing forms of land use. Immense variations likewise exist in the quality of the land and its potential for human exploitation. The "other" category includes such negative areas as deserts, arctic wastes, and mountainous terrain too rugged for human habitation. Consequently, the apparently generous land endowments of some regions are deceptive. [*Source:* Data from the *FAO Production Yearbook 1993* (Rome: Food and Agriculture Organization of the United Nations, 1995).]

Although a number of countries grow enough grain to satisfy their own needs and leave a balance for export, only the United States and Canada have surpluses large enough to produce a major impact on world markets (see Figure 4.12). With only 5 percent of the world's people—and approaching zero population growth—these two countries usually account for at least one-fifth of all grain output. The critical importance of this source area was underscored by the effect on world grain supplies created by the great North American drought of 1988, the most severe in that region since the "dust bowl" days of the 1930s. Following a smaller-than-usual grain harvest the previous year, the 1988 crop failure significantly reduced world grain stocks and aroused fears that global atmospheric warming was at last beginning to alter the climates of critical grain-producing regions. The North American crop returned to normal in succeeding years until 1993, when once-in-a-century floods again curtailed output.

Meanwhile, as we saw in Figure 4.4, many less-developed regions have lost the capacity to feed themselves and have had to turn to the surplus producers for help. If world food output is to keep pace with the continuing growth of these less-developed populations after the turn of the century, advances in agriculture production will have to take place. What are the possibilities?

Two main ways exist for increasing world output of agricultural commodities: (1) expanding the cultivated area and (2) increasing the output per hectare (yield). Some estimates suggest that the possibilities for expanding the world's cultivated land are substantial—that perhaps twice the present total quantity of land in use is potentially arable. But the unused land is generally not in the same places as the people with the greatest need for it, and major economic, political, and social obstacles limit the wholesale transplanting of populations required to redress the imbalance. The Food and Agriculture Organization of the United

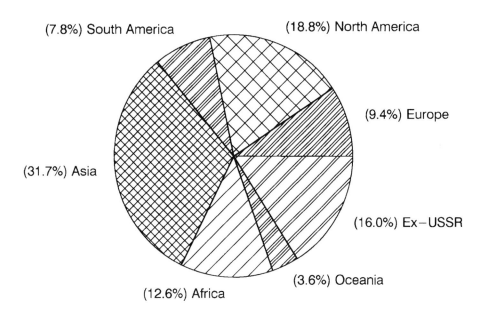

FIGURE 4.7 Regional shares of world cropland. Asia contains nearly one-third of the total global supply of cropland (arable land and land under permanent crops). North America and the former Soviet Union also enjoy large endowments. Africa, South America, and Oceania (mainly Australia and New Zealand) have much smaller shares of the world's land under crops than might be expected from the size of their total land areas. Because the regions differ greatly in population densities, a more useful indicator of their potential for food production is cropland per capita (see Figure 4.6). [*Source:* Based on data from the *FAO Production Yearbook 1993* (Rome: Food and Agriculture Organization of the United Nations, 1995).]

Nations (FAO) anticipates, therefore, that no more than 10 or 20 percent of this potential cropland will be in use by the end of the present century.

The greatest need, according to a study conducted jointly by the FAO and the International Institute for Applied Systems Analysis (IIASA), is concentrated in a group of 57 countries, all of which lack sufficient arable land, at present levels of agricultural technology, to feed the populations projected for them for the year A.D. 2000 (Shah and Fischer, 1984). Of these "critical" countries, 27 are in Africa, the region that has only just begun to signs of progress toward bringing its population under control during the twenty-first century (Figure 4.13). Most of these rank among the poorest lands on earth, with per capita gross domestic products less than $300. Ten critical countries are in Middle America: El Salvador on the mainland and nine island nations of the Caribbean. Five are in southern and southeastern Asia, Bangladesh being the most difficult case. All but four countries in the Middle East are on the list, and of these four only Turkey has substantial potential for further agricultural development. Elsewhere in the Mediterranean, and in most of Asia, reserves of unused arable land are essentially exhausted.

Another reason that estimates of unused land are misleading is that in most major areas where potential arable land is supposedly available, obstacles stand in the way of its development. One such obstacle is excessive aridity. One-fourth of the earth's land surface is classified as desert—areas where rainfall averages less than 10 inches per year. Most of the unused potentially arable land of Asia is desert. Only a small fraction of such land can be irrigated.

One problem with irrigating desert lands is that many of these are covered either by shifting sands or by "desert pavement," stony surfaces devoid of soil. Equally difficult is the problem of finding enough irrigation water in the right places. Much of the irrigated agriculture in desert areas occurs along "exotic" streams, such as the Nile or the Colorado, which flow into these dry lands out of rainy mountainous regions. Many other irrigation districts make use of ground waters available through an unusual combination of geological conditions that link such areas with rainy uplands. Besides being rather uncommon, these artesian systems have an exceedingly slow rate of natural recharge—usually thousands of years. In many places, such as the American Southwest, water tables in artesian basins are falling precipitously from overuse. A further problem

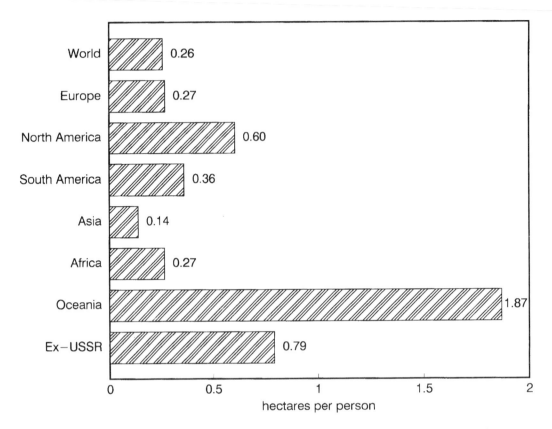

FIGURE 4.8   Cropland per capita, by world regions, hectares, 1992. On average, each inhabitant of the earth can draw on 0.26 ha (0.57 acre) of cropland. For an Asian, the quota is only 0.14 ha. Cropland per person in both Europe and Africa closely approaches the world average, but the output of that land is exceedingly different: Europeans enjoy ample diets from the output of their farms and have a surplus of agricultural goods for export; many Africans are undernourished and the continent as a whole has become a net importer of food. In most years, the United States, Canada, and Australia have big farm surpluses and are leading suppliers to the world. Latin America is a region of great disparities: Argentina, Brazil, and Chile are important exporters of farm products; the three Andean countries of Ecuador, Peru, and Bolivia are unable to produce sufficient food for their citizens. Farm output in the former Soviet Union, which has 0.79 hectare of cropland per person, is highly variable from year to year. The country is therefore an unpredictable, and often major, factor in the world agricultural trade. [*Source:* Data from the *FAO Production Yearbook 1993* (Rome: Food and Agriculture Organization of the United Nations, 1995).]

with irrigating deserts is the very high cost of constructing dams, canals, and roads, preparing soils, and administering these systems. One of the most unsettling aspects of the aridity problem is the mounting evidence that some of the world's major deserts are growing, encroaching on neighboring lands where large populations gain their livelihood from agriculture and grazing. For a discussion of this "desertification" process, see Box 4.2.

In addition to the virtually rainless desert areas, nearly one-third of the earth's surface is steppe land, where rainfall averages between 10 and 30 inches per year. Because of high evaporation, steppe lands in tropical latitudes are usually suitable only for grazing, but in temperate

areas, commercial grain farming may be possible, using "dry farming" techniques that conserve the available moisture. Although the upper-latitude steppes have some of the world's best soils—excellent for wheat or grain sorghum—the lack of dependable rainfall makes the farming of these areas highly uncertain. The tragic dust bowl conditions of the American plains during the 1930s and the failure of Premier Nikita Khrushchev's "virgin lands" project in the USSR dramatize the problems of relying on the steppe lands for substantial additions to the earth's total arable area. Nevertheless, as we shall see shortly, many areas of uncertain rainfall have provided important opportunities for increasing the output of existing farmlands

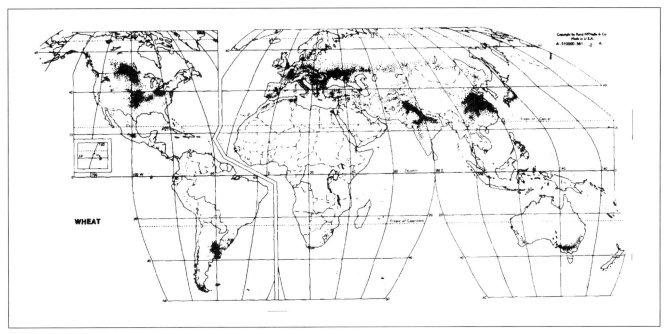

FIGURE 4.9   World wheat production. One dot = 1 million bushels (27,200 metric tonnes). [*Source:* Adapted from *Goode's World Atlas*, © 1988 Rand McNally R.L. 92-S-217-Revised.]

through the introduction of new agricultural technology, including irrigation.

Many of the lands commonly classified as potentially arable lie within the vast tropical rain forests of the Amazon and Congo basins. The agricultural capabilities of these areas are much overrated because the heavy downpours of rain leach essential plant food elements out of the surface layers of soil, rendering them unproductive for ordinary shallow-rooted crops. An even more serious obstacle to the use of the tropical areas of Africa, where population pressures in neighboring lands are intense, is the prevalence of such diseases as river blindness (onchocerciasis) and sleep-

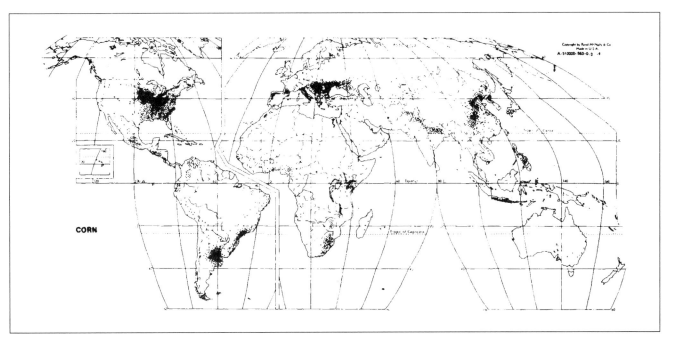

FIGURE 4.10   World corn (maize) production. One dot = 1 million bushels (25,400 metric tonnes). [*Source:* Adapted from *Goode's World Atlas* © 1988 Rand McNally R.L. 92-S-217-Revised.]

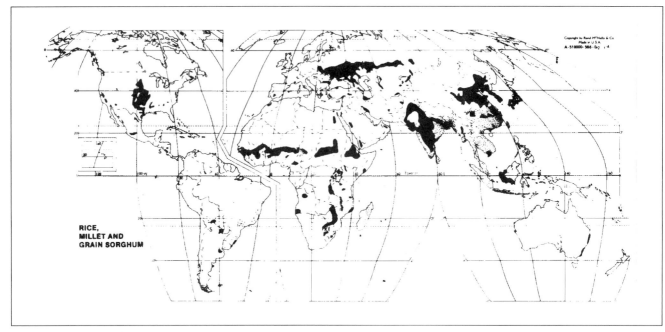

FIGURE 4.11   World rice production. One dot = 5 million bushels (102,000 metric tonnes). Also shown on this map (solid patterns) are major producing areas of millets and sorghums, members of another large and diverse class of grains grown chiefly for local animal and human consumption in semi-arid lands not suitable for rice culture. [*Source:* Adapted from Goode's World Atlas © 1988 Rand McNally R.L. 92-S-217-Revised.]

ing sickness (trypanosomiasis). Great areas in the valleys of the Volta, Niger, Congo, Gambia, and Upper Nile rivers remain unfarmed owing to fear of river blindness, which persists despite concerted efforts of governments and world organizations to eradicate it. Sleeping sickness, carried by the tsetse fly, has excluded the usual types of farming from 1 billion hectares of tropical Africa. Experiments with insecticides have been largely unsuccessful because of their high cost and because of the fly's resistance to them.

The best hope for increasing the world food supply from agriculture, therefore, does not lie in expanding the amount of arable land, but in more intensive use of existing farmlands: applying more labor and capital in order to raise yields per hectare. Recent technological advances in North America, Western Europe, and Japan—as well as in certain developing countries—point the way. The problem of transferring agricultural technology to new areas is, however, an intricate one because every locality has distinctive soil and climatic conditions and its own combination of land, labor, capital, and customs. Plant varieties that work well in one place usually have to undergo substantial modification before they can be introduced on the farms of another locality.

The appropriate strategy for raising yields differs for a country with an abundance of farmland but a small supply of farm labor—such as the United States—and a country

with a relatively large number of farm workers but a limited amount of arable land—as in the case of Japan. The situation is still different for a less-developed country with large quantities of both land and labor but lacking management skills and capital. Nevertheless, Japan's solution offers much hope because, initially at least, that country's population/food supply problems so closely paralleled those of today's less-developed countries. During the first half of this century Japan's arable land area increased by only 18 percent, but average yields rose by two-thirds and total national farm output nearly doubled.

The intensification of agriculture entails two kinds of technologies, and Japan used both: mechanization and the introduction of improved plant varieties in combination with increased fertilizer use. In addition to adopting new high-yielding seeds and making optimal use of chemical fertilizers, the Japanese developed special types of machinery suitable for use on their tiny, garden-size farms. In this way, they were able to maintain and increase output even as industrialization lured more and more farm workers to the cities. Thus, in Japan, farmers substituted machinery for labor, just as their counterparts did in the United States, except at a different scale. Japanese agriculture also benefited from governmental protection from import competition. This kept domestic food prices very high, enabling farmers to continue operating despite high production costs.

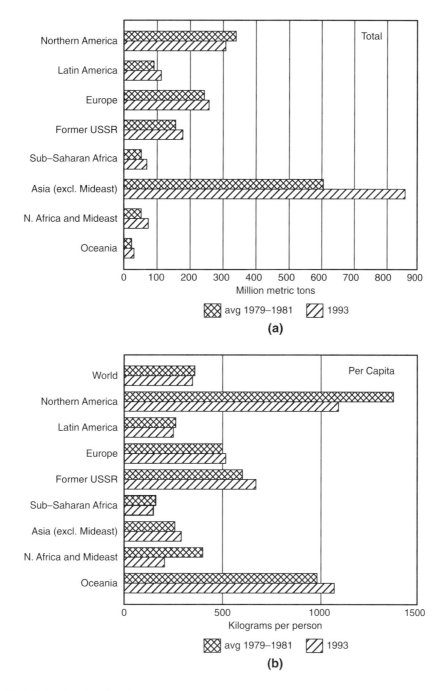

FIGURE 4.12 Total and per capita cereal production, world regions, 1980 and 1993. Total world output of all cereal crops (Figure 4.12a) rose substantially between 1980 and 1993, aided by higher yields produced by the green revolution in Third World agriculture, especially in Asia. U.S. grain production was held in check during this period as a result of federal farm policy. By contrast with this picture of ostensible progress by the Third World in raising total grain output, per capita figures (Figure 4.12b) show only slight gains for LDCs during the period; indeed, the average person in sub-Saharan Africa was actually worse off. Thus, when the numbers of people to be fed in the various regions are taken into account, it is clear that the world must look mainly to Northern America (the United States and Canada) for future grain supplies. Other surplus areas do not have sufficient total output to make important contributions to world supplies. [*Source:* Data from the FAO Production Yearbook 1993 *(Rome: Food and Agriculture Organization of the United Nations, 1995).]*

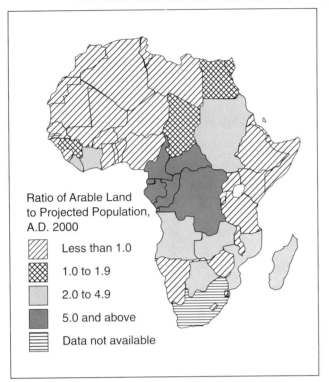

FIGURE 4.13 Land-short countries of Africa. Ratio of population-supporting capacity to projected population, A.D. 2000. Today, Africa as a whole is a food-deficit region, and many African countries depend on food imports to sustain often inadequate diets (compare with Figure 4.3). By the end of this century, at least 29 African countries are expected to lack sufficient arable land to produce the food required by the populations they are projected to have by that date, according to a study jointly sponsored by the International Institute for Applied Systems Analysis (IIASA) and the United Nations Food and Agriculture Organization (FAO). The land shortage is especially critical in 27 of the 29 countries. The Republic of South Africa was excluded from the study. [*Source:* Data from Mahendra Shah and Günther Fischer, People, Land, and Food Production: Potentials in the Developing World, in *Options,* (International Institute for Applied Systems Analysis, IIASA), 2 (1984): 1–5.]

Japanese farmers remain a strong and influential political lobby that fights to prevent the lowering of protectionist barriers.

Though most less-developed nations have little incentive to replace their abundant rural labor with machines, they can increase farm output by introducing machinery for certain operations. For instance, at harvest time, when all workers are needed in the fields, a few trucks can transport the crop to market more quickly, economically, and with less spoilage than could any number of human porters and draft animals. Also, mechanical pumps are much cheaper

and more effective in raising irrigation water than are primitive hand pumps and waterwheels.

The greatest opportunities for increasing yields come from the second of these technologies, however: the introduction of new, higher-yielding varieties of plants, together with the chemicals and water supplies that these require for the full realization of their potential. The scientific selection and breeding of plants, which had done so much to raise farm yields in the industrialized countries since the beginning of plant genetics a century earlier, are now being applied successfully to increasing the output of wheat, rice, and other cereal crops in the Third World. International research centers have led the way by developing new plant strains and spreading them throughout the tropics and subtropics. This has required adapting these crops to an enormous variety of local soil and climatic conditions. Plant breeders have concentrated on producing sturdy, short-stemmed plants capable of supporting the large cereal heads that yield greater output per hectare. They have also bred these plants to mature more quickly, to be resistant to pests and diseases, and to have better flavor and storage qualities. Agricultural biotechnologists promise that these will be succeeded by a new era of *transgenic crops,* products of gene splicing that will be cheaper to grow, taste better, and be even more effective in resisting spoilage and pests.

Unlike the hardy but poor-yielding native varieties they are replacing, the new types of grains that have been introduced to date require large amounts of fertilizer. Accompanying the introduction of the new seeds, therefore, has been a large increase in the use of chemical fertilizers in developing countries, where they were virtually unknown prior to the 1960s. Half the increase in grain yields in the past three decades is attributable to greater fertilizer use. The fertilizers are effective, however, only when sufficient moisture is present in the soil to dissolve these nutrients so that they can be taken up by the plant roots. Hence, the other part of this new agricultural technology is the provision of adequate water supplies. In much of the world, natural rainfall is either inadequate or comes at the wrong times. In southern Asia the timing and amount of the monsoon rains have been crucial to the success or failure of harvests in the past. Supplementary irrigation therefore has been a third essential element in the drive to raise farm output in developing lands.

In some tropical and subtropical countries irrigation has been the largest single contributor to improved yields. Under certain conditions, it has doubled and even trebled yields during the main growing season and has made possible the growing of a second or third crop in the remainder of the year. The irrigated area has increased steadily since the 1960s until it now encompasses about a fifth of the arable lands in the developing countries. China and India alone account for half of this. Unfortunately, the extensive irrigation systems and storage reservoirs required for such projects are not feasible in many other areas, especially those parts of sub-Saharan Africa suffering from drought and famine.

On the whole, agriculture has made substantial progress in the less-developed parts of the world during the past three decades. Yields and total output of staple crops have risen markedly. These advances have greatly improved the lot of millions of people in some less-developed countries, where it has been termed the *green revolution* (see Box 4.3 for further discussion of the achievements and problems of the green revolution).

Unfortunately, this revolution has not yet reached all parts of the world. Many poorer countries have been unable to avail themselves of the new technology, and even within those countries that have profited from this development are regions that have not had access to it. In some countries, the overall results hardly more than offset the growth of population during that same period. Thus, whereas per capita output was rising by 1.2 percent a year in South and East Asia during the 1980s, it remained static in Latin America and actually shrank in some other areas. In Africa, per capita food output rose by 0.2 percent per annum during the 1960s but declined at an annual rate of -0.7 percent in 1980s.

Clearly, questions of time and cost arise. Enormous expenditures are required for opening new lands, building new fertilizer factories, and distributing the fertilizer and new seed varieties. Much time is needed to develop the seeds and to train farmers and technicians in their use. What, then, are the prospects for supplementing future food supplies through alternative approaches?

Food from the Sea.   The seas supply about one-fifth of the world's high-quality animal protein, and this source of food is particularly important to certain fishing nations such as Japan, the former USSR, China, Norway, and Iceland. Yet the nearly 80 million metric tons of food obtained from seas, lakes, and rivers provide less than 1 percent of the world's total food. Public statements on this subject often overestimate the unused potential of food from the sea: Informed sources insist that the present catch cannot be increased by much more than 15 percent on a sustained-yield basis.

This last qualification identifies the real problem, for overexploitation today means reduced catches in the future. Indeed, stocks of many varieties of food fish have greatly diminished and some species are virtually depleted. Certain types, such as salmon, are especially vulnerable. Overfishing is one result of the "open seas" principle, which treats the world's oceans as common property, as we shall see in Chapter 6—see, especially, Box 6.4. This means that no one is responsible for maintaining the "fertility" of fishing grounds; indeed, the open-seas concept encourages intense competition among national fishing fleets, which

develop increasingly sophisticated gear to capture larger quantities of dwindling stocks of fish. Another unfortunate feature of commercial fishing is the practice among less-developed nations of exporting their catches instead of retaining this valuable protein to feed their own undernourished populations. Currently, nearly one-seventh of the world catch is exported.

The seas thus contribute only a small part of global food needs, and the supply of conventional sea foods appears unlikely even to keep pace with the rate the factors spurring the search for unorthodox forms of food.

More Radical Methods of Increasing Food Supplies

From time to time the Sunday newspaper supplements report spectacular scientific discoveries that will multiply the world's food supply limitlessly. Many such claims are mere science fiction, but certain recent developments are genuinely encouraging to a world concerned with the challenge of feeding future billions. Let us explore the possibilities offered by some of the proposals now being advanced.

One of the paradoxes of world agriculture is that some of the driest deserts are adjacent to huge bodies of water; however, the salinity of these oceans and seas precludes their use for irrigation. The technology of desalination is sufficiently advanced to provide large quantities of water for household use, but the process is still much too costly for ordinary agricultural and industrial purposes. One proposal is to construct large multipurpose nuclear installations whose costs are largely borne by the sale of the electric power they generate but that have sufficient additional capacity for the production of fertilizer and desalinated water for adjacent farmlands. Another alternative for seaside agriculture in dry lands is to breed food plants that tolerate salt water. Research on this problem has already shown some promise.

A second approach to augmenting the global food supply is for the world as a whole to adopt the traditional Oriental practice of bypassing animals in the food chain. Under this plan, everyone would eat the products of the soil directly rather than first convening them into animal products. These "direct calories" are much more efficient in their use of the land because at best only 14 percent of the plant food value per hectare reaches the meat eater. This would require radically altering the eating habits of most people, especially in the richer nations, but it might also subject them to the same high-starch, low-protein diets that keep so much of the world's population malnourished.

A likely solution for this nutritional problem is to develop high-protein foods from plant sources. Research has focused on soybeans, and to some extent cottonseeds, both of which are already important sources of nutritious animal feed. An acre of land can supply 10 times as much

BOX 4.2 Desertification

By attracting worldwide sympathy to their suffering, the victims of famine in sub-Saharan Africa have served to focus attention on a worsening global problem: the continuing spread of deserts into adjacent populated lands, a process called 'desertification.' Though a severe, prolonged drought was the immediate cause of the crop failure and resulting starvation in Africa's Sahel in the 1980s, drought is a temporary condition that has come and gone many times in that part of the world; more worrisome is the evidence that drought is merely furthering the long-term, virtually irreversible process of desertification already under way in the region. Furthermore, the deserts of Africa are not the only ones that are advancing: Desertification is also proceeding at an accelerating pace in other subhumid areas of the world, especially the Middle East and parts of northwestern Asia (see Figure 4c). Each year an additional 200,000 square kilometers are rendered useless in this manner—an area equivalent to all of New England plus New Jersey. Altogether, the threat extends to 20 percent of the earth's land surface, home to possibly 80 million people.

This destruction of productive land is largely a result of prolonged human use and misuse of a vulnerable natural environment. Soils form slowly in are lands, and they are usually deficient various important plant nutrients. Because of the scarcity of moisture, plant cover is sparse, and the shallow soils are susceptible to rapid deterioration through erosion and guilying. In these areas of ecological instability, the chief agents of land degradation are overcultivation, overgrazing, and deforestation. Over the ages poor farming practices, trampling and close cropping of vegetation by goats and sheep, and stripping of woodlands for timber and fuel have so reduced the natural ground cover that the soils lie exposed to erosion from sun and wind.

Human pressures on this fragile ecological system are intensifying, for the rates of population growth in these areas are among the world's highest. As they struggle to feed their expanding numbers, the farmers and grazers of the semiarid lands struggle to get more and more out of the land until finally the soil is so exhausted that it yields nothing. The onset of a drought therefore finds the land stripped of its natural defenses, and the process of desertification quickens. Eventually the inhabitants must abandon their farms and seek food wherever they may hope to find it.

The most recent drought in subSaharan africa began in the 1970s, abated slightly in 1980, then resurged with new vigor in the following years to become the worst in a century and a half. In the process, an estimated 70,000 square kilometers succumbed to desertification each year. The band of most intense drought stretched uninterruptedly for 6000 kilometers from Dakar on the Atlantic to the Horn of Africa on the Indian Ocean, an area twice the size of the continental United States. The severest impact fell on Chad, Ghana, Mali, Ethiopia, Somalia, and Senegal. Farther to the southeast, Mozambique was among the hardest hit in still another area of drought.

The human tragedy was immeasurable: More than 150 million people lacked sufficient food, and countless numbers died of disease and starvation. By 1983, grain output in the affected countries had fallen 35 percent below normal, a decline further accentuated by severe insect infestations of crops. Adding to the misery were outbreaks of cattle disease and brushfires, as well as wars and revolutions in Chad, Ethiopia, and Somalia.

The great African drought of the 1980s ended with the return of ample rainfall during the 1985 season. Recurrent crop failures, however, continued in subsequent years to plague

---

protein in the form of soybeans as it can in the form of beef and at a far lower cost. One difficulty has been to make soybean and cottonseed products sufficiently palatable for human beings. Thus far these products have served mainly as additives to meat and bread. Among other radical experiments are attempts to convert alfalfa leaves, forest leaves, pea vines, and other common green plant parts into high-protein human food. Scientists have also worked at developing a palatable human and animal food from single-celled organisms cultured on petroleum.

Possibly the greatest promise lies in the deoxyribonucleic acid (DNA) that describes all life-forms. As scientists gain a better understanding of DNA, they are able to create new varieties by manipulating the genetic code. Although genetic engineering is only in its infancy, plant scientists have already succeeded with certain experimental techniques, notably *tissue culture*. This is a method for multiplying plants starting with only a single part—a piece of root or leaf—and developing completely new genetically identical plants. Tissue culture is a much quicker way of multiplying plants than seeding or grafting, and the resulting clones are completely uniform in all important respects, such as yield, quality, and maturing times. The technique also permits the engineering of plants that are resistant to disease and that are adapted to particular environments. Considerable success has already been achieved with various temperate and tropical tree crops. The potential for quantum increases in world food supplies through these and other recently developed techniques of plant engineering offer much hope for the next century.

Meanwhile, other scientists are seeking ways to multiply the food-producing potential of the seas. One product attracting attention is *fish protein concentrate*, a flour made by grinding whole fish and using it as an additive to fortify low-protein diets in poorer countries. Not only does this method employ more of the fish for food but it also makes

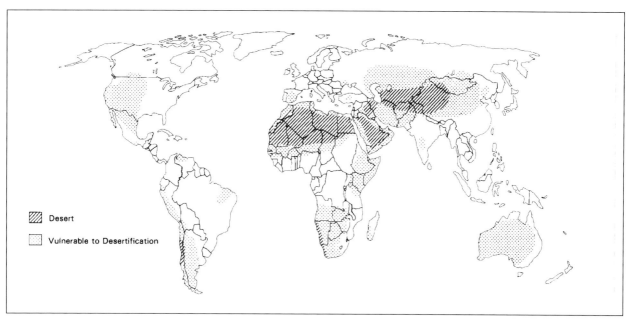

FIGURE 4c World map of desertification. [Source: United Nations Conference on Desertification, 1977.]

the north of Ethiopia, where the loss of life from famine was exacerbated by a brutal civil war that prevented food shipments from reaching the troubled areas.

If the past is a reliable guide, the recent siege of droughts in sub-Saharan Africa will not be the last for that tormented region. The record shows that, for reasons not yet well understood, droughts in this region occur in cycles averaging 7 years in length, with especially severe episodes having reappeared in each of the past three centuries. An episode of intense droughts occurred between 1820 and 1840, according to historical records; and a still earlier one took place between 1758 and 1773, as indicated by geological evidence. It seems unlikely, however, that the end of the drought of the 1980s will return the sub-Sahara to previous levels of food output. The lands most recently swallowed up in the process of desertification are probably lost for good.

possible the use of fish not ordinarily caught for human consumption. Thus far, however, fish protein concentrate has not been well received by consumers.

Despite the sophisticated techniques employed by some fleets, commercial fishing is still essentially little different from the activities of food gatherers and hunters. Modern fishing fleets merely seek out what nature has provided, with little or no thought for cultivating or replenishing the breeding stock. For the long run at least, it would seem logical for the fishing industry to follow the example of agriculture or animal husbandry by devising methods for commercial fish farming. Oriental rice farmers have traditionally cultivated carp and other fish in their irrigation ditches, ponds, and flooded fields as a source of much-needed protein in their starch-filled diets. In the same way, rice farmers in the lower Mississippi valley and delta successfully produce catfish and shrimp as by-products of their irrigated rice growing. Oyster farming is a long-established industry in the brackish waters of Chesapeake Bay and

various other coastal waters of the United States. These techniques are now being adapted to the cultivation of other relatively sedentary forms of sea life, such as lobsters, clams, and crabs.

Several fishing nations of Western Europe have begun to expand "mariculture" by cultivating nonsedentary species, especially certain high-quality food fish found in the open seas. Norway's fish-farming program is already far advanced: By 1984, it was earning a substantial income from trout and salmon and had begun production of cod, turbot, and flatfish. Spain, France, and Germany have developed techniques for growing fish and shellfish in aquaculture plants and releasing the hatchlings into their coastal waters for restocking. Japan and other fishing countries have long used such methods for rebuilding their salmon fisheries.

As in agriculture, opportunities exist for short-cutting the food chain of the seas. Harvesting seaweed is already a well-established industry, especially along the coasts of

BOX 4.3 The Green Revolution

The dramatic development in world agriculture called the *green revolution* traces its origins to a unique international research network introduced initially in Mexico by the Rockefeller Foundation in 1943. The world first became aware of this work during the 1960s with the release of new high-yielding varieties of wheat and rice to the farmers of less-developed countries by two of these research institutes, the International Maize and Wheat Improvement Center (CIM-MYT), sponsored by the Mexican government and the Rockefeller Foundation, and the International Rice Research Institute (IRRI), funded by the Rockefeller and Ford foundations. These accomplishments represented the first worldwide efforts to extend the benefits of modern plant genetics to the problems of tropical agriculture. The early successes of this program led to the establishment of 13 international research centers under the auspices of the Consultative Group on International Agricultural Research (CGIAR) in Washington.

The significance of these developments is vividly shown by their effects on Indian agriculture. Following introduction of the new varieties in 1966, India's wheat output doubled within 6 years. Previously the world's second largest grain importer, India had become self-sufficient by the end of the 1970s, relieving its government of a drain on the national treasury and averting the tragedy of mass starvation.

Figure 4d illustrates the remarkable success achieved during those early years by wheat and rice farmers in the Indian state of Punjab, which lies on the semiarid Indo-Gangetic Plain. Although this district is subject to frequent droughts, its progressive and energetic farmers have availed themselves of local supplies of irrigation water and have applied the chemical fertilizers required by the new plan strains.

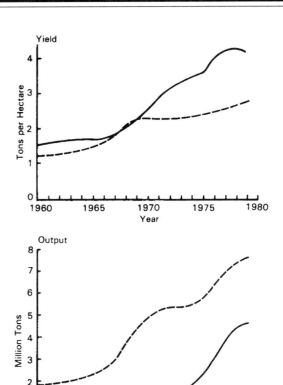

FIGURE 4d Results of the green revolution in the Indian state of Punjab (plotted as 3-year moving averages). Dramatic increases in yields and output of rice and wheat followed the introduction of new hybrid seeds in the mid-1960s. A brief decline in wheat yields during the early 1970s, owing to the appearance of wheat rust, was subsequently corrected by the development of disease-resistant strains. [Source: World Bank, World Development Report 1982 (New York: Oxford University Press.]

Other countries were quick to adopt these innovations, too. China, Pakistan, Turkey, and Bangladesh were among those to attain early success with the new strains of wheat. The new rice varieties likewise spread quickly throughout southern and southeastern Asia, although certain areas were unable to adopt them because of their exacting water requirements. Those districts with suitable conditions, however, enjoyed very large increases in rice output. Not only did farmers gain from the high yields but they also benefitted from the shod maturity times of the new strains, which make it possible to grow two or more crops within a single year.

Although the green revolution has had less impressive results with maize (corn) and grain sorghums, notable gains have occurred here as well. Maize varieties that produce exceedingly high yields in one district often fail in other areas. Nevertheless, improved types have succeeded in a number of countries, especially Argentina, China, Kenya, and Zimbabwe. Sorghums initially presented special technical problems and encountered some resistance from farmers, but they are now gaining wide acceptance in northeastern China, the drier parts of India, and some areas of Latin America.

The impact of the green revolution on Third World agricultural productivity has been striking. Mainly as a result of gains by less-developed countries, world grain output rose from only 620 million tons in 1950 to 1660 million tons in 1985, while yields increased from 1.1 ton per hectare to 2.6 tons—an unprecedented gain. Between 1970 and 1983 the area planted to the new varieties of wheat and rice expanded from 270,000 ha to 9.6 million ha. By the 1980s, half of the wheat and nearly three-fifths of the rice produced in less-developed areas came from land planted to high-yielding strains. The percentages in Latin America and China were even higher.

Despite these triumphs of the new technology, as viewed from a global perspective, it has helped some Third World farmers more than others. Indeed, the benefits have tailed to reach a troubling number of these farmers altogether. The program has therefore aroused much controversy.

Perhaps 230 million rural households have been passed over by the green revolution, many of these in Africa, where only 1 percent of the grain area has been planted to new high-yielding strains. Among those overlooked are the subsistence farmers, who produce only for their own needs on marginal, rain-fed land—diverse areas ranging from the arid savannas of sub-Saharan Africa to the high altiplano of Andean America. These farmers cannot get the irrigation waters required by the new strains, nor do they have access to markets for the sale of a surplus. In many areas lacking suitable physical conditions for wheat and rice, the traditional crops on which farmers must rely have not as yet caught the attention of agricultural research. Farmers on marginal land necessarily have a different set of priorities. For them, economic survival is the prime objective: Increasing yields is not as important as gaining security against drought and other natural calamities.

Even within those regions where the green revolution has been successful, many farmers have failed to gain from it. The main beneficiaries in these favored areas have been Western-educated farmers possessing fertile soils and the financial resources to pay for the fertilizer, irrigation equipment, and other capital and energy-intensive inputs essential to the new technology. Such communities usually hold large numbers of illiterate, impoverished smallholders who are unable to adopt the new strains and can no longer compete when the increased efficiency of their better-off neighbors drives down commodity prices. This situation creates a landless rural proletariate, many of whom

migrate to the cities, further swelling the urban slums.

Critics also point to the environmental damage caused by the intensive use of chemical fertilizers and pesticides. These have penetrated underground water supplies and have contaminated streams and lakes, creating health hazards for adjacent populations.

The CGIAR-sponsored research institutes have responded to these criticisms by devoting more research to ways of raising crop yields without degrading the environment and by directing more attention to the special needs of small farmers. Agricultural researchers have gained a new respect for traditional farming systems and are looking for methods to improve rather than replace them in submarginal areas.

Against the disappointments of the green revolution must be weighed the very substantial contribution it has made toward global food supplies at a time when Third World populations are still mounting. It is important to note that some of the greatest successes for the new technology have occurred in the most-populous less-developed countries, particularly India, China, Indonesia, and the Philippines. As some observers have stressed, without these advances, many millions of people would have died of starvation each year. Those who developed the new high-yielding strains never regarded their achievement as the answer to all the world's food problems; their best hope was that the increased productivity would provide time for solving the central problem: bringing population growth under control. However the green revolution is viewed, few would deny that one of its most significant accomplishments has been the creation of an international network of research institutes devoted to reducing world hunger and improving the lot of farmers in less-developed areas.

Japan and Canada's Atlantic provinces. The seaweed yields products widely used as food additives (e.g., ice cream stabilizers) and in the chemical industries. One frequently voiced proposal is to harvest plankton directly instead of concentrating on catching the fish that feed on it. Experiments have shown that this is an expensive operation, however, and consumers find the fishy flavor of the product distasteful. Moreover, some marine biologists argue that large-scale harvesting of plankton would merely deprive food fish of their main source of sustenance.

Feeding the World beyond A.D. 2000

The problem of feeding future populations raises questions that lack sure answers. Just how many people will have to be fed, and how much food will it take? Where will the greatest demand for food come from? Who will have to produce it and how? The world population will continue growing at a fairly high rate into the twenty-first century before it tapers off, and the less-developed countries will account for virtually all of that growth beyond the year 2000. The new additions to population will increasingly concentrate in the poorest of the poor countries.

The new demand for food will stem from two sources: (1) the increase in numbers of people to be fed and (2) greater per capita consumption as a result of rising incomes. Better diets for populations whose standards of living are improving probably mean more consumption of animal proteins, which in turn will substantially augment the demand for feed grains. This second source of demand increase—rising incomes—will center on the middle-income, less-developed countries. The poorest countries will probably continue subsisting on their accustomed high-starch diets and direct calories.

How will this new demand be supplied? The developing countries as a whole are already net importers of food: About 9 percent of current needs come from foreign sources. Only a select number of less-developed countries—notably the newly industrialized nations of the Pacific rim—can find the needed foreign exchange to pay for significant additional supplies of imported food. Realistically, therefore, most less-developed countries must count on producing their new food needs themselves.

Such future increases in food supplies will have to come from two sources: conventional agriculture and new developments in nonconventional food production. The seas currently contribute only a minor fraction of world food needs, and conventional fish catches have already leveled off. Agriculture remains the chief hope, especially with the encouraging rise in yields and output during the past two decades. If world agriculture is to continue keeping up with population, it must achieve ever-greater technological improvements. It must also minimize future losses of arable land to competing forms of land use—urban, industrial, transportation —and to soil deterioration from such causes as erosion, desertification, and alkalinity.

Agricultural experts concerned about the earth's future food supply have still another worry: the possibility of a major climatic change. This century has already seen unusual periods of global warming and cooling, leading some climatologists to speculate that this growing variability foretells the approach of another ice age, which they believe is about due. Others note that human activities may be actually producing a countertrend that could bring a general global warming. The combustion of fossil fuels causes carbon dioxide and other chemicals to accumulate in the upper atmosphere, where they create a "greenhouse effect" by trapping the incoming sun's rays and raising air temperatures. If either of these opposing trends were to materialize, crop production could be greatly affected, particularly in those areas that are unusually sensitive to temperature change: the higher latitudes, the upper elevations, and the semiarid regions. For instance, a 1°C decrease in mean annual temperatures, it has been estimated, would cut the potential wheat-growing area of Canada by one-third and would cause the U.S. corn belt to shift 140 km (85 miles) southward. Farmers in the South American Andes and other upland areas would have to abandon their lands at higher elevations and retreat to the lowlands. Conversely, a 1°C increase would move both crop production and arid zones northward and upward.

Aside from the threat of environmental change, agriculturalists can expect additional yield increases to become more costly if they require larger capital outlays for irrigation, machinery, and chemicals. Many of the measures on which we rely to augment world food supplies have the effect of intensifying the demand for other resources, many of which are nonrenewable. Minerals are essential for the manufacture of commercial fertilizers, for smelting metals used in making farm machinery and transport equipment, for the mechanical energy to propel this equipment, and for the construction of buildings, roads, dams, irrigation ditches, and other facilities. What are the prospects for maintaining an adequate supply of such resources? This is the question to which we turn in Chapter 5.

VOCABULARY

Listed are vocabulary items that appear for the first time in this chapter. They are defined in the Glossary. Be sure you know them:

artesian systems

chemical agriculture

"critical" countries

cultivated area

desert pavement

desertification

dry farming techniques

economists' views of future supply of critical resources

environmentalists' views of future supply of critical resources

flow resources

food-deficit region

gene splicing

green revolution

greenhouse effect

income disparity

intensification

land use

Lebensraum

malnutrition

mechanization

nonrenewable resources

"open-seas" principle

per capita food output

politics of resources

poverty

protectionist barriers

renewable resource

resource

spaceship earth

steppe land

subsistence

sustainable development

sustained yield

tissue culture

transgenic crops

yield

TOPICS FOR DISCUSSION

1. Explain the general trends affecting the numerator and denominator of the resources/population ratio. What do these trends tell us about the future spatial pattern of resource use? Why are government policymakers and the general public unable to sustain a long-range view of resource problems and to adopt the necessary measures to solve them?

2. What is meant by the term 'resource,' and why must any given resource be regarded as a changing concept? Define the various categories of resources. Why do the spatial patterns of supply and demand For most resources differ, and what political and economic problems arise from these differences?

3. Most experts no longer fear that the global food supply will be exhausted before the end of this century. What has happened to allay those fears? Why, then, do 1.5 billion people nevertheless remain hungry? Discuss the nature and spatial pattern of world hunger.

4. Give the reasons why many estimates of the world's potential cropland are misleading. Describe the process of 'desertification' and examine the various dimensions of the food problems of sub-Saharan Africa. Where must the world look for additional supplies of food that will be required beyond the year 2000?

FURTHER READINGS

Council for Agricultural Science and Technology. (1994). *How Much Land Can Ten Billion People Spare for Nature?* Ames, IA: Cast,

   Written by a team led by agricultural scientist Paul Waggoner, a scenario is developed in which a crowded planet can become simultaneously better fed and "greener"—the result of continuing advances in technology. Even with 10 billion people, one-third of today's cropland could revert to wilderness.

Evans, Lloyd T. (1980). The Natural History of Crop Yield. *American Scientist,* 68,: 388–397.

   A persuasive demonstration that improved varieties of crop plants and technological innovations continue to increase productivity, but that there may be limits set by biological constraints.

Glaeser, Bernard (Ed.). (1987). *The Green Revolution Revisited.* London: Allen & Unwin,

   An assessment of the economic, political, and social effects of the technological revolution in Third World agriculture. The contributors, experts in tropical farming methods, report their observations of the green revolution in the field. Some are critical of the widening income disparities that result from the tendency for the benefits of innovative techniques to favor the educated, more prosperous farmers to the competitive disadvantage of the others. They urge increased research on ways to improve traditional farming methods and to reduce the vulnerability of Third World farmers to periodic crop failures.

Kates, Robert W. (1983). *The Human Environment: Penultimate Problems of Survival.* Natural Hazards Research and Applications Center, Special Publication No. 6. Worcester, MA.: Clark University, The Center for Technology, Environment, and Development,

Thoughtful analysis of three related sets of issues: the Malthusian question regarding the adequacy of resources for a growing population, the problems of growing income disparities and their potential for widespread unrest and conflict, and the contrast between the growing technological capability for change (and destruction) and the meager ability of society to control it.

Meadows, Donella H., Dennis L. Meadows, Jôrgen Randers, and William W. Behrens III. (1972). *The Limits to Growth: A Report for the Club of Rome's Project on the Predicament of Mankind.* New York: Universe Books,

A very influential study commissioned by the Club of Rome, an international group of prominent industrialists, scientists, and economists. Using a dynamic world model linking population, pollution, resources, land, and capital generation, Dennis Meadows and co-workers at MIT predict that exponential growth will ultimately result in global collapse.

Shah, Mahendra, and Günther Fischer. (1984). People, Land, and Food Production: Potentials in the Developing World. *Options.* International Institute for Applied Systems Analysis (IIASA), 2: 1–5.

Assesses the output of particular food crops and their population-supporting potentials in the Third World. Synthesis of a study conducted by IIASA in collaboration with the Food and Agriculture Organization of the United Nations. This work finds that, of the 117 countries analyzed, 57 do not have sufficient land resources to feed the populations that have been projected for them in A.D. 2000.

Sadik, Nafis. (1990). *The State of World Population 1990: Choices for the New Century.* United Nations Population Fund. New York: United Nations,

Declaring that the world's population has arrived at a critical stage in this final decade of the twentieth century, the executive director of UNFPA contends that the ultimate check on population growth in the coming era may not be merely the earth's capacity to feed growing numbers of people but rather the poisoning of the physical environment that overcrowding would cause. Heedless overuse of material resources by great masses of humanity could render the planet uninhabitable.

Smil, Vaclav. (1994). How Many People Can the Earth Feed? *Population and Development Review.* 20: 255–292.

The world produces plenty of food: If the poor do not have enough money to buy it, or if it cannot reach them, those are different problems. There are many ways that food output could be increased, often with no more than the right price signals and a bit of education. Better growing techniques alone could feed up to 3 billion more people. Bringing 20 percent more land under cultivation and raising yields by 35 percent could feed a further 2 to 2.5 billion people by 2050. This could be achieved without further crop-boosting innovations such as those of the past 60 years, including synthetic ammonia, hybrid corn, and pesticides.

Wolf, Edward C. (1986). *Beyond the Green Revolution: New Approaches for Third World Agriculture.* Worldwatch Paper 73. Washington, DC: Worldwatch Institute,

A concise, informative, and balanced examination of international research in tropical agriculture. The author describes the evolution of the current worldwide system of research institutes and reports on the differing effects of technological innovations in various regions. He discusses the constructive responses of these research programs to criticisms of earlier phases of the green revolution and he proposes further steps that need to be taken to relieve the worsening circumstances of farmers living in remote areas under adverse physical conditions.

5

Energy, Minerals, and the Environment

OVERVIEW

Population growth and industrialization exert pressures on nonrenewable resources. Recurring oil crises since the early 1970s have focused attention on energy supplies. Like other minerals, the fossil fuels are concentrated in a few countries and regions, some politically unstable. Oil output will peak early in the new century; coal and natural gas should last much longer. In the longer run, new technologies will take over.

The outlook for other minerals is mixed. Although a few are plentiful, many have limited life spans, and all draw upon other scarce resources in their production and use. It appears unlikely that the world as a whole can ever consume many of these at current U.S. levels. The solution appears to lie in the development of silicon-based substitutes.

The intensifying use of the earth's resources threatens the quality of the environment. Pollution wastes valuable resources even as it poisons the atmosphere and water. Although costs of remedial measures are high, the future habitability of a crowded planet requires that these measures be taken.

OBJECTIVES

- to distinguish between short- and long-run political, economic, technical, and environmental problems of global energy supply
- to evaluate future prospects for mineral raw materials and possibilities for extending their life -spans
- to understand the role of technological change in impelling materials substitution
- to describe the impacts of population increase and industrialization on environmental quality

RESOURCE USE AND THE THREAT OF EXHAUSTION

Soils often can be restored to fertility, plants and animal stocks can be replenished, and some barren wastes can be afforested; but a mineral deposit, once exhausted, is gone forever. The rate at which nonrenewable resources are being used is rising steadily throughout the world and especially in the industrialized countries, raising environmentalist concerns. During much of this present century, the United States alone has accounted for one-third to one-half of total world consumption of these resources; United States mineral usage increased tenfold (reckoned in constant dollars) during the first 70 years of this century while population was rising only 2.7 times. Today, the United States, with fewer than 5 percent of the world's people, consumes resources at a per capita rate more than seven times the world average.

The U.S. experience has shown that per capita resource use rises steeply during the earlier stages of industrialization, but eventually tapers off at some higher level, describing an S-shaped logistic curve similar to that of population growth. This plateau is reached as an economy turns increasingly to the production of advanced-technology goods, which are less resource-intensive in their manufacture, and as the output of services claims a larger proportion of gross national product. Although U.S. consumption had leveled off by the third quarter of the century, the world as a whole was just entering the steepest part of the growth curve. This suggests that other countries have been following the path already taken by the United States. In recent decades, Western Europe and Japan have substantially increased their consumption of resources, and the newly industrializing countries of the Pacific Rim and Latin America have added further to the drain on global supplies. Thus, if the world as a whole were ultimately to attain the current American level of per capita production, vast quantities of energy and materials would be required.

The important question to be addressed in the following pages, therefore, is whether or not the total supply of these resources will be adequate for a world consuming at the United States rate. The resources to be examined will be mainly of the nonrenewable kind, but a few are of the flow type, such as water, which are constantly being renewed by nature but are limited in total amount and subject to deterioration in quality as a result of human use.

The Nature of Reserves.

Viewed in absolute terms, 88 known elements occur in the earth's crust in great amounts. Though some of these elements are indeed plentiful, others are relatively scarce (Figure 5.1). These less-abundant materials have become available to human beings only through the natural processes of concentration, which have caused comparatively large amounts of each to accumulate in a few places. This is the basis for the usual concept of a *reserve,* defined as that part of the naturally occurring-stock of a raw material that can be exploited commercially with existing technology and at current prices. A price rise makes it economically feasible to exploit deposits that are less accessible or poorer in quality. Thus, it took an OPEC crisis to add the high-cost deposits of Alaska's North Slope and Britain's North Sea to world oil reserves. Conversely, falling prices cause global reserves to decline as marginal deposits become uneconomical.

Considering the erratic, seemingly capricious way in which such concentrations have formed, what is the current state of world reserves? The consumption of most resources is growing more rapidly than the rate of population growth. Not only are more people consuming resources, but the average person is consuming larger quantities. According to some projections, the known resources of many vital materials will be used up within the next century, and some of the more important ones will become exhausted within only a few decades. Rarely, however, are natural resources totally exhausted; usually, their extraction is abandoned. This does not usually happen suddenly. More often, the use of substitutes causes the rate of use to diminish to the point where exploitation virtually ceases. Moreover, with improved knowledge, the reserve base of many materials has grown, not fallen, and now substantially exceeds rates of consumption (Tables 5.1 and 5.2)

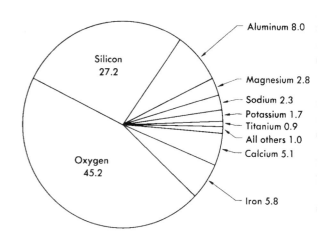

FIGURE 5.1   Elements in the earth's crust. Some of the most important industrial raw materials are included in the category "All others," which comprises only 1.0 percent of the earth's crust. [*Source:* Brian J. Skinner, *Earth Resources,* 2nd ed. (Englewood Cliffs, NJ: Prentice Hall, 1986).]

TABLE 5.1
Growth of the world reserves base of selected commodities [a]

Decade	Copper	Lead	Zinc	Aluminum [b]
1940s	91	31–45	54–70	1,605
1950s	124	45–54	77–86	3,224
1960s	280	86	106	11,600
1970s	543	57	240	22,700
1980s [c]	566	120	295	23,200
1993	590	130	330	28,000

Source: U.S. Bureau of Mines. "Reserve base," as used by the U.S. Bureau of Mines, includes reserves, which are currently economic to extract, as well as resources, which are currently subeconomic and marginally economic but can reasonably be expected to become economically available.

[a] In millions of metric tons of contained metal near the end of the relevant decade

[b] Gross weight of bauxite.

[c] Reserve base in 1989

Among the variables affecting the cost of exploiting a resource are *quality* and *accessibility*. In the case of a mineral resource, accessibility includes both the depth of deposits in the ground and their distance from markets. As exhaustion of a material approaches, miners pursue reserves of progressively poorer quality to greater depths and in more remote locations. Meanwhile, however, technological developments may slow the rise of production and processing costs, thereby postponing exhaustion; indeed, with technological change few resources are even exhausted: New production switches to substitutes, and extraction of the older resource is abandoned, as when the mining of anthracite, a hard, high-energy type of coal, ceased when the world's navies switched from coal-burning to oil-burning ships.

Spatial Distribution. Most natural resources are distributed very unevenly. This erratic spatial pattern results from the nature of the physical processes that cause mineral concentrations to form initially. In many cases, a single country, or two or three, possesses a major share of the world total. The leading producers of a material, however, are not always those with the largest reserves, but in the most industrialized countries, which are the principal markets for the materials and for the products made from them. On the other hand, some of the largest reserves of certain vital nonrenewable resources are in countries with economies too small—such as Canada or Australia—or too underdeveloped to make full use of what they possess. Russia and certain politically volatile areas, such as the Middle East and southern Africa, are leading producers of several essential fuels and raw materials.

This combination of spatial patterns of production and consumption holds many important implications both for world commerce and for global politics. These concerns will underlie our discussion of the present and future status of particular types of earth resources.

ENERGY

Ever since the dramatic events of the 1970s, energy has been a matter of intense international concern. When the

TABLE 5.2
Worldwide annual consumption in 1991 and reserve base in 1993 of selected metals [a]

Metal	Annual Consumption (10^3 metric tons)	Reserve Base (10^3 Metric tons of contained metal)
Aluminum	17,194	28,000,000 [b]
Copper	10,714	590,000
Iron	959,609	230,000,000
Lead	5,342	130,000
Nickel	882	110,000
Tin	218	10,000
Zinc	6,993	330,000

Source: U.S. Bureau of Mines

[a] Consumption includes primary and secondary (scrap) metal, except for iron, which includes only crude ore.

[b] Bauxite (crude ore).

Organization of Petroleum Exporting Countries (OPEC) seized control of global oil supplies and pricing late in 1973, it abruptly halted an era during which the world had come to believe that energy would remain cheap and abundant forever. Subsequent oil crises in 1979–1980 and 1990–991 again brought soaring prices and renewed fears of energy shortages. These episodes have posed two urgent questions: Will the world have enough energy for continued economic growth? If so, will those who control these supplies share them with the rest of the world—and at what political and economic price?

Accelerating Demand. Considering the central role of mechanical energy in modern technology, this concern for future supplies seems warranted. Indeed, the spread of industrialization throughout the world has called for ever-growing amounts of energy. Although some of the poorest lands may still depend on human porters, hand laborers, and craft workers for power, this is no longer true—or even possible—for those countries where modernization is well advanced. A little more than a century ago, for instance, the United States still relied on human labor for 94 percent of

its industrial power; today, less than 8 percent derives from this source.

As in other forms of resource use, the United States has led the way in the enormous expansion in energy consumption. How rapidly this growth took place in the United States is apparent from Figure 5.2, which shows the increase in total horsepower of the country's main prime movers (i.e., the various devices for harnessing mechanical energy, such as electric motors and steam and gasoline engines). Between 1870 and 1970, U.S. nonhuman energy capacity more than doubled in almost every decade. This means that in 1870, the average resident of the country could draw on only 0.4 horsepower, but a century later each American had access to 100.6 horsepower. Note, however, that the growth of energy consumption slowed sharply following the oil crises and economic recessions of the 1970s and slipped further during the 1980s.

The United States still leads the world in energy use, but it no longer has the highest per capita use. The current leaders in per capita terms are three small Persian Gulf states—Bahrain, Qatar, and the United Arab Emirates—all

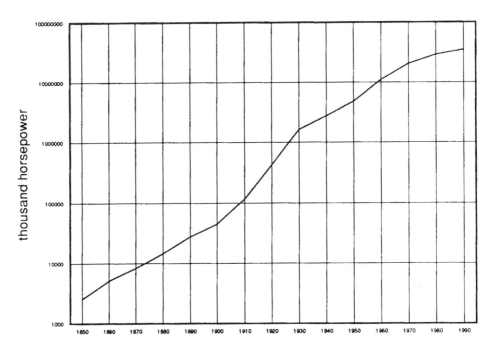

FIGURE 5.2 Total nonhuman energy of all prime movers, United States, 1850–1990 (horsepower). Except for a slight slowing in the depression years of the 1930s, the capacity for mechanical energy use in the United States more than doubled in every decade of this century until the 1970s, when the first Middle Eastern crises threatened foreign supplies of oil and raised its price. Since then, the growth of consumption has lagged, mainly as a result of increased energy efficiency in transportation, industry, and housing and a shift in the economy toward less energy-intensive forms of production. [*Sources:* U.S. Bureau of the Census, *Statistical Abstract of the United States: 1995,* 115th ed.. (Washington, DC: U.S. Government Printing Office, 1995) and *Historical Statistics of the United States* (Washington, DC: U.S. Government Printing Office, 1995).]

surplus energy producers. Although total world energy use has tripled since 1960, consumption rates vary greatly among countries at different levels of development. The relationship between energy use and economic development arises because the development process requires quantum increases in labor productivity. This is possible only through the replacement of human and animal power with inanimate energy. The closeness of this relationship is apparent from Figure 5.3, which shows how per capita energy consumption rises with increases in per capita national product. The world map of energy consumption (Figure 5.4) offers further confirmation of this.

During the 1960s and 1970s, per capita energy consumption climbed in Europe, Japan, Australia, and New Zealand, but it never reached Canadian and U.S. levels, owing in most cases to a lack of domestic oil supplies and high energy taxes imposed under government policies designed to restrain demand for costly imports. In the aftermath of the energy crises, per capita consumption actually lessened somewhat in most of those countries during the 1980s. Therefore, all major world regions continue to lag well behind North America in per capita energy use (Figure 5.5).

Consequently, the regions differ markedly in their shares of total energy consumption (Figure 5.6). The sharpest disparity exists between the developed and less-developed regions. With 77 percent of the world's population, the less-developed countries account for only 25 percent of all energy use. Except for the oil exporters, LDCs must spend the greater part of their export earnings for energy imports, even as their industrialization efforts call for ever-larger amounts of energy.

The various forms of inanimate energy upon which the world increasingly relies are drawn from five storage banks, all ultimately derived from that basic source, solar energy. The first of the five to be used by human beings was the living-plant bank, which was tapped through the domestication of herbivorous draft animals and the burning of wood. Exploitation of the water-storage bank came next, followed by development of the fossil-fuel bank, consisting of decayed and buried plant

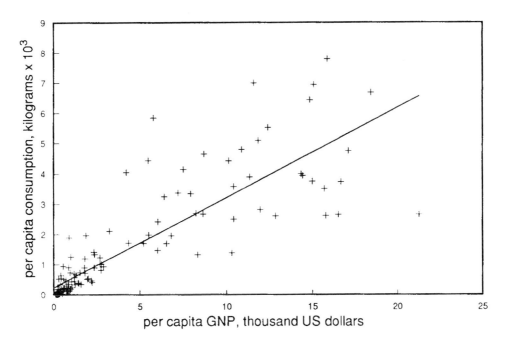

FIGURE 5.3 Per capita energy consumption and level of development. On the whole, a strong association exists between the amount of energy used per person and a country's per capita GNP ($R^2 = 0.724$), but the relationship weakens at higher levels of development. In this diagram, Japan and most of Western Europe form a cluster of energy-conserving nations in the lower right, below the regression line. To the right above the line is another group of prosperous countries that are more profligate in their use of energy, including Canada and the United States and a few oil-exporting countries. The former Soviet Union and the nations of Eastern Europe, with their economic emphasis upon energy-intensive heavy industry, also appear above the line, but at intermediate levels of per capita GNP. [*Sources:* United Nations, *Energy Statistics Yearbook 1987* (New York: United Nations, 1989), and *1990 Britannica Book of the Year* (Chicago: Encyclopaedia Britannica, 1990).]

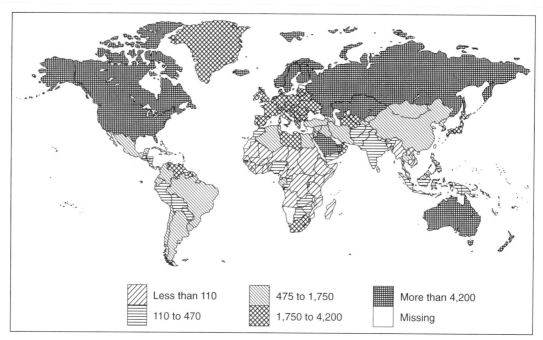

Less than 110		475 to 1,750		More than 4,200	
110 to 470		1,750 to 4,200		Missing	

FIGURE 5.4 World energy consumption per capita (kilograms oil equivalent), 1993. The countries with the least mechanical energy consumption per person are in Africa south of the Sahara, southern Asia, and Andean Latin America, all areas at generally low levels of development. Several OPEC members, notably those on the Persian Gulf, rank with the industrialized countries in per capita energy consumption. Those nations at the highest levels of development differ substantially in their rates of energy consumption, depending on a variety of economic, political, and cultural considerations. [*Source:* Data from *The World Bank Atlas 1996* (Washington, DC: The World Bank, 1996).]

remains in the form of coal, oil, and gas. More recently, the world has begun to draw on the nuclear-fuel bank through the harnessing of the products of nuclear decay. In some favored localities, heat generated deep in the earth itself is providing the basis for commercial development of geothermal power. Complementing these five, the power of ocean tides and direct solar energy are now also subjects of experimentation.

Since the middle of the nineteenth century, major changes have occurred in the relative importance of the different energy banks. In 1850, draft animals supplied the largest share of nonhuman animate energy in the United States, and these remained important well into the twentieth century. Fuel wood, however, was the leading source of inanimate energy in 1850, accounting for 87 percent of the total (Figure 5.7). In the latter part of the nineteenth century, electricity came into general use, followed quickly by the internal combustion engine. This meant increasing dependence first upon the water-storage bank for electric power generation and then upon the fossil-fuel bank, which subsequently gained overwhelming dominance. During this present century, however, the relative importance of the various fossil fuels has changed greatly. Coal was the

principal fossil fuel prior to 1910, but oil and gas have since overshadowed it. Today, our mounting needs force us to turn to the remaining energy banks.

In view of the accelerating demand for mechanical energy, we need to ask just how good are our reserves in each of the principal energy-storage banks, where these reserves are located, and who controls them. Considering our present heavy dependence on fossil fuels, let us begin by reviewing the status of each of these and examining the possibilities for maintaining a future supply.

Fossil Fuels

Today, the United States obtains nine-tenths of its mechanical energy from fossil fuels. The figure was even higher prior to the early 1970s, when the sudden crisis in global oil supplies and prices gave added urgency to the search for alternatives. As Figure 5.7 shows, the share of other forms of energy (hydroelectric, nuclear, geothermal, and solar) edged slowly upward during the late 1970s and 1980s. Nevertheless, fossil fuels offer so many advantages in cost and convenience that they continue to dominate the short-run, U.S. energy picture.

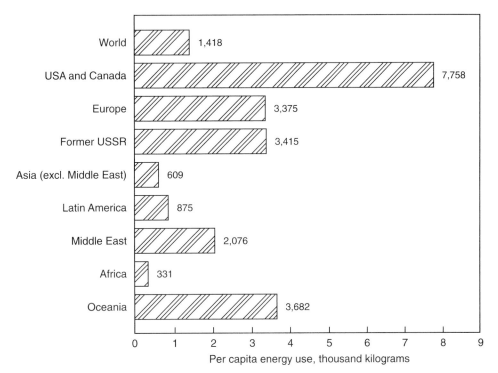

FIGURE 5.5 Per capita energy use (thousand kilograms of petroleum equivalent) of major world regions, 1994. The average earth inhabitant used the equivalent of 1,418 kilograms of oil in 1994. A typical African, however, consumed less than a quarter as much. Canadians and Americans, on the other hand, consumed energy at more than 5 times the world average. Consumption in the republics of the former USSR has declined markedly since the end of the communist era. Europeans are fairly restrained in their energy use. [*Source:* Based on data from the *BP Statistical Review of World Energy* (London: British Petroleum Company plc, 1995).]

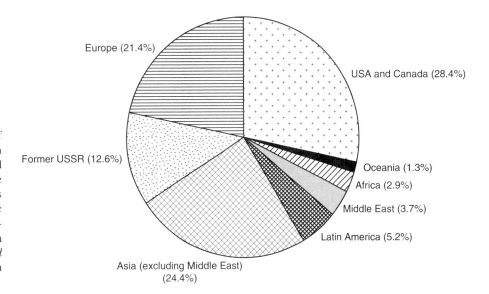

FIGURE 5.6 Regional shares of world energy consumption (petroleum equivalent), 1994. The less-developed countries currently use 29 percent of the world's energy, but this proportion is mounting as the pace of economic growth accelerates in the newly industrialized nations. [*Source:* Based on data from the *BP Statistical Review of World Energy* (London: British Petroleum Company plc, 1995).]

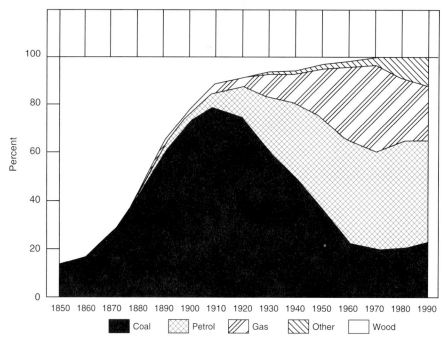

FIGURE 5.7   Percentage production of energy in the United States, by major sources, 1850–1990. ("Other" consists mainly of hydro, nuclear, solar, and keothermal power.) Wood supplied 87 percent of the country's inanimate energy in 1850, but it is little used for that purpose in the United States today. Its place has been taken mainly by fossil fuels—first coal, then oil and natural gas. The impact of the energy crises since the early 1970s is seen in the arrested growth of petroleum and gas output and the relative gains made by coal and such alternative sources as nuclear, geothermal, solar, and wind power. Falling crude prices in the 1980s engendered complacency and oil consumption began to edge upward again, until another Persian Gulf crisis in the second half of 1990 reminded the country once more of its excessive dependence on uncertain foreign sources of supply. [*Source:* U.S. Bureau of the Census, *Statistical Abstract of the United States: 1995,* 115th ed. (Washington, DC: U.S. Government Printing Office, 1995), and *Historical Statistics of the United States, Colonial Times to 1970* (Washington, DC. U.S. Government Printing Office, 1976).]

This is equally true in the world at large; some regions rely on fossil fuels to a degree even more extreme than that of the United States (Figure 5.8). This is especially true for that large group of resource-poor, less-developed countries dependent on imported fuels for all their energy needs. For them, the energy of choice almost invariably is oil, because of its transportability, ease of storing, and versatility.

Fossil fuels are derived from the fossil remains of plants and animals and represent the energy products of organic decay. Normally, these decay products escape into the atmosphere through radiation, but under certain special conditions they may be trapped and stored. This occurred ordinarily in swamps and bogs, where these materials later become preserved and concentrated under the pressure of layers of rock. The resulting hydrocarbons assume the form of solids (coal), liquids (oil), and gases. Although these formed in minute quantities each year, their total accumulation eventually became considerable during the millions of years of the Carboniferous era (between 280 and 350

million years ago). Because of their slow rate of formation, fossil fuels are essentially nonrenewable.

Oil and natural gas are more highly prized as fuels and as chemical raw materials than is coal because they are more easily transported and stored, have higher caloric content, and give more nearly complete combustion. Although oil is cheaper to transport than gas, which requires pipelines for overland shipment and specially designed vessels for movement by water, gas has the advantage of burning more cleanly. By contrast, because it is solid in form and has a high ratio of bulk to heating value, coal is expensive to ship, and its combustion creates many pollutants.

Much of the crude oil (a liquid) and natural gas (mainly methane) occurring in nature are found in association, both apparently having been derived from decayed organic matter in ancient sea basins. Crude oil is a complex mixture of hydrocarbons—hydrogen and oxygen chemically combined in many ways. It therefore occurs in many grades, some light and others very heavy. The lighter grades are naturally richer in gasoline and other valuable

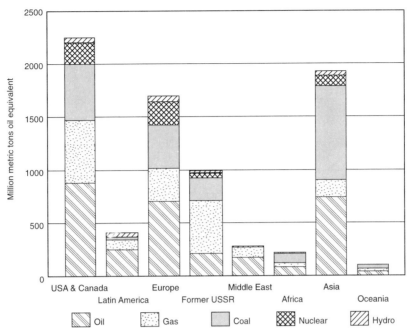

FIGURE 5.8 Primary energy consumption by fuel, world regions, 1994. By comparison with the rest of the world, the United States and Canada have a relatively balanced distribution of primary energy sources. The particular mix of energies in each region is attributable not only to availability of domestic supplies but also to the relative costs of imports and considerations of public policy. The European consumption pattern, for example, shows a preference for oil, found in and around the North Sea, and coal, mined in a number of European countries. In addition, hydroelectricity is abundant in Scandinavia and the Alpine lands. Nuclear energy is unusually well-developed in Europe also, a result of government policies designed to reduce dependence on unreliable foreign sources of energy. The former Soviet Union's consumption pattern reflects that country's large domestic reserves of all the fossil fuels, especially natural gas. The large consumption of coal in Other Asia (which excludes the former USSR and the Middle East) shows the influence of China, which has huge deposits of coal. [*Source:* Based on data from the *BP Statistical Review of World Energy* (London: British Petroleum Company plc, 1995).]

fractions, but modern refining technology makes it possible to "crack" the heavy fractions into lighter forms. Unlike coal, oil and gas often migrate from the rocks in which they originated. Moving upward toward the surface, they become caught in "traps," rock formations that act as barriers. There they accumulate in pools, with the gas partly dissolved in the liquid and partly resting on top. Oil and gas are also capable of lateral migration, sometimes moving many miles from their origin. As the lightest fraction, natural gas often migrates still farther and may become entirely separated from the oil. In addition, some natural gas is derived from organic materials that are incapable of yielding oil. Hence, some countries lacking the geological conditions for oil have sizable reserves of gas.

Today, every barrel of crude oil brought to the surface is used completely. Not only does it yield gasoline, kerosene, jet fuel, lubricants, and fuel oil, but it also serves as a feedstock for hundreds of thousands of petrochemical products in direct competition with coal chemicals. Natural

gas has a similarly wide range of uses. Modern urban-industrial economies therefore have grown heavily dependent on these convenient and versatile fuels, which until recently were so cheap. As a result, these two energy sources, which have been exploited commercially for only a little more than a century, are being extracted and consumed at a profligate rate. How much is left, and where is it?

Proven reserves of crude oil are widespread, but they are unevenly distributed (Figure 5.9). (*Proven reserves* are those quantities of a mineral that current geological and engineering information indicate with reasonable certainty to be capable of recovery from known reservoirs with existing technology and under present economic conditions.) The heaviest concentrations are in a select group of less-developed countries, most of which belong to the Organization of Petroleum Exporting Countries. The majority of OPEC's members are in the Middle East (Iran, Saudi Arabia, the United Arab Emirates, Kuwait, and Iraq),

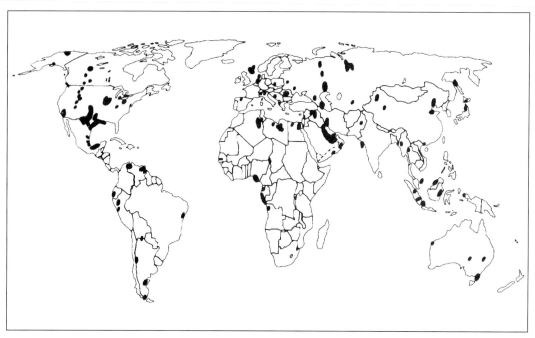

FIGURE 5.9   Principal oil fields of the world. Deposits of oil occur throughout the world and on all continents, but the reserves contained in those deposits vary greatly in size. Potential supplies for the future are therefore concentrated in only a few favored regions (see Figure 5.10).

centering on the Persian Gulf. and in North and West Africa (Algeria, Nigeria, Gabon, and Libya), but two are in South America (Venezuela and Ecuador) and another (Indonesia) is in South Asia.

OPEC's proven reserves represent more than three-fourths of the world total, and the Middle Eastern states alone account for 65 percent of that total (Figure 5.10). Saudi Arabia possesses more than a quarter of the world's proven reserves, and Iraq and Kuwait together have another fifth. Furthermore, every year brings upward revisions of these estimates as new discoveries are made in the Persian Gulf. At present rates of production, the Middle Eastern reserves are expected to last more than a century. Not only are these deposits vast, but the average output per well is many times that of North America, and costs of discovery, development, and production are only a fraction of those elsewhere.

Latin America holds the next largest block of proven reserves, which, reflecting significant new finds, now account for 8 percent of the world total. Some of these discoveries have been in Mexico, which now ranks second in reserves outside the Middle East. Substantial deposits of oil occur along the Andean margins of South America, especially in Venezuela. After many years of exploitation, Venezuela's oil fields still rank first in proven reserves among non-Arab producers, as indicated by recently revised estimates. The reserve life of Latin America's oil is judged to be some 50 years.

The prospects are less promising for the oil futures of the United States and Canada. After more than a century of intensive exploitation, proven reserves are dwindling, despite the development of large deposits along the North Slope of Alaska and continued exploration along the continent's Arctic margins, although there may be major deposits off the coast of Newfoundland.

Europe's oil fields are estimated to hold 1.8 percent of the world's proven reserves, enough to last into the first decade of the coming century. Although previously considered a have-not region with respect to petroleum, Western Europe has been the scene of important discoveries in recent years. High prices, resulting from OPEC's impact on world markets, provided the stimulus for intensive exploitation of high-cost North Sea deposits, principally those of Norway and the United Kingdom. Despite these developments, the continent must import large quantities of oil.

Asia, excluding the former Soviet Union and the Middle East, possesses another 4.3 percent of the world's proven reserves. However, significant strikes continue to be made in previously neglected parts of the continent, particularly China and Southeast Asia.

The spatial patterns of global oil production and consumption correlate poorly with the locations of world reserves. With 89 percent of reserves concentrated in less-developed countries and another 5.7 percent in the former Soviet Union, only 5.3 percent of the total is left for the developed market economies of North America, Europe,

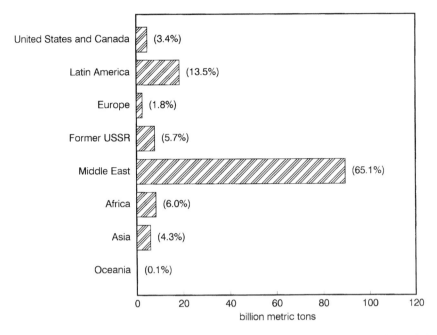

FIGURE 5.10 Proven oil reserves, major world regions, 1994. With two-thirds of the world's proven reserves, enough to last more than a century at present rates of production, the Middle East dominates world oil supplies, present and future. Latin America, which has more than one-eighth of the total, is second, bolstered by encouraging new oil strikes in Mexico and Venezuela. Former Soviet and African producers also have large reserves, with surpluses available for sale on world markets. Europe and Northern America have much smaller shares of total reserves and, at present rates of production, will have exhausted those supplies by the turn of the century. [*Source:* Based on data from the *BP Statistical Review of World Energy* (London: British Petroleum Company plc, 1995).]

and Oceania (Australia and New Zealand). Yet the latter continue to exploit their remaining deposits with growing intensity. As a consequence, the developed market economies still produce a quarter of the world's total output (Figure 5.11). This means, however, that they are depleting their reserves at a rapid rate. Even this is not enough to satisfy the enormous demand of this group; in all, these nations are responsible for more than half of global consumption. They therefore must make up the difference in imports.

By the early 1980s, the United States had slipped to second place among individual producers of oil, but at the end of the decade, it continued to lead in consumption. Together, the United States and Canada use 28 percent of world output, with the United States alone responsible for more than a quarter of world consumption. On average, an American uses oil at a rate five times that of the world as a whole, and the country must import more than half of its needs. Even so, the United States has avoided the extreme import dependence of most industrialized nations because of its generous supply of other fuels. With its smaller population, Canada produces sufficient oil to cover domestic consumption and provide a small surplus for export.

Other industrialized regions are less fortunate than Northern America. As a whole, Europe uses more than one-fifth of the world's oil (Figure 5.11) and must import three-fifths of its needs despite substantial production in the North Sea. Japan, the third largest oil user, has negligible domestic output and therefore is much worse off than other major industrial nations. The Japanese have long been acutely aware of their precarious dependence on foreign supplies of this vital energy source and, through conservation and industrial restructuring, they reduced their oil use by one-eighth during the 1980s. During this same period, however, the rest of eastern and southern Asia increased its consumption by more than two-fifths, as the nations of that region have quickened the pace of their industrialization. Japan's dominance of Asian oil consumption therefore is much reduced from a decade earlier, when it comprised more than half the total.

The Middle East as a whole furnishes 30 percent of global output. More than four-fifths of this goes into world markets. Latin America now supplies 13 percent of the world's oil. Asia, excluding the Middle East and the former USSR, now contributes 10 percent, and Africa provides a like amount.

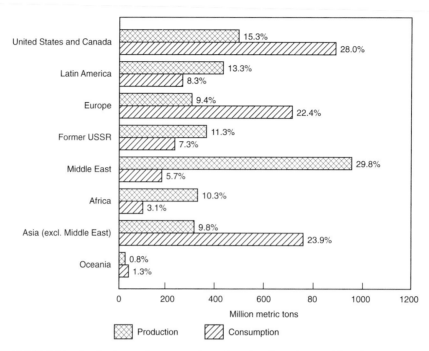

FIGURE 5.11 Production and consumption of crude oil, major world regions, 1994. The world relies heavily for its oil on four regions of surplus production: the Middle East, Africa, Latin America, and the former Soviet Union. The developed market economies of Northern America, Europe, and Oceania, plus Japan, all consume far more than they produce. Those nations within this latter group possessing domestic oil reserves continue to exploit their dwindling domestic resources with great intensity. Nevertheless, large deficits remain between production and consumption, necessitating massive imports from the surplus regions. [*Source:* Based on data from the *BP Statistical Review of World Energy* (London: British

World oil consumption peaked at 64 million barrels per day in 1979, the year of the second big OPEC oil-price rise. By 1983, it had dropped to 58 million barrels, owing to conservation measures by consuming nations and also to the global economic recession of the early 1980s. The most highly developed countries were responsible for most of this decline; consumption actually continued to rise among less-developed countries, especially the newly industrialized members of this group. The weakening world demand for oil, together with widespread cheating by some OPEC members against their agreed-on production quotas, subsequently caused a supply reversal—from the shortages of the 1970s to the glutted markets of the late 1980s. The accompanying fall in prices resulted in a slackening in exploration and retarded the development of alternative sources of energy.

Relaxed pressures on oil supplies and prices inevitably led to increased use, and by 1994, world consumption had risen to 67 million barrels per day. Then, just as predictably, another Persian Gulf crisis erupted in 1990 and oil prices climbed once more on a nervous world market. This time, however, the threat was a political and military one—the *fear* of a cut in supplies rather than an actual shortage.

Further helping to ease the pressures on world oil supplies is the growing availability of natural gas, which has a somewhat different global pattern (Figure 5.12). In all, natural gas has been found in some 30 countries that apparently have no oil. Gas is much better represented in the former USSR, North America, and Western Europe than is oil, but is relatively less abundant in the Middle East, Latin America, and Africa. Indeed, the former USSR, which possesses only 5.6 percent of proven oil reserves, has nearly 38 percent of the world's gas supplies. Recent estimates have raised the Middle East's proven reserves to 32.1 percent of the world total, and they show a fairly equal division of the remainder among Northern America, Latin America, Europe, Africa, and Asia (excluding the former USSR and the Middle East).

Estimates of proven gas reserves have risen steadily throughout the past decade, increasing by more than one-third in that period (Figure 5.13). Although these new reserves stem predominantly from major finds in Russia, Kazakhstan, and the Middle East, large discoveries also have been made in such widely scattered places as China, South Africa, and western Australia. Reserve estimates also have been revised upward in Western Europe, Latin America, and Northern America.

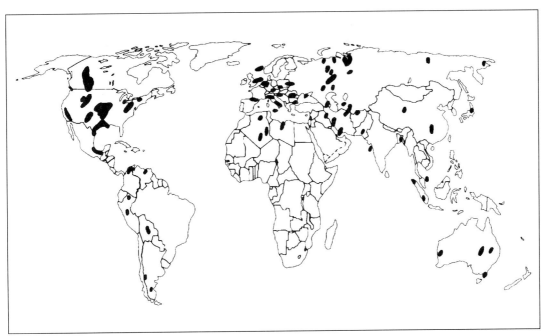

FIGURE 5.12   Principal producing natural gas fields. Natural gas is found in many parts of the world but, as in the case of oil, the most productive deposits are concentrated in particular areas. The major concentrations of gas, however, do not necessarily coincide with those of oil (refer to Figure 5.13).

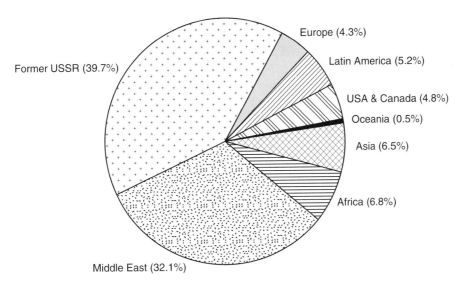

FIGURE 5.13   Proven reserves of natural gas, by region, 1994. Although natural gas frequently occurs in association with oil, this is not always the case. A comparison of this figure with the graph of proved oil reserves (Figure 5.11) shows a number of marked differences. The most striking distinction between the two distributions is the prominence of the former Soviet Union's gas reserves in the world picture. The political volatility of the world oil supply situation has further increased the attractiveness of this energy source and has led to an intensified search for new supplies. As a result, estimates of the world's proved gas reserves increased by 36 percent during the 1980s. [*Source:* Based on data from the *BP Statistical Review of World Energy* (London: British Petroleum Company plc, 1995).]

A comparison of Figure 5.11 and Figure 5.14 shows that natural gas also differs from oil in its spatial patterns of output and use. Some of the leading oil-producing regions—especially the Middle East and Africa—use only a fraction of their own petroleum output, whereas the major oil-consuming areas of Western Europe, the United States, and Japan have huge deficits. By contrast, quantities of gas produced and consumed are very similar at the regional scale (Figure 5.14). This close correspondence results mainly from the high cost of transporting gas by sea, which limits intercontinental movements. Within continental areas, however, this valuable fuel moves readily by pipeline and has become an important item of commerce.

Pipeline distribution systems, however, are feasible only in high-income areas where urbanization and industrialization provide mass markets. Gas came to be widely used in the United States during the postwar years, and by the early 1970s, it was supplying one-third of national energy needs. Conveniently served by an elaborate pipeline network direct from the producing fields, consumers obtained

this clean, efficient fuel very cheaply because of government-regulated prices. The low prices discouraged the search for new reserves, however, so that the energy shortages resulting from the OPEC oil crisis of the 1970s forced a relaxation of price restraints. Higher prices thereupon caused gas consumption to slip to one-quarter of U.S. energy use (Figure 5.7), but they also stimulated new drilling. The resulting new supplies, and imports from Canada and Mexico, have once more made gas plentiful; proven reserves amount to 160 trillion cubic feet (TCF), whereas annual consumption is about 20 TCF, and the estimated resource base exceeds 1,500 TCF.

Meanwhile, production and consumption of natural gas have increased in other industrialized countries as new fields have been discovered and linked by pipeline to industrial and consumer markets. During the 1960s, large finds were made in the British and Norwegian sectors of the North Sea and in Groningen Province of the Netherlands. As intra-European trade in this new energy source grew, the United Kingdom and neighboring lands on the continent

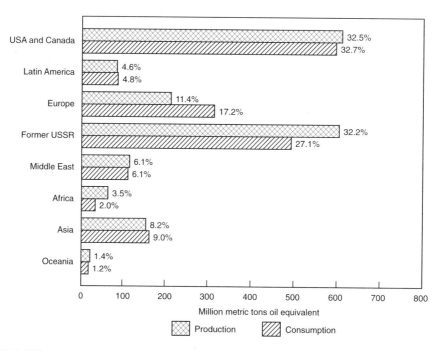

FIGURE 5.14   Production and consumption of natural gas, major world regions, 1994. Unlike oil, the pattern of natural gas production is generally similar to that of consumption, a consequence of the high cost of transporting gas by sea. Pipeline shipment between adjacent regions, however, occurs on an ever-larger scale. Thus, Europe, though a significant producer in its own right, imports large quantities of gas from the nearby former Soviet Union, and the United States receives gas by pipeline from contiguous Canada and Mexico. Some natural gas is indeed exported in pressurized ocean-going vessels from Africa, the Middle East, and Southeast Asia. World production and consumption of natural gas grew by one-third during the 1980s, the greater part of this increase taking place in the former Soviet Union. [*Source:* Based on data from the *BP Statistical Review of World Energy* (London: British Petroleum Company plc, 1995).]

switched from coal and oil to natural gas for many of their energy needs.

In recent years, Russia has found enormous quantities of natural gas, especially in northwestern Siberia. As pipelines are built, Russia has begun converting more of its economy to natural gas and exporting the growing surplus to Eastern Europe. A further extension of these pipelines has brought a large flow of Siberian gas into Western Europe, adding to the growing domestic supply and causing gas prices to fall.

As Figure 5.14 shows, the developing countries have lagged in their use of natural gas. Even the Middle East, which has nearly a third of world reserves, accounts for only 6 percent of consumption. Lacking effective consumer and industrial demand, producers in these countries merely burn off into the atmosphere much of the gas that naturally occurs in association with the oil. In the world at large, about 6 percent of this valuable resource is lost in this manner, and nearly half of this waste occurs in the Middle East. Some progress is being made, however. Saudi Arabia, for instance, has constructed two petrochemical complexes, one each on the Persian Gulf and the Red Sea, that use natural gas as a feedstock and an energy source.

New technology is also providing the developing countries with a way to export their natural gas to overseas markets. At special waterside installations, this bulky product is converted to the liquid state by reducing its temperature to −259°F. The liquefied natural gas (LNG) is very compact and can be transported long distances in tankers designed like thermos bottles. Algeria was one of the pioneers, exporting LNG to the United States, Britain, and other European markets. Japan, the most energy-deficient large economy, is receiving LNG from a growing number of sources, particularly Indonesia. Pipeline transport is much cheaper, of course, and a number of Third World producers are finding ways to export their gas by this means. Algeria and Libya ship gas to southern Europe through a trans-Mediterranean pipeline, Mexico has direct pipeline links to its U.S. markets, and Malaysia now pipes gas to Singapore.

Although more natural gas is being used productively rather than being burned off and wasted, the rate at which it is being consumed hastens the time when global reserves of this valuable nonrenewable resource will begin to diminish, as is already occurring with oil. Later, we shall look at the projected life-span of this and other energy sources, but let us first consider the status of some competing forms of mechanical energy.

One form of energy that appears to face no immediate global supply problem is coal, the most abundant fossil fuel. Although coal was the energy that powered the Industrial Revolution, it has been eclipsed in this century by oil and gas, which are much more convenient to extract, transport, and use. Thus, coal accounts for 70 percent of the world's energy reserves, yet it comprises little more than one-fourth of current consumption.

Coal is a solid fuel that evolved from the burial, compaction, and aging of peat, a process that progressively increased its density and carbon content. The energy-giving qualities of coal therefore rise with increasing age. Hundreds of coal types exist, ranging from the highest-quality anthracite (hard coal) and bituminous (soft coal) to the lowest-grade lignite (brown coal). Although the major coal basins of the world have apparently been identified, the full extent of these is only now being determined with any accuracy. The projected life-span of world reserves is estimated to be several hundred years at current rates of use.

Not only is coal more plentiful than the other fossil fuels but it is more evenly shared by the major world regions (Figures 5.15 and 5.16). Northern America is the leading source area with a quarter of the total, and the United States alone accounts for 23 percent. The former Soviet Union also has 23 percent of total reserves, though its largest deposits are inconveniently located in Siberia. Close behind is Asia, most of its reserves being in China (which ranks third behind the former USSR) and India. Europe, too, is well-endowed with coal, despite continuous heavy use of this energy source since the eighteenth century. Less than 15 percent of the estimated supply is found south of the equator, but this is substantially more than had earlier been thought. Both Australia and South Africa have large amounts—indeed, Australia's reserves rank fourth in the world.

Because of high transport costs, coal production has always been greatest in those regions where it is demanded (compare Figure 5.16 and Figure 5.17). Changes are beginning to take place in the world patterns of production and consumption, however. Several major coal-producing areas are either developing other fossil fuels or are gaining better access to them, and high oil prices have brought a resurgence of coal use in certain other regions. At the same time, intensified exploitation of coal deposits is occurring in some places in response to industrialization and in others because of export opportunities.

Figure 5.17 shows the resulting patterns of production and consumption. The prominence of Asia (excluding the former USSR and the Middle East), for instance, stems from the surge of coal use by China, which now surpasses the United States in coal output. Both China and India have had substantial growth in energy-intensive heavy industries that draw on their large coal reserves. Although the United States and Canada have more coal reserves than do the Asian lands, they rely more on other fuels. As oil and gas have become more expensive, however, their dependence on coal has risen somewhat. The same is true in Western Europe, which is not only a large producer of coal, but also a major importer. The growing availability of natural gas,

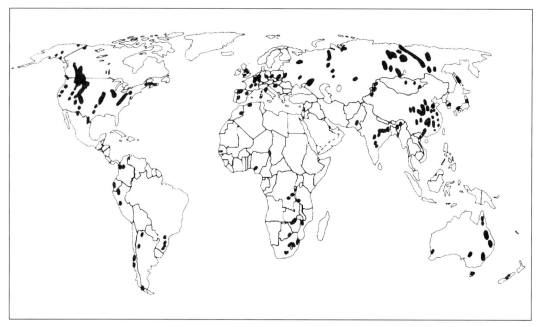

FIGURE 5.15 Principal coalfields of the world. Most abundant of the fossil fuels, coal is amply represented in several of the major world regions (see Figure 5.16).

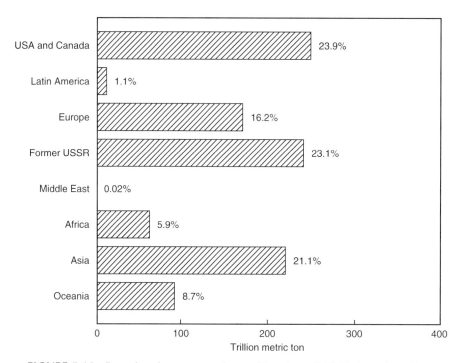

FIGURE 5.16 Proved coal reserves, major world regions, 1994. Estimated world reserves of coal have risen by nearly one-quarter during the past decade, and these increases have occurred in most major regions. By comparison with the other fossil fuels, coal is found in substantial amounts in most world areas. The only region lacking significant deposits of coal is the oil-rich Middle East. The calculated life of world coal reserves, at present rates of extraction, is nearly three centuries. [*Source:* Based on data from the *BP Statistical Review of World Energy* (London: British Petroleum Company plc, 1995).]

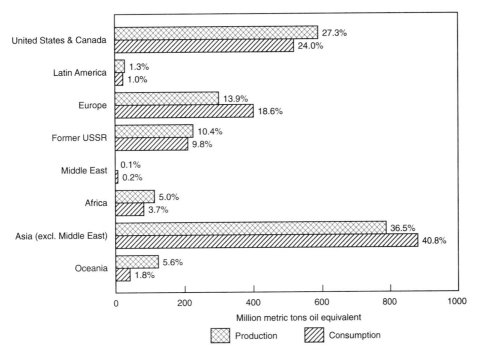

FIGURE 5.17 Production and consumption of coal, all types, major world regions, 1994. Because it is so costly to ship, most coal is consumed in the areas where it is produced. The spatial pattern of world production and consumption therefore corresponds to some degree with that of world reserves (Figure 5.16). China and some European countries lacking domestic oil supplies, however, rely on coal to a greater extent than their reserves might suggest. The former Soviet Union has reduced its previous dependence on coal, much of which is located in remote areas, in favor of abundantly available natural gas and oil. The chief exporters are the United States, Australia, and South Africa. [*Source:* Based on data from the *BP Statistical Review of World Energy* (London: British Petroleum Company plc, 1995).]

however, has prevented an even greater increase in Europe's coal use. Coal consumption in the former USSR and Eastern Europe has always been very great, but during the past two decades, it has been declining because of increased availability of gas and oil. Another country that has relied heavily on coal is South Africa, which exploited its sizable coal reserves as a way of achieving energy independence. To make up for its lack of oil, it has successfully synthesized liquid fuels from coal and has even become an exporter of its synfuel technology, as well as an important supplier of coal.

In the 1990s, the United States was replaced as the leading coal exporter by Australia, whose rich northeastern coalfields are well located near major sea lanes. Other major suppliers to the world are South Africa, Canada, and Poland.

Coal production and use in the industrialized world would be still greater were it not for the harmful effects of coal combustion on the atmosphere. Newly developing countries that rely upon coal, such as China and India, have yet to become concerned with this problem. Ironically, with all its problems as a pollutant, coal is the leading fuel for the generation of electricity, which is the cleanest form of energy.

Electricity

Of the conventional forms of energy, electricity has experienced the steadiest growth in demand during the modern era. Indeed, electric energy requirements have at times risen so fast that new generating capacity could not be installed quickly enough in some areas to avoid power shortages at peak periods of use. The popularity of electricity stems from its many special advantages. One of these is its mobility, which has given a new locational freedom to its users, especially light industry. It is clean to use, even though generating it can create a great deal of pollution. It also can be used in precisely the quantities needed, unlike the big steam engines that supplied power for factories in earlier times.

Because it is so flexible and versatile, electricity is ideal for an infinite variety of energy applications. In the United States, 35 percent of all electricity is consumed by residences, 28 percent by commercial establishments, and the remainder by industrial and other users. In many parts of the world, the percentage used by manufacturing is much larger. Electric motors account for much of the industrial consumption, but electrometallurgical and electrochemical companies also require great amounts of power.

Electricity is difficult to categorize, for it is really a hybrid. An electric current is essentially a movement of electrons and it therefore has many characteristics of a flow resource, except that it is used up. Also, unlike other flow resources, electricity is difficult to store and most of the output, except for transmission losses, is consumed as it is produced. It is easy to transmit over short distances, but long-range transmission entails higher costs and greater losses. The difficulty of storing electricity requires that the power industry attempt to anticipate demand, which can vary seasonally, daily, and even hourly.

Electricity is a derived form of energy rather than a primary source in itself. It is produced by generators that are powered by other (primary) energy forms. Thus, the force of falling water drives turbines, which generate hydroelectricity. In the production of thermoelectricity, heat from the burning of coal, oil, or gas is used to raise steam, which in turn drives the turbines. Generators may also be powered by internal combustion engines, which may burn either gasoline or diesel fuel. More recently, new types of primary power for generating electricity have appeared. Two thermal sources—nuclear and geothermal energy—are in commercial use, whereas solar and tidal energy are still experimental.

Per capita consumption of electricity varies widely (Figure 5.18), and so does the source of primary energy employed to produce it. The richer countries use far more electricity per person than do the poorer ones. For instance, in 1992, Ethiopia used only 24 kilowatt-hours per person, Chad only 15, and Haiti 70, whereas semi-industrialized Argentina consumed 1,778 kilowatt-hours per capita and the United States 12,160. In most less-developed countries, per capita electricity use is considerably lower than total energy consumption, much of which is in the form of motor fuels for transportation.

The correlation of electricity consumption and level of development is not perfect, however, mainly because advanced countries differ so greatly in their use of power. How much electricity a high-income country uses depends on its industrial structure, whether or not a particular cheap source of power is available, and the frugality of the populace. Thus, Canada uses 49 percent more electricity per person than does the United States, and Norway uses more than twice as much. Both Canada and Norway have small populations and unusually abundant supplies of inexpensive

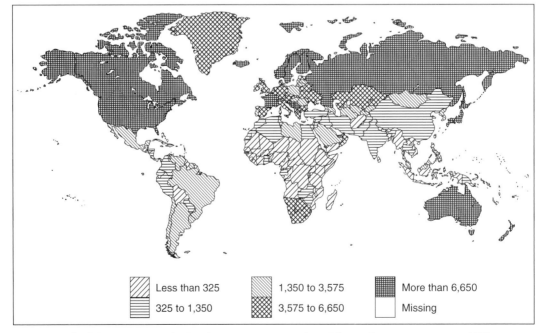

Less than 325	1,350 to 3,575	More than 6,650
325 to 1,350	3,575 to 6,650	Missing

FIGURE 5.18 Annual electric power consumption, kilowatt-hours per person, 1992. Northern America and Scandinavia have very high levels of per capita electricity use, and the other industrialized countries are close behind. The lowest consumption rates are in sub-Saharan Africa, southern Asia, and the Andean Americas, where annual usage levels are generally less than 325 kilowatt-hours per person. [*Source:* Data from the *1995 Britannica Book of the Year* (Chicago: Encyclopaedia Britannica, 1995).]

hydroelectricity, which has attracted large electrometallur-gical and electrochemical manufacturers requiring huge blocks of power.

In the world at large, nearly two-thirds of the primary energy for generating electricity is from thermal sources—mainly coal and petroleum (fuel oil and diesel) (Figure 5.19). Nearly a fifth of the world's electricity comes from falling water, and another one-sixth is from nuclear energy. Geothermal and other forms of primary energy provide the remainder, less than 1 percent of the total.

Of the thermal sources, the preferred fuel in much of the world is coal, despite the environmental problems it cre-ates. Because of the cheapness and availability of this form of primary energy, the United States and the majority of Western European countries rely on coal for three-fourths or more of their generating capacity. The proportion is much higher in Eastern Europe, Australia, and South Africa.

Petroleum is a leading fuel for electric generation in many places, especially the Persian Gulf countries, which

rely almost entirely on this locally abundant resource for their electricity. Moreover, Japan produces three-fifths of its electricity with oil-fired generators; and the United Kingdom, which obtains four-fifths of its electric power from fossil fuels, uses dual generators designed to burn either coal or oil, depending on availability and market con-ditions.

Water power is a main source of electricity in those countries fortunate enough to have the requisite physical conditions and the large supplies of capital needed to develop such resources. Norway obtains 99.6 percent of its electricity in this way, Switzerland 58 percent, Iceland 95 percent, and Canada 61 percent. Hydroelectricity is espe-cially important in certain pans of the Third World. A prominent example is Brazil, which, to reduce its depen-dence on imported energy, has embarked on an ambitious dam-building program; at present, the country relies on falling water for 93 percent of its electricity. Brazil's latest major project is the world's largest hydroelectric dam,

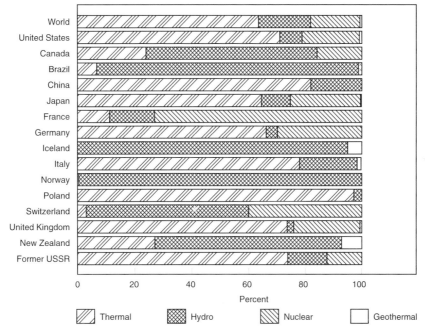

FIGURE 5.19   Production of electricity by type of primary energy source, selected coun-tries, 1992. As a derived form of energy, electricity relies on various primary energy sources for its generation. Of these, thermal generation (chiefly from coal, petroleum, or natural gas) leads in the world as a whole. Because of the growing trend toward dual generators, which can be switched quickly from one fossil fuel to another, the world statistics do not distinguish among thermal sources. Countries that depend on thermal generation to a high degree include Poland (97 percent), Italy, the United Kingdom, the former USSR, and the United States. Hydroelectricity predominates in countries with large supplies of falling water, especially Norway (99.6 percent), Iceland, Brazil, New Zealand, Canada, and Switzerland. Nuclear energy has its greatest development in France (73 percent), Switzerland, Germany, and Japan. A few countries are able to generate electricity from geothermal sources (the earth's heat), notably Iceland (5 percent), New Zealand (7 percent), Italy, the United States, and Japan. [*Source:* Data from United Nations, *Energy Statistics Yearbook, 1992* (New York: United Nations, 1994).]

Itaipu on the Parana River, which began delivering power in 1984. Among other large hydroelectric facilities in the Third World are Zambia's huge dam on the Zambezi River and Egypt's Aswan Dam on the Nile. Africa as a whole has 27 percent of the world's hydroelectric potential but only a tiny proportion of that has been harnessed. This is true also of Southeast Asia, which has 16 percent of the potential, and Latin America with 20 percent. In each region, the problems are lack of necessary capital and lack of a present market for the power. In the industrialized countries, on the other hand, the largest and most accessible sources of hydroelectricity have mostly been used up, especially in Western Europe, North America, and Japan.

In those countries lacking fossil fuels or water power, a common primary source of energy is uranium. The power of the atom is harnessed in two ways: nuclear *fission* (the process used by the atomic bomb), and nuclear *fusion* (the hydrogen bomb method). The former entails capturing the energy released by fissioning radioactive elements, a process that can be controlled to release steady amounts of heat for generating electricity. One pound of nuclear fuel can produce as much electric power as 5,900 barrels of oil. This fuel is uranium 235, a rare and costly element with the potential to create dangerous levels of radioactivity in the environment. Nuclear fusion, on the other hand, relies on cheap and plentiful raw materials, and the process is nearly pollution-free. The fusion reaction presents enormous technological problems, however, and it is therefore unlikely to become a commercial source of energy before well into the twenty-first century.

Despite its high cost and the hazards it poses, nuclear fission has gained widespread use throughout much of the world. By 1984, France had taken the lead in fostering this energy source, on which its state-operated utility system now relies for 73 percent of its electricity. The United Kingdom, which pioneered in the commercial development of atomic power, depends on this source for 24 percent of its electricity. Indeed, atomic energy has become a major supplier of electric power to nearly all parts of Europe, both West and East. Even Japan, the only country to experience wartime atomic destruction, depends on nuclear power for 25 percent of its electricity. Among developing countries with atomic power installations are India, South Korea, and Taiwan. The former USSR obtains 12 percent of its electricity from this source, and the United States, despite its many problems with nuclear power, generates 20 percent of its electricity in this manner.

Still another new technology that contributes significant amounts of electricity in several countries is *geothermal* energy. This method of generating power relies on heat that occurs naturally inside the earth; temperatures rise with increasing depth, reaching 5,000°C at the core. Over most of the earth's crust this heat remains too deep for it to be tapped in any useful way, but in a few areas, abnormally hot rocks approach the surface. Where groundwater comes into contact with these rocks it forms geothermal pools, which overflow as hot water or steam to create hot springs and geysers. Among countries successfully harnessing this earth heat to generate commercial quantities of electricity are Iceland, Italy, Japan, Mexico, New Zealand, and the United States (in California).

Today, increasing amounts of electricity are traded among countries as power-surplus nations sell their excess supplies to power-short neighbors. Regional and national power grids link adjacent countries in order to balance differing peak loads and to provide extra reservoirs in case of emergency. The continental countries of Western Europe have interconnected power systems of this sort, and a two-way cable links the United Kingdom and France under the English Channel. The leading exporting country of the Western Hemisphere is Canada, which sends large amounts of its cheaply produced hydroelectricity to nearby power-deficient areas of the United States. Among the chief exporters of Western Europe are Switzerland, Norway, and Austria—all with great surpluses of hydroelectricity—and France, which is rapidly expanding its supply of nuclear-generated power for export. A similar exchange of electricity takes place in Eastern Europe, Russia being the largest supplier. Some trade in electricity is even taking place among less-developed countries. Zambia, for example, finds sizable markets for its abundant hydroelectricity in neighboring Zimbabwe and South Africa.

Noncommercial Energy

In the developing countries, much of the inanimate energy comes from noncommercial sources. Ironically, it is in these lands that perhaps the most critical energy shortages of all are taking place, threatening not only local economies but also the physical environment itself, along with all those people who depend on it for support. The amount of energy obtained from fuel wood, agricultural wastes, animal dung, and other noncommercial fuels is immense. For instance, in India and Indonesia, two of the most populous less-developed countries, these sources contribute almost as much to total energy consumption as do commercial sources. In all, possibly 1.5 billion people rely solely on firewood for heating their water and cooking their food. Most have no access to alternative forms of energy and could not afford them even if they did. The total amount of firewood used in a year is likely more than a billion metric tons.

Although noncommercial energy constitutes a diminishing proportion of total energy consumed in the developing world—a result of increasing industrialization in some countries—the number of people still relying on traditional fuels remains very great because of the high rates of population growth in these lands, especially the poorest ones. Indeed, severe population pressure is a prime cause of the worsening energy crisis now facing major parts of the Third World. With growing numbers of people scavenging for wood, the forest cover is disappearing at an alarming rate over vast areas. Wood gatherers have to range farther and farther each day in search of wood, and in some countries, they are forced to take every sapling and twig and even the litter on the ground. As the forest floor becomes denuded, trees and shrubs are no longer able to reseed themselves and the bare soil is left to erode in the wind and rain.

When the firewood disappears altogether, as it has in much of Africa south of the Sahara and in southern Asia, the population must turn to the dried dung of their livestock for fuel. This deprives their fields of vitally needed animal fertilizers and thus reduces crop yields. Hence, the crisis in noncommercial energy adds to the crisis in food supply of poorer lands. This energy problem is little noticed in the general effort to ensure future supplies of commercial energy for the industrialized countries.

The Energy Future

Having examined the characteristics of conventional energy forms, and the spatial patterns of their reserves, production, consumption, and exchange, we now turn to the most pressing question: Is the supply of energy adequate for future needs? Public complacency on this subject gave way to deep concern after the oil price shocks precipitated by the Arab oil embargo of 1973–1974 and the Iran–Iraq War beginning in 1979. As oil prices rose, the prices of gas and other competing fuels rose in sympathy, introducing a new era of more costly energy and greater uncertainty. It brought with it economic recession and slower economic growth and it aggravated income and social inequities.

Considering the immense transfer of wealth from oil-importing to oil-exporting countries that took place during the 1970s and early 1980s, the world as a whole made a surprising adjustment. Energy consumption declined in response to higher prices and slower economic activity. And new sources of petroleum were vigorously sought and found in the North Sea, Alaska, Mexico, and other non-OPEC areas. Indeed, the adjustment was sufficient to lull many people, and their political leaders, into a false sense of security.

This illusion was abruptly snapped by Iraq's August 1990 invasion of Kuwait and the ensuing United Nations embargo, which deprived world markets of one-fifth of their usual supply. Crude oil prices soared, again reminding the world of its dangerous reliance on a vital resource tightly concentrated within a politically volatile region.

Looking to an uncertain energy future, therefore, we may ask: What can be done to avoid these recurring crises? And, even if further oil-supply interruptions can be averted, how long are the world's stocks of this and the other conventional forms of energy likely to last? What can we do to postpone the ultimate exhaustion of these nonrenewable resources? What are the prospects for replacing them with new kinds of energy? Before taking up these questions of future supply, however, we first must see how much energy the world can be expected to need.

Anticipating future world demand is difficult because countries at various levels of development use energy differently and react differently to price changes. Less-developed countries generally spend a higher proportion of their gross national products on energy than do advanced countries, and this proportion continues to diminish at the highest levels of development. Though per capita energy consumption is very low among the least-developed countries, this climbs steeply with rising GNP (refer back to Figure 5.3).

The effects of price on energy demand are complex. In the short run, the price elasticity of demand for energy is low in advanced countries; that is, a rise in price is not immediately reflected in reduced consumption (see Chapter 6 for a more detailed explanation of price elasticity of demand). Consumers do not instantaneously trade in their gasoline-wasting big automobiles for more energy-efficient ones when fuel prices rise, nor do factories immediately install new machinery or homeowners insulate their houses. More likely, a quick, sharp rise in energy prices will merely precipitate an economic recession. In the longer run, however, the price elasticity of demand is much higher: The next car purchased gets much better gasoline mileage, and so forth. On the whole, citizens of the richer countries have many opportunities for saving energy merely by making discretionary changes in life-style—living closer to work and recreation, traveling less, and turning off electric lights and appliances. The effects of price rises on the economic growth of advanced countries are generally less, too, because a larger part of GNP is derived from the services and high-technology industries that consume little energy.

The cost of energy and its availability have a severe impact on the economic growth of less-developed countries, however, because of the nature of their industrial and transport needs. Any rise in their level of development is directly reflected in increased demand for energy. High rates of population growth add further to this demand.

Projections of future energy needs therefore suggest that a doubling of total energy demand in the industrialized nations would be likely accompanied by a five- to seven-fold demand increase in the less-developed countries. Nevertheless, current levels of energy use in the LDCs are so low that even this gain in total amount would leave their per capita consumption six or seven times smaller than that of the richer ones. Thus, if in some manner all the world's nations could achieve the levels of prosperity now enjoyed by the industrialized countries, enormous increases in the total demand for energy would result.

Finding sufficient additional quantities of energy to supply this growing demand raises still other uncertainties. Although reserve estimates such as those appearing in Figures 5.10, 5.13, and 5.16 give some indication of near-term prospects, the more distant future is clouded by questions of data quality and changes in costs. Added to this is the problem of uneven world distribution and the political risks this poses for energy-importing countries, all of which carry great potential for future price fluctuations.

Based on what we know now, and assuming a minimum of political intervention in world commerce, we may expect oil production to peak during the final decade of this present century. Therefore, supplies will likely diminish gradually and production costs and market prices will rise accordingly. Because such a large proportion of known reserves is concentrated in the former USSR and the politically volatile Middle East, however, the political uncertainties surrounding this current prime energy resource are especially troublesome.

Natural gas production should rise substantially toward the year 2000, reaching a peak within the first two or three decades of the new century. Gas supplies are thus likely to last a little longer than oil. As in the case of oil, however, a major part of the world's natural gas is in the former USSR and the Middle East. North America and Western Europe are relatively better off in gas reserves than they are in oil, and the United States has a very large potential from high-cost sources. As we have seen, however, the sharing of this resource between have and have-not nations is more difficult than oil because gas is so costly to ship by sea.

As the most abundant fossil fuel, coal should be plentiful throughout the next century. Moreover, its reserves are more widely distributed, including very large stocks in the United States and China, as well as the former USSR, Europe, and Australia. This pattern is therefore much more favorable for the industrialized nations than other conventional fuels. Yet, those countries lacking coal are at a disadvantage because of its high shipping costs. Widespread future use of coal also requires finding an economical solution to the problem of atmospheric pollution now associated with coal combustion.

The remaining energy sources now making a significant contribution all pose problems for future expansion. With current technology, nuclear fission is unlikely to last beyond the turn of the century because of limited supplies of low-cost uranium. Environmental constraints also present a serious deterrent, especially in the United States. Hydroelectricity has a limited future among developed countries, where most of the existing waterpower potential has been exhausted. A very large unused potential remains in parts of the Third World, but obtaining the capital required to develop this resource will continue to be a great obstacle.

Beyond this present century, projections of energy demand and supply become increasingly uncertain. The distant energy future is easier to foresee in the case of the present group of industrialized nations because their populations have stabilized and their levels of resource use appear to have peaked and even to have begun a decline. The less-developed countries present an entirely different set of problems. We cannot be sure of their future demand for energy without knowing how far their development will proceed and what form their industrialization will ultimately assume. What we can be sure of is that the potential demand will inevitably rise as populations continue to climb before peaking in the latter part of the twenty-first century. At that point, the number of potential users of energy will probably have reached 11 or 12 billion. With the output of today's preferred forms of energy expected to dwindle soon after A.D. 2000, the search for new kinds of energy is already pressing. This is especially so because of the long lead time required for a new form of energy to supersede an older one; in the past, this has usually required about 50 years.

Experience gained from the energy crises of the 1970s demonstrated that one sure way of gaining additional time for developing radically new kinds of energy is to stretch out existing supplies of conventional energy. Conservation is now generally recognized as the cheapest and quickest method of obtaining energy in the short run. The OPEC crises slowed the rate of energy use far more than the most optimistic predictions of the time. The reaction was almost worldwide; between 1979 and 1983, consumption in the noncommunist industrialized countries actually fell by one-tenth, reversing the steady rise in energy consumption that had prevailed for decades previously (Figure 5.20).

This reversal in consumption trends was especially dramatic in the United States. By 1983, the country was using less energy than it had in 1973 on the eve of the first OPEC crisis, yet gross national product had risen at an average annual rate of 2.5 percent during that 10-year period. The United States achieved its 1983 GNP with 22 percent less energy than if 1973 levels of energy efficiency had continued unchanged.

The trend toward saving energy acquired a momentum of its own when people discovered that unlimited future supplies of cheap oil were no longer assured. As a result, energy efficiency has assumed a built-in quality. Purchasers

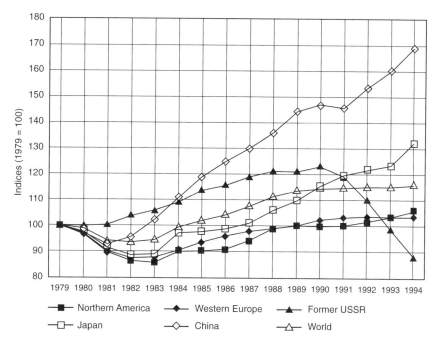

FIGURE 5.20 Changing consumption of primary energy, selected areas, 1979–1994, indices (1979 = 100). The sharp run-up in energy prices following the 1979 Persian Gulf crisis produced a worldwide drive to conserve energy. By 1983, total energy consumption in the noncommunist industrialized countries had dropped by a tenth. World consumption gradually rose thereafter until, by the eve of the 1990 Persian Gulf crisis, global energy use was 15 percent above its 1979 level. Since then, world consumption has remained static. The USSR, with its abundant domestic supplies, continued to increases energy use up to the collapse of the Soviet Union in 1990. Since then, energy consumption in the USSR's successor states has dropped precipitously. Rapidly industrializing countries such as China have recently added substantial upward pressures on world energy supplies. During the fifteen-year period, however, Western Europe's consumption rose only 3.7 percent, and Northern America's grew only 5.7 percent—a decline in per capita terms. Japan's energy use was 32 percent higher in 1994 than in 1979, but this represented a marked decline in relation to its GNP, which expanded considerably during the 1980s. [*Source:* Data from the *BP Statistical Review of World Energy* (London: British Petroleum Company plc, 1995).]

of home furnaces and household appliances now expect these to be energy-efficient, and builders routinely insulate new residential and commercial structures. In the United States, federally mandated standards for new automobiles had raised the average fuel efficiency from only 14 miles per gallon in the 1970s to 28 miles per gallon by the late 1980s. Though both consumers and government officials had grown increasingly complacent during that era, the Persian Gulf crisis of 1990 brought a return to realism. Following this event, the U.S. Congress imposed much stricter fuel standards on vehicle manufactures for future model years.

During the 1980s, industrial users intensified their efforts to improve energy efficiency. By 1982, industrial use of all types of energy was one-third less in the United States than would have been the case if 1973 consumption trends had persisted. Continuing this pursuit, industries have

reduced their share from 40 percent of total U.S. energy use in 1983 to only 36 percent by 1990. This has been achieved in part by installing better equipment, but it has also reflected slower industrial growth associated with structural changes in the economy. At a time when service activities have been contributing a larger share to GNP, older, energy-intensive industries have been declining—replaced by new high-technology enterprises with far lower energy requirements. Nevertheless, the potential remains for even greater improvement: The Department of Energy has declared that American industries actually could turn out the same amount of product with 50 percent less energy than at present.

In its conservation efforts, the United States continues to lag behind Japan and Western Europe, where energy has always been more costly. Even the Europeans and Japanese, however, had been lulled by the cheaper petroleum of the

1980s and had relaxed their vigilance. Jolted by the 1990 Iraqi invasion of Kuwait into renewed awareness of their vulnerability to oil-supply interruptions, these countries once again revived energy restrictions of the kinds imposed during earlier emergencies.

Viewed globally, some of the greatest opportunities for energy conservation are in the former Soviet Union, whose per capita consumption is 50 percent greater than Europe's (refer to Figure 5.5) despite a far-lower standard of living. Soviet energy use continued to rise steadily throughout the 1980s at a time when noncommunist countries were cutting consumption (Figure 5.20). The reasons for this high rate of energy use are to be found mainly in Soviet industry, which emphasized heavy, energy-intensive forms of production and relied on outdated plants and equipment. More recently, the economic dislocations forced by the fall of communism in 1990 have caused a steep decline in energy use by USSR's successor states.

Although in the short run conservation has proved unexpectedly effective, in the longer run substantial new supplies will have to be found. One way of doing this is to intensify exploitation of existing reserves and exploration for new ones in order to extend the life-spans of conventional fuels. Those producing countries that are net importers of energy are already pursuing this policy with considerable effect. Thus, the United States, which has only 3 percent of the world's proved oil reserves, accounts for 12 percent of total production, whereas the Middle East, with 65.4 percent of the reserves, yields only 29.8 percent of world output. Additions to U.S. production now come mainly through horizontal and vertical expansion of existing fields, that is, drilling new wells on the margins and going to greater depths.

The only truly important U.S. finds in recent times were in Alaska, and that region (which holds one-third of U.S. reserves) continues to be the country's main hope for new supplies to replace the now-dwindling output at Prudhoe Bay. An equally intensive and costly search for oil and gas is under way in the Canadian Arctic. Elsewhere in the world the effort to locate new supplies has continued since the first OPEC crisis, yielding important finds in the North Sea, southern Mexico, China, Australia, and Colombia. The former USSR, though known to have some of the world's largest energy resources, had to put massive new investments into oil exploration to compensate for declining output. The former USSR's main problem is that thus far the industry has been relying on only the richest and most accessible deposits, thus skimming off the cream of its huge energy wealth. As these older fields decline, new exploration has led ever deeper into remote and frozen areas of Siberia, where high costs and technical difficulties have slowed development. Meanwhile, the Middle East maintains its status as the richest area of all: Recent additions to Kuwait's proven reserves, for example, alone equal all the known reserves of the United States. The net effect of all this intensified exploration since 1973 is that the world has located more oil than it has used since the first oil crisis. In 1979, the world's proven oil reserves were calculated at 650 billion barrels; in 1994, they were estimated at 1,009 billion barrels, a 43-year supply at current levels of production and use.

The success of this feverish search for new energy has reduced the oil cartel's hold on world markets and has postponed the time when fossil fuels will become exhausted. Experts consider it unlikely that any new "Middle Easts" will appear to provide a quantum rise in world reserves. Given the long lead time for developing new types of energy, where do our best hopes lie for the more distant future?

All the options for other energy sources involve the development and refining of new technologies. One such option concerns the perfection of techniques for recovering the great amounts of oil left underground in an oilfield after the usual extraction methods have ended. When pumping of an oil pool ceases, as much as 60 to 70 percent of the oil remains behind, trapped in pockets and holes in the rock. The industry has developed secondary recovery techniques that can bring up some of the remaining oil, and so-called enhanced recovery contributes additional amounts; but these methods still leave possibly half of the total behind. The remainder represents an enormous resource, but finding ways of tapping it poses great technical difficulties yet to be solved.

Another huge resource that awaits further technological development before it can be fully utilized is coal. Its combustion releases into the atmosphere dangerous impurities that pose serious environmental hazards, but a truly effective treatment is costly because of the number and complexity of the pollutants that must be driven off. Present techniques—washing, fluidized beds, scrubbers—add 20 percent or more to the cost of generating electricity and therefore place this valuable fuel at a competitive disadvantage with respect to other forms of energy, especially in locations remote from coalfields. Developing an economical method that would give clean-burning coal should be of highest priority to the United States, which has very large reserves. Although such techniques appear within grasp, this type of research has been unable to attract the funding needed for a quick solution.

On the other hand, during and immediately after the energy crises of the 1970s, a great deal of attention focused on *synfuels*. These are produced by converting solid fuels to gaseous or liquid forms suitable for use in internal combustion engines. The most common raw materials are coal, oil shales, and tar sands. For at least 150 years, coal has been used for generating a low-grade fuel called "coal gas," or "town gas," which was common in Europe and North America until it was superseded by cheaper, hotter natural gas. More recently, attention has turned to obtaining liquid fuels from coal, to be used as substitutes for oil and gasoline. Processes developed in Germany during World War II are the bases for existing methods, which South Africa has adopted and further refined for its drive to achieve energy independence, as described earlier. Several experiments with these techniques were undertaken in the United States in the late 1970s but languished with the decline in world oil prices in subsequent years.

North America is likewise well-endowed with two other resources used for making synfuels—tar sands and oil shales. So plentiful are these that they have the potential for nearly doubling the world's fossil-fuel stores. Tar sands contain large-molecule hydrocarbons like those of crude oil, but they do not migrate as do oil and gas. Instead, this thick bituminous material adheres firmly to the sand grains among which it has lodged. Tar sands occur in limited quantities in several parts of the world, but the most important known deposits are in western Canada. The Athabaska tar sands of northern Alberta are 200 feet thick and extend over 30,000 square miles. Other large occurrences are the Orinoco deposits of Venezuela and the Olenek deposits in Russia. Recovery of this resource requires mining the sands and then heating them to cause the asphaltic hydrocarbons to flow.

Oil shales are rock formations that contain concentrations of bitumen that can be convened into petroleum products. Vast reserves of rich oil shales occur in the Rocky Mountains of the United States, extending over much of Colorado, Utah, and Wyoming. These Green River shales can be made to yield from 0.5 to 1.5 barrels of oil per ton; in total, the country's oil shales probably exceed the amount of its conventional oil reserves. Pilot plants have proved the technical feasibility of mining oil shale, but it is too costly to exploit at present price levels. In addition, current processing techniques threaten the vulnerable western environment with atmospheric pollution, water contamination, and problems of waste disposal. Nevertheless, both tar sands and oil shales represent potentially important supplements to future energy supplies.

To many experts, the ultimate answer to the world's energy needs lies with nuclear power—but not necessarily the form now in commercial use, nuclear *fission*. Though it is the basis of expanding power programs worldwide—by 1989, 429 commercial reactors were operating in 25 countries—fission poses such complex, and frightening, issues that its long-term prospects are in doubt.

Perhaps most serious of all are the grave environmental concerns that the commercial use of nuclear fission provokes. The siting of nuclear power plants in populated areas arouses fears of horrible nuclear accidents such as the 1986 Chernobyl disaster in the Soviet Union; controversy also surrounds the search for safe ways to dispose of radioactive waste products. Debate over these environmental issues has become so heated that atomic energy development has stalled in the United States and existing generating plants are being closed down in Sweden.

Also clouding the long-term future of fission is the prospect of rising costs. High-grade ores of U-235 are severely limited in occurrence, and continued exploitation of this scarce resource therefore will become increasingly costly. Solution of this supply problem depends on perfection of the fast-breeder reactor, which uses a lower-grade fuel and creates new fuel at the same rate or greater than the fissioning atoms are used up. However, the breeder reactor further heightens safety concerns; countering these would require elaborate measures that could make this form of energy prohibitively expensive.

Nuclear *fusion* promises a longer-term solution to the environmental safety problems surrounding atomic power. If and when research on this technology succeeds, nuclear fusion could supply limitless amounts of electric energy using one of the cheapest and most plentiful raw materials, hydrogen—and it would present no radiation dangers. Unlike fission, however, nuclear fusion has not yet been controlled to permit its use for generating electricity, despite intense research.

The energy emergencies of the 1970s precipitated a concerted worldwide drive to find commercially feasible alternative energies that would liberate the world from dependence on fossil fuels and the political, environmental, and long-term supply issues that surround them. Researchers have made important progress in several directions. See Box 5.1 for a list of the more promising alternative forms of energy now emerging. There appear to be many options for keeping the world supplied with mechanical energy in the future. This present period appears to be one of transition, a time when the end of the familiar and conventional forms of energy is approaching. In the short run, the result could be continuing crises. The long-run situation is another matter. After the transition is past, the world energy supply is not likely to be limited by an insufficiency of resources. Large amounts of coal, tar sands, and oil shales remain to be used. Meanwhile, radical new forms of energy are already becoming commercially feasible.

INDUSTRIAL MATERIALS

If the long-run outlook for energy is optimistic, the situation may be less secure for another class of nonrenewable resources, the industrial raw materials (Figure 5.21). This would seem to apply especially to certain metallic ores that must be teamed with mechanical energy if the modern economic system is to function. Further technological change will be needed to relieve supply constraints that are beginning to threaten some of these resources.

BOX 5.1 *Promising Energy Alternatives*

Among all the new forms of energy proposed as alternatives to the familiar types now in use, a select few appear to have at least some of the characteristics required of an eventual replacement for fossil fuels. A viable alternative energy would have to be (1) competitive in cost with existing types, (2) in abundant supply, and (3) widely available or cheaply and easily transported. Ideally, it also should be (4) nonpolluting and (5) safe to transport, store, and use. The present candidates tend to fall into two somewhat overlapping categories: (1) primary energies for generating electricity and (2) energies designed to propel motor vehicles.

GENERATING ELECTRIC POWER

A derived form of energy, versatile and convenient, electricity is indispensable to modern technology and society. Though the main uses for electricity are nonpolluting, the fossil-fuel-burning plants that generate it are among the worst of environmental offenders. Important advances have recently been made in the search for ways to make electricity cleanly from primary sources that promise energy

independence of foreign monopoly control.

Fuel Cells. The technology that supplies on-board electricity for U.S. space shuttles has now become commercially available for use in apartment complexes, office buildings, factories, public utilities, and, eventually, homes and motor vehicles. A fuel cell works much like a battery: Hydrogen atoms diffuse through an anode that strips off electrons, producing an electric current. Extracting the hydrogen from natural gas or coal entails no burning and is therefore an appealing way to use these fuels without creating pollution. Fuel cells are very efficient, converting up to 60 percent of the energy in natural gas into electricity as opposed to 30 percent for conventional boiler-fired generators. The early fuel cells had two disadvantages: high operating temperature and cost. Improved designs have now reduced temperatures, however, and unit costs are falling as larger numbers are produced for commercial installation.

Solar Energy. One of the most tempting energy alternatives involves extracting energy directly from its very

source—the sun's rays. For some time, solar collectors have been heating water and generating electricity in regions with cloudless skies, such as the Middle East and the American Southwest. By means of solar (photovoltaic) cells, made from silicon wafers, it is also possible to use incoming rays of the sun to generate electricity. Photovoltaic research has now raised the efficiency of solar cells to the point where they are close to being economically competitive with conventional methods of generating electricity.

Wind and Sea. A number of areas with sustained winds of high velocity have experimented with using wind turbines to generate electricity. Thousands of these are in operation in California, where they feed current into the state grid, sufficient to power a city of 350,000 (California gets 45 percent of its electricity from renewable sources). The ocean tides and currents also represent immense potential sources of energy. Several experimental efforts have been undertaken to harness these inexhaustible flow resources, but commercial applications remain in the more distant future.

Metals

Metals are a class of elements that are hard, heavy, and opaque, and are capable of being drawn into fine wire (ductility), hammered into thin plates (malleability), and melted by heat. Moreover, they are able to conduct both electricity and heat (conductivity). Each metal possesses these qualities in different combinations and degrees and therefore has its own set of uses. The versatility of many metals is enhanced by a capacity for *alloying*, that is, for combining with other metals in varying proportions. This multiplies the already extensive range of special purposes that these elements are able to serve.

An intimate relationship exists between metals and the consumption of mechanical energy. Indeed, metals are indispensable to all sectors of the modern economy. Although obvious in the case of manufacturing and transportation, this is equally true of the extractive industries,

including modern agriculture. Not only do the metals contribute to high agricultural yields through their use in farm tools, machinery, and transport equipment, but also in the production of agricultural chemicals. A great many metals are required by an increasingly complex modern technology, in which subtle differences in metallic qualities can be vital. Although some substitution of materials is possible, no feasible substitutes have been discovered for certain key metals.

For these reasons, a continuing supply of metals is vital. But how good is this supply? The answer is different for each metal: Some are still plentiful whereas others are nearing exhaustion. All are nonrenewable. One of the first things we discover when examining metallic reserves is that some of the most "common" metals are not really common at all. Of the so-called common metals, only iron and aluminum are among the first 10 elements in the continental earth crust, and these 10 represent 99 percent of the total

MOTOR VEHICLE PROPULSION

For any country that seeks to reduce its dependence on foreign energy, the prime targets for savings are its motor vehicles. At a time when the United States imports 50 percent of its oil (at a cost of $50 billion in 1990), the transport sector accounts for two-thirds of national consumption. Raising the average fuel efficiency of the country's automobile fleet to 40 miles per gallon would save 2.8 million barrels of oil per day. While this political issue is being debated, however, another option would be to convert cars and trucks to alternative fuels that are available domestically—and are less polluting than gasoline and diesel. Motor-vehicle manufacturers now recognize that the days of oil-dependent vehicles are numbered and are concentrating their research efforts on new forms of propulsion. Several alternative fuels now offer viable options.

Ethanol. Existing internal combustion engines work very well on grain alcohol. Alcohol made from corn and mixed with gasoline to produce 'gasohol' has become a popular motor fuel in the grain-producing American Midwest. Brazil uses pure alcohol distilled from its plentiful, cheap sugar cane to fuel its motor vehicles.

Methanol (Wood Alcohol). The nonpetroleum fuel that currently leads in contention for commercial use is methanol, which can be made from coal, natural gas, or even garbage. These are so abundant in the United States that they could soon completely emancipate the country from dependence on imported oil. Although methanol is corrosive and therefore requires some modification of the fuel system, it is powerful and cheap. American manufacturers expect to introduce several thousand methanol-burning cars into the California market by 1993.

Electricity. Pioneer motorcars that ran on electricity were so sluggish and restricted in cruising range that they soon lost out to gasoline models, Recent developments, especially in battery design, have now yielded electric cars with rapid acceleration and greater range. For the future, one of the likeliest prospects for electrically powered vehicles is the fuel cell (see previous discussion). California has mandated zero emissions by A.D. 2009, a standard that only electric cars can presently meet, and the state now has 10,000 of these on order.

Hydrogen. The cleanest energy of all is hydrogen, which is the staple fuel for rockets. One of the most abundant elements, it is made by passing an electric current through water. Vehicle engines run perfectly well on hydrogen, but it is still much too costly for commercial use. Steadily rising efficiencies of solar cells, however, offer the possibility of producing hydrogen in desert regions and piping it to markets at competitive prices.

Compressed Natural Gas (CNG). Compressed natural gas is cheaper than gasoline and it is abundant in the United States and several other industrialized countries. It is also cleaner than methanol. The only major problem of CNG is the huge pressurized tank that must be installed in the vehicle, making it costly and impractical for passenger cars. Nevertheless, CNG-powered trucks and buses are competitive in price, and half a million of these are currently operating in California, Florida, Alaska, and around the world.

crustal weight. Relatively speaking, therefore, the other commercially important metals exist in only small quantities. Considering the great mass of the earth's crust, however, the absolute amounts in fact are much greater than this would seem to indicate and a realistic dividing line between the abundant and the scarce metals is nearer the 0.01 percent level. The most plentiful metallic elements, therefore, are iron, aluminum, manganese, magnesium, chromium, and titanium, whereas the least plentiful include such familiar metals as copper, lead, zinc, and nickel. In many cases, the scarce elements are being extracted in large quantities despite severely limited reserves.

Some metals are much more widely distributed over the earth than others. In some instances this results from a generally greater crustal occurrence, but in others, it reflects the essential character of the ores from which they are extracted. Certain ores—such as iron, aluminum, and copper—have a metallic content that varies continuously from very rich to very lean. This variability is a boon to the mining industry, for the limits to practical exploitation are set simply on the basis of cost and available technology. Many other metals, however, are discontinuous in concentration; they either occur in a place or they do not. This is true of such important metals as lead, zinc, tin, nickel, tungsten, mercury, manganese, gold, and silver. Certain of these are concentrated in only a few places.

Still another problem of world mineral supply is that the countries consuming the largest quantities are not necessarily the ones that are best endowed with resources. The United States is the outstanding consumer of metals, but it lacks many vital metallic resources. Similarly, most European industrial nations are conspicuously deficient in metallic ores. Some of the largest reserves occur in less-developed countries and in those advanced nations with large territories and small populations, especially Canada and Australia.

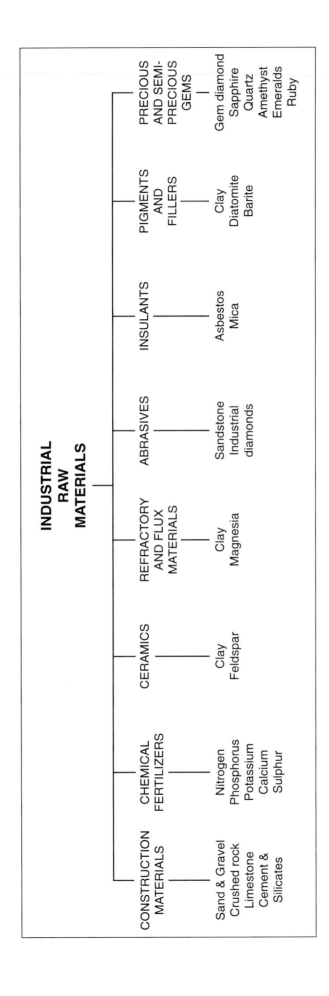

FIGURE 5.21 The industrial raw materials.

Among those metals required by world industry in very large quantities are iron and its close partner, manganese. Of the metals, iron is the overwhelming leader in total annual tonnage of output—constituting 95 percent of all metals extracted. One reason for the heavy production and consumption of iron is that it is plentiful and very cheap (only a few cents per pound). Another reason for its popularity is its great strength and its readiness to form alloys with many other metals. When added to iron in even minute quantities, these elements can cause it to assume a variety of desirable properties that contribute still further to the versatility of this metal. Iron technology is relatively easy, too, for the metal can be removed from its oxides (the most common occurrence in nature) by means of chemically simple processes.

Since the first discovery of a technique for making iron, about 2000 B.C., this metal has been one of the most important materials, used by virtually every society today. Nevertheless, per capita consumption of iron is closely related to level of development. Usage is exceedingly low in such underdeveloped countries as Somalia or Bhutan, but it climbs steeply with rising per capita income. Ultimately, however, per capita use reaches a saturation point, and consumption rates among the most industrialized countries are fairly similar.

Production rates of iron and steel likewise correlate fairly closely with level of development ($R^2 = 0.633$), but the relationship is changing. Though Russia, Japan, and the United States still lead in steel output, many newly industrializing countries in the Third World are now installing their own steel. With new facilities using the latest technology, and with abundant cheap labor and ample domestic supplies of raw materials, China, Brazil, and South Korea, among others, are challenging the leaders in world markets (Figure 5.22). Altogether, 76 countries were producing their own raw steel by the end of the 1980s, up from 50 in the early 1970s.

Many leading steelmaking nations, however, have little iron ore of their own, notably Japan, Germany, and most other European producers. Even the United States, which originally had large reserves, now imports much of its ore and rising amounts of finished steel. The richest Lake Superior deposits have long since been exhausted and lower grades of American ore are now being developed. Indeed, low-grade taconite iron deposits now contribute a major part of the ore mined in the United States. Prominent among today's largest producers of iron ore are such LDCs as Brazil, China, and India, as well as two advanced nations that have large areas and low population densities—Australia and Canada (Figure 5.23). Many of these are major exporters of ore.

Because iron is the second most plentiful metal in the earth's crust, and because nearly all types of iron ore are now successfully treated by iron technology, total reserves of this element are enormous. Consequently, iron is cheap for its bulk. Transportation costs and accessibility to market therefore are important determinants in the selection of deposits for exploitation, more so than for any other metal. But the smelting of iron ore also requires great tonnages of other ingredients, especially coal for fuel and for driving off oxygen, and limestone to carry off other impurities. Hence, transportation costs and accessibility of these other materials are likewise important locational considerations for the steel industry. For these reasons many large known deposits in remote areas remain ignored, whereas ores of indifferent quality but close to market and to other ironmaking materials are actively pursued.

The projected life of world iron ore reserves is thus much greater than that of most mineral resources (Table 5.2). In addition, vast resources of lower-grade iron ore are available. The main effect of future iron ore usage, therefore, will be to cause prices to rise as richer, more accessible reserves become exhausted. Because iron resources are in no immediate danger of depletion, the basic supply problem for iron becomes the adequacy of companion resources on which its production and use depend, namely, energy and alloying elements.

Manganese is a vital alloying metal for steel manufacture. It serves a dual function in the steel industry: (1) a process material acting as a "scavenger" to carry off sulfur and oxygen, an essential use for which there is no known substitute, and (2) an alloying element that imparts toughness to the metal. Although manganese has other industrial applications, they are minor. Because manganese is a relatively plentiful element in the earth's crust, its total world supply presents no immediate problem. Indeed, so large are current supplies that the metal tends to be overused.

The main difficulty of manganese supply is the spatial distribution of reserves: The best deposits are not always in the places where the metal is most needed (see Figure 5.24). The United States has virtually no domestic reserves of high-grade manganese ore and an inadequate supply of low-grade ore. Other big industrial nations also lack manganese, except for the former USSR, which has one-third of the known world supply. Except for Australia, the remaining reserves are mainly in the less-developed nations of Africa, Latin America, and Asia. Consequently, a major part of the world output of manganese moves between continents. Fortunately for the United States, very large quantities of manganese occur on the ocean floor. Nodules of manganese have been found at depths of 500 to 3,000 feet off the southeastern coast of the United States and at depths of 5,000 to 14,000 feet in the eastern Pacific. Commercial extraction, using dredges and vacuum devices, has proved feasible.

Several nonferrous metals essential to technologically advanced countries have been thought to be in relatively

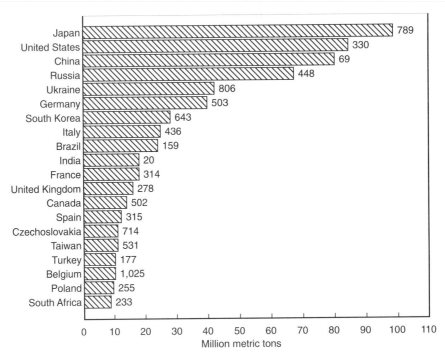

FIGURE 5.22 Largest producers of raw steel (million metric tons), with per capita output (in kilograms), 1992. Since the collapse of the former Soviet Union, Japan has been the leading steelmaker, currently with 13.6 percent of the world total. However, this is still exceeded by the combined output of two former Soviet republics, Russia and Ukraine, which account for 15.1 percent of global output. Many leading steel producers, especially Japan and the European nations, must import most of their raw materials. A longtime center of steelmaking, Europe now supplies 21 percent of the world total. Joining the leaders in recent times are third-ranking China and several other newly industrializing countries such as South Korea, Brazil, India, Taiwan, and Turkey. The more populous LDCs rank very low in per capita output, however. China produces only 69 kilograms per person and India a mere 20 kilograms. Compare these with the average Belgian's 1,025 kilograms. [*Source:* U.S. Bureau of Mines, *Minerals Yearbook 1992* (Washington, DC: U.S. Government Printing Office, 1994).]

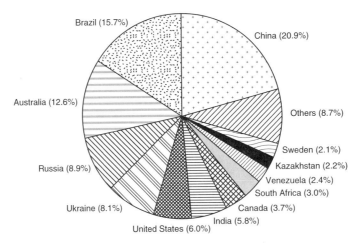

FIGURE 5.23 Major producers of iron ore, 1992. Iron ores are plentifully available and widely distributed around the world; hence, the prominence of countries with large land areas, such as China, Brazil, Australia, Russia, and Ukraine in this diagram. Several of the less-developed countries appearing here are also leading manufacturers of raw steel (see Figure 5.21). [*Source:* U.S. Bureau of Mines, *Minerals Yearbook 1992* (Washington, DC: U.S. Government Printing Office, 1994).]

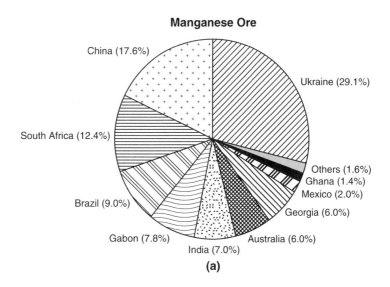

(a)

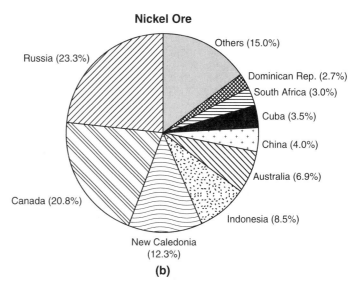

(b)

FIGURE 5.24 World production of manganese and nickel ores, 1992. Both elements are essential to the steel industry and both are erratically distributed in the world, as are most alloying metals. Together the former Soviet republics of Ukraine and Georgia produce 35 percent of all manganese. China also has become a major supplier. Much of the rest comes from Africa, Latin America, and southern Asia. Russia is the largest source of nickel, followed by Canada and the South Pacific island of New Caledonia. Australia is an important producer of both metals. [*Source:* U.S. Bureau of Mines, *Minerals Yearbook 1992* (Washington, DC: U.S. Government Printing Office, 1994).]

short supply, but some question this conclusion (refer to Tables 5.1 and 5.2). The members of this group—aluminum, copper, lead, and zinc—are widely used and consumed in large quantities. All the nonferrous metals normally occur in low-grade ore, except aluminum. These elements are also erratically distributed in the world, resulting in a large volume of world trade both in the metals and their ores. All four metals are more costly than iron, owing to the complexity of their ores, intricate technology of extraction, and expensive processing methods.

Aluminum is an exception in this group in several respects. First, it is the only nonferrous metal that appears abundantly in the earth's crust (8 percent of the total). Moreover, it is the only one of the four that occurs in high-grade ores, mostly over 32 percent metallic content (see Figure 5.25 for the leading producers of bauxite, the chief ore of aluminum). Consumption of this metal has grown very rapidly throughout the postwar period. Very large supplies of low-grade aluminum ore exist, but these are not commercially feasible to exploit with today's technology.

The other nonferrous metals are rare in crustal occurrence, copper being only 0.0058 percent, lead 0.0010 percent, and zinc 0.0082 percent. These three have become sufficiently concentrated for commercial extraction only through fortuitous acts of nature. Of the three, only copper occurs in continuously variable concentrations, which means that lower grades may be mined. Copper already is being extracted from exceedingly lean ores: only 0.9 percent metallic content in the United States, 1 to 2 percent in Canada and Chile, 4 percent in Zambia, and 6 percent in Zaire. Turning to still lower grades appears feasible, in view of the cheap open-pit mining that prevails in the copper industry. But this alternative does not apply to lead and zinc,

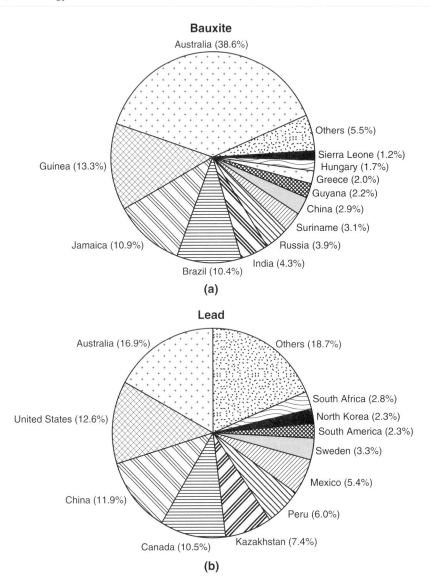

Bauxite

Australia (38.6%)

Others (5.5%)
Sierra Leone (1.2%)
Hungary (1.7%)
Greece (2.0%)
Guyana (2.2%)
China (2.9%)
Suriname (3.1%)
Russia (3.9%)
India (4.3%)

Guinea (13.3%)

Jamaica (10.9%)

Brazil (10.4%)

(a)

Lead

Australia (16.9%)

Others (18.7%)

South Africa (2.8%)
North Korea (2.3%)
South America (2.3%)
Sweden (3.3%)

Mexico (5.4%)

United States (12.6%)

Peru (6.0%)

China (11.9%)

Canada (10.5%)   Kazakhstan (7.4%)

(b)

FIGURE 5.25 World production of bauxite (the chief ore of aluminum) and lead, 1992. These nonferrous ores differ substantially in crustal occurrence and in the nature of their deposits. Aluminum is one of the most plentiful elements, being a main constituent of many common rocks, but only four countries account for more than two-thirds of the bauxite mined. Though the crustal occurrence of lead is relatively small, it is extracted commercially in many parts of the world. [*Source:* U.S. Bureau of Mines, *Minerals Yearbook 1992* (Washington, DC. U.S. Government Printing Office, 1994).]

which usually occur together. Their ores are generally much richer than those of copper, but their deposits are small and require costly underground mining. This cost tends to be partially offset by the valuable by-products, such as copper, gold, and silver, that are frequently obtained in lead and zinc mining operations.

Unlike many minerals, a substantial proportion of the nonferrous metals comes from advanced nations, especially Canada and Australia (Figure 5.25 and Figure 5.26). Australia has more than one-third of the known reserves of the chief aluminum ore, bauxite (aluminum hydroxide), and the industrialized countries as a whole have about one-half of the total. Africa and Latin America have most of the rest. Nearly half of the world's copper reserves are also in the

developed countries, particularly the former USSR and the United States. The rest is mainly in South America (principally Chile and Peru) and Africa's rich copper belt (Zambia and Zaire). Most of the world's larger deposits of zinc and lead are found in Australia, the United States, Canada, and the former USSR.

Although these metals cost more per pound than iron, they are surprisingly cheap, considering their relative scarcity. Nevertheless, the cost of extraction has risen as reserves have declined in size and richness. Despite this, uses continue to appear. Copper and aluminum are virtually indispensable in electrical applications because of their high conductivity. All four metals are used variously in the manufacture of important alloys such as bronze, brass,

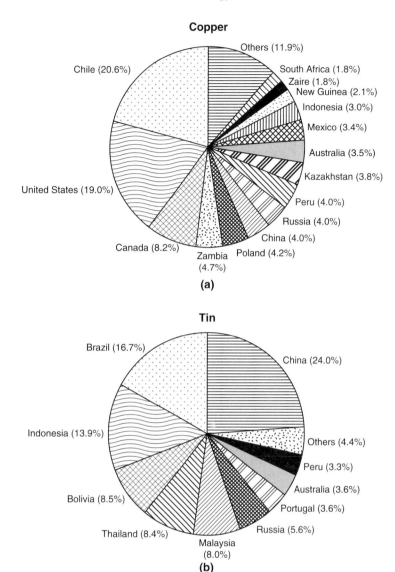

FIGURE 5.26 World production of copper and tin, 1992. Both of these elements are relatively scarce in the earth's crust. Copper is mined in many parts of the world, whereas most tin comes from two major source areas: a narrow belt extending from north to south through Asia and another zone in South America. [*Source:* U.S. Bureau of Mines, *Minerals Yearbook 1992* (Washington, DC: U.S. Government Printing Office, 1994).]

morel metal, solder, bearing metal, type metal, casting metal, and special alloys for aircraft applications. Aluminum, because of its lightness, is valuable as a structural metal. Copper and aluminum are used for cooking utensils, owing to their heat-conducting properties. Copper, lead, and zinc each have their special applications because of their resistance to corrosion: sheathing, storage batteries, and galvanizing, for example. All four have essential uses in the production of chemicals.

The nonferrous metals thus have a multitude of vital applications and have become interwoven into modern production in a variety of ways. With the possible exception of aluminum, their supplies are limited, however. Some substitution is possible, as, for example, the increasing use of aluminum in the place of more copper in applications requiring conductivity; unfortunately, such substitution is not always feasible. Note also that the production of nonferrous metals is a drain on other resources. In particular, a great deal of mechanical energy is used in their extraction and processing. Zinc processing requires much heat, and copper and aluminum refining use large amounts of electricity.

Most of the metals produced and consumed in small volumes also are limited in crustal occurrence, and all are relatively expensive. Several of these low-volume metals are obtained as joint products of mining operations designed to obtain simultaneously other metals occurring in the same ores. Despite their low levels of use, these metals are essential to modern industry. Among the many elements fitting this description, two categories are especially prominent: the alloying metals and the precious metals.

The alloying metals have many individual characteristics and a multitude of uses, but they all share one kind of application: their use in combination with other metals, especially steel, to give special properties to the finished product. For most of them, this is their main application. Because this is a derived use, their demand structures and price levels are usually derived also. If the price of one of the alloying metals should fall, for example, it is unlikely that any additional amounts of it would be consumed, for the quantity required depends on the current level of steel production. Pricing is further complicated for those alloying metals obtained as joint products. Because their output is tied to that of other metals with different demand conditions, changes in price have little effect on quantities produced. Although the alloying metals are often used in minute quantities, they have such an essential function that they are often referred to as *vitamin elements.* Some substitution among them is possible, but in many cases it is not.

Although a few of the alloying elements are plentiful in the earth's crust, others are rare. It is important here to distinguish between *rarity,* which is determined by an element's relative physical abundance in the earth's crust, and *scarcity,* an economic concept that refers to the costs of acquisition at a particular time and place. Three alloy metals appear to present no immediate problems of scarcity: chromium, titanium, and magnesium.

Because chromium helps steel to keep a sharp cutting edge even at high temperatures, it is employed in high-speed steels, a use for which chromium has no satisfactory substitute. Together with iron and nickel, it is also one of the principal constituents of stainless steels, a large and particularly important family of alloys. Chromium is fairly plentiful, four-fifths of total output coming from South Africa, the former USSR, Turkey, Zimbabwe, and the Philippines. Another abundant alloying element, titanium, comprises 0.86 percent of the earth's crust, and most of its current output is in Canada, Japan, the United States, Australia, and Brazil. It is a lightweight, high-strength, corrosion-resistant metal used as an alloy of steel as well as in aerospace applications and in paint pigments. Magnesium is the lightest of all the metals, yet it is very strong. It is used to produce lightweight, corrosion-resistant alloys and in chemical production. It, too, is widespread in occurrence. Magnesium is consumed in only small amounts and total output is not great. At present, most of the world supply is obtained through electrolysis of seawater. At current levels of demand, therefore, magnesium poses no supply problems.

Supply is more critical for most of the other alloying elements, especially nickel, molybdenum, tin, and tungsten. Shortages of tin and tungsten are possible in the near future.

Occasionally, these four elements occur separately; but these individual occurrences are in special metallogenic provinces—regions that have undergone a rare combination of geological events. More often they occur as by-products or joint products with other elements, which means that a shift in demand and price may have little effect on the supply.

Most of the nickel that is mined is used in stainless steels and high-temperature and electrical alloys. Its crustal occurrence is small and it is found concentrated in only a few places: Russia, Canada, New Caledonia, Indonesia, Australia, and China (Figure 5.24). Molybdenum imparts toughness and resilience to steel, and this is its chief use. Like nickel, its occurrence is highly erratic. Some of it is obtained as a by-product of copper, but most comes from a metallogenic province that extends north and south through the Canadian and U.S. Rocky Mountains.

Tin, long valued for its corrosion-resistant properties, is used for plating iron and steel and as an alloy of copper in the production of bronze. Most of its output comes from two metallogenic provinces—one in Southeast Asia and the other in South America (Figure 5.26). The tin supply from these sources is dwindling, however. Tungsten often occurs together with tin in its main source region, which extends in Asia from Korea to Malaysia. It makes exceedingly hard alloys with steel and is also used to manufacture tungsten carbide for cutting tools.

The precious metals—silver, gold, and the platinum group—are another important class of elements whose supply is diminishing. Since ancient times silver and gold have been prized for their beauty and indestructibility. The precious metals always have been rare but they are becoming increasingly scarce today as their demand grows. Silver has a number of very useful properties, and much more would be used if it were less costly. Its principal applications are in coinage, household silver, and jewelry, but industrial applications constitute its greatest market. Silver is the main ingredient of photographic film, and it is also used in critical electrical applications because of its conductivity, which is even greater than that of copper.

Silver is naturally rare (only 0.000008 percent of the earth's crust by weight). The world's major source area is the Great Cordillera of the western Americas; smaller amounts are found in the former USSR and Australia. Today, most of the newly mined silver is obtained as a by-product of lead, zinc, and copper operations. Very little is mined for its own sake, as the ore is rarely rich enough.

Because it occurs in the native state and is easily worked, gold was used for coinage and shaped into jewelry by the earliest civilizations. The antiquity, beauty, and rarity (0.0000002 percent of the earth's crust) of gold have endowed it with a mystical aura. This esoteric quality of gold is apparent in the tenacity with which modern governments cling to it as a basis for their currencies in the face of a steadily dwindling natural store of the metal. One of its principal commercial uses continues to be in jewelry making, where it is highly regarded for its lustrous appearance and great value. However, gold's inertness and resistance to corrosion account for many of its growing number of industrial applications. Although some gold is produced in 71 countries, 90 percent of the total output comes from South Africa (two-thirds), the former USSR (one-eighth), Canada, the United States, and Australia.

In modern times, gold and silver have been joined by another group of precious metals, the platinoids. In addition to platinum, the main member of the group, these include five other closely related metals that invariably occur together in nature. They are not quite as rare as gold, and the world supply seems fairly secure at present rates of consumption. The platinoids are acquiring a growing number of industrial applications, in addition to their use in jewelry, and current projections could prove excessively optimistic. The former USSR, South Africa, and Canada are the principal sources.

Another valuable element that does not fit into any of these categories is the industrial metal mercury, which appears in the liquid state at ordinary temperatures. Although mercury is generally regarded as indispensable to any number of industrial applications, its supply is dwindling. The ancient Spanish mines remain the leading source but their expected life is limited.

Other Nonrenewable Resources

Two other classes of nonrenewable resources remain to be considered: (1) the mineral raw materials used for the manufacture of fertilizers and other chemical products, and (2) the nonmetallic-mineral building materials. Both of these are essential to the functioning of a modern economy, and they affect every member of society either directly or indirectly. Will the supply of these be adequate to support a growing population?

As we noted earlier in the chapter on food supply (Chapter 4), the best hope for feeding the expected additions to the world population is to increase the yield of land currently under the plow. Chemical fertilizers are essential to achieving this increase, along with improved seeds and more water. Although every plant type has its own particular combination of requirements, all crops must have nitrogen, phosphorus, potassium, calcium, and sulfur. These are natural constituents of some soils but not all. Moreover, some plants make unusually heavy demands on certain elements and quickly deplete them from the soil. These nutrients must be replaced for subsequent plantings.

Farmers have traditionally restored plant food elements to the soil either by *fallowing*—that is, resting the soil so that it can recuperate naturally—or by *crop rotations* that alternate soil-depleting crops with soil-restoring ones such as the legumes. Another way of restoring nutrients to the soil is through the application of organic fertilizers, both animal manures and human wastes. This is inadequate for today's needs, however, and manufactured fertilizers therefore are essential.

The mineral raw materials for manufacturing fertilizers are also used to produce other chemical products and have a variety of other industrial applications. However, fertilizer manufacture is the largest single market for these materials. The United States is still the leading producer and consumer of chemical fertilizers, which were responsible for the quantum gain in agricultural productivity that occurred after World War II.

The original source of nitrogen for fertilizers was from naturally occurring compounds, the most important deposits being those in Chile's Atacama Desert. Today, Chile supplies only minor amounts. Much of the remainder is extracted directly from the atmosphere, of which nitrogen is the largest constituent element. In addition to large quantities of electricity, the other major requirement for synthesizing nitrogenous fertilizers is hydrogen, with which the nitrogen is combined to produce a water-soluble ammonia compound that plants can readily assimilate. Ammonia also is obtained as a by-product of coke-oven operations, most of which are associated with the steel industry.

Phosphorus is essential to plant growth, but it is easily exhausted by intensive cultivation. The chief commercial source of phosphorus is phosphate rock (apatite), which is treated with sulfuric acid to make it water-soluble and thus accessible to plants. The resulting superphosphate is very concentrated. Phosphorus is an abundant element, constituting 0.1 percent of the earth's crustal weight, but most phosphate rock is found among the marine sediments of old sea beds. Despite the large global reserve of this mineral, deposits of commercial size and quality occur in only a few places (Figure 5.27). The United States produces 27 percent of the total world output, most of the rest coming from the former USSR and North Africa. One consequence of the unequal distribution of this vital material is the large quantity of it that moves in international trade.

Another abundant element that produces a vital fertilizer is potassium, which comprises 1.68 percent of the earth's crust. Potassium is widely distributed throughout the world, but not in a readily usable soluble form. Most of it is obtained commercially from saline residues formed by the evaporation of inland seas that existed in previous geological eras. Total reserves are very great, but the chief source areas are the former USSR, Canada, various European countries, and the United States. Israel and Jordan also extract this chemical, among others, from the Dead Sea salts. See Figure 5.27.

Calcium is important to certain crops, especially corn and other grains. It is a natural constituent of certain soils in sedimentary regions and it reaches high levels of concentration in subhumid lands, such as the plains and prairies of western United States and Canada and the steppes of Russia. These are all extremely productive soils.

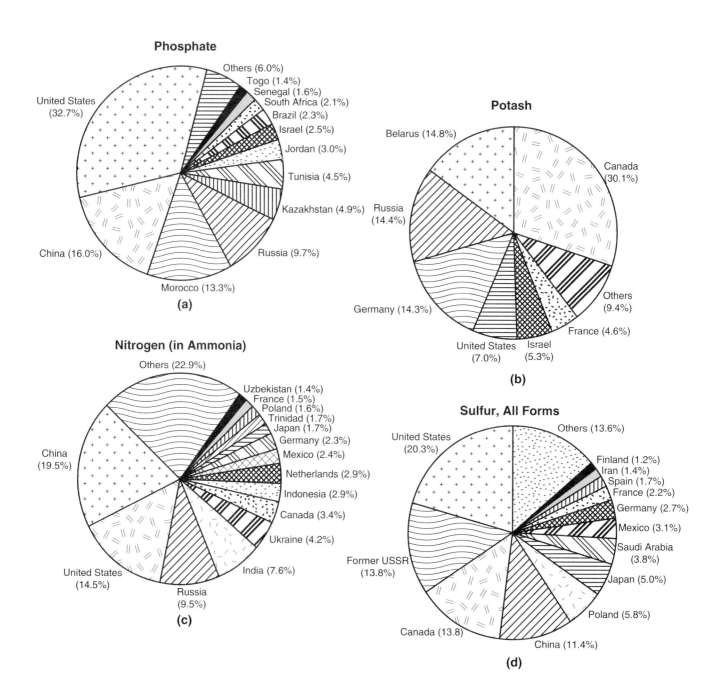

FIGURE 5.27   World production of mineral fertilizers, 1992. Three of the four principal fertilizer raw materials are mineral products; the fourth, nitrogen, is extracted mainly from the atmosphere, then combined with hydrogen to form ammonium nitrate. Only one-fourth of the world's sulfur now comes from native sulfur deposits. The remainder is extracted from mined pyrites or is obtained as a by-product of the oil and natural gas industries, coal treatment, and metal smelting. [*Source:* U.S. Bureau of Mines, *Minerals Yearbook 1992* (Washington, DC: U.S. Government Printing Office, 1994).]

The calcium content of many other soils is inadequate, however, and easily exhausted by intensive cultivation in humid areas. Lime needed for replacement of this lost element is easily obtainable in many parts of the world wherever limestone is available. Calcium is one of the most plentiful elements, and processing is simple.

The most basic chemical raw material is sulfur, which has an endless number of uses in chemical production and manufacturing in general. The largest single application, however, is fertilizer production, which consumes two-fifths of total output. Sulfur is used both in the manufacture of superphosphates and ammonia sulfates. In addition, much of the chemical industry's use of sulfur goes eventually into agricultural applications, including insecticides and herbicides. Sulfur is widespread and abundant, being united in nature with many other elements (Figure 5.27). Relatively pure elemental sulfur is also available in limited quantities and in specific places. Volcanic cones in Japan, Sicily, and the Chilean Andes provide a certain amount, but the largest sources are coastal salt dome deposits along the margins of the Gulf of Mexico. Increasing output is coming from fossil fuels, where it is obtained in the purification of oil and gas and collected from coal smoke. It also constitutes a by-product from the processing of sulphide metallic ores. These and other similar occurrences assure an ample supply of sulfur.

Total reserves of all the principal fertilizer raw materials are thus very large. No world shortage is apparent for the foreseeable future despite increasingly heavy demands for agricultural, chemical, and general industrial applications. The resource problem resulting from consumption of these minerals concerns the drain that their use imposes indirectly on other resources. Because the nations of the world are unequally endowed with fertilizer materials (except for atmospheric nitrogen), much long-range transporting of bulky commodities is required, thereby consuming much energy and other resources. Moreover, fertilizer production involves large inputs of capital and draws heavily on fossil fuels, electric power, and other chemicals.

The rocks and earthen materials that are used for building purposes are so common that their true importance is often overlooked. In volume of output they lead all the minerals, and in value they are second only to the fossil fuels.

Some of the building materials—such as sand and gravel, crushed stone, and dimension stone—are used directly with almost no further treatment after extraction. Others—including asbestos, clays, and the raw materials for glass and cement—receive considerable processing before final use.

Some of these commodities are among the most plentiful natural resources, and, with special exceptions, tend to be found in a great many places. As in the case of the fertilizer raw materials, therefore, the main long-run supply problem that the mineral building materials present is their effect on other resources. Their extraction is highly mechanized, using power machinery made of metals and burning fossil fuels. Most of the building materials are heavy and bulky, and their transportation makes further demands on the mechanical energy supply. Their processing, too, in some instances consumes large amounts of heat. Any projections of future use of these commodities therefore must take into account their substantial effects on the energy supply.

SOLUTIONS FOR MINERAL SUPPLY PROBLEMS.

Every mineral resource has its ultimate limit, yet the demand for minerals continues to grow steadily. In the past, the Americas, Africa, Asia, and Australia quickly yielded fabulous finds of rich ores occurring in deposits at or near the earth's surface. Today, exploration must proceed more painstakingly in the search for hidden deposits. Ultimate exhaustion of particular nonrenewable resources appears to many thus to be inevitable. According to Malthusian prophets of doom, approaching exhaustion will be signaled well in advance when growing shortages force prices upward until they finally become prohibitive. But the optimists who place their trust in technology think otherwise, arguing that instead of scarcity and skyrocketing prices, the end for such resources will be marked by alternatives, abandonment, and prices that collapse rather than skyrocket.

So far, the technologists seem to have the better of the argument. Stanford University biologist Paul Ehrlich, whose 1968 book *The Population Bomb* had predicted that by the end of the 1980s the population crisis would be on the world, and that hundreds of millions of people would have starved, wagered economist Julian Simon in 1980 that the price of five basic metals would rise. Ten years and 800 million people later, Ehrlich lost his $1,000 despite his prediction that a rising population would increase demand for and prices of the metals. In fact, as Simon had surmised, their prices had all fallen.

How is technology stretching out the life-spans of existing resources, and crafting substitutes? Among the new developments that are helping to keep known reserves from dwindling are new methods for discovering, mining, extracting, and refining minerals. In the past, such technological advances have had the effect of reducing costs (or at least preventing prices from rising unduly). They have also made feasible the exploitation of materials that had not previously been classified as resources because of their remoteness or poor quality.

Some optimists are predicting that technology will eventually provide such an abundance of very cheap electricity from new sources that it will become feasible to use this to extract and process minerals from sources now considered unorthodox. The costs of renewable energy are plummeting, according to a October 7, 1995, article in *The Economist*. With abundant cheap energy, one such source, it is suggested, could be the oceans, which cover 71 percent of the earth's surface to an average depth of nearly 2.5 miles. This great volume of salt water contains much dissolved material—as much as 160 million tons of solids per cubic mile. Salt, magnesium, sulfur, calcium, and potassium constitute 99.5 percent of this. Other, more valuable, elements in a cubic mile of seawater include 47 tons of zinc, 14 tons of copper, 14 tons of tin, 1 ton of silver, and 40 pounds of gold. Sodium, chlorine, magnesium, and bromine are already being extracted electrolytically from the sea. One of the problems with the proposal is the disposal of the enormous tonnages of waste materials. Even more serious is that the valuable metals are contained in extremely dilute solutions, which would require that huge quantities of water be treated. The most serious problem of all is the amount of energy needed to do the job.

Fanciful as such ideas may appear, certain other radical methods are being actively pursued with some success. One is the development of techniques for seeking out ores deep beneath the earth's surface and for determining the most promising areas in which to concentrate exploration. Many people insist that more resources are yet to be found, both in areas that have already been explored and in some that have not yet been thoroughly surveyed. These individuals believe that better exploration techniques and an improved knowledge of regional geology will substantially expand reserves of many commodities. Remote sensing of the earth's environment from orbiting satellites has had some success in accomplishing these ends.

Even the most confident of the technology optimists, however, are coming to agree that we should take better care of the mineral resources available now. The recent success in conserving energy described before has stimulated interest in this approach to enhancing other earth resources. A promising place to begin is the reduction of waste in extraction and processing. Indeed, surprisingly large quantities of valuable mineral materials are lost in the earlier stages of production. Underground mining is especially wasteful. Pillars left to support mine roofs are often rich in minerals, but these have traditionally been left behind after the mine is abandoned. Many minerals are overlooked, owing to ignorance of irregularities in the shape of the ore body; others are ignored because the ores are considered too lean for economical extraction. Although improved techniques may subsequently allow these residues to be of use, reopening an abandoned flooded mine is usually difficult.

Open-pit or strip-mining operations are ordinarily far more efficient in extracting most of the valuable mineral. Perhaps the best example of this is the mining and processing of porphyry copper ores, which result in virtually 100 percent recovery of the copper from ores averaging below 0.9 percent in the United States. In addition, these techniques yield valuable by-products, such as gold and silver.

Several techniques permit resources to be used more efficiently in manufacturing. The quantity of a metal that is required for a given application often can be reduced, for example, by producing the metal to closer tolerances or by adding alloys to increase its strength. Today, a ton of steel gives about 43 percent more structural support than the same amount would have provided a few years ago. Because of this, it is possible to make structural members and sheets thinner than before.

In addition to these advances, certain others are equally feasible but require changed social attitudes and goals. Thus, one way to husband large quantities of valuable resources would be to increase the durability of manufactured products. This is desirable not only for goods employing scarce materials but even those using abundant ones, for valuable energy resources are required for their manufacture in either case. Most advanced societies have opportunities for changes in life-style that would deemphasize high per capita levels of resource use.

The idea of reusing valuable metals and other materials has received much attention recently, but the notion is by no means a new one. Today, approximately 40 percent of the copper consumed each year has been reclaimed from discarded objects, as has a high proportion of the tin. Nearly half of the lead is recycled, most of it from old automobile batteries. More reclamation is possible, especially the materials from abandoned vehicles and household wastes, but ironically this is more likely to happen when prices increase rather than as now, decrease, or when recycled materials are cheaper than virgin supplies.

Ultimately, however, the solution may have to come via substitution—*transmaterialization*. According to resource economists Lorna M. Waddell and Walter C. Labys, transmaterialization is "a characteristic behavior of materials markets through time" in which minerals demand changes as materials linked to mature industries undergo periodic replacement by higher-quality or technologically more appropriate materials linked to new industries. The notion is clearly illustrated by Figures 5.28 to 5.30, which reveal demand shifts for materials as industrial transformation has occurred in the U.S. economy during the twentieth century. Undoubtedly, the most significant progress toward substituting new materials for old is the accelerating development of novel advanced engineering materials such as glass fibers, composites, and ceramics. See Box 5.2 for some of the innovative products now reaching world markets.

These and past achievements may seem to justify continued faith in the ability of technology to bring salvation to the problem of materials supply, but there are also those who argue that previous experience is no

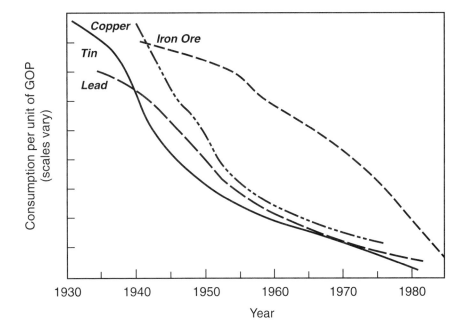

FIGURE 5.28 Consumption of Copper, Iron Ore, Tin, and Lead per Unit of GDP *Source:* (Adapted from L. M. Waddell and W. C. Labys, *Transmaterialization: Technology and Materials Demand Cycles* [(Morgantown: West Virginia University, 1987).]

longer a reliable guide to the future, feeling that excessive optimism diverts attention from the real problem of ultimate exhaustion of nonrenewable resources. The question hangs on whether human beings will assert their position as the "ultimate resource," using their brainpower to craft alternatives.

ENVIRONMENTAL QUALITY

Thus far, our attention has focused on the quantitative results of the increasingly intensive exploitation of our physical environment. The main question has been whether

sufficient resources exist to support large numbers of people at ever-higher levels of per capita consumption. Now we consider the qualitative aspects: How are rising levels of human activity affecting the world as a place in which to live?

The Physical Environment

Pollution is a problem with many facets. At the least, it concerns aesthetics; at the most, it poses a threat to the ecosystem involving the survival of human life itself. Pollution wastes important resources during the process of contami-

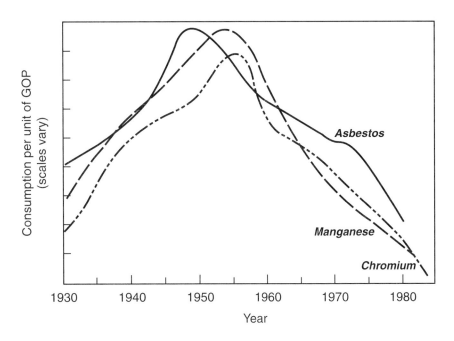

FIGURE 5.29 Consumption of asbestos, chromium, and manganese per unit of GDP.

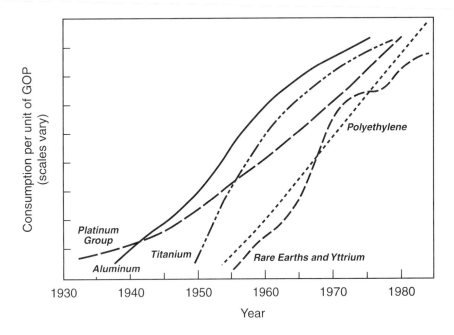

FIGURE 5.30 Consumption of aluminum, platinum, rare earths and yttrium, and titanium per unit of GDP.

nating the air and water. The compounds of mercury and lead entering the atmosphere and water supplies are serious pollutants, but they also represent the loss of scarce metals. And just as resource use is growing even more rapidly than the population, so also is pollution rising. This is evidence of the relationship that pollution bears to agricultural activity and industrialization.

The impact of pollution tends to be delayed, raising the danger that it will exceed the limits of safety before we become aware of the problem. Many long-lived toxic substances travel great distances and accumulate in unforeseen places.

Contamination of the Atmosphere

Air pollution occurs when waste gases and solid particles enter the atmosphere and spread. In the form of smog (smoke plus fog) it hangs visibly over large industrial cities, so thick at times that it shuts out much of the sunlight. It assails the other senses, too, irritating the eyes and lungs and issuing repulsive odors. Some other common effects of air pollution are corrosion of paint, steel, rubber, nylon stockings, and statuary.

To a major extent, air pollution is a product of the consumption of energy, especially the combustion of fossil fuels, and of many industrial processes. Among the greatest offenders are the internal combustion engines that power passenger cars, buses, trucks, and aircraft, all of which emit great quantities of noxious gases: carbon dioxide, carbon monoxide, sulfur oxides, nitrogen oxides, particulate matter (soot), and tetraethyl lead. The most serious industrial offenders are pulp and paper mills, iron and steel mills,

petroleum refineries, smelters, and chemical plants, which contribute enormous tonnages of carbon monoxide, sulfur dioxide, nitrogen oxide, and fly ash to the atmosphere.

The cleanest form of energy, electricity, is the source of some of the worst pollution. Thermal generating plants contribute one-fifth of all the particulates and nitrogen oxides and half the sulfur oxides sent aloft from the United States annually. Sulfur compounds emitted from coal-burning plants become dissolved in particles of moisture within the upper atmosphere to form sulfuric acid. Drifting with the prevailing winds from its industrial source, this airborne moisture subsequently falls as "acid rain," which is accused of destroying forests and other vegetation and of killing water life in ponds and lakes. Increasingly, this is becoming the subject of international disputes. Canadian provinces downwind of the Ohio River Valley's coal-burning industries protest the environmental damage attributed to this source, and several Western European countries are in contention over the acid rain that crosses their borders from elsewhere to kill forests and water life. Nuclear power plants, which contribute a growing proportion of the world's electricity, avoid the atmospheric pollution problems of conventional power plants but add new environmental hazards of their own.

A further source of atmospheric pollution is *space heating.* The use of fossil fuels to heat homes, offices, and factories adds much to the total load. The burning of trash by householders and also by municipalities, commercial junk dealers, and others is an additional source.

Each of the principal contaminants of the atmosphere is capable of becoming extremely hazardous to human beings. These toxic substances in the atmosphere tend to be

BOX 5.2 *Nonmetallic Substitutes for Scarce Metals*

One of the most encouraging solutions for the imminent depletion of crucial metallic elements is the trend toward substituting new classes of nonmetallic materials for these. Intensified efforts to develop *advanced engineering materials* have yielded a variety of synthesized substances with properties that match or even exceed those of conventional metals now in use. The success of this work is suggested by the degree to which plastics are replacing metals in a growing variety of uses, from plumbing pipes to automotive pads. Further augmenting the usefulness of these advanced plastics has been the recent development of *composites,* products in which high-strength fibers of such materials as graphite or glass are embedded in a plastic matrix. Worldwide demand for these extraordinarily strong, light materials has burgeoned as their technical merits and cost effectiveness in automotive, aerospace, and other industries have come to be appreciated.

Another group of engineered materials that holds great promise for advanced applications is *ceramics*—a type of production that is rooted in one of the most ancient of human technologies, the making of pottery and bricks. Ceramics are products manufactured from a nonmetallic mineral by firing at high temperatures. One of their prime attractions is that they are made from some of the commonest, cheapest, and most widely available earthen materials, such as clay and silicon.

Advanced ceramics have quickly forged a global market, totaling $12 billion in 1990. An early triumph of advanced *electronic ceramics* was fiber optics, which, because of their superior efficiency, are replacing copper and aluminum cables in communications. Equally bright are the prospects for advanced *structural ceramics,* whose applications include automotive heat engine components, cutting tools, and wear- and corrosion-resistant industrial components. The first ceramic-intensive auto and truck engine s(containing at least six ceramic components) are scheduled for the Japanese and US markets by 1999. The Japanese now dominate the world market for advanced ceramics with 57 percent of the total in 1988, as against 31 percent for the United States and 12 percent for Europe.

Despite the recency of these radical new human-made materials, they appear destined to relieve much of the pressure on conventional metallic elements, especially the increasingly scarce alloying metals. The fact that their raw ingredients are so widespread and cheap is an obvious boon to Japan and other resource-poor industrialized countries on the Pacific rim. Advanced engineering materials would thus seem to be a case favoring the technological optimists.

---

slow-acting with people of normal health, but they may affect with tragic suddenness the very old, very young, or those with respiratory ailments.

Evidence is mounting that atmospheric pollutants may even affect the weather and perhaps alter climatic patterns. Because all energy is ultimately dissipated as heat, the cumulative effect of energy consumption on a large scale is to warm the atmosphere. It has been estimated that by the year 2000, the amount of heat released by human activities may be equal to 18 percent of incoming solar energy. This may eventually impose a limit to the amount of mechanical energy that can be safely used.

Probably the most valuable resource of all is water. The total amount on the earth's surface, below it, or above it, is vast; but 99.35 percent of this is in the oceans or locked in the polar ice caps and thus not directly accessible for human consumption. The remaining 0.65 percent is all that we have to use (except for navigation); this occurs as ground water or is in lakes or streams. When viewed on a global scale, water is a renewable resource; at the local level, it can be a vanishing resource.

During its stay on earth, water is often used and reused many times for municipal purposes, industrial cooling, process water, or irrigation. Almost every time that water is used, contaminants are added to it. Flowing water has natural recuperative powers, but these can be easily exceeded under intensive use. It must usually then be treated before reuse, but much of the water that contains municipal and industrial wastes is incompletely treated, and some is dumped into streams with no treatment at all.

The Cost of Growth

The accelerating pace of modern living has thus brought with it a multitude of problems. Increasing numbers of people and rising volumes of industrial production have resulted in contamination of the atmosphere, pollution of water, disfiguration of the landscape, and deterioration of human relationships within an environment that is being used with ever-greater intensity. These are the complications that have accompanied our efforts to reach successively higher levels of material well-being measured in terms of more and better transportation, housing, appliances, clothing, recreation, medical care, and other specialized services of a proliferating variety—in other words, all that is contained in that familiar measure called the gross national product (GNP). More formally defined, GNP represents a country's total annual output of goods and services.

Today, some people are saying that the GNP has been misleading us, that it does not take into account hidden costs exacted by problems of the kinds just described. Such costs, it is said, actually reduce the total benefits gained from rising output. As a more realistic index of how well off a population may be, economists William Nordhaus and James Tobin have proposed a Measure of Economic Welfare, MEW. This is derived by adjusting the GNP to allow for the costs to a society resulting from environmental deterioration and the problems of contemporary urban life. More euphoniously, and perhaps more accurately, Paul Samuelson has relabeled this measure Net Economic Welfare, or NEW.

Figure 5.31 illustrates the relationship between GNP and NEW as this evolved during a four-decade period. Note how steeply per capita GNP climbed following World War II. On the other hand, NEW rose much more slowly, owing to the cumulative effects of modern urban problems. Because the two curves are rising at different rates, the gap between them is widening. If effective steps should be taken to solve the problems caused by growth, NEW would begin to rise more steeply; however, the costs of such remedial measures—for example, sewage treatment plants and devices for precipitating pollutants in factory stack gases—would reduce the slope of the GNP curve. In this way the gap between the two would begin to close and GNP would thereby gain increased reliability as a measure of a society's well-being.

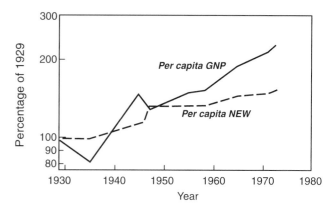

FIGURE 5.31   Differential growth of net economic welfare and gross national product. Note that as per capita GNP dropped during the Great Depression, net economic welfare (NEW) remained little changed. When war production brought a sharp rise in GNP during the 1940s, NEW lagged behind until the period of postwar readjustment. Since that time, GNP has continued to rise more rapidly than NEW. (Drafted from trends suggested by Paul Samuelson.)

VOCABULARY

The new vocabulary items, defined in the Glossary, are

afforestation	environmental constraints	living plant bank
alloying	environmental damage	Measure of Economic Welfare (MEW)
animal stocks	exhausted	metallic ores
animate energy	exploitation	metallic reserves
atmospheric pollution	fallow	metals
by-product	fission	mineral deposit
coal	fossil-fuel bank	natural gas
conservation	fossil fuels	Net Economic Welfare (NEW)
crop rotation	fusion	noncommercial energy
dematerialization	geothermal energy	nonferrous metals
electricity	geothermal power	nuclear-fuel bank
energy	hydrocarbons	oil reserve
energy crisis	hydroelectricity	per capita energy consumption
energy efficiency	inanimate energy	plant stocks
energy shortage	liquefied natural gas (LNG)	pollution

power of ocean tides	scarcity	transmaterialization
precious metals	solar energy	uranium
price elasticity of demand	spatial distribution of resources	waste disposal
proven reserves	synfuels	water contamination
rarity	thermoelectricity	water-storage bank
reserve		

TOPICS FOR DISCUSSION

1. Discuss the relationship between resource use and development, and suggest the implications this holds for future supplies of nonrenewable resources. Define "reserve," indicate why reserve estimates fluctuate from time to time, and describe the process of resource exhaustion.

2. How do oil, natural gas, and coal differ in their spatial patterns of occurrence, exploitation, consumption, and trade? Account for these differences. How was OPEC able to gain command over world oil markets, and what caused this control to slip by the mid-1980s?

3. Where is future demand for energy likely to be greatest and why? What sources of energy are likely to predominate in the short-run future? In the longer run? Explore the various measures available to us for extending current supplies of energy and for ensuring future supplies. Should we be optimistic or pessimistic about the short-run and long-run prospects for energy?

4. Why are many observers more worried about world supplies of industrial raw materials than they are about energy? What classes of industrial materials give the greatest cause for concern and why? Discuss the political and economic implications of the erratic spatial distribution of minerals. Why have OPEC-like cartels failed to develop in the case of industrial materials?

5. Not only does pollution poison the physical environment and threaten human health but it also constitutes a waste of scarce and valuable physical resources. Explain. Discuss the implications of pollution for international politics and for economic development. Interpret Samuelson's concept of Net Economic Welfare.

FURTHER READINGS

Chameides, W. L., P. S. Kasibhatla, J. Yienger, and H. Levy II. (1994). Growth of Continental-Scale Metro-Agro-Plexes, Regional Ozone Production, and World Food Production. *Science,* 264:74–77.

The authors claim that three regions of the northern midlatitudes, the continental-scale metro-agro-plexes, presently dominate global industrial and agricultural productivity. Although these regions cover only 23 percent of the Earth's continents, they account for most of the world's commercial energy consumption, fertilizer use, food-crop production, and food exports. They also account for more than half of the world's atmospheric nitrogen oxide (NOX) emissions and, as a result, are prone to ground-level ozone (O3) pollution during the summer months. On the basis of a global simulation of atmospheric reactive nitrogen compounds, it is estimated that about 10 to 35 percent of the world's grain production may occur in parts of these regions where ozone pollution may reduce crop yields. Exposure to yield-reducing ozone pollution may triple by 2025 if rising anthropogenic NOX emissions are not abated.

Darmstadter, Joel, Hans H. Landsberg, Herbert C. Morton, and Michael J. Coada. (1983). *Energy Today and Tomorrow: Living with Uncertainty.* Englewood Cliffs, NJ. Prentice Hall.

This concise review and analysis of contemporary energy issues is based on the authors' work at the Center for Energy Policy Research at Resources for the Future. Included is a useful examination of the contrasting views of "limitationists" and "expansionists" on resource questions.

Hodges, Carroll Ann. (1995). Mineral Resources, Environmental Issues, and Land Use. *Science,* 268:1305–1312.

Argues that contrary to predictions from the 1950s through the mid-1980s, persistent shortages of nonfuel minerals have not occurred, despite prodigious consumption, and world reserves have increased. Global availability of raw materials is relevant to policy decisions regarding mineral development and land use. Justification for environmental protection may exceed that for mining a specific ore body. Demand for environmental accountability is rising worldwide, and new technologies are enabling internationalization of costs. Mineral-rich developing nations plagued by inefficient state-owned mining enterprises, high population growth rates, and environmental degradation could realize substantial benefit by reforming government policies to encourage foreign investment in resources and by appropriate allocation of mineral rents.

Skinner, Brian J. (1986). *Earth Resources.* 2nd ed. Englewood Cliffs, NJ: Prentice Hall.

Succinct discussion of the geology of existing and potential sources of energy and industrial raw materials. Describes the spatial pattern of their occurrence in the earth crust, and provides estimates of reserve size and relative scarcity.

6

Price and Other Mechanisms for Regulating Exchange

OVERVIEW

People regulate the exchange of goods and services that they require by mechanisms that are primarily social, economic, or political. Social mechanisms were dominant in the traditional economies that prevailed before the Industrial Revolution. These economies were largely self-sufficient, at the scale of the household, the region (with redistribution among households), or a set of regions (with reciprocity between regions). Reciprocity involved trade, often disguised as gift giving.

The expansion of trade to include more goods shipped over greater distances was associated with the gradual emergence of peasant economies. Peasant economies are intermediate in nature. Necessities are home-produced and are distributed according to social custom. Surpluses and specialty goods are traded on economic principles.

Full-exchange, free-enterprise economies use price to regulate exchange. Goods command a price when they are both useful and scarce. The market equilibrium price attracts just enough output to meet demand and just enough buyers to clear the market of output. Supply and demand come into balance because they have opposite relationships to price. Supply increases with price; demand decreases. If supplies are short, the price tends to rise, augmenting supplies and cutting demand. The rate of response of supply and demand (or elasticity) varies for different goods, and for market conditions such as income levels and consumer and producer preferences.

Price, supply, and demand vary systematically across regions because of transportation costs. Prices increase outward from production or market centers generating price funnels. The price funnel is the consumer price ceiling. Consumers pay central market price plus transportation costs unless local producers can sell at lower prices. Demand drops, in step with price increases, producing corresponding demand cones. The outer limit of the market area is the base of the cone, where demand falls to zero. The price floor for producers is the central market price minus transportation costs. The limit of the central market supply area is where the price floor is too low to attract supplies. The spatial market equilibrium price brings aggregate demand and supply over the market and supply areas into balance.

These economic principles and resulting geographies can be distorted by imperfect competition. Producers or consumers can distort prices at a market and across its region using basing-point price systems or uniform pricing.

Government regulation of free-enterprise economies rose sharply after the 1930s, either to strengthen competition or, conversely, to modify it. Some regulations embody explicit regional goals, such as diminishing income disparities and high unemployment in lagging regions. Other policies, though not explicitly regional, have regional impacts, because of the regional concentrations of the target commodity or target population.

Government regulation has fallen victim to failures of its own. All regulations give advantage to some group at the expense of others. Often, that advantage can be converted into a value capitalized by some group. This group is not necessarily the group intended to benefit from the

161

legislation. Regulations then become entrenched in the price system.

Political administration of the economy reached its extreme in communist countries. In principle, communist economies have no private ownership or profit. Prices are set by a central authority on the basis of assumed average costs, without taking demand or market equilibrium into account. The emphasis is on achieving production levels set by planners rather than satisfying the demands expressed by consumers.

No comparative assessment of various mechanisms of regulating exchange has yet been offered. Different mechanisms reflect different goals. Traditional societies were not oriented to growth, producing only what was needed. "Chayanov's rule" applied: the greater the productivity, the less the hours worked. Communist economies produced

more social equity than economic growth, albeit at low levels, and to achieve some growth they neglected the environment with disastrous consequences. Market economies, to encourage innovation and stimulate economic growth, have reduced governmental intervention and privatized state-run enterprises, but this has had adverse consequences too: inequality has increased, and there have been growing complaints about "fairness."

What is increasingly clear is that different types of political economies deliver different mixtures of growth, equity, and environmental integrity. What also is clear as the world approaches the twenty-first century is that one system has prevailed, that of markets. It is the triumph of this system that is driving globalization, but the very success is also leading cultures to try to introduce some sense of difference, based on alternative sets of values.

OBJECTIVES

- to describe the householding, redistribution, and reciprocity mechanisms for regulating exchange in preindustrial economies

- to discuss differences in exchange mechanisms among the principal types of political economy that divided the world prior to the collapse of communism

- to explain the mechanisms by which price regulates exchange in market economies

- to define and interpret the basic economic concepts underlying price theory and illustrate how they can be extended to apply to geographic variations in prices paid by consumers and received by producers

- to examine the role of governments in distorting market forces

- to provide a foundation for the discussion of theories of location, exchange, and interaction

COMPARATIVE ECONOMIC SYSTEMS

American anthropologists have tried to develop a classification of the many different socioeconomic systems that have emerged during the long evolution of humanity. During this evolution, they argue that change has been expressed in two ways: a steadily rising level of development, involving increasing control of the environment; and progressively more complex organization, permitting larger and larger groups to work together to mutual advantage. Up to the modern transformation of the world beginning in the Industrial Revolution, they argue, human social systems have evolved through four stages, examples of which, persisting to the present, preserve earlier patterns of exchange and distribution:

1. Hunting and gathering societies

2. Seminomadic groups engaging in simple slash-burn ("swidden") agriculture without animal husbandry

3. Settled villages of tropical agriculturalists with animal husbandry

4. Northern Hemisphere plow and irrigated agricultures dominated by complex forms of social stratification.

Fundamental transformations in these systems occurred in the past three centuries as the result of a succession of industrial, political, and social revolutions, and five types of *political economies* evolved, differing significantly in how growth takes place and how locations and land use are determined. These are, as follows.

1. Free-enterprise, decentralized, market-directed systems. In such classic laissez-faire systems, decisions are made by individuals, groups, and corporations. These decisions interact in the market through the interplay of the forces of demand and supply. Economic power and political power, vested in claims of ownership and property, are widely dispersed and competitively exercised, leading to pluralistic societies in which many groups exercise influence. Government action protects and supports the central institutions of the market and maintains the decentralization of power. In the last four decades, these market systems have first moved toward Types 2 or 3, discussed next, and then back, as economies experienced both large-scale industrial development and pressures for welfare-state redistribution, and then were downsized, deregulated, and privatized.

2. *Organizational market-negotiated systems.* In these systems, which are outgrowths of large-scale industrial development, decisions are made by negotiation among large-scale organizations-—corporations, labor unions, special-interest groups, and governments. A classic case is the alliance in Japan among business, labor, and government in what is often called "Japan Incorporated." Pitted against each other, these organizations, which are profit-oriented but not necessarily maximizers, bargain together and exist in a context of negotiated relationships. Decision-making power is determined as a matter of policy or is agreed upon by the counterbalancing of power. Listing the characteristics of these systems, we obtain the following:

(a) Organization of production is by large corporations run for the benefit of stockholders. Labor negotiates wages through large-scale unions.

(b) Consumption of end products is determined partly by individual choice, partly by special interests working through the courts, and partly by governmental policy.

(c) The power of organizations, the collective power of the government, and the free choice of individuals are all part of the system.

3. *Redistributive welfare states.* In such states, the result of liberal reactions to the problems accompanying capitalism, the free-enterprise system is modified by government action to reduce social and spatial inequities, to provide every citizen with minimum guarantees of material welfare—medical care, education, employment, housing, and pensions. This redistribution is usually achieved through differential taxation and welfare payments, but sometimes is accompanied by nationalization of industries and by direct governmental investment. There was a progressive increase in the welfare functions of governments throughout the world, but particularly in Western Europe, after the Great Depression, with an associated extension of more centralized decision making designed to make the market system satisfy social as well as economic goals. After 1980, however, the inefficiencies associated with centralization led to the countervailing move to "privatize" state-run enterprises and to reduce taxation and redistribution in the interests of efficiency.

4. *Communist economies.* This group, which is an outgrowth of twentieth-century political revolutions, took welfare-state liberalism one step further, reconstructing society around principles antithetical to those of capitalism. Dominated by single-party political systems, there was state operation of nonagricultural industries (in some, agriculture, too), centralized direction of the economy, semi-industrialized production structures except in defense, yielding per capita incomes more variable than in the West. This group included the former USSR and Eastern Europe, and still includes China, Cuba, Vietnam, and North Korea (although China and Vietnam have permitted markets to emerge while maintaining centralized political controls). In such systems:

(a) The *plan* rather than the free movement of market prices controlled production, consumption, and distribution.

(b) The essence of the plan was centralized decision making; the few decided for the many, and the activities of the many were carried on under the directives of the few.

Central direction proved incapable of guiding increasingly complex economies, however, resulting in lagging growth, continuing poverty, and mounting environmental degradation. Former Soviet President Mikhail Gorbachev recognized that communism had to be replaced by free-enterprise markets and began a reform program in 1985 that contributed to the elimination of communism in Eastern Europe and the collapse of the Soviet Union. Russia and other newly independent states such as Ukraine and Kazakhstan began to introduce market reforms and private property at the end of 1991, starting a wrenching process of economic and political transformation.

5. *Authoritarian political economies of the developing countries.* A collection of partly preindustrial and partly modernizing societies, this group still persists, characterized most commonly by one-party governments or military dictatorships and political instability, with limited capacity for public administration, small public sectors, fragmentation of the economy along geographic and modern-versus-traditional lines, imperfection of markets, limited development, continued predominance of agriculture, lower per capita product, and market dependence on foreign economic relations. This group comprises many nations in Latin America, Africa, Asia, and many small island economies.

No single theory can bridge the fundamental differences between the four types of traditional socioeconomies listed at the beginning of the chapter and the equally diverse range of modern political economies that evolved after what Karl Polanyi called "the great transformation." In traditional economies, the economy was submerged in social relationships. Several types are described in Box 6.1. Laboring was motivated by social mores and custom, and it was not for cash income. Trade was not primarily undertaken for economic gain, but to acquire prestige items, although early trade networks contributed to the subsequent growth of markets, as discussed in Box 6.2. Life was not

---

BOX 6.1 Householding, Redistribution, and Reciprocity in Smaller Scale Societies

All economic systems known up to the end of feudalism in Western Europe were organized either on the principles of reciprocity, redistribution, or householding, or on some combination of the three:

Householding

Householding is a literal translation of the Greek word *oeconomia*, the etymon for our word 'economy.' Householding means 'production for one's own use.' The economic historian Karl Polanyi has described householding in his book *The Great Transformation* as follows:

> Whether the different entities of the family or settlement or the manor form the self-sufficient unit, the principle is invariably the same: that of producing and storing for the satisfaction of the wants of the members of the group....Production for use as against production for gain is the essence of householding.

The householding unit was a self-sustaining entity. The medieval *manor,* the Roman *familia,* and the South Slav *zadruga* are all comparable examples of such householding economic systems. Large numbers of these independent economic units were the basis of feudal society in Europe.

In the householding unit, division of labor was based on age, sex, social standing, and tradition. Only when kinship or political organization demanded was *Chayanov's rule* overridden. This rule states that "the greater the relative working capacity of the household, the less its members work." The rule indicates that householding production is designed to meet the household's needs and nothing more.

Thus, the medieval manor consisted of a series of families who worked cooperatively in cultivating their communal fields, woods, pastures, and ponds. Each family had an established right to the output from certain strips of land, to pasture a certain number of animals, to use a certain amount of wood, and so forth, but it also had the responsibility to produce a surplus for the feudal lord, who in turn was responsible for security. Equity was maintained by these rights. Local demands and supplies were kept in balance.

Redistribution

In some societies equity was maintained through the institution of a strong central authority, whose function was *redistributive*. Products were delivered to this head person, or chief. They were then parceled out by this person to members of the social group as determined by custom.

Many of the ancient empires, such as the New Kingdom of Egypt, were founded upon this principle of redistribution. It remains common among many of the cattle-raising tribes of East Africa. One interesting manifestation was found in the *potlatch* of the *Kwakiutl* Indians of the Pacific Northwest, in which the chief assembled the wealth of the tribe and redistributed it by giving to others in elaborate gift-giving ceremonies.

Redistribution by government is, of course, also the fundamental difference between modern market and socialist societies, and it was the organizing principle of the now defunct communist state.

Reciprocity

The third pattern of exchange was *reciprocity*. Needs were met by exchange between complementary producers. In the Trobriand Islands of Western Melanesia, for example, inland communities were paired with coastal villages in a pattern of exchange of inland breadfruits for coastal fish. The pairing extended to particular individuals being responsible for the direct exchange, in symmetrical arrangements of remarkable regularity and persistence. Many such exchanges were disguised in the form of reciprocal giving of gifts, but the principle was the same.

In each of these socially determined exchange patterns, the orderly production and distribution of goods were secured through the discipline of general principles of behavior. Custom, law, magic, and religion cooperated to induce individuals to comply with the rules of behavior that ensured the functioning of the socioeconomic system. As long as social organization ran in the ruts of tradition, no individual economic motives needed to come into play; nor was the shirking of personal effort to be feared. Division of labor was automatically ensured. Social and economic obligations were duly discharged. Material means for an excellent display of abundance at all public festivals were guaranteed. Such were the basic considerations guiding the simplest forms of exchange, not simply in feudal Europe, but in all societies in which the marketplace is absent.

BOX 6.2 The Role of Trade in the Evolution of Peasant Markets

The gradual emergence of trade was responsible for the transition of self-sustaining groups into peasant societies and, in turn, the transformation of peasant societies into full-fledged exchange economies. A *peasant society* is one in which the household or local social group remains self-sustaining with respect to necessities such as food and shelter, but trades a surplus or a specialty for outside manufactured goods or luxuries. A full *exchange economy* is one in which the principles of the division of labor apply to every producer. In an exchange economy, very few producers, even farmers, consume more than a small part of their own specialized output, for they come to produce only that for which they have a comparative advantage, not everything.

Perhaps the earliest longer-distance trade was exploration beyond the limits of the local area, involving warlike forays or intermittent exchange for ritual goods associated with the temple, the early focus of society, and the god-king who maintained social controls. As long as the resulting exchange of goods was sporadic, market centers did not develop. Only when regular trade connections emerged was there justification for the establishment of permanent marketplaces.

One regular form of long-distance exchange was between comple-mentary production zones, for example, between plains dwellers and hill folk, each trading surpluses of their own specialty for those of the other. Market sites developed along the territorial boundary zone. At the appropriate season, often in conjunction with religious festivities, people from surrounding areas would converge on the market sites to barter surpluses. Where relations between the different groups were strained, a truce would be called and the market site would constitute neutral ground.

Local trade also emerged on the basis of regular intercourse between peasants, local craftsworkers and specialists, and town merchants and intermediaries. Surpluses would be traded for such necessities as salt, iron, or durables, and merchants would have available some luxuries and trinkets obtained from the great fairs. To fit in with work on the land, the markets would be held periodically. Links connecting long-distance trade, great fairs, and local periodic markets were provided by the town merchants, whose travels would transport the goods from one place to the other.

It was only with the emergence of local and longer-distance trade that market sites and trading posts became widespread in peasant societies. For example, in Yorubaland in West Africa, the earliest markets were located along the contact zone between forest and savanna, along coastal lagoons and creeks, or at the boundaries between different peoples. The larger markets were situated along the chief trade routes, and changed in importance with these routes. One important origin of Yoruba markets was the resting place where local populations provided services to passing groups of traders. If such resting places became popular, a market into which farmers brought their wares sprang up, and periodic market days developed. Extra-large meetings would be held less frequently, when large numbers of traders converged.

Initially at these meeting places, *bartering* was the dominant means of exchange. But gradually, some form of *money* took over as the medium of exchange, and goods began to move at prices determined by *higgling*, that is, face-to-face bargaining between buyer and seller with both trying to maximize their advantages, ultimately agreeing on mutually satisfactory payment. Under such conditions, prices are highly variable and flexible from time to time and place to place, although in each case, they reflect a balance or agreement between buyer and seller that transfers a commodity or a service from one to the other.

directed by principles of economic efficiency or distinct economic institutions. The great transformation changed all this. Initially, market systems developed in which price regulated exchange, and social motivations yielded to economic imperatives. The early markets gave way to the five different types of political economy, but as a consequence of the equally great transformation that has occurred in the last 20 years, it is one, the free-enterprise market system, that now prevails. It is therefore to the geography of price in market systems that we now turn, because this geography has much to tell us about the manner in which the forces of globalization are reshaping the world economy, as we shall see in the chapters that follow.

THE GEOGRAPHY OF PRICE IN FREE-ENTERPRISE SYSTEMS

Basic Economic Concepts

Four important microeconomic concepts enable us to develop a geography of price: the nature of *price*, the relationship of *supply and demand* to price, *market equilibrium*, and *elasticity*.

Price. Price is the rate at which a good, service, resource, or factor of production can be exchanged for any other good, service, resource, or factor of production in a manner that clears the market of available supplies and satisfies demand at that price. Goods have prices because they are *useful* and *scarce.* When something has no use, it does not command a price; when it is useful but available to all in unlimited amounts, it cannot command a price. Whether a good is useful is determined by consumer demand. Scarcity, on the other hand, is determined by the supplies generated by producers. Price, then, is determined by the demands and supplies of consumers and producers jointly interacting in a market where goods and services are exchanged for each other.

The most fundamental characteristic of free-enterprise markets is that because there are large numbers of small-scale producers and consumers, none of whom accounts for a substantial share of what is bought or sold, the individual buyer or seller is a "price taker," having no control over the price he or she must pay or can receive. The prices are determined competitively in the market. The actions of any particular individual cannot change them. Very elaborate legal safeguards (antitrust legislation) have been developed in free-enterprise societies to preserve this situation as the way of conducting business. Free-enterprise markets work best in agriculture, the precious and nonferrous metals industries, the stock exchanges, and the markets for land, homes, and other kinds of property. In some types of economic activity, however, because of the possibility of achieving economies of scale, there has been the transition to *market negotiation.* In negotiated situations, large-scale businesses are able to exercise some influence on price. These situations are said to be *imperfectly competitive.*

Demand and Supply. The relationship between demand and price is quite simple. The theory of demand postulates that, *as the price of a product falls, more of it will be bought.* This is because some people who could not buy at the higher price will begin to make purchases as prices fall, and because many buyers are likely to increase their purchases of the cheapening commodity in place of alternative goods that have become relatively more costly. In addition, if nothing else changes, the price decline will increase people's real incomes, and they will consume more because they are relatively better off.

The theory of supply postulates that *the higher the price, the more of a good that will be offered for sale* because existing sellers are eager to sell while conditions are good, and rising prices will make it attractive for new producers to enter the market. If prices fall, supplies will be withheld in the hope that prices will rise again, and some producers may go out of business. Entry and exit are affected by the relative efficiency of different producers. If prices are low only the more efficient, lower-cost mines, power-generating plants, railroad rolling stock, and so forth will be used. When prices are high, less-efficient facilities will be brought into use because the higher prices will cover the higher costs.

Demand and supply can be represented in tables (or schedules) or by graphs. Hypothetical data are given in Figure 6.1 to illustrate how the demand and supply for imaginary "thingamabobs" might react to price changes, and the typical downward-sloping demand curve and upward-sloping supply curve that result. An example, using

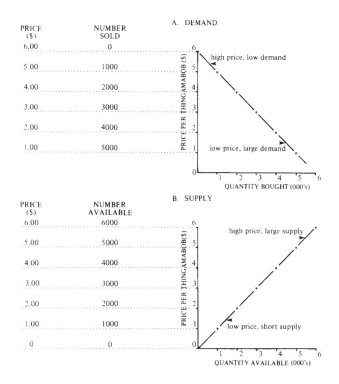

FIGURE 6.1 Demand, supply, and price. Demand has an inverse relationship to price: The higher the price, the lower the demand. Supply has a direct relationship to price: The higher the price, the greater the supply. These relationships are illustrated in table form (the demand-and-supply schedules) and by graphs.

real data, may help to emphasize that demand, even of such basics as specific food items, can be very sensitive to price. The U.S. Department of Agriculture, for example, attempted to estimate demand for a variety of meats, based on prices for 1948-1962. This period is particularly suitable for illustrating real-world demand curves because food expenditures were a much higher proportion of family budgets than is the case today, and so consumers were more sensitive to differences in food prices. (For comparable information from UK food surveys, read Appendix 6.1.) There was a fairly progressive drop in the price of chicken throughout this entire period. As prices fell, demand increased, apparently tracing out a smooth downward-sloping demand curve (Figure 6.2). Chicken consumption doubled in just 15 years in response to a halving in price (adjusted for cost of living). This change can be observed because the demand curve for chicken remained constant over the entire study period, whereas the supply curve shifted progressively.

Figure 6.3 provides a second example, the estimated demand curve for gasoline using data for 21 countries, 1970–1971. In this case, countries' supply curves vary because of differences in industrial organization and tax policy, but the 21 market equilibria trace out the demand curve.

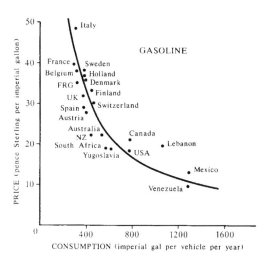

FIGURE 6.3 The demand curve for gasoline. Given the relatively small changes in gasoline prices that had occurred in Canada and the United States, Dennis Reynolds used data for some 21 countries to estimate the demand curve for gasoline. The data are for 1970–1971. Reynolds notes that the results may be affected by substantial differences in incomes, geography, history, demography, and road layout. [*Source:* D. J. Reynolds, *Consumer Expenditures on Auto Use: Income, Price Elasticities of Demand and Gasoline Rationing.* Role of the Automobile Study, Working Paper No. 17. (Ottawa: Transport Canada, 1979), p. 17]

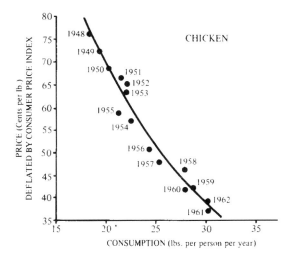

FIGURE 6.2 The demand curve for chicken, United States, 1948-1962. The demand curve for chicken remained constant in the United States over the study period: 1948–1962. The supply curve, however, kept shifting, because producers were able to produce more chicken at lower prices (in constant dollars) as the years went by. The demand curve is traced out as a sequence of market equilibrium points (see Figure 6.4). [*Source:* U.S. Department of Agriculture, Economic Research Service, Neg. ERS 2147–63(7)]

Market Equilibrium. In order to understand how demand and supply are brought into balance to produce equilibrium, it is helpful to plot supply-and-demand curves back to back on a single graph. The results for the "thingamabob" example are shown in Figure 6.4.

If suppliers are prepared to increase the quantity of a good they market as price increases, and if consumers reduce the amount they buy as price increases, then there should exist a *price at which supply equals demand.* This price, which "clears" the market of available supply and also satisfies demand, is the point of *market equilibrium.* Market equilibrium is identified on a graph of back-to-back supply and demand curves as the point of intersection (*E* in Figure 6.4).

Price will tend to fluctuate around the market equilibrium in a free-enterprise economy. If the price rises above the equilibrium, price reductions will be needed to clear the market of excess supply resulting from the price rise. If demand rises above supply, disappointed customers will scour the market, offering higher prices. Any deviation from the market equilibrium price thus triggers corrective action that pushes the price back toward the market equilibrium level.

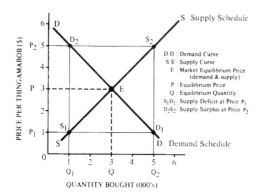

FIGURE 6.4 Market equilibrium. The market equilibrium is the point of intersection of the supply-and-demand curves (E). The market equilibrium determines the price (P) of the good, the quantity (Q) bought and sold, and total demand ($P \times Q$). At price P, buyers and sellers match purchases and sales and are just able to clear the market of available supplies. In the case of thingamabobs, $P = \$3.00$ and $Q = 3,000$, so that total demand is $\$9,000$. If the price were $\$1.00$, demand would rise to 5,000, and supply fall to 1,000, leaving a deficit ($S_1\ D_1$) of 4,000 thingamabobs. Disappointed customers would bid up the price. If the price rose to $\$5.00$, demand would fall to 1,000 and supply would increase to 5,000, leaving a surplus (S_2D_2) of 4,000. The market glut would force down prices. Thus, the market price will tend to remain at the market equilibrium level.

The natural tendency of prices to hover around the market equilibrium level makes it difficult to observe the full demand-and-supply schedules in real market conditions. Hence, the chicken and gasoline examples are of special interest. Actually, what Figure 6.2 shows is a series of market equilibria, one for each year! These market equilibria join to pick out the demand curve because the shifting supply curves intersected an unchanging demand curve at a progression of different price-and-quantity equilibrium levels. Similarly, what Figure 6.3 shows is a series of 21 market equilibria for each country that trace out the demand curve because supply conditions vary across countries, whereas the responsiveness of demand to price changes is much more consistent.

Price Elasticity of Demand. Elasticity (e) is a measure of response to price changes. The magnitude of response in demand to changes in price can vary a great deal depending on the good. For some items, such as tobacco, there is little drop in demand with increase in price. But consumers are, for example, conscious of seasonal swings in the prices of fresh fruits and vegetables and are highly responsive to these changes.

The *price elasticity of demand* is the percentage fall in demand for a product that results from a 1 percentage point increase in price. (Symmetrically, the *price elasticity of supply* is the percentage increase in supply of a product that results from a 1 percentage point increase in price.) If there is no change in demand with a change in price, the price elasticity is zero. If small changes in price produce massive shifts in demand, the price elasticity of demand approaches infinity, as is shown in Figure 6.5. An elasticity of 1.0 means that a 1.0 percent change in price results in a 1.0 percent change in quantity.

Some examples for goods in low- and high-income countries illustrate the factors affecting price elasticity of demand (Table 6.1). Luxuries tend to have higher elasticities of demand than basic goods. Meat is much more price-sensitive than rice in a low-income country. Big-ticket items such as automobiles are much more price-sensitive in high-income countries than cheap items such as matches. The availability of substitutes is important, too. Fresh foods can be replaced by dried foods (in low-income countries) or canned and frozen foods (in high-income countries) and so are price-sensitive. Liquor and tobacco, lacking effective substitutes, are not and so they have low elasticities of demand.

Income Elasticity of Demand. Demand also changes with variations in income (Table 6.2). These changes—the income elasticities of demand—are measured as the percentage change in the demand for a food item that occurs with a 1 percent increase in income. The change in demand can be negative as higher income consumers switch from less desirable foods to more desirable ones or it can be positive if demand increases with income. The United Kingdom's National Food survey has identified the changes over the years in the British consumer's shopping list and the effects that increases in income have had on it. The results are summarized in Appendix 6.1.

The Geography of Supply

Each of the basic microeconomic concepts (supply and demand, price, elasticity, and equilibrium) needs to be extended by introducing ideas of the market as a *place,* of location relative to this place, and of transportation costs, if they are to be useful in understanding the structure of the global economy. The result of such extensions is a *geography of supply,* a *geography of demand,* and a *geography of market equilibrium* in free-enterprise economic systems.

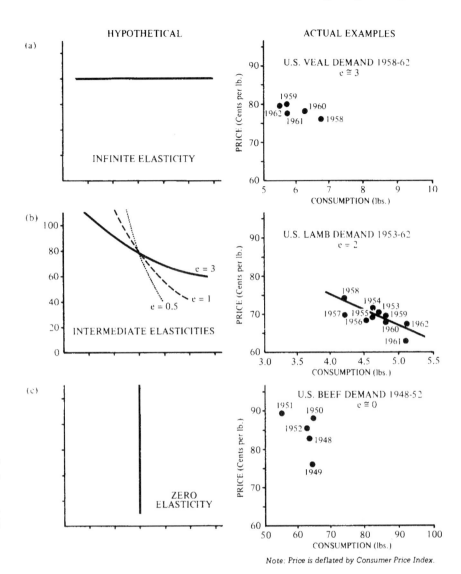

FIGURE 6.5 Price elasticity of demand. This figure shows a variety of price elasticities from zero to infinity. Note that the more sensitive consumers are to price, the higher the elasticity and the gentler the demand curve is.

Note: Price is deflated by Consumer Price Index.

TABLE 6.1

Price elasticity of demand in high- and low-income countries

| Elasticity | | Result of a Price Increase on | | Examples for | |
		(a) Total Amount of Good Purchased	(b) Total Amount Spent on Good	Low-income Countries	High-income Countries
High	2.0	Decrease is more than proportional to price increase	Decreases		Automobiles Furniture
Unitary	1.0	Decrease is exactly proportional to price increase	Stays the same	Vegetables Meat Fruit Maize Fresh fish Wheat	Clothing Gasoline Food
Low	0.5 0.2	Decrease is less than proportional to price increase	Increases	Rice	Liquor Tobacco Matches

Note: The high-income countries' elasticities are drawn from many different sources. The low-income countries' elasticities are adapted from Angus Deaton (1990). Price elasticities are nearly always negative, so the sign is usually ignored and elasticities, are given as absolute values.

TABLE 6.2

Variation in food expenditure by income level

	Income Level in $ per Annum						
	Under 5000	5000 to 9000	10,000 to 14,999	15,000 to 19,999	20,000 to 39,999	30,000 to 39,999	40,000 and Over
Household characteristics							
Age of householder (years)	44.2	51.8	59.6	45.5	42.5	41.5	43.7
Children < 18 years per household	0.29	0.58	0.57	0.61	0.77	0.97	0.90
Vehicles per household	0.6	0.9	1.1	1.4	1.7	1.9	2.3
Home ownership (%)	26.0	39.0	48.0	48.0	63.0	71.0	85.0
	Average Weekly Expenditure in Dollars						
Food eaten at home							
Flour	0.05	0.07	0.06	0.04	0.03	0.03	0.03
White bread	0.30	0.32	0.32	0.31	0.27	0.25	0.24
Doughnuts	0.10	0.11	0.13	0.15	0.13	0.16	0.18
Sirloin steak	0.07	0.04	0.06	0.10	0.11	0.10	0.16
Lamb	0.04	0.05	0.04	0.08	0.07	0.05	0.05
Fresh whole chicken	0.15	0.21	0.17	0.17	0.16	0.14	0.16
Sugar	0.15	0.16	0.15	0.15	0.11	0.10	0.10
Candy	0.22	0.19	0.26	0.22	0.31	0.40	0.44
Roasted coffee	0.23	0.22	0.26	0.23	0.26	0.24	0.27
Instant coffee	0.19	0.20	0.17	0.14	0.17	0.11	0.14
Food away from home							
Dinner	2.63	2.08	2.82	3.37	4.33	4.15	6.42
Wine	0.14	0.09	0.13	0.14	0.17	0.17	0.28
Total food expenditure	20.19	19.09	20.83	22.08	25.44	24.95	31.15

Source: David M. Smallwood, *Food Spending in American Households, 1980–1986*, Statistical Bulletin No. 791, (Washington, DC: U.S. Department of Agriculture, Economic Research Service,1990), pp.69–71. Table is for urban households. 1986

Basic Concepts. Supply curves of the type presented in Figure 6.1 ignore the systematic impact of transportation charges on the delivered cost of a good. Transportation costs increase with the distance a good has to be transported, causing selling price to increase with distance from the point of production. The result is a *supply–price funnel* of the kind illustrated in Figure 6.6.

August Lösch (1954), who introduced the term *price funnel,* provided maps and data to illustrate such price variations for a wide variety of goods in North America prior to World War II. Agricultural products were cheapest, he found, in the centers of production and increased in price outward from these centers. Potatoes in 1936 were 18 cents a pound on Prince Edward Island, for example, but 25 cents a pound in Toronto. Orange prices were 16 cents a pound in California, but 37 cents a pound in Chicago. Lösch also examined nonagricultural goods and found significant price funnels for newspapers with large market areas, automobiles, and soap, for example.

Similarly, and quite surprisingly, given the large number of small producers and the short distances milk is transported, even for milk there was in 1957–1958 a single, countrywide price funnel centered on Eau Claire, Wisconsin, at the heart of the dairy belt (Figure 6.7).

The Role of Central Markets in Setting Prices Received by Suppliers. Lösch's price funnels, rising upward and outward from supply regions, do not tell us what individual suppliers receive for their output, however. Within the supply region, there will be one or more *central markets,* and the price received by a given supplier will be the price established in that market minus the costs of transporting the product to that market. The farther the supplier is from that central market, the lower the price received, as shown in Figure 6.8.

Suppliers have a choice of selling to consumers in their local market or disposing their supplies in the central market. The supplier will sell to local consumers only if the price they are willing to pay exceeds the central market price less transportation costs. Prices in the central market minus costs of transportation therefore set a *producer's price floor,* the price that may be obtained by selling in the central market when local demand is weak.

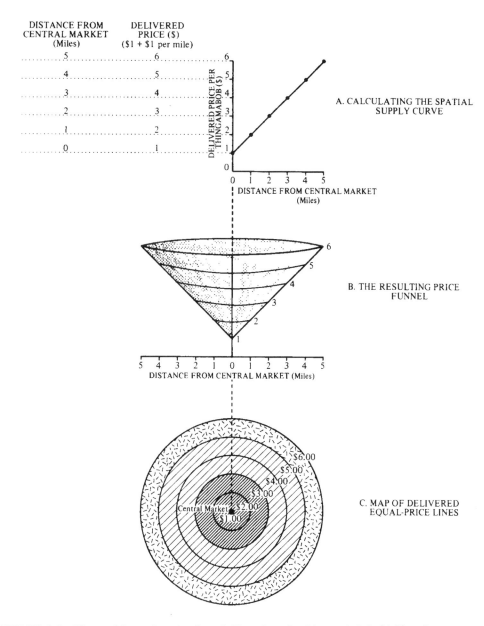

DISTANCE FROM CENTRAL MARKET (Miles)	DELIVERED PRICE ($) ($1 + $1 per mile)
5	6
4	5
3	4
2	3
1	2
0	1

A. CALCULATING THE SPATIAL SUPPLY CURVE

B. THE RESULTING PRICE FUNNEL

C. MAP OF DELIVERED EQUAL-PRICE LINES

FIGURE 6.6 The spatial supply–price funnel. The price of a thingamabob is $1.00 at the market plus a transportation charge of $1.00 per mile. The result can be shown in four equivalent ways: table, graph, price funnel, and map. Becoming familiar with all four is helpful in understanding the geography of supply. Note that a price funnel shows price against distance, whereas an ordinary supply curve shows price against quantity.

Each central market has its own *supply area.* Individual producers will sell to the central market that offers them the greatest *on-site return* (on-site return is another way of saying central market price minus transportation costs). The supply area boundary is located where the producers' price floor gradients intersect, as at *X* and *Y* in Figure 6.9. The boundary between the supply areas of competing central markets traces out the locus of minimum

on-site returns. How low that minimum is depends upon the locations of the central markets, the prices in those markets, and transportation costs. Compare the prices at boundaries *X* and *Y* in Figure 6.9.

Why Did Central Markets Emerge? Central markets are a creation of modern economies and transportation systems. In the United States, for example, until the 1850s,

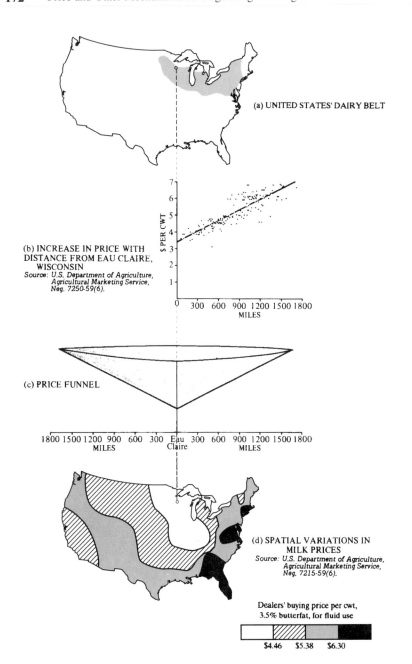

(a) UNITED STATES' DAIRY BELT

(b) INCREASE IN PRICE WITH DISTANCE FROM EAU CLAIRE, WISCONSIN
Source: U.S. Department of Agriculture, Agricultural Marketing Service, Neg. 7250-59(6).

(c) PRICE FUNNEL

(d) SPATIAL VARIATIONS IN MILK PRICES
Source: U.S. Department of Agriculture, Agricultural Marketing Service, Neg. 7215-59(6).

Dealers' buying price per cwt, 3.5% butterfat, for fluid use

$4.46 $5.38 $6.30

FIGURE 6.7   Milk prices in the United States, 1957-1958. The center of milk production in the United States is Eau Claire, Wisconsin. Milk prices increase regularly with increasing distance from Eau Claire, creating a price funnel. Prices climb from less than $4.00 per hundredweight (cwt) to more than $5.00 in California and nearly $7.00 in Florida. Prices increased on average by 2.2 cents per 10 miles.

agriculture was characterized by small production units. Transportation, communication, and marketing were local, and trading was very often a face-to-face matter between producer and consumer in a weekly market. In the last half of the nineteenth century, many changes took place that led to the development of a nationwide, commercial marketing system. Cities grew rapidly, western lands were brought into production, railroad mileage expanded quickly, and communications improved. These developments facilitated the long-distance flow of commodities from specialized production regions to food-deficit areas, but required that some other institution replace weekly face-to-face trading.

Trading therefore progressed from the informal weekly markets to formal clubs that provided a common meeting place for traders. The next step was for *commodity exchanges* to emerge and provide organized trading. Commodity exchanges are nonprofit associations of persons acting as principals or agents in the transfer of ownership of agricultural or other primary commodities. *Futures* markets are the major part of most exchange activities, trading contracts for future deliveries at agreed-on prices. *Cash* or *spot markets,* where available commodities are sold and delivered within a few hours, also are part of the commodity exchange function.

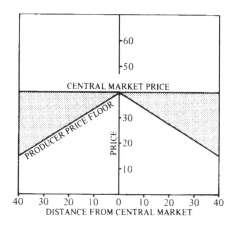

FIGURE 6.8   Producer price floors. For many agricultural products and industrial raw materials, a base price is competitively determined at one or more central markets. The supplier receives the central market price minus transportation and related charges, but may be able to sell locally at a price higher than this price floor.

What do such commodity exchanges do? Both spot and futures markets provide continuous market trading for those who wish to buy or sell. They involve large numbers of buyers and sellers, maintain quality standards, and permit a free flow of information, so that competitive prices can be determined. In effect, they are the prime example of "the market" in classical free-enterprise economies.

Commodity exchanges function as central markets for many products including livestock, grains, fruits and vegetables, wool, cotton, hides, and tobacco. For example, in the United States, corn prices are set by the price of No. 3 Yellow Corn on the Chicago Board of Trade. The prices of oats and soybeans are also set there. Barley prices are set by the quotations for No. 3 Barley in Minneapolis. Sorghums are based on No. 2 Yellow Milo at Kansas City. American cheese at factories in Wisconsin is priced at the Wisconsin Cheese Exchange. On the world scene, many metals are priced on the London Metals Exchange. Rotterdam now functions as the world's spot market for petroleum.

Chicago and London are examples of the large *terminal markets* where products from wide areas were concentrated, and it is for this reason that they developed their market concourses. Another example is that of Liverpool, which was the major international market for wheat until 1940. It first acquired this role when most of England's grain imports came from Ireland. Wheat prices registered on the Liverpool market later came to be looked on as the world price. From 1840 to 1940, the United Kingdom was the world's largest importer of wheat, and Liverpool served as the central market, setting prices for wheat regardless of its origins.

Logically, of course, the world price of wheat should be determined chiefly by the world supply of wheat and the general level of world commodity prices. From 1924 to 1938, virtually all the variation in the price of wheat at Liverpool, commonly referred to as "British parcels." was tied to variations in the world supply of wheat and British wholesale prices. A 1 percent change in supply in this

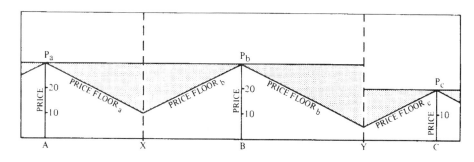

FIGURE 6.9   Supply areas of central markets. The boundaries of supply areas are set by the intersection of producer price floors from competing central markets. The boundaries are thus lines of indifference along which producers receive the same price from competing central markets. The lower a central market's price is, the smaller its supply area will be. Thus, *C*'s primary supply area (*CY*) is reduced and *B*'s (*BY*) is extended.

period was associated with a 1.4 percent change in the price of wheat in the opposite direction. A 1 percent change in the index of prices was associated with a 1.2 percent change in the index of wheat in the same direction.

United States wheat prices tended to depend directly on British wheat prices. Thus, from 1922 to 1939, three-quarters of the variation in the price of wheat in the United States at the domestic wheat-price basepoint, Kansas City, was associated with variations in the price of British parcels of wheat at Liverpool. Prices in wheat-producing areas elsewhere in the United States reflected transportation charges to Kansas City. In most years since then, however, U.S. domestic prices have been determined chiefly by the level of price support established by the government or by other governmental policies.

Role of the Market Traders. How are prices set in central markets? It is the market traders who make the whole process of balancing demands and supplies work. To illustrate, consider a trader who has been put in charge of a grain "desk" at the Continental Grain Company. A cable arrives from one of Continental's overseas offices—say, Paris. A buyer has bid for 10,000 tons of soybeans for July delivery in Rotterdam. Before accepting or countering with an offer, the trader considers future prices, world news, freight quotations, vessel bookings, the crop outlook, and the competition.

Then the trader makes a simple calculation. The basis for the final price is the "futures" quotation on the Chicago Board of Trade for July soybeans. The trader adds in the barge freight to New Orleans, the cost of handling at Continental's grain elevator there, and the ocean freight to Rotterdam. Then the trader cables the Paris office with a CIF price offer—cost, insurance, and freight.

If the trader gets an "accept" from the other side, the trader begins the task of seeking out a profit. First, the trader "hedges" by buying July futures in Chicago. Because the futures price is the basis for the actual soybean sale, the trader can limit losses this way. Then the trader tries to find cheaper soybeans. If found, July futures can be sold, and the trader's speculative profit will be the difference between the Rotterdam contract price and what the trader paid for the cheaper soybeans, less any cost of reselling July futures.

The chartering department, meanwhile, will be speculating on shipping, trying to get the best deal possible for the July delivery in Rotterdam. It may take a section of a ship under charter by another company. Or it may charter a tanker for the 10,000-ton sale; 30,000 tons excess may be filled by another sale, or it may figure on selling the space later to a competitor at a profit.

All these facts, and more, determine what Continental's profit on the sale will be. It will be months before the trader will know if the sale to Rotterdam was a success, but it is the possibility of making speculative gains that motivates the traders who maintain the free-enterprise system of buying, selling, and price determination.

The Geography of Demand

Under perfect competition, the price paid by a *consumer* increases with distance from a central market, in the manner of Lösch's price funnels (Figure 6.6). Central market price plus transportation costs from the central market sets a ceiling on the price that local consumers have to pay. They can always buy from local suppliers if prices are lower, of course, but they need never pay more than the ceiling price determined by the central market plus transportation (Figure 6.10).

Where goods or services are available from competing central markets, consumers will buy from the market offering the lowest ceiling price if they do not buy locally. Market prices plus transportation costs thus lead to ceiling price gradients that trace out *market area* boundaries where they intersect (as at X and Z in Figure 6.11). Such boundaries trace out the locus of maximum ceiling prices between adjacent central markets. There is, as a result, a direct relationship between welfare and distance: The most distant consumer pays the highest prices (Figure 6.11), just as the most distant producer receives the least (Figure 6.9). Those on the periphery are doubly disadvantaged!

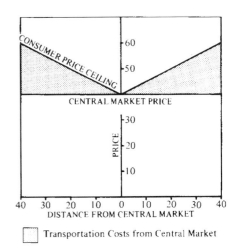

FIGURE 6.10   Consumer price ceilings. Under perfect competition, the maximum delivered price equals the central market price plus transportation. This price sets a consumer price ceiling. The consumer may be able to buy locally for lower prices, but will not pay more. Figure 6.10 can be thought of as the top half of Figure 6.8. Combined, they show two price gradients fanning out from central markets, a consumer price ceiling and a producer price floor.

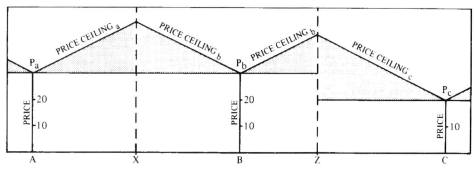

A, B, C : Locations of Central Markets
X, Z : Market Area Boundaries
AX : Primary Market Area of A
XBZ : Primary Market Area of B
ZC : Primary Market Area of C
P_a, P_b, P_c : Prices at Central Markets
▢ Transportation Costs from Central Market

FIGURE 6.11 Definition of market areas. The market area of a central market is the area in which central market price plus transportation is less than (or equal to) the delivered price from competing central markets. The lower the price at the central market area, the larger the primary market area. Thus, *C*'s primary market area (*CZ*) is increased at the expense of *B*'s (*BZ*).

The Spatial Demand Cone. Demand for a good sold at a central market can be expected to drop progressively outward from that market as transportation costs add to the price of the good. This relationship follows from the basic relationship of demand to price (see Figure 6.1). Using the demand schedule, which indicates the amount bought at each given price, and the delivered price at each distance band from the market, one can draw a *demand cone* centered on the market. The outer perimeter of the cone, where demand drops to zero, would be the market area boundary in the absence of competitive centers, and is called the *range of the good.* (See Figure 6.12.)

Consider the case of thingamabobs discussed earlier (Figures 6.1 and 6.12). The price of these delicate gadgets increases from $1 at the central market to $6 at a radius of 5 miles. Each dollar increase in price produces a decline of 1,000 in demand. Demand drops from 5,000 at the central market to zero at 6 miles distance.

A map of the market area can be drawn showing the demand contours for thingamabobs. The demand at the market boundary itself is zero. A succession of contours at $1,000-thingamabob intervals can be drawn with a spot height of 5,000 at the central market itself. The table, graph, demand cone, and map are equivalent. They all show the same information, but in different forms.

Incomes and Demand. Demand for most goods is sensitive to income, as we saw in Box 6.3. In general, lower-income families are more sensitive to price than higher-income families. Demand curves can, therefore, be drawn according to income. An example using our familiar thingamabobs is provided by Figure 6.13. In this example, the demand curve for low-income families, D_L, has a greater elasticity than that for high-income families, D_H. The total demand curve is formed by adding up the quantities demanded at each price by high- and low-income families.

These differences also may reveal themselves spatially. Suppose the market for thingamabobs is divided into high- and low-income sectors. The demand cone is steeper and the market area smaller in the low-income sector (Figure 6.14). This example demonstrates the general principle that the higher the income level is, the farther out the market area can extend.

Demand is affected by many other factors, too, besides price and income. The demand for food in Canada, for instance, has been shown to be affected by the aging of the population (older people spend less on food); the increasing proportion of women who work and smaller families (resulting in more restaurant meals and less spent on grocery food); and the increasing ethnic diversity of the population (so more food is bought in specialty food shops) (Johansen et al., 1989).

Spatial Market Equilibrium

The balancing of supply and demand in the case depicted in Figure 6.14 is a straightforward exercise. The supply-and-demand curves are drawn back-to-back and the equilibrium

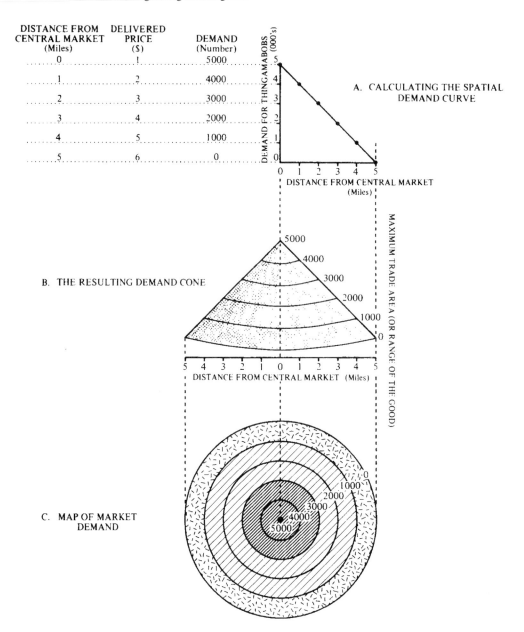

FIGURE 6.12   The spatial demand curve, or demand cone. The construction of a demand cone requires data on the delivered price with increasing distance from the market (the price funnel) and the quantity bought at each price (the demand schedule). Delivered price at each distance band is then translated into demand at each distance band. The maximum market area in the absence of competition (called the range of the good) is set by the radius at which demand falls to zero. It is important to understand that the table, graph, demand cone, and map are four equivalent ways of presenting the same information. Compare this figure with Figure 6.6.

price and quantities indicated by the point of intersection. This exercise is repeated every day in central markets throughout the world (Figure 6.15a). Suppliers can expect to receive, at the minimum, central market price *less* transportation costs (Figure 6.15b). Consumers can expect to pay, at the maximum, central market price *plus* trans-portation costs (Figure 6.15c). The total supply-and-demand curves at the central market (Figure 6.15a) are, however, an amalgam of many individual supply-and-demand curves. If you wish to understand how a combined supply curve is derived, refer to Figure 6.16. Suppose there is a central market at *M*. In the manner of Figure 6.15a the

FIGURE 6.13 Income level and market demand. Aggregate demand schedules, such as those presented in Figures 6.1 and 6.2, ignore differences in income level among consumers. Disaggregating the schedule for low- and high-income areas reveals in this hypothetical example that low-income areas are more sensitive to price. They stand to gain most with any fall in price (as in Figure 6.2), but conversely to suffer most with any increase in price. Note that the market equilibrium remains at E as in Figure 6.4 with the low-income area purchasing 1,200 and the high-income area 1,800 thingamabobs, to make a total of 3,000 as before.

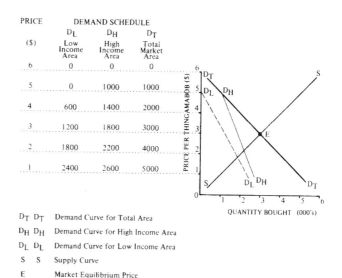

PRICE	DEMAND SCHEDULE		
($)	D_L Low Income Area	D_H High Income Area	D_T Total Market Area
6	0	0	0
5	0	1000	1000
4	600	1400	2000
3	1200	1800	3000
2	1800	2200	4000
1	2400	2600	5000

D_T D_T Demand Curve for Total Area
D_H D_H Demand Curve for High Income Area
D_L D_L Demand Curve for Low Income Area
S   S   Supply Curve
E   Market Equilibrium Price

right-hand side of the graph in Figure 6.16 shows how the combined supply curve of two producers is derived at the central market. The producers are shown at A and B on the left-hand side of the graph (Figure 6.16), which corresponds to Figure 6.15b. The problem is one of combining the two producers' individual supply curves, taking into account transportation costs. This process is described in the caption accompanying Figure 6.16.

MANAGED PRICES IN IMPERFECTLY COMPETITIVE SITUATIONS

The foregoing discussion refers to free-enterprise dynamics. But what about less-competitive situations? A market is imperfectly competitive when the actions of individual buyers or sellers can affect the equilibrium price. Such individuals are not "price-takers" forced to accept the price determined by the free play of market forces. On the contrary, in the extreme case, just one or two sellers or buyers set the market price themselves.

A situation of *monopoly* exists where a single *seller* sets the selling price, and a situation of *oligopoly* exists where relatively *few sellers* determine the price. This may be the case where a large proportion of total output of some product is accounted for by just one, or a few, manufacturing firms. *Monopsony* is where a *single buyer* dominates the market for the product and so dictates the purchase price. *Oligopsony* is where a *few buyers* dominate. A firm may be both monopsonist and monopolist. It may dominate the market for some raw materials, or components, hence setting the purchase price for them. It may also dominate the market for the finished product and so set the selling price. An automobile manufacturer, for instance, may dictate the price to parts manufacturers at which components such as

tires will be bought, and, as a *price leader,* the price at which cars will be sold on the market. Or one large firm acting as a monopsonist may *countervail* the power of another large firm, as where a retail chain accounts for a large proportion of sales of household appliances and is thus able to bid down the manufacturer's price of these items.

In conditions of imperfect competition, the industry may follow a price leader or engage in price collusion or in other discriminatory practices. Smaller firms with a local market must follow the price lead set by a dominant firm with a national market. To do otherwise would be to invite lethal retaliation, because the large firm can wipe out local competition by undercutting prices in that local area. Large firms in competition with each other realize they must restrain competition or be ruined by it. But whatever the precise circumstances, the general objectives are always the same, namely, to maximize returns either by manipulating the firm's sale price or negotiating its purchasing prices, and to stabilize the prices and volumes of goods bought or sold.

The Basing-Point System

The most common form of noncompetitive pricing is the *basing-point system.* Consumers pay a producer-dictated price quoted at a given place, the *basing point,* plus a transportation charge from that location—even if the good is produced and shipped from a nearer and lower-cost site. The purpose of the basing-point system is, of course, to entrench the advantages of the site selected as the basing point, and the producers whose facilities are concentrated there.

An example may be used to clarify the details of basing-point pricing. We have selected the British cement industry as described by Moyes (1980). Prices are administered by the Cement Maker's Federation (CMF), an

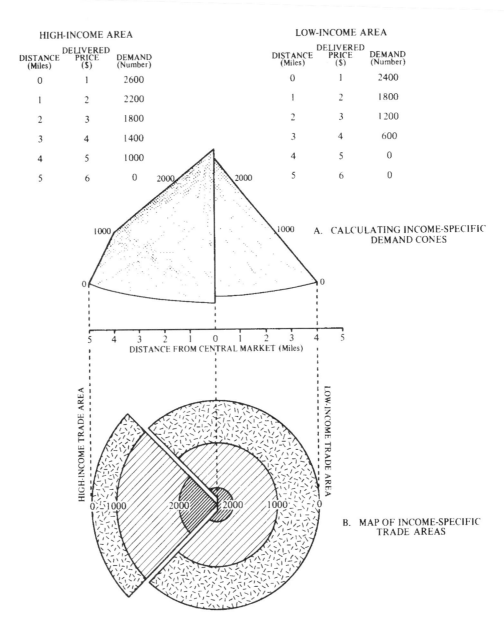

HIGH-INCOME AREA

DISTANCE (Miles)	DELIVERED PRICE ($)	DEMAND (Number)
0	1	2600
1	2	2200
2	3	1800
3	4	1400
4	5	1000
5	6	0

LOW-INCOME AREA

DISTANCE (Miles)	DELIVERED PRICE ($)	DEMAND (Number)
0	1	2400
1	2	1800
2	3	1200
3	4	600
4	5	0
5	6	0

A. CALCULATING INCOME-SPECIFIC DEMAND CONES

B. MAP OF INCOME-SPECIFIC TRADE AREAS

FIGURE 6.14   The demand cone for high- and low-income market areas. The demand schedules differ between high- and low-income areas (Figure 6.13). Therefore, the demand cone will be different for high- and low-income areas. The trade area is larger for the high-income area and smaller for the low-income area. Aggregate demand for a good within any given distance band of the central market equals the sum of the demand in the high- and low-income areas shown separately in this figure. The market boundaries occur at the price where demand falls to zero.

industry association to which all producers of any consequence belong. The price at the nominated basing points varied in March 1978, from £22.51 to £26.90 per ton, reflecting to some degree differences in production costs. Delivery charges were added to the basing point using a standard formula based on 5-mile steps. The first four steps cost 20.7 pence each. The next three cost 18.1 pence, after which all steps cost 12.9 pence each. The result was a regular concentric pattern of delivered prices radiating out from each basing point (Figure 6.17).

These results look very similar to the central market pricing discussed in the previous section. The two should not be confused, however. They differ significantly in the way in which prices are set. In basing-point systems, the price level at the basing point, the transportation cost schedule, and the number of basing points are all preset by the

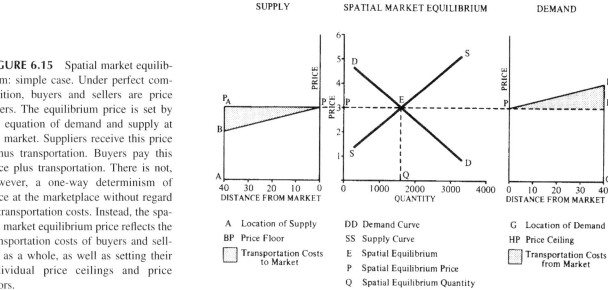

FIGURE 6.15 Spatial market equilibrium: simple case. Under perfect competition, buyers and sellers are price takers. The equilibrium price is set by the equation of demand and supply at the market. Suppliers receive this price minus transportation. Buyers pay this price plus transportation. There is not, however, a one-way determinism of price at the marketplace without regard to transportation costs. Instead, the spatial market equilibrium price reflects the transportation costs of buyers and sellers as a whole, as well as setting their individual price ceilings and price floors.

A   Location of Supply
BP   Price Floor
▨   Transportation Costs to Market

DD   Demand Curve
SS   Supply Curve
E   Spatial Equilibrium
P   Spatial Equilibrium Price
Q   Spatial Equilibrium Quantity

G   Location of Demand
HP   Price Ceiling
▨   Transportation Costs from Market

industry. With the free-enterprise central market system, these three elements of delivered cost—the price level at the central market, freight rates, and the number of central markets—are all determined by the free play of supply and demand. Industry-determined basing-point price systems were used as early as 1880 in the United States, but they did not come into widespread use until after 1901, when such a system was applied to steel by the U.S. Steel Corporation.

The U.S. Steel scheme was known as "Pittsburgh plus." Delivered prices for steel and steel products were quoted throughout the United States as the sum of a basing-point price at Pittsburgh plus a transportation charge from Pittsburgh, regardless of the actual plant price or freight costs incurred from the actual producing point. Nearer or lower-cost plants, which could actually deliver at lower cost than Pittsburgh plus, thus were able to earn extra profits. These profits were called "phantom freights" (Figure 6.18). The overall effect was to raise prices, reduce demand, and protect U.S. Steel's Pittsburgh investments.

Soon after the adoption of the basing-point plan by the steel industry, the practice was extended to the cement industry. Then, after 1912, the single basing-point practice spread rapidly to a variety of other industries; for example, cast-iron pipe, glucose, malt, maple flooring, welded chain, zinc, lead ("St. Louis plus"), and copper ("Connecticut Valley plus"). The practice became worldwide. In Russia, for example, before the communist revolution, steel was priced according to a "Chelyabinsk plus" basing-point system.

In some industries, multiple basing points were established. The principle is the same, except that two or more producing centers are quoted as bases, and the market is divided among them according to base-price-plus-freight charges. Some of the industries adopting multiple basing points have been iron and steel (in 1924, following U.S. government antitrust action declaring a single basing point illegal), cement, hardwood lumber, gasoline, sugar, chemical fertilizers, milk and ice cream, cans, asphalt roofing material, small-arms ammunition, corn products, gypsum products, hard-surface floor coverings, linseed oil, rigid steel conduit, firebrick, lubricating oil, and plate glass.

An example of basing-point pricing on the international scale is provided by petroleum (Melamid, 1962). The United States was the largest petroleum exporter at the turn of the century and its major producers set world prices on a "Gulf-plus" system. Delivered prices anywhere in the world equaled the price at the Gulf of Mexico plus transportation costs, regardless of the origin of the oil. Iranian oil shipped to the United Kingdom was priced at the U.S. Gulf price plus transportation rates from the Gulf of Mexico to the United Kingdom. Today, the world petroleum price is set by OPEC on the basis of Saudi Arabian light crudes at Dhahran, on the Persian Gulf, plus transportation.

Uniform Pricing

Consumers may be quoted prices FOB (free on board), meaning they pay the basing-point price and whatever they can arrange for transportation charges, or CIF (cost, insurance, and freight), in which case the supplier guarantees the delivered price at the consumer's location.

Another form of price quotation is *uniform pricing,* according to which suppliers quote consumers the same

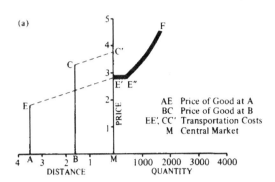

(a) As price increases above *ME'* and *MC'*, each supplier will be willing to produce and ship more to the market. Assume that the supply curve for producer is *E'E"F*. (This takes into account transport costs from *A* to *M*. At *A*, the supply curve would be lower because no transportation costs need be added in at the point of supply.) As the price at *M* increases, a level will be reached at which *B* becomes willing to supply the market, in competition with *A*. That price is *C*.

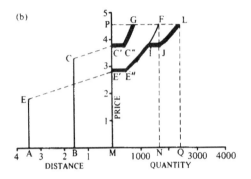

(b) Once the price at *M* exceeds *C'*, *B* begins to supply the market. *B*'s supply curve is shown in (b) by the upward-sloping line *C'C"G*. Since both *A* and *B* supply the market at prices above *C'*, their combined supply curve in the market has to be derived. This is *E'E"IJL* and it is formed by adding *B*'s supply curve *C'C"G* to *A*'s supply curve *E'E"F* horizontally, to show the total amount the two producers are willing to supply at each price level. *E'E"IJL* is the combined supply curve.

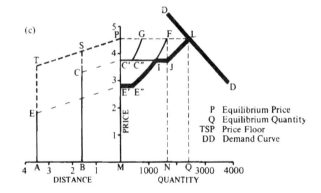

(c) The combined demand curve in the market is *DD* (note: *DD* can be derived in a manner analogous to the foregoing). The point of equilibrium is *L*. The resulting market price is *MP*. The total quantity *MQ* will be supplied. *PST* is the local producer's price floor. At the price *MP*, *A* supplies the quantity *MN* (given by the intersection of *A*'s supply curve *E'E"F* and *PL*) and *B* supplies the balance, *NQ*.

FIGURE 6.16   Spatial market equilibrium: a more complex case. The spatial market equilibrium price must take into account transportation costs of all suppliers and consumers as a whole. To simplify, imagine there are just two producers, at *A* and *B*, respectively. The local price at which *A* is able to start production is *AB*. At *B* it is *BC*. Notice that although *A* is more distant from the market, it can supply *M* more cheaply (*ME'* rather than *MC'*).

delivered price regardless of location. Such pricing is much more common than is generally realized. A number of reasons exist for its use. Transportation costs are often a very small fraction of total delivered price, and improvements in transportation make the scheme more logical (see Figure 6.19). Uniform pricing is also sensible when a commodity is moved in very small quantities to a large number of places, if transportation costs themselves vary little or not at all with distance, and if the administrative costs of determining the proper transportation charges are high.

Uniform pricing may also be used to extend the market area. Customers near the plant are charged more than FOB prices to subsidize customers beyond the FOB market area. Industries sometimes argue that advertising campaigns are more effective where a uniform price can be quoted, and that the additional sales achieved permit economies of scale. The practice is widespread in, for example, the United Kingdom, even in cases where transportation costs are substantial. British Oxygen, which accounts for virtually all oxygen and acetylene sales in the

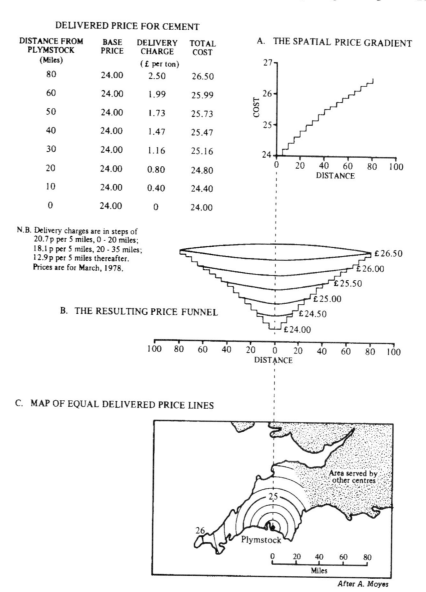

DISTANCE FROM PLYMSTOCK (Miles)	BASE PRICE	DELIVERY CHARGE (£ per ton)	TOTAL COST
80	24.00	2.50	26.50
60	24.00	1.99	25.99
50	24.00	1.73	25.73
40	24.00	1.47	25.47
30	24.00	1.16	25.16
20	24.00	0.80	24.80
10	24.00	0.40	24.40
0	24.00	0	24.00

DELIVERED PRICE FOR CEMENT

N.B. Delivery charges are in steps of 20.7p per 5 miles, 0 - 20 miles; 18.1 p per 5 miles, 20 - 35 miles; 12.9p per 5 miles thereafter. Prices are for March, 1978.

A. THE SPATIAL PRICE GRADIENT

B. THE RESULTING PRICE FUNNEL

C. MAP OF EQUAL DELIVERED PRICE LINES

After A. Moyes

FIGURE 6.17 The delivered price of cement in southwest England. The price of cement was £24 a ton in Plymstock in March 1978. Delivery charges were based on distance from Plymstock. The result was the regular concentric pattern of delivered prices shown in the map. For more details, see Moyes, (1980).

United Kingdom, charges uniform prices even though transportation costs average one-fourth of the total delivered price. Studies have shown that the practice is becoming more widespread, especially as improvements in transportation and communications reduce the share of delivered price accounted for by these factors.

PRICE REGULATION BY GOVERNMENT

Regulation by Western Governments

Strengthening Perfect Competition. Governments as well as industry associations try to influence prices. Western governments intervene in the marketplace under two opposite circumstances: (1) to strengthen the free play of market forces where free enterprise is considered beneficial; or (2) to modify the ordinary price mechanism where competitively determined outcomes are deemed socially or politically inappropriate. The result of governmental intervention of the latter kind has been a growing body of regulations that have the detrimental side effects of adding significantly to the cost of doing business and weakening market signals, thus distorting the effectiveness of market mechanisms. The goals of intervention include such policy objectives as encouraging economic growth, stabilizing prices, increasing productivity, and guaranteeing social welfare. Virtually all regulation explicitly or indirectly affects the supply and demand for goods and the prices at which they trade, as well as the size and the location of supply and market areas.

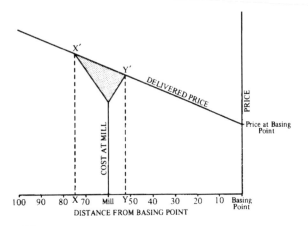

Phantom Freight

XY Distance from Basing Point over which Delivered Cost from Mill is less than Quoted Delivered Price.

FIGURE 6.18 Phantom freight with basing-point pricing. Under the basing-point price system, customers pay price at basing point plus transportation costs from that point. A local mill may not undercut the basing-point price structure. Its delivered price is boosted to the basing-point price level, yielding it a "phantom freight." The phantom freight negates any locational advantage of the mill. Thus, market area XY is shared between the local mill and mills at the basing point. Under FOB pricing, the local mill at M could expect to dominate the market area XY.

Governments strengthen market forces by three sets of policies. First, all Western governments are concerned with the degree of concentration of production or purchasing of goods, and the danger of price fixing (as in basing-point systems) that may result. When there is sufficient evidence of price fixing, governments may seize company documents and initiate legal proceedings against the companies involved.

Second, governments strengthen the competitive market mechanism by increasing market information. Labor exchanges provide both employed and unemployed persons with job information. A wide array of information is made available to industrialists, ranging from technical, to general management, to trade information. One function of censuses and surveys is to provide information on labor and markets that can be used to improve the working of the economy.

Third, special attention is given by governments to ease adjustment to secular (long-run) change. Industry may be locked into obsolete technology, regions overreliant on declining industries, and workers immobilized in declining regions. Government may offer industry investment incentives to retool. Research and development incentives are also sometimes available. Labor-retraining programs and relocation benefits may be introduced. Rural land-use programs may be developed where farmers have locked into inefficient practices.

The objective of such government intervention is to bring market prices closer to what they would be under perfect competition, free from oligopoly and oligopsony, and to ensure more perfect knowledge and an economy that adjusts more freely to market changes. Governments thereby strengthen the working of the price system as a mechanism for regulating production and exchange.

Economic Problems with Market Prices. Governments may, however, want to modify the free play of market forces for reasons that are economic, social, or regional. Economic issues arise: in pricing goods with a high social cost; in paying for collective goods; when maintaining quality takes priority over minimizing price; and in countervailing seasonal and cyclical fluctuations for particular commodities or for the economy generally.

The clearest case is when producers can pass some production costs onto society. One example is what Hardin

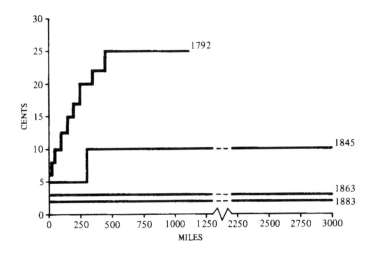

FIGURE 6.19 Toward uniform pricing: The example of postal rates. Note: National postal rates tend to be uniform, which makes delivery costs for industries shipping smaller goods by post also uniform. [*Source:* Ronald Abler, "What to Do While the Isolines Converge," paper prepared for the first Conference on the Geography of the Future, London, Ontario, October 15–18, 1970.]

calls the "tragedy of the commons." Appendix 6.2 discusses a particularly graphic case, that of Newfoundland's Grand Banks fisheries. The market price does not include the costs of pollution or resource depletion. Government may then regulate pollution levels, or set production levels, or it may tax the industry to recover part or all of the social costs involved. A particular problem arises in transportation. Subsidies for public transportation are justified because road and fuel taxes may fail to recover the full social cost of private travel to work. Similarly, subsidies for rail haulage are justified because rail companies must build and maintain their own lines, whereas road haulage companies do not. In each case, the concern is that optimizing on the basis of private plus social costs may lead to different decisions and prices than optimizing on the basis of private costs alone.

Some goods are collective and are not purchased in individual market actions. Examples are national defense forces, police and fire protection, meteorological services, city parks, and the cost of government itself. The cost of collective goods cannot be recovered effectively on a "user" basis. Governments are elected in part on the level of such services that they promise to provide, and they pay for them by taxes and public borrowing. The cost of these services to the individual is based on ability to pay (where taxes are progressive, that is, increase with income) and not on use or need. The price is determined by the level and quality of the service set by government policy.

Government also establishes the quality of service and regulates price when consumers cannot be expected to judge quality of service for themselves, as in the case of goods and services for which minimum standards are essential for consumer protection. Many regulations come under this third category, whether government-imposed or industry-controlled: fire protection, building codes, and zoning ordinances; regulations controlling foods and drugs; transportation services and equipment, whether automobiles, airlines, or ships; professional services and trades, whether medical, legal, insurance, electrical, or plumbing.

The fourth economic circumstance where free-market prices are considered inappropriate is when there are serious fluctuations in supply or demand, with concomitant fluctuations in price. To stabilize welfare in face of recessions or booms, the government may, for example, set minimum prices for farm products and store surpluses. Countercyclical measures also may be taken: These may be *fiscal,* as when tax rates are reduced to stimulate demand, or *monetary,* as when interest rates are raised to relieve inflationary pressures.

Social Needs versus Economic Efficiency. In certain cases, governments may conclude that the ordinary price mechanisms are inappropriate because they put economic efficiency above social need. Governments identify three broad cases of such social priority: the provision of minimum living standards and of social security; the distribution of benefits and responsibilities; and the maintenance of cultural levels. As Western countries industrialized, they found that the existing mutual-aid schemes failed to meet the needs of urban, industrial workers. Five basic sets of welfare policies were introduced in country after country, generally in this order: (1) injury related to employment; (2) sickness and maternity; (3) old age; (4) unemployment; and (5) family-income supplements. Governments have added regulations on working conditions, housing, education, and health and welfare, all of which affect the supply and cost of labor. Location decisions in the case of labor-intensive industry may well be influenced by the level and cost of such regulations in regions competing for the industry.

Social equity may also override market considerations when goods are in short supply. In times of war, particularly, governments and the public are not prepared to accept the allocation of food and other supplies on the basis of the ability to pay. A rationing system then is used to hold prices below their free-market level and to allocate supplies equitably, without regard to income. Duties such as military service are parceled out on the basis of ability, and individuals are not permitted to buy out. At such times, even the most free-enterprise country is prepared to abandon the very economic principles on which its society is based and argue instead, "from each, according to one's abilities; to each, according to one's needs."

Governments also feel a need to support cultural activities that could not survive the rule of the marketplace. The young writer seeking the wherewithal to write her first novel, the symphony orchestra that has established an international reputation, and live theater groups are all dependent on public funding to some extent. They give artistic expression to the sentiments of a nation and add to its culture and traditions in ways that cannot be measured in the marketplace. In such cases, it is agreed that support should be based on excellence and not commercial viability.

Regional Goals. Finally, the free play of market forces may be incompatible with the desires of Western governments for balanced regional growth and development. This set of goals may take three forms. Initially, in the case of New World countries, the concern may be with the spread of settlement and the development of resources across the entire national territory. Governments are sensitive to the dangers of large empty tracts of national territory and historically have encouraged immigration, settlement, and the building of railways. Canada is very sensitive about the presence of any foreigners in its Arctic regions and concerned that oil and gas developments there involve a much higher degree of Canadian ownership and control than in previous Canadian oil developments.

More recently, governments in all Western countries have become concerned with the problems of lagging or depressed regions. Until the 1930s or even later, governments believed that if they maintained strong national economic performance, then the regions would be able to take care of themselves. The reality of severe and persistent regional disparities forced a change in this attitude and the adoption of policies, often tied to directing the location of new manufacturing activity, to diminish regional disparities. As with social policies, the argument is one of equity, not efficiency.

In other cases, governments are concerned with locational aspects because of the nature of the specific activity. In wartime, governments may give higher priority to security than to economic efficiency in the location of industry. In peacetime, the recreation needs of the population may dictate the setting aside of lands for park use that may have a much higher economic value as industrial or commercial land. Beaches, cross-country ski trails, camping grounds, and adventure playgrounds are all established by government on the basis of geographic supply and demand rather than economic laws. Governments are finding that they must be even more sensitive to location issues when dealing with hazardous or potentially hazardous activities. The location of nuclear power stations close to, and upwind from, large urban concentrations is difficult to justify on grounds of cost efficiency. The regulation and control of the dumping of industrial waste products is another example where safety must be given precedence over convenience and cost.

Augmented Government Impact. The impact of government regulations on the economy and its regions is augmented by direct involvement of governments in the economy. Three measures of this direct involvement are (1) the amount of spending by all levels of government in a country; (2) the percentage of labor force employed in the civil service; (3) and the surface area of the national territory owned by government. Usually the first measure is employed, with government spending quoted as a percentage of gross national product or of total consumption expenditures. Western governments usually account for about a fifth of consumption expenditures and about a quarter to a third of gross national expenditures. Shifts in government expenditure patterns therefore can have a very significant impact on the economies of the regions affected, and indeed on the national economy as a whole.

The direct impact of government is further augmented and complicated where industries are owned by the government. Such industries are generally considered to make some special contribution to the nation, over and above their direct economic worth. Hence, their survival may not depend entirely on profitability as in private enterprise. In the United Kingdom, for example, most nationalized industries, including steel, shipbuilding, automobiles, and rail transportation, lost great sums of money and would not have survived at the scale they did without the umbrella of government ownership coupled with heavy subsidies. There were major restructurings when Prime Minister Margaret Thatcher's Conservative government returned them to private ownership in the attempt to restore efficiency to British industry.

Diminished Effectiveness. Both public and governmental attitudes on the effectiveness of government regulation of the economy underwent rapid change in the 1970s. Theoretical analysis and actual experience suggest that government regulation is far less effective than was previously thought. Far from correcting economic failures in the marketplace, government regulations can suffer their own failures. Far from achieving a wide range of economic, social, and regional goals, these goals can sometimes conflict with each other and policies can sometimes prove countervailing rather than reinforcing. And far from improving the working of the economy, government regulations can sometimes run into jurisdictional and administrative problems, consume resources, and sap enterprise.

The economic failures of government regulations are drawing increasing attention. The basic economic problem is that government regulations to control price inevitably affect quantity or quality, and regulations to control quantity or quality affect price. Economists have discovered that such regulations create a *transitory-gain trap*. The regulations create advantages or disadvantages that are quickly identified and capitalized. The advantages (or disadvantages) are temporary, or "transitory." Three examples, taxi regulation, housing policy, and transportation regulation, illustrate how this trap undermines government efforts to achieve economic, social, and regional goals in cases where free competition was considered inappropriate.

In many cities, local governments regulate the taxi business and limit the number of taxis by use of permits or medallions, to protect users and provide some security for drivers. But the number of permits issued is usually below the competitive level, giving them a scarcity value. As a result, taxis can earn extra income. That extra income can be converted into a capital value (based on current interest rates), or "capitalized." The price of a license is then equal to the city fee plus this capitalized value. The price varies from city to city depending on the level of undersupply. Thus, one study of the Canadian taxi industry found 1972 going prices of $18,000 in Toronto and $30,000 in Vancouver. The extra profits accrued to the original holders of permits (often taxi companies). The taxi driver, burdened with the cost of renting a licensed vehicle, or of buying a license, may find it as hard or harder to earn a living than it was before the regulations were introduced. The advantage was indeed transitory. But to deregulate the business would cause losses to those who paid high prices for permits in good faith that the regulations would remain in force. On the contrary in 1980, Montreal taxi drivers, misunderstanding the nature of the problem, complained that there were too many taxis to make a decent living and wanted a reduction in the number of licenses granted.

The same fundamental supply relationship between price and quantity has triggered a transitory-gain trap in rent controls. Government attempts to help low-income families by imposing rent controls create increasing distortions in the marketplace. In the short run, the supply of rental housing is inelastic, although rent controls do reduce supply as apartments are converted into condominiums and sold, and as construction rates fall. The most frequent market response to price controls where supply is inelastic is to allow quality to fall. Thus, profit levels can be redressed by postponing or eliminating customary maintenance. The demand for rental accommodation, however, can be expected to increase as rental controls make home ownership less attractive. In this case, families must vie with one another for possession of apartments on grounds other than rent. These grounds may include paying key money, offering to buy or rent furniture from the owner at high prices, agreeing to paint the apartment or provide other work at no income, or at less than market wage, or simply waiting in a long queue with little hope of success. When key money is the principal factor, the amount paid will be related to the capitalized value of the subsidy. It is thus equivalent to the medallion price paid by prospective taxi drivers.

The transitory-gains trap also afflicts regional policy, becoming a particularly contentious issue in the case of statutory grain rates in Canada. The development of Western Canada after confederation of the British North American colonies in 1867 was based on a National Economic Policy of railway building, agricultural settlement, and tariff protection for industry. In spite of the National Policy, rich mineral discoveries in the Kootenays and British Columbia drew American entrepreneurs northward by the 1890s. Railways and many other economic linkages began to form north–south along the natural routes of the cordilleran landscape. The Canadian government wanted the Canadian Pacific Railway to build a second rail line across the Rocky Mountains from Lethbridge, Alberta, through the Crowsnest Pass to Nelson, British Columbia, to preempt the American influence. To accomplish this goal, the government offered a cash subsidy and land rights to the CPR in return for 15 to 20 percent on eastbound grain shipments. These statutory rates on grain, known as the *Crow Rate* remained in place (except for a brief interlude during World War I) until 1983.

The result of Crow rates on wheat shipments was that it cost a farmer less to ship a bushel of wheat to Vancouver or Thunder Bay than to post a letter. Controlled prices reduced the quality of service as the railways were understandably reluctant to invest in rolling stock or line mainte-

nance for shipments that paid about a quarter of their real transportation costs. But farmers resisted many attempts by the Canadian government to raise rail rates, even if new rates were coupled with major improvements in speed and quality of service.

The problem was that the price of farmland in the Canadian prairies was related to yield, to wheat prices at central markets, and to the costs of shipment to those central markets (formerly dominated by Liverpool, as we saw earlier). The value of the Crow rate had already been capitalized and added an estimated $30 to $40 per acre to prime grain-growing farmland. The subsidy had thus created a sort of "key money" that farmers had to pay to gain access to the land. If the freight rate for wheat were to be increased, the capital worth of some farms would be reduced by tens of thousands of dollars, especially painful for farmers contemplating retirement or needing collateral to finance expansion. The failure of grain freight rates to keep in step with inflation created capital values that were captured primarily by the original farm owners.

The Crow Rate had other unintended side effects. By subsidizing grain transportation, it encouraged a grain-based monoculture in the Canadian west. Thus marginal land better suited to grazing was exploited for grain cropping that created soil erosion problems over the long term. The market-oriented cattle and hog feeding industry in Eastern Canada benefited from subsidized western grain and made the natural resource–oriented western cattle and hog feeding less competitive. And finally, as inflation in the 1970s made the Crow Rate more costly, the railways responded by failing to reinvest in rolling stock and track improvement. Thus the grain transportation system became progressively undercapitalized as its assets depreciated.

In 1983, the government permitted the gradual increase in grain transportation rates but had to pay a seven hundred million dollar annual subsidy to induce the railways to reinvest in rolling stock. Concerns over the rising federal deficit and the gradual realization that the Prairies could manage without transportation subsidies finally led to the end of the Crow Rate on August 1, 1995, some 98 years after its inauguration. Since the ending of the Rate parts of the Prairies have reverted from grain to range animals, putting pressure on East Ontario beef producers, and cheaper Canadian grain has moved southward to compete in United States markets.

These examples of government regulations suffering market failures of their own are very specific, but the principle of the transitory-gains trap is very broad. It applies, and has geographic implications, whenever quotas are set on farm acreages for specific crops or minimum prices are established for commodities. It applies when industries are subsidized with grants or special loans, or protected by tariffs. It applies within cities where development is regulated by zoning or other controls. And it applies as well to all regulation of transportation and of fuel charges. Regulations tend to create special profits that can be capitalized, sometimes by the owners of the resource, sometimes by labor, and sometimes by a third party. The benefits cannot be held always by those intended to gain from the regulations. They can end up serving private interests rather than the common good.

Regulation in Communist States

The economic theory and political objectives that govern prices in communist states have been quite different from those in Western countries. Recall how these "command" economies were described at the beginning of the chapter. Monolithic, authoritarian governmental systems were dominated by a single party. The state owned the means of production, operating nonagricultural industries, and in some communist countries, agriculture, too. There was centralized direction of the economy. In the classic communist scheme, each industry was supposed to produce according to preset physical targets. Performance——at least until the late 1960s——was measured by output rather than sales, which meant that commodity movements were managed through rationing systems rather than the interplay of demand and supply. Prices played little, if any, role in economic management. Communist economies were geared to ensuring rapid growth above all else.

Strong central direction did prove effective in running high-priority projects, such as space exploration and weapons development, which demand considerable concentrations of skills and resources regardless of cost. It failed in the ordinary economic management of where to invest resources, how to identify and exploit each competitive economic edge, how to achieve quality as well as quantity, how to balance supply and demand, and, in short, how to run efficient and productive economies. For years, Western economists assumed that the growth rates of gross domestic product (GDP) in communist states matched or exceeded that in the West. The reality was quite different. Productivity growth (GDP per man hour) lagged increasingly behind the Western countries. The Soviet Union reduced its productivity gap with the United States in GDP per worker hour until 1973, but retrogressed thereafter. Energy consumption per unit of output increased after 1973, and there was negative total factor productivity after 1984 (i.e., there was decreasing output, notwithstanding increasing inputs). As Russian workers jibed, "We pretend to work, they pretend to pay us."

The extent and the causes of the economic failure of communist economies are now quite evident. The economic problems arose from the huge party-controlled bureaucracies needed to devise plans for economic growth, to enforce economic planning decisions, to determine the allocation of resources and set production quotas, as well as to fix prices on millions of categories of goods, determine their distribution, and conduct all foreign trade.

How Prices Were Set. Prices were set without any reference to demand or supply, but only to production costs (themselves reflecting administered prices for inputs) and to some concept of "social value." Basic foodstuffs and rents were heavily subsidized. In the case of manufactured goods, retail prices were ultimately related to the pricing of labor and of industrial materials, taking into account standard markups and a turnover tax that varied between commodities to reflect social desirability. Industrial materials in turn, were, priced so that the return equaled the average production cost plus a limited planned profit. Because average costs change with the scale of output, this pricing policy had the effect of ultimately relating all prices back to the nature, scale, location, and efficiency of production—all of which were set by the command structure of economic planning in the state. Demand played no role whatsoever in price determination in this scheme.

In the 1960s, Soviet economic planners relied increasingly on mathematical programming methods to estimate more-efficient relationships among planned targets, output levels, and commodity flows. They thought that mathematics could substitute for free market prices. The methods produced what the Soviet planners called "objectively determined values" for products. Similar values are called "shadow prices" by Western scholars; if charged, these prices would ensure that the economic relationships sought are achieved. Such shadow prices can be calculated in ways that reflect both scarcity and productivity, and if they had been so estimated, some of the problems of shortages and surpluses that exist in the former USSR might have been avoided. However, because consumption targets were preset by the planners before the mathematical methods were used, Soviet shadow prices still reflected only production-and-supply considerations. The free play of consumer preferences and demands that characterize Western societies played no role in determining the mix of things produced. Persistent problems of deficits of items desired by the Soviet citizenry and surpluses of inferior-quality, unwanted goods that merely met production quotas were central to the decision to restructure and let market prices serve as the thermostat controlling the economy. The system simply did not work and ultimately collapsed.

Restructuring Communist Economies. The transition from socialist to free-market-oriented economies involves a number of immediate issues. Should the change be gradual, as in Hungary, or sudden as in Poland? How does one place a market-economy value on socialist state assets? How are these assets to be allocated among the employees, the public, and foreign investors? How do the new governments deal with the transition costs, which may include severe inflation, unemployment, trade deficits, and government budget deficits? The long-term benefits of the economic changes are not in question. Unfortunately, the price of bad economic management in the past has yet to be paid in full.

Living standards have fallen back to the levels of the 1950s when they were still depressed by the effects of World War II. The winter of 1993 witnessed outbreaks of diphtheria and cholera. Investments of foreign capital have lagged far below needs and have sometimes ended up in Swiss bank accounts.

The capital needed to rebuild the former communist world's neglected infrastructure, to modernize backward technologies, and to deal with the environmental consequences of uncontrolled pollution is immense, and the capital requirements must be accompanied by comprehensive economic restructuring. Massive state enterprises need to be broken into manageable companies, overstaffing must be eliminated, and the rights to private ownership need to be legally entrenched. Financial and stock markets need to be established and an efficient banking system must be created to channel savings into investment. Drastic currency reforms are crucial. Perhaps even more challenging are the changes needed in the attitudes of management, workers, and the population generally, first to forgo the privileges bestowed party members, second to accept the rights, responsibilities, and risks of running businesses competitively, and third to permit the accompanying inequalities in the distribution of wealth and income that are related to business success and failure to occur. Only then will marketization really work.

APPENDIX 6.1

Demand for Food in the UK and the Income Elasticity of Demand

The United Kingdom has had a national food survey for over 50 years, providing a long perspective on the changing demand for food (including drink) and on some of the factors responsible. These surveys reveal the relationship of such things as prices, income level, personal preferences, social attitudes and the desire for convenience, to the quantities of different food items that are bought.

However, the relative importance of each factor has changed over time. The 1940s were a period of wartime and postwar austerity in Britain with food rationing. Demand was restricted by limited availability. The 1950s saw the drive to return to normal diets. The 1960s are of particular interest for two main reasons. First, the proportion of family incomes spent on food was comparatively high, so the prices of different foods was an important consideration in making choices. Second, incomes were rising rapidly and the relative popularity of different foods emerged clearly as consumers were able to exercise their preferences more effectively. The 1960s thus revealed the food items for which demand rises with income, and those for which it falls. Consumption patterns in the 1970s were buffeted by strong fluctuations in food prices. The 1980s and 1990s

have seen personal preferences assume a growing importance on food purchased.

A particular interest of the UK's National Food Surveys has been the effect of increases in income of consumers, and of differences in income among consumers, on the basket of food items bought. For instance, the impact of rising incomes on the popularity of different food items, which began to emerge in the 1960s in the United Kingdom, was as follows:

Consumption Has Risen with Income	Consumption Has Fallen with Rising Income
Cheese	Canned meats
Canned salmon	Sausages
Shell fish	Herrings
Beef	Margarine
Pork	Lard
Chicken	Canned milk puddings
Salad vegetables	Potatoes
Salad oils	Dried pulses
Frozen vegetables	Canned vegetables
Fresh fruit	Tea
Chocolate biscuits	White bread
Brown & wholemeal bread	Oatmeal products
Rice	
Coffee	
Ice-cream	

The specific change in demand for a food item given a change in income can be measured as the *income elasticity of demand*. The elasticity equals the percentage change in demand divided by the percentage change in income. If increase in demand is proportionate to increase in income, then the income elasticity of demand is +1.0. Sometimes there is virtually no change in demand, so the income elasticity of demand is 0. When consumption falls with increasing income, the elasticity will be negative. See p. 188 for income elasticities for some foods for selected years:

These elasticity figures, together with the more complete tables published by the Ministry, reveal that expenditure increases vary little with income. For instance, a 10 percent increase in income in 1985 would, on average, produce a 2.6 percent increase in spending on beef and veal, no change in spending on bread, a 3.2 percent fall in the purchase of tea and a 2.3 percent fall in the purchase of potatoes. If income fell by 10 percent, the absolute figures would remain the same, but the signs would be reversed, and purchases of tea and potatoes would increase. Furthermore, elasticities have tended to fall over the years. Frozen peas are an example. Their elasticity has fallen from a quite high +1.53 to +0.33 between 1960 and 1985. (So a 10 percent rise in income level produced a 3.3 percent increase in spending on frozen peas in 1960 rather

Food Item	Income Elasticity of Demand		
	1960	1975	1985
Beef and Veal	0.16	0.25	0.26
Mutton & lamb	0.38	0.21	0.19
Pork	0.46	0.39	0.14
Frozen peas	1.53	0.43	0.33
Bread	-0.09	0.01	-0.06
Tea	0.03	-0.10	-0.32
Potatoes	0.07	0.01	-0.23

Source: Ministry of Agriculture Fisheries and Food, National Food Survey (Annual) (London; HMSO, various years).

Note: More recent surveys have not given elasticities of demand. In 1985, the highest were for fruit juices (+1.09), fresh fruit (+0.71), and yogurt (+0.64). Tea was the lowest.

than 15.3 percent as in 1960.) Fruit juice also can be expected to become a part of the regular shopping list, irrespective of income. The price elasticity of fruit juice fell from 1.07 to 0.94 in just 1 year from 1985 to 1986. Unfortunately more recent reports have not given elasticity of demand.

The low elasticity of demand for food has been reinforced by the falling proportion of the family budget spent on food. Almost a third of all family spending was on food items in 1950. That had fallen to less than 15 percent by 1985. The figures are plotted in Figure 6.20.

The main conclusions to emerge then for the long series of British food surveys thus are as follows:

- The proportion of the family budget spent on food has fallen steadily over the past 50 years.
- The family shopping list is no longer highly sensitive to income levels (with some notable exceptions such as fruit juice).

- Differences between high- and low-income families in the total amount spent on food have narrowed considerably over the same period.
- The dominant factor in the food choices made is no longer income or price, but rather consumer preference and convenience.

Sources: See particularly the following reports of *Fifty Years of the National Food Survey, 1940–1990.* Ministry of Agriculture, Fisheries and Food (MAFF). (London: HMSO, 1991); idem,

Household Food Consumption and Expenditure 1985 (London: HMSO, 1987, Sec. 5). More recent reports, such as idem, *National Food Survey 1993* (London: HMSO, 1994), no longer provide a detailed demand analysis, although the 1990 report (published 1991) does give the trends for 1940-1990.

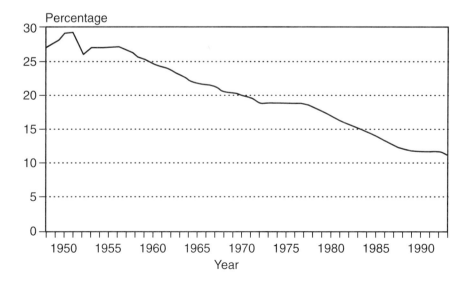

FIGURE 6.20   Household food expenditures as a percentage of total consumers' expenditure.

APPENDIX 6.2

The Tragedy of the Commons: Newfoundland's Grand Banks

The most important case when government intervention is needed, but usually fails, is when resources are not managed by any single organization, but are held in common ownership. What then results, all too often, is the "tragedy of the commons" to use the term of Garrett Hardin. We shall first define this term and then illustrate the principle with the events leading up to the dramatic seizure of a Spanish fishing boat in international waters by the Government of Canada in March 1995.

The "tragedy of the commons" is the mismanagement of resources that are common property for maximum short-term gain without regard for the long-term consequences. Imagine an area of common land open to herders who may keep as many cattle as they choose. It is in the collective interest of all to ensure that the commons are not overgrazed, and in the individual interest to graze a maximum number of animals. Therefore, the commons are likely to be overgrazed. Isolated action, by a single herder, to reduce overgrazing would serve only to reduce that individual's income without substantial benefit to the general community. Because individual action would fail, and there is no organization to manage collective action, the commons deteriorates to an irreducibly low carrying capacity and all lose. The tragedy of the commons applies not simply to herders on common land. We live in a global commons comprising the air, rivers, lakes, and the sea. It was in an effort to avert such a "tragedy of the commons" and to coerce all countries involved to take effective action to preserve the fishing stock of the Grand Banks off Newfoundland, that the Government of Canada took strong unilateral moves against the Spanish.

The Grand Banks, off Newfoundland has been one of the world's greatest fishing grounds for centuries. Indeed, the cod fisheries in the Grand Banks provided the first of the great staple exports that stimulated the settlement and economic development of Canada. However, falling catches in recent decades have drawn international attention to the need to restrict the total catch to a sustainable level. This issue was discussed in the meetings leading to the Law of the Sea in the 1970s and in the Earth Summit at Rio de Janeiro in 1992. Fishing quotas have been established under the Northwest Atlantic Fisheries Organization (NAFO) for some 10 years. Fourteen moratoria have been established in different areas of the Grand Banks on ground fish stocks including cod in 1986 and plaice and flounder in 1994. The commercial fishing of cod, red fish, American plaice and yellow and witch flounder would have been brought to an end in any case because of severe depletion of these stock. As a result of the fishing moratoria, and the restrictions to commercial fishing, some 40,000 fishermen in Newfoundland have lost their livelihood, affecting half the population of the province.

These moratoria, established by the Government of Canada, apply only within the 200-mile limit of Canadian shores. The straddling stock that move back and forth across this limit are not effectively protected when they move into areas of the Grand Banks beyond the limit. NAFO sets limits to catches beyond the 200-mile limit, but individual members of NAFO have been free to object to these limits and to set themselves new quotas far above the safe limits recommended by NAFO's own fisheries experts. There have been other problems, too. Compliance with NAFO regulations is known to be very lax with actual catches often 60 percent above declared catches. Legislation on the minimum size of fish net meshes is routinely disregarded and fine-mesh knits are used to catch juvenile fish before they reach spawning age. Furthermore, some fishing boats sailed under flags of convenience to avoid national quotas and regulations altogether.

The matter came to a head in March 1995 when Canadian fisheries patrol vessels, acting under the doctrine of necessity, fired on and seized a Spanish boat, the *Estai,* outside the 200-mile limit. The Canadian Fisheries Minister explained that the Spanish fishing fleet was out of control and threatening what little remains of the straddling stock.

The problem with the Spanish fishing fleet off Canada's east coast began when the African country of Namibia won independence in 1990 and immediately prohibited foreign fishing within its 200-mile territorial limit. Their action was taken to stop further depredations of Namibian fish stock by the Spanish fleet. Rather than decommission the boats, the Spanish boats were dispatched to the Grand Banks, where they simply ignored fishing quotas and regulations. NAFO had set a quota of 3,400 tons for turbot (Greenland halibut) for all European Union fishing boats for the whole of 1995. Yet by Canada's calculations, Spanish boats alone had caught 7,000 tons in the first two weeks of 1995. They had caught about 50,000 tons in 1993 and 1994. Meanwhile Canada had reduced its catch from a peak of 38,000 tons in 1979 to just 6000 tons in 1992.

After tense diplomatic negotiations, a new Canada–European Union fisheries enforcement agreement has been signed that includes among its regulations the placing of full-time observers on board vessels at all times, satellite tracking of fishing vessels, and significant penalties to deter violations. What is also needed, is first, a scaling down of government subsidies to the fishing industry that enhance its capacity and efficiency. These subsidies have reached the extraordinary level of about $60 billion in an industry whose annual catch is worth about $75 billion. Second, there will need to be a change in attitude. Among the remarks of Spanish fishermen reported at the time the *Estai* was seized were "our expertise found the fish, so the fish belong to us," "everyone cheats," "we are not doing the fish any harm."

Canada's action may have served to halt further depletion of the fishing stock on the Grand Banks. General action is needed if we are to conserve:

- hake and squid in the southwest Atlantic on Argentina's Patagonian shelf
- orange roughy on the Challenger plateau off New Zealand
- tuna in the south Pacific
- blue whiting and jack mackerel in the east-central and southeast Pacific off Chile and Peru

- pollock in the Doughnut Hole in the Central Bering Sea and in the Peanut Hole in the center of the Sea of Okhotsk off Russia's Pacific coast
- herring and salmon in the doughnut holes of the Northeast Atlantic
- cod, flounder, and redfish on the Grand Banks of Newfoundland off Canada's Atlantic coast outside Canada's 200-mile limit.

Destructive overfishing in all these fishing grounds can be stopped only by effective management of all participants.

VOCABULARY

This chapter introduces a considerable vocabulary, which you should do your best to command. The definitions are in the Glossary.

animal husbandry
antitrust legislation
authoritarian political economies
barter
basing-point pricing
basing-point system
British parcels
capital requirements
capital values
capital worth
capitalization
cash markets
ceiling price
central market
central market price
centralization
Chayanov's rule
collective goods
combined supply curve
command economy
commodity exchanges
communist economies
consumer
consumption expenditures
controlled prices
cost, insurance and freight (CIF)
countercyclical measures
countervail
Crow Rate

decentralization
demand
demand cone
deregulation
diminished effectiveness
direct involvement of government in the economy
division of labor
downward-sloping demand curve
economic efficiency
economic restructuring
elasticity
energy consumption per unit output
environmental consequences
equilibrium price
equity
exchange economy
exchange theory
federal deficit
feudalism
fiscal measure
free on board (FOB)
free-enterprise market systems
futures
geography of demand
geography of market equilibrium
geography of price
geography of supply
global commons

governmental investment
"the great transformation"
gross national expenditures
higgling
householding
imperfect competition
income disparity
income elasticity of demand
individual demand curve
individual supply curve
inelastic
inferior goods
interaction theory
"Japan incorporated"
"key money"
labor exchange
lines of indifference
location theory
luxury items
manor
market area
market-directed system
market equilibrium
market failure
market mechanism
market negotiation
market signal
market traders
maximum ceiling prices

TOPICS FOR DISCUSSION

1. What are the nearest central markets (or auctions) to where you live? Describe their operation.

2. How do demographic, ethnic, social and economic factors affect the typical shopping list for food in your community? (Is there a food survey covering your area? You may want to consult it, and the article by Johanssen, et al. [1989] for ideas).

3. Draw a graph showing the relationship between prices for beans and kerosene and distance from Kano, Nigeria, on the basis of the maps in Figure 6.21. How do spatial variations in price relate to areas of surplus and deficit?

4. The greater the costs of transportation, the less important are differences in central market base prices in determining the boundaries of market areas. Demonstrate this assertion by redrawing the consumer price ceilings for central markets *B* and *C* in Figure 6.11 with slopes at 10°, 25°, 40°, and 55°. Note the location of the supply market boundary at each of these gradients.

5. Continue to test the assertion in Topic 4 by determining the boundaries of the supply areas for central markets *B* and *C* given producer price floors at slopes of 10°, 25° and 55° on the same diagram in Figure 6.11.

6. How low can transportation costs get before central market *C*, with its lower prices, loses all its supply area to central market *B*? At this price, which central market loses its market area, *B* or *C*? Evidently a central market can attract supplies from a competing central market, paying higher prices, only if the transportation costs are greater than the price difference between them. What is the corresponding conclusion regarding the existence of separate market areas?

7. List the major government price controls in effect in your area and very briefly assess their effectiveness.

8. Discuss and illustrate the assertion that government support prices for individual commodities cause shifts in the location of production.

9. Is there a potential "tragedy of the commons" in your area? How can it be averted?

10. Describe current problems and prospects of the shift to a market economy in China, Russia, or one of the Eastern European countries.

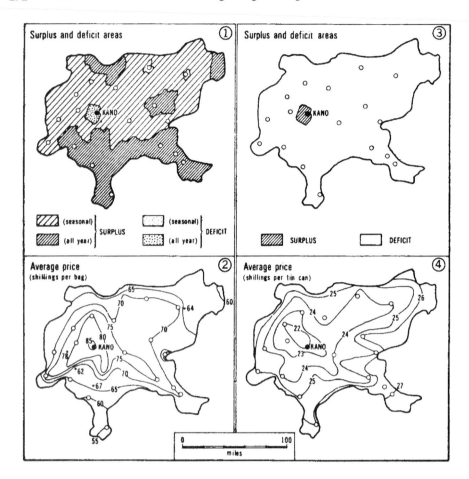

FIGURE 6.21   Pricing of beans (maps 1 and 2) and kerosene (maps 3 and 4) with respect to Kano, Nigeria, together with indication of zones of suplus and deficit.

FURTHER READINGS

Bressler, Raymond G., and Richard A. King (1970). *Market, Prices, and Interregional Trade.* New York: John Wiley.

A description of economic development and regional specialization in the United States from colonial settlement to mid-twentieth century is provided (pp. 3–70), as an introduction to an advanced theoretical treatment. See Figure 102, p. 191, for a map of optimal interregional movements of dairy products in the United States and compare it with Figure 6.6 in this chapter.

Brown, Michael Barratt (1995). *Models in Political Economy,* 2nd ed., London: Penguin,

An authoritative and balanced assessment of the Soviet and the Chinese models is given on pp. 193–248.

Chisholm, Michael (1970) *Geography and Economics.* 2d ed., London: G. Bell & Sons,

Provides a key reading on the economic fundamentals of economic geography. For this chapter, see "Relations Between Geography and Economics," pp. 4–7, and "Pricing Policies," pp. 163–194.

Deaton, Angus (1990). *Price Elasticities from Survey Data—Extensions and Indonesian Results.* Living Standards Measurement Study. Working Paper No. 69. Washington, DC: The World Bank,

Deaton has written numerous papers on price elasticities in low-income countries that make clear the methodological problems involved. This paper is based on surveys of rural households in Java in 1981.

Greenhut, Melvin L. (1964). When Is the Demand Factor of Location Important? *Land Economics* 40: 175–184. Reprinted in Gerald J. Karaska and David F. Bramhall

(Eds). *Locational Analysis for Manufacturing.* Cambridge, MA.: The MIT Press, 1969, pp. 339–348.

Greenhut has published extensively on location theory and the theory of spatial pricing, often at a very advanced level. This article presents a basic nonmathematical treatment of the three industrial pricing systems: CIF. FOB, and basing point. A recent mathematical treatment is provided in M. L. Greenhut et al., *The Economics of Imperfect Competition: A Spatial Approach,* Cambridge: Cambridge University Press, 1987.

Johannsen, E., L. Robbins G. Hewston, M. Zafirou, and L. Hunt. (1989) Demography and Socioeconomic Bases of Food Demand—What Does the Future Hold? *Food Market Commentary.* 11: 27–44. Canada: Department of Agriculture. Policy, Planning and Economic Branch Food. Markets Analysis Division.

A very readable account of the ways in which demographic, ethnic, social, and economic factors affect the demand for food in a country where immigration is becoming increasingly important in population growth.

Lösch, August (1954). *The Economics of Location.* 2d rev. ed. Translated by William H. Woglom. New Haven: Yale University Press,

This great classic always makes rewarding reading. See particularly Chapter 26 "Price Levels in Space," pp. 452–495, which demonstrates the continuing importance of regional differences in prices, notwithstanding reduction in freight rates and many cases of uniform pricing.

Melamid, Alexander (1962). Geography of the World Petroleum Price Structure. *Economic Geography:* 283–298.

A most interesting account of the basing-point price system from before World War II (Gulf plus) and the changes made following World War II.

Moyes, A. (1980). Can Spatially Variable Prices Ever be "Fair"? Some observations on the Price Commission's Judgments on British Cement Prices. *Regional Studies* 14: 37–53.

Not only an excellent case study of the basing-point price system, but also an exemplary geographic analysis.

Polyani, Karl (1975). *The Great Transformation.* New York: Octagon Books,

An impressive and wide-ranging work of synthesis that emphasizes the social and economic changes wrought by the Industrial Revolution and the fundamental differences between traditional and modem economies. See particularly Chapter 4, "Societies and Economic Systems": Chapter 5, "Evolution of the Market Pattern"; and Chapter 6, "The Self-Regulating Market," pp. 43–76.

Radford, R. A. (1945). The Economic Organization of a P.O.W. Camp. *Economica.* 12, 1945. Reprinted in Paul A. Samuelson et al. (eds.), *Readings in Economics.*7th ed., New York: McGraw-Hill, pp. 21–29

As a prisoner of war in World War II, Radford saw in microcosm the emergence of a price system based on cigarettes. Samuelson notes that, "The very simplicity of the story he tells has made this article a minor classic in economics. To understand its full flavor is to know the world around us better."

Wagner, Philip (1960). *The Human Use of Earth.* London: The Free Press of Glencoe,

This book is primarily concerned with the ecological expression of different cultures and social arrangements. Chapter 5, "The Economic Bond," pp. 60–87 restates and develops Polyani and presents a geography of economic forms. The themes of the text are summarized masterfully in Chapter 10, "A Geographic Outlook," pp. 228–237.

7

Rent Gradients, Land Use, and the Structure of Global Systems

OVERVIEW

The uses to which people put land reflect, in part, differences in physical factors, such as soil fertility and climate. These differences were recognized by David Ricardo when he attributed differences in land use to comparative advantages derived from natural resource endowments.

But even on a homogeneous plain, where there are no physical differences, the efforts of farmers to maximize their returns produce systematic land-use patterns. The exciting discovery of these spatial patterns was first presented by J. H. von Thünen in his study Der Isolierte Staat (The Isolated State) in 1826. The importance of von Thünen's contribution cannot be overemphasized. He provided the earliest theory of the spatial organization of land use. Although the world's economic geography has changed dramatically in the two centuries since von Thünen made his seminal

contribution, the basic principles that he stated still apply to the zonation of land use at scales from that of the village to that of the globe itself, appropriately adjusted for the map of transportation facilities and accessibility.

As the global economy has evolved, two processes have guided land use. During the nineteenth and early twentieth centuries, when accessibility differences were substantial, "Thünenization" produced a broad zonation of global land use from the world's urban-industrial core regions outward to open rangelands on the periphery. As transport costs have been slashed in the past quarter-century, however, "Ricardian Development" has guided increasing differentiation based upon both natural resource endowments ("basic factors") and the endowments created by culture and technology ("advanced factors").

OBJECTIVES

- to develop an understanding of the laws of returns
- to explain the concept of rent, and why the differential rents described by David Ricardo arise
- to present the problem posed by J. H. von Thünen, the deductive model he developed to solve the problem, and the application of his principles to the modern world
- to introduce the concepts of Thünenization and Ricardian Development
- to demonstrate that land-use determinants have moved from Ricardian Development tied to basic factors to Thünenization, and thence back to Ricardian Development tied to advanced factors.

WHY STUDY RENT?

As was seen in Chapter 6, in market economies with significant transport costs, marketplace-centered gradients structure the prices paid by consumers and received by producers. *Rent* is a particular kind of price, the price paid to use a factor of production, land—either the payment by a renter to a landowner or the cost to a landowner-user of capital tied up in the land that might have been used to generate income from investments in assets other than the land.

Rent differences arise from either resource productivity or transport gradients:

Differential rents are the product of fertility differences caused by differences in natural endowments. This was the conclusion of English economist David Ricardo as he wrote about the relationship between returns to landowners and the marginal productivity of land in *Principles of Political Economy and Taxation* in 1817. Ricardo's theories, important when societies lived close to their endowments of basic resources, have acquired new importance at the global scale as transportation and communications costs have been slashed in the past quarter century.

Transport-cost related rent gradients structure land use. This was the central conclusion of the first body of location theory ever written, J. H. von Thünen's theory of agricultural location, outlined in *Der Isolierte Staat* in 1826. Initially conceived as a theory of land use around a market town under conditions of horse-and-buggy transportation, Thünen's concepts are central to an understanding of how global systems of land use emerged during the nineteenth century, although their salience is diminishing today as transport costs decline.

We will explore both of these theories in this chapter. *Ricardian Development* and *Thünenization* have both played important roles in structuring land use, but their relative importance has shifted over time.

THE LAWS OF RETURNS

Strictly, economic rent is the payment for a factor of production that is in perfectly inelastic supply. To understand this point, we must make an excursion into the *laws of returns.* The principle applies not simply to finite supplies of land with given degrees of accessibility, as argued by von Thünen, but to finite supplies of land of particular quality, as was argued by David Ricardo. Indeed, the principle applies to any factor of production in imperfectly elastic supply: nonrenewable resources, and even supplies of brainpower and creativity. After the excursion, we return to concepts of land rent, to Thünen's theory of agri-cultural

location, to Ricardo's alternative, and then to the application of the ideas to an understanding of evolving regional and global systems.

Inputs, Outputs, and Isoquants

Consider the specific example of a dairy farmer in the state of Iowa who wants to know what combination of grain and hay should be fed to cattle to maximize milk output, and how to crop land to feed the cattle in an optimal manner. Following the advice of the Iowa State Agricultural Experiment Station, the farmer's herd of larger-sized Holstein and Brown Swiss cows (each of which has an expected output capacity of 300 to 400 pounds of butterfat annually) is fed varying combinations of legume hay, corn silage, and grain (the "inputs"). The resulting variations in milk production (the "outputs") are recorded and charted, as in Figure 7.1. The two axes record amounts of grain and hay fed to the cows. Each dot represents a cow, with its milk output noted. Interpolated contour lines reveal the

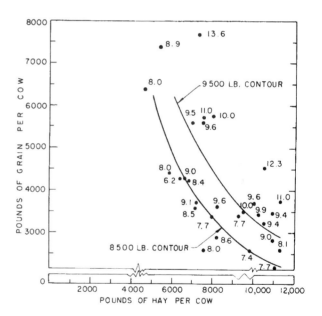

FIGURE 7.1 Equal-product contours (feed combinations) at 8,500 and 9,500 pounds of milk per cow. Contours interpolated using the production function, $Y = 3.56X_1^{.5035}X_2^{.4}$, where Y is the output of milk and X_1 and X_2 are hay and grain, respectively. Thus, for 8,500 pounds of milk, the input combinations yielding the 8,500-pound contour are given by $X_2 = (8500/3.56X_1^{0.5035})^{2.5}$. [*Source:* Earl O. Heady and Russell O. Olson, *Substitution Relationships, Resource Requirements and Income Variability in the Utilization of Forage Crops,* (Research Bulletin 390, Ames, Iowa State University, Agricultural Experiment Station, 1952).]

combinations of feed inputs that result in given levels of milk output (*isoquants* or *equal-product curves*). For example, the 8,500-pound isoquant traces out those combinations of grain and hay that yield 8,500 pounds of milk per cow as output.

Many such isoquants could be interpolated in the graph (the figure also charts one for an output of 9,500 pounds per cow). The mathematical equation that summarizes the shape of these curves, a *production function* describing the input–output relationship, is recorded in the caption for Figure 7.1. A set of isoquants describing the array of *production possibilities* open to the farmer could be drawn in the graph using this equation, with higher levels of output on the successive curves appearing upwards and to the right. These isoquants are all convex to the origin because grain and hay are not perfect substitutes for each other in feeding the cattle. For example, if a cow is producing 8,500 pounds of milk and it is being fed 5,000 pounds of hay and 6,154 pounds of grain, 1 pound of hay can be substituted for 1.55 pounds of grain and the milk output will remain the same. At the other extreme, however (reading along the isoquant), if 11,000 pounds of hay and 2,281 pounds of grain are being used to produce 8,500 pounds of milk, 1 pound of hay only does the same job as only 0.26 pounds of grain. This example illustrates the principle of *diminishing marginal utility*, which states that when a great deal of any one item is being used or consumed, its relative worth is much less than if a little of it is being used.

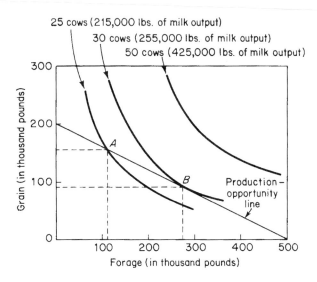

FIGURE 7.2 Determination of cropping pattern and herd size. The milk output contours are isoquants: lines of equal output from each possible combination of inputs. The maximum possible combination of inputs the farmer can produce is given by the production opportunity line. Hence, the largest isoquant the farmer can sustain is indicated at *B*, where the isoquant for 30 cows just touches (is tangent to) the production-opportunity line.

Production Possibilities and Farm Output

Figure 7.1 describes the input–output relationship for individual cows. What of the farm unit? Suppose that the farmer has 100 acres available to grow hay, grain, or some combination of the two feedstuffs, and that this will yield 200,000 pounds of grain (2,000 pounds per acre) or 500,000 pounds of hay (5,000 pounds per acre) if the land is used exclusively for one or the other. If the herd is restricted to 8,500-pound milk yielders, what size herd can be maintained? Multiples of the grain-hay inputs to an 8,500-pound yield cow shown by the lowest isoquant in Figure 7.1 yield the inputs to feed a 25-, 30-, and 50-cow herd: 25 times the input combinations that can be read off the isoquant give the total inputs required for 25 cows, for example.

These combinations can be plotted in a second graph, Figure 7.2, which shows a set of isoquants for different levels of farm output, that is, the feed combinations required for the different-sized herds. How large a herd can the farmer's 100 acres support, and how should these acres be cultivated? A second line is drawn in the graph, the *production-possibility* or *production-opportunity* line showing the combinations of inputs that can be grown on the 100 acres. If the land is used exclusively to grow grain,

200,000 pounds can be produced; if exclusively for hay, the output is 500,000 pounds; or there can be some combination of the two, depending on how much land is used for one or the other. These production possibilities are the ones charted in the second line.

The graph reveals that it is impossible to feed a herd of 50 cows and expect 8,500 pounds of milk per cow: The relevant isoquant in the graph requires far more inputs of feed than can be produced on 100 acres of land, lying as it does above the production-possibility line. The land *could* be cropped in a way that would just feed a 25-cow herd of 8,500-pound producers (point *A* in Figure 7.2), but the farmer can do better than this. The production-possibility line extends above the 25-cow isoquant in places. By producing somewhat more hay and less grain on the 100 acres, the farmer can still get 8,500 pounds of milk per cow, but can support a herd of 30 cows (point *B* in Figure 7.2). At this point—the highest isoquant reachable with the production-possibility line—some 270,000 pounds of hay and 90,000 pounds of grain need to be produced on the farm. These inputs will yield a total output of 255,000 pounds of milk.

Price Changes and the Price Consumption Curve

Now suppose that the farmer operates a feed lot instead of cultivating the land, buying forage and grain on the open market. Herd size and feed mix will be subject to fluctuations in grain and hay prices. The effects are illustrated in Figure 7.3. The graph shows a succession of isoquants for the feed lot. For purposes of this example, it is assumed that the farmer spends a fixed sum on forage and grain. If all the money is spent on forage, OF can be purchased.

Now, let forage prices remain constant, but grain prices change. When grain prices are high, only G_4 can be bought, and the farmer's *price-possibility line* is G_4F. This line, in a manner analogous to the production-possibility line discussed earlier, describes what can be purchased with the funds available. The optimal herd size and mix of input purchases is given by point A. If the price of grain falls, however, purchases of grain can be increased to G_3, G_2, etc. The equilibrium moves from A to B, C, and D on higher isoquants. Because grain prices are lower, more milk can be produced, and relatively larger shares of grain will appear in the feed mix. The line charted by the successive points A, B, C, and D is a *price-consumption curve*. If the information on how much grain will be purchased at different grain prices is plotted in a price-quantity graph, the farmer's demand schedule for grain will be apparent: As the price falls, the quantity consumed increases.

Price Effects, Income Effects, and Substitution Effects

Movement along the price-consumption curve as prices fall is called a *price effect*, which has two parts:

1. An *income effect*, that is, as price falls, the farmer moves on to a higher isoquant, maintains a larger herd, produces more, and is better off.

2. A *substitution effect*, that is, because the relative price of grain and forage changes with a move along the curve, the farmer tends to use more of the input that has become relatively cheaper, substituting it for the other in his input mix (see Figure 7.4).

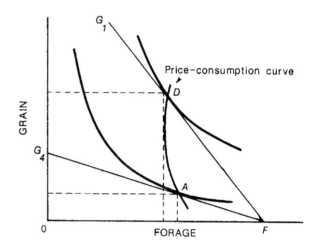

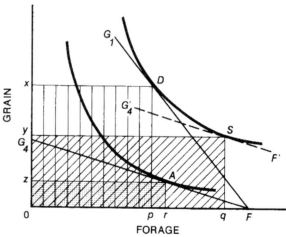

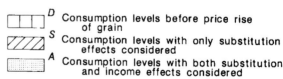

$\boxed{}^D$ Consumption levels before price rise of grain

$\boxed{}^S$ Consumption levels with only substitution effects considered

$\boxed{}^A$ Consumption levels with both substitution and income effects considered

FIGURE 7.4 Separating the income and substitution effects. The increase in grain price from G_4 to G_1 changes the ratio of grain to forage crops from G_4F' (parallel to G_4F) to G_1F. The substitution effect moves consumption from D to S (on the same isoquant), reduces grain consumption by yx, and increases forage consumption by pq. The income effect takes the farmer from S to A, on a lower isoquant, reducing grain consumption by zy and decreasing forage consumption by rq.

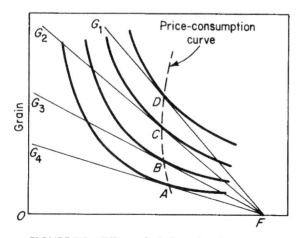

FIGURE 7.3 Effects of relative price changes.

Consequences of Spatial Variations in Prices

In Chapter 6, we saw how many prices increased with increasing distance from market centers because of the effect of transportation costs. We now are ready to explore the consequences. Restricting ourselves to the example presented before, when grain is shipped to the feed lot from a central market, grain price will increase with distance. As a result, the more distant farmers:

1. Will use more forage, substituting the cheaper input for the more expensive one
2. Will keep smaller herds, producing less milk
3. Will earn less

Because there are both income and substitution effects of price changes, as prices increase with distance, the quantity consumed decreases, producing a *spatial demand cone* of the kind discussed in Chapter 6.

Regional Variations in Welfare

The price effects of increasing distance thus include both income effects (people are less affluent) and substitution effects (activities are less intensive). The resulting regional variations appear and reappear in a variety of aspects of life throughout the world, where one of the most marked spatial differences is between affluent core regions where prices are determined, and lagging peripheries with greater poverty and with less intensive production.

To illustrate, Figure 7.5 presents a series of graphs constructed as part of a study of regional development in the United States using data from the 1960 census. The year is significant: it was before the construction of the interstate highway system significantly reduced transport costs and reduced many of the core-periphery differences within the United States. The horizontal axis in each of the 12 subgraphs covers the 270 miles from Dallas to Houston-Galveston, Texas. The vertical axis of each shows how different characteristics vary from place to place along this 270-mile stretch. For example, the first graph on the second row shows that income levels dropped with increasing distance from Dallas, rose around Bryan, fell again, then rose toward Houston. This is the income effect. Similar patterns will be found in each of the other graphs. In each case, the distance gradients reflect spatial adjustments resulting from the income and substitution effects of price increases. For example, as the extent of commuting to jobs in the metropolitan centers declines with distance from the metropolises (top left-hand graph), population densities, the proportion of the population classified as urban, the value of land and buildings, income, amount of schooling, rate of population increase, and percent change in the population through migration all decline. The percentage of the population classified as *rural nonfarm* rises and then falls. Both the percentage of families with incomes less than $3,000 (the 1960 poverty line) and the unemployment rate increase with distance from the central city.

These repetitive patterns create a spatial rhythm, the *regional welfare syndrome:* The lowest levels of welfare are to be found at the peripheries of major metropolitan regions, where prices of consumption items are highest and economic opportunities are least. That people were responding to these variations in welfare in 1960 also is evident: Population was decreasing at the outer edges of the metropolitan regions, responding to differences in incomes and opportunities by migrating from areas of low opportunity to the metropolitan centers that were perceived to offer greater advantages.

MARGINAL PRODUCTIVITY AND THE CONCEPT OF RENT

Let us now return to the situation charted in Figure 7.3, and derive the concept of *marginal productivity.* Begin with the input–output situation described in Figure 7.6. There are two inputs, X and Y, and the isoquants show the combinations of these inputs needed to produce 10, 20, or 30 units of output, respectively. Now assume that there is a fixed supply of one of the inputs (X), so that output may only be increased by increasing the use of the other input (Y). Let OA be the input in fixed supply (say, land). Then AB traces out the different scales of output that may be obtained by increasing inputs of Y (by using more capital or labor on the fixed amount of land). For example, increasing inputs of Y from 2 to 3 units on OA land enables output to be increased from 10 to 20 units. However, the next unit increase in Y, from 3 to 4, produces a lower increase in output, as does the one following, from 4 to 5, because of the way the line AB intersects the isoquants. The increase in output that results from adding a unit of the variable input Y is called the *marginal* increase in output, or the *marginal productivity* of Y—

FIGURE 7.5 Socioeconomic gradients along a 270-mile traverse from Dallas to Galveston, Texas. The graphs have been plotted using U.S. census data from 1960, before the Interstate Highway System smoothed accessibility differences. Each graph illustrates the same 270 miles from Dallas through Bryan, to Houston and Galveston. Locations of the towns are indicated at the bottom of each column. Note how incomes rise and fall in relation to the intensity of commuting to urban centers. Other characteristics rise and fall in the same manner.

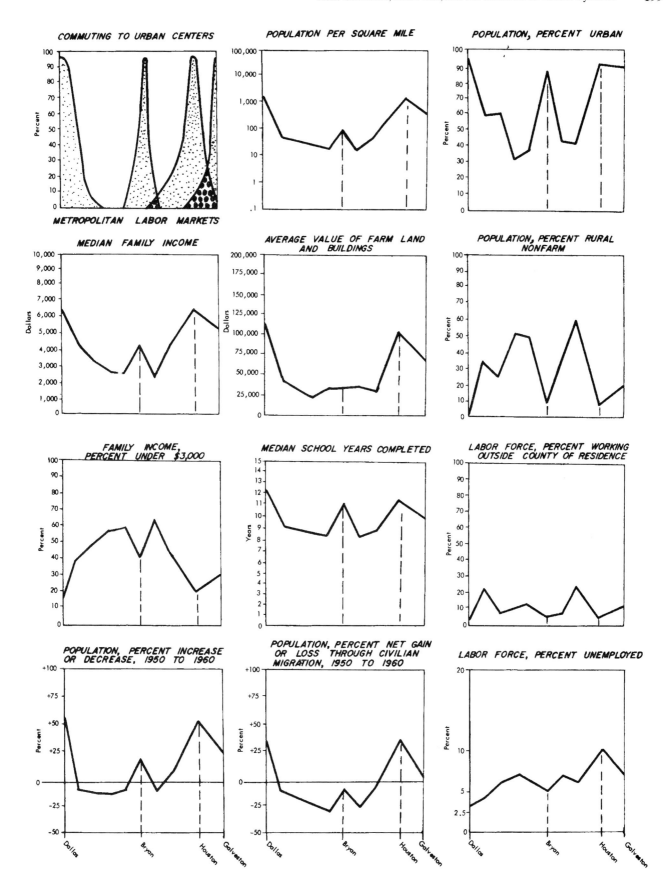

*marginal **physical** productivity* if it is measured in physical units of output, such as bushels of wheat, and *marginal **revenue** productivity* if it is measured in the dollar value of the output. The concept of marginal productivity is central to understanding the laws that govern returns to changing scale of output. The example just given illustrates *decreasing returns to scale.*

The marginal revenue productivity curve can be interpreted as the demand curve for the variable factor. In Box 7.1, if labor costs $10.00 per unit, then the farmer will maximize returns by consuming 9 units of labor at a cost of $90.00. If the price of labor were to double, two things would happen. First, all the numbers in the second column of the box would change. But, second, reading down column 5, so would the point at which the farmer could maximize returns: By consuming only 7 units of labor at a cost of $140.00, the resulting maximum net returns would be $6.00 ($146.00 – $140.00). In other words, the marginal revenue productivity curve also records how many units of an input should be used to maximize revenues as the price of the input changes. The relationship between quantity demanded and price is the demand curve for the input.

We can now use this relationship to develop the idea of the marginal revenue productivity of land (i.e., the demand curve for land), and from this the concept of land rent. To do this, we turn the analysis around and treat land as a variable input and the other inputs as fixed.

Rent as a Scarcity Payment

Assume we are dealing with an island that contains a fixed amount of homogeneous land (*OS* in Figure 7.7). The first farmer settles on the island, bringing a fixed amount of capital and labor. How much land will be used, and what rent will be paid?

Suppose this is a grain farmer selling wheat on the world market. Because of the nature of that market, the farmer must be a price taker, accepting a fixed world price. Let the marginal-revenue-productivity curve for land (demand curve) be *NM* in Figure 7.7, as output is increased by increasing inputs of land. The price paid by the farmer for the land (the land rent) and the quantity of land consumed will be determined by the intersection of the demand-and-supply curves for land. The demand curve is the marginal-revenue-productivity curve *NM*. The supply curve is line *OST*. Thus, the farmer will use *OM* land. The rent will be zero because there is land to spare. The farmer could always move if a landlord tried to charge rent.

Rent is payment to landowners for use of their factor of production, land, which arises solely because land is *scarce.* This relationship can be seen in Figure 7.7 as we let additional farmers arrive on the island. The total demand

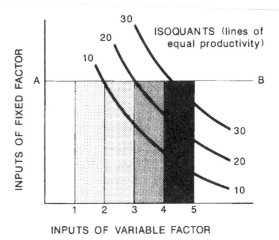

FIGURE 7.6 Production possibilities with one fixed and one variable output.

curve increases as each individual's marginal-revenue-productivity curve is added to that of the others. For example, *PQ* might be the total demand curve for land of one group of farmers (the summation of their individual marginal-productivity curves). *PQ* intersects the supply curve *OST* at *Q*. Because there is only *OS* land available—the land is in perfectly inelastic supply—farmers compete for the land, balancing demands and supplies at price *OR* (= *SQ*). The marginal cost curve for land is thus the price line *RQ*, and our first farmer, maximizing profits by equating marginal revenues and marginal costs, will cut land consumption to *OF*. The other farmers will cultivate the rest of the island, *FS*.

Differential Rents Due to Productivity Differences

Although the preceding example suggests that rents are uniform across the island, in reality rents do differ. Differential rents arise because

1. The productivity of different parcels of land varies
2. Land is located at different distances from market

First, let us take the question of productivity differences. The idea of rent variations being attributable to productivity of the soil was, as noted earlier, first discussed by David Ricardo in 1817. Ricardo said that high rents were due to the "niggardliness of nature" (or scarcity) and were related to the "original and indestructible power of the soil" (or differences in natural resource endowment). Further, he said that the most fertile lands are put to use first, with production extending to less favorable lands only as demand increases.

BOX 7.1 Equating Marginal Cost and Marginal Revenue

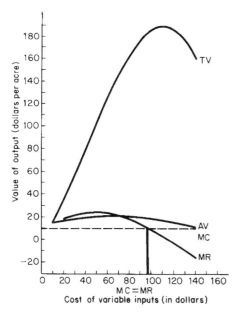

FIGURE 7a Total, average and marginal value of output per acre under conditions of increasing and decreasing returns. This figure compares the cost of variable inputs with total value of output, the average value of output at the scale of output reached, and the marginal value of the last $10.00 increase in outputs. The data from which the graph is plotted are shown below. Marginal cost (MC) is fixed at $10.00

Units of Land Used	Cumulative Cost of Inputs of Variable Factor (labor, per acre)	Yield (bushels per acre)	TV: Total Value of Output at $1.50 per Bushel	MR: Value of Additional Output per $10 Input per Acre (marginal value of product)	AV: Average Value of Output per Acre per $10 Input of Variable Factors
1	$ 10.0	10	$ 15.0		$15.00
2	20.0	22	33.0	18.0	16.50
3	30.0	36	54.0	21.0	18.00
4	40.0	52	78.0	24.0	19.50
5	50.0	68	102.0	24.0	20.40
6	60.0	83.3	125.0	23.0	20.83
7	70.0	97.3	146.0	21.0	20.86
8	80.0	109	163.5	17.5	20.45
9	90.0	118	177.0	13.5	19.67
10	100.0	124	186.0	9.0	18.60
11	110.0	126	189.0	3.0	17.18
12	120.0	124	186.0	−3.0	15.50
13	130.0	117.3	176.0	−9.0	13.54
14	140.0	106.6	160.0	−16.0	11.43

It is assumed that the farmer has a fixed amount of land in grain production, and the output of grain can be changed by using more labor. Column 2 in the table shows the dollar value of the inputs of labor that could be used (per acre) in increments of $10.00; column 3 shows the resulting yield in bushels per acre; column 3 shows the dollar value of output per acre; column 4 shows the marginal value of output per acre for each successive $10 of inputs applied—the marginal revenue productivity of each labor unit—and column 6 shows the average value of the output per acre per $10 of inputs. The three lines in the graph of Figure 7a show how the total (TV), average (AV), and marginal (MR) value of output per acre change as the total value of the labor inputs per acre increases. As more labor is applied to the land, the value of output first increases (i.e., there are *increasing returns to scale*) and then decreases (i.e., there are *decreasing returns*).

At what point should the farmer stop trying to increase output? This depends on both the marginal cost of the inputs and their marginal returns. As long as each successive $10.00 worth of labor input produces a greater marginal increase in the value of output, the farmer should add inputs. But if an extra $10.00 of input produced less than $10.00 worth of output, it should not be made. The general rule is that the farmer should keep on adding labor inputs to the point where the marginal *cost* of the inputs equals the marginal revenue produced, but no further. At this point, returns are maximized. Go beyond this point, and returns will decrease. Can you find this point in Figure 7a? Subtract from the total value of output the cost of inputs needed to produce that output. The resulting net returns (profits) will increase from $5.00 to a maximum of $87.00 when $90.00 of inputs are used. But the next $10.00 of input yields only $9.00 in output and, indeed, total value ($186.00) less total inputs ($100.00) produces only $86.00 in net returns.

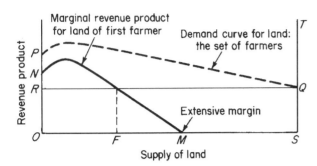

FIGURE 7.7 Marginal revenue product and the emergence of land rent.

Why is this so? Productivity differences change the marginal-revenue-productivity curve for land because they change marginal physical productivity. For example, in Figure 7.8, the marginal revenue productivities of two grades of land, *A* and *B*, are shown. Assume situations in which both are in equal supply *OS*. The lower-quality land will not command a rent, whereas that of higher quality will command rent *OR*. In agricultural terminology, the lower-quality land is "marginal" because it does not pay any rent, and the rent charged for the superior-quality land is due to its greater productivity.

A generalization of Ricardo's idea has been provided by geographers H. H. McCarty and J. Lindberg in the form of an "optima and limits" scheme (see Figures 7.9, and 7.10. In Figure 7.9, two variables—temperature and moisture—provide the basis for their hypothesis. In some restricted area, these variables are presumed to combine ideally for producing a particular crop. That area is identified as having "optimum" conditions. Outward from it, conditions become less and less favorable until, finally, the physical limits are reached, beyond which production of the crop is impossible. In most cases, however, greater significance attaches to the "economic limits," which appear in Figure 7.10. When the productivity data of Figure 7.9 are translated into unit costs of production and when these unit-costs are convened into rent (per unit of output), the areas of production that will appear in response to various price levels for the commodity can be estimated. Assume that a price of "7" will cover costs in the four inside zones of the model. No production will occur outside that zone (in the "no-rent" areas). Further, rent will increase toward the optimum.

What will happen if the price rises because of increasing demand? Marginal revenue productivity will rise, and the extensive margin of production will move into uncultivated lands. By the same token, the higher-rent land will also be used more intensively, because—recalling the earlier discussion of input substitution—if rents are higher

for better-quality land, and if other factor prices are constant, it will pay farmers to substitute inputs of the other (cheaper) factors for inputs of the more expensive land to achieve the same resulting output. Farm sizes can decrease and population densities will increase.

Rent Differences due to Locational Differences

The same relationship holds in the case of rent differences due to transportation cost. As we saw in Chapter 6, the at-farm price is calculated as market price less transportation cost. By holding land quality constant, the effect of an increase in transportation costs is to reduce the more distant farmer's marginal revenue productivity curve (even when marginal physical productivity remains unchanged), and thus to reduce the rent he pays for a given amount of land. See Figure 7.11, in which a farm of size *OL* pays OR_1 at the market, declining to OR_3 20 miles away. The difference (R_1, R_3) is accounted for by the reduction in revenues due to the cost of transporting output the 20 miles to the market.

In such a situation, rents display a pattern of *distance decay* from the market center. Just as higher-quality land will be used more intensively, so will more accessible land. We should expect to see both farm costs and returns decline with increasing distance from markets, and this is exactly the case in the agricultural example depicted in Table 7.1. Note that as rents fell with increasing distance from Louisville, Kentucky, in 1918, farm size increased because farmers substituted the cheapening factor of production (land) for others in their productive process.

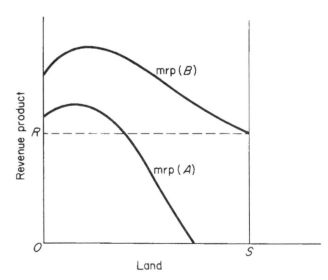

FIGURE 7.8 Marginal revenue product differences for differing land qualities.

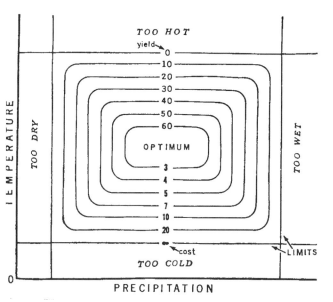

FIGURE 7.9 The optima and limits schema. [*Source:* H. H. McCarty and James B. Lindberg, *A Preface to Economic Geography* (Englewood Cliffs, NJ: Prentice Hall, 1966), pp. 61–62.]

Relationship of Land Rent to Everyday "Rents" and to Land Values

Is land rent the same thing as the rent paid to a landlord for an apartment? There is an important difference that must be clearly understood. What we call *rent* in an everyday sense is a payment to a landlord for a variety of things: the land, but also the building, furnishings, and other services. Only a portion of this payment is the land rent. The rest is the price paid to the landlord for the capital, labor, and enterprise involved in constructing and maintaining the apartment. The difference is clearly seen on local property tax bills, which separate assessments for the land from those for the "improvements."

The assessor talks of land and building *values,* not rents, however. What is the difference? Land value is the price paid to purchase the land; land rent is the payment to an owner to use the land. There is a simple accounting relationship between the two: Land rent capitalized at the current rate of interest equals land value.

VON THÜNEN'S ISOLATED STATE: THE FIRST ECONOMIC MODEL OF SPATIAL ORGANIZATION

The simple idea that rents decline with distance from market was the basis of the first economic model of spatial organization, Johann Heinrich von Thünen's 1826 classic *Der Isolierte Staat.* It is worth spending some time with von

Thünen's model, not simply out of historical curiosity, but because of the systematic way he linked the economic logic of rent theory to the spatial organization of land use.

Von Thünen had a university education in philosophy, biology, economics, and languages, and in 1810, when he was 27, he bought an 1,146-acre estate at Tellow, southeast of Rostock in Mecklenberg, Germany. As he operated and managed Tellow he kept meticulous records, and his early training led him to speculate about the best way of using his land.

Nature of the Abstraction from Reality

Von Thünen found it most helpful to develop the abstract ideas underlying the everyday operation of Tellow, pointing out to the readers of *Der Isolierte Staat* that "the reader who is willing to spend some time and attention" to his work should not "take exception to the imaginary assumptions…because they do not correspond to conditions in reality." Instead, he said, they would allow the reader "to establish the operation of a certain factor, whose operation we see but dimly in reality, where it is in incessant conflict with others of its kind." This is to be said of all location

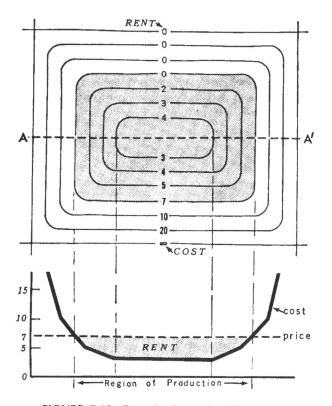

FIGURE 7.10 Rents in the productivity schema. [*Source:* H. H. McCarty and James B. Lindberg, *A Preface to Economic Geography* (Englewood Cliffs, NJ: Prentice Hall,) 1966.]

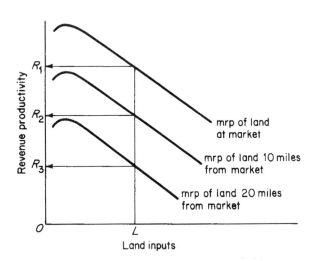

FIGURE 7.11 Marginal revenue productivities (mrp) of land of identical quality at different distances from market.

theories, which are abstract because they seek to understand the basic processes at work shaping the complex reality of the everyday world. Von Thünen was unremittingly logical. He stated his assumptions, posed his problem, deduced the consequences, and tested the deductions with empirical evidence that he collected on his estate over many years. As such, he was a model scientist.

The Assumptions

The assumptions enabled von Thünen to focus on spatial differences, and in particular on the effects of transport costs on land use:

> Imagine a very large town, at the center of a fertile plain that is crossed by no navigable river or canal. Throughout the plain, the soil is capable of cultivation and of the same fertility. Far from the town, the plain turns into an uncultivated wilderness that cuts off all communication between this State and the outside world.
>
> There are no other towns on the plain. The central town must therefore supply the rural areas with all manufactured products, and in return it will obtain all its provisions from the surrounding countryside.
>
> The mines that provide the State with salt and metals are near the central town which, as it is the only one, we shall in future call simply the "Town."

These assumptions are severe: a plain with complete physical homogeneity; a single market, the "Town"; a single source of food supply, the plain; transportation costs related only to volume and distance shipped; and decisions made by an economic maximizer, relentlessly organizing space in an optimal way. But these assumptions are needed in order to establish the role of distance, whose operation in reality is in constant conflict with other factors affecting land use, including variations in climate, soil fertility, management, and the transportation network with its freight-rate structure.

TABLE 7.1

Some variations in agricultural characteristics with increasing distance from Louisville, Kentucky, 1918

Distance from Louisville (miles)	Rent of Land per Acre	Value of Land per Acre	Percentage of Receipts from		
			Truckand Potato	Dairy	Other
8 or less	$11.85	$312	68	10	22
9–11	5.59	110	35	12	53
12–14	5.37	106	34	20	46
15+	4.66	95	20	27	53

Distance from Louisville (miles)	Average Area of Improved Land (acres)	Operating Expense per Acre	Gross Receipts per Acre	Land Earnings per Acre	Value of Fertilizer Used per Acre
9	44	$73	$96	$23	$19.25
12	121	36	45	9	6.50
13	212	15	20	5	5.20
16	420	14	18	4	4.25

Source: J. H. Arnold and Frank Montgomery, *Influence of a City on Farming*. Bulletin 678 (Washington, DC: U.S. Department of Agriculture, 1918).

The Problem

Von Thünen then presented the problem that concerned him.

> The problem we want to solve is this: What pattern of cultivation will take shape in these conditions? How will the farming system of the various districts be affected by their distance from the Town? We assume throughout that farming is conducted absolutely rationally.
>
> It is on the whole obvious that those products will be grown near the Town that are heavy or bulky in relation to their value and that are consequently so expensive to transport that the remoter districts are unable to supply them. Here also we find the highly perishable products, which must be used very quickly. With increasing distance from the Town, the land will progressively be given up to products cheap to transport in relation to their value.
>
> For this reason alone, fairly sharply differentiated concentric rings or belts will form around the Town, each with its own particular staple product.
>
> From ring to ring, the staple product, and with it the entire farming system, will change; and in the various rings, we shall find completely different farming systems.

Von Thünen is suggesting that locational differences alone are sufficient to cause a complete system of spatial organization of land use, embodying concentric circles of crop production and farm types. But he did not stop there. Once the effect of distance had been observed, the assumptions were relaxed and other variables were introduced into the model to see how they modified the "ideal" pattern of rural land use that results from distance effects alone.

Location Rent for a Single Crop at a Single Intensity

Let us proceed stepwise through von Thünen's model. He recognized that land inputs embody two different goods, *space* (physical area) and *location* (accessibility). The basic assumption in *Der Isolierte Staat* is that space is physically homogeneous, so that all variations in land inputs involve the second quality, accessibility to the Town. The impact of diminishing accessibility on net income per unit land area is thus measurable as total income minus production and transportation costs. Because production costs for any single farm commodity were also assumed to be virtually invariant with distance from the Town, variations in net income could then be attributed to differences in accessibility alone. Von Thünen called income net of all costs *location rent*. The question he then asked was how location rent differences were related to transport costs.

Von Thünen essentially calculated location rents as follows, where

R = location rent per unit of land
E = output per unit of land
p = price per unit of output
a = production expenses per unit of output (including labor)
f = transportation costs per unit of output per mile
k = miles from market

then

$$R = E(p - a) - Efk$$

To illustrate the change in rent gradient with distance, let us assume production of a crop such that $E = 40$ bushels per acre; price $(p) = \$2.00$ per bushel; expenses $(a) = \$1.00$ per bushel; and the transportation rate $(f) = 2$ cents per bushel per mile. For farm A, directly at the market and with no transportation costs, $k = 0$, and the equation reduces to

$$R = E(p - a)$$

Substituting gives

$$R = 40(\$2 - \$1)$$
$$= \$40 \text{ per acre}$$

For a second farm, B, 25 miles from the market:

$$R = 40(\$2 - \$1) - 40(\$0.02 \times 25)$$
$$= \$20 \text{ per acre}$$

At 25 miles, the rent has fallen to half. At what distance will it fall to zero? If

$$R = E(p - a) - Efk = 0$$

then

$$k = (p - a)/f$$

Substituting our hypothetical values gives

$$(2 - 1)/0.02 = 50 \text{ miles}$$

Figure 7.12 shows how the components of gross farm income will vary with distance from the Town. A rent gradient, sloping downward with increasing distance from the Town, can be identified. Rotating the rent gradient around the Town produces a rent cone, the base of which maps out the extensive margin of farm land, as demonstrated by Figure 7.13.

Who receives the location rent? Imagine that all the farms are rented out each year on a fully competitive basis at an auction. The farmers know that net return increases with accessibility and bid up the rents for farms closer to

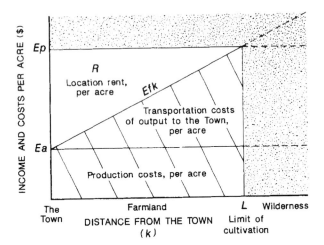

FIGURE 7.12 Components of gross farm income with increasing distance from the Town. Gross income per acre is invariant with distance from the Town. The residual amount, R, left after production costs, a, and transportation costs, Efk, are paid, diminishes with distance. This residual is called location rent and is a measure of market accessibility

market. It pays to continue bidding until the bid rent equals the location rent; indeed, it is necessary for the farmer who wants to occupy the land to do so. At that price, the farmer just recovers production expenses (including what he expects to receive for his own labor and enterprise) and transportation costs, and the landowner receives the location rent as a payment for his land. The competitive bidding eliminates the income differential to farmers that otherwise would be attributable to accessibility; and the bid rent, or contract rent, is the location rent. This bid rent produces a spatial equilibrium situation in which bid rent falls just enough from market to cover additional transportation costs so that the farmer is indifferent as to distance from market. In essence, there is a trade-off between transportation costs and accessibility rent.

Location Rent for a Single Crop at Differing Intensities

The higher location rent paid for land with greater accessibility is an incentive to increase output per unit of land by increasing inputs of capital and labor. Even in von Thünen's day when technology was limited, distinct intensities of grain production existed involving different proportions of the three factors of production—capital, land, and labor. As noted earlier, however, factor substitution is imperfect. The incremental output for each additional unit

of input of labor and capital is not uniform. At some point in the intensification of production, extra units of labor, machinery, or fertilizer add a smaller amount of product than the previous unit. Total physical product may continue to rise, but marginal physical product begins to fall.

This law of diminishing returns has important spatial ramifications. Consider the location rent formula again, $R = E(p - a) - Efk$. The difference between market price (p) and production costs (a) diminishes per bushel as intensity increases, and the transportation cost per bushel (fk) increases with distance. The optimal level of intensity occurs where the marginal addition to yield by the final increment of capital and labor just pays for the transportation of that marginal yield to market. The lower the transportation costs are, the lower that marginal addition to yield need be to pay for itself. The closer the farm is to market, the farther along the marginal physical product curve the farmer can proceed and the more intensive the farming system can be.

The spatial ramifications in the case where two intensity levels reflect two different types of farming organization (the *improved* and the feudal *three-field* systems) were explored in some detail by von Thünen. The data came from the Tellow accounts for 1810–1819, but were standardized for an area of 100,000 rods, or 217 hectares, an area slightly smaller than Tellow, and for soils a little poorer. See Box 7.2.

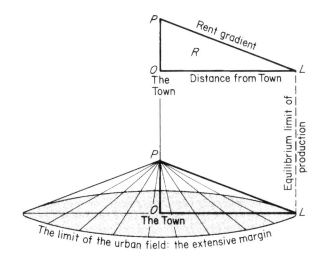

FIGURE 7.13 The rent cone and the extensive margin of production. The rent gradient is derived from Figure 7.12. Economic rent at the Town is *OP*. At *L*, the equilibrium limit of production is, *O*. The *OPL* is rotated to describe the rent cone and to map the extensive margin, where farm land gives way to wilderness.

BOX 7.2 Location Rent for a Single Crop at Two Different Intensities

The improved system yielded a gross product of 3,144 bushels of grain with costs of 1,976 bushels and 641 thalers. Location rent fell to zero at 28.6 miles, at which distance the 1,168 bushels of grain for sale (3,144 - 1,976 bushels) just fetched enough to pay the town-based costs (641 thalers).

The three-field system produced a much smaller gross product—1,720 compared with 3,144 bushels—but both farm-based and town-based costs were smaller. A 45 percent reduction in yield contributed a 48 percent reduction in grain costs and a 49 percent reduction in town-based costs. The economic rent was lower, but it fell more slowly with increasing distance because the ratio of the 327 thalers of town-based costs to the 696 bushels for sale at the market in the three-field system was smaller than the corresponding ratio for the improved system. Plotting these data indicates that at 24.7 miles from market, the three-field system provides the same location rent as the improved farming system (Figure 7b). The improved system is better up to 24.7 miles from the market, and the three-field system from there to the extensive margin at 31.4 miles.

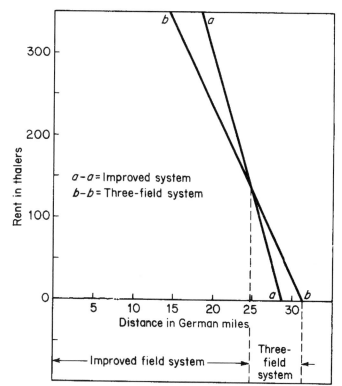

Figure 7b Rent gradients for the improved and three-field systems. (Source: Data are derived from Hall, 1966, p. xxvii.)

A spatial separation of the two farming systems occurs, with an inner circle of more intensive grain farming and an outer ring of more extensive farming. This separation illustrates the principle of highest and best use, which states that land is allocated to that use earning the highest location rent.

Land Use Organization in the Multicrop Case

The most prominent contribution of von Thünen's study was to demonstrate the spatial organization of land use for the multicrop case. Activities are ordered according to the principle of the highest and best use as measured by their location rent at each distance from the market. Market price, transportation costs, and production expenses vary between crops, so that the simple intensity law that applies to any single commodity is inappropriate. Instead, the general rule becomes that land uses are sequenced outward

from the market in the order of the price spreads they achieve between market price and production plus transport costs. The site nearest the market will be appropriated by the product that can pay the highest location rent.

The details are complex but the basic operation of these principles may be illustrated by using hypothetical data for four commodities—milk, potatoes, wheat, and wool (Table 7.2). To graph the rent gradients, only the rent at the market and the limit of cultivation need be computed. Thus, wheat commands a rent of $75 per acre at the market and can extend 60 miles from market.

The rent gradients for the four crops, based on their market rent and distance values shown in Table 7.2, are superimposed to construct the rent diagram, Figure 7.14. In accordance with the law of highest and best, the land use with the largest location rent at any given distance from market outbids the others. The four competing land uses are sequenced outward from the market to form concentric zones of milk, potato, wheat, and wool production.

TABLE 7.2

Location rent for competing crops

	Milk	Potatoes	Wheat	Wool
Annual yield, E	725 gal	150 bu	50 bu	50 lb
Market price, P	$ 0.65 per gal	$ 1.75 per bu	$ 1.70 per bu	$ 0.060 per lb
Production cost, a	$ 0.05 per gal	$ 0.25 per bu	$ 0.20 per bu	$ 0.10 per lb
Transport rate per mile, f	$ 0.05 per gal	$ 0.075 per bu	$0.025 per bu	$ 0.005 per lb
Location rent at town	$435.00	$225.00	$75.00	$25.00
Rent becomes zero at	12 mi	20 mi	60 mi	100mi

Note: The data are hypothetical

Von Thünen's Farming Systems with Relaxed Assumptions

Von Thünen's model of land use in the Isolated State had six farming systems sequenced outward from the Town (Box 7.3). In the simplest case, under the rigorous assumptions of homogeneity of fertility and transportation costs, the systems were concentric.

Von Thünen recognized that his assumptions needed to be relaxed to approximate actual conditions more closely, even in 1826. He wrote:

"Actual countries differ from the Isolated State in the following ways:

1. Nowhere in reality do we find soil of the same physical quality and at the same level of fertility throughout an entire country.

2. There is no large town that does not lie on a navigable river or canal.

3. Every sizable state has in addition to its capital many small towns scattered throughout the land."

What changes in spatial organization result from taking account of these factors? And what effects do increasing prices or yields have on the pattern? The central diagram in Box 7.3 represents von Thünen's description of the effects of increasing prices and yields on crop zonation. The effects maintain the concentric zones.

An irregular pattern of natural soil fertility, on the other hand, might completely disrupt the ordered pattern of concentric land-use zones, as Ricardian rents came into play. A pocket of fertile soil beyond the limit of cultivation for low-yield soil might support the intensive crop alternation system. Such variations in soil fertility distort the spatial pattern formed by simple rent gradients under conditions of resource homogeneity.

Finally, as shown in the bottom diagram of Box 7.3, substantial reorganization in the land-use pattern occurs with the introduction of a navigable river, for which von Thünen assumes a transportation rate of only one-tenth the land rate. A farm 100 miles from the Town but located on this river has the same relative accessibility as a farm 10 miles from the Town by road. A farm 5 miles from that riverside farm has the same relative accessibility as one 15 miles by land from the Town. Von Thünen pictured the crop alternation system that results extending along the banks of the river to the limit of the cultivated plain with the land-use zones changing from a concentric to a sectoral pattern. In the same vein one can imagine radiating expressways producing a "starfish" pattern.

Von Thünen also raised this question: What determines the relative position of the towns in the Isolated State in respect of size and distance from each other? For example, towns of one size, distributed evenly throughout the country would support higher location rents and farm population density. But a number of disrupting factors are discussed by von Thünen. Mineral deposits, notably ore, salt, and coal, are unevenly distributed, resulting in an irregular distribution of mining towns and of the manufacturing towns processing raw materials of little value in relation to

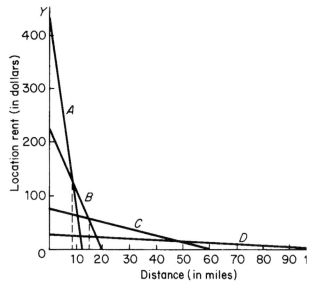

FIGURE 7.14   Rent gradients for competing crops.

their bulk. The largest town, on the other hand, as the focal center of the country, would attract those industries enjoying large economies of scale, as well as functions and amenities such as government administration, institutes of higher learning, and art collections associated with the capital city of a state.

Von Thünen was satisfied, then, to leave the Isolated State with one primary center, introducing only one small town to illustrate the effect resource-oriented centers would have on land-use pattern, as in the bottom of Box 7.3. The small town would compete with the large town for food supplies, and have a region skewed away from the big town.

How might one determine the market area boundary between the large and small town? Figure 7.15 provides the answer. First, market price is lower in the small town because of lower population and, hence, demand. Rents fall with distance from each town, as in the top diagram of Figure 7.15. The spatial pattern of rents is shown in the middle figure, as is the market "indifference" line (i.e., that line along which rents from selling in the two centers are equal). The bottom diagram thus illustrates the subdivision of the plain into market territories, and the rent patterns that result.

FROM VON THÜNEN TO GLOBALIZATION

Von Thünen wrote about a world in which grain was rarely transported overland more than 20 miles. Thus, a typical economic system was limited in scale to the population that could be fed on the output produced within a 20-mile radius of its market town, an area of approximately 1,250 square miles within which a full set of Thünen rings would develop. Most towns living off such microeconomies were small. Few exceeded 5,000, and in Germany in A.D. 1500, the average town size was 400. Even today, in those parts of the world where people still walk or use animals for their principal motive power, similar microeconomies persist. An example is provided by the villages in north India explored by P. M. Blaikie. Minute adjustments of land use to distance are in evidence because self-sustaining farmers existing close to the basic survival level economize on use of their time traveling to and from their fields (Figure 7.16).

In the early days of the Agricultural Revolution in Europe, during the sixteenth and seventeenth centuries, Dutch and English farmers enabled their microeconomies to grow by inventing new crop rotations that improved yields and left less land fallow than in the medieval two- and three-field systems. The new crop rotations were supplemented by new crops, especially the potato and corn (maize), introduced from the Americas after 1600. Potatoes were particularly important, generating three times the calories per acre as grain, enabling land to be freed up to produce animal protein and materials for town industry.

The urban growth that resulted was enhanced in the northwest European towns that had access to water transportation by the technological improvements in merchant shipping introduced by the Dutch in the sixteenth century. Urban specialization could increase with the increasing size of markets made possible by cheaper water transportation. Outward expansion took two paths: *Thünenization*, by which ringlike *world economies* developed and expanded around Amsterdam and London; and *Ricardian Development*, by which the growing urban economies reached outward for high-quality resources.

Thünenization

Amsterdam was the first major city to reach outwards, for Danish and Polish grain, to be followed by London, whose growth pushed agricultural zones outwards across England and Wales, and thence across the sea to Ireland. H. M. Schwartz (1994) writes that prior to British colonization,

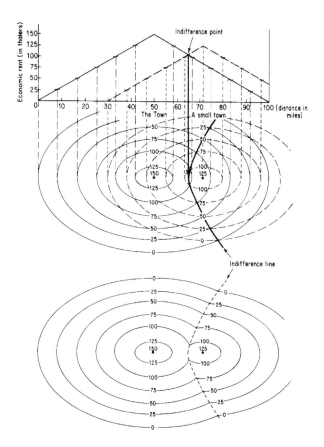

FIGURE 7.15 The impact of a second town on rent gradients and supply areas in the isolated state. The data are hypothetical and assume a single-crop, single-intensity land use with simple transportation cost-to-distance relationships.

BOX 7.3 Von Thunen's Farming Systems

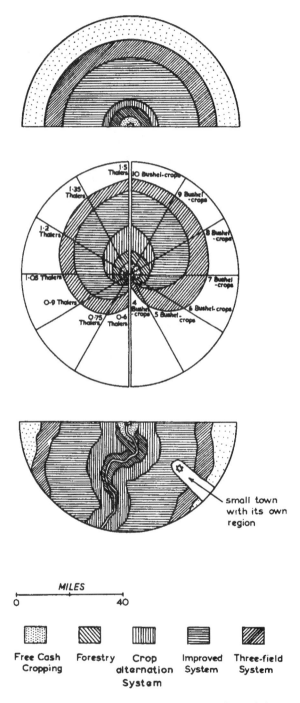

MILES

0   40

Free Cash   Forestry   Crop   Improved   Three-field
Cropping   alternation   System   System
System

Figure 7c   Agricultural regions in the Isolated State, showing effects of changing prices or yields, and of a navigable river and a small second town. (*Source*: Hall, 1966, pp. 216–217)

Von Thünen described six farming systems in the Isolated state, ordered outwards as follows (Figure 7c):

1. *Free cash cropping* included horticulture and dairying for which perishability dictated a location as close as possible to market. Land use is intensive, involving large labor inputs, multicropping, and heavy fertilizing; its outer limit of 4 miles is the maximum range of manure shipments from the city, where horses provided the principal motive power in von Thünen's day. The land is too valuable for open grazing and the milk cows are stall-fed.

2. *Forestry.* The location of forestry in the second zone comes as a surprise from the perspective of modern technology. It was logical at a time when forestry products were in great demand for both building and fuel and when transportation costs, by the primitive means available, were high so that it achieved a substantial cost reduction by proximity to market.

3. *Crop alternation system (Belgian system).* Rings 3, 4, and 5 represented decreasing intensities of crop and livestock farming modified by von Thünen from contemporary agricultural practice. The crop alternation system involved a 6-year crop rotation without fallow in which a given field was devoted for two years to rye, the staple grain crop, and for 1 year each to potatoes, barley, clover, and vetch (a legume fed to livestock). Rye and potatoes were cash crops, and the others used for livestock production, which also provided some cash income. Soil fertility was maintained under this intensive crop system by the rotation, which included two soil-builders, clover and vetch, and by farm manure.

4. *The improved system (Mecklenburg-Koppel system).*

5. *The three-field system.* Both the improved and three-field systems were used to illustrate von Thünen's crop intensity theory earlier. The improved system involved a 7-year rotation, 6 of crops and 1 year fallow. The crops were rye, barley, and oats for 1 year each and 3 years of pasture. The three-field system commonly entailed the division of the farm area into a permanent pasture and an arable area with a rotation of winter grain, spring grain, and fallow. Production costs and yield were about halved in this system compared with the Koppel system (ring 3). Cash income in both systems came from rye and livestock products, the same commodities as the crop alternation system, with the exception of potatoes.

6. *Grazing,* the farthest zone functionally linked to the town, extended outward to a 50-German-mile radius (230 English miles). In von Thünen's day, this zone was too distant for economic shipment of most grain and other crops, and beyond it the land was wilderness. The grazing zone was devoted primarily to permanent pasture, although surprisingly, it could successfully market some intensive cash crops such as oilseeds, hops, tobacco, and flax.

Interestingly, zones 1, 3, 4, and 5 also tell us about economic history. The zones closest to the town were reserved for the most modern "improved" agricultures of the early nineteenth century, whereas those farthest away were the most traditional: Feudal agriculture still persisted in the more remote regions.

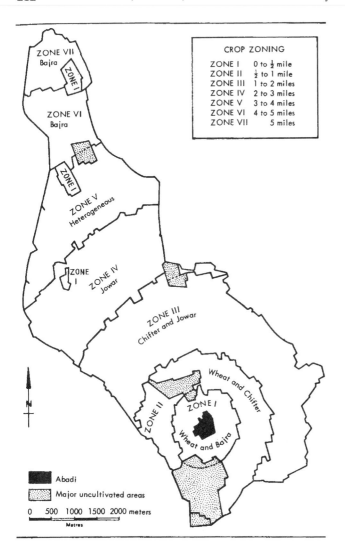

CROP ZONING

ZONE I	0 to ½ mile
ZONE II	½ to 1 mile
ZONE III	1 to 2 miles
ZONE IV	2 to 3 miles
ZONE V	3 to 4 miles
ZONE VI	4 to 5 miles
ZONE VII	5 miles

Abadi

Major uncultivated areas

0   500 1000 1500 2000 meters

Metres

FIGURE 7.16   Crop zoning in a northern Indian village. [*Source:* P. M. Blaikie, "Organization of Indian Villages," *Transactions of the Institute of British Geographers, London,* No. 52, (March 1971):p 15.]

the Irish peasantry subsisted by herding cattle and growing oats. After the English conquest, however, the new Anglo-Irish landlords began to provide range-fed salt beef to the British market, using former peasant land, as the outermost Thünen ring was pushed overseas by rising rents in England. Meat began to disappear from the Irish peasants' diets. As markets for cattle grew, the landlords raised rents to force the peasantry on to inferior land so they could expand the grazing area. Only the arrival of the high-yielding potato enabled the peasants to subsist on the limited and inferior acreage to which they had been relegated. By the middle of the eighteenth century, half of local food consumption was accounted for by potatoes, and virtually all meat was exported.

As the first stage of the Industrial Revolution played itself out, continuing urban growth in Britain led to grain shortages and motivated the writings of Rev. Thomas Malthus about the pressure of growing population on food supply. These shortages initially were met by the shift of the second Thünen ring to Ireland, pushing the first ring farther afield. In 1780, Ireland had exported little grain. By the early 1800s, Ireland provided half of Britain's grain imports, and the nearby port city Liverpool emerged as the market center at which overseas grain prices were established. Within Ireland, grain replaced cattle as the principal export commodity. This change placed even greater pressures on the Irish peasantry. Landlords again raised rents, forcing the peasants into even more marginal environments where they became even more dependent on the potato. The dependence was such that a million died when the potato blight hit in the 1840s. Other millions left for the New World, even while Ireland's grain exports to England increased.

This loss of labor might have been disastrous to the Anglo-Irish landowners, especially in light of new cheap grain supplies entering the market from Prussia and the Ukraine, which had also been brought within the radius of the second Thünen ring by the railroad. They were, however, saved by yet another movement of the Thünen rings as the urban-industrial markets continued to grow in England. Grain acreage fell from a peak of 272,000 hectares in 1846 to only 18,000 hectares in 1887 as the Irish landowners switched from grain to fresh beef and cream production—activities requiring far smaller labor inputs.

Ireland was but one small part of the process of Thünenization. Table 7.3 provides graphic evidence of the expansion of Thünen rings outward from Britain between 1831 and 1895. J. Richard Peet writes that a coherent *Thünen World City* appeared in Britain, Western Europe, and northeastern North America during the nineteenth century, surrounded by a series of concentric agricultural zones that, by the end of the century, extended worldwide. With the growth in food and raw material demands in the "city" market, the zones were pushed outwards across the globe, causing the agricultural frontier to invade the continental interiors. Movements of the frontier, and of all the zones behind it, he said, were explicable through an analysis of changes in demand-and -supply conditions in the system.

There are many examples of the ringlike zonation produced by Thünenization. For example, W. R. Mead shows how exploitation of the forest resources of Scandinavia responded to "the discipline of distance" in the early nineteenth century (see Figure 7.17). The sailing vessel, with complementary horse haulage or riverboat transport, gave rise to a distinctive regional zonation of farmland and woodland use. There was a sharp gradient in softwood timber values from coast and tributary waterway to the interior, with corresponding differences in their use.

TABLE 7.3
Average distance traveled by agricultural imports to Britain, in miles, 1831–1895[a]

Thünen Ring	1831–1835	1856–1860	1871–1875	1891–1895
Ring 1				
Fruit and vegetables	0	324	535	1,150
Ring 2				
Butter, cheese, eggs	262	520	1,340	1,610
Live animals	0	630	870	3,530
Ring 3				
Feed grains	860	2,030	2,430	3,240
Flax, linseed	1,520	3,250	2,770	4,080
Ring 4				
Wheat and flour	2,430	2,170	4,200	5,250
Ring 5				
Meat and tallow	2,000	2,900	3,740	5,050
Wool and hides	2,330	8,830	10,000	11,010

[a] "Imports" from Ireland are not included.

Source: Adapted from a table in J. Richard Peet, "The Spatial Expansion of Commercial Agriculture in the Nineteenth Century: A von Thünen Interpretation," *Economic Geography* 45, 4 (October 1969): p. 295.

Accessible woodlands tended to provide the bulkier, less-refined materials, whereas less-accessible woodlands produced the refined more transportable commodities. Norway, closer to Western European demand, produced relatively more of the transport-sensitive forest products than Finland.

Another example of the response to differential transport costs is provided by the U.S. dairy industry. In the United States, a hundredweight of 4 percent milk can be converted approximately into (1) 10 pounds of 40 percent cream, and 8 pounds of skim milk powder, or (2) 10 pounds of American cheese, or (3) 5 pounds of butter and 8 pounds of skim milk powder. These differences in weight and perishability cause substantial differences in the costs of shipping milk in the different forms. The ratio of transportation costs of milk to an equivalent amount of cream is roughly 7 to 1, to skim milk powder 15 to 1, to American cheese 12 to 1, and to butter 25 to 1. Concentrated dairy products, whose values are high relative to their weight, can be shipped economically for longer distances than relatively bulky and perishable fluid milk. The result has been a concentric zonation of milk specialization around urban-industrial markets, as illustrated in Figure 7.18.

In continental Europe, the intensive cash-cropping areas that had extended only four German miles from the Town in 1826 had expanded by 1950 to encompass much of Europe (see Figure 7.19). The stock farming belt and the extensive grain production regions had, by this time, migrated to countries in the New World and the Southern Hemisphere, which developed as their export-oriented agricultures expanded. Beyond the extensive margin of the global economy, peasant agricultures remained in remoter regions, and hunting and gathering societies only in the world's remotest peripheries. By the middle of the twentieth century, the Isolated State had become the world, and the urban-industrial complexes of northwest Europe, northeast North America, and Japan had become great "World Thünen-Towns," reinforcing the tripolar structure or "triad" of the global economy that we first encountered in Chapter 1.

The process continues. The December 11, 1994, issue of *The Economist* reports on a study of the Machakos District of Kenya by Britain's Overseas Development Institute and the University of Nairobi. Machakos is located east of the capital city of Nairobi. The period studied was 1930–1990.

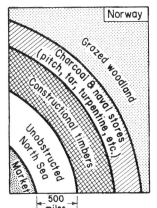 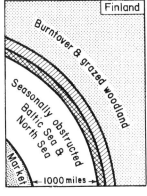

FIGURE 7.17 Zones of softwood exploitation in Scandinavia in the early nineteenth century. [*Source:* W. R. Mead, *An Economic Geography of the Scandinavian States and Finland* (London: University of London Press, 1958), p. 95.]

Sixty years ago, most farmers kept cattle for milk, meat, and as a bride price, and grew some grain and pulses. The region faced periodic food shortages: During the 1940s and 1950s, it needed regular famine relief. There was pressure of population on resources, and soil erosion deeply scarred the landscape. But by 1990, the population has swelled fivefold, to 1.4 million. Was the result a Malthusian disaster? No. Total output had risen fifteenfold: More land was under cultivation (by 1979, there was no unclaimed land left) and yields per square kilometer were up tenfold. The "badlands" of the past had been transformed into a landscape of neatly terraced hills and fenced fields.

How did it happen? Decent road links to Nairobi, dating from the 1950s, made a huge difference. As Thünenization occurred, it became profitable to grow fruit and vegetables. Asian traders began to travel to Machakos to buy crops—and later other goods—for city markets. Better communications also helped government advisers spread news about new farming methods. Most important, Machakos became integrated fairly early—during the 1960s—into the market economy. Farmers diversified from subsistence crops into ones they could trade: coffee, bananas, peas, and pawpaws. Under British rule, the region's Kamba people had not been allowed to grow coffee in competition with white farmers, or to sell grains outside the area without a permit. After independence, in 1963, land reform and the lifting of some state controls encouraged smallholders to invest in higher-value crops and to conserve soil and water so that the land could support them.

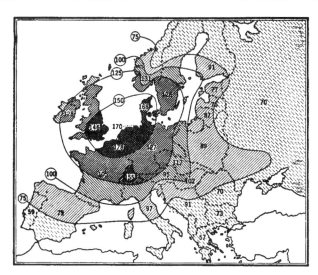

FIGURE 7.19   Intensity of agricultural production in Europe. The index of 100 is the average European yield per acre of eight main crops: wheat, rye, barley, oats, corn, potatoes, sugar beets, and hay. 1937 political boundaries. [*Source:* Michael Chisholm (1962), p. 108, reproduced from S. van Valkenburg and C. C. Held, *Europe* (New York: John Wiley, 1952).]

Capital for investment came from new opportunities to earn money outside farming. By 1990, most farm families in Machakos had at least one son or daughter earning money from nonfarm work. This income helped families buy better tools, fertilizer, drought-resistant strains of maize, and seed for second crops to plant among first ones to take advantage of Kenya's second seasonal rains.

Ricardian Development

Much of what happened in Machakos was Thünenization as the frontier of commercialization arrived, but the switch of Machakos farmers to coffee production is an example of the second land-use determinant, Ricardian Development. Ricardian Development is growth based on the comparative advantage provided by superior resource endowments. Ricardian strategies typically use agricultural or other primary product exports to drive economic development. Their success depends on the ability to locate and exploit new resources. Inevitably, however, such resource-based growth encounters diminishing returns unless new technologies can be brought to bear (Figure 7.20). Thus, Ricardian Development is also technology-dependent.

As the European powers reached outwards in the sixteenth, seventeenth, and eighteenth centuries, early Ricardian Development was state-sponsored. Trading

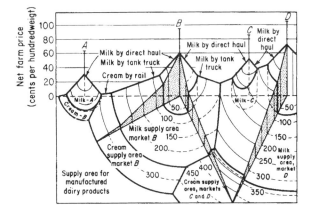

FIGURE 7.18   The net farm prices and supply areas for fluid milk, cream, and manufactured milk products, four-market model, relative to base price for milk sold in manufacturing outlets. [*Source:* William Bredo and Anthony S. Rojko, *Prices and Milksheds of Northwestern Markets,* Bulletin No. 470, (Amherst: University of Massachusetts Agricultural Experiment Station, 1952).]

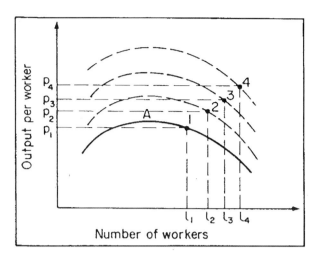

FIGURE 7.20 Diminishing returns and technical progress. Output per input (in this example, workers) is seen to increase to a maximum at *A*, and then decrease, with application of more inputs (workers)—solid line. However, new technologies can raise the input–output relationships to higher levels—successive dashed lines—so that with technological change, even if diminishing returns are setting in, output per worker can increase, as illustrated by the path 1–2–3–4. The idea is developed by Ester Boserup in her 1981 book *Population and Technological Change*, where she suggests that the onset of diminishing returns with population growth created the conditions for the transitions that have occurred in human history from hunting and gathering to slash-and-burn cultivation, thence to extensive field agriculture, and finally to more intensive sedentary agricultural systems.

companies such as the Dutch and the British East India Companies and the Hudson Bay Company were granted government monopolies to encourage them to reach overseas for such transportable high-value commodities as furs, silks, precious metals, spices, and other tropical products. Later, as the overseas territories were colonized, administrators brought crops that could not be produced at home to favored climatic zones: rubber to Malaysia and West Africa, tea to India and Sri Lanka, and cacao to West Africa.

To facilitate this expansion, indigenous populations were displaced, as they had been in Ireland. Railroads, ports, and administrative centers were built. Plantation labor was imported. A colonial development pattern evolved, with urban-industrial heartlands surrounded by Thünen rings and by specialized resource-producing hinterlands created by Ricardian Development.

Later, Ricardian Development arose in different ways, as a consequence of technological change. Railroads and refrigeration increased the transportability of fruits and vegetables, enabling the specialized agricultures of Florida and California to develop in regions possessing special climatic advantages. The process has continued. Today, the reach of American, European, and Japanese supermarkets is worldwide: including, for example, grapes from Chile and Kiwi fruit from New Zealand. The effects are profound. The continuing fall in transportation and communication costs is eroding global Thünenization. Instead, rent differentials are more likely to arise from either natural or created resource endowments. Hence, future land use is likely to be determined by Ricardian Development.

VOCABULARY

Be sure that you add the following items to your vocabulary:

accessibility rent	differential rents	income effect
average product	diminishing marginal utility	increasing returns to scale
average value of output	distance-decay pattern	indifference line
bid rent	economic rent	indigenous populations
commercialization	equal-product curve	input substitution
comparative advantage theory	fixed factor	isoquant
contract rent	fixed price	land rent
core	heartlands	land-use patterns
decreasing returns to scale	hinterlands	land value
demand schedule	income differential	laws of returns

location rent
location rent formula
marginal cost
marginal cost curve
marginal physical productivity
marginal product
marginal productivity
marginal revenue productivity
market price
marketplace-centered gradients
"optima and limits" scheme
output
periphery
price effect
price-consumption curve
price-possibility line

principle of highest and best use
production function
production opportunity
production possibilities
regional welfare syndrome
rent
rent cone
rent gradient
resource productivity
returns to landowners
returns to scale
Ricardian Development
spatial equilibrium
spatial organization of land use
substitutes
substitution effect

three-field farming system
Thünen World city
Thünenization
total demand curve
total product
total value of output
transport gradients
unit cost of production
urban-industrial core
world economies
zonation of land use

TOPICS FOR DISCUSSION

1. Describe the contributions of Ricardo and von Thünen to understanding land use. Discuss the assertion that technological developments enforce Ricardian Development but undermine Thünenization.

2. If the fixed factor Y is equal to 1 and a firm's production functions are

$$\text{total product (TP)} = 6x^2 - x^3$$

$$\text{average product (AP)} = 6x - x^2$$

   (a) What is the marginal product (MP) function?

   (b) From the three production functions, construct a table and a figure showing graphically the three production functions for six successively larger increments to the variable factor X.

   (c) It should be possible then to divide the figure into three stages, a phase of increasing average returns to the variable factor, a phase of diminishing average returns to the variable factor, and a phase of negative marginal returns. Give the characteristics of each function at each stage.

3. Holding land quality constant, what is the effect of increasing transportation costs on marginal revenue productivity? In such a situation, what kind of a pattern do rents display? What happens to farm size with increasing distance? Why?

4. In what sense has von Thünen's Isolated State become the world? Is there anything wrong with this interpretation? If so, what?

5. Consider the location rent formula,

$$R = E(p - a) - Efk$$

   (a) As intensity of land use increases, what happens to the difference between market price (p) and production costs (a)?

   (b) What happens to transportation costs per unit as distance increases?

6. Refer to Figure 7.21. To what extent do you expect urban land use to follow the principles initially formulated by von Thünen? What other factors are likely to influence the spatial organization of cities?

7. Environmentalists complain that urban expansion is consuming the world's "best" agricultural land. Use what you know of rent theory to demonstrate that this is not necessarily so.

8. After the Civil War, steam-heated greenhouses became a feature of the agricultural landscape around the largest cities in the Northeastern United States, but by the Great Depression, the greenhouse economy was largely defunct. Applying what you know of Thünenization and Ricardian Development to explain this rise and fall.

9. Might Frederick Jackson Turner's theory of the role of the frontier in American history, and of stages of development, be rewritten as a process of Thünenization?

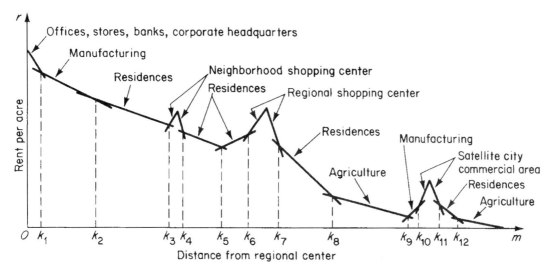

FIGURE 7.21 Hypothetical land rent profile in a multicentered urban area. [*Source: William Goldner, A Model for the Spatial Allocation of Activities and Land Uses in a Metropolitan Region* (Berkeley: Bay Area Transportation Study Commission, 1968).]

FURTHER READINGS

Beckmann, Martin. (1968). *Location Theory*. New York: Random House.

A succinct treatment of the theories of industrial location, land use, and central places, together with the locational impact of economic growth. See especially Chapter 4, "Allocation of Land," which summarizes von Thünen's main ideas and extends these to include the effects of changes in demand, wage differentials, the appearance of urban rings, the introduction of transportation routes, and other complicating elements.

Chisholm, Michael.(1962). *Rural Settlement and Land Use: An Essay in Location.* New York: John Wiley.

Simply and interestingly written, this classic was the first to bring von Thünen's ideas to the attention of modern audiences.

Gregor, Howard F. (1970). *Geography of Agriculture. Themes in Research.* Englewood Cliffs, NJ. Prentice Hall.

A general treatment of the geography of agriculture. Chapter 4, "Spatial Organization," contains a brief exposition of rural land use theory.

Hall, Peter (Ed.). (1966). *Von Thünen's Isolated State.* Translated by Carla M. Wartenberg. Oxford: Pergamon Press.

This translation of von Thünen's classic work on agricultural land use theory covers the essential portions of the original. The book provides invaluable access to von Thünen's seminal writings for English-speaking students of location theory. A substantial introduction by the editor supplies revealing background information on von Thünen and his times and includes an especially helpful guide to the main features of his theory.

Hoover, Edgar M. (1948). *The Location of Economic Activity.* New York: McGraw-Hill.

An influential and comprehensive statement of location theory for four decades, this very readable work remains a valuable sourcebook on the subject. See particularly Chapter 6, "Land Use Competition."

Kellerman, A. (1989). Agricultural Location Theory 1: Basic Models. *Environment and Planning A.* 21: 1381–1396; and Agricultural Location Theory 2: Relaxation of Assumptions and Applications, 1427–1446.

A straightforward and thorough review of von Thünen that is well illustrated and fully referenced.

Peet, J. Richard. (1969).The Spatial Expansion of Commercial Agriculture in the Nineteenth Century: A von Thünen Interpretation. *Economic Geography* 45:283–301.

A clear exposition of the spread of Thünen rings outward from northwestern Europe to cover the globe by the end of the nineteenth century.

Schwartz, Herman M. (1994). *States versus Markets. History, Geography, and the Development of the International Political Economy.* New York: St. Martin's Press.

A graphic account of Thünenization and Ricardian Development in international development.

8

Comparative Costs and the Geometry of Industrial Location

OVERVIEW

The classical theory of the location of industry is concerned with the optimal location for an individual plant in a given industry. It assumes an economic maximizer seeking the plant location that minimizes costs or maximizes some benefit, and focuses on the role of transport costs in locational choice

Early theorists, such as Alfred Weber, thought that the most important criterion for a firm in a competitive indus-try was to minimize transport costs, leading to either raw material or market orientation. All other location factors were thought to "distort" locations from this optimum

Later theorists used transport costs to develop "laws" of market areas and to construct generalized measures of accessibility that better express the growing importance of markets.

OBJECTIVES

- to identify the essential features of least-cost location theory as developed by Weber and others
- to present laws of the market area that can be derived from least-cost location theory
- to review Harris's approach to measuring the importance of markets as a factor in location

WHY STUDY INDUSTRIAL LOCATION?

Not only have transport costs been determinants of rents and therefore of the spatial organization of land use; they also have been key variables in industrial location. But as in the case of land use, as transport and communications have been transformed in recent decades and as their costs have fallen, other factors have come to the fore as locational determinants. In this chapter, we focus on the transport-centered elements of locational choice by manufacturing industry, and on the resulting geometry of industrial location. Chapters 9 and 10 deal with questions of scale, externalities, and agglomeration, and the advanced factors driving locational choice in a global economy dominated by multinational enterprise.

The questions we address in these chapters are important because locational decisions by manufacturing industries are central to the economic growth and health of regions and nations. Manufacturing is the dominant economic base of many regions, and a large proportion of employment in the service industries meets the need of manufacturing workers and their families. Within regions, manufacturing tends to be a *city-forming* activity, whereas traditional service industries tend to be *city-serving.* The distribution of the urban population in most developed countries therefore has largely been an echo of the distribution of manufacturing, until, that is, the onset of "fifth-wave" technologies described in Chapter 10. Differences in employment growth rates between cities and regions are largely a function of their industry mix: Areas enjoying a disproportionate share of fast-growth industries usually have relatively fast rates of employment growth.

But manufacturing also can be relocated more readily than other economic activities, and is moving out of high-labor-cost locations in developed countries to countries with lower labor costs, "deindustrializing" the developed world even as it industrializes less-developed parts of the world. Because manufacturing provides higher-paid, more secure jobs with better fringe payments than employment in service industry, fears of deindustrialization raise concerns not only about the loss of jobs, but also about income levels and the standard of living.

The deep concerns about the *global shift* of industry that have been expressed since the late 1970s stand in sharp contrast to the benefits anticipated from the *national shift* of industry thought desirable by policy makers after the Great Depression. If a country's declining regions were only slightly less competitive in costs than regions with concentrations of fast-growth industries, it was thought that national governments should attract industries into the declining regions with incentives, and prop up declining industries with subsidies. Such national policies to direct the location of industry to serve the objective of balanced regional growth have raised a host of problems, however. How are disadvantaged regions to be defined and delimited?

Do subsidies prevent or just delay closures in declining industries? Do incentives merely offer windfall profits to firms that intended to open in these regions anyway? And much more serious is the speculation that the use of manufacturing as a national policy lever in fact only serves to delay necessary adjustments and rationalization of industry, so that when change finally comes, it is not only more abrupt and severe, but also contributes to global shift.

If incentives and subsidies have failed to secure a lasting industrial base in declining regions in Western countries, what are the growth prospects of the newly industrializing countries? Can their lower labor costs secure for them a lasting industrial base at the global scale in competition with new "lean producers" using information-age technologies in new locations? (Lean production is discussed in Chapter 9.) Is deindustrialization a passing phase, with labor costs becoming less important as a location factor? And what is the role of multinational enterprises in this global shift of industry? They have less attachment to particular countries than do small single-establishment firms, and they can subdivide and move production with relative ease to take advantage of global differences in production costs. So are MNEs "snatchers" (concerned with short-run profits) rather than "stickers" (concerned with building up long-term business)? If foreign multinationals have proved to be an unstable element in manufacturing location, this shift may also explain the resurgence of small manufacturing firms in the Western world. Thus, to the general question of the factors that affect location and locational mobility must be added the specific question of differences between the locational decisions and choice of large multinational manufacturing enterprises and of small owner-managed firms.

LOCATION DECISIONS AND THEIR OBJECTIVES IN THEORY

Beckmann's Classification of Optimal Location Types

An active decision by a firm to select a location for a new manufacturing plant must, in theory, take into account whether or not production costs and the factory selling price are affected by the location of the plant. Martin Beckmann has accordingly classified locations into four types (Table 8.1). The classical theory deals with Type A, which occurs when the costs of assembling raw materials and shipping the finished goods to market vary significantly with location. It is assumed that selling price does not vary with scale of output (i.e., a competitive situation in which the firm is a "price taker"), although consumers will buy from the lowest-cost supplier. The concern of the firm is thus to find the location at which the combined costs of procuring raw materials and shipping the product to market are minimized. The firm will deviate from this least-cost location

TABLE 8.1

Beckmann's classification of location types

	Selling Price (FOB)	
Production costs	*Locationally Variable*	*Locationally Invariant*
Locationally variable	Type B Optimal location maximizes difference between production costs and sales revenue—for example, Smith (1981).	Type A Optimal location minimizes costs to maximize profits—for example, Weber (1909).
Locationally invariant	Type C Optimal location maximizes profits by maximizing sales—for example, Harris (1954).	Type D Plants are footloose. However, theories relating to small-firm birth rates and survival apply.

Source: After Martin Beckmann, *Location Theory* (New York: Random House, 1968), p. 11.

Note: See Further Readings at the end of the chapter for references to the authors cited.

only if some other advantage offsets the additional transportation costs that the competing location entails. Historically, the iron and steel industry has been a good example of a Type A industry.

In the reverse locational type, assembly costs of components or raw materials are insignificant, so that manufacturing costs are spatially uniform. Accessibility to market is crucial because demand is sensitive to selling price, and selling price is sensitive to location. So Type C industries maximize their profits by locating close to market. Soft-drink bottling plants are an example.

Some industries may combine elements of both Types A and C. Production costs and selling price may both be sensitive to location. The solution is to find the location that maximizes profits by making the best trade-off possible between production costs and selling price offered by each location (Type B). The New York apparel industry, for example, has to weigh the advantages of the lower labor costs that would result from moving out of New York City with the design and marketing advantages of remaining there. Activities not governed by rapid style changes have moved out of New York City, but the style-sensitive components have remained.

The fourth locational type, Type D, occurs when neither production costs nor market prices vary spatially. Industries in this group tend to be dominated by standardized production processes, and firms may be "footloose." However, those that depend on a high level of innovation for continuing competitiveness tend to agglomerate, endowing locations with local economies of scale and a support network of services that can increase sales and enhance the survival chances of new firms starting up. Silicon Valley, California, is an example of such a location where such *external economies* have developed. This location type is of growing significance and is dealt with in detail in Chapter 9.

Emergence of Beckmann's four types may be understood historically. The earliest phases of the Industrial Revolution involved the growth of large numbers of small manufacturing firms converting raw materials to finished products that were sold in highly competitive markets. As price takers, these firms depended on minimizing production costs for their successful competition and long-term survival. Toward the end of the nineteenth century, scholars began to observe that "survival of the fittest" had produced quite distinctive industrial location patterns. Industrial location theory developed as these scholars codified their understanding of the market's guiding hand. The first of the theories that sought to explain Beckmann's Type A locational choice was that of Alfred Weber, discussed later..

As the Industrial Revolution progressed, plant sizes increased, along with scale of industrial organization and the ability of oligopolies to manipulate prices in different markets. Type A locational choice was joined by Type B behavior, and then by Type C decisions in industries creating high value-added products from standardized components produced by other manufacturing industries. By the middle of the twentieth century, as a consequence of this economic evolution, location theorists such as August Lösch and Melvin Greenhut were adding demand, price, and markets to their extensions and reformulations of Weber.

Since World War II, economic evolution has progressed to even higher levels of technology with the creation of products selling at uniform prices in national markets, using inputs and manufacturing processes that cost the same wherever the plant is located. Type D situations have emerged in which qualitative factors not entering into the plant's cost or profit equation seem to have dominated locational choice; predominant among these have been the regions and the environments where business people and their key personnel prefer to live. Some of these locations have acquired considerable industrial concentrations and developed external economies that have lowered cost or increased returns for those located within the clusters.

COST MINIMIZATION AS A DETERMINANT OF OPTIMAL LOCATION

A manufacturing firm must go through several stages in getting its product onto the market:

1. Procurement of raw materials
2. Processing of raw materials into finished products
3. Distribution of products to the consumer

The first and third stage involve transportation costs. The second involves the productive operations—capital inputs and economies of scale—plus labor costs.

Transportation costs may dictate a plant location near the sources of raw materials where the following exist:

1. The raw materials are highly localized.
2. The processing of the raw materials involves a considerable reduction in their weight.
3. Transportation costs form a significant proportion of the manufacturing costs and the value of the finished product per unit weight is low.
4. Large volumes of raw material are used per worker.

Examples are the heavy industries such as iron and steel, shipbuilding, and chemicals that formed the economic base of many towns during the late nineteenth and early twentieth centuries.

Under the converse conditions, a plant will be more likely to locate near the market. Such industries might use raw materials that are almost ubiquitous or for which there is little or no weight loss in processing, or produce bulky, fragile, or perishable goods, making distribution costs much higher than procurement costs. Other factors supporting a market location include a requirement for frequent or rapid contact with consumers, as in the high-fashion industry, or differential transportation rates that favor bulk goods and discriminate against finished products.

WEBER'S THEORY OF PLANT LOCATION

These transport cost considerations were the basis of the original theory of plant location, formulated in 1909 by a German location economist, Alfred Weber, in a book entitled *Über den Standort der Industrien* (The English Translation is *Theory of the Location of Industries*, 1929)—basically a theory of transport orientation. Weber sought a theory of industrial location that, he believed, would represent "one of the keys to understanding the current general social phenomenon of population concentration along with a host of other social and cultural changes which characterize our period."

Assumptions and Definitions.

The assumptions on which Weber's argument is based are as follows:

1. A uniform country with equal transportation rates like that of von Thünen's uniform plain
2. The locations of sources of raw materials were assumed to be known and available at equal cost throughout
3. The location of points of consumption also were assumed to be known
4. Labor was geographically fixed. Weber assumed that there exists a number of places where labor at definite, predetermined wages could be had in unlimited quantities
5. Transportation costs were assumed to be a function of weight and distance and were the key locational determinant. Differences in topography are allowed for by appropriate additions to distance and differences in transportability by additions to actual weight

Limited by the science of his time, Weber conceived of his model as a mechanical system of pulleys and weights that resolved competing pulls within a field of forces.

Terms defined included the following:

1. *Ubiquities*—materials available practically everywhere, and presumably at the same price everywhere.
2. *Localized materials*—materials obtainable only in geographically well-defined localities.
3. *Pure materials*—materials that enter to the extent of their full weight into the finished product. Thread to be woven into cloth is perhaps an example of this category.
4. *Gross materials*—materials that impart only a portion of, or none of, their weight to the finished product. Fuel is the extreme type of gross material, for none of its weight enters into the product.
5. *Material index*—indicates the proportion that the weight of localized materials bears to the weight

of the finished product. A productive process that uses pure material has an index of 1.

6. *Locational weight*—the total weight to be moved per unit of product. An article made out of ubiquities would have a locational weight of 1 because only the product itself would be moved; if it were made from pure material the locational weight would be 2 because an equivalent weight of materials would be required for transportation of the product

7. *Isodapane*—the locus of points of equal transportation cost. The meaning of the term will become clear in the discussion.

Seeking in the first instance to measure the effect of transportation on location, Weber then imagined certain cases and developed conclusions about them.

Case 1: One Market and One Source of Raw Materials

The first case supposes a raw material to be produced at *A* and the finished product made out of the material to be consumed at *B*. The problem is to determine where the manufacture or processing is to take place. Weber states four possibilities:

1. If ubiquities only are used, the processing will occur at point of consumption *B*, because the selection of *B* will make transportation unnecessary.

2. If one pure material is used, processing may occur at *A*, at *B*, or at any point between *A* and *B*. This conclusion is based upon the fact that the weight to be transported and the distance to be covered is the same in all instances.

3. If pure material plus ubiquities is used, the processing will occur at the point of consumption *B*, because the pure material will be without influence, and the ubiquities will govern.

4. If one weight-losing material is used, processing will occur at point of production, because the weight that is lost will not have to be transported.

Case 2: One Market and Two Raw-Material Sources

Weber's second case assumes that raw materials are available at two places, *A* and *B*, at equal prices. The finished product is to be consumed at *C,* and the problem as before is to determine where manufacture or processing is to take place. Three possibilities are now considered:

1. If ubiquities alone are used, manufacture will occur at the point of consumption for the same reasons as when only two points were involved.

2. If several pure materials are employed, manufacture will also take place at point of consumption. On this supposition, the weight of materials exactly equals the weight of the product. All weights, whether in the form of materials or in the form of product, have to be moved from their deposits to the place of consumption. They should not deviate unnecessarily; therefore, each material will proceed along the straight line that leads from the origin to the point of consumption. Unless the way of one should lead, by chance, through the deposit of another, all these ways will meet for the first time in the place of consumption. Because the assembly of all materials at one spot is the necessary first condition of manufacture, the place of consumption is the location where manufacturing will be carried on; a productive enterprise, using several pure materials alone, will always locate at the place where its products are consumed.

3. The conclusion is different if several localized weight-losing materials are used. In analyzing this case Weber sets up what he calls a "locational figure." Let us suppose a process that uses two weight-losing materials produced at *A* and *B*, and let us suppose that the product is to be consumed at *C*. Manufacture will not take place at *C* because it is undesirable to transport from *A* and *B* to *C* the material weight that does not enter into the weight of the finished product. It will not, according to Weber, occur at *A* or *B* unless the importance of one material happens to be so great as to overcome the influence of all other elements. Instead, it will usually be found somewhere *within* the triangle, at that location determined by the relative balance of the locational weights.

The "Distortions"

Weber treated labor costs as "a first distortion" of the industrial locations determined by transport costs (for a more detailed consideration of the role of labor costs, see Box 8.1). The second step of his locational analysis was to plot the spatial variations in transport-cost away from the optimum transport-cost location in order to observe the background against which differences in labor cost operate. If, at some other place in the region, the cost of labor per unit of product is less than it is at the optimum transport location,

BOX 8.1 Types of Labor Orientation

Labor costs are dominant locational forces in certain types of industries. If transport costs are a low proportion of total costs, if the ratio of labor to total cost is high, and if labor costs vary a good deal from place to place, plants tend to be most competitive when they are located in areas in which labor cost is least. It is under such conditions that plants are described as being *labor-oriented*. In the world today, there are major industrial shifts taking place in labor orientation as part of a global scramble for cheap labor. Accelerating wage inflation in established industrial areas is pushing manufacturers into new efforts to tap the vast pool of willing and cheap labor in poorer countries. Manufacturers are farming out production of component pads, subassemblies, and even finished products sometimes for export to other areas but often for use back home. In the process they are not only cutting their own costs but speeding the industrialization of underdeveloped countries, some of which are coming to relish the role of workshops for distant, richer lands.

TRADE-OFFS BETWEEN MONEY WAGES AND SKILLS

What are the bases of this movement? Clearly, the prime reason is labor costs, but studies of labor costs show how important it is to recognize that labor costs involve not only money wages. There are many situations in which money wages vary apparently without effect on industrial locations because the benefits of lower wages are offset by a lack of skill and lower productivity of the lower-wage labor force. In such cases, skills are far more important in determining the least-labor-cost location than money wages alone. However, the importance of labor orientation to skills may be offset by technological advances that make unskilled and semiskilled workers as productive as the skilled workers who previously dominate the industry. In such cases, an orientation to low-wage areas rather than to skills has arisen, and is apparently the source of the world trend noted before Labor costs, therefore, vary, first, in terms of money wages, and, second, in terms of productivity and skills.

SHORT- AND LONG-RUN LABOR ADVANTAGES

If the supply of labor is great relative to local demands for labor, wages will be low compared with areas where competition for labor is relatively greater. But research has shown that low wage-conditions tend to be ephemeral: If industry comes to an area in search of the low wages, the very act of movement changes the local supply-and-demand schedules for labor and raises the price. Also, labor tends to migrate from areas of low opportunity to areas of higher opportunity, tending to equalize geographic differentials in wages for that reason, too. Thus, labor-cost variations due to money wages tend to be short-run differentials that can only persist in longer periods of time either because there is a substantial immobility of labor due to ignorance, poverty, or local social ties, or political barriers between countries that inhibit the free movement of labor. But even such immobilities will tend to be eroded in longer periods of time.

Persistent long-run, money-wage differentials have been studied in two types of conditions. First, are those cases in which money-wage differences do not represent differences in real wages; for example, in areas where the cost of living is low. Second, there can emerge those dynamic conditions described by Gunnar Myrdal in *An American Dilemma* for the United States or in his work *Asian Drama* for conditions on an international scale. Myrdal argued that processes of "circular and cumulative causation" can be identified such that labor-cost differentials, rather than being equalized in the long run, tend to increase over longer periods of time. The principal reasons that he cited were the differential nature of the migration flows from areas of low to areas of high economic opportunity. Put simply, the most able people move to find better jobs, leaving behind an older and less able population group. This migration decreases the economic viability of the home area, although it increases the quality of skills available in the reception area. These skills impart advantages for further growth, so that the reception areas gain more and more relative advantages.

REGIONS WITH MONEY-WAGE ADVANTAGES

Money wages have been shown to be low in four kinds of areas, which therefore represent the most attractive zones for industry decentralizing in search of low labor costs.

1. *Where the supply of labor is increasing more rapidly than the demand for labor.* This is typical in rural and backward areas where net reproduction rates are substantially greater than elsewhere. Such a condition was typical of the rural parts of the United States in which particular minority groups lived. On an international scale, this is the characteristic of the South Asian countries. In each of these cases, migration rarely tends to offset the natural increase completely, so that a persistent labor surplus develops, which keeps the price of labor at a minimum.

2. *Where economic opportunities are declining in relation to a sizable local labor force.* Such a condition is typical of any kind of economically depressed areas. The coalfields, for example, were in this position during

the peacetime between the world wars. For a long time, the anthracite towns of eastern Pennsylvania have faced this situation, as have many other mining areas. This was the history of the cotton textile towns of New England when the cotton textile industry moved to the Piedmont area of the Carolinas and Georgia. Of course, where economic opportunities are declining in relation to the labor force, wage rates will drop.

3. *Where employment opportunities are available only for part of the population.* This has been a general characteristic of female labor in heavy industrial areas where the demand is traditional only for male labor—in the coalfields, in mining areas, in fishing towns, or in railroad towns. In these areas of heavy industry, female labor has traditionally been available at very low wage rates. Where the size of the local female labor pool is large, however, labor-intensive, low-wage industries have been attracted.

4. *Where the cost of living is low so that real wages are high relative to money wages.* For example, housing prices in the American South and Southwest are much lower than in the Northeast because homes in the Northeast must be protected against the very severe winters. Lower housing prices mean that people can maintain the same real level of living at lower money-wage rates because they need to put less into the housing that they purchase. A similar situation is where superior residential amenities create a substantial "psychic income" that people are willing to take instead of the higher wage rates offered in areas with fewer residential advantages. In such conditions, of course, money wages will tend not to reflect the real level of living, and the money-wage differential will act to the competitive advantage of labor-oriented firms.

TECHNOLOGICAL CHANGE AND THE TIES OF LOCALIZED SKILLS

Money wages are only significant locational factors where skills are relatively insignificant. We will turn later to instances in which the advantages of certain highly localized skills lead to the long-term ties of particular industries to particular locations, and we will discuss the reasons for the development of these localized skills. What is significant is the condition under which skill factors have been shown to exert a diminishing pull on industries. Localized skills are usually relevant to only one industry and are relatively immobile. They are thus very powerful causal factors in geographical inertia. Many operations can only break out of the bonds of localization in a skilled labor area by diminishing reliance on the skill factor. Only when higher productivity is not related to skills will lower labor cost mean lower wages.

Industry has been shown to shift into areas of lower money wages most generally only under conditions of technological change, when increased mechanization, routinized operations and processes have tended to diminish the importance of skills. The introduction of line methods of production facilitates the use of relatively 'green' labor, for example, so that operations can become routinized and can be performed efficiently with only a short period of training. Thus, when semi-skilled labor-force requirements become increasingly uniform, decentralization of routinized operations is facilitated in the direction of low-wage areas, and a wider source of labor is available. But, of course, we have to repeat that this movement to low-wage areas is essentially a movement of routinized operations. Quality products have to stay in the traditional areas, for style cannot be routinized

and the skills required for production of high style are localized. In the clothing industry, for example, ready-made clothing production has moved to cheap labor areas, but style lines remain in the world style centers—New York, London, Paris, and so on.

In routinized operations, on the other hand, low-wage areas may even have an advantage in productivity. First of all, a new plant coming into a previously nonindustrialized area can "skim the cream" off the local labor force by offering higher wages than those offered by the alternative occupations of the previously nonindustrialized area. This new labor force in general, having no previous experience in factory employment and no preconceived notions about the organization of the industry, or about work loads, is more plastic to requirements of a changed technology, and will be willing to operate with more pieces of machinery than the worker in the traditional industrial areas. Also, too, low-wage areas tend to be those areas that have the least restrictive labor codes—we are all well aware of the substantial differences in legislation relating to employment and labor conditions among the states. The areas that have the most restrictive forms of legislation also tend to be the areas in which the trade union movement is strongest. In the United States, this reflects, in general, the differences between North and South and between large city and small town. The relative abundance of labor in the South and in small-town locations means the inability of trade unions to establish themselves. Smaller towns, too, will tend to be dominated by one producer, who controls whatever he or she does not own locally. There, work loads are likely to be higher, employee benefits lower, and employers much freer to adapt the productive process to their wishes.

perhaps because an established industry closed down or an unusually high rate of population growth occurred, or a pool of particularly skilled workers is available, and if the increment to transport costs at this alternative location is less than the labor savings, a "deviation" from the "optimum" least-transport-cost location will arise.

Weber suggested that *isodapanes* be used to determine whether deviations from an optimum least-cost location could occur. Isodapanes are curves of equal transportation cost. All places on the same isodapane thus have transportation costs equally higher than the least-cost location. A *critical isodapane* can be identified along which the additional transportation costs are equal to the savings in labor costs. A plant can move to an alternative labor-saving location only if it is within the critical isodapane.

Having combined the effects of transport and labor costs, Weber then turned to the problem of determining how that location may be deflected within the region by the tendency of firms to agglomerate. In Weber's view, there are two main ways in which a company can gain the benefits of agglomeration. First, it may increase the concentration of production by enlarging its factory, thus obtaining savings through a larger scale of operation. Second, it may benefit by selecting a location in close association with other plants. This "social" agglomeration yields benefits from sharing specialized equipment and services, greater division of labor, and large-scale purchasing and marketing.

As a "second altering force," agglomeration acts to divert manufacturing from either a least transport-cost location or a least-labor-cost location. For an establishment that would normally be transportation-oriented, the savings from locating close to other firms may be sufficient to justify some sacrifice of transport cost. To determine whether or not such a diversion from the least transport-cost location was feasible, Weber employed a similar logic to that previously used for weighing the counterattractions of transport and labor locations.

Because, in Weber's view, the attractions of agglomeration and labor-cost savings both represent deviations from the least-transport-cost location, however, these two influences may conflict. The decision will go to the one that provides the greater savings. Weber indicated that the winner is more likely to be the labor location because that is a place where "accidental" agglomeration may be expected to occur as a result of a concentration of population or the presence of special transport features.

Weber's conclusion that scale and agglomeration are the least important "distortions" of optimal transport orientation may have been appropriate for the years prior to World War I. With declining transportation and communications costs, had he written today, his conclusions would certainly have been different, as we shall see in Chapter 9.

THE LAUNHARDT–PALANDER SOLUTION OF THE LEAST-COST LOCATION

Weber was concerned with finding the least-cost location when the market was located at certain known points of consumption. A useful contribution to understanding the importance of the location of the raw materials in determining the least-cost location for a plant had already been worked out in a general way by Wilhelm Launhardt in 1882 and was elaborated by Tord Palander in 1935. The Launhardt–Palander construction is summarized in Box 8.2 and its application to the U.S. steel industry is illustrated in Box 8.3.

The Launhardt–Palander solution leads to three principal conclusions about the location of industry under Weberian assumptions. First, there cannot be as many least-cost locations as points of consumption. Indeed, the number of least-cost locations is much more limited than might be expected. So even under the strict assumptions of Weber, industry will tend to concentrate in a *manufacturing belt* delimited by the location of the raw materials and by the numerical value of the material index. Furthermore, the higher the material index, the more limited the possible number of least-cost locations and the narrower the manufacturing belt will be. Second, only raw-material locations can offer the lowest transportation costs for any extensive area, and they are the only locations that can command a large market area. The advantages of a location at the raw materials is further enhanced by the economies of scale that production for a large market area make possible. Third, and perhaps most important, the Launhardt–Palander solution provides a clear demonstration of the impact of technological advances on the location of industry.

If inputs of both raw materials per unit of output are reduced, then both lose market area to the points of consumption. However, any change in the material index has the effect of changing the actual location of an intermediate least-cost location. This change occurs because the location of the pole (P) on the weight triangle (Box 8.2) changes, and hence the line from the pole to the point of consumption (PC). The vulnerability to technological change of the least-cost status of an intermediate location enhances the advantages of a location at the source of raw materials. Intermediate locations are further disadvantaged if more realistic assumptions are introduced about transportation costs involving terminal costs and line-haul economies (Box 8.4).

The evidence about the importance of sources of raw materials as stable least-cost locations for large market areas is very important. It serves to correct the impression given by simple applications of Weber's principles involving ubiquitous and localized pure materials that the

BOX 8.2 The Launhardt–Palander Solution of the Least-Cost Location

1. Launhardt and Palander provided a simple geometric construction that demonstrates the market area served, given Weber's assumptions. In particular, assume that the firm must minimize transportation costs and that M_1 and M_2 are the only sources of the raw materials needed for production.

2. Construct a weight triangle M_1M_2P in which the sides of the triangle are proportional to the weights of the raw material inputs and the weight of the finished product output.

   (a) M_1 M_2 is translated from a geographic distance, set by the scale of the map, to a geometric distance equal to the unit weight of output.

   (b) M_1P equals the weight of the M_2 input per unit of output

   (c) M_2P equals the weight of the M_1 input per unit of output

3. Draw the circumscribing circle through M_1 M_2P.

4. Extend PM_1 to A and PM_2 to B. The least-cost location for any point of consumption above M_1M_2 can now be determined.

5. Assume the point of consumption, C_1, is beyond the circumscribing circle. The manufacturing location that minimizes transportation costs is L, where line PLC_1 intersects the circumscribing circle. Repeat for C_2 *also on the line PLC_1.* The least-cost location is still at L. For A, the least-cost location is M_1 and for B it is, M_2

6. Market areas can be determined that are served from least-cost locations on or within are M_1 LM_2. M_1 and M_2 have the largest areas. Arc M_1 L M_2 is the locus of points serving markets beyond the arc. The area within the are is served by plants at each point of consumption.

7. To complete the map of market areas, the construction (steps 2 to 6) is repeated with the weight triangle above M_1M_2. In this example, M_1 has the largest market area because it has a larger input, by weight, than M_2.

The Location of M_1 and M_2

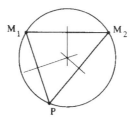

The Weight Triangle with Circumscribing Circle

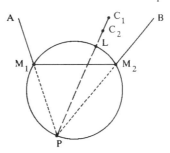

Note: the material index equals

$(M_1P + M_2P)/ M_1M_2$

The Least-cost Location for C_1 and C_2

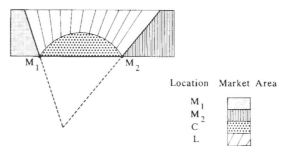

Market Areas Above M_1M_2

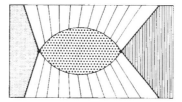

Location	Market Area
M_1	
M_2	
C	
L	

The Complete Map of Market Areas

BOX 8.3 Locational Implications of a Reduced Material Index: The Case of the U.S. Steel Industry

1. In 1900, the U.S. steel industry averaged 1.85 tons of coal and 1.83 tons of iron ore per ton of finished steel. The MI (material index) was 3.68 and given the primary locations of coal at Connellsville and ore at Mesabi, the market area map is easily constructed using the Launhardt-Palander construction. Pittsburgh had the largest market area and had been the leading steel producer since 1875.

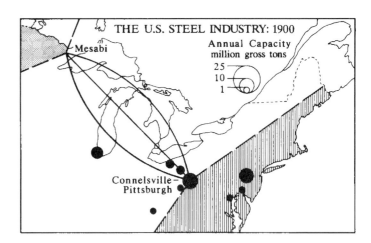

2. By 1960, coal inputs had dropped to 0.79 ton and iron ore to 1.10, reflecting technological advances and the greater use of scrap. The MI was 1.89. Pittsburgh had tried to retain its market share with Pittsburgh-Plus Pricing, but the industry was moving closer to the markets, particularly along the Eastern seaboard, and to Detroit and Chicago.

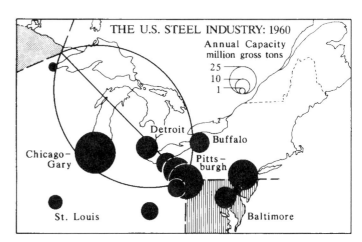

3. Superimposing the two sketch maps illustrates the locational implications of the reduction in the MI.

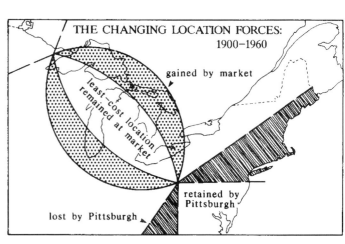

Note: This example is based on an unpublished idea of Richard Lamb.

BOX 8.4 Plant Location with Line-Haul Economies and Transshipment

Consider an industry using one raw material located at *X* and serving one market located at *Y*. The farther a plant from the raw materials, *X*, the higher will be its procurement costs. So procurement costs, *ab*, increase from *X*. Conversely, the farther the plant from the market at *Y*, the higher will be its distribution costs. So distribution costs increase from *Y(cd)* The transport cost curves assume there are terminal or loading charges (*cY* for *Y* and *aX* for *X*), and line-haul economies so that the cost per kilometer decreases with distance.

Procurement and Distribution Costs

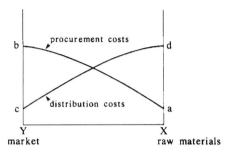

A plant minimizes its transportation costs, under these assumptions, by locating at either the market (*Y*) or at the raw materials (*X*). At either of these locations it eliminates one set of terminal charges and gains the maximum long-haul economies.

Total Transportation Costs

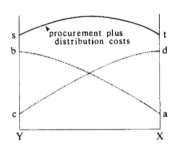

The cost structure changes if there is a break of bulk point *T* where goods must be transshipped, say, from railroad to canal. Both procurement and distribution costs jump at *T* because of additional unloading–loading charges. A plant at *T* avoids these charges, and in fact, on the freight rate scheduled as shown, *T* is a lower transportation cost point than *X*, the raw-material location.

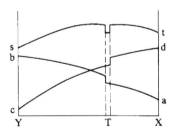

point of consumption may often be the least-cost location. Under the more realistic case of localized gross materials, the point of consumption loses much of its attraction as a location for industry. Conversely, the evidence about the impact of technological change is very different. It helps to explain why markets have had an increasing attraction on the location of industry, and why location theory has moved away from a concern with cost minimization (Type A, Table 8.1).

Industry may not always shift location in response to these changing location forces, however. In the case of the United States steel industry, for example, a stagnant market

demand and the large capital costs required to set up new integrated mills combined to lead to a process of "in situ restructuring" virtually pinning the industry to its 1960s location pattern (Box 8.5).

ECONOMIC LAWS OF THE MARKET AREA UNDER LEAST-COST LOCATION

Assuming that any given consumption point will be served from whichever plant can deliver at the lowest combined production cost plus freight, it is possible to determine laws

BOX 8.5 The U.S. Steel Industry Since 1960

Surprisingly little change in the location of the U.S. steel industry has occurred since 1960, and the present distribution of the industry is still governed by the Weberian forces acting up to 1960. From 1960 to 1980, the industry suffered from a short-term investment strategy and *industrial inertia.* After 1980, substantial Japanese investment occurred and a process of *in situ restructuring* took place (Florida and Kenney, 1992).

INDUSTRIAL INERTIA: 1960–1980

Investment in the U.S. steel industry trailed off between 1960 and 1980. The last integrated steel mill built by a U.S. corporation in the United States was Bethlehem Steel's Burns Harbor Works built near Chicago in the 1960s. During this period, the industry expanded by making additions to existing mills. This process was called "rounding out." It was a short-term strategy that resulted in cluttered facilities with a technology and location pattern that had been frozen since the 1950s. Meanwhile, Japan's steel industry was following a diametrically opposed scrap-and-build strategy that enabled Japan to overtake the United States in steel production technology, production capacity, and in quality by 1980. U.S. steel corporations began to diversify in an attempt to shift out of steel production. For example, U.S. Steel purchased Marathon Oil and changed its name to USX. Since the 1980s, U.S. steel producers have improved the quality of their products, but a recent survey of users, the most important of which is the automobile industry, indicates that the gap in quality between steel produced by Japanese and U.S. corporations persists. Only Japanese corporations are perceived as achieving overall excellence in quality and the steel delivered to the Big Three auto manufacturers is generally below the minimum standard considered acceptable by

Japanese car makers. It was partly for this reason that Japanese steel corporations began to invest heavily in the United States during the 1980s.

IN SITU RESTRUCTURING: POST-1980

Florida and Kenney, (1992) introduced the term "in situ restructuring" to describe the comprehensive technical, economic and social reorganization of industry produced by this Japanese investment in the U.S. steel industry.

Why did the Japanese invest in the U.S. steel industry when U.S. corporations had virtually stopped investing in it and were trying to exit? Among the reasons identified, the most important were (a) limited future prospects in Japan, (b) U.S. trade protectionism that limited imports from Japan, and (c) the needs of Japanese car markers already in the United States. Japanese steel corporations were suffering increasing import penetration into their home market from low-cost producers in the developing world, which exacerbated a fall in demand in Japan. The steel industry has historically been regarded as vital to national interests and the United States was becoming very sensitive to import levels of steel from Japan, alleging "dumping." Japanese car makers in the United States needed a more consistent and higher-quality range of inputs than United States steel corporations could provide. Steel is the dominant component of a car, accounting for three quarters of the weight of the typical Japanese automobile. Particularly important is galvanized steel, about half the total steel used in a car, where U.S.-made products lagged in quality.

Japanese steel firms chose to invest in the United States mainly by linking up with United States steel firms in a series of joint ventures. American management and unions might well have been opposed to

independent Japanese production in the United States but Japanese joint ventures were welcomed in an industry that recognized the benefits gained as being essential for survival. Joint-venture capital investment helped to resolve the quality problem without creating a surplus quantity problem

The result was to produce a geographic pattern of in situ restructuring oriented largely to the needs of the automobile industry. The form and organization of the integrated steel mills and galvanizing and coating mills were changed, but not their location, with the exception of some galvanizing and finishing lines that were set up close to new Japanese automobile assembly lines.

To the extent that locational shifts occurred in the United States steel industry, they were dictated by where the Japanese did *not* invest. The automobile-oriented restructuring contributed to a retention of the steel industry along the Chicago–Detroit axis, close to the major automobile assemblers. In the Pittsburgh district, on the other hand, there was little Japanese investment and the integrated mills closed. What remained were mini mills producing specialty steels using electric arc furnaces, and relying on scrap as the raw material. Thus, whereas at the global scale Japanese preeminence in achieving lean, high-quality output has shifted world steel and automobile production from Western Europe and North America to Japan, within the Untied States, the combined effects of industrial inertia from 1960 to 1980, and of in situ restructuring since 1980, have been to entrench part of the pattern of industrial location established byWeberian forces acting up to the 1960s.

Source: Richard Florida and Martin Kenney (1992). "Restructuring in Place: Japanese Investment, Production, Organization and the Geography of Steel," *Economic Geography* 68 (2):146–173.

of the market area. The principal contributors to such laws have been Tord Palander in *Beiträge zur Standortstheorie* and Frank Fetter in "The Economic Law of Market Areas" (Box 8.6).

In the simplest case of producers with identical production and freight costs, the market boundary between them will be an *equidistant straight line.* The delivered price from either producer is equal along this market boundary and consumers are indifferent as to which firm they buy from. However, the delivered price is not the same all along the market boundary. The more distant a consumer is from the production point, the higher the transportation cost is. The two plants thus deliver at an equal but higher price.

In the case where transportation costs are equal but production costs are not, then the lower-cost producer extends its market area. The market boundary then becomes a hyperbola pointing toward the high-cost producer. As in the case before, consumers are indifferent along the market boundary as to which firm they buy from, but the price increases along the market boundary as distance and transport costs from the firms increase. If one producer were able to progressively reduce production costs, the market boundary would encroach on the second producer in a succession of hyperbolas. Provided, however, that the difference in production costs remains less than the shipping costs between the two producers, then the higher-cost producer will always retain the local market together with the area facing away from the lower-cost producer. It is only when a producer has lower transportation costs than a competitor that the competitor's market area can be reduced to an enclave. This can happen even though their production costs are lower.

Some excellent examples of the preceding cases can be drawn from Britain's Labor government's post–World War II "White Papers" on the sand and gravel, brick, and cement industries. These examples reveal increasing concentration of production as relative transport and production costs declined from one case to the other.

Sand and gravel are widely available in superficial deposits in Britain. They are usually worked together, because gravel aggregates are found surrounded by sand. The product has a very low value in relation to bulk: In 1948, the pit price was 5 shillings per ton, including all costs of excavation and dressing. Pit price did not vary much from one part of the country to another. Transportation costs loomed large in final delivered prices: Transportation of only 2 miles increased selling prices by 30 percent (the markup being for the fixed costs of loading and the variable costs of carriage) and shipment of 13 miles doubled the pit price. Because consumers make their purchases on the basis of final delivered price, it is easy to see how small sand and gravel pits multiplied, each serving small market areas limited by increasing transportation costs. Few pits sold sand and gravel farther than 30 miles from the pit in Britain; the few exceptions are where cheap water transportation is available.

In 1950, there were almost 1,500 brickmaking plants in Great Britain. There are very few clays in the country that have not been worked for brickmaking. Transportation costs were lower in relation to production costs than for sand and gravel. Prices increased 20 percent with shipment of 50 miles, and doubled if shipped 150 miles. Lower transport costs imply larger market areas, and more latitude in location of the brickmaking plants. Thus, plants tended to concentrate on the best brickmaking clays. One-third of the productive capacity of Great Britain was found at the time of the White Paper in 46 plants at Bedford, Bletchley, and Peterborough in the Midlands where the superior Oxford clays were used to make "Fletton bricks," the familiar red bricks that characterize the English landscape. This concentration was made possible because production costs on the Oxford clays were lower than elsewhere. Peculiar advantages are thick homogeneous beds that reduce excavation costs, the fact that 5 percent of the volume of the clay is carbonaceous, which reduces the amount of coal that has to be purchased to bake the bricks, and the plastic qualities of the clay, which eliminate pretreatment, such as pulverization, normally required before bricks can be molded. The Fletton producers sold over longer distances by virtue of lower production costs.

A third case is illustrated by the British cement industry. There are two kinds of cement: (1) Portland cement, formed by burning clay and chalk together until they fuse in a clinker, which is crushed to make cement, and (2) blast-furnace cement, a by-product of the steelmaking industry. The former is most common in England and provides this third example of the joint role of transport and production costs in reducing the diffusion of industry.

Several raw materials are needed to produce Portland cement. To obtain 100 tons of cement requires 225 tons of chalk, 75 tons of clay, 60 tons of coal, and 5 tons of gypsum. Clay and chalk are usually found close together in England, and because chalk inputs are greatest, cement plants tend to be tied to sources of chalk. But because costs of transporting cement are high, cement plants tended to be small, located centrally to small scattered markets. Price increases with overland transport were such that the cement was not sold farther than 25 miles overland from the cement plant.

In spite of such obvious pressures for diffusion, however, 50 percent of Britain's Portland cement was produced in the Thames–Medway area, southeast of London. Why

BOX 8.6 *Laws of the Market Area Under Transport-Cost Minimization*

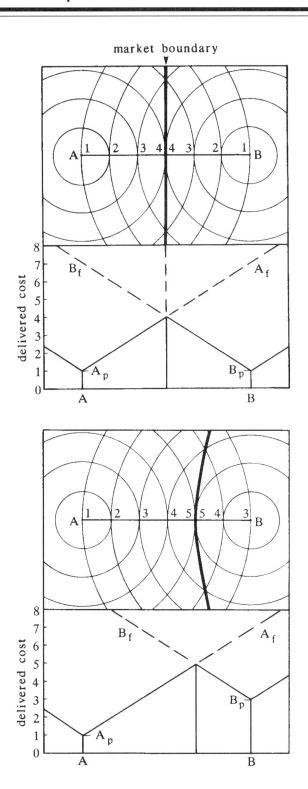

MARKET AREA LAWS WHERE TRANSPORTATION COSTS ARE EQUAL

The Law of the Equidistant Market Boundary

Assume that equal products are made at *A* and *B* and shipped at equal transportation rates. The delivered cost will increase concentrically outwards from A and B. If consumers always buy the product sold at the lowest delivered price, then *the market boundary between A and B will be an equidistant straight line.*

The Law of the Hyperbolic Line of Indifference

If the price at $B(B_p)$ is higher than the price of $A(A_p)$, and assuming goods are shipped at equal transportation rates, then the market boundary is a hyperbolic curve, which cuts into market area of the higher-cost producer.

The Law of the Encroaching Hyperbolic Market Boundaries

If the price at B were to increase in progressive increments, then the market area of A would steadily encroach on B. A sequence of hyperbolic curves would result. The penultimate case is when A can deliver to B at only slightly more than B's FOB price. The market area of B then collapses to a line extending from B away from A. Finally, B exits from production, when its FOB price is higher than the delivered price from A.

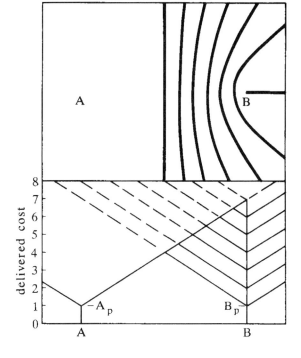

MARKET AREA LAWS WHERE TRANSPORTATION COSTS ARE NOT EQUAL

The Law of the Parabolic Market Enclave

Market areas are sensitive to differences in transportation costs. If the plant at B faces higher freight rates than A, in addition to a higher FOB price, the market area around B can shrink to a parabolic market enclave.

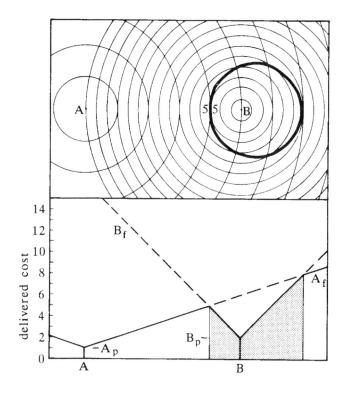

Source: Frank Fetter, "The Economic Laws of Market Areas," *The Quarterly journal of Economics* 38 (1924):520–529.

should there have been this concentration? First, the Greater London market, accounting for 25 percent of Great Britain's consumption of cement, lay within a 25-mile radius of the Thames–Medway cement plants. Second, the chalk of lower Thamesside is pure, easily extracted, and convened into cement so that production costs are lower than elsewhere. As in the use of Fletton bricks, this led to increases in the market area of the cement plants. Third, the plants were located by the river Thames, and cheap water transport was available to cement markets around the coasts of England. Thamesside was able to dominate the coastwise cement trade for several hundred miles. The lesson is that the size and shape of market areas, and the amount produced in any area, may be modified by the size and shape of market areas, and the amount produced in any area, may be modified by the size of local markets and by differentials in transportation rates.

THE MARKET AS A FACTOR IN THE LOCATION OF INDUSTRY

Chauncy D. Harris drew attention to the increasing importance of the market as a factor in the location of industry in a seminal essay published in 1954, and proposed a "market potential" concept to measure the aggregate accessibility of any location to all consumers within a given area (Box 8.7 and Type C, Table 8.1).

Harris's argument was as follows. Markets are growing in importance as a factor in the location of industry. But freight movements decrease systematically with increasing distance from a market. Total shipments to a market must, of course, increase in direct proportion to the size of a market. No industrial plant is restricted to serving a single market. Hence an abstract measure is needed of possible contacts with all markets taking into account their size and their distance. Physics provides such a measure for calculating the strength of a field, whether electrical, magnetic, or gravitational. Harris calls this measure *market potential* and notes that it is analogous to population potential, which had been introduced to the social sciences by John Q. Stewart. The market potential of any location is the sum of its interactions with each market (including itself). These interactions are proportional to the size of each market and inversely proportional to the distance from that market. Hence market potential (P) is defined as the summation (Σ) of markets (M_j) accessible to a point (i) divided by their distance from that point (d_{ij}).

$$P_i = \sum_j \frac{M_j}{d_{ij}}$$

There are many reasons why the market has increased in importance as a factor in the location of industry. One is the technological advance that has decreased the amount of material inputs per unit of output in most industries (Box 8.3). Another is increasing productivity of labor, which frees an increasing proportion of the labor force to move from primary activities to manufacturing, and from both into services. Products, too, are becoming more sophisticated. The horse and buggy gives way to the automobile, and the automobile incorporates over time more and more features to increase ease of driving, safety, and comfort. The icebox is replaced by the mechanical refrigerator, which also incorporates, over time, additional features. As another example, compare the amounts of materials used in a microwave oven and a conventional oven. As a consequence of these changes, a shift of the labor force is taking place from activities that are raw-material-oriented to those that are market-oriented.

Not only are the material inputs being reduced in manufactured products, but the research and design, the engineering, and the sales and marketing components are all increasing. These components are generally concentrated at major market centers. Furthermore, as manufacturing processes become more sophisticated, waste products become by-products, as when scrap metal is used by the new "mini mills" to produce specialty steels, reducing still further the attraction of raw material locations for industry. To add to the shift, as manufacturing becomes vertically integrated and multistage, the final stages comprise the assembly of components in which there is no weight loss. So as Harris notes, major agglomerations of population become self-reinforcing networks with a growing concentration of facilities and services, management and labor force, and transportation and marketing in addition to their actual market sales.

Whether or not declining transport costs will erode these networks is a matter of much debate (Box 8.8). The correlations between market potential and aggregate measures of manufacturing activity, such as the total number employed in manufacturing, remain high and many former peripheries still lag. This result is to be expected. Market potential reflects the distribution of the large urban centers, and manufacturing continues to be an important component of the economic base of many large cities. The principal contributions of the market potential concept may, therefore, be in drawing much-needed attention toward the market as a factor in the location of industry and in demonstrating the feasibility of producing what is, in effect, a demand surface.

BOX 8.7 Market Potential

ASSUMPTIONS: Market potential makes two simple, basic assumptions:

1. Larger market centers generate more sales at a location than smaller market centers at equal distances from that location.
2. The sales made in a given market diminish with distance from that market.

DEFINITION: The market potential (P) of any location (i) is proportion the sales (M) of every location (J) weighted by their distance (d_{ij}) from that location.

$$P_i = \sum_j \frac{M_j}{d_{ij}}$$

Market potential was defined by Chauncy D. Harris, who introduced the concept, as *an abstract measure of the intensity of possible contact with the market.* That is, it indexes each location's aggregate accessibility to the national market.

MARKET SHARE: The market-share assumption of market potential is in sharp contrast to that made in Laws of the Market Area under Transport-Cost Minimization, Box 8.6.

Spatial monopoly within market area

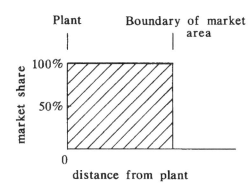

Market share under transport-cost minimization

Distance decay in market share

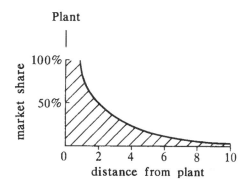

Market share with market potential

Calculating market potential

1. Data

Town	A	B	C	I	J	K	L	M	N
Sales	250	1000	250	100	500	100	250	100	100
Distances to:									
From:									
B	5	1.5	5	5	10	15	20	25	25
J	15	10	15	5	1.5	5	10	15	15
M	30	25	30	20	15	10	5	1.5	10

continued on next page

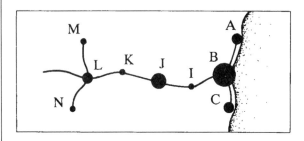

Map of Locations

2. Calculations (sales divided by distance

	A	B	C	I	J	K	L	M	N	Total	Index
B	50	667	50	20	50	7	13	4	4	865	100
J	17	100	17	20	333	20	25	7	7	546	63
M	8	40	8	5	33	10	50	67	10	231	27

3. Explanation

The calculations are illustrated for an area with nine towns, three on the coast (A, B, and C), and the remainder inland (1 through N). All towns are 5 miles from their nearest neighbor. Average travel distance within towns is set at 1.5 miles. The sales at B are $1,000, at J $500, at A, C, and L $250, and at the rest $1 00.

These totally unrealistic figures facilitate the arithmetic.

The data are set out in the form of a matrix with sales in the first row, followed by the *ij* distances for each *ith* town.

The calculations are given for three of the towns: B, J, and M. For each town, the sales at every other town are divided by the distance to

that town and the results recorded. B is 5 miles from A, so that contribution of A to B's potential is its $250 of sales divided by 5 miles equal 50. The sum of all B's values is 865—the highest value for the area. Indexing to a 100 on this value gives a market potential index of 63 for J and 27 for M. The indexes for the complete set of towns are as follows:

Town	A	B	C	I	J	K	L	M	N
Potential	84	100	84	83	63	47	41	27	27

The market potential index values can be plotted on the map and isolines (or contours) of equal value plotted.

Market Potential Index

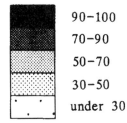

90–100
70–90
50–70
30–50
under 30

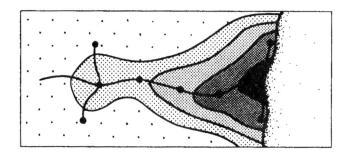

Source : Chauncy D. Harris, "The Market as a Factor in the Localization of Industry in the United States," *Annals of the Association of American Geographers* 44 (1954): 315–348.

BOX 8.8 The Continuing Importance of Accessibility to Market

The market potential index of Chauncy D. Harris was developed more than 40 years ago. Since then transportation costs have declined in relative importance, perhaps reducing the importance of accessibility to market as a factor in location. An opportunity to test the current importance of accessibility is provided by a survey of the Confederation of British Industry (CBI) in 1995 of 1,000 senior executives in top UK companies. The survey was in two parts. First, executives were asked to indicate the single most important factor influencing the location decision if they had recently relocated or that would influence their decision if they did move in the future. Then they were asked to rate six peripheral regions in England and Wales as a possible location for their industry or business.

What the executives stressed was the importance of accessibility as a factor influencing location decisions, and this applied to both groups of executives, those who had relocated recently and those who had not. More specifically, the answers to the question about the single most important factor were, for those who had moved and in descending order of importance, (1) proximity to markets, (2) proximity to other depots and branches of the company, and (3) lower costs. Other factors cited were (4) the availability of sites and premises, (5) good communication and transport links, and (6) the availability of a high-quality work force. The answers were much the same for those executives who had not relocated.

Given the emphasis placed on accessibility, how should we expect them to rate peripheral regions? According to the market potential index, peripheral regions should suffer a low rating. However, Michael Chisholm has pointed out that over the past 40 years, improvements in transportation have reduced the disadvantage of distance. Let us examine

these two viewpoints before returning to the CBI survey.

Market potential is the best single indicator of proximity to markets. It is also, indirectly, a good indicator of the availability of skilled workers and of good transportation and communication links. Such an index was computed for the UK by Colin Clark in 1966. Clark used personal income to produce an "economic potential" index. His map showed a corridor of high potential from London to Liverpool with a progressive decline in accessibility with increasing distance from this corridor. Clark then compared regional employment growth from 1931 to 1964 with regional economic potential. One of his key conclusions was that the potential isoline of 1,150 marked a clear division in employment growth rates. He wrote that beyond the 1,150 isoline lay the whole of Scotland, most of Wales, the remoter parts of Northern England, Devon and Cornwall, and East Anglia (Norfolk and Suffolk). He then concerned himself with measures that government might take to accelerate the general lack of economic progress in these peripheral areas. In a subsequent article (1969), Clark and others recalculated the index for Britain as a member of the European Common Market. Continental Europe served to add a sloping plateau of economic potential to Britain, to the particular advantage of southeast England. The peripheral areas remained the same.

Nor have they changed in extent since then. A more recent calculation of economic potential by David Keeble, reprinted in Chisholm (1995), shows the peripheral regions extend across the same areas. Five of the six peripheral regions selected for the CBI survey fall below the critical 1,150 economic potential index, namely, North Wales, West Cumbria, County Durham, Cornwall, and East Norfolk. One, the East Riding of Yorkshire, straddles the 1,150 isoline.

Michael Chisholm (1995) questions the continuing importance of accessibility. He finds, for instance, that the average distance that freight is shipped has increased from less than 70 km during the 1960s to about 100 km since 1981. This increase is due in part, of course, to the building in the UK of high-speed motorways and the use of larger, more economical trucks. It reflects the generally rising productivity in the transport sector that has outstripped productivity gains in the British economy as a whole. Chisholm also finds that transport costs are now such a small proportion of total industry costs that they cannot directly affect, to more than a minor extent, the relative prosperity of different regions.

Nevertheless, the evaluations of senior executives place a very emphatic emphasis on the disadvantages faced by the peripheral regions as locations for business or industry and strongly argue for the continuing importance of market accessibility, whether measured by the market potential or the economic potential index. Cornwall, with the lowest economic potential of the six regions surveyed, ranked lowest among the business executives. Some 50 percent rated Cornwall as poor and an additional 30 percent rated as very poor as a location for business or industry. Cornwall's two key disadvantages were said to be distance from customers and poor communication by road and rail. Additional disadvantages cited were distance from suppliers and lack of an experienced work force. The East Riding of Yorkshire, with the highest market potential of the peripheral regions, did the best of the six regions surveyed. Only 10 percent of executives rated it as poor or very poor, compared with the 80 percent for Cornwall. Five percent rated it very good as a location for business and industry compared with 1 percent for Cornwall. Those executives who liked the location of the East Riding of

continued on next page

Yorkshire cited accessibility factors as their reason.

A clear gap exists between the actual minor cost disadvantages that peripheral British regions face and the very severe subjective disadvantages perceived by senior executives. Can it be that accessibility is not simply a matter of cost, but also of lost time and considerable inconvenience, as well as missed opportunities because of business contacts not made and of amenities and quality services not available? Or can these subjective evaluations be merely obsolete ingrained habits of thought established when accessibility really was a key locational factor? Right or wrong, executives will continue to treat accessibility as a key factor in making their locational decisions and in shaping the pattern of future regional economic development.

References

Chisholm, Michael (1995).*Britain on the Edge of Europe*. London: Routledge, 1995.

Clark, Colin (1966). Industrial Location and Economic Potential. *Lloyds Bank Review*. 82: 1–17.

Clark, Colin, F. Wilson, and J. Bradley (1969). Industrial Location and Economic Potential in Western Europe. *Regional Studies*. 3: 197–212.

Confederation of British Industry (CBI) (1995). *Go West Cumbria! Perceptions of West Cumbria as a Destination of Inward Investment*. Newcastle-Upon-Tyne: CBI Northern Region.

Manners, Gerald (1980). Inter-regional Development and Planning. In Gerald Manners et al., (Eds.), *Regional Development in Britain*. 2nd ed.., Chichester: John Wiley, p. 29 has reprints of the Clark potential maps.

MAXIMIZING PROFITS

It is possible, conceptually at least, to combine the results of least-cost location theory (Type A) and market-potential theory (Type C) to determine locations that maximize the differences between production costs and sales revenue (Type B). David Smith has developed such an approach by drawing on the idea of Weber's isodapanes, the measurement of spatial variations in demand, and E. M. Rawstron's concept of margins of profitability.

The isodapane was used by Weber simply to describe the additional transportation costs in moving from the least-cost location. It served to deal with the effects of lower labor costs and agglomeration economies on location. Its significance is far greater than this, however, for it changes the focus from the identification of a single least-cost location point to the map of production costs. From the isodapane as a contour map of transportation costs, it is a small conceptual step to a map of total production costs for any given level of output, incorporating all relevant costs. Similarly a revenue map can, in concept at least, be produced showing the revenue a producer could expect to derive at each location, given the market area such a location would confer and the sales that could be expected.

Profits are revenues minus costs. Subtract the cost map from the revenue map and the difference equals the profit map. The areas in which the industry can make a profit are delimited by the spatial margins of profitability. Plants that open within these spatial margins survive. Those that open beyond it will fail.

Conceptually, this approach to location theory is more appealing than either least-cost or market-maximization approaches. But by combining these two partial approaches, it combines their measurement problems and has proved empirically intractable. Furthermore, by the time that Smith was developing his approach, a number of fundamental questions were being raised that called into question the whole search for a location theory that looked for the optimal location for single plants by single-establishment firms operated by economic maximizers. These theories do continue to provide useful insights and practical solutions, but interest of location theory is now turning to questions of scale, externalities, agglomeration, and the differences in location choice by small firms and by multinational enterprises. These are the topics to which we turn in Chapter 9.

VOCABULARY

The vocabulary items introduced in this chapter follow. You will find the definitions in the Glossary.

accessibility
agglomeration
balanced regional growth
cheap labor
circular and cumulative causation
city-forming activity
city-serving activity
critical isodapane
deindustrialization
demand surface
distortion
dumping
economic maximization
economic potential index
fifth wave
footloose industry
generalized measures of accessibility
global shift of industry
green labor
gross material
in situ restructuring
industrial inertia
industrial location theory
information-age technologies
input
isodapane

labor costs
labor oriented industry
labor pool
Launhardt–Palander solution
Law of the Equidistant Market Boundary
Law of the Encroaching Hyperbolic
  Market Boundaries
Law of the Hyperbolic Line of
  Indifference
Law of the Parabolic Market Enclave
laws of market areas
lean producers
least cost location
least-cost location theory
line-haul economy
localized material
location determinants
locational choice
locational figure
locational weight
long run
manufacturing belt
margins of profitability
market boundary
market potential
market-potential index

market share
material index
national shift of industry
optimal transport orientation
point of consumption (PC)
pole
population potential
production cost
production point
productivity of labor
"psychic income"
pure material
"rounding out"
short- un
snatchers
social agglomeration
spatial margins of profitability
stickers
terminal cost
Type A industry
Type B industry
Type C industry
Type D industry
ubiquity
Weber's Theory of Plant Location°

TOPICS FOR DISCUSSION

1. Why is Weber's *Theory of the Location of Industries* still relevant to location of the United States steel industry?

2. In the world today, major industrial shifts are taking place in labor orientation as part of a global scramble for cheap labor, yet there are many situations where money wages vary apparently without effect on industrial locations. Why? Why do labor cost variations due to money wages tend to be short-run differentials? In what circumstances can these differentials persist over longer periods of time?

3. Why did accessibility to market become increasingly important as a factor in the location of industry?

4. Have there been any surveys in your region of how executives rate it as a location for business and industry? How do you assess their evaluations?

FURTHER READINGS

Harris, Chauncy D. (1954). The Market as a Factor in the Localization of Industry in the United States. *Annals of the Association of American Geographers* 44:1954 315–348.

The seminal statement that led location studies on from a preoccupation with least-cost location.

Smith, David M. (1981). *Industrial Location. An Economic Geographical Analysis,.* 2d ed. New York: John Wiley.

The most authoritative source on traditional location theory.

Watts, H. D. (1987).*Industrial Geography.* Harlow: Longman Group UK.

The first of the new-look textbooks on the subject. Makes an interesting contrast with R. C. Riley's *Industrial Geography* of 1973 and exemplifies how rapidly the field is changing.

Weber, Alfred. (1929). *Theory of the Location of Industries.* Translated by Carl J. Friedrich. Chicago: University of Chicago Press.

Where location theory begins, it is far more comprehensive in its scope than can be portrayed in a textbook summary.

9

Scale, Externalities, and Agglomeration: The Evolving Structure of Global Industry

OVERVIEW

Economies of scale are the reductions in unit costs that result from an increased level of output. These cost reductions may be internal economies of scale, gained within a single plant in the manufacture of a single product such as shoes. They may be internal multiplant economies achieved by a chain of bottling plants, shops, or hotels in many different locations. They may also be external economies of scale achieved by the agglomeration of many different firms in a particular region, thereby attracting specialist services and knowledgeable customers and gaining a national or even international reputation.

However achieved, economies of scale are important to the survival of firms and essential to achieving an international competitive edge. Understanding the various ways in which economies of scale can be achieved, why diseconomies of scale set in, and how they can be measured for

production in a single plant thus helps to explain the location and growth of economic activity and patterns of trade, both regional and international, in goods and services.

Significant differences have emerged between the locational behavior of small firms, operating a single plant, and multinational enterprises (MNEs), which may operate several firms, each with numerous plants. The location of small firms may reflect an "adoption" process in which surviving firms map the margins of locational choice. The location of MNEs is better understood as a process of "adaption" by oligopolies contending for market share. Both, however, involve economies of scale. Small firms find their greatest advantage where there are agglomeration economies and where industrial districts produce "dynamic externalities" that lead to increasing returns. MNEs organize their activities to internalize economies of scope.

OBJECTIVES

- to identify and describe the various kinds of internal and external economies and diseconomies of scale

- to explain the relationships among scale, industrial concentration, and barriers to entry in oligopolies

- to differentiate between short- and long-run cost curves

- to incorporate the effects of transportation costs into the measurement of economies of scale

- to explore the phenomenon of increasing returns in the development of specialized industrial districts

- to describe the resurgence of small firms, the components of change in firm numbers and their employment, and the characteristics of small-firm owner-managers and their contribution to employment growth at the urban, regional, and national scales

- to distinguish between locational "adoption" and "adaption" and to suggest how far the geography of the births and deaths of firms may reflect these processes
- to outline the growth and distribution of the multinational manufacturing enterprise and the organization of mass production, and to note the contrasts with lean, just-in-time production that is beginning to replace it

THE IMPORTANCE OF ECONOMIES OF SCALE

If Alfred Weber had written today instead of 90 years ago, he probably would have written about economies of scale, externalities, and the new significance of increasing returns, rather than about transport orientation. As the costs of transportation have plummeted, as revolutionary changes in communications have transformed the information environment within which companies operate, and as human skills—the ultimate advanced factor of production—have replaced cheap labor as a cost-reducing element in many industries, the size of the firm and the nature of the industrial cluster within which it locates have become increasingly important determinants of locational choice. Significant differences have emerged between the locational behavior of small firms and of multinationals.

It is to these questions that we now turn. We discuss the economies and diseconomies of scale, compare and contrast the locational behavior of small firms and large multinational enterprises, and consider the relationships among externalities, agglomeration, and increasing returns.

Economics of scale are the reductions in the average per-unit costs of production (hereafter *unit costs*) that result from an increased level of output. There are three kinds. Such cost reductions are easiest to identify and to measure in the case of *internal economies of scale,* which involve the increased output of a single good or service in a single establishment. But internal economies of scale also can be achieved by a multiestablishment enterprise. When the enterprise's activities are broadened to include several goods and services, any resulting reductions in average per costs for any of the products are said to arise from *economies of scope.* Thirdly, cost reductions can be achieved by an enterprise as a result of the clustering of enterprises in the same area. These are called *external economies* because they arise in the environment surrounding the enterprise rather than inside the enterprise itself.

It was thought until the 1950s that competitive "price-taking" firms could only maximize profits if located where the joint transportation costs of assembling raw materials and marketing the finished product could be minimized. Additional labor savings might shift the firm from this location. External economies were only thought to be achievable in the special case where such economies exceeded the additional transportation costs of clustering in an alternative location. Because competitive industries are made up of similarly sized cost-minimizing firms, internal economies of scale were not considered by industrial location theorists.

Increasing importance is now being attached to economies of scale in understanding the location, survival, and growth of industry, however. Michael Porter (Chapter 1) remarks on how frequently international competitive advantage is restricted to a narrowly defined set of industries, such as the manufacture of printing machines or ceramic tiles, concentrated in particular regions or even a particular city. The external economies generated by such spatial concentration provide a cost advantage that makes it possible to export to international markets, even in the absence of comparative advantages in the costs of labor or raw materials. Scott and Angel (1987) made similar observations about the U.S. semiconductor industry some years earlier. Just why the industry should have developed in Santa Clara County (Silicon Valley), California, in the 1950s is open to question. But once the process of growth had begun, accumulating external economies created a privileged location for the industry. Many further examples are given by Paul Krugman (1991a), including the origin of the U.S. carpet industry in Dalton, Georgia. Cliff Pratten (1991a) found that 40 percent of small firms employing less than 500 workers regarded proximity to firms producing similar products or providing similar services as important for their competitiveness. Furthermore, a similar proportion (40 percent) of the firms surveyed thought that economies of scale are now more important than 10 years ago, compared with only 4 percent who thought they were less important.

The pervasive importance of the subject has stimulated a continuing flow of research, with detailed studies of a wide range of industries and with instructive international comparisons. These studies have sought to identify the factors responsible for economies of scale, to measure the minimum efficient size (MES) for various industries, and to evaluate the economic, geographic, and policy consequences that follow. Perhaps the most exciting of these studies' discoveries has been the finding that *dynamic externalities*—in particular the externalities associated with "knowledge spillovers"—have become the "engine" of recent urban and regional growth, producing *increasing returns* to scale. We spend some time discussing these new discoveries after we review the nature of internal economies. The locational behavior of small firms and large multinational enterprises is discussed in Appendices 9.1 and 9.2.

IDENTIFYING INTERNAL ECONOMIES OF SCALE

Average per-unit production costs (unit costs) usually decrease with increasing output until a minimum unit cost is achieved. This output level is the minimum efficient size (Figure 9.1). Unit costs rise, in the short run, if production is increased above this level. Hence, if a firm is operating at or near its MES, with the selling price set accordingly, it will increase supply only if prices increase.

Internal economies of scale include all increases in efficiency and improvements in productivity that occur with increasing output within a single firm. These efficiencies may result, for example, from better, faster production; the use of specialized machines; concentration on the production of a single, standard item; and longer production runs. A distinction should be drawn, however, between economies of scale and *pecuniary advantages*. A large corporation may be able to obtain special rates for raw materials, energy, transportation, advertising, and bank loans as a result of the bargaining power bestowed by size. When such price advantages involve no physical resource saving or change in productivity but only a redistribution of income between buyers and sellers, the advantage is *pecuniary*, rather than a *real* economy of scale.

Internal economies of scale are pervasive and can be cross-classified in a variety of ways. They are sometimes distinguished by the level in the corporate hierarchy at which they are achieved. That is, economies of scale can result from the concentration of resources on the manufacture of particular *products*, within specialized *plants*, integrated in a single *corporation*. Economies of scale also are described according to the function involved: product development, labor savings, technical improvements, managerial economies, and marketing and finance advantages.

Because the economies for these functions are achieved largely at some given level of the corporate structure, we discuss them under the headings of product-specific, plant-specific, and multiplant economies.

Product-Specific Economies

Product-specific economies are associated with spreading startup costs over a large output, with product standardization, with improved labor efficiency as production runs increase in *length,* and with technical efficiencies as production runs increase in *rate* of output.

Product Development Costs. The production of any good involves initial design and development costs. These may be very small, as in the case of shoes, or may be an important element of total cost, as in aircraft manufacture. Economists call these costs *indivisible* with respect to output. That is, the cost required for development and design is the same whether 10 or a thousand units are produced. Design and development costs can be averaged out, however: the greater the output, the smaller the cost per unit of output (Figure 9.2). The economies of averaging such fixed costs over increasing scale of output are tending to increase in importance over time, as products become more sophisticated, embodying much greater design and development expense. The semiconductor industry exemplifies this trend: Fixed overhead costs can run up to 75 percent or more of the total costs of manufacturing microchips.

Labor Economies. Specialization of production on a single good permits *labor efficiencies*. These efficiencies arise from the *division of labor*, first described by Adam

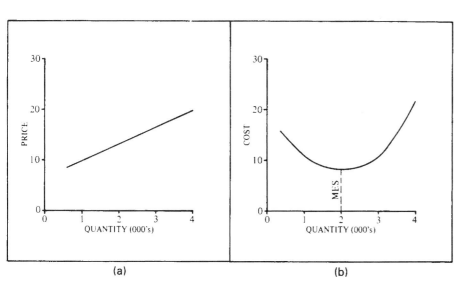

(a) (b)

FIGURE 9.1 The industry's supply curve and the firm's unit-cost curve. (a) The supply curve. Supply curves such as were used in Chapter 6 show how industries respond to price changes by offering more or less goods. Higher prices are needed to cover the increased costs of additional output by existing firms and to attract new producers into the field. (b) The unit-cost curve. Unit-cost curves show the relationship of production costs to scale of output. Initially, increasing output is accompanied by economies of scale, and unit costs fall to a minimum efficient size (MES)—in this case, at an output level of 2,000. Thereafter, costs per unit of output may rise if diseconomies of scale are incurred.

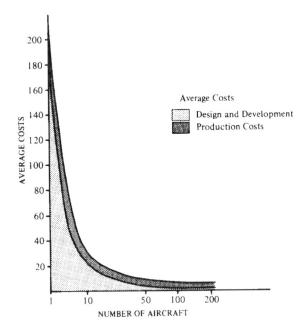

FIGURE 9.2 Economies of scale in the aircraft industry. Development costs include research and development, and the cost of special tools. These figures are representative of aircraft costs in the early post–World War II period. Development costs quickly fall to a small fraction of total production costs. [*Source:* After C. F. Pratten, *Economies of scale in Manufacturing Industries* (London: Cambridge University Press, 1971), p. 152.]

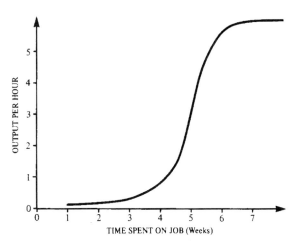

FIGURE 9.3 The learning curve. The longer a worker remains on the job, the higher is his or her productivity. Productivity tends to rise at an accelerating rate to the average level of efficiency, and from then on at a decelerating rate. The importance of experience is dramatic in highly technical activities. In the manufacture of large-scale integrated circuits, fewer than 2 in a 100 made by an inexperienced worker may function properly. With experience, this proportion may rise to 80 out of 100.

Smith over two centuries ago in his *Wealth of Nations* (Box 9.1). If instead of each worker making the entire good, production is divided into particular processes, output can be increased substantially. There are three reasons for this. First, there is increased dexterity in performing the work. Second, time is not lost, as it would be by a single worker passing from one process to another. Third, machinery can be specialized, adding *technical economies of scale* to labor economies.

Practice makes perfect. Experienced workers gain a rhythm and an economy of motion and division of labor facilitates the allocation of workers to jobs at appropriate skill levels. Output tends to follow a *learning curve* (Figure 9.3). Labor costs in aircraft production during World War II were found to fall by 20 percent for each doubling of output. The British Textile Council reported that output per worker increased by 167 percent when average rayon cloth-weaving runs increased from 3,800 to 31,000 yards. The most dramatic examples of increased output are in highly technical industries such as integrated electronic circuits, where much experience is needed before good parts exceed rejects.

The second economy in the division of labor is the time saved in passing from one job to another. The manufacture of a relatively simple product like a pair of shoes requires a hundred or more distinct operations, divided into five sets. First is "clicking"—the highly skilled work of cutting the uppers. Decoration, stitching, and cementing of the uppers takes place in the "closing" room. The bottoms are

---

BOX 9.1   *Adam Smith on Producing a Pin*

A workman not educated to this business…could scarce, perhaps, with his utmost industry, make one pin in a day, and certainly could not make twenty…but it is divided into a number of branches. One man draws out the wire, another straightens it, a third cuts it, a fourth points it, a fifth grinds it at the top for receiving the head; to make the head requires two or three operations; to put it on is a particular business, to whiten the pins is another; it is even a trade by itself to put them into the paper….I have seen a small manufactory of this kind where ten men…could make among them upwards of forty-eight thousand pins in a day. Each person, therefore,… might be considered as making four thousand eight hundred pins in a day.
—The Wealth of Nations (1776).

made in the "preparation" room. Ten different machine operations are employed in the "making" room, completing the shoe. The final shoe process is inspection and packing. The work is passed from room to room on conveyor belts, or on trolleys or trays.

Third, the division of labor, when concentrated on the production of a single commodity, justifies the development of special machines that would be quite uneconomic unless kept continuously in production over long periods of time. For instance, the decoration of the uppers in the closing room of a shoe factory may involve a pattern of perforations. When a small number of shoes is to be made, this work must be done by hand. Press stamping is much faster, but the machine cost can be justified only for long production runs.

Ball-bearing production provides an example of three technology levels according to output volume. On the largest runs of standard-size bearings (perhaps a million a year), a computer-controlled, fully automated process is justified. At intermediate levels (about 10,000), simpler automatic equipment can be used, but unit costs may be double. Even so, unit costs are much less than for very small runs (of perhaps a 100). These small runs must be done on general-purpose lathes by skilled operators because the 8 hours it takes to set up an automated machine cannot be justified.

Plant-Specific Economies

It is at the level of the establishment, or plant, that most internal economies of scale can be attained. Many *fixed costs* are incurred at the plant level and can be averaged down as output is increased. Major technical economies come into force involving a number of different principles. These technical economies produce concomitant labor economies. Management economies are achieved with a larger operating scale as well.

Averaging Down the Fixed Costs.   Operating a factory incurs *fixed costs.* The magnitude of these costs is unaffected by the volume of output. Fixed costs include property taxes and rents, interest payments, depreciation of buildings and equipment, maintenance costs, and insurance. All functions, from labor and maintenance, to marketing and finance, involve some component of fixed costs (Table 9.1). The larger the factory output, the lower are the average fixed costs per unit of output.

Economies of Scale in Variable Costs.   Plant-specific economies of scale are also achieved for *variable costs.* Variable costs are those costs that vary in magnitude with the level of output. These economies of scale occur when an increase in variable cost is less than proportional to the increase in output. Most of these economies are technical and involve three principles: the *cube-square law,* the *principle of multiples,* and the *principle of reserves.* A fourth principle, *bulk transactions,* may also apply.

The cube-square law states a simple and obvious relationship between the volume of a container and its surface area. Surface area increases as the square of the dimensions. Volume increases as the cube of the dimensions. Double the dimensions and the area is four times larger (2^2), but volume is eight times greater (2^3). The "container" may be a blast furnace, a storage tank, a compressor, a turbine, or even a ship. The cube-square law (or *two-thirds rule* as it is sometimes called) still holds. If costs increase in proportion with area, as they can be expected to do, and output increases in proportion with volume, then significant economies can be

TABLE 9.1

Examples of fixed costs in the manufacturing industry

Type of Cost	Partly or Wholly Indivisible with Respect to
Product development costs:	
Designing a new aircraft	Number of aircraft built
Labor:	
Factory cleaning staff	Variations in daily output
Management:	
Arrangement of fringe benefits for employees	Number of employees
Marketing:	
Preparation of advertisements	Number of advertisements printed
Financial:	
Issuing a prospectus to raise capital	Size of issue

Source: C. Pratten, 1971, p.11; and idem, 1991a, p. 15. Pratten's research indicates that, for smaller firms at least, fixed costs yield greater economies of scalethan do variable costs, and that the two major economies of scale in fixed costs are in product development and marketing (presently for export orders).

achieved by scaling up equipment. Thus, chemical engineers often apply "the 0.6 rule," which states that if equipment is scaled up, capital cost increases at a rate of 0.6 (rather than the 0.66 of the cube-square, or two-thirds rule). The same rule applies to breweries. Of course, the figure (whether 0.6 or 0.66) is only a rough guide and the specific characteristics of the industry modify the actual economies of scale substantially.

The cube-square law has been widely used in shipping to capture economies of scale with growth in traffic. Ferries may be cut horizontally to add an extra deck, as British Columbia Ferries Corporation did to the *Queen of Victoria* to double its capacity from 192 to 400 cars. This work cost only a third the price of a new ferry. Similarly, P&O European Ferries have progressively increased the size of their ferries as passengers, cars, and freight increased. The original Viking class ferries, introduced in 1964, were about 1,800 net tons. The Venturer class introduced in the 1970s were about 3,000 tons. In the 1980s, these ships were cut to add both a new deck and a larger bow section increasing their tonnage to 7,000 (Box 9.2). The new Pride class, first introduced in 1987 with the *Pride of Dover* and *Pride of Calais,* are over 26,000 tons. The increase in car and truck capacity at each size increase has been in line with the cube-square law. Passenger capacity has increased at a lesser rate to enable facilities to be enhanced. Some companies design their freighters so that they can be cut in two and a computer-measured prebuilt section fitted within a few days, enabling increased demand to be met by larger ships rather than more ships. Information supplied by *Lloyd's Register of Shipping* in London for the period 1993–1995 shows that the cost of new bulk carriers and of new tankers varied respectively at close to the 0.6 power of tonnage.

The *principle of multiples* is also straightforward. The design of special equipment for each specific process in making a commodity raises a problem. The machines are not all likely to run at the same rate. Those that complete their step in the production chain at the slowest rate will hold all faster machines back to their speed unless a principle of multiples is applied. This principle states that the minimum efficient scale (MES) at the technical level is the lowest common multiple (LCM) of the individual machines. If three steps are involved, with machines processing 4, 3, and 6 units per hour, the LCM is 12. The MES requires three of the 4-unit, four of the 3-unit, and two of the 6-unit machines, respectively, to produce 12 units per hour (Box 9.3). Most situations are seldom as neat.

The third explanation of greater efficiency at higher output levels is the *principle of reserves.* The smooth operation of a plant, including production and marketing, requires maintaining some minimum level of stock, raw materials, fuel, spare parts for equipment repair and maintenance, and perhaps even spare machines, to guarantee supply security–for example, the ability to withstand a sup-

plier's strike. These economies are harder to document although their existence is easy to understand. They are most evident when equipment must be taken out of service at regular intervals for maintenance. A basic oxygen furnace in the steel industry must be relined with refractory bricks every 25 to 40 days. Two furnaces are needed to keep a steady flow of steel. Adding a third furnace, however, increases output by 50 percent for a 33 percent increase in cost.

An alternative to scale economies of reserves is provided by *just-in-time delivery* of stock, which reduces inventory handling costs. Very substantial sums are tied up in manufacturing industry stock: Interest and other costs of holding stock have been estimated to be as high as a quarter of the purchase. Chrysler Corp. saved $1 billion in the first year it adopted just-in-time inventory, which was more than its reported profits. Recent innovation in transport and communications has facilitated the transition from massing of reserves to just-in-time delivery.

Finally, a *principle of bulk transactions* sometimes applies. Economists distinguish between the case when size is used to bargain for better rates, which is a pecuniary advantage, and when real increases in efficiency occur. Shoe manufacturers often sell their shoes through their own outlets. A complete range of sizes in each color for each style must be carried. When sales are large, the size distribution of the stock can more nearly approximate the size distribution of the market. Volume sales thus reduce overhead costs and the risks of being left with extreme sizes at the end of the season.

Management costs, not all of which are fixed, also rise less than proportionately with size. Management economies at the plant level are very much like labor economies at the product level. Division of management tasks permits allocation of duties according to aptitude. The principles of the learning curve, specialization of duties, and development of specialized management aids become feasible in larger plants. Management economies are thought to continue beyond the scale where technical economies are exhausted and continue on up to multiplant firms. Just how great these economies can be is seen in Table 9.2.

Multiplant Economies

The organization of industry into multiplant firms permits production economies over and beyond those attributable to the sizes of the individual plants. These economies of scale for multiplant firms involve primarily the financial and marketing functions.

Production Economies.   Multiplant firms can allocate particular products to specific plants, increasing product-specific economies. The 1969 merger of three British

BOX 9.2   *The Cube-Square Law: Economies of Large Machines*

THE CUBE-SQUARE LAW

This is also called the engineering principle. It states that area increases at a rate of two-thirds the increase in physical volume of the equipment. In industries where output is proportional to volume, and capital costs are proportional to area, substantial economies are offered by scaling up equipment. Chemical engineers thus sometimes use a "rule of 0.6" to estimate the ratio of capital cost increase to volume increase when scaling up equipment.

This example of the conversion of the *Venturer* to a jumbo ferry by adding a new deck and bow reveals that when length is doubled, area is squared, and volume is cubed.

Sources: Miles Cowsill and John Hendy, *The Viking Saga: Celebrating 25 Years of Services* (Kilgetty, Wales: Ferry Publications, 1989); and information supplied by P&O.

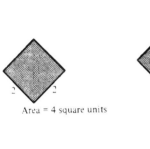

Area = 4 square units

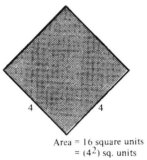

Area = 16 square units
= (4²) sq. units

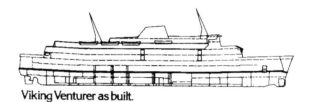

Viking Venturer as built.

length	128.7 meters
net tons	2,918
passengers	1,200
cars	275

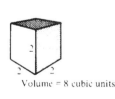

Volume = 8 cubic units

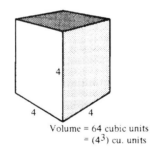

Volume = 64 cubic units
= (4³) cu. units

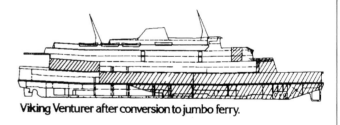

Viking Venturer after conversion to jumbo ferry.

length	143.7 meters
net tons	7,014
passengers	1,316
cars	380

companies manufacturing antifriction bearings provides an example of just how great such economies can be. Two of the companies had manufactured overlapping lines of general-purpose bearings. The merger permitted production assignments that ended duplication and permitted longer production runs. Output per employee jumped 50 percent in 1 year, and even greater improvements in productivity were expected with the introduction of new equipment justified by longer runs. Two Canadian companies, each making broad lines of home appliances, merged in 1971, ending duplication and achieving major, if less spectacular, economies.

Marketing Economies. Multiplant firms can also achieve important marketing economies. Companies sometimes spend large amounts on advertising to hold or extend their share of sales, or to market a new product. Advertising

BOX 9.3   The Principle of Multiples

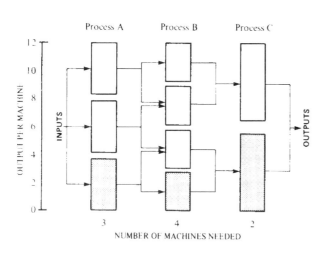

Machines Used Numbered in Sequence	Output per day Per machine
1	1550
2	4360
3	820
4	1000
5*	2300
6	1300
7	1150
8*	2300
9	3130
10	2180

Source: Data provided by a British shoe factory, 1995.

THE PRINCIPLE OF MULTIPLES

Given a number of processes involving machines operating at different rates, the technical minimum efficient size is the lowest common multiple of the rates

Note: These figures are for joining the uppers to the bottoms of a ladies court shoe. Output is in pairs of shoes. Machine processes #5 and #8 are unmanned conditioning machines and are interchangeable. Why is the minimum efficient scale of output about 3000 pairs of shoes a day? How many of each machine are needed for this output? Which machines are most underutilized at this scale of output?

costs are particularly high in the case of soaps and detergents. Unilever's new detergent *Power,* introduced in 1994 in Europe, had to be withdrawn when it was found that under a particular set of circumstances, the new stain-removal catalyst in the detergent could damage clothes. The development and marketing costs for this new detergent had amounted to £57 million, but they had to be written off as an exceptional item. In addition, Unilever sales of concentrated fabric powders suffered from the bad publicity. Volume was down by 13 percent in Western Europe and profits were down significantly. Unilever, with global operating profits (before exceptional items) in 1994 of £2,618 million could take this setback in its stride, but the example illustrates the level that fixed costs can reach and the need to average down these costs through multiplant production and multi-market sales. Some threshold level of expenditure must be made on advertising before the product catches public attention, word spreads, and sales take off.

An effective sales campaign can reshape an industry, as it did in the case of the U. S. brewery industry. After the repeal of Prohibition in 1933, a few breweries chose to set their prices high relative to local and regional beers, and to promote a national image as "premium" Milwaukee beers.

The big three, Anheuser-Busch, Schlitz, and Pabst, captured an increasing share of the market. The consequent economies of scale then enabled them to reduce their prices and to start driving out smaller-scale local producers, thus enlarging their market share still further.

Financial Economies. Multiplant firms also achieve important financial economies of scale. They can concentrate their financial resources on the expansion of each plant in turn as the market grows. This strategy is impossible for single-plant firms. When an industry is composed largely of single-plant firms, all firms will try to expand competitively, usually resulting in initial overexpansion and then of failure by the least efficient.

Multiplant firms are also better able to raise capital through stock issues because the financial community views them as better risks. Many of the costs of negotiating a loan are fixed, and it has been found that costs can vary from as little as 5 percent of share value to as much as 44 percent according to the size of the corporation.

Underlying these multiple economies are the same set of principles as in the plant-specific and product-specific cases, and they apply to all functions. First is the principle

TABLE 9.2

Estimates of internal economies of scale for small single-plant firms

Source of Economies of Scale	Index of Costs Per Unit at Given Output Level		
	Existing Level	Extra 25%	Extra 100%
Fixed costs:			
Product development (R&D)	10	2	2
Marketing, sales, after sales	10	8	8
Delivery	2	2	2
Management overhead	12	10	9
Total fixed costs	34	22	21
Labor costs	16	14	12
Total product-specific costs	50	36	33
Unit purchase price of materials	42	40	38
Total product-specific costs	92	76	71
Profit	8	?	?
Sale price	100	?	?
Economies of Scale as a % of Existing Total Cost	-	152%	185%

Source: After Pratten, 1991a, p. 86.

Note: Small firms are defined by Pratten as having less than 500 employees. The firms were in the computer systems, machinery, electrical and electronic goods, instruments, chemicals and allied products, and food industries in East Anglia, England. The values are very generalized: Large variations occurred both within and between different industries

The sources of economies of scale are drops in the unit fixed costs and in unit labor costs from 50 to 36 to 33. (Savings in the unit purchase price of materials are a pecuniary advantage, not a true economy of scale.) These savings represent an 18.5% savings if output is doubled [(50-33)/92 x 100].

of averaging down the fixed costs over larger volumes. Next are the sets of principles applying to variable costs: the cube-square law, multiples, massed reserves, and bulk transactions. The last two are particularly important. The economies of scale at the firm level depend in part, however, on the relationship among the plants. This relationship in turn depends on any mergers by which the plants were acquired.

The Merger Movement in the United States.
Multiplant corporations dominate most industries in most Western countries. A 1963 U.S. survey of 417 industries revealed only 22 industries in which the four leading sellers operated only single plants. This dominance of the market by multiplant firms is the result of three great merger periods. The first period was dominated by *horizontal integration*, the second by *vertical integration*, and the third by *conglomerate mergers*. Let us look at each of these.

The first period, which lasted from 1887 to 1904 in the United States, saw the consolidation of thousands of firms into relatively few multiplant corporations dominating the market they supplied. The mergers were triggered by changes in transportation, communications, manufacturing technology, and legal institutions. Standard Oil captured 90 percent of the petroleum market by acquiring competitors. U.S. Steel was formed in 1901 by the merger of 785 plants accounting for 65 percent of the country's steel capacity. The American Can Company, organized the same year, involved 120 firms with 90 percent of the national market. Other leading corporations established during the great

merger wave were U.S. Rubber (Uniroyal), Pittsburgh Plate and Glass (PPG Industries), International Paper, United Fruit (United Brands), Eastman-Kodak, and International Harvester. Almost all industries were affected: copper, lead, railroad cars, tobacco, chemicals, and shoe machines were among them. The first great merger period was halted only by a combination of a depression and the enactment of antitrust laws, but some significant mergers still occurred. IBM was established in 1911. General Motors was formed from Buick, Cadillac, and Oldsmobile, added Chevrolet a few years later, but was unable to raise the cash to buy out Ford when Henry Ford offered to sell out in 1908 and 1909.

The second great merger period, from 1916 to 1929, involved more companies but created fewer industrial leaders. It did, however, create important "number two" firms, such as Bethlehem Steel and Continental Can. One authority distinguished this second period as "mergers for oligopoly" as compared with first-wave "mergers for monopoly." In addition, the second merger period saw much more *vertical integration* of industry than the first, during which *horizontal integration* predominated.

Horizontal integration involves the combination of firms producing similar items and selling in the same market. Industry concentration is involved. The leading firms may account for most of the sales in a given industry. Competition is reduced as former competitors become integrated partners in a single firm. Vertical integration combines successive production activities into a single firm. The firm's plants now serve each other in sequence as the product is carried through a progression of processes. In steel, the succession of steps involves making pig iron, converting it to steel, and shaping the steel into semifinished products. In other cases, vertical integration involves separate components of a good, as when a soft-drink producer buys out a bottle manufacturer. Vertical integration is *backward* when a firm buys out its suppliers. A steel company may acquire coal and iron ore mines to secure raw materials. Vertical integration is *forward* when the purpose is to secure markets and outlets for the production of the dominant partner in the integration. Breweries in Britain own their own pubs, the film industry operates its own cinema chains, automobile companies sell through franchised dealerships.

The impact of vertical integration on competition is more subtle than in the case of horizontal integration, and it can involve clear economies when the production steps are technologically complementary, as in the steel industry. Mergers that produce sizable shifts in market shares are increasingly frowned on, however. As a result, the post-World War II period witnessed a third wave of *conglomerate mergers,* in which the firms that joined together had no obvious complementarities other than those of financial and tax manipulation. A case in point is the 1982 acquisition of Marathon Oil Co. by U.S. Steel (renamed USX). When some small complementarities do exist, the mergers are described as *lateral integration.* The British aircraft industry has thus moved into a variety of engineering ventures.

The urge to merge springs from a variety of motives. Among these are the search for financial security, the instinct to jump at a good business opportunity, tax advantages, and hoped-for economies of scale. Horizontal integration increases security by reducing competition, vertical integration reduces vulnerability by controlling supplies and markets, and conglomerate mergers spread product and financial risk by diversity. Integration may be good business when another company's stock is underpriced, when new management can revitalize a lagging corporation, or when its physical plant can be acquired at a low price. But mergers also offer economies of scale. These are most obvious in horizontal mergers. Vertical integration can improve the flow of output through the sequence of processes and facilitate the management of quality and design of components, and size always bestows financial and marketing advantages. Indeed, a company may be acquired for its good will, even if the physical plant is not needed. An extreme example is in the case of U.S. breweries when the G. W. Heileman Co. paid $10.7 million for the Blatz trademark, 32 trucks, and the Blatz marching band (but see Box 9.4). In the case of commodities with high transportation costs, when the market area that can be served by any one plant is as a result restricted, horizontal integration offers nationwide sales: Several factories in different market areas produce and sell the same nationally advertised product. This is an important factor in cases like beer (not all "Milwaukee" beers are produced in Milwaukee), cement, petroleum refining, and the soft-drink industry. Coca-Cola, Pepsi-Cola, and others are bottled in a myriad of small plants serving particular urban-regional markets.

DISECONOMIES OF SCALE

Average costs of production tend to fall with increased scale of output because of economies of scale, but there is reason to believe that once a minimum efficient size of production has been reached (the MES), costs may not fall any farther, and may rise thereafter, at least in the short run (see Figure 9.1).

Internal Diseconomies of Scale

Labor Diseconomies of Scale. The reductions in labor costs per unit of production end when all the economies of the division of labor have been achieved. As workers become skilled in operating their equipment, the learning curve flattens out and no further economies can be expected from this source (Figure 9.3). There is a one-time savings in keeping workers at a single specific task using specialized equipment. Overspecialization of jobs makes the work repetitive and boring. As workers find their jobs less satisfying and challenging, they must be paid higher wage rates. As a result, many industries have been reorganized to make work more varied and interesting. The sales offices of Rowntree & Co. in York, England, reintegrated the handling of correspondence and the granting of credit into a single division, thus giving wider responsibilities for fewer customers to each section head. Their tasks thereby became less monotonous, and as section heads became familiar with their own batch of customers, the time lost on consulting records was reduced. In Sweden, long assembly lines have been replaced in some industries by smaller work groups carrying the product through to completion, resulting in greater worker commitment and higher-quality products.

The sheer size of the labor force in a single plant also produces problems. Workers in large plants tend to find their work less satisfying than workers in small plants for reasons not yet properly understood by psychologists. Large plants find they must therefore pay a wage premium. As the size of the labor force grows, it must begin to attract workers from greater distances. The added transportation costs faced by workers are reflected in wage rates. A point will be reached when increases in wage rates associated with increasing size of plant cannot be offset by increased efficiency. At that point, labor economies of scale give way to labor diseconomies of scale.

Technical Diseconomies of Scale. In the case of technical factors, many firms find that a size is reached

BOX 9.4   Big Brand Names Face Trouble

Brand names are one of the great assets of successful consumer goods industries, enabling them to deter entry into production by competitors and to enhance their profit levels. More recently, brand names have had problems as consumers have moved "down market." Let us examine these issues and how companies are coping with more competitive markets.

Consumers may use the brand name as a generic term of the product. Do you call a vacuum flask a "Thermos?" Do you vacuum a carpet or "Hoover" it? Do you "Xerox" or photocopy? Such associations of products with their leading brands reinforce market dominance. Pepsi and its associated soft drinks account for nearly a third of the U.S. market. Cadbury Schweppes has 20 percent of the UK chocolate market. Recently, Guiness has established market leadership in low alcohol beers, with its brand Kaliber taking a 30 percent share of the market.

Brand names can be sold at a premium price but require strong and consistent marketing, up-to-date production and distribution facilities to ensure very high quality at competitive costs, and careful repositioning to hold market share as demands shift. Brand name products are sold and often produced worldwide, creating important economies of scale, particularly in research and development and in marketing.

But brand names have had problems in the 1990s as consumers have tended to move down market and stores have responded by selling their own label goods at "everyday low pricing." In response, brand name prices have had to be reduced. Philip Morris, the world's largest brand name goods company, lowered the price of Marlboro cigarettes by 20 percent in 1993 in the face of stiff competition. "It would be irresponsible to our shareholders," a senior executive said, "not to defend Marlboro, the world's most valuable trademark." BSN, France's largest food manufacturer is cutting prices and eliminating weaker brands. Procter and Gamble has cut the price of Tide and Cheer and closed 30 of its 147 production plants worldwide, reducing employment by 14 percent. Expenditure surveys in the UK show that supermarket sales of brand name goods fell from half of total sales in the early 1980s to just a third by the early 1990s.

Brand names are fighting back. One possible strategy is to produce the retailer's own brand products for them. They then gain added economies of scale, help to eliminate small-scale, higher-cost, branded competitors, and win extra shelf space. Against this they may rescue the distinction enjoyed by their brand name, trigger a price war, reveal confidential information on costing to the retailers, and divert the attention of management from their central tasks. Unilever has decided it will not provide own-label products. Most of its products are in the top two of their particular markets (including, in the UK, Walls, Persil, Surf, Birds Eye and Brooke Bond). Coke and Pepsi will not.

Some large enterprises are countering with a strategy of alternative brands marketed more widely. PepsiCo introduced All Sport in 1991 (already the number two sports drink in the United States), ready-to-drink Lipton's tea in 1992 (now the best-selling iced tea), Pepsi Max in 1993 for the international market (already sold in about 60 countries), and Aquafina in 1994. Grand Metropolitan has enjoyed great success with Häagen-Dazs, now the leading brand in the U.S. premium ice-cream market and developing fast in Europe.

International investment has become of growing importance. PepsiCo formed a new bottling company in 1993 to expand sales in Brazil and Argentina, two of South America's biggest soft-drinks markets; it is building 10 new bottling plants in China, and has already expanded to most major cities in India, capturing a third of that country's fast-growing soft-drinks market. Cadbury Schweppes also sees most growth potential in international investment. It has set up a joint venture to produce chocolate in China, and has established extensive interests in South America and the Pacific Rim. Cadbury Schweppes also has a joint venture with Coca-Cola in the UK, giving it market leadership there, and recent acquisitions in the United States make it number three in that market.

Finally, and most basically, the survival and growth of the big brands has depended on their relentless efforts to cut costs by streamlining their organizations, by achieving further economies of scale, and by aggressive marketing, including major promotions and more convenient packaging.

Sources: Can the Big Brands Survive, *Investors Chronicle* 105(1139): 10–14. See also the annual reports of major brand name companies.

where technical economies of scale are exhausted. The cube-square law faces sheer size limits beyond which technical problems and costs exceed possible economies. Cement lime kilns experience unstable internal aerodynamics above 7 million barrels per year capacity. Machines and equipment become increasingly unwieldy. Parts may have to be strengthened in proportion to volume rather than size once strength limits are approached, offsetting any possible scale economies. When the size of a new plant is above the usual size range for the industry, there may also be substantial design costs and initial difficulties in getting into production.

The principle of multiples confers fixed rather than continuous economies of scale. Costs are a minimum when the product of output per machine times the number of machines is the same for each step in a process. If output is increased beyond this level, costs rise until production reaches a new multiple of machine capacity. But the average costs per multiple may be the same unless increased scale permits larger and more efficient machines to be introduced.

The other principles underlying technical economies of scale also run into diminishing returns. The *principle of reserves* may not apply fully if several smaller production lines are replaced by a single large production line. In the chemical industry, for example, continuity of production is essential. Supplies are more vulnerable for a large single-stream plant than for many small ones. The danger of disruption can be reduced by storage, but the storage costs reduce the economies of scale of a larger plant.

A firm may run into actual technical difficulties in increasing scale of output. Limited physical space available for expansion may cause increasing congestion. There may be physical limits imposed by availability of water for production or cooling processes from nearby rivers and lakes. Environmental pollution may become more difficult to cope with at larger output levels. In sum, technical considerations tend to set a minimum efficient scale of production, but once this scale has been reached, further technical economies of scale may be difficult to win. Technical diseconomies of scale can be avoided by operating a number of separate plants. In this case, however, the firm is still faced with management diseconomies of scale.

Management Diseconomies of Scale. Management diseconomies of scale occur because of the increasing difficulty of coordinating larger firms. Supervisory and management personnel grow disproportionately with output, in fact, at a 3/2 power of the growth in production. Many functions that can be taken care of informally in small plants must be organized formally in larger organizations. Parking, eating facilities, medical care, and security are examples. Coordination becomes more complex with increasing size and division of labor. What was managed by a worker as part of the job routine becomes a new and wholly separate function. Hierarchies of management control evolve, with the attendant danger that top management becomes increasingly remote from day-to-day production problems. Decision making becomes more difficult, takes longer, and becomes less flexible. Bad decisions are more difficult to detect but may be more damaging and difficult to reverse. One need only to look at the giant corporations in difficulty today to see examples of this.

Marketing Diseconomies of Scale. The most serious diseconomies of scale may be in marketing. More output requires more sales. Advertising can be used to promote additional sales, but too much advertising can backfire. Budweiser found that advertising increased its sales of beer up to a maximum, beyond which further advertising appeared to reduce sales: Consumers deluged with Budweiser ads asked their liquor dealers to give them *anything but a Bud* (Figure 9.4).

Sales may be increased by extending the market area, but more distant sales incur greater delivery costs. Beyond a certain distance, these increased costs can be expected to exceed the economies of scale.

Of all the factors contributing to internal economies of scale, only finance appears to be immune to diminishing returns, and hence to diseconomies of scale.

MEASURING SCALE ECONOMIES

The Theoretical Approach

The many ingredients contributing to economies and diseconomies of scale can be usefully melded into a composite picture by focusing on the relationships of costs to output. Costs can be measured in various ways, but if these various measures of cost can be identified for a particular industry, then the most efficient size can be identified very precisely. Actual cost data for a comprehensive range of outputs and industries are not generally available. Even if they have such comprehensive data, industrialists are naturally reluc-

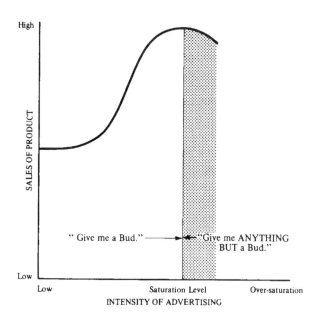

FIGURE 9.4 Diseconomies of advertising. Saturation advertising of a product beyond consumer tolerance levels can turn off potential buyers, as Budweiser found. [*Source:* Suggested by F. M. Scherer, *Industrial Market structure and Economic Performance* (Chicago: Rand McNally, 1980), p. 109.]

tant to part with information that might help competitors. The cost curves shown in most books are, therefore, based more on the theoretical understanding of economies of scale than on actual cases. In this text, too, the data are hypothetical and employed only to illustrate the key relationships among cost, output, and economies of scale.

Costs can be classified in two distinct ways. First, there is the distinction between *fixed cost* and *variable cost:* This distinction was noted in describing plant-specific economies. Second, there is the distinction between *total, average,* and *marginal costs.* It is this second classification that is crucial to the theoretical approach to understanding economies of scale.

Total costs of operating a plant at a given output level are equal to the fixed costs plus the total variable costs. If fixed costs are $100 and total variable costs are $180, then total costs are $280. Fixed costs do not change with output. However, variable costs must always *increase* with output (Box 9.5). If they did not, an industry could find itself in the enviable but bizarre position where it cost less to produce more.

Economies of scale are easier to identify from average costs than total costs. Average costs are simply total costs divided by output. Average fixed costs always decrease with higher output (Box 9.5). Average variable costs decrease until diseconomies of scale come into play. Diseconomies in variable costs may be offset by continuing economies in fixed costs. Thus, the output level with minimum average total costs may be higher than for the minimum average variable costs. It is the output level with *minimum average total costs* that marks the point of *maximum economies of scale.*

There is a simple test of whether output has reached the point of maximum economies of scale, which depends on calculating *marginal cost.* Marginal cost is the added cost of producing just one more unit of output (Box 9.5). As long as the marginal cost is less than the average total cost, producing more will lower the average. For example, if the average cost of six units is $50, and the marginal cost of producing one more unit (the seventh) is $42, it pays to do so. The average cost for seven is less than for six. But it turns out in the example that the marginal cost for the eighth unit jumps to $60, which is higher than the average. Hence, the average cost starts to rise. The rule is, therefore, that *average total cost is a minimum where it equals marginal cost.* At lower output levels, marginal cost is less than average cost and pulls average cost down. At higher levels, it pulls average cost up (Figure 9.5). Thus, economies of scale are maximized when average total cost equals marginal cost.

In summary, costs can be classified into fixed, variable, and total costs, and further classified into total, average, and marginal costs (Figure 9.5). The behavior of the cost curves in this two-way classification identifies the point

of maximum economies of scale. This point is the MES (minimum efficient scale). The point occurs *after* marginal costs have started to rise, and *after* average *variable* costs have started to rise. The MES occurs where average *total* costs are minimized.

Complicating Factors: Transportation Costs. A number of complications need to be considered. Increased output may require a larger market area and involve higher transportation costs. If transportation costs are substantial, they can reduce the MES. Each marginal unit sold involves higher and higher transportation costs, forcing up average total costs (Box 9.5). Another layer of costs is added to production so that average costs comprise average fixed, average variable, and average transportation costs (Box 9.6). Comparing the output levels with and without transportation costs thus permits an exact determination of the impact of transportation costs on the point of maximum economies of scale (Box 9.6).

Hoover's Margin Lines. Edgar Hoover (1937) introduced the concept of *margin line* to deal with the effect on economies and diseconomies of scale of extending the marketing area and incurring transportation costs. The concept is fairly straightforward. At each distance from a plant a calculation is made of what the delivered price would be at that point when transportation costs are added. As long as economies of scale outweigh transportation costs to each given distance, the margin line slopes down and it pays to extend the market area. Once the transportation costs outweigh the economies of scale, the margin line begins to slope up (Figure 9.6). The actual delivered price at each location is determined by the margin line at the actual market boundary. The price paid at each location is this price at the boundary, less the savings in transportation.

The Age and Scale of Equipment. Actual calculations of operating costs are affected by the age, or *vintage,* of equipment used and the scale of the operation. The age of factory equipment affects capital costs for a variety of reasons. Newer equipment tends to be relatively expensive because of inflation and added controls (whether for pollution, safety, or comfort). New equipment sometimes runs into teething problems, which can take years to correct. And the impact of these costs may be aggravated by accounting practices of heavily depreciating equipment in the early years. On the other hand, old equipment may be inefficient, raising labor costs. Based on his survey of British industry,

BOX 9.5 *Measuring Internal Economies of Scale*

OUTPUT	TOTAL COSTS ($)		
Number of Units	FIXED	VARIABLE	TOTAL
0	100	0	100
1	100	50	150
2	100	90	190
3	100	123	223
4	100	152	252
5	100	180	280
6	100	210	310
7	100	252	352
8	100	311	411
9	100	405	505
10	100	550	650

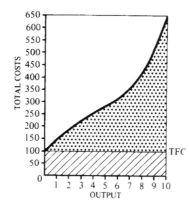

CHANGE IN TOTAL PRODUCTION COSTS WITH SCALE

Total production costs comprise two components, fixed costs and variable costs. These figures are entirely imaginary and are chosen to display, first, increasing economies of scale and then increasing diseconomies of scale in the figures that follow.

OUTPUT	AVERAGE COSTS ($)		
Number of Units	FIXED	VARIABLE	TOTAL
1	100	50	150
2	50	45	95
3	33	41	74
4	25	38	63
5	20	36	56
6	17	35	52
7	14	36	50
8	13	39	52
9	11	45	56
10	10	55	65

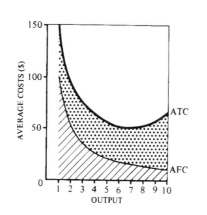

CHANGE IN AVERAGE PRODUCTION COSTS WITH SCALE

These figures are obtained simply by dividing the totals by the output levels involved. The total fixed cost for five units is $100, so the average is $20. Total variable for five units is $180, so the average is $36. The average total cost is cost divided by output.

OUTPUT	TOTAL VARIABLE COSTS	MARGINAL COSTS	INCREASE IN OUTPUT
Number of Units	($)	($)	from
0	0		
1	50	50	0 to 1
2	90	40	1 to 2
3	123	33	2 to 3
4	152	29	3 to 4
5	180	28	4 to 5
6	210	30	5 to 6
7	252	42	6 to 7
8	311	60	7 to 8
9	405	93	8 to 9
10	550	145	9 to 10

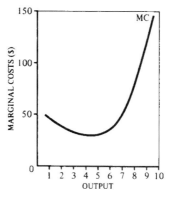

CHANGE IN MARGINAL PRODUCTION COSTS WITH SCALE

Marginal cost is the additional cost of producing one more unit. It can be calculated as the difference in variable costs in increasing output by one unit. The result is the same if total cost is used. The marginal cost of increasing production from five units to six is $30. The marginal cost is $210 in variable costs for six units minus $180 for five. Equally, it is $310 in total costs for six minus $280 for five.

| | Variable costs | ATC | Average Total Cost | TFC | Total Fixed Cost | | |
| | Fixed costs | AFC | Average Fixed Cost | TC | Total Cost | MC | Marginal Cost |

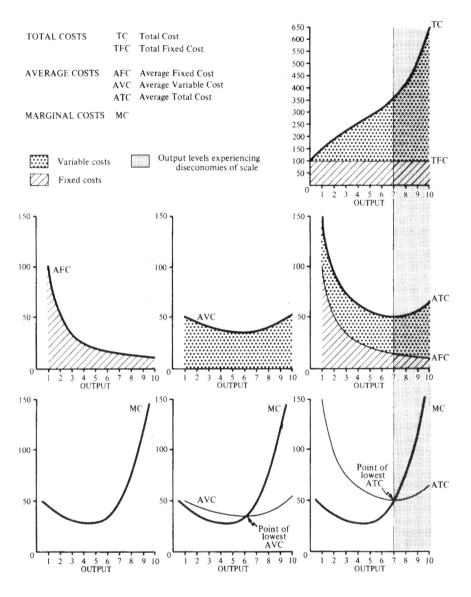

FIGURE 9.5 Finding the divide between economies and diseconomies of scale. This figure essentially brings together the figures shown in Box 9.5. Note that the marginal-cost curve MC for a product always intersects the average variable-cost curve AVC, where AVC is a minimum. It also intersects the average total costs ATC, where these costs are a minimum. The divide between economies of scale and diseconomies of scale is at this point of intersection, where ATC is a minimum and where there is an inflection in total costs. Total costs are rising at a decreasing rate if there are economies of scale, and at an increasing rate if there are diseconomies of scale.

C. F. Pratten (1991a) thus found the structure of industry varied with the age of equipment in a characteristic way (Table 9.3; Figure 9.7). Moreover, the characteristic change between labor and capital costs with age of equipment was the same whether the equipment had a short life, as some machine tools and textile equipment, which can wear out within 10 years, or a long life, as in the case of cement or soap whose machinery can continue to operate for over 40 years.

The newer the equipment is, the lower the average total costs tend to be, and the higher the output at which minimum average costs are achieved (Figure 9.8). Thus, the

vintage of equipment affects not only the structure of operating costs but also the average level of operating costs, and the minimum efficient scale.

LONG-RUN VERSUS SHORT-RUN UNIT COSTS

Most of the previous discussion refers to the shape of *short-run* unit cost curves. *Long-run* average-cost curves (also called *planning curves*) differ from these, because the assumption of a fixed investment in a given plant is dropped; all costs can be considered variable. In the short

BOX 9.6   *Adding in Transportation Costs*

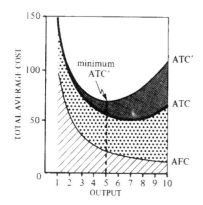

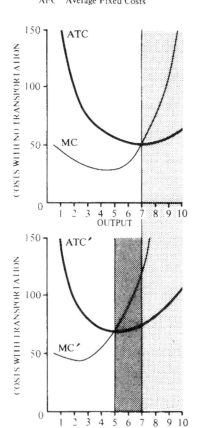

Average transportation costs

Average variable costs

Average fixed costs

ATC′   Average Total Costs
       plus Transportation
ATC   Average Total Costs
       not including Transportation
AFC   Average Fixed Costs

Average costs of:

Output Number of Units	Transportation	Production	Transportation and Production
		ATC	ATC′
1	0	150	150
2	3	95	98
3	5	74	79
4	9	63	72
5	14	56	70
6	20	52	72
7	26	50	76
8	33	52	85
9	40	56	96
10	48	65	113

Marginal costs of:

Output Number of Units	Total Transportation Cost	Transportation	Production	Transportation and Production
0	0 > . . .	0 . . .	50 . . .	50
1	0 > . . .	5 . . .	40 . . .	45
2	5 > . . .	10 . . .	33 . . .	43
3	15 > . . .	20 . . .	29 . . .	49
4	35 > . . .	35 . . .	28 . . .	63
5	70 > . . .	50 . . .	30 . . .	80
6	120 > . . .	65 . . .	42 . . .	107
7	185 > . . .	80 . . .	60 . . .	139
8	265 > . . .	95 . . .	93 . . .	189
9	360 > . . .	120 . . .	145 . . .	265
10	480			

MC   Marginal Costs
ATC   Average Total Costs
MC′   Marginal Costs plus
      Transportation Costs
ATC′ Average Total Costs plus
      Transportation Costs

Diseconomies of scale

Impact of transportation costs:
diseconomies of scale if
transportation costs incurred

Note: Total transportation costs are given and assume that increasing production levels require a growing sales area and increasing transportation costs. The average and marginal costs are both calculated from total costs as before. Then total average costs plus transportation (ATC′) equals the total average production cost from the top figure plus the average transportation cost. Marginal production cost and marginal transportation cost are summed to give the combined marginal cost (MC′).

Average total costs plus transportation are given in the accompanying table. This figure adds one more layer of costs to the average production costs presented in Box 9.5. Note that the minimum average costs occur at an output level of 5 units when transportation costs are added in.

The middle figure, repeated from Figure 9.5, shows the output level at which diseconomies of scale set in without transportation costs. The lower figure shows that diseconomies set in at a lower production level if transportation costs are incurred. The difference between the two levels indicates the impact of transportation costs on economies of scale.

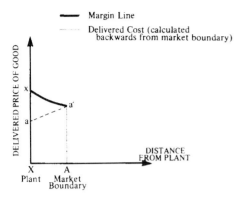

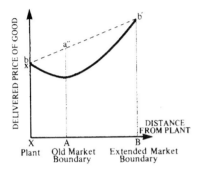

TABLE 9.3

Vintage of equipment and structure of costs in brick production

	Old Works (%)	New Works (%)
Clay	2.6	2.6
Fuel and power	31.5	28.6
Wages and salaries	41.5	20.1
Repairs	9.6	10.5
Rates (local taxes)	2.6	2.8
Office expenses	5.5	5.6
Depreciation	6.8	30.0
Total	100.0	100.2

Source: Pratten, 1971, p. 97.

Note: Costs include depreciation but exclude interest on capital. Total costs are approximately the same for the two works. The new works has a capacity of about three times the old works, which is 40 years old.

FIGURE 9.6 Diseconomies in extending the market area. Edgar M. Hoover (1937) introduced the concept of margin line to deal with the economies and diseconomies in extending the market area. The margin line shows what the delivered price would be at each distance from a plant, taking into account the economies of scale given the market available within that distance, and the transportation costs of shipping the good that distance. Given a plant at X, which ships as far as A, the delivered price at A is Aa'. If the market is extended to B, transportation costs outweigh economies of scale. The price at B is Bb', and the price at A rises to Aa'. The price at any location is the price at the market boundary minus the transportation costs from that boundary.

run, it is assumed that one is dealing with cost variations from operating a *given* farm or factory at different levels of output. In the long run, the business can be modified or sold, or a new unit with a different amount and configuration of investment can be planned and built for a different scale of output.

In practice, the distinction between short run and long run is not as clear and simple as the foregoing might indicate, however. For example, Rhys (1971–1972) has estimated that in heavy commercial vehicle manufacturing, only 5 percent of total costs are variable within a week's

time, but in a 6-month period 80 percent may be variable (Table 9.4).

One way of looking at the long-run average-cost curve is by comparing average cost levels for a variety of different facilities, as in Figure 9.9, which deals with the costs per patient per day for hospitals in Chicago in the late 1960s. Each of the individual facilities, representing different investment "packages," has its own short-run cost curve; the relationship between the short- and long-run curves is expressed by a relationship in which the long-run cost curve

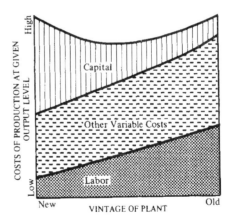

FIGURE 9.7 The effect of age of equipment on the structure of costs. New plant involves heavy capital costs, which in economic terms are incurred when it is installed, but which, for accounting purposes, may be depreciated over a number of years. An older plant is likely to have higher variable costs, for a given level of output. The structure of costs, therefore, varies according to the vintage of the equipment. [*Source*: Adapted from Pratten, 1971, pp. 306–307.]

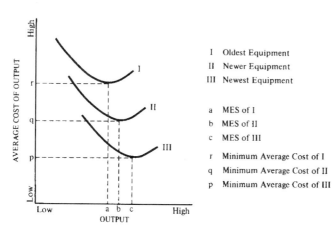

I	Oldest Equipment
II	Newer Equipment
III	Newest Equipment

a	MES of I
b	MES of II
c	MES of III

r	Minimum Average Cost of I
q	Minimum Average Cost of II
p	Minimum Average Cost of III

FIGURE 9.8 Vintage of equipment and economies of scale. Newer equipment tends to achieve its most efficient scale at higher output levels than older equipment. Thus, the vintage of equipment affects not only the structure of operating costs but also economies of scale. [*Source:* After Pratten, 1971, p. 5.]

appears as an "envelope" embracing the many possible short-run curves, as in Figure 9.10.

The "Lazy-J" Long-Run Unit Cost Curve

The most important feature of Figure 9.10 is that it shows that long-run returns to scale may not be U-shaped, but may instead form an envelope that has the shape of a reverse- or "lazy-J." The figure begins by plotting the short-run cost curves for each of several types of dairy farms in Minnesota. The characteristics of the least-cost farm are described in each case. For example, the least-cost three-person dairy farm (farm D) is one with an investment of $325,000, working 623 acres of land with a 100-head herd, and producing a net return of $16,925 per annum on a gross income of $80,000. A long-run curve is added that traces the best achievable cost per unit of output at each scale of production by forming an envelope beneath the short-run curves. Each individual type of dairy farming has a short-run unit-cost curve that is U-shaped, with economies and diseconomies of scale, and an MES when costs are mini-mized. The long-run curve continues to slope downward to the right, however, indicating continuing cost advantages of increasing farm size. Similar behavior of the long-run curve has been observed elsewhere (Table 9.5). Agriculture is pursuing these long-run cost advantages, resulting in rapid decline of smaller farms and a progressive increase in numbers of larger operations. Cost advantages to larger-sized farms, accruing as they did throughout most of American agriculture, were responsible for the decline in the U.S. farm population from 15 million in 1960 to 10 million in 1970 and to 5 million in 1990 as the small-scale farmers moved into urban occupations.

Returns to Scale and Threshold Size

Lazy-J long-run cost curves indicate a particular pattern of returns to investment. First, for the reasons cited in the case of short-run curves, there will be economies of scale, and the long-run unit-cost curve will fall with increasing output. But only if there are long-run constraints will there be diseconomies of further increases in scale, producing a U-shaped long-run unit-cost (LRUC) curve. What occurs with the lazy-J is that the zone of increasing returns to scale terminates at a critical *size threshold,* the minimum size at which the lowest attainable unit costs are achieved. There is no onset of decreasing returns beyond this point because of the flexibility of different investment configurations that may be designed and built. Instead, beyond the threshold, average costs per unit of output tend to be relatively stable, and there is no apparent cost advantage of operating at either one scale or another. The *threshold size* sets the *condition of entry* for new firms to be able to compete. Entry at smaller scales means higher costs, lack of competitiveness, and ultimate failure, but firms may grow to several multiples of the threshold without cost penalty.

TABLE 9.4

Cost flexibility in heavy commercial vehicle manufac-

Proportion of Total Costs Variable Within		
1 week	1 month	6 months
5	35	80

Source: D. G. Rhys, (1971–1972, p. 233).

Note: Cost flexibility is not symmetric. If orders increase in a 6-month period, then 80 percent of costs will increase directly in proportion with output. If orders fall, the manufacturer may become locked into some costs.

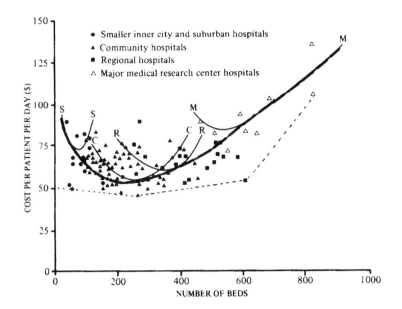

FIGURE 9.9 Cost data for hospitals in metropolitan Chicago. Each point in this graph shows the average patient-day cost for a hospital in the Chicago region. The solid line shows the average relationship for all the hospital averages. The dashed line is an envelope tracing the silhouette of the best possible long-run average-cost curve suggested by the data. The degree to which a hospital's costs lie above this silhouette is an indication of that hospital's relative inefficiency. [*Source:* Adapted from Gerald F. Pyle, *Heart Disease, Cancer, and Stroke in Chicago,* Department of Geography Research Paper No. 134, (Chicago: University of Chicago, 1971).]

The Relationship of Threshold Scale to Industrial Concentration

Measurement of Size Thresholds. One economist, J. S. Bain (1956), has identified the size thresholds associated with lazy-J cost curves in a variety of industries in North America. By expressing the scale of individual manufactur-

ing plants as a percentage of the total national capacity of an industry, costs were shown to decrease with increasing scale, and then to level off. This enabled threshold size to be measured in relation to the proportion of national industrial capacity contained in one plant of minimal efficient size, by selecting as the threshold the point at which costs leveled off. It also enabled the capital requirements for a new plant to enter the industry at the minimum efficient cost threshold

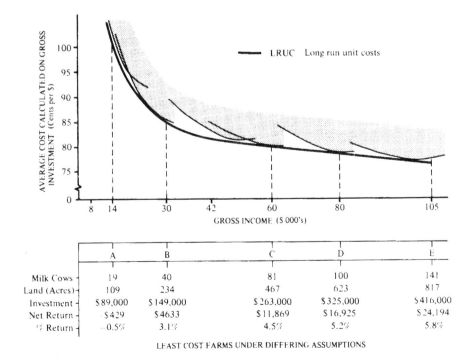

FIGURE 9.10 Short- and long-run cost curves in Minnesota dairy farming, c. 1970. The cost curves are a "lazy-J" shape in this example rather than the "U" shape of the earlier discussion of economies and diseconomies. The principles are the same, however. For each investment package, there is an optimal output, as shown by the short-run unit-cost curve. Alternative farm sizes reveal that the long-run unit cost curve favors larger farms. Farms of 100 acres operate at a net loss.

	A	B	C	D	E
Milk Cows	19	40	81	100	141
Land (Acres)	109	234	467	623	817
Investment	$89,000	$149,000	$263,000	$325,000	$416,000
Net Return	-$429	$4633	$11,869	$16,925	$24,194
% Return	-0.5%	3.1%	4.5%	5.2%	5.8%

LEAST COST FARMS UNDER DIFFERING ASSUMPTIONS

TABLE 9.5

Long-run economies of scale: cement industry

Item	Capacity (1000 tons)	100	200	500	1000	2000
	Number of kilns and mills	1	1	2	2	2
Fuel, power, and materials		100	98	97	96	95
Wages and salaries		100	70	55	40	35
Depreciation and return on capital		100	80	70	58	47
Overhead		100	90	82	75	70
Average total costs		100	85	77	69	62

Source: Pratten, 1971, p. 92

Note: Costs are given as an index of production costs in the smallest plant (100,000 tons per annum). Costs of transportation and selling are excluded. All plants are new.

to be calculated. The threshold conditions for entry in many of the industries that Bain studied were substantial.

Emergence of Oligopolies and Administered Prices.

There are several consequences of such reverse-J long-run cost curves with high conditions of entry. Generally, high conditions of entry limit potential new competition and tend to create oligopolies in which the industry is controlled by a small number of multiplant firms.

An example of a typical oligopoly in which a few firms have consistently controlled a large share of the market is that of the sulfur industry, in particular the Frasch sulfur industry, which produces sulfur from brimstone deposits found in the salt domes of the United States and Mexican Gulf coasts.

The Frasch sulfur industry is oligopolistic because of the high conditions of entry, and the LRUC is reverse-J. The difficulties faced by potential new competitors in gaining entry to the industry are threefold:

1. *Absolute cost barriers.* Established firms control existing Frasch sulfur deposits, and there is great competition for new deposits when discovered. A new sulfur firm enters this arena by having to raise capital for the cost of entry at the same time that it competes with existing producers owning less costly deposits. The effect is to raise the price that must be paid for the new deposits.

2. *Product differentiation barriers.* Firms who have an established reputation with their customers have a sales advantage over new competitors.

3. *The economy-of-scale threshold.* The minimal scale at which a new firm may achieve the lowest attainable cost is a significant fraction of the total capacity of the industry. The entry of an additional firm may induce established firms to lower their price to preserve their market share. In this case, the newcomer must compete against a price that is even lower than the prevailing price when the

firm entered. This discouragement is often sufficient to turn away potential new entrants.

Relatively free from new competitors, Frasch sulfur producers let their prices be determined by administrative decisions rather than allowing them to fluctuate with market conditions. First, prices were determined by the industry in response to long-run criteria, rather than with respect to short-run economic changes. Second, the industry practiced price discrimination, charging one price in domestic markets and a second, higher basing-point price for foreign markets. The higher price was quoted FOB vessels, Gulf port through the Sulfur Export Corporation, to which all Frasch producers belonged. The domestic price was established competitively by producers; the foreign price, however, was an arranged one producing a world pattern of Frasch sulfur prices rising with transport costs from U.S. Gulf ports.

Product Differentiation as a Barrier to Entry.

In most such oligopolistic circumstances, product differentiation is as powerful a force in restricting entry as is the condition of entry itself. The most obvious sources of product differentiation are differences in quality of design among competing outputs. For example, one brand of shoes may have better materials and workmanship than another, or one make of clothes may be fashionable whereas another may not. In either case, different buyers may rank the competing products differently. One buyer may be fashion conscious, looking for the latest styles. Another may be quality conscious, willing to pay a considerable premium for quality shoes. Yet another may be price conscious, accepting the lower quality if there is only a relatively small price concession.

A second source of product differentiation is the ignorance of buyers regarding the essential characteristics and qualities of the goods they are purchasing. This is likely to be an important consideration particularly with durable consumer goods, which are infrequently purchased and complex in design or composition. In this situation, the buyer is likely to rely on the "reputations" of the various products or their sellers—on popular lore concerning the product's performance and reliability, or on whether or not the seller has successfully remained in business for a long time.

Third, buyer preferences for certain products are developed or shaped by the persuasive sales-promotion activities of sellers, particularly by advertising of brand names, trademarks, or company names.

J. S. Bain (1956) has classified industries according to degree of product differentiation. He concludes that product differentiation is generally negligible in the producer-good segments of the agricultural, forestry, fisheries, and mining industries. Because goods produced by these industries are likely to be standardized at various grades and qualities, the sellers' efforts to introduce product differentiation have generally been unsuccessful. Moreover, these industries have many small sellers, thus providing a close approximation to the theoretical "pure competition."

On the other hand, in manufacturing and processing industries—particularly those producing consumer goods—product differentiation becomes very important. The consumer-buyer tends to be poorly informed, especially when faced with choosing among goods with complex designs. Even when the goods are not complex, buyers are susceptible to persuasive advertising campaigns that emphasize the sometimes nominal differences among products. In addition, producers can purposely vary the designs or quality of their goods in ways whose significance is not easily understood by consumers.

In some consumer-goods manufacturing industries, however, product differentiation is relatively unimportant. This seems to be especially true of basic necessities—food, clothing, and household supplies. In these industries, the efforts of competing sellers to differentiate their products significantly have not been too successful. Thus, the establishment of brands and their support by advertising has not been automatically efficacious in creating strong product differentiation within a consumer-goods industry.

In manufacturing industries making producer goods, product differentiation is most frequently slight or negligible, and for the usual reasons—expert buyers, and goods that may be produced to standards or specifications. Basic industrial chemicals, for example, clearly come under this heading. Buyers purchase to specification or rely on established grades and generally do not prefer one seller's output to another sufficiently to induce them to pay a higher price for it. The slight buyer preferences that do introduce some product differentiation generally depend on ancillary services that the seller performs for buyers, such as promptness in filling orders or making deliveries. But with producer goods for which the provision of services by the manufacturer is an important element of the transaction (often when the producer-buyers represent rather small firms) and with

large, complex producer goods (specialized machinery of various sons), product differentiation may become as important as it is in consumer-goods categories. This would be true, for example, of farm machinery and business office machines of various sorts.

Other sectors of the economy may be characterized more briefly with respect to the incidence of product differentiation:

1. *Wholesale and retail trade (groceries, clothing stores, pharmacies, and so on).* In retail distribution, product differentiation based on type and quality of service offered by the retailer and on the convenience of location to the buyer is generally quite important. Product differentiation is evidently less important in wholesale markets in which retailers purchase from wholesale distributors.

2. *Service trades (barber shops, dry cleaners, entertainment enterprises, and so on).* Product differentiation is again important, for the same general reasons as those that apply to retailing.

3. *Contract construction.* On large-scale construction for industry or government when contracts are awarded after a process of bidding to specifications, product differentiation is a minimal factor. In residential construction, product differentiation based on design and location is generally quite important.

4. *Finance (real estate firms, insurance companies, banks, and so on).* Product differentiation is important in some cases and not in others.

5. *Public utilities and transportation.* In most utility industries, including suppliers of electricity, gas, and communications services, local monopoly by a single firm typically forestalls the emergence of product differentiation. In the transportation field, product differentiation among the services of competing types of carriers and between competing carriers of the same type is present, but is evidently more important in passenger transportation than in freight transportation.

Conditions of Entry and Pricing Behavior. The degree of difficulty that a new firm has in entering a field of industry determines how much the already established firms can raise their prices above the defined competitive level without attracting new competition. In effect, the established firms administer a geography of price, with their selling prices restrained according to the barriers of entry. In industries where the conditions of entry are not difficult, the established firms can exceed only slightly the competitive selling price before new competitors will enter; if entry conditions are difficult, the established firms can perhaps attain a monopolistic price—substantially higher than the competitive level—without attracting competitors; if entry conditions are moderately difficult, the established firms can only raise their prices moderately to keep out new competitors.

Thus, J. S. Bain found the following in his studies:
1. When barriers to entry are either high or moderate, then
(a). among industries of high seller concentration, *limit pricing* to exclude entry is likely. This will result in higher prices and greater monopolistic output restriction according to the height of the barriers to entry.
(b). among industries of moderate to low seller concentration, the preceding tendency is likely to be modified or obscured because intra-industry competition will frequently keep price fairly close to the competitive level.
2. When barriers to entry are low, then
(a). among industries of high seller concentration, periodic high prices and monopolistic output restriction are likely to emerge, followed by induced entry, and further followed by excess plant capacity. The ultimate result may be a significant decrease in seller concentration, an increase in intra-industry competition, and a lessening or elimination of monopolistic tendencies.
(b). among industries of moderate to low seller concentration, the pressure of entry plus the inherent tendencies toward strong intra-industry competition are likely to produce close approximations to competitive pricing and output.

Costs, prices, and the degree of concentration of production thus are closely interdependent.

EXTERNAL ECONOMIES

Given the importance of economies of scale, one wonders how so many small firms survive. There is no definitive answer. Sometimes small firms concentrate on a niche product or service for which total demand is too small to support large firms. The small firm may have proprietary knowledge of the product. It may survive because of the level of service it offers, perhaps to a highly specialized market. It may have acquired a leading reputation for quality or style. Or the small firm may survive because of subsidies, perhaps from governments providing low-cost premises, or loans or grants to encourage the enterprise culture. The subsidy may be from the owners themselves, risking all in the hope of future returns. The subsidy may be by workers prepared to accept below-average wages. Whatever the ostensible reason, one factor is clear, however: Small firms that survive are a few among many, and most of the survivors are those lucky enough to be "adopted" by a competitive "survival of the fittest" environment. In this environment, they must be sure they reach threshold and quickly seek out their MES.

For many small firms, the relevant environment may be one that contains both competitors and specialist auxiliaries in close spatial association. The *external economies* provided by such an environment have grown in significance as factors guiding locational choice by small firms, an importance that stands in sharp contrast to the preference of large MNEs for *internalizing* the economies of scale and scope within the corporation. Dramatic small firm "churning" (i.e., high rates of entry and exit) leads to survival-of-the-fittest adoption of successful small businesses, and one of the environments where success can be most rewarding is the cluster of firms involved in the same industry, where networks of information, specialists, and venture capital are available. Multinationals, on the other hand, skillfully "adapt" their structure and operations to global markets, and in turn structure these markets, taking advantage of internal economies of scale and the use of market power. Appendices 9.1 and 9.2 offer more detailed discussions of small-firm churning and locational adoption, and of locational adaption by MNEs. Read these appended materials thoroughly once you are comfortable with the ideas of internal and external economies of scale.

What clusters and networks offer to small firms are external economies that contribute to the lowering of average production costs. They may also offer the opportunity to increase returns by creating demand and increasing market share, a topic to which we turn in the section that follows. External economies are the gains in efficiency resulting from the concentration of different firms in a single location. They derive from the environment surrounding the firm—from *spatial association*—rather than being "internalized" via corporate integration. External economies may be *industry-specific*, depending on the concentration in one location of different firms involved in the manufacture of similar products (called *localization economies*), or they may be *place-specific* and result from efficiencies that arise not from the particular nature of the industry, but from the local scale of economic activity of all kinds (called *urbanization economies*). They produce what the great English economist Alfred Marshall called *industrial districts*.

Localization Economies

Localization economies arose historically from the clustering of plants engaged in similar activity in a restricted geographical area. The local scale of the industry benefits individual plants and tends to perpetuate the localization of the industry. Several kinds of economies have been identified:

1. The reputation acquired by goods produced in a given locality leads to *product differentiation*. Goods produced in some localities, whether or not they meet the standards of that locality, carry with them the aura of high standards of workmanship and quality. A noteworthy case is that of the cutlery and steel produced in Sheffield, England; others are Brussels lace, Irish linen, and Milwaukee beer. Whether or not the products are superior, the image is that they are. Their product is therefore differentiated from the same goods produced elsewhere, giving a distinct market advantage.

2. The creation of a pool of skilled labor strengthens localization economies. Because the local labor force becomes uniquely adapted to the needs of the local industry, local productivity is enhanced. Local educational institutions may offer special training programs, which further benefits local industry by ensuring a flow of new workers, and by upgrading the skills of those already employed.

3. The adaptation of local utilities and services to the particular needs of the industry also produces efficiencies that reduce costs. Banks, insurance agencies, and transportation companies supplying special facilities appropriate to the needs of the industry dominate the kinds of service provided in the locality, and their costs are lower because they become expert in the problems and needs of the industry.

4. Most important, the local scale of industry permits the subdivision of operations. Auxiliary specialists emerge, meeting the requirements of several firms. The specialists provide components of needed services more cheaply than if the individual firms had to provide their own. Within a localized industry, then, vertical disintegration is important. It arises from the close geographical association of firms, short hauls, speedy delivery, and the lessening of stock requirements. The resulting local interdependence is the hallmark of successful localization. Outstanding historical examples include the clothing industry and the cutlery trades, for example, the garment districts of New York and the East End of London, and the concentration of cutlery makers in Sheffield. In the metal trades of the West Midlands of England, the localization was composed of three main types of activity: (1) a large number of firms performing common metal processes, but not producing finished goods; for example, the foundries, reorders, forgers, welders, and galvanizers; (2) a large number of firms making common components, screws, bolts, nuts, tools, and springs; and (3) service trades, for example, small establishments making wooden patterns or machine tools, the scrap merchants, and so on. These three main types of activity supported metal goods manufacturers who assembled and further processed the components. Good examples were motor vehicles, bicycles, motorcycles, and guns in Birmingham, locks at Wolverhampton, and so on. In the United States, a similar complex fed Connecticut's gun, lock, tool, and clock makers. Such localization economies accomplish through geographic juxtaposition the same kinds of linkages as are achieved through corporate integration in internal economies of scale.

Urbanization Economies

Urbanization economies derive from the close association of many different kinds of industry in large cities. Among the advantages identified are the following:

1. *Transportation Costs.* Large cities usually have superior transportation facilities, offering significantly lower transportation costs to regional and national markets. A city located at a focal point of transportation networks is especially suited for easy assembly of raw materials and for ready distribution of products. Historically, there thus were market advantages for speedy and cheap distribution from big-city locations, accentuated by the advantages arising out of the size of the local consuming market. The local population may in fact form a large part of the total national market. In the 1960s Greater London comprised one-fifth of the British consumer market and the New York metropolitan area was called "one-tenth of a nation." In both cases, significantly larger proportions of higher-quality and fashion-oriented demands were accounted for. Where transport costs are significant, the large city may be the ideal plant location: Local demands are substantial and the rest of the plant's output is easily distributed.

2. *Labor Costs.* The big-city labor market is diverse and dynamic, and the labor demands of single firms are only a small part of the total demands for labor. This labor pool is especially important when firms have seasonal variations in labor needs. The big-city labor market also offers a wide range of skills. Facilities for workers that are readily available in the large city (restaurants, transportation) may also have to be provided by the firm in the small town, which raises the real labor costs.

3. *Quality of Services.* The larger the city, the higher the scale of services it can supply. Services such as firefighting, police, gas, electricity, water, waste disposal, education, housing, and roads are generally better in the larger city than in the small town, and they are provided publicly. Firms located in otherwise unindustrialized areas may be forced to spend much more of their capital on infrastructure and social facilities. These kinds of advantages first came into play in the industrial development of the largest metropolitan areas in the period following World War I. Service economies had a magnetic effect on industries in which coal was replaced as motive power by electricity, and in which rail and water transportation was replaced by the truck. Light industry, manufacturing consumer goods, was attracted to large cities not only by their markets and marketing facilities, but also by their services. In turn, the accumulation of light industry in large cities further enhanced the attractiveness of the cities, creating positive conditions for further growth. In this way, urbanization economies fed on themselves in a process of *circular and cumulative causation.*

External Diseconomies

There also may be external diseconomies of scale. They set in, for example, once the costs of urban congestion begin to exceed the benefits of industrial concentration. Precise definition is more difficult than in the case of internal diseconomies, but the general nature of these diseconomies is not difficult to understand. Some cause industries to seek lower-cost regions, as when rising big-city wage rates force labor-intensive industries such as textile producers to exploit lower-wage labor forces elsewhere, in a process of "filtering" (refer back to Box 8.1). Others produce a shifting of activities between central and suburban locations. High land values in inner-city areas, rising tax rates, increasing crime, cramped and restricted sites, parking difficulties, deficiency of light and air, and environmental pollution lead industries to go to the periphery of the big city, to smaller towns, or to nonurban areas; often a relocation is planned to bring the plant closer to the owner's or manager's preferred place of residence. Carefully selected, the peripheral area can avoid the diseconomies of centrality while retaining the advantages of proximity.

This movement to the fringe took place slowly in the industrial areas of the United States and Western Europe before World War II. Despite more widespread use of electric power and the development of road transportation and of improved highways, reducing the locational pull on industrial locations of rail terminals and docks in central areas, a long period of economic depression prevented wholesale relocation or many new suburban plant locations, although new outlying planned industrial estates were pioneered in many countries. The great change came after World War II: Highways were improved and new large-scale trucks came into operation, in combination with rail transport ("piggyback"). Rapid decentralization of industry from the central cities began in force.

Initially, decentralization operated selectively. For some kinds of activities, central locations remained so crucial that they outweighed the disadvantages of congestion. Industries decentralizing were those using road transportation and preferring single-story facilities or expansive sites. Industries moving out of big cities altogether did so in sequence: First were those seeking low labor costs (especially textile producers and a variety of assembly operations), next were the machine tool industries serving those that left first, then integrated production complexes that were capable of standing alone, and then a variety of new computer- and communications-based industries that were relatively immune from the pulls of the central city but highly dependent on being able to attract skilled scientists and technicians to attractive residential environments. With the advent of information technologies, the decentralizing movement became a flood, as we shall see in Chapter 10, only stemmed by the emergence of new localizations based not on external economies, which operate on the cost side, but on *increasing returns,* which are a revenue-side phenomenon.

INCREASING RETURNS AND THE NEW GEOGRAPHY OF CONCENTRATION

One conclusion to emerge from Michael Porter (1990) is that firms that achieve world class are likely to have built their international competitive edge on the continuum of economies of scale from internal to external. The process of accumulating these economies of scale to create a privileged location for a particular industry may begin with the location of a single firm, as when Koenig and Bauer (K&B) moved from England to Oberzell, Bavaria, Germany, in 1818 to manufacture printing press machines (Porter, 1990, p. 182). The firm grows, achieving internal economies of scale: product-specific, plant-specific, and firm-specific, step by step (Table 9.6). The firm may then promote technological developments among local supply industries to enhance its competitive position, as when K&B helped local paper producers to develop the stronger papers needed by the printing machines and the German chemical industry

TABLE 9.6
Internal and external economies of scale: The continuum

	Type of Economy of Scale	Economy of Scale Depends on	Example of an Economy of Scale Achieved
External (Different firms)	Place-Specific (urbanization)	Size of city	Range of urban services
	Industry-specific (localization)	Size of of industry	Research and development
Internal (Same firm)	Firm-specific	Size of firm	Advertisement and marketing
	Plant-specific	Size of plant	Larger machines(cube-square law)
	Product-specific	Length and volume of production run	Division of labor

Note: External economies are in part a continuum on the range of economies of scale. They are industry- or place-specific, rather than specific to a particular firm, or to a plant or product within that firm. Sometimes they are a partial substitute for internal economies. Firms internalize economies of scale by integration and they externalize them by disintegration.

to develop synthetic printing inks. Spin-off companies may be created as employees leave the firm to set up businesses on their own, as when an ex-K&B foreman set up Helbig and Muller in Vienna in 1836, which after various mergers again become part of K&B in 1921. The growing importance of the industry in the region may lead to the establishment of specialized apprenticeship programs and vocational schools. The industry may gain an important voice in regional and even the national government, ensuring that attention is given to its public infrastructure needs and ensuring public funding of industry-related research in regional universities, to help it maintain its technological and quality advantages. The growing international reputation of the region attracts world-class suppliers of related products to move to the region—as when Linotype moved its headquarters from the United States to Germany in the 1980s. The external economies of scale achieved by the industry then began to constitute a barrier to the entry of competing firms in different regions. Germany has maintained a competitive edge in the manufacture of printing presses for 160 years. It accounts for half the world's exports of these machines. The explanation for the dominant position does not lie in the local availability or cost of raw materials, or in cheap labor. Instead, it depends on the *created advantages* of internal and external economies of scale mutually reinforcing themselves in an increasingly privileged location.

The fundamental ingredients of the success story of the German printing press industry can be replicated for many different industries in many different countries, and serve to underline the importance of economies of scale as a primary factor in the survival and growth of economic activity. There is a growing realization that this is only part of the story surrounding the emergence of new industrial concentrations, however. The most notable of these new concentrations in the United States are California's Silicon Valley and the Boston region's Route 128, which emerged together in the 1960s and 1970s, but have had contrasting experiences since.

In the 1970s, both of these regions featured fast-growing start-up companies, a growing stable of entrepreneur celebrities, abundant venture capital, world-class universities, and a seemingly endless ability to generate wave after wave of breakthrough innovations that created an environment of *increasing returns* for their participants. They also provided the source of new ideas and innovations for increasingly global high-technology production systems. One aspect of this is the movement of routine factory production to places like Mexico, Malaysia, Thailand, and even India and China. Another is the out-migration of advanced semiconductor and computer production to new industrial complexes in and around Austin, Texas; Phoenix, Arizona; Albuquerque, New Mexico; and Portland, Oregon. See Box 9.7. Silicon Valley's global dimensions are also evident in

---

BOX 9.7   *Locational Determinants for High-Tech Plants*

Chicago's Fantus Corporation, perhaps the major location research firm in the United States, believes that locational determinants for high-tech plants depend on the developmental stages of the high-tech product. Three developmental stages are recognized: theory, product, and market.

Theory-driven firms are usually embryonic, involved in advanced theoretical research. These firms are at the advanced cutting edge of ideas, innovations, and inventions. For them, the key criteria for selecting a plant location are

1. availability of venture capital
2. ease of technological transfer
3. ease of start-up

Product-driven firms are the second stage of high-technology development. At this stage the product is viable, but must be closely monitored for quality and must be often

modified before sale. Companies at this stage employ a blend of research and manufacturing personnel. The location requirements are

1. availability of technicians and skilled workers
2. demonstrated high worker productivity
3. accessibility to theory-driven R&D facilities
4. attractive living conditions
5. a favorable business climate, such as low business and personal taxes

Market-driven facilities emerge as the product becomes routinized, imitators enter the market, and price competition enters the selling process. Location requirements for competitive facilities switch dramatically, emphasizing

1. cost, availability, and attitude of labor
2. cost, availability, and dependability of utilities
3. incentives, inducements, and exemptions

Labor costs will rise to exceed 50 percent of all locationally variable costs at this stage, but where labor costs and available utilities are approximately the same, it is often special local inducements and giveaways that dictate the final locational choice.

The speed with which new innovations move from theory to product to competition is producing an increasingly fluid global industrial landscape.

an inflow of foreign capital to many of its most innovative companies—General Magic, Kaleida, Silicon Graphics, and 3DO are examples.

In the early 1980s, both Silicon Valley and Route 128 suffered severe economic downturns. But over the course of the 1980s and early 1990s, Silicon Valley was able to recapture much of its technological and economic dynamism, leading to new rounds of increasing returns, whereas Route 128 could not. The difference was the emergence in Silicon Valley of a decentralized *network system* of technological and industrial organization that encouraged innovation, collaboration, and collective learning among companies and enabled them to respond quickly to changing markets and technology. Indeed, the reemergence of Silicon Valley was based on a new generation of start-up firms such as Cypress Semiconductors, Chips and Technologies, Cirrus Logic, Maxim Integrated Products, Silicon Graphics, Sun Microsystems, MIPS, and countless others that were flexible and diversified enough to capitalize on the continuing revolution in high-technology products and markets. Route 128, in contrast, remained dominated by a few large, relatively independent companies like DEC, leaving the region less able to adapt to these dramatic changes.

In understanding the emergence and continuing success of new industrial concentrations such as Silicon Valley we therefore need to understand both the phenomenon of increasing returns and the emergence of network organization.

Increasing Returns

Kaldor's Model and Verdoorn's Law. The possibility that individual firms might be able to continue to experience increasing returns to scale was brought to the attention of contemporary scholars by economist Nicholas Kaldor in an innovative model of economic growth (1966, 1978), although it had been suggested as early as 1928 by Allyn Young. Rediscovering an essay written by the Dutch economist P. J. Verdoorn in 1949, Kaldor restated what he called *Verdoorn's Law* (*"The greater the rate of increase of output inside a firm, the greater the increase in productivity"*), and made it a central element of his new macrodynamic theory of economic growth.

To Kaldor, the more a firm produces of a good, the more experience it gets as it learns by doing, and the more efficient it becomes at producing not only that good, but others like it. Productivity increases not only because of economies of scale, but also because improved techniques arise out of increased knowledge. Echoing a famous essay on learning by doing by Nobel-prizewinning economist Kenneth Arrow (1962), Kaldor argued that the two factors are interrelated: Technological knowledge is acquired by

experience, which is in turn a function of the cumulative volume of gross investment.

In Kaldor's scheme, such technological progress is internal to the firm, or *endogenous,* and it results in a self-propelling spiral of growth, enhanced productivity, and increasing returns. Other terms used to describe such a process are "positive feedback" and "circular and cumulative causation." At the core of Kaldor's theory of increasing returns is the view that the dynamic relationship between productivity change and output change involving economies of large-scale production and technical progress is the key to the growth of capitalist economies, and that the relationship is self-propelling and therefore endogenous.

Dynamic Externalities

Students of recent small-firm growth view externalities, particularly externalities associated with knowledge spillovers, as the engine of this growth, however. This seemingly conflicts with Kaldor's belief that the essential play between economies of scale and technical progress is endogenous. The difference is one of scale. Subsequent theorists, notably Paul Romer (1986) and Robert E. Lucas, Jr. (1988), winner of the 1995 Nobel Prize in Economics, argue that whereas the interplay occurs external to the firm, it is internal to regional industrial clusters, such as Silicon Valley: The self-propelling growth mechanisms remain endogenous, but to the regional cluster as a whole. The recent emergence of the phenomenon of increasing returns has rested on an increase in the geographic scale at which Verdoorn's Law operates—from the firm to the region.

Romer's work builds not only on Kaldor and Verdoorn, but also on the early ideas about industrial districts within cities spelled out by Alfred Marshall (1890), and Arrow's learning-by-doing model (1962): Concentration of industry in a region facilitates knowledge spillovers between firms through spying, imitation, and rapid interfirm movement of skilled labor. Ideas are quickly disseminated among neighboring firms, promoting productivity enhancement, and therefore the growth of the industry within the region. Growth adds new firms, new experiments, and new ideas, and the process continues.

The modern theorists differ about the requirements for growth of regional clusters in the long run, however. Romer believes that, in the longer run, growth can only be maintained if the industry becomes dominated by a very large firm that is able to "internalize" the externalities, in the manner of Microsoft with computer operating systems or Intel with processors and integrated circuits. Only by internalization, he says, will the interplay between economies of scale and learning by doing continue to propel growth. Michael Porter believes otherwise. Citing such cases as the Italian ceramics industry, he insists that it is

BOX 9.8   *The Cycle of Manufacturing*

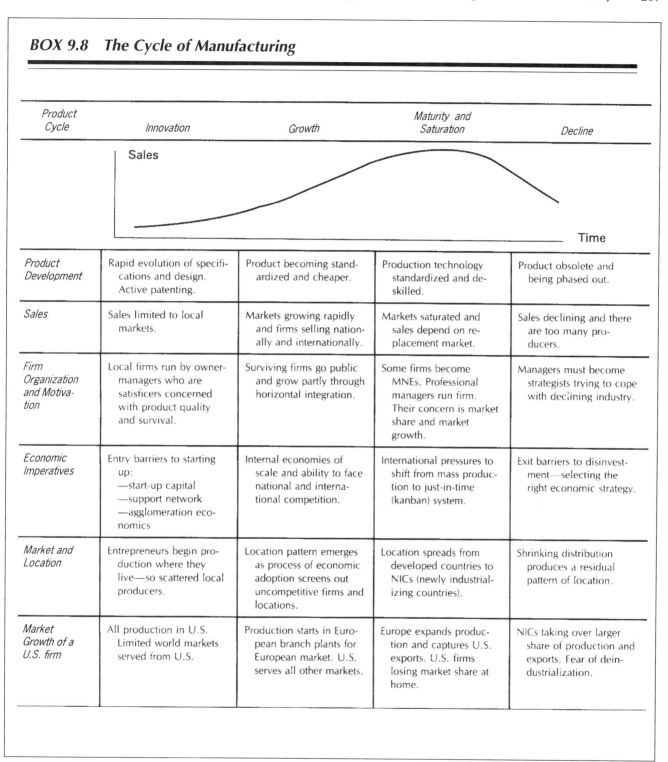

Product Cycle	Innovation	Growth	Maturity and Saturation	Decline
Product Development	Rapid evolution of specifi-cations and design. Active patenting.	Product becoming stand-ardized and cheaper.	Production technology standardized and de-skilled.	Product obsolete and being phased out.
Sales	Sales limited to local markets.	Markets growing rapidly and firms selling nation-ally and internationally.	Markets saturated and sales depend on re-placement market.	Sales declining and there are too many pro-ducers.
Firm Organization and Motiva-tion	Local firms run by owner-managers who are satisficers concerned with product quality and survival.	Surviving firms go public and grow partly through horizontal integration.	Some firms become MNEs. Professional managers run firm. Their concern is market share and market growth.	Managers must become strategists trying to cope with declining industry.
Economic Imperatives	Entry barriers to starting up: —start-up capital —support network —agglomeration eco-nomics	Internal economies of scale and ability to face national and interna-tional competition.	International pressures to shift from mass produc-tion to just-in-time (kanban) system.	Exit barriers to disinvest-ment—selecting the right economic strategy.
Market and Location	Entrepreneurs begin pro-duction where they live—so scattered local producers.	Location pattern emerges as process of economic adoption screens out uncompetitive firms and locations.	Location spreads from developed countries to NICs (newly industrial-izing countries).	Shrinking distribution produces a residual pattern of location.
Market Growth of a U.S. firm	All production in U.S. Limited world markets served from U.S.	Production starts in Euro-pean branch plants for European market. U.S. serves all other markets.	Europe expands produc-tion and captures U.S. exports. U.S. firms losing market share at home.	NICs taking over larger share of production and exports. Fear of dein-dustrialization.

local competition and rapid churning that foster the pursuit and rapid adoption of innovation. When hundreds of firms are located together, competition to innovate will be intense; the alternative to innovation is demise, as the large firm moves through a characteristic life cycle (Box 9.8).

Network Organization

If the experiences of Silicon Valley and Route 128 are indicative, the evidence appears to support Porter. What is involved, according to Italian scholar R. Camagni, are dif-

TABLE 9.7

Camagni's organizational models

	Territorial	Competitive	Network
Nature	Firm aims at local market	Firm involved in international market	Network firm
Crucial function	Production	Marketing	Innovation
Strategy	Control local market	Control market shares	Controlling innovation
Internal structure	Unique location	Specialized functional units	Integrated functional units
Barriers to entry	Distance	Competitiveness	Continuous innovation

Source: Adapted from R. Camagni, Organizational économique et réseaux de villes, in P. H. Derycke (Ed.), *Espace et dynamiques territoriales* (Paris: Economica, 1992), pp. 25–52.

ferences in industrial organization. He suggests that there are three basic models, *territorial, competitive,* and *network*. Refer to Table 9.7. Territorial firms seek to dominate markets using the umbrella of transport costs (Chapter 6). Competitive firms are concerned about their shares of multiple markets. Network firms are concerned about maintaining their position on the leading edge of innovation. When located in geographic proximity, technological progress and growth are endogenous to the network: Member firms thrive in what Camagni calls the *milieu innovateur* (innovative environment). Increasing returns and cumulative growth are characteristic of such networks, and *human capital* plays a significant role in the growth process alongside local entrepreneurship, close interaction, and cooperation among firms, and the specialized nature of the local labor market. Economist Paul Krugman (1991a), who we will encounter in Chapters 11 and 12, restates the relationship in terms of the interplay of geography and history: Proximity of firms facilitates synergies from which spring technological innovation. Firms permeate the environment in which they locate, and the growth of cities and regions cannot be understood without recalling history. Territory and space influence the development of firms, a recognition of the feedback relations between firms and the place in which they locate. Space becomes endogenized in the explanation of regional growth. The dynamics of growth cannot rely solely on explaining location decisions by firms but must incorporate an understanding of the functioning of local-regional milieu. The role of increasing returns and circular self-reinforcing mechanisms emphasize the importance of history in addition to technology and business strategy in explaining development.

Camagni is more specific. The elements that characterize the *innovative milieu* are, he says:

(a) *District economies* that promote an industrial atmosphere capable not only of reducing the cost disadvantage of small local firms with respect to large firms, but especially of helping them in their innovation process (*dynamic efficiency elements*). An element that belongs to

this category is the educational and training process that takes place within the *innovative milieu;*

(b) *Proximity economies* that reduce "transaction cost" and the "use cost of the market" through easier information circulation, face-to-face contacts, and lower information-gathering costs within the local economy (*information elements*). Examples of this include easy processes to exchange information between customers and suppliers that are mainly informal in nature,

(c) *Synergy elements* that enhance local innovation capability through imitation processes, interaction between local agents, private-public partnerships for infrastructure and service projects, interaction between research centers and potential adopters of inventions and customer–supplier cooperation.

The preceding factors play a twofold role. They reduce the *uncertainty elements* that are particularly evident in innovation processes, while minimizing the obstacles to economic change and enhancing the creativity of the local environment. The functions of information collection, information screening and transcoding, selection of decision routines, control over competitors' moves—functions aimed at reducing static and dynamic uncertainty, usually performed by the R&D or strategic planning departments in big companies—are performed in a collective way by the *milieu* itself, through fast information circulation, imitation and cooperation processes. The innovative milieu also performs a second, crucial function in the innovation process, that of ensuring the transfer of tacit know-how among firms. These same functions are secured, in the big firm, through internal interaction between the R&D and engineering departments, and can take place thanks to the long-term permanence of the firm. Within districts of small firms, characterized by turbulence and shorter life cycles of the single units, these functions take place in a collective way and find their continuity in the local labor market, in the local institutions and in the interpersonal and intergenerational links.

APPENDIX 9.1

The Dynamics of Small Manufacturing Firms

What are "small" manufacturing firms? They were defined in a 1971 landmark study, the Bolton *Report of the Committee of Inquiry on Small Firms,* as firms employing 200 workers or less, having a relatively small share of the market, administered in a personalized way by their owners or part-owners, and independent and free from outside control in making their principal decisions. Most manufacturing firms in the United Kingdom and North America employ less than 20 workers, however, and Canadian data use this number as the upper employment limit to define small firms. In fact, the typical manufacturing firm in Canada is very small, employing less than five workers, and is only about 5 years old.

The birth of new, small firms is now recognized as a major source of job creation in Western countries. In fact, a number of studies have shown that employment growth rates decrease with increasing firm size. Many larger firms have been cutting their employment levels over recent years and so small firms are accounting for an increasing proportion of total manufacturing employment. Hence, regional differences in the birth rates of firms are critical to understanding differences in levels of regional health. Studies

coordinated by Paul Reynolds, David Storey, and Paul Westhead (1994) found that only those regions in Western countries with high birth rates of firms could hope to have high rates of employment growth and economic development—and not always then. It is time to revise the old rule that large firms grow larger and small firms grow more numerous, implying that small firms are of little economic consequence. In the 1978 to 1986 business cycle in Canada, for example, small manufacturing firms increased in both average size and in numbers to outperform large firms. It was the large manufacturing firms that declined, in numbers as well as in total employment (Figure 9.11).

The remarkable contribution of small firms to employment growth in Western countries may not be due to the economic sectors or regions in which small firms are concentrated, as some have thought. When these attributes are factored out in Canadian longitudinal data, the disparity in employment creation between small and large firms is increased, not decreased. Such data as are available for other developed countries support this conclusion. For half a century, economists and geographers have been schooled to believe that employment growth in a region is determined by the industry mix in the region and regional shifts of industry in and out of that region. However, the resurgence of small firms is becoming so important, both directly and indirectly, that regional differences in employment growth, industry mix, and economic development are coming to reflect regional differences in the size mix of firms. The extreme case is where the size mix of firms statistically biases industry growth rates so that composite industry performance levels are the opposite of size-class-specific performance levels. This case is known as Simpson's Paradox (Box 9.9). Comparisons of employment growth rates that fail to correct different industry rates for their firm-size composition can lead to quite erroneous conclusions. Equally, regional comparisons of employment growth rates need to be adjusted for their industry-firm-size mix as well as by industry-type mix.

Some are concerned about the magnitude of the contribution of small firms to employment growth and hence to the changing location of industry. One concern is triggered by the higher *exit* (or death) *rates* of small firms. The *churning* of small firms—the combination of high entry and exit rates—may create two classes of firms and jobs: temporary jobs in unstable small firms and permanent jobs in stable large firms. And even if small firms have higher net job creation rates, job loss through plant closure may involve greater dislocation and inefficiency than do layoffs from continuing plants. Furthermore, the gross employment creation by new small firms may be less than the gross employment growth by large firms. These concerns involve the components of employment change in industry, which are not always properly understood (Box 9.10).

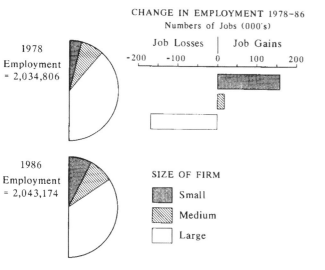

CHANGE IN EMPLOYMENT 1978–86
Numbers of Jobs (000's)

1978
Employment
= 2,034,806

1986
Employment
= 2,043,174

SIZE OF FIRM

- Small
- Medium
- Large

FIGURE 9.11 Employment change in manufacturing industry in Canada by size of firm, 1978–1986. [*Source:* Special Tabulation, Statistics Canada]. Note: 1. Firm sizes are: small—0 to 19.9 employees; medium—20 to 99.9 employees; large—100 and more. 2. Firms are classified by their size in 1978.

BOX 9.9 The Size Mix of Firms and Simpson's Paradox

The longitudinal tracking of individual firms in Canada enables us to tabulate employment growth rates by industry. Consider the forestry, wood, and paper industries over the last business cycle, 1978–1986. Firms in the paper industry had by far the largest growth rate for all three size classes, small, medium, and large. Forestry had by far the lowest in all three. Yet when industry totals are computed, the industry rankings are completely reversed: Forestry did best, paper worst. Crude industry growth rates are biased by the heterogeneity in their size mix.

Employment growth in the forestry, wood, and paper industries, by size class: Canada, 1978–1986

	Forestry		Wood		Paper	
	Percent Growth	Rank	Percent Growth	Rank	Percent Growth	Rank
Size Class						
Small (0–20)	52	3	80	2	179	1
Medium (20–100)	−28	3	−6	2	29	1
Large (100+)	−40	3	−19	2	−14	1
Industry growth rate	−3	1	−4	2	−9	3
Percent employment:						
in small firms	36	1	12	2	1	3
in large firms	35	3	65	2	94	1
Industry standardized growth rate	−54	3	17	1	−7	2

Note: Growth rates ar standardized at the two-digit SIC level, by province, by size class, and by country of control of firms. The standardized growth rate is the industry growth rate corrected for size, and regional and ownership mix. It is equivalent to the growth for each industry size—class-region-ownership group of firms multiplied using standardized weights.
[*Source*: D. Michael Ray, *Standardizing Employment Growth Rates of Foreign Multinationals and Domestic Firms in Canada: From Shift-Share to Multifactor Partitioning.* Working Paper No. 62. Geneva: ILO Multinational Enterprises Programme, 1990).]

The reversal of the rankings of the crude and standardized growth rates for the forestry and paper industries is an example of Simpson's paradox. Simpson's paradox occurs when crude rates or averages computed for two heterogeneous groups are the opposite rank of the standardized rates corrected for their heterogeneity. Other examples have been given for crude and standardized female death rates for Costa Rica and Sweden (Cohen, 1986). Observed examples of Simpson's paradox emphasize that crude rates confound true underlying rates with compositional differences. For instance, firms have many attributes that affect their growth rate such as their industry type, size class, location, and country of control. Simply to use a crude national growth rate for an industry is to attribute to industry type all the growth that has occurred without taking any account of the other factors involved. This is rather like comparing regional growth rates, without taking into account their industry mix.

Reference: Joel E. Cohen (1986), An Uncertainty Principle in Demography and the Unisex Issue, *The American Statistician* 40:(1) 32–39.

The Components of Change in Manufacturing Firms and Their Employment

Almost half the 1978 stock of small manufacturing firms in Canada had gone out of business by 1986, just 8 years later (Table 9.8). More new small manufacturing firms were established between 1979 and 1986 than existed in 1978, but about 40 percent of these new firms also had closed by 1986. The net result was that each addition to the stock of small manufacturing firms was the balance of four new firms opened and three closed. The rate of firm entry and exit diminishes with the size class of the firm: Larger firms are more likely to decrease employment than to close. But the proportion of firms that either closed or reduced their

BOX 9.10   Components of Change in Firms and Their Employment

An industry begins a period with an existing stock of firms (A). Existing firms either grow (P) or decline in employment (Q) or they exit (R) during the course of a period. Whether they grow or decline, they are called continuing firms (P + Q). The stock of firms at the end of the period equals continuing firms plus new firms (B), opened during the period, that survive to the final year (I). New firms that open and close during a period (J) are not usually tabulated and their employment impact is not included in job turnover.

Gross job gains occur from continuing firms that grow (P) and new surviving firms (I). New surviving firms have, by definition, grown: They had zero employment in the initial year.

Gross job losses occur from continuing firms that decline (Q) or existing firms that close (R).

The net employment record of all continuing firms is P + Q. This record is sometimes compared with the net employment created by (surviving) births (I) and (continuing firm) deaths (R). Such comparisons may have little meaning. Strictly, the employment records of existing firms (P, Q, and R) should be compared with that of new firms (I and j). The data on new firms are incomplete: j is not tabulated. The net employment contribution of new firms that close is zero. But they did create jobs and those jobs were lost and they are part of the job churning caused by the entry and exit of firms.

Job turnover is the sum of the absolute value of (tabulated) jobs gained or lost (P + Q + R + I, with sign ignored).

Job losses from declining firms can be divided into temporary or permanent. Temporary layoffs are sometimes defined as lasting 2 years or less. Temporary layoffs cause fluctuations in the employment of continuing firms. Job gains from surviving firms must increase, the longer the period is. Hence, the relative importance of employment creation by continuing firms and new firms is not independent of the length of period.

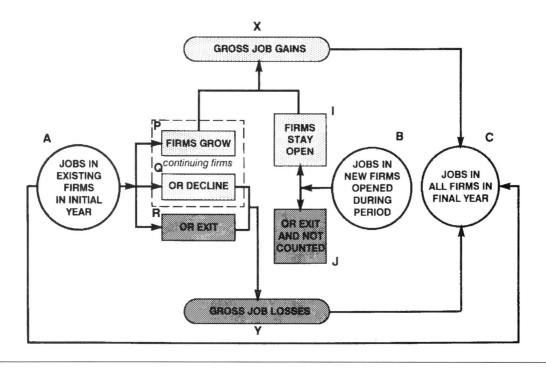

employment is about the same for all size classes of manufacturing firms (Table 9.9).

The proportion of jobs lost through firm declines and exits combined is higher for smaller firms than for larger ones, according to the Canadian data. But size-class differences in gross job losses are very much less than differences in gross job gains. The better performance of small manu-

facturing firms in net job creation and in the efficiency of job creation can be credited to their much higher gross job-creation rates bought at the cost of somewhat higher gross job-loss rates.

What of the quality of jobs created? Smaller firms tend to pay lower wage rates and fringe benefits than larger firms. Some of the increased employment in small firms

TABLE 9.8

The components of change in manufacturing firms and employment: Canada, 1978–1986

Life Status of Firms	Number of Firms			Change in Jobs 1978–1986, in 1000s		
	Small 0–19.9	Medium 20–99.9	Large 100+	Small 0–19.9	Medium 20–99.9	Large 100+
Existing firms 1978	31,076	7,463	2,724			
Continuing firms, 1978–1986	16,104	4,930	2,003	67.6	54.8	-85.8
Increased jobs	9,737	2,607	933	85.0	92.5	196.1
Decreased jobs	6,367	2,323	1,070	-17.4	-37.8	-281.9
Exits of 1978 firms	14,972	2,533	721	-53.0	-98.4	-176.6
Net job change, 1978 firms				14.6	-43.6	-262.4
New firms, 1979–1986	43,320	1,144	248			
Exits, 1978–1986	18,121	387	68			
Entries (surviving in 1986)	25,199	757	180	144.0	61.0	81.6
Totals						
Net growth	10,227	-1,776	-541	158.7	17.4	-180.7
Gross job turnover				299.4	289.7	736.2
Job-creation efficiency				0.53	0.06	0.25

Source: Special Tabulation, Statistics Canada

Note: Data: Employment figures are in standardized labor units. Employment losses from exits are tabulated only for firms operating in 1978. Firms opening after 1978 and closed by 1986 are not included in employment tabulation for the period.

Reading the table: There were 31,076 small firms in 1978, of which 16,104 survived (were continuing firms 1978–1986). Of these continuing firms, 9,737 increased their employment, 1978–1986. Some 6,367 small continuing firms decreased their employment and another 14,972 of the 1978 firms closed.

During the period (1979–1986), 43,320 new small firms opened, of which 18,121 closed in 1986 or earlier, so only 25,199 firms survived past 1986. The new small firms that closed are not usually included in components of change tables.

The employment consequences of this considerable firm churning is that *net* changes are small compared to the underlying components of employment change; The gross turnover in employment serves as an indicator of the ability of manufacturing to adjust to change.

Job-creation efficiency is the quotient of net growth in jobs divided by gross job turnover. The maximum value is +1.0 when there are no job losses from decreasing firms of exits. The minimum value is –1.0 when there are no job gains from firms increasing or entering.

may also represent a shift of jobs from large firms subcontracting production as a means of evading labor standards. But tracking individual workers by industry in Canada demonstrates just how high worker turnover is even in industries dominated by large firms (Boxes 9.11 and 9.12). The general evidence in Canada is that worker turnover is heavily concentrated among young workers with no evident reduction in average length of job tenure by the work force as a whole.

The extent of job churning in the manufacturing sector has now been measured on a comparable basis for the US and Canada and the results show a remarkably high and similar rate in both countries (Table 9.10). Approximately one job in ten that existed in any one year in the manufacturing sector has been lost by the next year. And one job in ten existing in any one year did not exist the previous year. Net job gains and losses are a fine balance between the rates of job gains and job losses. Moreover, job-turnover rates are

TABLE 9.9

The proportion of manufacturing firms that decreased employment or closed: Canada, 1978–1986

Employment Size Class in 1978	Less than 4.9	5 to 19.9	20 to 49.9	50 to 99.9	100 to 499.9	500 or more	Total
Percent decrease	17.8	28.3	31.3	33.2	36.7	54.2	24.8
Percent exits	50.7	35.7	32.1	32.8	27.3	13.3	41.4
Total decreases and exits	68.5	64.1	63.4	66.0	64.0	67.5	66.2

Note: There is a remarkable symmetry in the table. The figures for the percentage of firms that closed is almost the reverse series of the figures for firms that decreased. And the sum of the two is always equal to about two-thirds of the firms in the size class.

BOX 9.11   *Worker Turnover in the Canadian Steel and Automobile Industries 1978–1983*

Worker turnover is very high even in industries dominated by large firms as this example of the steel and automobile industries shows. Individual workers in these industries were tracked from 1978 to 1983. Both industries reduced their actual number of workers by about 10 percent, but in each case about one-third of the 1978 labor force had left 5 years later (which would include voluntary quits and retirements as well as permanent layoffs).

Workers	Steel	Automobiles
Actual number		
1978 total	97,270	116,667
Indexed numbers		
1978 = 100	100	100
1978 workers		
Left (1978–1983)	34	38
Remained	66	62
New workers (1979–1983)		
Total hired	n.a.	79
Left	n.a.	51
Net additions	23	28
1983 total	89	90

Note: These special tabulations from Statistics Canada are for iron and steel mills (SIC 291), steel pipe and tube mills (SIC 292), and wire (SIC 305): and for motor vehicle manufacturers (SIC 323) and motor vehicle parts and accessories (SIC 325). The numbers are for individual workers (full-time, part-time, or temporary) and are not converted to average labor units as in earlier tables. Some tabulations for the steel industry are not available (n.a.).

---

high for every sector of manufacturing, the highest rates being for apparel and lumber, the lowest for paper, chemicals, petroleum, and primary metals (Table 9.11). Western Europe may have comparable job turnover rates. Davis et al. (1995) report figures ranging from 16.0 in Germany to 23.5 percent in Sweden. Less developed countries may have higher rates. Figures of 26.2 to 30.6 percent have been reported for Colombia, Chile, and Morocco. It needs to be borne in mind that the figures on employment creation are very sensitive to the length of the period tabulated. Job turnover rates for a 10-year period would be much less than 10 times the average annual rate because job fluctuations in continuing firms would be partly netted out, as workers laid off in one year, for instance, were rehired a year or two later.

Comprehensive longitudinal data on manufacturing firms and employment are just becoming available for other developed countries. Such data for Western Europe and Japan point to a shift in production and in employment in all these countries to small manufacturing firms, so that a 1990 report of the International Labor Office is entitled *The Re-emergence of the Small Firm* .

The Location of Small Firms

Where small firms open and where they survive are becoming increasingly important for the health of regions. The factors influencing their birth and death rates do not, however, point in any simple or direct way to a geography of industrial change. The geographic consequences of firm births and deaths arise indirectly from the factors involved. A Darwinian process of *economic adoption* —survival of the fittest —occurs in which the surviving new firms map the margins of locational profitability, and firms become concentrated in those regions best able to meet their prerequisites for birth and survival.

Three stages have been distinguished in the entrepreneurial process leading to new firm formation (Reynolds et al., 1994): (1) *conception*—the decision by one or more

BOX 9.12   *The Industry Shift of Workers Who Leave Their Jobs*

What happens to workers who separate—that is, voluntarily or involuntarily leave a job in manufacturing? Box 9.11 shows that 34 percent (actually 21,093 workers) of the 1978 work force in iron and steel in Canada left the industry 1978–1983. Tracking these workers showed that most of them had found a job by 1983 at incomes slightly lower than they had previously earned, but only about a third stayed in manufacturing. The same proportion held for all Ontario workers who left the independent automobile parts industry 1981–1982. And for Ontario auto workers, thee figure was lower—only one-fifth.

Percentage distribution of workers out of steel and automobiles who found another job

To:	*From:*	*Canada Steel (1978–1983)*	*Ontario Auto Parts (1981–1982)*	*Ontario Motor Vehicle (1981–1982)*
1. Primary (+ mining)		6	5	3
2. Manufacturing		32	36	19
3. Construction		8	6	12
4. Transportation		7	2	4
5. Retail and wholesale trade		14	19	13
6. Finance, insurance, and real estate		6	10	9
7. Services (community, business, and personal)		19	18	32
8. Public administration		8	4	8
Total		100	100	100

Source: Special Tabulations, Statistics Canada.

TABLE 9.10

Job churning in the manufacturing sector in the United States and Canada, 1979–1986

Year	United States				Canada			
	(1) Job Gains	*(2) Job Losses*	*(3) Net Change (1 – 2)*	*(4) Total Turnover (1 + 2)*	*(5) Job Gains*	*(6) Job Losses*	*(7) Net Changes (5 – 6)*	*(8) Total Turnover (5 + 6)*
1979	10.3	−7.0	3.3	17.4	12.1	−8.5	3.6	20.6
1980	8.0	−9.1	−1.1	17.1	9.8	−10.1	−0.3	19.9
1981	6.3	−11.4	−5.0	17.7	9.8	−9.6	0.2	19.4
1982	6.8	−14.5	−7.7	21.3	7.6	−15.4	−7.8	23.0
1983	8.4	−15.5	−7.2	23.9	10.7	−12.9	−2.2	23.7
1984	13.3	−7.6	5.7	20.9	12.4	−9.3	3.0	21.7
1985	7.9	−11.1	−3.2	19.0	12.0	−9.4	2.6	21.3
1986	7.9	−12.1	−4.2	20.1	12.9	−10.5	2.4	23.3

Sources: These figures are based on special tabulations by the U.S. Bureau of the Census and Statistics, Canada, as published in John Baldwin et al., *A Comparison of Job Creation and Job Destruction in Canada and the United States*, Research Paper No. 64 (Ottawa: Analytical Studies Branch, Statistics Canada, n.d.), p.15. See also S. J. Davis, J. Haltiwanger, and S. Schuh, *Job Creation and Job Destruction in U.S. Manufacturing: 1972–1988* (Washington, DC: U.S. Government Printing Office, 1995).

Note: The job gains and losses are tabulated firm by firm, comparing employment levels at the end and beginning of each year. The changes are given as a percentage of employment at the beginning of the year. U.S. manufacturing firms that grew added an average of 9.2 % to their employment in the year they grew. Those that declined in a year cut employment by 10.4%. Canada performed better than the U.S. primarily because of higher job-creation rates. Job losses include layoffs and plant closures. Mergers, divestitures, takeovers, etc., are not included except in so far as they affect employment totals.

TABLE 9.11

Job churning in selected industries in the United States: Annual average for 1973–1986

Industry	Job Gain	Job Loss	Job Change	Job Turnover
Apparel	10.9	−14.6	−3.7	25.5
Lumber	12.6	−14.6	−2.0	27.2
Printing	8.9	−8.2	0.8	17.1
Chemicals	6.6	−7.4	−0.8	14.0
Petroleum	6.3	−8.4	−2.1	14.6
Primary Metals	6.5	−9.7	−3.3	16.2
Average of all manufacturing industries	9.2	−10.3	−1.1	19.5

Note: The numbers are for the industries with the highest and lowest job-churning rates.

entrepreneurs to start a new business; (2) *gestation and birth*—the establishment of a new firm, purchasing parts and supplies, renting space, paying wages and other bills, and, it is hoped, selling goods and services; and (3) *infancy and growth* (or decline and exit). The research program which Reynolds, Storey, and Westhead have coordinated has revealed a reasonably consistent range of average, annual birth rates of new firms in Western Europe and the United States, and consistent regional factors associated with regional variations in new firm formation rates. For example, the average annual birth rate of manufacturing firms varied from 5.6 per 100 manufacturing firms for German regions to 16.5 for regions in the United Kingdom. The highest regional rates in a country are generally two to three times the lowest rates. The United States shows a much greater variation, perhaps reflecting the sheer size of the country and the great diversity among its 382 labor market areas. The average regional rate of births of manufacturing firms in the United States was 6.0 for 1986 to 1988. The figure varied from 2.1 to 14.2, giving a quotient of 14.2. However in all countries, Western European and the United States, three characteristics consistently and significantly correlated with high birth rates of firms: (1) a regional economy dominated by small firms, (2) growth in demand as measured by population growth and per capita income growth, and (3) a highly urbanized population able to offer external economies of scale.

No published surveys of the motivations of entrepreneurs have ever found that they are driven by a single, dominant goal of profit maximization or that they explicitly locate on the basis of location theory, however. Some, the "classical entrepreneurs," may include profits and growth high on a list that includes many other motivations. The most typical case is the "artisan," or "craft entrepreneur," setting up a business close to home with the help of loans from family and friends, because of the personal satisfaction they derive from autonomy and quality workmanship. These craft entrepreneurs are probably prepared to work longer hours for a lower return on their investment than would be acceptable to a large firm. They may also have

less formal education than senior executives in large firms and hence feel socially marginalized. They may want to keep their business small, concerned that growth would threaten their independence. A third group, "management entrepreneurs" may have a superior education and industrial experience, setting up their own business perhaps with a contract from the firm where they previously worked, to supply it with components previously made in-house. Or perhaps they have identified a new product that fills a neglected need.

Likewise, no comparable research has been completed on the death rate (or exit) of firms. However, the death rates are high. Probably a third of small new manufacturing firms close down within 3 years, and one-half fail within 5 years. As with the reasons for their entry into business, so, too, the reasons given for their exit lack any obvious geographic logic. Some of the reasons given for closing are unique to small firms, such as the death of the managing director or owner-manager; fire; end of lease on premises; or voluntary liquidation. By contrast, large firms cite a less varied list of causes; most common are a fall in demand, uneconomic production, and concentration of production elsewhere.

Concern about company failures has grown in recent years and the Institute of Chartered Accountants of England and Wales asked Cliff Pratten to review the situation. His evaluation is of broad interest because company failures highlight the factors that, in less acute form, can lead to plant closures within firms or to layoffs within plants. Pratten (1991b) found four principal groups of reasons for corporate failure.

(a) *Business Failure.* Business failures can occur for a number of reasons. A high rate of business failures is almost inevitable among firms starting up to make a new product. As the market winners emerge, they can use the economies of scale they achieve to undercut weaker competitors, leaving an industry composed of a few large firms and some niche-market suppliers. This process was exemplified in the personal computer industry. Business failure may also result from a marked decline in demand for a product, competition from newer products, the failure of newly installed equipment, and so on. The reality is that every firm, no matter how secure now, can expect to have to face severe business problems at some time in the future. These challenges are a concomitant of industrial progress, and part of a process by which assets are moved from less productive uses in companies that fail to more productive uses in companies that grow.

(b) *Macroeconomic shocks*, which cannot be predicted in advance, also cause company failure. Specific shocks in recent decades have included (i) oil price increases in 1973/4 and 1979/81, (ii) periods of rising inflation and interest rates, and (iii) exchange-rate fluctuations. Companies may fail because they have entered into fixed-price long-term contracts just as inflation and interest rates begin to rise, or because their production commitments are based on an extrapolated boom at the start of a recession.

(c) *Financial Failure.* In one sense, the immediate cause of all company failure is the lack of cash to pay bills. Financial failure occurs because of (i) a mismatch in the timing of cash receipts and trade debts that cannot be bridged by borrowing, (ii) inadequate equity capital to run the business, and (iii) an overrapid expansion entailing unsustainable cash-flow demands.

(d) *Management failures* are the most varied group and the one probably most common for small firm failure. This group includes failures to foresee problems early enough to take effective action and fundamental management misjudgments. Pratten did not add a fifth group of firms that filed because of a *wrong locational choice*. Nevertheless, one underlying cause that may well lead to the closing of a firm is locational imperative. Firms that have failed to pursue an active policy of economic adaption (making rational and correct decisions on product, location, and technology) will be subjected to a process of economic adoption (selection by the "guiding hand" of the market).

Locational Adoption. *All new firms must compete for venture capital, workers, premises, equipment, supplies, and customers. This competition for survival ensures the survival of only the fittest. The location pattern of the beginners may be haphazard and random. The process of adoption has a large enough cohort of new firms each year, and high enough death rates, to produce a residual pattern of rational location for the survivors, for survival depends on competitiveness in product, price, and marketing, and these in turn are influenced by location.*

The longitudinal tracking of firms in Canada makes the point emphatically. Establishments or firms that close are less productive and less profitable on average than either surviving firms, or the new establishments of existing firms that are opened. Economic adjustment and locational adoption are continuous processes, relentlessly transferring resources from less-productive and less-profitable uses to firms that are more competitive. The rapid turnover of firms

and the churning in the job market that is generated exist on a much larger scale than was imagined from simple net change data, and they emphasize the major role played by locational adoption in the economy.

Locational Adaption. *The opposite of locational adoption is locational adaption. Locational adaption is the rational selection of an optimal location for a firm, or for a new plant of an existing firm, based on the evaluation of competing locations. Firms enhance their chances of success by a careful analysis of market trends and locational factors. The result is that the initial location pattern is rational and consistent with location theory.*

In principle, it is to be expected that small firms with more limited resources and more complex motivations are subjected to locational adoption, and that large firms with more to lose and more comprehensive management structures achieve economic adaption. The longitudinal tracking of manufacturing firms in Canada by initial size does provide indirect support for this dichotomy of adoption of small firms and adaption by large firms, though the distinction is blurred:

1. The differences in death rates between small and large firms is greatest during the first 3 years after start-up (Table 9.12). After the high death rates in these early years, the death rates for small firms fall to the steady low level experienced by large firms right from their start-up. The concentration of firm deaths among small firms in their infancy points to a swift process of economic and locational adoption.

2. The death rates of large firms are much more sensitive to this stage in the business cycle than small firms are. New small firms fail at a high rate even when the economy is booming, suggesting that causes other than the general business climate are responsible for their failure. Among these other causes is locational adoption.

3. The simplest evidence of adoption among small firms is the sheer number of births and deaths involved. Half the existing small manufacturing firms in Canada in 1978 made it through to the end of the business cycle in 1989. For every 10 firms that did survive, another 25 had opened between 1979 and 1986. But 10 of these new firms closed by 1986. Nevertheless, the 1986 cohort of small manufacturing firms was made up of 15 new small firms for every 10 survivors established 1978 or earlier. For large manufacturing firms, three-quarters survived. For every 10 that survived, one more opened and it, too, probably survived. The 1986 cohort was thus made up of one new large firm for every 10 survivors. These figures allow for locational adoption to be a powerful force among small firms, but not among large ones.

Adoption and adaption are two extremes marking the limits of a continuum. In reality, the locational decisions of firms are some mixture of the two, with the balance favoring adoption in the case of most small firms, shifting to

TABLE 9.12

Exit rates of small and large manufacturing firms: Canada, 1978–1986

Existing firms	Total Firms		Total Deaths			*Year in Which Firms Died as Percent of Total*								
	No.		No.	%	1978	1979	1980	1981	1982	1983	1984	1985	1986
1978														
Small	31,976		14,972	48	10	7	6	6	5	4	4	3	4
Large	2,724		721	26	2	2	2	2	3	4	3	4	3
Firms started up in:														
1979					1978	1979	1980	1981	1982	1983	1984	1985	1986
Small	5,462		3,196	59	—	11	13	11	8	5	4	3	4
Large	37		15	41	—	0	14	5	5	3	5	5	3
1980														
Small	5,052		2,816	56	—	—	10	15	10	6	5	5	4
Large	24		14	58	—	—	33	0	0	21	0	0	4
1981														
Small	4,906		2,454	50	—	—	—	10	14	9	7	6	5
Large	25		11	44	—	—	—	8	12	8	8	0	8
1982														
Small	4,208		2,068	49	—	—	—	—	11	13	11	8	7
Large	14		6	43	—	—	—	—	14	14	0	7	7
1983														
Small	5,399		2,466	46	—	—	—	—	—	12	15	10	8
Large	21		7	33	—	—	—	—	—	14	5	10	5
1984														
Small	5,655		2,198	39	—	—	—	—	—	—	13	15	12
Large	47		10	21	—	—	—	—	—	—	6	9	6
1985														
Small	6,106		1,859	30	—	—	—	—	—	—	—	14	16
Large	35		5	14	—	—	—	—	—	—	—	9	6
1986														
Small	6,532		1,064	6	—	—	—	—	—	—	—	—	6
Large	45		0	0	—	—	—	—	—	—	—	—	0

Source: Special Tabulations, Statistics Canada.

Note: The recessions years, 1981–1983, affected laarge firms more severely than small. The difference in death rates between large and small firms tends to narrow after the first 3 years. For the complete set of new firms opened 1978 to 1986, the period death rate was 42% for small firms and 27% for large, a difference of 15 percentage points: Almost all that difference was accounted for by the difference in the death rates for the first 3 years (for which the rates were 32% and 19%).

adaption by most large firms. But whichever the dominant process, surviving new firms reinforce the locational advantages and strengthen the economic support network of their region. The survival of new firms, particularly new small firms, depends on the network of voluntary associations, trade associations, venture capital groups, public agencies, university research centers, and informal meeting places where information and ideas are exchanged, production problems solved, venture capital raised, and markets identified. Such networks build very slowly. Several decades may be needed before a high density of ties is established where actors and decision makers know each other and influential persons have emerged with an established reputation for reliable opinions and judgments. It is this regional network that selects which new firms will survive. But the surviving firms add new competence to the region's pool of management and technology and new products and industries to its economic base. So although new firms must be adopted by the region in which they locate, they can serve to enhance the competitiveness of that region and help it to adapt to increasing world competition.

APPENDIX 9.2

Multinational Enterprises: Trends in Location, Organization, and Employment

We devoted a considerable portion of Chapter 1 to a discussion of the nature of multinational enterprise and the role of MNEs in the globalization of production. MNEs are probably the dominant economic organizations in the world today, transcending most nation-states in importance. They have a significant direct and indirect impact on employment, trade, and technology transfer, and hence on the location of industry. MNEs are strategic planners, acting by design, practising locational adaption. They may, for example, open a branch plant in a foreign country as an

BOX 9.13   Why Do Firms Invest Abroad?

A distinction is made between an investment by a firm in another firm in a foreign country, without gaining control of that firm (this is called a portfolio investment), and foreign direct investment. Foreign direct investment includes opening a new, greenfield branch plant or gaining a controlling interest in an existing firm in a foreign country. In general, the following three conditions must be met before a firm will make a foreign direct investment.

1. The foreign country must offer specific advantages, or *country-specific endowments*, such as raw materials and growing markets.
2. The firm must have relevant assets, called *firm-specific advantages*.
3. There must exist *market imperfections* that make it better for the firm to use its own assets in its own foreign branch plant rather than to sell them to a foreign firm.

See Chapters 11 and 12 for additional foreign trade conditions relating to barriers to trade that lead to foreign direct investment.

There are three classes of firm-specific endowments:

TYPES OF FIRM—SPECIFIC ADVANTAGES

1. *Barriers to entry by domestic firms.* MNE has patents and trademarks and has established significant product differentiation.
2. *Branch plant advantages over new firm.* MNE offers a convenient, market-tested package of product, technology, and capital with costless access to MNE's research and development, advertising, and marketing know-how, and to product-specific economies of scale.
3. *MNE's access to international markets.* MNE can take fuller advantage of country-specific advantages in costs of materials and labor because of its knowledge of international market conditions and international marketing network.

EXAMPLES OF INDUSTRY TYPES

Brand name consumer goods such as soft drinks, breakfast cereals, and automobile tires.

Product with high fixed costs and large economies of scale such as automobiles (although trade barriers are a key additional factor). Capital-intensive resource industries such as the oil industry, and R&D-intensive products such as computers.

Manufacture of components or goods in a foreign branch plant largely to serve export markets, taking advantage of host-country low labor costs.

---

alternative to foreign trade. Therefore, a full understanding of MNEs requires an eclectic approach involving elements of both location theory and international trade theory. Classical location theory may explain why an industry is located where it is; it does not attempt to explain whether the industry will be run by a domestic firm or a foreign multinational. The classical theory of international trade deals with flows of products between countries; it does not deal with transnational intra corporate flows of parts and components, labor, innovations, and expertise. A new kind of theoretical blend is needed.

An Eclectic Theory of International Location

Why do companies open branch plants in foreign countries? John Dunning has identified three specific requirements:

1. The host country must offer the MNE some advantage specific to the country. These assets may be raw materials or domestic markets. But these *country-specific endowments* or advantages are presumably more readily accessible to domestic firms in the host country than to the MNE. Therefore, there is a second condition.

2. The MNE must have technologies, patents, or some other *firm-specific advantages* that are relevant to the country-specific endowments of the host country. But the MNE could sell these assets to a domestic firm in the host country.

3. There therefore must exist *market imperfections*, which make it difficult for the MNE to capture the true market value of its firm-specific endowments, and which drive it to internalize these assets within the enterprise by operating a branch plant in the host country.

In addition to firm-specific advantages that foster the establishment of a foreign branch plant, there are general advantages to multinational operation that apply to all MNEs regardless of their firm-specific advantages. These advantages are

- Protection from trade barriers and currency shifts. The weak U.S. dollar from 1987 to 1989 badly hit the profits of luxury European car exporters such as Jaguar, for example, and underlined the competitive advantages of global enterprises.
- Achieving cross-regional product flows. The three major world markets, Europe, North America, and Japan, tend to demand different types of products and to have different images of what constitutes luxury. So an MNE can produce regionally for the region volume markets and export to the other two regions serving their luxury niche markets. An example is the Honda Accord, marketed as a middle-range, high-volume automobile in the United States, and sold as a luxury product in Japan.
- The sophistication and knowledge of market and product trends gained by MNEs in comparison to local firms.
- Further, although all regional markets experience business

cycles, they are not necessarily synchronic. The Japanese and North American business cycles, for example, are often at different stages with respect to each other. MNEs can alleviate the effects of fluctuations in demand by use of cross-regional product flows.

- Finally, producing in the foreign country should increase local knowledge of the firm, recognition of the firm's commitment to the local market, and acceptance of the quality of its products. This enhanced reputation of the MNE should boost the sale of the MNEs products, whether locally produced or imported.

There may be additional advantages that apply to all MNEs from a particular home country and that support their expansion abroad. These include

- A large, stable home market
- Superior education facilities providing R&D facilities, quality business school graduates, and engineers and scientists, as well as a generally skilled and productive labor force
- Highly efficient services, including financial markets and transportation and communication facilities
- A generally supportive and stable government with a liberal

attitude towards mergers and industrial concentration.

Alternatively other factors such as high labor costs and an unfavorable home-currency exchange rate may push a firm to seek a foreign location for production.

The host country may also offer a number of general attractions to MNEs, including

- A rapidly growing market
- Comparatively few competitors
- Export processing zones where manufacturing is free of duties and taxes
- Access from that host country to a larger regional market forming a free-trade area.

References:

John H. Dunning, "Trade, Location of Economic Activity and the MNE: A Search for an Eclectic Approach." In *The International Allocation of Economic Activity*, B. Ohlin, P.-O. Messelborn, and P. M. Wijkmann, (Eds.),London: Macmillan, 1977, pp. 395–418.
———, Towards an Eclectic Theory of intentional Production: Some Empirical Tests, *Journal of International Business Studies* 2 (1980): 9–31.
U.N. Center on Transnational Corporations, *Transnational Corporations in World Development* (New York: United Nations, 1988).

There are further conditions relating to barriers to international trade, discussed in Chapters 11 and 12, which also make it better for the firm to establish foreign production facilities rather than shipping goods to that country.

MNEs can have three different kinds of firm-specific endowments: (1) endowments that constitute barriers to entry by domestic firms, (2) advantages of an existing firm over a new firm attempting to set up operations, and (3) advantages of a multinational with international connections over a domestic firm (see Box 9.13).

The most obvious firm-specific advantages of MNEs are such assets as patented technologies, trademarks, economies of scale and scope, and their international experience and networks, together with superior management and organization, which endows a firm with decisive cost and sometimes quality advantages. Management and orga-

nization advantages proved telling in the changeover of organization from craft production to mass production at the turn of the century. They have played an equally important role in the contemporary changeover from mass production to "lean" production. This new production organization has pervasive implications for the management and labor force of a firm, its suppliers, and its distribution network, and although it is taking much longer to incorporate and assimilate than might be thought, during its diffusion, it is giving lead firms a clear advantage over laggards, providing them with an unequaled opportunity to capture larger market shares and expand production internationally at the expense of lagging firms. The expansion of lead firms has important consequences for subsequent location of industry. The automobile industry provides a graphic example.

BOX 9.14   *Competing Production Methods of Automobile Production*

Attribute	Craft Production	Mass Production	Lean Production
General Characteristics of Production Method	Small-scale craft producers relying on highly skilled work force to produce a low volume of output	Use of specialized machines to turn out big volumes of interchangeable parts that can be assembled by unskilled workers, eliminating need for crafts people	Flexible batch production by multiple-skilled workers using flexible machinery and just-in-time inventory delivery
History	Developed in late 19th century with innovations such as the high-speed gasoline engine of Daimler (founder of Mercedes–Benz)	Production technique developed by Henry Ford with Model T after 1908. Management and marketing by Alfred Sloan of General Motors after 1920	Developed by Toyota Motor Co. in Japan after World War II, based on analysis of problems with Ford plant at Detroit
Objectives	• High quality • Innovativeness • Customized features	• Ease of manufacture • Low price • High volume • "Good enough" quality	• Eliminate waste • Reduce capital equipment costs • Achieve flexible cost-effective batch production • Constant improvements
Principles	• One-at-a-time, even one-of-a-kind, customized products	• Standardization of parts • Division of labor and reduction of task cycle time • Economies of scale • Vertical integration to regulate inputs and control sales	• Just-in-time inventory • Identify and solve assembly line problems immediately • Component suppliers organized into tiers • Decentralized design and decision making
Achievements	• Pioneered basic technology • Demonstrated usefulness of product • Tested market reaction • Established basic design features of product	• Reduced product costs—Model T fell in price steadily from 1908 • Easier to drive and maintain than craft-produced vehicles • Helped to make automobile production the largest industry in the world	• Assembly time halved • Design effort halved • Design time reduced by a third • Assembly faults almost eliminated • Much higher-quality level
Problems	• No standard gauge—so dimension creep in fitting parts together • Problems of reliability and replacement parts • Averaging down the cost of R & D • Tradition versus new technology	• Labor problems, frequent layoffs, and worker boredom • Long product development times	• Requires great commitment and acceptance of responsibility by all workers and management • Requires paradigmatic shift in management thinking

The Evolution of Automobile Production

Craft Production. The dramatic improvements that industrial organization can have on productivity and quality and hence on competitiveness and location of industry have been documented by James P. Womack and his colleagues (1990). A key-points summary of their findings about the history, objectives, principles, achievements, and problems of craft production, mass production, and lean production, all of which coexist today, is provided in Box 9.14.

Automobile production began in the late nineteenth century as a small-scale, made-to-specification, custom industry. There was no standard product. One company, Panhard et Levassor, established the *Système Panhard,* with the engine in front driving the rear wheels and passengers placed in rows in the middle. Technical problems with the cutting of steel parts meant that skilled fitters were required to file down adjacent parts, one after the other, to fit them together, producing "dimensional creep." The amount of dimensional creep varied from car to car—no two were identical even if produced using the same blueprints. Craft production did achieve pioneering advances in technology, such as the development of the gasoline engine. It did demonstrate the usefulness and practicality of the product and tested market reaction. But it did not solve the problems of replacement parts, reliability, large output volumes, and cost, the essence of the American System of manufacturing based on interchangeable parts that began in the mid-nineteenth-century gun industry.

Some cars are still made today on a craft production basis. Aston Martin, for instance, turns out only one car per working day. The aluminum panels are shaped by skilled panel beaters who pound them onto the dies with wooden mallets. But Aston Martin has produced less than 10,000 cars in its 65 years compared with a current industry total of 50 million cars made each year. And even Aston Martin has had to link up with Ford to gain specialized technical information at reasonable cost on a range of subjects from emission controls to crash safety.

Mass Production.   It was Henry Ford who spelled out the end of craft production as the dominant organization of car production, sensing the essential ingredients of mass production and laying the foundation of what is today the world's largest industry.

A key principle of mass production is the *standardization of parts* achieving simple fitting of adjacent parts, and complete interchangeability of corresponding parts (the American System). This principle could be realized because of Ford's introduction of standard gauges to measure part sizes and of advanced machine tools that could cut hardened steel. A second key principle was the reduction of the task cycle and moving the assembly line at an optimal speed, based on *time-and-motion studies* pioneered by F. M. Taylor. In 1908, Ford's task cycle (the time required by an assembler to complete one set of operations) was 8 h, 56 min. By 1913, parts were delivered to workers and with further division of labor the task cycle had been reduced to 2.3 min. That year Ford introduced the moving assembly line and reduced the task cycle to 1.2 min. A third principle of mass production is economies of scale. Ford built his first car, the Model A, in 1903, and it was not until he reached his twentieth model (and the twentieth letter of the alphabet) with his Model T in 1908 that he had a car that was easy to assemble, drive, and repair. Production soared, reaching over two million in 1923. Prices fell continuously throughout the company's production history. The increases in industry efficiency were extraordinary. Between 1913 and 1914 alone, the time to assemble a vehicle fell from 12 h, 30 min, to 1 h, 33 min. Because of the productivity increase. Ford was able to double wages to an unheard of $5 a day.

The achievement of economies of scale and the efficient use of very expensive, highly specialized equipment required that production lines be kept moving without interruption. Consequently, buffers had to be built in: extra supplies and parts, extra workers, and extra space. Vertical integration was used to control the flow of parts with closer tolerances and tighter delivery schedules than ever before thought possible.

There was one key ingredient of mass production and the large corporations it created that was introduced not by Ford, but by Alfred P. Sloan, Jr., president of General Motors: the concept of the *multidivisional company with decentralized divisions.* Five of the divisions were each allocated one of the product ranges, from Chevrolet to Cadillac; others were given responsibility for component groups such as steering gears and generators. The divisions reported to the senior executive on sales, market share, inventories, profit and loss, and capital budgets. This organizational decentralization was crucial for combining the economic advantages of mass production with the product diversity demanded by the market.

Given the willingness of Henry Ford to show European carmakers around his Highland Park plant and to explain the clear cost and productivity advantages of his system, and the establishment by Ford of European subsidiaries, beginning with Trafford Park, Manchester, in 1911, it might have been expected that mass production would have diffused quickly and smoothly to Europe. It did not. The story of Europe's failure to emulate American mass production and productivity is long and involved. One fundamental cause was the resistance of European skilled craft workers, who saw nothing in mass production to benefit them, versus the unskilled immigrant workers to the United States used by Ford at Highland Park, many of them barely able to speak English. Another was the endemic weakness of British management, which, unable to cope with operational routines, surrendered them to "shop stewards" (themselves often skilled craft workers) who were deeply suspicious of mass production. Indeed, it was not until the financial crisis of the 1990s that Rover, successor to the original Austin and Oxford Motor companies, adopted standard hourly rates (rather than the craft piece rates) and set out explicitly to match U.S. productivity. But by 1990, U.S. productivity and quality had long since been overtaken by Japanese lean production. On the European continent, it was the 1960s before Detroit-style mass production was mastered and European carmakers could successfully challenge U.S. producers.

Lean Production.   Womack and his colleagues use the term *lean production* to describe the revolutionary management system first introduced by the Toyota Motor Co. of Nagoya, Japan, after World War II. One important aspect of the system is the "just-in-time" *(Kanban)* delivery of parts to the assembly line, which contrasts to the "just-in-case" buffer of spare parts in mass production. The organizational revolution triggered by Toyota was fully comprehensive, however, affecting the organization and management of labor, design, and production at the intrafirm and interfirm levels. The approach appears to contradict the logic and principles of mass production, the division of labor, and the economies of scale. It seems to revert to some of the ideas of craft production in its use of multiple-skilled labor responsible for the quality as well as the quantity of output, in the level of commitment it requires of all workers in the assembly plant and in part supplies to track down the causes of any faults, and to eliminate them, and in its concern with flexible batch production rather than long uninterrupted production runs. The most important attributes of lean production are the contrasts in its productivity with those of mass production. Lean production enables Japanese cars to be designed in about two-thirds the time, with about half of the engineering design input as the U.S. and European cars. The products are universally ranked highest in ease of assembly and take only about half the time to assemble. Lean-produced cars have a much lower incidence of defects than do mass-produced cars, with virtually no reworking at the end of the assembly line, even though fixing assembly-line faults accounts for up to one-quarter of their total production time. So not surprisingly perhaps, the United States lost 20 percent of its domestic market to Japanese cars in just 8 years. Moreover, as lean-production techniques spread to other Japanese industries, the success story of Japanese cars was repeated in motorcycles, machine tools, consumer electronics, and others in which the firm-specific advantages were not hard technology, but organizational superiority.

Toyota began its organizational changes with rethinking the process by which mass production uses hundreds of expensive, highly specialized presses to stamp the individual parts of cars and trucks. It takes up to a day to change the dies on these machines to produce a part with a different shape, so typically very large quantities of any one part are stamped out and stockpiled before the dies are changed. Toyota redesigned the presses so that the assembly-line workers could change the dies in just a few minutes and make the parts on an as-required basis. The results were surprising. Flexible batch production was achieved at lower costs, without the space and carrying costs of large inventories and with very quick feedback on stamping mistakes, eliminating the waste of large numbers of defective parts. Capital costs were reduced, too, because only a few presses were needed for an entire car. This kind of lean principle was carried through the entire automobile manufacturing chain, from assessing the wants of customers, through design, development, engineering, manufacturing of components, assembly, and distribution.

Lean production depends on and promotes quality work. For instance, inventory in a mass-production system is several weeks' supply. Under lean production, it may be several hours'. Lean production is hand-to-mouth: A string of defective parts would halt production. Workers have to be concerned constantly with quality, to anticipate problems and to devise solutions. And they must do these things themselves. Under lean production, there are no supervisors or shop stewards to turn to.

Lean production does not accept the "move the metal" mentality of mass production under which the assembly line is kept running with a rework area at the end to correct errors. Lean production treats rework areas as a waste that should be made redundant. Workers are expected to stop the production line if they detect an error they are unable to correct. It is argued that it is better to correct defects before they become embedded in the vehicle and at the point where they occur so that the ultimate root causes responsible for the defect can be solved. (Workers are taught to ask the "five why"s"—"And why did that go wrong?" is asked and answered five times.)

Lean production began in Japan, but not all Japanese producers are equally lean, and the worst have lower plant productivity than the average in North America. North America has been improving its productivity, but in two cases, General Motors and Chrysler, this has come from closing the least-efficient plants. It is Ford Motor Co., the pioneer of mass production to the world, that is the first Western automobile company to begin incorporating the lessons of lean production. Just how far North American and European car producers still have to go in catching up with a continually improving Japanese industry is illustrated by Womack's figures on the average assembly hours needed per vehicle in the three major world markets (Table 9.8).

The Impact of Lean Production on the Location of the Automobile Industry

The impact of lean production on cost, quality, and upgrading of product range achieved by Toyota and subsequently by other Japanese carmakers has resulted in a shift of automobile production from North America to Japan, and of North American and European production from domestic companies to Japanese companies. The locational impact is most visible in the list of domestic assembly plants closed and of foreign branch plants opened, but it goes beyond the components of industrial change to include indirect effects as well.

The direct locational effects of lean production are startling. The Japanese share of world motor vehicle production rose from a couple of percent in 1955 to 30 percent in 1980. The world recession and the Japanese shift of production offshore reduced Japan's share in the 1980s. Nevertheless, about one car in four is now made in Japan. That figure is about equal to the current North American share of world production, but North America dominated world output in 1955 with about three-quarters of world production.

The Location of Japanese Assembly Plants in the United States. The reduction in world market share by U.S. producers is even greater than the North American total production figures indicate. Starting in 1982, when Honda opened the first Japanese overseas assembly plant in Marysville, Ohio, Japanese companies have created a second automobile industry in the United States. Their output is about equal to that of Britain, or France, or Italy and accounts for about a quarter of all automobile production in the United States.

The decision by Japanese firms to open assembly plants in the United States was a direct response to the trade friction caused by Japanese import penetration (Dicken, 1991, p. 294). Japan had accepted a voluntary restraint on the number of automobiles exported, but there was pressure for Japan to improve the U.S. trade balance and to save jobs by assembling automobiles in the United States.

Japanese assembly plants have all been located in the U.S. midwest, to minimize costs of serving the entire national market from a single location. The dispersion of secondary assembly plants by the big three U.S. auto producers to the East Coast and to California, to manufacture big-volume standard automobiles, thus was reversed. Following Honda's Ohio plant in 1982, Nissan located an assembly plant in Tennessee in 1983. Mazda located in Michigan in 1987, Toyota in Kentucky in 1988, Mitsubishi in Illinois also in 1988, and Subaru and Isuzu jointly in Indiana in 1989.

The location of Japanese companies in different states was not a coincidence. Japanese firms each established an individual relationship with a particular state government. This bonding had begun with the visit to Japan by the governor of Ohio to seek industrial investment in his state. Honda's decision to locate there led to the identification in Japan of Ohio as Honda territory (Rubenstein, 1991, pp. 130 and 136). State governments offered Japanese firms substantial financial incentives toward the costs of highway improvements, site developments, and worker training. Honda received $30 million from the State of Ohio, and the amounts subsequently offered by other states increased as the competition for Japanese investment intensified. Local governments, too, made financial contributions to attract investment, including money for local improvements and property tax concessions.

However, government financial incentives have not generally been the most critical factor in the site selected for a Japanese assembly plant. More attention was given to local attitudes toward a major Japanese presence, and to the attitudes and aptitudes of the local work force. One concern was that some older Americans, with memories of the war in the Pacific, might be hostile to a dominant Japanese presence in their local community. Others might not want the change in life-style imposed by a large factory. Any dealings with the U.S. autoworkers union were shunned and communities were selected where single-union agreements, critical to just-in-time production methods, could be signed. Once a community was selected, great care went into the interviewing, screening, and selection of the work force, who then underwent thorough preparatory training, including, in some cases, visits to Japan.

All the Japanese firms except Mazda were built on greenfield sites. Mazda, 25 percent owned by Ford, located in an existing plant originally built by Ford. Otherwise, they located in small communities, typically with a population of about 10,000, on a major interstate highway, and with good rail connections. Small towns offer the advantages of easier land assembly and lower land costs,.

The Location of Japanese Parts Suppliers. Japanese assembly plants originally expected to be served by American parts suppliers but quickly discovered that American firms could not adopt just-in-time delivery and quality requirements (Kennedy and Florida, 1993, p. 129). American suppliers often considered Japanese quality requirements to be unrealistic and sometimes preferred to abandon the business rather than attempt to meet new, higher standards. Conversely, Japanese assembly plants found the defect rate of American suppliers was many times higher than that of domestic suppliers in Japan. A second concern of the Japanese automakers was the extent to which the manufacture of parts in the United States was controlled by dependent subsidiaries of the big three. Outsourcing (the buying of parts from independent suppliers) averaged a comparatively low one-third the value of an auto. To the extent that they were tied to the big-three suppliers would be less able to meet the needs of Japanese assembly plants. Consequently, Japanese automobile firms encouraged their Japanese suppliers to set up production in the United states and now have a network of over 300 Japanese, and Japanese-U.S. joint venture suppliers, 250 of which are located in the six midwest states.

The location of these suppliers has been dictated by the location of the assembly plants that they serve. The just-in-time system requires close geographic links. The two most important factors cited by suppliers for their site selection were proximity to their customers and access to major transportation routes (Kennedy and Florida, 1993, p. 146). About 40 percent of suppliers are within a 2-hour shipping radius of the firm they supply, and 80 percent within the 8-hour radius that conforms to just-in-time delivery requirements. Typically, they are located on, or close to, the main interstate highways. So many are located on Interstate 75 that it is frequently referred to as Kanban Highway, and the region stretching from southern Ontario, through Michigan, Illinois, Indiana, and Ohio to Kentucky and Tennessee has been described as the transplant corridor. Within the corridor, there is a clear state affiliation between assembly plants and their suppliers. Rubenstein (1991, p. 136) quotes the case of southwestern Ohio, which is within 90 minutes of the Toyota plant at Georgetown, Kentucky. However, Ohio is regarded as Honda territory and Toyota suppliers are strongly discouraged in Japan from locating there.

Parts suppliers, like automobile firms, have usually preferred small towns with a population of about 10,000 that do not already have a Japanese firm. They do not want to have to compete for labor and financial benefits. Alternatively, they have located on the edge of a metropolitan area, near an airport, as in the case of Detroit and Chicago. In general, they have avoided heavily industrialized areas. The complex network of suppliers that has evolved is illustrated by Honda's Ohio distribution of suppliers, and it portrays part of the new geography of automobile production built up within the very backyard of existing U.S. producers.

The Japanese Presence in the UK.   Japanese investment in assembly and parts has been quite different in Europe (Saddler, 1994). The European industry is more fragmented and parochial, with greater allegiance to national brands, such as Fiat in Italy and Volvo in Sweden. Japanese automobiles have made slower market progress in Europe and Japanese firms have been slower to establish branch plants. Honda had again led the way with a joint-venture agreement with British Leyland (subsequently privatized as Rover, and then bought out by BMW). Nissan was again second, beginning production at a greenfield site in Sunderland, N.E. England in 1986, which has become the largest Japanese direct investment in Europe. In 1989, both Toyota and Honda announced plans for both assembly and engine plants, followed by investment announcements by other Japanese firms.

Japanese parts suppliers have also been much slower to invest in Europe. In part, this resulted from the slower growth of the Japanese automobile production in Europe. It also reflected the much stronger indigenous components industry in Europe. Typically, a half to two-thirds of European cars by value are made up of outsourced parts and the major parts suppliers are large MNEs in their own right. There was strong political pressure for Japanese automobile assembly plants to incorporate a very high level of European-made parts before they could be exported freely within the European Economic Community.

Nissan chose to use the existing network of suppliers, but monitored them closely for quality, cost, design capability, delivery performance, and management. Nissan also developed a relationship with suppliers, based on the Japanese model, but taking account of cultural differences. Most suppliers did not relocate, partly because the West Midlands, the center of the UK parts industry, is only a 3- to 4- hour drive to the Nissan plant. Those that did locate plants close to Nissan fell into two categories (Saddler, 1994, p. 44). The majority supplied low-value, high-bulk components requiring considerable variation in the product range, such as plastic moldings, trimming sand seats. The second category located close to Nissan to supply parts not previously made in the UK By 1992, when Nissan was producing the Micra and Primera ranges of Sunderland, it had 180 suppliers, 27 in the northeast of England, 102 in the rest of England, with most of the rest in Germany, France, and Spain. Some external warehousing of parts was therefore necessary and the just-in-time system could not be implemented to full Japanese standards. Other aspects of lean production are being achieved and UK parts suppliers have been leapfrogging their European competitors in technology, development, design, and quality. The British parts industry is thereby achieving an in situ restructuring and providing a new variant of Japanese lean production.

Assessing the Direct and Indirect Impact of MNEs

The immediate reaction by host-country governments and labor organizations to foreign direct investment (FDI) and to the opening of branch plants by MNEs tends to be enthusiastic. But if foreign direct investment grows rapidly or if foreign subsidiaries are sold or closed, then serious concerns begin to be expressed about their effects. Assessing the direct and indirect effects of MNEs is difficult, but a framework for doing so has been developed by the International Labor Organization (ILO) (Box 9.15).

It might be thought that the direct effect of foreign branch plants is simply the new employment created by those plants. But is the contribution of a foreign branch plant to employment growth and industrial output the same when the MNE buys out a going concern as when it builds a new factory at a greenfield location? The new Nissan plant at Washington, England, would appear to contribute more to the British car industry than did Chrysler's ill-fated buyout of the British Rootes group. However, Rootes was in trouble when Chrysler bought a controlling interest in it in the 1960s. The new Rootes small car, the Hillman Imp, had smaller sales than expected and was not generating the profits needed to update the aging product line or the outdated inefficient engines. Had Chrysler not bought in, Rootes probably would have closed. No other corporation had shown an interest. In 1978, after Chrysler found it was unable to turn the losses around and was facing mounting financial difficulties in the United States, it sold out to Peugeot. Again, had Peugeot not bought out Chrysler's European interests, the former Rootes' factories would have had to close. Indeed, Peugeot did close one assembly plant in 1981 at Lynwood, Scotland, which had been newly opened at the time of the Chrysler takeover. Even if it is argued that the Chrysler and Peugeot buyouts did not directly create employment, they did save employment and preserved industrial locations. So considerations of employment effects, direct or indirect, are always bedeviled by the

---

BOX 9.15   *The Direct and Indirect Employment Effects of Branch Plants of MNEs in the Host Country*

Type of Effect	*Definition and Example*
A. Direct	Total labor force in all plants in the host country owned or controlled by MNEs.
B. Indirect	Employment generated in the country as a result of spending by the MNE (for parts and services from enterprises in that country) and by its employees on domestically produced goods and services.
1. Horizontal	Employment displaced from similar industries in the host country that may be locally owned, labor-intensive.
2. Vertical	
(a) Backward linkages	Employment generated by the MNE among domestic suppliers of raw materials, parts, components and services.
(b) Forward linkages	Employment generated in the distribution and service networks.
3. Macroeconomic	Second-round employment generated by the spending on domestic goods and services by MNE workers and reinvested MNE profits.

Source: N. Jéquier, *Measuring the Indirect Employment Effects of Multinational Enterprises: Some Suggestions for a Research Framework*, Working Paper No. 56 (Geneva: ILO, Multinational Enterprises Programme, 1989).

"alternative hypothesis": What would have happened if the foreign direct investment had not taken place?

Even if the direct employment effects are accepted, three concerns have been raised about the limitations of the direct contributions of foreign direct investment. First, branch plants are often truncated firms, performing a number of the production and assembly operations, but seldom involved in the full hierarchy of corporate activity. Strategic planning, research and development, and design and engineering tend to remain in the MNE's home country. Japanese foreign investment typically begins with an assembly plant, followed later by a plant to assemble engines. Nissan, Honda, and Toyota each now have an engine plant both in the United States and United Kingdom. The design and engineering are still mainly performed in Japan. One concern with MNEs is then that they export the production jobs, but keep the best jobs at home.

A second concern is with exports. An MNE may expressly locate a branch plant in a country to serve a free-trade area to which the host country belongs. More usually, the branch plant is limited to serving the host-country mar-

ket. Even when the branch plant secures export orders, these shipments may be contrary to government policy in the MNE's home country. Problems of "extraterritoriality" may then occur in which the branch plant finds itself subject to laws of the MNE's home country. This problem has occurred in Canada, for instance, when one Canadian subsidiary planned to export buses to Cuba. Exports are job-creating and when they are restricted, the growth of the branch plant is limited.

A third concern is whether foreign branch plants are "snatchers," concerned mainly with seizing a quick profit and ready to close a plant if profit levels fall (Box 9.16). Certainly, the exit barriers (i.e., the costs of closing down operations in a host country) are lower for MNEs than for domestic firms. They can transfer equipment to another country rather than liquidating. Intangible assets, such as goodwill and proprietary knowledge, which can be of considerable value, need not be lost in an MNE transfer of production as they usually are in the closing of a domestic firm. Furthermore, MNEs may be under political pressure to maintain employment levels at home during a recession,

BOX 9.16   *Plant Closings*

Classical location theory is concerned with the optimal location for production. It was traditionally assumed that the outcome of the process would be investment in plant and equipment, the creation of employment, and production of new goods to meet growing demand. But since about 1980, economic geography has begun to acknowledge that disinvestment of plants, the layoff of workers, and the cessation of production have become powerful forces shaping industrial regions. Industrial relic landscapes such as Lackawanna, New York (steel); Akron, Ohio (tires); Detroit, Michigan (automobile assembly and parts); and Chicago's Packingtown or Toronto's stockyards district (meatpacking) illustrate these disturbing forces. As the structure of costs, trade barriers, and technology change, previously optimal locations become less desirable, new opportunities are revealed, and plants may be closed.

Plant closure has become a political issue and has been viewed as an assault on an immobile working class by hypermobile capital accumulated by large corporations. One engrossing account along these lines is *The Deindustrialization of America* by Barry Bluestone and Bennett Harrison (1982). They describe the changing geography of job creation and job destruction in the United States and argue that most of the

plants were profitable at the time of closing. The trouble is that their conglomerate corporate parents believe that they can disinvest in one location, shift resources to a second location, and earn even higher returns on their investment. Their policy prescription demands greater accountability by the owners of capital, who may have extracted profits from places for many years without every reinvesting.

The motivation for plant closings depends on the size of the firm and the number of plants and products it produces. Small businesses often have limited capitalization and are vulnerable to the vicissitudes of the business cycle, loss of key customers, or management blunders. Thus, small businesses are constantly being created and nearly as often are wound up. They may go out of business after the death of the proprietor or their plants may be padlocked with a bankruptcy trustee's notice taped to the door.

Notwithstanding the constancy of the "churning" of the small business sector, it is the large-scale plant closings by well-known multilocational firms that gain the most notoriety in the local press and have the most acute impact on the local economy. Multilocational firms have greater flexibility than small businesses to respond to a generalized recession or to declining demand for a particular

product. (For example, per capita consumption of beef has declined continuously in North America since 1980, bias ply tires have become unattractive to fuel-economy-minded motorists, and electric typewriters have been almost completely supplanted by microcomputers and word processing software.) Thus, a firm may simply decide to exit from a particular market and close a plant that was at one time optimally located to produce a product.

Economics of scale remain very important in the location of production of standardized goods for mass markets. In many materials processing industries, the cost savings accruing from economies of scale exceed the added transportation costs incurred to supply a grater market area. In the 1940s, virtually every Canadian city had a locally owned and operated brewery that supplied the immediate vicinity with a local beer known for its distinctive regional flavor. One by one these small breweries have been closed as beer production has become concentrated in a small number of very large breweries that operate at national or global scales. The same may be said of other beverage industries such as soft-drink bottling, dairies, and distilleries.

whatever the employment cost to branch plants in other countries.

The evidence on the strategies of MNEs regarding foreign branch plants is complex, but does not generally support the "snatcher" argument. MNEs tend to follow a long-term strategy such as portfolio adjustment based on their share of market and the growth expectations of that market. Mark Casson argues that when an MNE closes a branch plant as opposed to selling it as a going concern, the most likely reasons are these.

1. The facility may be in the wrong location.
2. The plant is obsolete.
3. The plant has incorrigible management and working practices.

4. The plant may have high costs in an industry faced with falling demand.

A plant may be in the wrong location for many reasons. The sources of inputs may have changed, leaving the plant stranded. Tariff and nontariff barriers may change, opening the plant to new sources of competition. Transport costs and facilities may have changed. Manufacturers located in older industrial districts may be disadvantaged by traffic congestion. Or the plant may be a victim of government policy that has lured the plant to the wrong location or left it unable to compete with plants benefiting from incentives in another location.

The Lynwood plant in Scotland, closed by Peugeot, is an example of a plant in a wrong location selected to obtain government subsidies. Lynwood did have poor industrial

Some plant closings are the result of intense competition from low-wage producers operating in the developing countries of Latin America and the Pacific Rim. Typically, the closed plant's equipment is packed up and shipped to a developing country where it will be used to even further intensify trade pressure. Known as a "runaway shop," these closings often motivate calls for increased protection to maintain the wage position of manufacturing workers in the developed countries. In some cases, foreign competition is the catalyst for concession bargaining in which management offers workers a choice: accept a 10 or 20 percent cut in wage rates or be prepared to be laid off as the plant is shut down. This presents a difficult decision to workers and their families. Management argues that concessions are the price that western workers must pay in a competitive global economy. Labor unions take the position that plants are likely close in any event thus workers should oppose attempts to lever their wages downward.

Intensified competition is one of many motives that may prompt multi-

locational forms to undertake strategic planning that may reveal the opportunity to effect significant cost savings by "rationalization." Rationalization reorganizes the way products are allocated to plants at different locations. For example, one clear trend has been for plants to specialize and increase the scale of production while increasing the size of their market areas. This is especially true when trade barriers between provinces or states are reduced.

Rationalization does not necessarily involve plant closings and job losses but it often does. For the wage-earning labor force, the results are often tragic as blue-collar workers may no longer have marketable skills in other sectors of the economy and they may be too old to undertake retraining. Closed plants may be unattractive for other activities and lie idle for many years, a blight on the economic landscape and a symbol of the economic decline in industrial regions.

Ian MacLachlan
University of Lethbridge

References:

Baldwin, John R. (1995). *The Dynamics of Industrial Competition: A North American Perspective.* Cambridge: Cambridge University Press.
Baldwin, John R., and Mohammed Rafiguzzamen (1995). *Restructuring in the Canadian Manufacturing Sector from 1970 to 1990: Industry and Regional Dimensions of Job Turnover.* Research Paper Series No. 78, Analytical Studies Brand, Ottawa: Statistics Canada.
Bluestone, Barry, and Bennett Harrison (1982). *The Deindustrialization of America*: Plant Closings, Community Abandonment, and the Dismantling of Basic Industries. New York: Basic Books.
MacLachlan Ian (1992). Plant Closure and Regional Dynamics: Competitive Strategy and Rationalization. *Economic Geography* 68:128–145.
Pratten, Cliff (1991). *Company Failure.* London: the Institute of Chartered Accountants in England and Wales.

relations too, but the decisive factor in its closing was high transportation costs. Engines were cast at Lynwood, and then shipped to Coventry in the Midlands, England, to be bored. The completed engines were transported back to Lynwood for final vehicle assembly. The vehicles then were shipped south again to their main markets. It seems unlikely that Lynwood could have survived regardless of country of control. The investment–divestment sequence fits more closely to the portfolio strategic-planning explanation than to any "snatcher" hypothesis.

The indirect employment consequences of MNE foreign direct investment are more difficult to sort out. In general, the horizontal indirect effects are likely to be negative. The opening of a new branch plant, perhaps using state-of-the-art technology and able to draw on the resources of the

parent company, may lead to closure of domestic plants making similar goods. The closure of U.S. automobile assembly plants in North America is an example of such negative horizontal effects. Once established, branch plants may constitute barriers to entry by domestic firms.

Vertical indirect effects are likely to create jobs, though probably less than had the plant been domestically owned. The vertical effect depends on the local content of the product made in the branch plant. Japanese car plants in North America had only 20 percent North American content in the early 1980s. That figure has now reached 60 percent and may reach 75 percent by the late 1990s. The many individual case studies point to a wide array of factors that influence the vertical effect of MNEs on employment. They vary with the industry type, the home country of the MNE, the industrial policies in the host country, and the length of operation of the MNE in the host country. Capital-intensive industries tend to create more indirect employment. So do export industries that are growing rapidly. European countries, particularly the smaller ones like the Netherlands, Sweden, and Switzerland, do better than the United States, which in turn does better than Japan. But Japan's poor performance may reflect the recentness of its direct foreign investment. It takes time for a branch plant to establish linkages, and so longer-established branch plants tend to generate more indirect employment than new ones.

In addition to the industry-specific horizontal and vertical indirect employment effects, MNEs have broad macroeconomic effects on employment. The wages spent by branch plant workers help to create more jobs. And retained profits reinvested in the host country can stimulate the economy. But there are concerns that these macroeconomic effects can be reduced by repatriation of profits and by *transfer pricing.* Transfer pricing can occur because the dealings of a branch plant with sister plants in other countries are not at arm's length, so that prices are not determined in the marketplace. An MNE can, therefore, set the prices so as to transfer the apparent profits of its various operations to those countries where corporate tax rates are lower, for example. If an MNE transfers profits out of a host country, it reduces the macroeconomic benefits of its operations. Transfers of declared profits can also have implications for the macroeconomic contributions of the branch plant, for exchange rates, and for balance of payments.

All these employment effects, direct and indirect, affect the amount, the type, and the location of industry. MNEs affect the distribution of industry on a global scale through their investment policies. In addition to the country-specific endowments that attract branch plants mentioned by Dunning in his eclectic theory, it is clear that in the initial stages of foreign direct investment, MNEs exhibit a strong preference for similar cultures in nearby countries. For U.S. branch plants, the most frequent order of investment is Canada, United Kingdom, Mexico, West Germany, Brazil, France, Columbia, Spain, Japan, and Italy. Compare the global distribution of U.S. MNE manufacturing activity in the 1950s when it first began its major expansion, with that for Japan in the 1980s at the onset of its major expansion: In 1955, U.S. foreign direct investment in manufacturing was concentrated in Canada (45 percent), Europe (30 percent), and Latin America (15 percent). For Japan in 1983, the distribution was quite different: Asia (33 percent), North America (27 percent), Latin America (20 percent), and Europe (7 percent). It takes experience before foreign direct investment by a country's MNEs is an efficient response to global economic opportunities and conditions, rather than reflecting a mix of economic opportunity, cultural similarity, and geographic proximity. The rapid growth of Japanese foreign direct investment is an important force for change in a pattern previously dictated by U.S. MNEs.

VOCABULARY

Additional items to add to your vocabulary are as follows:

absolute cost barriers	cube-square law	financial economies of scale
administered prices	diseconomies of scale	fixed costs
average cost	district economies	forward linkages
backward linkages	division of labor	Hoover's margin line
barriers to entry	dynamic externalities	horizontal indirect effects
bulk transactions	economic adaption	human capital
churning	economic adoption	increasing returns
classical entrepreneur	economies of scope	indirect employment consequences
competitive firm	economy-of-scale threshold	indivisible costs
competitive model	endogenous	industrial districts
condition of entry	engineering principle	industry-specific economies
conglomerate mergers	exit barriers	internal diseconomies of scale
cost-minimizing firms	exit rates	internal economies of scale
craft entrepreneur	external economies of scale	internal multiplant economies
craft production	"filtering"	job-turnover rates

"just-in-case" delivery

just-in-time production

kaizan

Kaldor's model

kanban

"knowledge spillovers"

labor diseconomies of scale

labor economies

labor efficiencies

lateral integration

"lazy-J"

lean production

learning curves

limit pricing

localization economies

locational adaption

locational adoption

long-run average-cost curve

long-run unit-cost (LRUC) curve

lowest common multiple (LCM)

macroeconomic shocks

management diseconomies of scale

management economies

management entrepreneur

margin line

market-driven facilities

marketing diseconomies of scale

marketing economies

mass production

massed reserves

maximum economies of scale

merger

mergers for monopoly

mergers for oligopoly

milieu innovateur

minimum average total cost

minimum efficient scale (MES)

minimum efficient size

multidivisional company with decentralized divisions

multiplant economies

network firms

network model

network system

nontariff barrier

organizational decentralization

pecuniary advantages (contrast with real economies of scale)

place-specific economies

planning curve

plant-specific economies

positive feedback

price discrimination

principle of bulk transactions

principle of multiples

principle of reserves

product differentiation

product-driven firm

product-specific economies

production economies

production run

profit snatcher

proximity economies

pure competition

returns to scale

reverse-J cost curve

runaway plants

scale economies of reserves

scope of operation

short run unit cost curve

Simpson's Paradox

size threshold

spatial association

standardization of parts

standardized growth rate

synergy elements

tariff barrier

task cycle

technical diseconomies of scale

technical economies of scale

territorial firm

territorial model

theory-driven firm

three stages in the entrepreneurial process

time-and-motion studies

total cost

transfer pricing

two-thirds rule

urbanization economies

variable costs

venture capital

Verdoorn's Law

vertical indirect effects

worker turnover

TOPICS FOR DISCUSSION

1. List some of the small manufacturing firms in your area. If economies of scale are so important, then why do these small firms survive? Prepare a short questionnaire and do some field work.

2. Select one of the principles (cube-square, multiples, reserves, and bulk transactions) by which internal economies of scale are achieved and show how it applies to one industry in your area.

3. What economies of scale does an entrepreneur achieve by buying a franchise? Make inquires, perhaps from a local fast-food franchise.

4. Select either an industrial park or your central business district and make a list of the specific external economies of scale that it offers.

5. What are your nearest brand-name manufacturing plants? What market areas do they serve? Can you explain the size and spacing of plants in that industry?

6. Read the story of Catherine Evans in Krugman (1991b, Chap. 2). Are there similar stories of how one person or event helped to trigger an industry in your area?

7. Can you find any local evidence to support the claim that economies of scale are becoming more important either in service industry or in manufacturing?

8. "Internal economies of scale are important to large firms, external economies to small firms." Discuss, using some of the evidence gathered in your local field work.

9. Why are economies of scale relevant to the geography of manufacturing? For instance, what is the set of relationships among minimum efficient scale in a given industry, the maximum number of efficient plants in that industry in a given industry, the maximum ubiquity of that industry among a given set of cities, and the urban hierarchy.

10. Prepare a leaflet explaining to industrial firms why they should choose your area in which to locate their next branch plant.

11. When would job losses, whether through the closure of individual firms, individual plants within different firms, or layoffs in different plants, be likely to have a severe regional impact? Why is a region dominated by small firms likely to adjust more quickly than one dominated by a few large firms?

12. What effect is the North American Free Trade Agreement likely to have on firms and their employment levels in Canada or the single European market on Britain? Is peripheral location still a serious disadvantage? Or are other factors more important?

13. Select a case of a decision to open or buy, or to sell or close a branch plant that has received attention by government and labor. How well were the direct and indirect employment effects identified? What effects were missed altogether?

14. What organizations are there to assist small firms in your area? Do they maintain a research and publication program? What assistance could you obtain in starting your own small manufacturing business? How well do you think your region does compared with others in helping small firms? Describe the key elements of the Japanese system of lean production. Organize your answer under the headings just-in-time (*kanban*), continuous improvement (*kaizen*), and the organization of work teams. Compare it with mass production using the example of the impact of Japanese investment in an industry in either North America or Europe.

FURTHER READINGS

Arrow, K. J. (1962). The Economic Implications of Learning by Doing. *Review of Economic Studies* 29:155–173.

This article lays one of the foundations of the modern theory of dynamic externalities.

Bain Joe S. (1956). *Barriers to New Competition.* Cambridge, MA: Harvard University Press.

A pioneering work that laid an intellectual foundation for much that followed on the engineering approach to measuring the minimum optimal scale as a percent of national capacity, and on product differentiation and other barriers to entry.

Baldwin, John R. (1995). *The Dynamics of Industrial Competition: A North American Perspective.* Cambridge: Cambridge University Press.

A pioneering work using the components of change (firm birth growth, decline, and exit) and the associated job turbulence to trace the reallocation of resources and the dynamics of competition.

Birch, D. L. (1979). *The Job Generation Process.* Cambridge, MA: The MIT Program on Neighborhood and Regional Changes.

This study sparked North American interest in the role of small firms in employment creation.

Burns, Paul, and Jim Dewhurst (Eds). (1989). *Small Business and Entrepreneurship.* London: Macmillan.

Written for practical guidance as well as academic study, the combination of literature review and case studies makes this book fascinating as well as instructive.

Camagni, Roberto P. (1995) The Concept of *Innovative Milieu* and Its Relevance for Public Policies in European Lagging Regions. *Papers in Regional Science* 74:317–340.

Provides an excellent review of the circumstances that produce increasing returns.

Casson, Mark (1984). *International Divestment and Restructuring Decisions (with Special Reference to the Motor Industry).* Working Paper No. 40. Geneva: International Labor Office, Multinational Enterprises Programme.

One of a series of working papers dealing with individual countries in the industrialized and developing countries, and with special topics such as export-processing zones, indirect employment effects, and the employment effects of technology choice. It is a key source of information. Casson is useful because he provides a detailed typology of divestment decisions as well as the Chrysler-Peugeot case study.

Davis S. J., J. Haltiwanger and S. Shuh (1995) *Job Creation and Job Destruction in U.S. Manufacturing: 1972–1988.* Washington, DC: U.S. Government Printing Office.

An analysis of the newly available longitudinal employment files for the United States.

Dicken, Peter (1991). *Global Shift: Industrial Change in a Turbulent World.* London: Harper & Row.

A comprehensive survey of the growth of MNEs and their role in the major industries, and an assessment of their costs and benefits to host countries. Essential reading.

Fothergill S., and G. Gudgin (1982). *Unequal Growth: Urban and Regional Employment Change in The UK.* London: Heinemann.

A key reading on the changing factors in regional development, particularly employment creation by new small firms.

Harrigan, Kathryn Rudie (1985). *Managing Maturing Business, Restructuring Declining Industries and Re-vitalizing Troubled Operations.* Lexington, MA: Lexington Books.

Harrigan is a seminal contributor to the extension of Bain's structure, conduct, and performance paradigm to include exit barriers and suboptimal decision making in declining industries.

Hoover, Edgar M. (1937). *Location Theory and the Shoe and Leather Industry.* Cambridge, MA.: Harvard University Press.

One of the great classics on location theory, this book is in two distinct parts: Part I, pp. 3–111, provides a systematic review of location theory within the framework of Alfred Weber (with the developments of Wilhelm Launhardt and Tord Palander). The rest of the book is devoted to two case studies. Economies of scale, discussed in Chapter VI, "Economies of Concentration," pp. 39–111, focuses on Hoover's concept of the margin line and on the balance of additional production economies less additional delivery costs.

Kaldor, N. (1966). *Causes of the Slow Rate of Growth of the United Kingdom: An Inaugural Lecture.* London: Cambridge University Press.

——— (1978). *Further Essays on Economic Theory.* New York: Holmes & Meier.

Kaldor lays out Verdoorn's Law and his theory of endogenous growth.

Kennedy, Martin, and Richard Florida (1993). *Beyond the Age of Mass Production: The Japanese System and Its Transfer to the U.S.* New York: Oxford University Press.

A seminal contribution based on detailed field work offering a comprehensive review of the Japanese system and incisive case studies including steel, automobiles, and auto parts. The authors introduce the term "innovation-mediated production" in preference to "lean production."

Krugman, Paul (1991). Increasing Returns and Economic Geography. *Journal of Political Economy.* 99:483–499.

——— (1991). *Geography and Trade.* Cambridge, MA.: The MIT Press.

An economist writes simply and thinks spatially in a series of lectures given at Leuven University. He provides many examples of agglomeration economies in Chapter 2 pp. 35–67.

Lucas, Robert E., Jr. (1988). On the Mechanics of Economic Development. *Journal of Monetary Economics.* 22:3–42.

Lays out his theory of endogenous growth.

Maclachlan, Ian (1993). Plant Closure and Regional Dynamics: Competitive Strategy and Rationalization. *Economic Geography* 68:128–145.

The fortunes of individual firms can differ from industry trends, with firms simultaneously opening and closing plants on either side of the United States–Canada border in an effort to capture market share or simply to remain in business.

Marshall, Alfred (1890). *Principles of Economics.* London: Macmillan.

Includes a classic discussion of the role of external economies in the development of Industrial Districts.

Mason, Colin M., and Richard T. Harrison (1985). The Geography of Small Firms in the U.K.: Towards a Research Agenda. *Progress in Human Geography.* 9:1–37.

A useful review of a rapidly growing literature and some unanswered questions.

Porter, Michael E. (1990). *The Competitive Advantage of Nations.* New York: The Free Press.

A widely reviewed book by an economist. Its numerous case studies show how localization economies improve the cost and quality performance of industry.

Pratten, C. F. (1971). *Economies of Scale in Manufacturing Industries.* London: Cambridge University Press.

A detailed study of some two dozen industries, which describes the production process, the structure of the industry, cost components, and economies of scale. An excellent source book to use as a foundation for further field study.

——— (1991). *Company Failure.* London: Institute of Chartered Accountants, Financial Reporting and Auditing Group.

A brief overview with case studies and a review of the literature.

——— (1991).*The Competitiveness of Small Firms.* Cambridge: Cambridge University Press.

A straightforward account of internal economies of scale based on a survey of 235 firms in East Anglia, England, employing less than 500 employees in six industries.

Reynolds, Paul, David J. Storey, and Paul Westhead (1994). Cross-National Comparisons of the Variation in New Firm Formation Rates. *Regional Studies* 28:443–456.

A special issue of *Regional Studies* with articles on birth rates in individual European countries and the United States and a concluding article by the guest editors. The issue documents the importance and contribution of firm births and identifies common factors associated with high birth rates.

Rhys, D. G. (1971–1972). Heavy Commercial Vehicles: The Survival of the Small Firm. *Journal of Industrial Economics.* 20:230–252.

A well-documented case study of economies of scale.

Romer, Paul M. (1986). Increasing Returns and Long Run Growth. *Journal of Political Economy.* 94:1002–1037.

Lays out an alternative to classic theories of economic development.

Rothwell, R., and W. Zegveld (1982). *Innovation and the Small and Medium Sized Firm.* London: Francis Pinter.

Chapter 7, "SMEs and Employment," is particularly interesting, but the whole book provides pithy summaries of the literature, a good bibliography, and the general economic context for employment trends through the 1970s.

Rubenstein, James M. (1991). The Impact of Japanese Investment in the United States. In Christopher M. Law (Ed.), *Restructuring the Global Automobile Industry.* London: Routledge.

A useful complement to Florida and Kenney. Other good chapters include Miyakawa's fascinating account of how Japan's automobile industry started and the chapters on the UK.

Saddler, David (1994). The Geography of Just-in-Time: Japanese Investment and the Automotive Components Industry in Western Europe. *Economic Geography.* 70:41–59.

The Japanese System takes a modified form as it adjusts to the presence of a well-established parts industry in Western Europe.

Saxenian, Annalee (1994). *Culture and Competition in Silicon Valley and Route 128.* Cambridge, MA: Harvard University Press.

A careful and provocative comparison of similarities and differences in the structures and institutions contributing to the growth of two new industrial regions.

Scherer F. M., Alan Beckenstein, Erich Kauffer, and R. Dennis Murphy (1975). *The Economics of Multi-Plant Operation.* Cambridge, MA: Harvard University Press.

See Chapter 2, "The Economies of Multi-Plant Operation: Interview Evidence," pp. 237–355. A thorough and systematic discussion, enriched with a continuous stream of examples that bring the topic alive.

Scherer, F. M. and David Ross (1990). *Industrial Market Structure and Economic Performance* 3rd ed. Boston: Houghton Mifflin.

See Chapter 4, "The Determinants of Market Structure," pp. 55–96. A readable, well-referenced book intended for courses in industrial organization and public policy. Chapter 4 covers economies of scale and mergers, providing many examples and brief reviews of key articles on the subject.

Scott A.J. (1988). *New Industrial Spaces: Flexible Production, Organization and Regional Development in North America and Western Europe.* London: Pion.

The three case studies of agglomeration economies are particularly interesting. The Japanese system takes a modified form as it adjusts to the presence of a well-established parts industry in Western Europe.

Scott A. J., and D. P. Angel (1987). The U.S. Semi-conductor Industry: A Locational Analysis. *Environment and Planning A* 19:875–912.

A case study of how localization economies create privileged locations for specific industries and enable them to achieve a competitive edge.

Wood, Jonathan (1988). *Wheels of Misfortune, the Rise and Fall of the British Motor Industry.* London: Sidgwick and Jackson.

Do firms always know their production costs? Apparently not. Read, for instance, about the Mini and how it was priced in a book by a car enthusiast written for the general public. Its failure to track unit costs was one more nail in British Leyland's coffin.

Young, Allyn (1928). Increasing Returns and Economic Progress. *Economic Journal.* 38:527–542.

The initial statement of a theory of increasing returns.

Young, Steven, Neil Hood, and Ewen Peters (1994). Multinational Enterprises and Regional Economic Development. *Regional Studies* 28:657–678.

A key review of the literature on the potential role of MNEs in the European community and their contribution to the regional economy.

10

Technology Transitions and Patterns of Growth

OVERVIEW

The Industrial Revolution, by which a world composed of largely self-sustaining agrarian societies was transformed into a progressively more interdependent global economy, was neither gradual nor continuous. Key innovations came in a succession of bursts at roughly 50-year intervals: in the 1770s and 1780s, the 1820s and 1830s, the 1870s and 1880s, and the 1920s and 1930s. Each swarm of innovations introduced new industries and transformed older ones, signaling the end of a period of "stagflation" and precipitating decades of new growth. Each wave of development ended with the onset of the next stagflation crisis as the former growth industries overshot needs and saturated markets. New types of industry, new industrial regions, and new forces affecting industrial location emerged in each period of growth. Depressed areas suffering from the collapse of their base industries appeared in each depression.

This chapter presents the related concepts of "technoeconomic transitions" and "long waves of prices" to enable you to understand the waves of growth and the industrial types, industrial regions, and location factors that emerged. It then explores the "Fifth Wave"—the technology transition that followed the 1980–1981 stagflation crisis and is now transforming industrial systems and growth processes.

OBJECTIVES

- to understand the nature of the "long wave" phenomenon, and the theories that explain Kondratiev waves
- to learn about Mensch's "metamorphosis model," and of the triggering mechanisms for the clusters of innovations that drive long waves
- to learn about the currently unfolding Fifth Wave, including the nature of the advanced services sector, and the role of information technology in the transformation that is now occurring

TECHNO-ECONOMIC SYSTEMS AND THE LONG-WAVE PHENOMENON

In the first chapter, we learned that a combination of technological and institutional changes has led to the triumph of markets and to accelerating globalization. Chapter 2 revealed that globalization has weakened the role of the nation-state, leading to the emergence of new transnational policy regimes and to the intensification of efforts by cultures and regions to express their individuality and their differences. Economies can be now classified by stage of development into those that are factor-driven, those that are investment-driven, those that are innovation-driven, and those that are wealth-driven. It is the factor-driven economies that are in the earlier stages of the demographic transition; innovation- and wealth-driven economies are reaching a new low-fertility, low-mortality equilibrium. As the demographic transition runs its course, promising a global demographic equilibrium at 11 to 12 billion people in the second half of the twenty-first century, the Malthusian specter seems to have been avoided as the key human resource—brainpower—assumes ascendance in the production process. As a result, we learned in Chapters 4 and 5 that natural resources no longer impose limits to growth as escalating demand forces deadly price spirals; rather, there is transmaterialization as smarter, smaller, lighter products are manufactured from commonly available materials to which considerable brainpower has been added.

Globalization is, of course, not a new process. World economies have been emerging for several centuries, following the tentacles of world trade. The first truly global organization evolved during the nineteenth century as the new urban-industrial heartlands of Western Europe and the northeastern United States grew into great "Thünen towns." Price gradients radiated from these regions (chapter 6) and Thünenization structured most land use and resource utilization (Chapter 7), save for Ricardian Development of tropical resources. As costs of transportation have fallen, Thünenization has become less important, however, and Ricardian Development has emerged as the more significant factor in land use: Environmental differences are of increasing importance to world patterns.

As transportation and communications technologies have been improved, the determinants of industrial location have shifted, too. Formerly transport-oriented to raw materials or markets (Chapter 8), internal and external economies of scale now are critical variables in industrial location (Chapter 9), as are the differences between small-firm and large-firm behavior. Many of the advantages that regions possess are created by dynamic externalities, rather than endowed. As a result, the new globalization appears to be producing new combinations of specialization and dispersion. What are evolving are new and unfamiliar modes of spatial organization, with attendant opportunities for educated people to shape this organization.

Technoeconomic Systems and Long Waves of Prices

Restructurings of the kind that is currently unfolding have occurred at 50 to 60 year intervals at least since the early stirrings of the Industrial Revolution in England in the 1770s and 1780s. To understand the underlying rhythms, it is necessary to understand the concepts of "technoeconomic systems" and "long waves of prices" and their interrelationships.

A *techno-economic system* is an interrelated set of technologies with which are associated particular sets of raw materials, sources of energy, and distinctive products. The emergence of a new technoeconomic system also involves the development of supportive infrastructures that open additional product and factor markets and contribute to the major surge of economic growth that new technoeconomic systems generate. Thus, the steam engine and the steel converter were interrelated technologies that depended on coal as an energy source, that generated a swarm of "downstream" metal-using industries and related technologies, including the steel-frame skyscraper that made the high-rise core of the industrial city possible, and required the development of the transcontinental railroad networks as their key transportation infrastructure. Deployment of this system drove economic growth in the second half of the nineteenth century, opening new resources and regions to development. But too much growth has its adverse consequences, placing pressures on raw-material supplies, and driving up prices. Decreasing returns set in. As growth opportunities vanish, all that is left of the rising tide is the inflationary pressure, resulting in a *stagflation crisis*—a combination of stagnation and inflation. It is in the aftermath of stagflation crises that technology transitions occur as new technoeconomic systems take over from those whose growth has ended.

U.S. history has been marked by the rise and fall of successive technoeconomic systems centering first on wind, water, and wood, next on coal, steam, and steel, and most recently on petroleum, internal combustion, and electricity. The interval from takeoff to market saturation of each of these new technologies has averaged some 50 to 60 years (Figure 10.1). Linked with these technoeconomic systems have been 50 to 60 year *long waves of prices*, shown in Figure 10.2. These waves are named for the Russian economist Nikolai Kondratiev, who first discovered them. As Figure 10.2 reveals, Kondratiev waves are characterized by accelerating rates of price increase from deflationary depressions (the 1840s and the 1890s) to inflationary peaks (1815, 1865, 1920, and 1980–1981), followed by decade-long plunges from the peaks to primary troughs (1825,

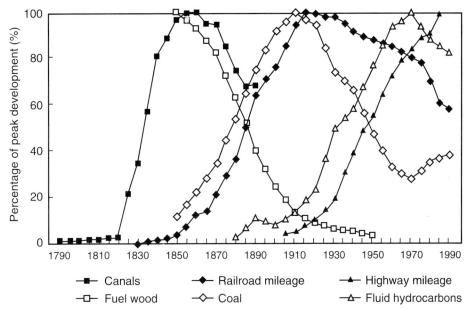

FIGURE 10.1   The rise and fall of successive technoeconomic systems in the United States. The canal, railroad, and highway networks are charted as their mileage increases to a peak, and then declines. The energy sources—fuel wood, coal, and fluid hydrocarbons—are charted as they rise to a maximum share of the nation's energy budget, and then decline. [*Source:* Berry, et al., 1993, pp. 111–135.]

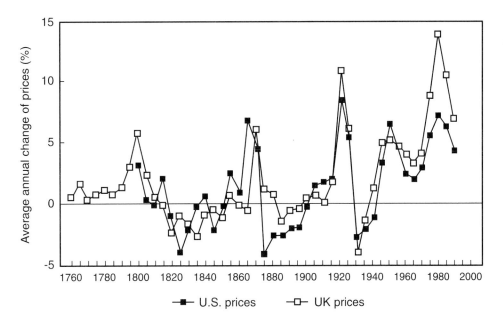

FIGURE 10.2   Long-wave price rhythms. Annual growth rates of prices are plotted, smoothed by a 10-year moving average, to reveal the long-wave pattern. Separate analyses for the United States and the UK produce remarkably similar results, suggesting that the rhythms are global, not confined to particular nation-states. [*Source:* Berry, et al., 1993, pp. 111–135.]

1873, 1929, and 1991), by weak recoveries, and then by sags into the next deflationary depressions. Figure 10.2 also reveals that the UK and U.S. long waves have been synchronized for at least 200 years. As more economies have joined the global system of markets, they, too, have come to experience the same rhythms.

The connection between technoeconomic systems and long waves of prices is the *growth logistic,*—a decadewide band of change that progresses along a half-century-long S-shaped path from "takeoff" in the decade following one long-wave peak to market saturation in the decade preceding the next peak. The growth logistic for the U.S. coal–steam–steel technoeconomic system is charted in Figure 10.3 against the backdrop of the long wave of prices. Note how the logistic topped out as the railroads reached their maximum development and further investment opportunities in the railroad and related industries dried up in the period of stagnation and rapid inflation (i.e., "stagflation") that lasted from 1907 to 1920. *Technology stalemates* are associated with stagflation crises. Box 10.1 presents Gerhard Mensch's "metamorphosis model," which postulates a critical role for technology stalemates in economic evolution, separating the growth logistic of successive technoeconomic systems.

Why should growth logistics and long waves last 50 to 60 years? The controlling variable is the time it takes to plan, finance, and develop the supportive infrastructure networks—the system of canals and inland waterways, the railroad network, the highway system. Why should growth logistics be separated by stagflation crises and technology stalemates? The controlling variable is the exhaustion of market opportunities for the old system, and the search for and deployment of alternatives.

Following a long-wave peak, the older technoeconomic system retrenches, and a substitute technoeconomic system begins its path of growth. The substitutions involve not only the resources that are demanded (producing transmaterialization in the primary sector) and the mode of production (e.g., the shift from steam to electricity in the secondary sector), but also the structure and mode of satisfying final demand (seen, e.g., in shifts in the tertiary sector, about which we will say more later). The crossover between the declining and the rising systems occurs midway between the long-wave peaks, in the deflationary depressions that separate successive long waves of prices. Thus, the 1890s saw the crossover between the wind–water–wood system and the coal–rail–steam system in the United States (Figure 10.1). The 50 to 60 year period of *market dominance* of technoeconomic systems thus corresponds with the depression-to-depression extent of successive long waves; their growth logistics, from innovation to maximum deployment, extend between adjacent pairs of long-wave peaks.

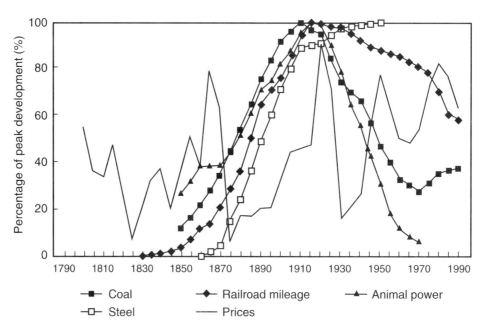

FIGURE 10.3   Relationship of technological expansion and the long wave. The coal–steel–railroad system's expansion to market saturation is plotted against the U.S. long wave of prices. Inflationary spirals follow market saturation of a technological regime and signal the decline of that regime and its replacement by a successor. Note the decadewide logistic of technological change. [*Source:* Berry, et al., 1993, pp.111–135.]

The First Wave

Each of the successive technoeconomic systems to emerge since the middle of the eighteenth century brought a wave of industrial revolution. As shown in Figure 10.4, the first wave unfolded in Great Britain in the 1770s. The major technologies triggering the change were in textile production, which was a cottage craft at the beginning of the eighteenth century. The key inventions mechanized the production of yarn and thread. By the end of the century, the handicraft cottage industry had given way to mills located where the power of falling water could be tapped to drive the new spinning machines. By 1812, the waterpowered spinning mule enabled a single worker to produce yarn 200 times faster than the pre–1770 spinner could. During the same period of time, major innovations also took place in the metal industries. These involved the substitution of coke (from coal) for charcoal (from progressively scarcer wood) in iron smelting, and the development of the "puddling furnace," which was used to convert crude pig iron into vastly superior wrought iron. The small furnaces of the old iron industry had been scattered in forested areas where charcoal could be produced; the new coke-using furnaces were located on the coalfields to minimize the costs of transporting that bulky raw material.

Coal mining expanded rapidly to meet the demand for the cheap alternative to charcoal. But more coal could only come from deeper mines, mines that were often waterlogged, a problem solved by James Watt's (1769) steam engine and his succeeding improvements to it. The steam engines burned coal and when, later, they were used in the new textile factories instead of waterpower, they produced yet another relocation of the textile industry from the scattered sites where falling water was available to the coalfields or to other spots where cheap water transport for coal was available. Mill towns developed around these locations.

The new spinning factories, with their central source of power, their batteries of expensive machines, and their large permanent working force, moved into lowland towns that were close to markets, to sources of supply, and to labor. Manchester had its first steam mill in 1787. By 1800, dozens of great mills were in operation, and Manchester had already become the prototype of the modern industrial city, along with the rapidly growing ironmaking towns of Birmingham and Sheffield in Britain's "Black Country."

The growing demand for cotton also led the economy of the recently formed United States to be fundamentally altered. The new nation quickly became the largest customer for British textiles and hardware and by far the largest supplier of the basic raw material for the spinning and weaving mills of Lancashire. Prior to 1786, the year before the first spinning mill was built in Manchester, no cotton was grown commercially in the United States. At first, it was grown only on the moist sea islands of Carolina and Georgia, the only areas suitable for the production of smooth-seed, long-staple cotton. The burry, prickly seeds in short-staple cotton made its cleaning too costly for commercial application. By 1792, however, farmers in the continental south were planting short-staple cotton in anticipation of the invention of an engine that could efficiently remove the burry seeds, however. The following year, Eli Whitney obliged, providing a classic example of an "induced invention." His cotton gin and the others that followed made possible the rapid spread of cotton culture, and with it slave labor, throughout the lower south. Because climatic and soil conditions prevented the production of other crops suitable to cultivation by slaves—rice, sugar, and tobacco—historians have often maintained that the cotton gin, by spreading slavery into these regions, was at least partly to blame for the American Civil War.

The factory and the industrial town spread rapidly in Great Britain and brought with them an enlarged urban

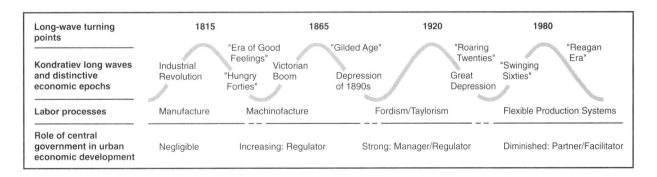

Long-wave turning points	1815	1865	1920	1980
Kondratiev long waves and distinctive economic epochs	Industrial Revolution	"Era of Good Feelings" Victorian "Hungry Boom Forties"	"Gilded Age" Depression of 1890s	"Roaring Twenties" "Swinging Great Sixties" Depression	"Reagan Era"
Labor processes	Manufacture	Machinofacture	Fordism/Taylorism	Flexible Production Systems
Role of central government in urban economic development	Negligible	Increasing: Regulator	Strong: Manager/Regulator	Diminished: Partner/Facilitator

FIGURE 10.4   The long waves summarized. [*Source:* Adapted with permission from Paul L. Knox, *Urbanization: An Introduction to Urban Geography* [Englewood Cliffs, NJ: Prentice Hall, 1994. p.9.]

BOX 10.1 *Mensch's Metamorphosis Model of Economic Evolution*

Following Nikolai Kondratiev's identification of 50 to 60 long-wave rhythms of prices, an Austrian economist, Joseph Schumpeter, argued that technology plays a key role in the long-wave phenomenon, writing that the "fundamental impulse" that sets and keeps the capitalist engine in motion comes from the new consumers' goods, the new methods of production and transportation, the new markets, and the new forms of industrial organization that the capitalist enterprise creates. The central driving force of long waves of prices was, he thought, *technological revolutions.* This idea has been systematized by a German economist, Gerhard Mensch, who has advanced a *metamorphosis model of industrial evolution* as the essential explanation for Kondratiev's long waves.

Mensch distinguished *scientific discovery and invention*—both of which, as S. C. Gilfillan pointed out in the 1930s, appear as a more or less steady stream in response to well-articulated social needs—from *innovation,* the practical application of the invention or idea. Innovations, Mensch discovered, tended to come in clusters or surges. Charting the dates of inventions and the basic innovations that followed them in the early nineteenth century (e.g., rolled wire invented 1773, innovation 1835, steam locomotive invented 1769, innovation 1824), he discovered one clustering of innovations in the period 1814–1828. Likewise, there was a clustering of innovations in electricity and chemistry in the period 1870–1886, and of early twentieth-century innovations in the years 1925–1939. Surprisingly, the periods of innovation appeared to begin in periods of depression that accompanied world economic crises.

Two questions therefore emerged: Why do innovations cluster? Why have the clusters coincided with depressions?

Mensch's important contribution was to cast light on these questions, tying together in an explanatory framework the empirical observations of Kondratiev and the technological innovation hypothesis of Schumpeter. His key concept was that of a *technological stalemate,* out of which an economy is ultimately eased by clusters of innovations implemented by a society from a reservoir of investment opportunities formed by a continuing stream of scientific discovery and practical inventions. New clusters of innovation produce a *structural metamorphosis* as old activities are cast off and replaced by revolutionary new ones.

Mensch's metamorphosis model postulates the following causal sequence:

1. A cluster of *basic innovations* introducing new branches of industry, and *radical improvement innovations,* which rejuvenate existing branches, occurs in response to a technological stalemate. Venture capital is attracted to the new lines of business. New demands are awakened.

2. Parallel S-shaped *product growth cycles,* perhaps substituting for older goods or services, characterize the new branches of industry. Initial entry is followed by rapid upswing, and then by accelerated growth until market saturation is reached.

3. During the new product upswing, investment, employment, and incomes increase rapidly, well ahead of prices and inflation, and lifestyles may well be revolutionized.

4. The revolutionary pioneering innovations are then followed by *routine improvement innovations* that rationalize production and increase capital intensity. But they find themselves subject to diminishing returns on the demand side and diminishing marginal utility on the supply side. The growth curve grades over from acceleration to deceleration. This is a natural phase of the *product life cycle of manufactured gods,* discussed by Raymond Vernon in 1966. As Vernon saw it, new products will tend to be introduced and produced initially in the biggest, richest markets, but as the market grows, the basis for competition gradually shifts from *performance* to *price.* To exploit economies of scale, this evolution requires standardization of the product and of the production technology. When the latter is sufficiently standardized, the optimum location for mass-production facilities moves away from the rich market to areas with lower labor or material costs. The predicted emigration of production (and jobs) is clearly visible in the case of textiles and shoes, cameras, watches, consumer electronics, steel, autos, bulk chemicals, and many other standard products. As the jobs are transplanted, so is the purchasing power of the workers. Thus, unless the emigration of older industries is more than compensated for by growth in newer, more innovative industries, economic stagnation is the consequence. It cannot be reversed by increased capital formation per se because the capital itself—being mobile—will also tend to move where returns are higher. The stagnation can only be reversed by the creation of new, more dynamic industries. In this view, the fundamental problem is a technological one.

5. But *corporate growth tends to overestimate domestic markets and produces excess supply and heated competition.* Almost inevitably, an industrial economy tends to overinvest in any new technology—capital goods industries in particular. For example, the latest wave of overinvestment began in the 1960s; worldwide overcapacity in steel, autos, diesel engines, chemicals, shipbuilding, and machine tools became apparent in the late 1970s. The automobile industry is the best recent illustration of how overinvestment occurs. In the postwar period, autos not only became one of the nation's largest industries, but also helped spur the growth of highways and spawned suburbs, which created new markets for homes, shopping centers, schools, and hospitals. Automobiles also influenced the location of plants and distribution centers. In the 1970s, however, with the stock of cars near a saturation

level and with consumers keeping them longer, autos became primarily a replacement market in which sales grew slowly if at all. Meanwhile, the nation had spent 25 years building up an enormous investment in industries—steel, machine tools, cement, glass, forest products—needed to produce cars and the many other products they helped create. As the auto industry waned, much of this investment became unusable.

6. There are two responses to excess supply:

(a) attempts to reduce competition by market segmentation and industrial mergers.

(b) attempts to segment domestic and foreign markets, "dumping" excess output.

Overinvestment breeds *pseudo-innovation* that benefits neither buyer nor seller, reflecting rather the attempt on the part of existing industries to protect their market shares by *product differentiation* in which the "image" or "packaging" of the product is changed, but no longer any of its basic qualities. The pace of change means that individual products have limited life cycles. This results in rapidly vanishing returns for a given product and intense competition to substitute new products. Ultimately, however, after repeated attempts to substitute new products by packaging "pseudo-innovations," the opportunities for further technological improvement are exhausted—the usable fund of ideas runs out. The economy enters a period in which output stagnates and industry leaders merge with other firms to create *oligopolies* that try to maintain their revenue growth by increasing prices. Definite *limits to growth* are encountered, markets are often flooded, key resources may be scarce, there is a slowdown in income and employment growth, and spreading stagnation. Rates of return decline, and capital is therefore not reinvested in existing lines of business: A huge money and capital market builds up instead. Funds move into currency speculation and paper investment and

there is a standstill in industrial investment, with money flowing into capital markets where returns are greater than in existing industries, but ceasing with rapid price inflation. Satiated markets also are accompanied by a *"dinosaur effect"* because the largest companies are the least innovative. Pseudo-innovations are a device by which producers seek dominance over a market segment. Consumers' choices become more limited as production concentrates in a few oligopolies. Producers can maximize profits and keep prices increasing by eliminating price competition. The attempt is to secure the bastions of established producers, because diminishing returns in existing branches of industry first lead to capital being used to protect markets via pseudo-innovations/market segmentation and acquisitions to limit competition.

7. The end result is a *technology stalemate* in which growth is replaced by stagnation and in which large-scale organizations seek to maintain the appearance of growth by controlling output and raising prices, inducing *stagflation*—the apparently antithetical but simultaneous conditions of recession and inflation. It is during this period that one sees increasing protectionism, yet it is overconcentration in leading industries that sets the price spiral into gear. Large-scale organizations that grow in the period of pseudo-innovation require and promote conservative patterns of investment: Risk taking in new ventures is minimized.

8. But as returns in older established industries are eliminated during the period of stagflation and vanish in the ensuing depression, new *venture capital* becomes available, seeking high-growth investment opportunities. The appearance of venture capital at this time results in a rush of attempts to convert many of the speculative inventions that had appeared since the preceding period of basic innovation into useful techniques or products. Much of investment produces a new upswing of growth. During the

upswing, dormant basic innovations attract capital and, via entrepreneurship, some begin to diffuse into economic use, although others will fail. The resulting new industries attract capital and labor from stagnant sectors, circumvent older resource scarcities, stimulate demand for new kinds of goods and services, and generally introduce the reinvigorating effects of a *structural transformation* of the economy.

This key idea that basic innovations produce structural changes in the economic system and drive the business cycle has, as we noted earlier, been most closely associated with the German economist Joseph Schumpeter. Mensch's contribution was to identify the precise circumstances when Shumpeter's "fundamental impulses" occur. He noted that "they do not simply fall from heaven." What determines them is the degree of stagnation of old technologies and the attractiveness of new alternatives. Stagnation reduces the usefulness and profitability of labor and capital in overgrown traditional business fields and induces the implementation of cost-saving and product-adding innovations. Labor is displaced and older privileged groups lose self-confidence. Sociopolitical conflict increases, and a variety of groups look to revolutionary change in the period of temporary instability—not only innovators looking to profit from new ventures, but also radical political reformers, because conditions of instability offer the opportunity for talented individuals to circumvent established social and power structures. The cycle appears to be approximately 50 years, or two generations.

References

Mensch, Gerhard. *Stalemate in Technology*. Cambridge, MA: Ballinger Books, 1979.

Note: This is a translation of Mensch's work, published earlier in German.

middle class, an industrial bourgeoisie, and a much larger working class. But the spread of this first Industrial Revolution beyond Britain was at first surprisingly slow. The French Revolution and the Napoleonic Wars and then-existing economic, political, and social structures delayed its spread to the Continent. But when it came, it came fast, as Britain moved into the second wave after 1815. In the United States, first-wave, urban-industrial development arrived only after canals had been built to open up the anthracite fields in eastern Pennsylvania. As coal began to course through the economy in the 1840s, the New England textile industry—largely waterpowered—reached maturity and an American iron industry boomed in eastern Pennsylvania. Once the railroad reached Pittsburgh, that city became America's Birmingham. By the 1850s, the U.S. northeast was undergoing as profound an economic and social transformation as Britain had half-century earlier, and the outlines of the nation's economic heartland, the northeastern manufacturing belt, took shape.

The Second Wave

The second wave of industrial revolution occurred in Britain, France, and Germany after the defeat of Napoleon. The key technological innovations were the application of steam power to water and land transportation and its diffusion throughout manufacturing, resulting in increased regional specialization and trade, the rapid growth of coalfield-, waterside-, and railroad-oriented industry, and the acceleration of urbanization and rural-to-urban migration.

The coming of the steam-powered "iron horse" running on iron rails (see Box 10.2), plus the coal-fired iron steamship, also produced a fundamental organizational invention, the formation of the modern multiunit enterprise with its hierarchy of salaried managers. This happened because the new forms of transportation and communication made possible a speed, regularity, and certainty in the movement of goods, messages, and people that had been unavailable before. The new speed and volume forced the railroads to build centrally controlled managerial organizations, if only to prevent trains from running into each other. Then much larger hierarchies became absolutely essential to guide the flow of millions of tons of a vast variety of raw materials and goods over distances of hundreds and even thousands of miles, to thousands of different destinations. One manifestation was the development of urban hierarchies to manage distribution (Box 10.3). The new speed, regularity, and reliability of transportation also made possible mass marketing of goods. Completely new types of enterprises—department stores, mail-order houses, and chain stores, all operated through managerial hierarchies—appeared, marketing an unprecedented volume of goods at very low prices from "high level" central places in the emergent urban hierarchies.

Application of steam power lagged in the United States, however, because of the impracticality of long hauls of coal or other bulk commodities with the comparatively light equipment and iron rails of the time. As a result, water-power sites continued to dominate industrial location. By 1870, waterwheels were still providing roughly half of the inanimate energy for manufacturing. Steam was not universally used in cotton mills in the United States until the railroads were sufficiently developed to transport coal cheaply. That ability came in the 1870s.

Nonetheless, important foundations for the future were being laid as the United States pioneered the *American System of Manufactures,* building a successful machine-tool industry to create interchangeable parts and, simultaneously, exploring notions of mechanical and press production. The United States was short of both machine tools and skilled machinists, and Britain refused to export machine tools until after 1843. Manufacturers in New England therefore concentrated on simplifying product design and rationalizing the production process to minimize the need for "fitting" parts together. The use of standardized interchangeable parts was perfected in the gun-manufacturing industry, where Eli Whitney of New Haven put into practice his idea that if gun parts were machined accurately enough, guns could be assembled from the first parts that came to hand, rather than from parts tailored to the individual gun, as was previously the custom. At the same time, the city engineer of New York, Marc Brunel, saw how to break down the job of making wooden blocks used in the rigging of men-of-war into a series of specific shapings. He took the idea to England and commissioned 43 specialized machines for the tasks from Henry Maudslay; with them, 10 men could do the work of 100.

Whitney's concept of interchangeable parts spread from the arms business to farm machinery, and then to almost all mechanical production. It required ever more precise machining to work; and ever more precise machining became available thanks to Henry Maudslay's lathes. Brunel's notion of cutting up work and creating specialized tools for each of the functions this division produced eventually led to twentieth-century mass production.

The Third Wave

The third wave of industrial revolution, shared by the United States and Germany, unfolded in the 1870s. Industrial growth also spread to new centers in Eastern Europe, Western Russian, and Japan. The key innovations were those permitting low-priced steel production, the harnessing of electric power, and the emergence of the modern chemical industry. Geographically, the consequence was the *heartland–hinterland pattern* of regional development within the United States and in the European nations' relations with their colonial empires (Box 10.4). An equally important ingredient was the creation of institutional arrangements that permitted the systematic application of science to the improvement of existing processes and products and to the development of new ones. By the 1890s, successful technological innovation was beginning to require more than just an individual innovator to develop the product and one or two entrepreneurs to build the organization to mass produce and to distribute it to national and world markets. In a few industries, technological advances became increasingly dependent on people trained in science and working in well-equipped laboratories to do the innovating, and then on teams of professional managers and engineers to bring the new product into full-scale production and widespread use.

During this wave, steel rails replace iron on both newly built and existing lines. Heavier equipment and more powerful locomotives permitted increased speed and the long haul of bulk goods on rail for the first time. Refrigerated cars made their entry, ushering in a new era of regional specialization in agriculture. For the first time, massive forces were arrayed that favored market orientation of industry. At the same time, the long rail haul spelled the doom of most passenger traffic and cargo movement on the inland waterways, especially the rivers.

As important in the long run as the introduction of the steel rail were inventions in electricity and magnetism. Electric street railways and lights were the first major applications, followed by such things as electric elevators, which along with steel permitted the development of the modern steel-framed skyscraper. After 1895, progress in electrification was extremely rapid. The cost of electricity fell rapidly as generating plants grew larger and increased in efficiency. By 1910, the major cities of Europe and the United States were electrified. Many urban homes had electric lights, and some had other electric appliances such as electric sewing machines, electric carpet sweepers, electric washing machines, and electric talking machines. However, the spread of the electric appliances into the average home took place mostly in the 1920s.

Another important new technology was the telephone, an outgrowth of research to improve the telegraph. The first switchboard went into operation in New Haven in 1878. By 1900, there were 1,500,000 phones in the United States, or 8 phones for every 100 persons, compared to 4 in Canada, 3 in Sweden, 2 in Switzerland, fewer than 1.5 in Germany and the United Kingdom and only 0.5 in France.

Accompanying these shifts, the modern industrial enterprise came into being by integrating the new mass production with the new mass distribution. In those industries where the existing wholesalers and the new mass retailers were unable to sell the output of the new processes in the volume that they were able to produce, enterprises began to build their own national wholesaling, and occasionally retailing, networks and their own extensive purchasing organizations, which often included control of raw materials: A strategy of vertical integration occurred in which independent marketers were unable to satisfy manufacturers' requirements.

In both the United States and Germany, organized research and development expanded during the third wave in private industrial laboratories. The process began in electricity. The most notable innovators, Thomas Edison and Werner von Siemens, worked in large, carefully organized laboratories, and soon the giant multifunctional organizations such as Edison, General Electric, and the Siemens Company in Germany, which had been created to make and sell their innovations, were relying, as were their competitors, on large research facilities to improve existing products and processes and to develop new ones.

Enterprises in other scientifically based industries quickly adopted the same strategy. In the chemical industries, the Germans led the way. Bayer, BASF, AFA, Hoechst, and other firms built their research laboratories in the 1880s and 1890s. In the United States, Du Pont and General Chemical followed suit in the first years of the new century. By the 1920s, laboratories in large chemical companies in the United States and Germany were turning out a stream of new synthetic products—dyes, pharmaceuticals, fertilizers, fabrics, plastics, detergents, paints, and films. By the 1920s, comparable laboratories were appearing in metals and machinery industries. Two-thirds of the personnel employed in industrial research in the United States were concentrated in five technologically advanced industries— 50 percent were in just two of these, electrical machinery and chemicals—and in these industries, by far the largest numbers were working in large, multifunctional corporations.

The Fourth Wave

Following World War I came a fourth spurt of technological change that finally ended in the stagflation crisis of the late 1970s. The foundations had been laid in Henry Ford's mass-production assembly lines—hence, the term "Fordist" to describe fourth-wave production—and in the great research laboratories that forged a clear link between research and development (R&D) and economic growth, a relationship that has persisted and that differentiates the economic performance of nation-states today (Box 10.5). The greatest impulse came with the rapid growth of industries based on new technologies—electronics, petrochemicals, and pharmaceuticals. These technologies created new markets. There was a rapid growth in demand for capital equipment, often of a new kind. The wealth generated caused an associated boom in demand for consumer durables, leading to the rapid growth of the automobile, aircraft, and consumer goods industries, of the supporting superhighway and airline infrastructures, of shopping centers and suburbs, and the decentralization and dispersion of growth.

BOX 10.2 *Diffusion of the Railroads*

Diffusion is the term used to describe the spread of innovations outward from centers of innovation. The time sequence involves a small band of "early adopters," followed by accelerated acceptance as a "bandwagon effect" takes hold, succeeded by a slowing rate of adoptions as laggards finally join in, and the potential market is saturated. The spatial pattern involves two elements: *hierarchical diffusion* and *spread effects*. Hierarchical diffusion is the tendency for inventions to be adopted in larger cities and markets first, and to diffuse down the urban hierarchy. A spread effect is the wavelike pattern of acceptance outwards from an urban center into a surrounding rural area.

Together, time-space sequences incorporate the following features of geographical diffusion:

1. Outwards from heartlands where circular and cumulative causation occurs into progressively more remote hinterlands
2. From large cities to small, down the urban hierarchy
3. From urban areas into their rural hinterlands

In each case the laggards benefit least.

An example of a typical time–space sequence is provided by the diffusion of the railroads, without which industrialization probably could not have run its course. Railroads represented the fastest means of transportation in the century preceding World War I (Fig. 10a). During the period that railroads were the best means of transportation available, railroad mileage grew in a logistic fashion of increasing then of decreasing rates of construction (Fig. 10b). The logistic increase of railroad mileage was accompanied by a lagged outward spread from the original center of the innovation, Great Britain, at an accelerating growth rate (Fig. 10b). The sequence was from the original headland of the Industrial Revolution, outwards into the world's hinterlands.

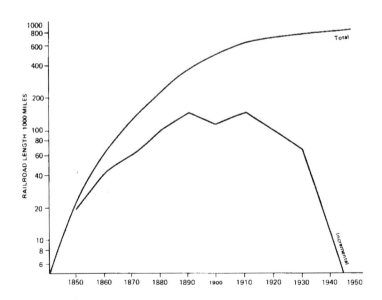

FIGURE 10a   World railroad building, 1840–1950. Most railroad mileage was built in the period when railraoads enjoyed a speed superiority over other modes. [*Source*: Alfred J. Lotka, Population Analysis as a Chapter in the Mathematical Theory of Evolution in W.E. Le Gros Clark and Peter P. Medawar (Eds.) *Essays on Growth and Form*, Oxford: Clarendon Press, 1965), p. 380.]

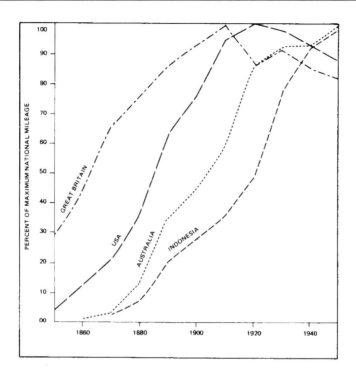

FIGURE 10b The logistic curves of railroad building for selected countries. [*Source*: W .S. Woytinski and E. S. Woytinski, *World Commerce and Governments*: Trends ane Outlook (New York: Twentieth Century Fund, 1955).]

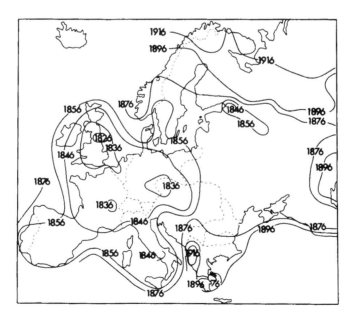

FIGURE 10c The diffusion and growth gradient of railroad building in Europe, 1826–1916. [*Source*: Sven Godlund, *Ein Innovationsverslauf in Europa, dargestellt in einer vorläufigen Untersuchung über die Ausbreitung der Eisenbahninnovation*, Series B in Geography, Human Geography Royal University of Lund, No. 6 Lund, Sweden:Department of Geography, 1952).]

BOX 10.3 The Concept of Urban Hierarchies and Central-Place Theory

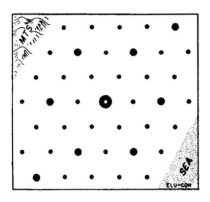

Theoretical distribution of central places. In a homogeneous land, settlements are evenly spaced; largest city in center surrounded by 6 medium-sized centers that in turn are surrounded by 6 small centers. Tributary areas are hexagons, the closest geometrical shapes to circles that completely fill area with no unserved spaces.

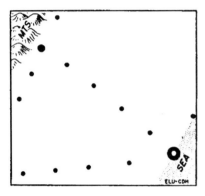

Transport centers, aligned along railroads or at coast. Large center is port; next largest railroad junction and engine-changing point where mountain and plain meet. Small centers perform break-of-bulk principally between rail and roads.

Specialized-function settlements. Large city is manufacturing and mining center surrounded by a cluster of smaller settlements located on a mineral deposit. Small centers on ocean and at edge of mountains are resorts.

There are many reasons for cities. *Transportation centers* perform break-of-bulk and allied services along transportation routes and tend to be arranged in linear patterns with respect to railroads, highways, coastlines, and rivers. *Specialized-function cities* perform services such as mining, manufacturing, or recreation. Because the principal localizing factor is often a particular resource such as a coalfield or a sandy beach and a warm sunny climate, such cities occur singly or in clusters. *Central places* organize retail and service business into *urban hierarchies*, which involve

1. a system of cities, arranged in a hierarchy according to the types of business provided by each
2. corresponding areas of urban influence or urban fields surrounding each city

The size and functions of a city and the extent of its urban field are proportional. Each region within the national economy focuses on a center of metropolitan rank. A network of intermetropolitan connections and interregional tradeflows links the regions into a national whole. The spatial incidence of economic growth within these regions is a function of distance from the metropolis. Troughs of economic backwardness lie in the most inaccessible areas along the intermetropolitan peripheries. Each major region is, in turn, subregionalized by successively smaller centers at progressively lower levels of the hierarchy—smaller cities, towns, or villages that function as market centers

FIGURE 10d   Differing patterns of urban location.[*Source*: Chauncy D. Harris and Edward L. Ullman, The Nature of Cities, reprinted from *Annals of the American Academy of Political and Social Science* (November 1945): 7–17, in Harold M. Mayer and Clyde F. Kohn (eds.), *Readings in Urban Geography* (Chicago: University of Chicago Psress, 1959), pp. 278–279.]

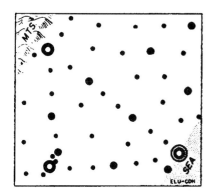

Theoretical composite grouping. Port becomes the metropolis and, although off center, serves as central place for whole area. Manufacturing-mining and junction centers are next largest. Railroad route in upper left has been diverted to pass through manufacturing and mining cluster. Distribution of settlements in upper right follows central-place arrangement.

for the distribution of goods and services to the region's consumers. The theory relating to urban hierarchies is called *central-place theory*.

Although many antecedents can be cited, the first explicit statement of central-place theory was made by the German geographer Walter Christaller in 1933 in a book entitled *Die zentralen Orte in Süddeutschland*. The Central Places in Southern Germany. The essential features of Christaller's argument may be summarized in six points.

1. The main function of a market town is to provide goods and services for a surrounding market area. Such towns are located centrally within their market areas, and hence they can be called "central places"'
2. The greater the number of goods and services provided, the higher is the *order* of the central place.
3. Low-order places offer convenience goods that are purchased frequently within small market areas and hence the range of low-order convenience goods (i.e., the maximum distance consumers are willing to travel) is small.
4. Higher-order places are fewer in number and are more widely spaced than lower-order places, providing goods with greater ranges. Generally, the greater the range, the greater is the *threshold* (i.e., the minimum sales level necessary for the seller to make a profit).
5. A *hierarchy* of central places exists to make as efficient as

possible the arrangement of convenience and shopping goods opportunities for consumers who have a basic desire to travel as little as possible to obtain the goods and services they need to maintain their households and persons, and for producers, who must earn at least a minimum 'threshold' to survive.
6. Hierarchies have three spatial forms, organized according to
   (a). a marketing principle
   (b). a transportation principle
   (c). an administrative principle

Christaller proceeded, in the manner of von Thünen and Weber, to a case in which extraneous variables were controlled by simplifying assumptions. Assume, he said, identical consumers distributed at uniform densities over an unbounded plain on which access is equally easy in any direction. Under such circumstances, the range of any good has a constant radius. How can centers be located so as to provide for the most efficient marketing of the goods? Given the homogeneity of the plain, Christaller concluded that each good should be supplied by a uniform net of equidistant central places, close enough together so that no part of the plain is left unsupplied.

The resulting distribution is one in which the central places are located at the apexes of a network of equilateral triangles, with each set of six centers forming a hexagon. This organization permits the maximum packing of central places into the plain.

BOX 10.4 Heartlands, Hinterlands, and Polarized Growth

Harvey Perloff, an American planner, together with several associates, has described the process by which *heartland-hinterland organization* emerged within the United States. They point out that North America's oldest cities were mercantile outposts of a hinterland resource area whose exploitation was organized by the developing metropolitan system of Western Europe. The initial impulses for independent urban growth came at the end of the eighteenth century when towns were becoming the outlets for capital accumulated in commercial agriculture and the centers of colonial development of the continental interior. Regional economies developed a certain archetype: a good deep-water pod as the nucleus of an agricultural hinterland well adapted for the production of a staple commodity in demand on the world market.

New resources became important from 1840–1850 onward, and new locational forces came into play. Foremost was a growing demand for iron, and later steel, and along with it rapid elaboration of productive technologies. Juxtaposition of coal, iron ore, and markets afforded the impetus for manufacturing growth in the northeastern United States, localized both by factors in the physical environment (minerals) and by locational forces created by prior growth along the East

Coast (linkages to succeeding stages of production, in turn located closer to markets). The heartland of the North American manufacturing belt therefore developed westward from New York in the area bounded by Lake Superior iron ores, the Pennsylvanian coalfields, and the capital, entrepreneurial experience, and engineering trades of the Northeast. This heartland became not only the heavy industrial center of the country, but remained the center of national demand, determining patterns of market accessibility through the 1960s. The heartland had initial advantages of both excellent agricultural resources and a key location in the minerals economy. With development, it grew into the urbanized center of the national market, setting the basic conditions for successive development of newer peripheral regions by reaching out to them as its input requirements expanded, and it thereby fostered specialization of regional roles in the national economy. The heartland experienced cumulative urban-industrial specialization, while each of the hinterlands found its comparative advantage based on narrow and intensive specialization in a few resource subsectors, diversifying only when the extent of specialization enabled the hinterland region to pass through that threshold scale of market necessary to

support profitable local enterprise. Flows of raw materials inward, and of finished products outward, articulated the whole.

Perloff concluded that the American economy could be divided into

> ...a great heartland nucleation of industry and the national market, the focus of large-scale national-serving industry, the seedbed of new industry responding to the dynamic structure of national final demand and the center of high levels of per capita income....[1]

and, standing in a dependent relationship to the heartland,

> ...radiating out across the national landscape...resource-dominant regional hinterlands specializing in the production of resource and intermediate outputs for which the heartland reaches out to satisfy the input requirements of its great manufacturing plants...in the hinterlands, resource-endow-

[1] Harvey S. Perloff, Edgar S. Dunn, Jr., Eric E. Lampard, and Richard F. Muth, *Regions, Resources and Economic Growth* (Lincoln: University of Nebraska Press, 1960), p. 51.

What was at the heart of the fourth wave? The spread and continued improvement of institutional arrangements and the exploitation of vast new sources of fossil fuels were probably the most important factors. Two fundamental institutional developments that influenced the continuing application of science to industrial activities were critical. One was the rapid spread of the multidivisional form of corporate organization, or "M Form" invented by Du Pont shortly after World War I. This form, by replacing the centrally controlled functional departments with autonomous, self-contained product or regional divisions, permitted enterprises to move rapidly into new products and new markets. Facilitating product diversification, the M Form greatly enhanced the potential value of the industrial research laboratory and furthered the continuing flow of new products into the economy. The other basic institutional development was the creation of new ties

between corporations, universities, and the government The prototype was the Manhattan Project, where the technology of the atom bomb was developed in the universities, the facilities for production as well as the product itself were created by industrial contractors such as Du Pont, and the federal government funded and coordinated the project as a whole.

The continuing military demands of the Cold War stimulated other forms of institutional linkages among business, government, and the universities. In rapidly moving technologies, faculty members and Ph.D.'s from places like MIT and Stanford built their own enterprises to serve specialized markets. Once technologically advanced products were mass produced for national and international markets, large enterprises took over, however, as IBM demonstrated in computers, Boeing in the aircraft industry, and Xerox in copying machines.

ment is a critical determinant of the particular cumulative advantage of the region and hence its growth potential.[2]

Others have argued similarly with respect to both the European and the global case. V. I. Lenin, for example, presented a *colonial model of world spatial organization* in which he argued that since the early nineteenth century the economic geography of the world has been organized by and for the benefit of the industrial countries. The German location economist Andreas Predöhl gave the notion more substance when he described how, during the early nineteenth century, Britain became the focus of a unicentric world economy that, with the growth of new industrial core regions, has now become multicentric, with the rest of the world organized to produce raw materials for and to consume the products of the industrial heartlands. Europe was divided into an industrial heartland and agricultural hinterland by F. Delaisi in 1929 in a book with the graphic title *Les Deux Europes: Europe industrielle et Europe agricole (The Two Europes: Industrial Europe and Agricultural Europe)*. Subsequent researchers have identified a regular pattern of distance decay in agricul-

[2] ibid

tural productivity and per capita income from the European heartland, as was noted in Chapter 7, so that agricultural productivity is actually higher in 'industrial' Europe than in "agricultural" Europe.

More recently, international heartland-hinterland contrasts have been identified by Raul Prebisch, who divides the world into an industrial center and a primary-producing periphery, and who blames much of the economic difficulties of the periphery on what he considers to be a long-term deterioration of the periphery's terms of trade. John Friedmann, in turn, attempted to elaborate the heartland-hinterland model as a general theory of polarized growth applying at all geographic scales.

Friedmann's paradigm was presented as an intellectual framework for the study of the processes—economic, social, and political—that act to create heartland-hinterland contrasts. Heartlands are defined by Friedmann as territorially organized subsystems of society possessing a high capacity for generating innovative change. Hinterlands are all the regions beyond the heartlands whose growth and change are determined by their dependency relationships to the heartlands. Heartlands share in common a heavy concentration of their

labor force in manufacturing (secondary) activity and advanced (quaternary) services, representing a shift from development based on natural resources to development based on human resources.

At both national and global scales, heartlands set the developmental path for the hinterlands, stimulating economic growth in the peripheries differentially according to the resource needs of heartland industries and consumers. Complementarities in the availability of factors of production between heartland and hinterland lay the foundations for interaction. Improvements in transportation and the organization of trade increase the transferability of staples from hinterland to heartland. Intervening opportunities impose spatial regularities in the timing of hinterland development and sequence the order in which unsettled areas and areas with a subsistence economy are drawn into the heartland's sphere of influence.

Friedmann saw the diffusion of innovations from the core as controlling system growth and the form of the heartland-hinterland relationship affecting economic activity and settlement patterns, sociocultural traditions and values, and the organization of power not only in the core, but also in the periphery. The periphery is thus dependent on the core in all respects.

These institutional developments provided one pillar for postwar economic growth. The coming of cheap oil was another essential pillar. Because oil and gas were less costly to extract, transport, and deliver than coal, and because they were more concentrated and flexible fuels, they had already begun to replace coal in the interwar years. Nevertheless, it was only after World War II that advanced industrial economies became addicted to petroleum. In 1945, coal still accounted for 53.4 percent of the energy consumed. Then the oil fields of the Persian Gulf came into full production, and the crossover from coal- to oil-based energy occurred. As the supply poured out, the price dropped. Suddenly everyone was converting to oil. The utilities did so massively. By the 1960s, the diesel locomotive had made the steam locomotive an historic relic. Chemical companies that had relied almost entirely on coal for the feed stocks in the rapidly growing production of synthetics turned to oil,

and oil companies integrated forward into chemicals. By the mid-1950s, coal had become a sick industry. By 1960, it produced only 28 percent of U.S. energy. The figures for the transformation in Europe are even more striking.

THE FIFTH WAVE

The mass-production technologies of the fourth wave reached market saturation in the 1970s and began their decline after the long-wave peak of 1980–1981, confirming yet again the relationship between the rise and fall of successive technological systems and the 50 to 60 year long waves of prices. Simultaneously, the spread of markets enabled individual countries' long waves to become increasingly tightly interlocked on a global basis. During the 1980s, yet another technological transition took shape

BOX 10.5 R & D and Economic Growth

In an article entitled Why Growth Rates Differ in Giovanni Dosi, et al.,(Eds.), *Technical Change and Economic Theory* (London: Pinter Publishers 1988), pp. 432–438, Jan Fagerberg provides startling graphic evidence of the relationship between per capita GDP, R&D expenditures as a percentage of GDP, and the magni-

tude of patent applications. His data, which deal with 27 North American, European, Central and South American, and East and South Asia industrial or industrializing nations for the period 1973–1983 are presented in the two graphs (Figures 10e and 10f). The R&D percentage goes up at an increasing rate with higher levels of

economic development (the GDP data are in thousands of dollars). The relationship is even sharper for levels of patenting activity, the results of R&D, indicating that increases in the magnitude of a nation's research effort stimulate even greater increases in the volume of useful (that is, patentable) inventions.

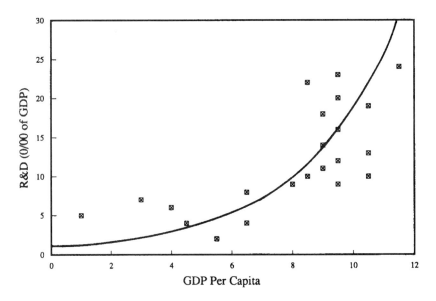

FIGURE 10e   SRelationship between R&D expenditures and levels of economic development.

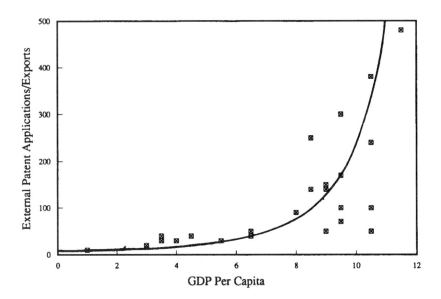

FIGURE 10f   Relationship between patenting activity and economic development

as innovative firms brought a new thrust of growth to the economy. As the old manufacturing industries collapsed, the principal contributions to growth have come from the *advanced services sector* whose defining feature is that it *creates and uses knowledge products* in exactly the way that older manufacturing industry transformed raw materials into finished products. The supporting infrastructure is that of *cyberspace* on the *Internet,* the global "information superhighway."

The Service Industries: An Historical Aside

Another term that has been used to describe the service industries is the *tertiary sector,* but as we shall see, this term fails to capture the nature of advanced services. The term was introduced in the 1920s by Irving Fisher, and popularized in 1940 by economist Colin Clark in a book entitled *The Conditions of Economic Progress.* Clark argued that

> for convenience in international comparisons production may be defined as primary, secondary and tertiary. Under the former we include agricultural and pastoral production, fishing, forestry and hunting. Mining is more properly included with secondary production, covering manufacture, building construction and public works, gas and electricity supply. Tertiary production is defined by difference as consisting of all other economic activities, the principal of which are...commerce and distribution, transport, public administration, domestic, personal and professional services . . . Studying economic progress in relation to the economic structure of different countries, we find a very firmly established generalization that a high average level of real income per head is always associated with a high proportion of the working population engaged in tertiary industries....Low real income per head is always associated with a low proportion of the working population engaged in tertiary production and a high percentage in primary production....High average real income per head compels a large proportion of producers to engage in tertiary production even in countries which are supposed to be predominantly agricultural....The reasons for this growth of the relative number of tertiary producers must largely be sought on the demand side. As incomes rise the demand for such services increases, and being non-transportable they must be supplied by workers within the country concerned.

Clark's argument certainly seemed to be borne out when the first data on employment patterns across the globe became available in 1950 (Figures 10.5 and 10.6). All world regions have experienced rapid tertiary-sector growth in the four decades since 1950 (Figure 10.7).

Problems with Clark's definition were soon identified, however. P.T. Bauer and B.S. Yamey (1953) wrote that "Tertiary production is an aggregation of many dissimilar

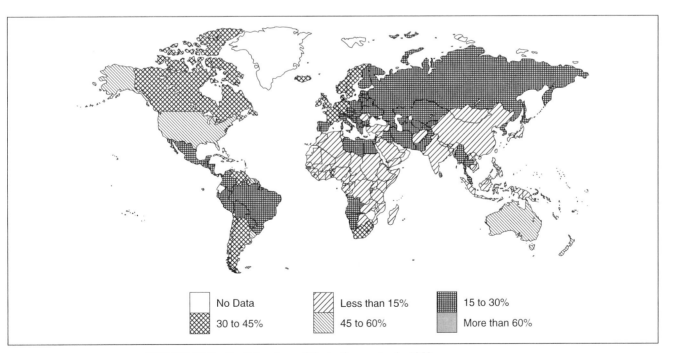

FIGURE 10.5   Spatial pattern of the tertiary sector in 1950.

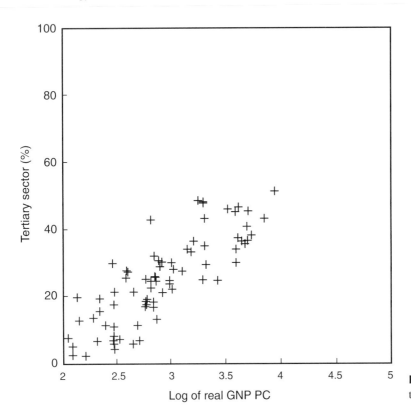

FIGURE 10.6   Relationship of the tertiary sector to levels of income of nation-states in 1950.

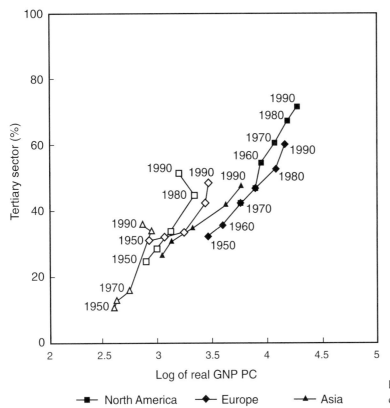

| ■— | North America | ◆— | Europe | ▲— | Asia |
| –□– | Latin America | –◇– | Middle East | –△– | Africa |

FIGURE 10.7   Mean levels of the tertiary percentage and of real per capita GNP for continental groups for the years 1950–1990.

activities.…There is no reason why the demand for every one of these should follow a common trend. The only feature common to all tertiary production is that the output is non-material."

A solution to this problem of heterogeneity came when Nelson Foote and Paul Hatt (1953) argued that the tertiary sector should be broken down into three distinct categories:

The first of these categories we shall call *tertiary* industries, defined as domestic and quasi-domestic services: restaurants and hotels, and beauty shops, laundry and dry cleaning, repairing and maintenance, and the sprinkling of handicrafts.…Next, under the caption of *quaternary* industries we shall group transport, commerce, communication, finance, and administration. The principle governing this grouping is that these are the industries which facilitate or effectuate the division of labor. Their office is to knit together in a working system the specialized producers of raw materials, manufactured goods, and other services. Logically and empirically, *quinary* industries as we shall define them…comprise medical care, education, research, and recreation (including the arts). The principle which guides this grouping is that they all have to do with the refinement and extension of human capacities. They differ from the domestic and quasi-domestic tertiary industries in that they are not devoted simply to the maintenance of individuals in the style to which they are accustomed but to the cultivation of behavior to which they are not accustomed. It might almost be said that in the sequence of social and economic development, their office has emerged as that of *engendering social and economic development itself. The product of their operations is to feed back into the working of the (economy) new increments of ability, skill, and knowledge* [italics added].

In 1974, sociologist Daniel Bell associated the quaternary and quinary sectors with what he called "the coming of postindustrial society"—an emergent transformation of the United States that was evolving along a series of dimensions:

- *Economic sector:* the change from a goods-producing to a service economy.
- *Occupational distribution:* the preeminence of the professional and technical class.
- *"Axial principle:"* the centrality of theoretical knowledge as the source of innovation and of policy formulation for the society.
- *Future orientation:* the control of technology and technological assessment.

- *Decision-making:* the creation of a new "intellectual technology."

Bell forecast the emergence of a new form of society with new leading sectors and geographies that contrasted sharply with those of preindustrial and industrial society. Table 10.1 summarizes and extends Bell's construct. Postindustrial society is seen as an outgrowth of the emergence of the quaternary and quinary sectors as the driving forces in economic growth.

If the changing sectoral composition of employment in the United States between 1900 and 1990 is examined using the five-part sectoral subdivision, an interesting pattern emerges (Figure 10.8). The proportional share of the *tertiary sector, providing services directly to the consumer,* has remained relatively constant throughout the twentieth century. The major shift in shares after the 1920 long-wave peak involved significant expansion of the *quaternary sector, the sector responsible for effectuating and transforming mass production,* whereas the most significant changes athwart the 1980 long-wave peak have involved rapid expansion of the *quinary sector, the sector responsible for engineering new social and economic development.*

With each of these shifts has come a new and different geography. That of the traditional tertiary sector, providing goods and services directly to consumers, is described by central-place theory (Box 10.3), and consists of urban hierarchies. That of the quaternary sector, providing services directly to producers, emerged from the increasing economies of scale made possible by mass-production technologies. Increasing internal economies of scale resulted in a shift of managerial emphasis from the level of the individual firm to that of the multiestablishment enterprise. Such functions as inventory control, purchasing, advertising, promotion of brand names, and long-term financing could be shifted to the level of head offices, restricting the functions of individual firms to the delivery of the main line product or service. As a result, a new geography of nodal centers emerged, sitting atop local hierarchies of central places still predominantly involved in the face-to-face delivery of goods and services to the consuming public at the tertiary level. Stanback et al. (1981) argue these high-level quaternary sector nodes include

(i) *National nodal centers,* metropolitan complexes in which there is a massive concentration of corporation headquarters, banking activity, and great intensity and diversity of specialist producer services, including advertising, consulting, and investment banking.

(ii) *Regional nodal centers,* smaller metropolitan bases from which large corporations can

TABLE 10.1

Contrasting attributes of preindustrial, industrial, and postindustrial societies (modified from Bell, 1974)

	Preindustrial	Industrial	Postindustrial
Principal economic sector	Primary Extractive Agriculture Mining Fishing Timber	Secondary Goods producing Manufacturing Processing Tertiary Transportation Utilities Trade	Quaternary Finance Insurance Real estate Quinary Health, education, research, government, recreation
Technology	Sun, wind, and water	Inanimate energy	Information
Occupations	Farmers Miners Fishermen Unskilled	Semiskilled worker Engineers	Professional and technical workers Scientists
Methodology	Common-sense experience	Empiricism and experimentation	Abstract reasoning, decision theory, systems analysis
Time perspective	Orientation to past practices	Ad hoc adaptiveness	Future orientation, simulation
Axial principle	Traditionalism: land-resource limitation	Economic growth	Theoretical knowledge

administer their industrial and commercial operations in a country's main regional markets.

Figure 10.9 captures the resulting spatial pattern in the United States both in terms of the metropolitan areas in which corporations valued at more than $1 billion by the stock market in 1991 were headquartered (upper map) and in terms of the total market values of these corporations (lower map). The preeminence of New York is evident, together with Chicago, Los Angeles, Dallas, Atlanta, and San Francisco—the nation's key national-level hubs. Complementing these are 77 other metropolitan areas that serve as either regional nodes or the centers of specialized production districts that have arisen out of external economies, the second of the arenas in which producer services have emerged. As we saw in Chapter 9, external economies involve the growth of specialist firms that undertake part of the production process on more favorable terms than internal departments or divisions, providing "intermediate" goods and services that are delivered to producers rather than to final consumers. The economies are either industry-specific ("localization" economies) or place-specific ("urbanization" economies).

Advanced Services-Sector Expansion

With the structural transformation that occurred astride the 1980 Kondratiev peak has come yet another type of service-sector growth. What is distinctive about this growth is that it is not caused by increasing wealth, as was the case with the traditional tertiary sector. Nor does it arise out of the economies of large-scale production, as was the case with the initial rounds of quaternary-sector growth. The services that have been growing have not been services in the traditional sense at all, but new kinds of specialized technical and business activities, and a variety of public and not-for-profit organizations. Their defining feature is that they create and use knowledge products in exactly the way that the manufacturing industry transforms raw materials into physical products. They have become the driving forces of the modern *thoughtware economy,* the leading sectors that, simultaneously, are helping to restructure the geography of the manufacturing industry because they are the root sources of most of the productivity increases in manufacturing: technological innovation, better resource allocation, and better education.

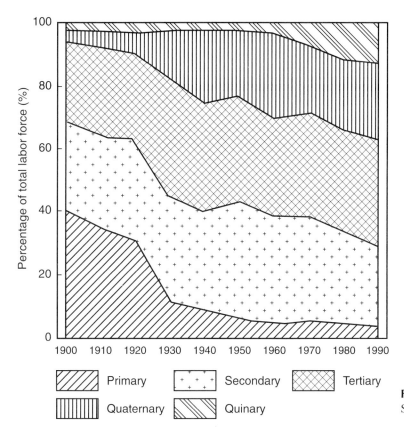

FIGURE 10.8 Sectoral shifts in the United States, 1900–1990.

According to Nusbaumer (1987), the major functions of these advanced services are (1) *knowledge carrying,* including education and training, producer services, business services and other forms of advisory services; (2) *linkage forming,* including establishment of channels of communication and the means for carrying information, as well as creation of markets; (3) *communication,* the actual information transmission process, which combines with the linkage function to reduce distance and support the market system; and (4) *information,* the content that is transmitted. The advanced services sector permits business to be conducted more efficiently and effectively, bringing resource use closer to the theoretical maximum. Thoughtware production involves research-and-development activities in the broadest sense of the term: management and management support; analysis; and activities that seek to identify and reduce risk, to assure health and safety, to simplify products, to assure performance, and to increase both quality of product and of life (Table 10.2). The fruits are in "high-tech" industry: micro processors, robots, genetic engineering, and space, together with better information processing and management built around computers and inexpensive electronic communicators.

Cyberspace and the Internet

Central to the emergent thoughtware economy is *information.* What microelectronics does is to process and generate information. What telecommunications does is to transmit information at increasingly greater speed and lower cost, completing the process of compression of time and space that began early in the Industrial Revolution (Figure 10.10). What automation does is to introduce preinformed devices in other activities. What genetic engineering does is to decode the information system of living matter and to try to reprogram it. Whereas traditional manufacturing produced "congealed resources" like iron and chemicals that faced diminishing returns, the new thoughtware economy creates products that are largely "congealed knowledge" that display increasing returns.

Critical to the growth of thoughtware technology is a new information infrastructure, *cyberspace,* the emerging electronic culture of computers and networks, information systems and software, that exists on the *Internet.* Cyberspace, a term coined by William Gibson in his 1984 novel *Neuromancer,* is to the fifth wave what railroads were to the third and highways/airways were to the fourth. The Internet is a worldwide system of computer networks, a "network of networks." It had its origins in the U.S. Department of Defense's Advanced Research Projects Agency Network, the *Arpanet,* and was made possible by Vinton G. Cerf, senior vice president of data architecture for MCI's Data Services Division, who, in 1973, began work on *TCP/IP* (Transmission Control Proctocol/Internet Proctocol), the set of rules used by networks on the Internet

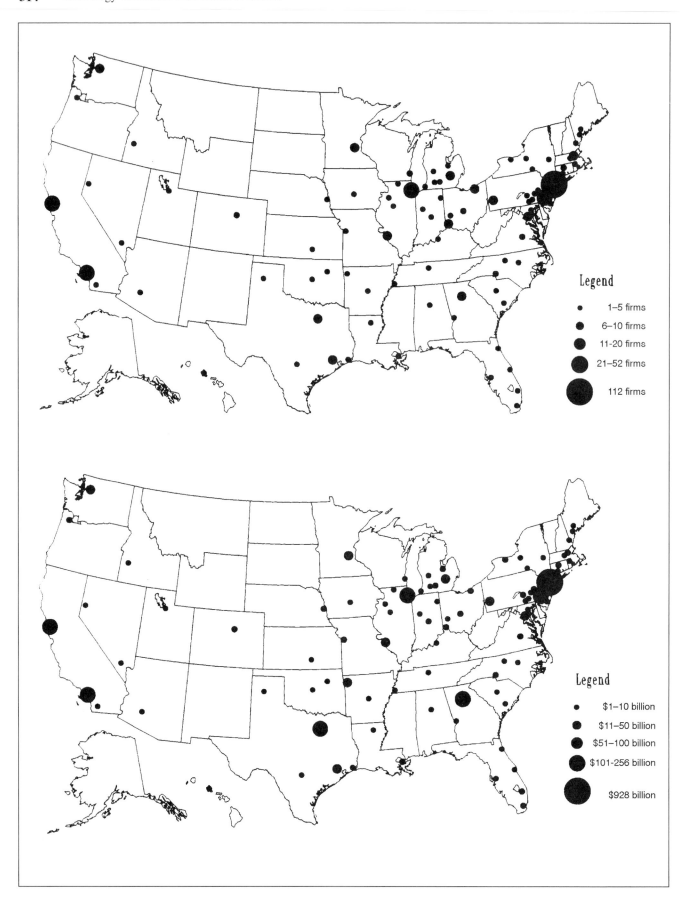

TABLE 10.2
Advanced services classified by function

Knowledge-Carrying Function	Linkage Function	Communication Function	Information Function
Education	Brokerage	Fiberoptics and satellites	Databases
Training	Rentals and leasing	Telephone and telegraph	Data processing
Painters, sculptors, composers	Banking and other	Mail services	Marketing
Consultancy	financial services	Performing arts	Cultural services
Engineering	Insurance, and	Radio and TV broadcasting	News services
Religious services	reinsurance	Advertising	Business management
Medical services	Diplomatic services	Franchising	Library services
Defense services			
Legal services			
Sports instruction			
Supervisory services			
Computer software and data-processing services			
Laboratory services			
Architecture and design			
Administration, including police			
Accountancy and audit			

Source: Adapted from Nusbaumer, 1987.

to communicate with each other. Evolving rapidly, the present Internet bears a relationship to the global networks of the future that the nation's highways of 1920—a loose and only partially improved agglomeration of farm-to-market roads—bore with respect to today's Interstate Highway System. It currently is connected via a diverse set of copper-wire channels, supplemented by the fiber-optic cables that breakthroughs in laser design made possible in the 1980s, by microwave communications, and prospectively by global satellite networks that will be connected directly to the Internet via small satellite dish antennas and that will provide medium- and high-speed data transmission. Currently U.S. connections to the Internet are doubling every few months.

The Internet Society gives the following members for Internet "hosts"—computers connected to the net—in August 1995:

North America	4,541,470
Western Europe	1,463,870
Pacific	251,320
(Australia 207,426)	
Asia	299,854
Eastern Europe	66,998
Africa	41,416
(S. Africa 41,329)	
Latin America	27,069
Middle East	19,548

What is evident are the distinctions between the "connected" and the "unconnected," causing many to worry about another source of inequality between the world's rich and poor. Currently, the Internet is the tool of the world's English-speaking societies.

But today's Internet is but a precursor of the global information structure of the future. Diffusion will take place, even if it unfolds over decades, and the net itself will be reshaped and enhanced many times over. Nonetheless, certain characteristics of cyberspace already have emerged that seem likely to shape its future evolution, just as Stevenson's early "standard gauge" came to structure railroad development. The fundamental property is that the information accessible on the *World Wide Web*, the multimedia branch of the Internet invented by Englishman Tim

FIGURE 10.9 Metropolitan locations of "billion dollar plus" corporations in the United States in 1991. The upper map plots numbers of corporations valued in the market at more than a billion dollars in 1991 by the metropolitan areas in which their headquarters were located. The lower map shows the total market value of these corporations. [*Source:* The Top 1000 U.S. Companies Ranked by Stock-Market Value, *Business Week*, 1992 Special Bonus Issue.]

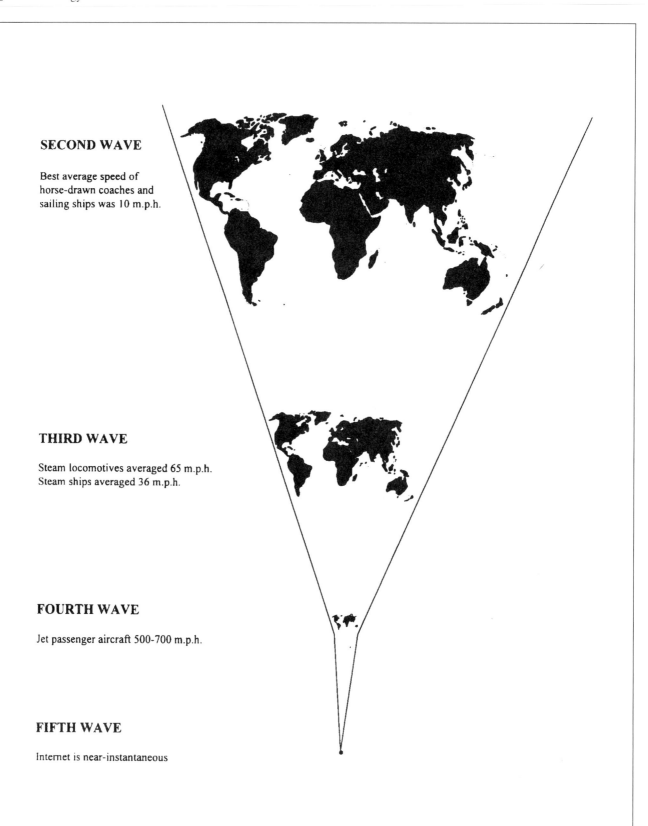

SECOND WAVE

Best average speed of
horse-drawn coaches and
sailing ships was 10 m.p.h.

THIRD WAVE

Steam locomotives averaged 65 m.p.h.
Steam ships averaged 36 m.p.h.

FOURTH WAVE

Jet passenger aircraft 500-700 m.p.h.

FIFTH WAVE

Internet is near-instantaneous

FIGURE 10.10   Time–space compression in successive waves of the Industrial Revolution

Berners-Lee, is available instantaneously and universally, without regard to origin. Soon, software will also reside in the net rather than in individual workstations. As the costs of communication continue to plummet and the means and quality of interchange to improve, a second property is that cyberspace is developing a particular culture—a radical libertarianism that is devoted to preventing regulatory control of a domain in which location, class, hierarchy, race, gender, or physical disability matter for little. Cyberspace has already become egalitarian, democratic, and individualistic, projecting core Western values. As such, it threatens tradition and authority. It is a domain that is easy to enter. It is one where people can connect directly to other people using *e-mail,* or via special interest *Bulletin Boards, Chat Lines,* and *Usenet Groups* without the influence of mediating institutions, an environment where frankness is not constrained by social convention. Participants are simultaneously everywhere and nowhere: The Internet is universal and ubiquitous.

This led *The Economist* for September 30, 1995 to opine that "As a result, one of the most important limits imposed by geography on human activities will eventually vanish. *The demise of distance as the key to the cost of communication may well prove to be the most significant economic force shaping the next half century"* [p. 15; italics added]. "It will alter, in ways that are only dimly imaginable, decisions about where people live and work; concepts of national borders; patterns of international trade" [p. 5, special section entitled *The Death of Distance*].

Cyberspace not only provides access to information resources, it also enables multiple communities of interest to coexist without competing territorial claims. It is offering increasing numbers of opportunities to meet in *virtual spaces* where alternatives can be experienced before choices must be made, and it even enables individuals to seek pleasure and enlightenment, or to hone special skills, in virtual worlds that might never be. Just as the first steam engine, developed in Devonshire, but first applied to lifting water out of coal mines in Staffordshire, ultimately transformed transportation, factory production, and energy use, the low-cost communication potentialities of cyberspace are changing both what is produced and consumed, and how and where people learn, work, shop, and relax in ways that the innovators could never contemplate.

What will this new world be like? *The Economist* continues (pp. 27–28):

> The death of distance will mean that any activity that relies on a screen or a telephone can be carried out anywhere in the world. Services as diverse as designing an engine, monitoring a security camera, selling insurance or running a secretarial paging service will become as easily exportable as car parts or refrigerators. Already, first glimpses of this world are beginning to appear. A flourishing computer-software industry has grown up around Bangalore, India, following initial investments in the area by Texas Instruments Inc., and later by Digital Equipment Co. (DEC), Hewlett-Packard, Siemens, and Motorola, drawn by low-cost high-quality English-speaking Indian software engineers. Its exports more than doubled between 1990 and 1993, to $270m, and its 800 software companies are now attracting back-office work from airlines such as Swissair and British Airways. Similarly, some of Hong Kong's paging services are manned from China. In Perth, in Western Australia, EMS Control Systems monitors the air-conditioning, lighting, lifts and security in office blocks in Singapore, Malaysia, Sri Lanka, Indonesia and Taiwan....

> All this will expose white-collar workers in rich countries to the same competitive pressures that have already squeezed manufacturing workers. But it will also offer educated workers in poor countries the chance to attain a standard of living that they can now get only by emigrating.

> Countries that want to take a share of such markets have a huge incentive to make telecommunications as inexpensive as possible. That is a lesson few developing countries have yet learnt. Among the exceptions are some Asian countries such as Malaysia and South Korea, which are installing state-of-the-art telecommunications networks and have a relatively high density of telephone lines....

> Within countries, work-related travel may decline, and so may the demand for office buildings, as people increasingly work from home....

> Many services now provided by government will be changed out of recognition. Welfare and social-insurance payments will increasingly be made by plastic card rather than by relays of officials....

> But some caveats also are offered:

> Predicting the future of a new technology is a mug's game. Marconi thought radio would be useful mainly for ship-to-shore calls. Guessing the social impact of a new technology is even more hazardous. Who would have foreseen that the invention of the post box would contribute to women's liberation—by enabling new generations of young ladies to post letters to their sweethearts without their parents' knowledge?

Flexible Manufacturing Systems

One important outcome of more and better thoughtware is the growth of flexible manufacturing systems (FMS), which complete the process of factory automation that began back in the 1950s and support new kinds of *economies of scope* that arise not from multiproduct multidivisional organization, but on the production line itself. First came numerically controlled machines driven by coded instructions on paper or Mylar tape. Then came computer-aided design and computer-aided manufacturing, or CAD/CAM, which replaced the drafting board with the CRT screen and the numerically controlled tape with the computer. The new production systems integrate all these elements. They consist of computer-controlled machining centers that sculpt complicated parts at high speed and with great reliability, robots that handle the parts, and remotely guided carts that deliver materials. The components are linked by electronic controls that dictate what will happen at each stage of the manufacturing sequence, even automatically replacing worn-out or broken drill bits and other implements.

Flexible automation provides the capacity to manufacture goods cheaply in small volumes. Ever since Henry Ford's organizational innovation, the unchallenged low-cost production system has been Fordist "hard automation" that stamps out look-alike parts in huge volume. Under hard automation, the greatest economies were realized only at the most massive scales. Flexible automation makes similar economies available at a wide range of scales, so that fragmented and fast-changing markets can be served quickly and efficiently. The key is the embodiment of the necessary information inside the machine tools. A flexible automation system can turn out a small batch or even a single copy of a product as efficiently as a production line designed to turn out a million identical items.

This capability has transformed economies of scope. The manufacturer is able to meet a far greater array of market needs, including quick-changing ones, and to reduce or eliminate warehousing in anticipation of future demand. Manufacturers can keep up with changing fashions in the marketplace by taking full advantage of computer-aided design free from the tyranny of large-scale investments in hard automation. This allows construction of smaller plants and permits fast-thinking manufacturers to move swiftly into new fields and to leave them just as swiftly if need be, at the expense of less agile and older producers.

Interestingly, there are international differences in these new thoughtware-driven, high-performance workplaces. The April 9, 1994 issue of *The Economist* summarizes them as follows:

- The most familiar model is the Japanese one of "lean production," spread by car makers like Toyota, which whittled down stocks and used teams of workers to eliminate bottlenecks, guarantee quality, and institutionalize continuous improvement. It has resulted in a dramatic fall in how long it takes to make things.
- The (northern) Italians excel at "flexible specialization," using industrial networks to combine the virtues of small firms (timeliness, customization) with the advantages of giant organizations (economies of scale, global reach). Benetton, a clothes firm, uses its fluid relationship with a myriad of suppliers, some specializing in design, others in manufacturing, to pander to the public's whims.
- The Germans specialize in "diversified quality," producing short batches of luxury goods such as cars and machine tools. German managers insist that their traditional advantage in this area, their highly skilled work force, is being reinforced by information technology, which is making it easier to combine the virtues of craft and mass production.
- The Swedish approach centers on autonomous teams of highly skilled craftsmen. In Volvo's Uddevalla plant, teams are responsible for assembling entire cars and have direct contact with customers.
- The American approach is eclectic, combining the best of the preceding: quality circles from Japan, apprenticeships from Germany, and especially lean production and team production. The two latter models have a lot in common, notably an enthusiasm for sacking middle managers and introducing computers. But they differ in the power they devolve to workers. The lean-production model relies on centralized coordination and performance indicators. Marlow Industries, a Dallas-based manufacturer of thermoelectric coolers, has improved quality through extensive measurement of performance. The team model relies on workers to make decisions and produce innovations. At IBM's plant at Charlotte, North Carolina, 40-person teams work on production lines designed to make as many as 27 products simultaneously. Around each workers are "kits" of parts that people in a nearby parts cage have assembled to match production orders; more kits arrive as the day progresses. To keep things moving efficiently, each worker has a computer screen hooked into the factory network. It displays an up-to-the-minute checklist of the parts that must be installed on the product guiding the worker through the assembly steps. When the work is finished, the worker punches a button and the computer system moves the product via conveyor to the next bench on the line. The new automation paradigm reflected in this arrangement involves an ingenious balancing in which software and computer networks have emerged as more important than production machines, in which robots play supporting role, and in which human workers are back in

force. The digital factory, for its dependence on information technology, or the soft factory, for its mix of the human and the mechanical, is setting the tone of manufacturing for years, to come.

Globalization of Services

Knowledge-based industries are not only becoming the mainsprings of innovation-led growth, encouraging learning by doing and the emergence of increasing returns. They also lead to a reevaluation of the factors determining international competitive advantage (discussed in Chapter 11), which now appears to be driven by differences in human capital (i.e., the intellectual abilities of the labor force), and by differences in the availability of thoughtware, rather than by natural factor endowments or domestic capital availability. They also force a new and different look at the major functions of services. The traditional tertiary sector provided local services. Advanced services are becoming important components of international trade and globalization. In part, this globalization is the result of the activities of MNEs (Table 10.3), but it also involves a much broader range of banking, telecommunications and data services, insurance and reinsurance, transportation, and a number of types of professional, business, and scientific services.

The key role of banks (and of related financial services in deregulated markets) is that of financial intermedi-ation, and globalization has been accompanied by considerable innovation: diversifying the sources of funds, making expected returns attractive to different fund providers, and making funds available to balanced portfolios of would-be users in a variety of productive activities. A consequence has been the emergence of financial conglomerates that seek to maximize advantage across countries, providing global competition for loanable funds. Their activities have been facilitated by the emergence of electronic fund transfers, which not only have transformed a labor-intensive activity into a standardized information-driven one, but also have enabled banking transfers to take place immediately at close to zero marginal cost.

Globalization of international financial markets of course, has, also been accelerated by such specific factors as increasingly open financial markets, participation in international tax treaties, and financial instrument innovation, as well as telecommunication network development. The portfolio market has been the greatest beneficiary. Because there is now total integration of global financial markets, Richard O'Brien (1992) sees a resulting "end of geography," in the sense that location does not matter any more to the participants. This financial market integration he says, will, inevitably be followed by integration at the economic and political levels: Capital mobility creates more competition, which results in similar monetary policy among countries. As a result, the government type becomes similar as voters react to common stimuli.

TABLE 10.3
How multinational enterprise encourages globalization of business services

Type of Foreign Production by MNEs	Advantage of the MNE	Assets Sought	Advantages to the MNE	Types of Business Services Attracted
Resource-based	Capital, access to markets, managerial skills, international reputation	Resources (e.g.,skilled labor, information)	Secure supply of skilled labor, protection and exploitation of specialist information, quality control	Engineering design, insurance and reinsurance, management consultancy, investment banking
Import-substituting services	Capital, specialist knowledge, international reputation, access to markets	Labor and other costs, size of local market, need to protect market	Protection and exploitation of knowledge and business contracts, buyer uncertainty, high information costs, quality control	Reinsurance, executive search and accountancy, management and engineering consultancy, branch banking
Trade and distribution	General merchandising knowledge, access to supplers and market outlets	Size of market, access to customers, suppliers and commodity, exchanges, liberal attitudes toward trade	Secure market share, exploitation of business and market contacts	Import and export merchanting

Source: Adapted from Daniels, 1985.

Supporting O'Brien's hypothesis, telecommunication and data services, still evolving, are moving rapidly toward universal real-time personalized global connections that integrate voice, image, text, and data, transmitted via satellite and fiber optics. These developments seem destined to transform the nature of professional, business, and scientific services that heretofore have involved lengthy hours of consultant travel. Many knowledge-intensive services now are functioning in a progressively more "spaceless" world that minimizes on expensive and exhausting travel: A medical specialist does not need to be on the spot to evaluate patient diagnostics; a researcher does not need to consult a manuscript by traveling to a distant archive. What appears to be emerging is a spaceless universality of access for those with the training and opportunity to connect.

On the other hand, the global integration produced by modern telecommunications also appears to be resulting in new forms of centralization that foster the growth of *global cities* according to Sassen (1991). These new global cities (the major examples are New York, London, and Tokyo) now perform four key functions: (1) they are highly concentrated "command points" in the organization of the global economy, marked by major clusters of multinational headquarters; (2) they are key locations for finance and specialized service firms; (3) they are sites for the production of innovations in these leading industries; and (4) they are the leading markets for the innovations produced. The dispersal of many types of routinized secondary activity to low-wage areas, and of heavy industry to already industrialized developing countries, Sassen says, has created the need for expanded central control and management, not simply of multinational enterprises, but also of financial markets. Accompanying the centralization of control has been a new level of development of the specialized services needed by complex organizations for running spatially dispersed networks of factories, offices, and service outlets. Accompanying the concentration of financial markets has been the emergence of a range of financial innovators. The key trait of global cities is that they are the most advanced production sites for creating the high-level business and other services that shape and transform the global production process. In this sense, global cities have emerged as a new level of structure that exists above Stanback's national metropoles. National nodes have been forced to adapt, losing ground with respect to international legal and accounting services, management consulting, financial services, and the like, but enhancing their specialized service functions with respect their immediate economic bases.

INFORMATION TECHNOLOGY, FUNCTIONAL DISINTEGRATION, AND LOCATIONAL CHOICE

These shifts suggest the need for a closer look at the ways in which the new information technologies (ITs) are affecting industrial organization and locational choice. The linkages were explored in a study completed in 1995 by the Office of Technology Assessment of the Congress of the United States (OTA), entitled *The Technological Reshaping of Metropolitan America.* The balance of this chapter is based upon this report.

OTA's investigators began by pointing out that information technologies are of three kinds: (1) those that transfer information into electronic form; (2) those that distribute and route information; (3) and those that transmit this information to different locations. Because they can capture, store, and transmit information in digital form, electronic and therefore instantaneous, transmission is possible. Rapid adoption of information technologies is being driven by the significant increases in productivity they make possible. The extent to which widespread diffusion of the technologies is affecting the location of industries, employment, and residential choice is a function of

- the degree to which functions can be cost-effectively transformed into electronic flows facilitated by telecommunications
- the degree to which spatial proximity is still required to suppliers, customers, competitors, and other units in the firm
- the degree to which externalities remain important in reducing costs or in increasing returns

Because many services involve manipulation of physical objects (auto repair, restaurants, barbers), their location continues to be bound by the location of their customers. For many activities, the information share is increasing, however, as the new IT produces a shift from face-to-face transactions and goods shipment to systems based on electronic communications. Electronic communications loosen the spatial linkages among firms, suppliers, customers, competitors, and other units within the firm. The IT therefore is likely to

(a)   *reduce urbanization economies* by freeing many activities from the need to interact face to face, and therefore to require proximity

(b)   *provide greater economies of scale* by permitting service from a single or a few rather than multiple locations—in new high-tech markets consumers seek security by flocking to the products of the market leader

(c)   *enable firms to restructure,* concentrating on their "core competencies" and *outsourcing* other activities to independent service providers

(d)   *permit workers to "telework"* in these new service facilities from widely dispersed locations

How technological change will spatially reorder economic activity will depend on the type of function involved.

On the one hand, the possibilities of achieving economies of scale are precipitating a new wave of horizontal mergers in the banking, utilities, computer medical devices, paper and paint industries (to cite $19 billion dollars worth of "megamergers" announced on November 6, 1995), making possible extensive substitution of information technology for middle-range management. On the other hand, what is permitted is corporate restructuring that includes "functional disintegration." The process may be understood by examining several different functions: front office (customer interaction), routine back office (no direct customer interaction), goods production and distribution, and complex office work.

Front office functions require interaction with the consumer. Historically, they have been oriented to local market demand, and central-place theory has served as a useful guide to their location. Developments in computing technologies, database access, and telecommunications have increased the share of services that can be conducted without physical proximity to the customer, however, although functions involving some transmission or manipulation of physical things are likely to continue to be bound by customer location. Examples of functions centralized out of immediate customer orientation include banks' customer-service and check-processing centers, telemarketing and telephone-based services, and other activities in which direct consumer access via information networks is possible.

Routine back office functions, office activities not involving direct contact with customers, were traditionally located behind the front office because the large volume of paper and personal transactions required proximity with both front office and back office managerial and professional functions. The back office was like an assembly line where paper was processed and information added at certain places. Because the linkages between routine back office functions and customers and other firms are relatively limited, they are more footloose than front office or managerial and professional back office work, however. The routinized nature of the work has meant that information technologies were applied early. The growing share of information in digital form able to be transmitted electronically, along with effective intrafirm communications, has enabled many back office functions to be physically separated from front office and complex back office work. Companies have been able to split off routine functions from more complex functions and put each in its optimal location, thus promoting functional disintegration, or they have outsourced to independent suppliers that develop their own core competencies as outsourcers, creating a daisy chain of service relationships.

Goods processing involves four main components: production, transportation, distribution, and sales. Within production, it is worthwhile to distinguish between technologically advanced, complex production and more routine production. The development of mass-production technologies has allowed decentralization of a considerable share of routine production. Many manufacturing firms have spun off low-skill assembly and warehousing functions to low-cost regions, in part because telecommunications facilitates communication between physically distant headquarters and these branch facilities. In contrast, as manufacturers shift to more flexible production, localization economies become more important, favoring core locations closer to markets, suppliers, and a skilled, adaptable work force. The creation of these technologically based production complexes, referred to by some as *technopoles,* is driven in part by the need for technologically based manufacturers to interact on a close basis with suppliers, customers, competitors, and other institutions (including universities and research institutes). Within wholesale trade and distribution, information and telecommunications capabilities allow firms to deliver goods much faster than before, allowing in turn a consolidation of distribution facilities outside large metropolitan areas, in areas with lower land and labor costs. Similarly, technological change allows freight transportation functions to consolidate and serve wider markets from fewer areas.

Complex office work, nonroutine in nature and often still requiring face-to-face proximity, is usually undertaken by managers, professionals, and executives in industries such as accounting, law, consulting, R&D, and corporate and regional headquarters offices. In addition, innovation and development of new products and services is a nonroutine function. Information technology appears to be bringing about an increase in the share of more complex functions and employment by changing labor requirements, product and service offerings, the product cycle, and the innovation process. Traditional localization economies of clusters of firms in similar industries continue to be important for these nonroutine and more innovative functions. Although information technology is increasingly being used in these activities, it does not substitute for close physical proximity or face-to-face contract, but supplements it due to the complex and highly varied nature of the interactions and information being transferred. Face-to-face interactions are still critical in many industries and functions. In some industries, such as accounting and consulting, professionals usually meet in the offices of their clients. In contrast, in industries such as banking and legal services, clients usually meet in the service provider firms.

OTA explored how these differential pulls of IT on different functions have reshaped locational choice in a number of information-based service industries. The following are its conclusions.

Financial Services

IT has, as noted earlier, altered the geography of finance. Some functions long associated with major financial centers have been progressively decentralized; others now take place on a global scale; and some seem to have escaped the boundaries of space altogether.

Back office functions include check clearing, remittance processing, credit card processing, and wholesale banking processing. Telecommunications and information technology have allowed these processes to be routinized and physically separated from other bank functions. In many cases, this separation has resulted in migration of routine processing operations away from high-cost urban areas. This relocation away from major financial centers to areas with lower labor costs, less expensive office space, and in some cases lower taxes, has been one of the most visible and most commonly noted impacts of IT on location. These new locations have included new suburban sites and more remote locations.

In some cases, such as credit card payment processing and international money transfers, automation has also created new economies of scale, with dominant providers concentrating routine processing activities in a few very large processing centers. Chase, the world's leading provider of international money transfer services, processes all such transactions in just two locations—Brooklyn, New York, and Bournemouth, England.

As the trend toward disaggregation of financial functions has progressed, the facilities of third-party processors also have become an important element of the financial services industry processing infrastructure. These third-party processing activities are dispersed in many locations that are often far removed from the country's leading financial centers.

In contrast, IT seems to have reinforced centralization of corporate banking. Firms can now gain access to more, better, and more timely information. These advances have greatly reduced the cost and increased the speed of international financial transactions, and have made possible the development of new techniques for managing the risks involved in lending, borrowing and investing across national borders. Opportunities for globalization and new technologies have reinforced the important role that major cities play as centers of financial innovation.

IT also has facilitated the creation of a whole new range of financial products. Beginning in the late 1970s, U.S. financial institutions began to use computer technology to support the creation of new products and services—a process that continues to this day. Early examples of new products made possible by computer technology include adjustable-rate mortgages, money market accounts, and cash management accounts. As the process of technological innovation accelerated, so did the introduction of new products.

In contrast to routine processing functions, most financial institutions keep the development and launching of new products and services closely tied to headquarters.

And just as innovation has become more important to the competitive position of individual firms, so the role of leading cities (especially New York, Charlotte, Chicago, and San Francisco) as centers of innovation has become more important to their role in the financial services sector. Firms located in established centers usually have easier access to the specialized skills, detailed market knowledge, and supportive services needed for the development and introduction of new products and services.

New product development often requires highly specialized skills, such as the ability to model how a new type of security will perform under a variety of conditions, that may not be readily available outside the leading financial centers. Those who develop and launch new products often require the assistance of other specialists, experts in banking and securities law, market research or risk management, for example. Such expertise is usually found most readily in areas where the financial services industries already are concentrated. So are the formal and informal sources of information, from meetings of trade and professional associations to conversations at the gym or local watering hole, that help to foster continuous innovation. For all of these reason, much of the activity related to innovation in finance has, to date, remained concentrated in just a few major cities.

Agglomeration economies also remain important to corporate banking functions, which are largely wholesale and nonroutine, requiring a concentration of highly specialized knowledge and ready access to up-to-the-minute information, together with an infrastructure of supporting facilities and services both within individual firms or institutions and in the community at large, international legal and accounting expertise, access to satellite connections, and to major international airports. Firms often seek to syndicate bank loans or new securities issues, or otherwise bring partners into their deals. This process works most efficiently when the principal players are concentrated in one location.

Insurance

Insurance companies once dominated the cores of American cities with their downtown skyscrapers within which their many functions were concentrated, although central headquarters were complemented by decentralized consumer access and service. Today, these same companies are largely restructured and relocated as a consequence of the new IT. During the 1980s, insurers introduced database management systems to collect interrelated data, minimize data redundancy, allow updates regardless of the data's physical storage location, and enhance recoverability and security. Online access to policy and claim files has weakened the traditional need for proximity in insurance operations. Optical scanning and imaging technology has reduced paperwork barriers to distributed work because virtually all information can be online. Scanning is widely used now to process policy applications and premium collections, and is being applied to claims processing as well. Finally, more companies are relying on phone and mail to communicate with policyholders. Branch offices serve less purpose when a telephone call accomplishes the same task, whether it is over 20 miles or 2,000 miles.

IT is reducing the need for face-to-face contact between company employees. Claims processors can tap into underwriting computer files when they process claims. Agents and field adjusters can communicate electronically with the claims office through fax machines, e-mail, and modems linked to portable computers. This permits consolidation. State Farm Insurance Co. is consolidating policy processing currently undertaken in 27 offices into three centers (Dallas, Atlanta, and Phoenix), and is reducing life and health insurance operations from 27 to 9. A principal motivation for such consolidation is to achieve economies of scale and save money on overhead such as buildings, management, and support staff, and to spend a greater share of resources on operations.

IT is changing the insurance industry's front office functions as well, allowing more work to be done in centralized service centers. Insurance companies use two main systems to reach customers with their products, local agents and direct response (e.g., direct mail, media advertising). Local agent distribution systems are expensive, and because of increased cost competition in the industry, insurance firms are trying to find ways to reduce agent functions or to bypass them altogether. Automated kiosks in places such as shopping centers are proving to be cost-effective distribution channels for routine lines of personal insurance. Direct response functions are being expanded, too, with toll-free numbers providing access to centralized consumer-service centers.

Securities Trading and Investing

The securities trading and investment industry has undergone shifts similar to other information-based service industries. Selling functions were distributed around the country close to customers, whereas back office and trading and investment functions were concentrated in the downtowns of the largest cities, particularly New York. Both these patterns have changed, in part due to the introduction of information and communications technology.

IT has given rise to new modes of delivering financial products and services. In recent years, innovations such as digital call distribution systems, telephone keypads, and screen phones have enabled banks, brokerage firms, and mutual funds to broaden the range of services that clients can access by phone. In addition, online brokerage accounts are allowing investors to place "buy" and "sell" orders from a PC at home.

But in contrast to banks and insurance companies, the securities industry has tended to keep its automated back office operations closely tied to headquarters. For example, in New York, the largest firms all developed processing facilities in Manhattan, although not at the same site as their headquarters.

Securities trading and investment has been a face-to-face enterprise, largely concentrated downtown. Technological change is reinforcing this, but also threatening it. IT has facilitated the creation of such new products as stock index futures, derivatives, and synthetic securities. One of the most important financial market trends of the past decade, *securitization,* or the conversion of all kinds of assets from home mortgages and credit card receivables to commercial real estate into securities that can be bought and sold, would not have been possible without the use of sophisticated computer programs. In the mutual fund industry, intense competition has fueled a spiral of new product introduction; between 1985 and 1990, the 20 leading mutual fund companies in the United States introduced more than 500 new funds. As in banking, these innovative activities tend to be located in the downtowns of central cities of major metropolitan areas.

However, advances in information and communication technology as well as the standardization of real-time market information and research available online have the potential to change this. The Securities and Exchange Commission's (SEC's) electronic filing requirements for companies have meant that researchers and stock analysts do not have to be in the core to gain the information. The advent of computer and high-speed telecommunications technology also has made possible the creation of a widening range of options for investors to buy and sell securities without going through the established exchanges. The National Association of Securities Dealers Automated Quotation System (NASDAQ), launched in 1971, triggered the rapid growth of the "over-the-counter" market.

Automation of trading systems has the potential both to reduce trading employment and to allow it to relocate. For example, Bernard L. Madoff Investment Securities handles about 5 percent of the daily trading volume of stocks listed on the New York Stock Exchange. But rather than going to the floor of the Exchange, the trades are routed through Madoff's own proprietary trading system. An even more revolutionary system was launched in 1991 by the Arizona Stock Exchange, which handles only a fraction of 1 percent of the volume of shares traded each day on the New York Stock Exchange, but does so in a completely automated way. At a prescribed hour, participating firms and institutions can post bid and asked prices for blocks of a specific stock. The system then arrays bids and offers into textbook-style demand-and-supply curves; the price at which the curves intersect is the price at which trades are executed. Such systems are coming into direct competition with today's face-to-face markets.

Telecommunications

The telecommunications industry is in the middle of a transformation, from a set of regulated utilities to that of a more competitive and high-tech market, and in this transformation the large telephone companies are reorganizing and looking to cut costs and increase labor and capital productivity in every part of their businesses. These companies are therefore cutting and relocating workers in the face of increasing competition, enabled by new technologies that allow more centralization and control of activities.

Employment in the telecommunications industry can be divided into three areas: (1) routine front and back office (e.g., operators, billing and repair inquiries, customer service); (2) nonroutine front office (e.g., repair, maintenance, and marketing); and (3) complex back office.

The telephone companies have automated many customer-service and other functions by using new call-processing equipment, and transferring inquiries to large megacenters via the industry's own telecom infrastructure. Automated call management (ACM), voice mail, and interactive voice response (IVR) equipment allow telephone companies to play recordings to callers, accept touch-tone or voice inputs, and triage calls in complex ways. Calls can be transferred to the next available assistant and even across time zones as the need requires. These applications are linked to other technologies. For example, centralized billing allows customer-service representatives to call up information on the customer's account and process it in real time: Any service representative in the company can gain online access to any customer record. Much of the call-completion, directory assistance, and customer-service functions are automated and computer-assisted, so that workers in those positions do not have to be located near the customer and are not limited by a local paper-based, record-keeping system. Most companies are moving to computerize all records.

The technology, as well as the reorganization of the industry, has led most companies to create larger, centralized customer-service centers. These centers are usually specialized in five activities: call-completion operators, directory assistance, network management, customer-service representatives (for ordering, billing, and queries), and accounting and billing. Companies are centralizing into megacenters in order to gain economies of scale—trimming employees and other costs. In addition, a smaller number of managers can more easily manage consolidated functions. As companies downsize management, remaining managers have increased spans of control, making management of dispersed offices more difficult.

Long-distance providers have also consolidated operations. AT&T has six megacenters for its residential customer-service line, several more for small businesses, network management, and call-completion operations. Relatively new competitors such as Sprint and MCI built megacenters into their networks from the beginning, locating them in lower-cost regions of the country. Sprint, for example, has centers located in Jacksonville, Florida; Dallas, Texas; Kansas City, Missouri; Phoenix, Arizona; and Winona, a small city in Minnesota.

Before central electromechanical switches, many operators for the former Bell system worked out of their homes with mechanical patchboards. Today, after a series of centralizations, the telecom industry is once again returning to home work. Such decentralization is enabled by the same technology that enabled the current centralization. Calls and information can be transferred to virtually anywhere, whether to a central megacenter or to dispersed homes or telework centers. Because many of the activities are already monitored by computer, oversight of employees in a common location may not be necessary and tasks therefore can be performed at home or in *telework centers* (discussed in what follows). Telework is particularly attractive for filling off-shift positions as companies turn toward 24-hour service, as well as for ordinary routine and nonroutine workers. Such a pattern of decentralization allows companies to combine the benefits of centralization (e.g., economies of scale of operations, centralized customer access) with the benefits of decentralization (lower space-utilization costs and lower wages).

Nonroutine front office functions in the telecom industry include customer sales, especially business marketing, plant operations include installing and maintaining the local telecommunications infrastructure, engineering, network administration, testing, and other tasks associated with the switches and the main trunk lines. Roughly one-third of the jobs in telecommunications are plant-related jobs involved in the production, construction, and maintenance of equipment and lines.

New technologies are altering the number and location of plant operation jobs. The greatest relative decline in employment for the industry is for installers and repairers as a result of such technological improvements as fiber optics, digital switches, modular equipment, quick-connect features on cables, and the off-loading of many tasks to the customer.

In addition, technology allows many of these functions to be performed remotely. In the past, installers wired buildings and homes, and had to go into the field for most of the diagnostics and repair. Today, installers perform many functions remotely at the central office. Much of the network management, including troubleshooting and adding new features, can be supervised and performed in remote locations.

There are a number of technologies that enable this. The most striking is the digitization of internal telephone operations, which allows providers enormous flexibility in the management of their systems. Digitization means that voice communications are converted from analog signals coming into the switching office to binary ("on/off") signals, which usually are converted back to analog before they reach the other user. Yet another development in digitization and switching leads to the centralization of the operating system software. This development, called "advanced intelligent network" (AIN), eliminates the need to replace the software in all the (standardized) switching equipment, itself a costly process. Instead, the carrier can change the software in only certain central "nodes" within a region. The effect of the developments in digitization is a net decrease in installation and maintenance using analog switching equipment. Remote switches, for example, can be controlled through larger switches at central facilities, removing the need for on-site personnel.

Automation of system troubleshooting allows computers to diagnose problems so that humans do not have to intervene. If there is a break in a fiber-optic transmission line, for example, a computer in the command center can detect the interruption, reroute all following transmissions through new paths, and narrow down the possible failure modes. In many cases, a failure in a switching facility can be identified, and a technician is sent only to replace or repair the part. In the past, local technicians were on call to identify and repair such problems.

One result is the growth of network management centers. These centers monitor local switching and switching between company facilities, manage emergency routing, monitor weather and disaster information, diagnose network problems, and so forth.

Finally, complex back office functions include planning, accounting and finance, procurement, information management, legal services, and so forth. These operations are almost always located in major metropolitan areas, and often in downtown locations. The headquarters of the regional Bell operating companies and major long-distance providers are all located in large metropolitan areas, and most are in central business districts. For example, Bell Atlantic (Philadelphia), Bell South (Atlanta), U.S. WEST (Denver), Pacific Telesis Group (San Francisco), and AT&T (New York) are all located in the central business districts of these cities. Some others, such as MCI (Arlington, Virginia) and Southwestern Bell (Irving, Texas), are in edge cities of large metropolitan areas.

Professional Services

Professional services—legal, accounting, engineering, computers and software—continue to grow rapidly. Some sectors, such as legal services, appear to have been impor-

tant components of central business district revitalization. Other sectors, such as computer services, appear to have contributed to the increase in suburban office growth.

Much of the work in services such as law, architecture, accounting and consulting involves individualized, non-routine craft work. Many employees are "front office" professionals—lawyers preparing individual cases, accountants auditing accounts to produce financial statements, consultants producing reports. These functions are impossible to automate, but technology, such as the personal computer, can increase efficiency. Back office support includes clerical and paraprofessional jobs.

Because of the nonroutine and complex nature of these functions, professional services are still overwhelmingly located in metropolitan areas. Law firms, especially large firms, are predominantly located in central cities of large metropolitan areas.

There are several reasons for this concentration in metropolitan areas. First, firms want to be near clients. One survey of legal, architectural and engineering, and management consulting firms found that face-to-face conversations with clients or in-person delivery of documents was a principal way of delivering services to clients. Accountants must visit clients and in some cases spend considerable time on their premises going through financial records for auditing and tax work.

Second, a high percentage of firms (legal, 83 percent; accounting, 76 percent; and engineering, 77 percent) collaborate with other service firms and institutions in producing their services. The importance of collaborative work within law firms, and also interactions with clients, courts, and other law firms, has led law firms to concentrate in metropolitan areas. Moreover, legal work involving litigation must maintain close linkages with district and federal courts, whereas legal work related to financial transactions maintains linkages with banks, both of which are located principally in central cities of metropolitan areas.

In addition, unlike banking and insurance sectors, professional service firms are less likely to move support and back office functions to separate locations outside the Central Business District (CBD). For example, lawyers want support staff nearby because the staff directly support legal work, unlike back office work in insurance and banking, which processes transactions. However, some accounting firms have moved some back office functions such as computing facilities to suburban locations.

There are four technological developments in professional services that are, however, affecting location. First, an increasing share of work and information is in electronic form, making it possible for professionals to do some remote working. Second, *expert systems* are improving productivity in some sectors, particularly in the more routine segments. For example, computers can mechanize and automate relatively simple work such as estates and trusts. Expert systems are also emerging that make legal knowledge available to novice legal practitioners. Knowledge-based systems can be used to outsource the production of some legal documents to "document sources," reducing locally based legal employment, which tends to do more routine legal work. Third, information networks and shared work systems are increasingly allowing professionals to cooperate on work in different locations. For example, the accounting firm Price Waterhouse uses Lotus Notes to allow personnel from different offices to work collectively on one project. Similarly, scientists and engineers are using such tools to collaborate across distances. "Virtual" experimental communities, or *collaboratories,* that permit real-time interaction among researchers have emerged. For example, Xerox has created an internal research group of researchers in Britain, Los Angeles, Rochester, and Palo Alto to cooperate on a particular technical problem that Xerox earlier had not been able to address because the expertise to do so was distributed among these four sites. The researchers communicate via video conferencing and e-mail. Finally, the increased use of electronic mail and fax and growth in telephone and video conferencing are making communication between clients and professionals easier. Because such technologies make it easier to communicate, they will allow increased movement of these activities out of high-cost central business districts to suburban sites.

Data Entry and Processing

The computer services industry, including data entry and processing, employed 233,000 people in 1994 in routine tasks such as keying mailing lists and receipts and more complex tasks such as payroll and tax-return processing. Routine data-entry jobs already have relocated to exurban and rural areas and developing nations, because they consist of more labor-intensive, low-skill data-entry tasks, especially when labor cost is a key factor and contacts with clients are routine. Firms generally are able to communicate with clients through mail and courier services to obtain hard copy, which they in turn enter into the computer. Companies then return data either by telephone line (larger companies) or by mailing computer tape or disks (smaller companies). Firms in urban areas are not competitive in data entry because of the high labor costs. Rural areas in the United States are generally competitive in work that requires a quick turnaround, whereas overseas locations such as Barbados and Jamaica, where wages are about half of rural U.S. wages, compete in work that does not require immediate response. More complex work, which makes up the bulk of data-processing work, occurs largely in metropolitan areas, in large part because of the need for close communication with clients.

Technological change is reducing the amount of routine work, while increasing its overseas share, and increasing the proportion of work that is complex and done largely in large and midsize metropolitan areas. First, improvements and cost reduction in image technologies are eliminating the quick-turnaround advantage currently held by rural firms and allowing overseas locations to be competitive. Images of documents increasingly are being sent cheaply to offshore locations for data entry. Jamaica, for example, has invested in image transmitters and satellite transmission, and has access to digital switching and fiber-optic circuits to the Untied States. Second, new technologies are displacing manual data-entry tasks. For example, developments in optical character-recognition (OCR) technology have the potential to reduce manual data entry. Moreover, point of transaction data-entry will reduce subsequent manual data entry. Finally, as routine data-entry operations become more automated, data entry firms are offering more specialized services, such as tax preparation and consulting and software development. As firms do more of these functions, they choose metropolitan locations, in part to be close to clients, but also to attract more skilled labor.

TELEWORK AND THE DISTRIBUTION OF JOBS AND HOMES

Even as IT is changing the nature of the economy and the structure and locational choices of firms, it also is changing the relationship between employers and employees, particularly the place of employment. Current forecasts of the extent of telework in the United States place the likely number of workers who will work out of their homes, or out of telework centers, at between 15 and 25 million by the year 2000. Companies such as AT&T are not only reorganizing themselves to increase the amount of telework, but are selling the technologies that make it possible to others: high-speed data transmission; long-distance, dedicated, and private lines; enhanced fax and satellite communication.

What is telework? The terms "telework," "telecommuting," "distributed work," and "teleprocesses" all refer to the substitution of transportation by the use of telecommunications and other information technologies, but they mean different things. The terms "telecommute" and "telework" were coined by Jack Nilles in 1973 and are better known than the others.

Telecommuting means the partial or complete substitution of an employee's normal working hours in a traditional office or other workplace by the home or alternative workplace such as a neighborhood *telework center.* Telecommuting reduces commuting time and is accomplished through information technologies.

Telework is the broader concept, and includes telecommuting, but also includes some self-employed people who work at home, and mobile workers who use information technologies and telecommunications to do their jobs. A teleworker may use a laptop and modem at the customer's site to conduct business; a telephone, fax, computer, and/or modem to work out of a permanent office located in the home; or a cellular telephone to conduct business while in a vehicle.

Hoteling is often a component of telework and refers to two or more mobile workers sharing office space in a traditional office or telework center. Hoteling saves office costs but requires special workspace arrangements, as well as sophisticated telephone and computer networking tools. The offices offer temporary or portable storage for the rotating workers, and are able to route calls and electronic transactions to the workers, wherever they may be.

Distributed work is the use of telecommunications and other information technologies to perform work at a distance but not necessarily outside an office. It includes group activities, such as videoconferencing and networked information resources, that allow people from distant locations to work together. Distributed work can cut travel costs, and perhaps more importantly, permits work to be done that previously could not have been done at all, or only at great expense or inconvenience. In contrast, telework emphasizes the *substitution* of a home or other remote or mobile environment for the traditional office.

Finally, a *teleprocess* is an arrangement in which a remote transaction is performed by anyone, not just a worker (e.g., a customer who makes an airplane reservation via the Internet), and is facilitated through the use of telecommunications.

There are several reasons why IT is resulting in rapid growth of telework. Workers benefit through reduced commuting time, a more flexible work schedule, more time with family, lower fuel costs, and more freedom of choice in where to live. Telework also increases opportunities for disabled workers and others who are limited in mobility. Organizations benefit. Telework improves individual productivity, improving employee morale, reducing employee turnover, and reducing office space. Metropolitan regions and society at large benefit from widespread telework because of reductions in traffic congestion, pollution, and energy use.

Three categories of jobs are responding most rapidly to the opportunities for telework:

1. *Routine Information-Handling Tasks.* Workers in these positions perform well-defined tasks using telephones, facsimile machines, or computers with modems in such a way that their tasks are not tied to a physical location.

2. *Mobile Activities.* Field service representatives, delivery personnel, field salespersons, and others perform their duties at the customers' or vendors' site and do not require an office environment except for occasional meetings or to use shared resources. Many employers use telework arrangements for such workers to encourage more direct contact with customers and to save on the costs of unoccupied offices while the workers are offsite (hoteling).

3. *Professional and Other Knowledge-Related Tasks.* "Knowledge workers" manipulate, analyze, or otherwise process information in a non-routine manner and may spend many hours with telephone, facsimile, computer equipment, and/or paper documents. Consultants, translators, marketing personnel, authors and editors, software engineers, executives, and others may telework from home or while traveling.

The technologies required for home-based telework are relatively commonplace. For most teleworkers, a laptop or personal computer with a modem, e-mail software, facsimile equipment, and traditional telephone service are enough. For the employer, current computer networking and/or call-distribution equipment is often adequate. Some applications, however, benefit from or require faster data transmission for file transfers or videoconferencing. In such cases, current digital telephony services, including ISDN (integrated services digital network) service, is generally adequate. Desktop videoconferencing equipment may facilitate the further adoption of telecommuting.

More advanced telework applications also are possible, including advanced technologies for high-performance computing and networking. For example, a scientist may wish to process data entered from a collaborator at another location using software resident on a computer at a third location, and display the results on his or her computer. Such applications use the most advanced information technologies available today. The widest range of information technologies can be applied to telework, just as they are currently applied to the wider set of teleprocesses, including cryptographic tools; advanced-data transmission protocols for special applications; satellites for distance education, remote sensing, or geographic positioning; and virtual reality tools.

The shift from paper-based to computer-based document systems within industry facilitates telework. Electronic file-management systems that rely on electronic imaging allow an increasing share of back office workers to review customer and other files, make comments and changes, and send the files to another worker for the next step in processing, all on desktop computers. Similarly, "groupware" programs facilitate the sharing of electronic resources for workers who collaborate on projects. Transforming the work itself so that an increasing share can be conducted using personal computers increases the mobility of the work and makes telework cheaper.

Expansion of telework is likely to have a profound effect on the structure of regions. Not only are there likely to be direct effects, such as reductions in traffic congestion, pollution, and energy consumption, via reduced commuting, there also are likely to be a range of indirect effects that include savings in office space and a change in office loca-

tions; relocation of telecommuters to preferred residential settings in the outer suburbs, exurbs, small towns and rural areas; and changes in travel patterns. Some go as far as to suggest that telework itself will globalized, so that a significant future component of transnational "trade" will be the work performed by teleworkers within firms that have reached the ultimate stage of globalization. This possibility leads to the call for a new body of international trade theory as globalization progresses, to be addressed in Chapters 11 and 12.

VOCABULARY

The new vocabulary items added in this chapter are as following:

advanced intelligent network (AIN)
advanced services sector
American system of manufactures
Arpanet
axial principle
bandwagon effect
bulletin boards
central-place theory
chat lines
collaboratories
communication services
congealed knowledge
congealed resources
cyberspace
diffusion
dinosaur effect
distributed work
diversified quality
e-mail
expert systems
externality
fifth wave
first wave of Industrial Revolution
flexible automation
flexible manufacturing systems
flexible specialization
Fordist
fourth wave of Industrial Revolution
front office functions
functional disintegration

general theory of polarized growth
global cities
growth logistic
hard automation
heartland–hinterland pattern
hierarchical diffusion
hierarchy of central places
hoteling
human capital
induced invention
information services
information technology (IT)
intellectual technology
Internet
Internet hosts
knowledge-based industry
knowledge carrying-services
knowledge products
knowledge workers
knowledge-based systems
Kondratiev cycle
libertarianism
limits to growth
linkage-forming services
localization economies
long-wave of prices
M-form
Manhattan project
market dominance
megamerger

metamorphosis model
national metropoles
national nodal center
national nodes
network of networks
nodal center
O'Brien hypothesis
optical scanning (optical character-recognition technology, or OCR)
order of a central place
per capita income
pioneering innovation
postindustrial society
primary sector
product growth cycles
pseudo innovation
quaternary industries
quaternary sector
quinary industries
quinary sector
radical improvement innovations
real time
regional nodal center
routine improvement innovations
rural-to-urban migration
second wave of Industrial Revolution
secondary sector
securitization
service industries
specialized function cities

spread effects
structural transformation
take-off
technoeconomic system
technological revolution
technology stalemates
technopoles
telecommuting
teleprocess
telework

tertiary sector
third party processors (in the financial
    services industry)
third wave of Industrial Revolution
thoughtware economy
time–space sequence
transmaterialization
transmission control protocol/Internet
    protocol (TCP/IP)
transportation center

triage
urban hierarchies
urbanization economies
usenet groups
vertical disintegration
virtual spaces
World Wide Web (WWW)

TOPICS FOR DISCUSSION

1. What were the leading industrial sectors and the types of organizational change that characterized the first four Kondratiev cycles? In which regions did the changes occur first? What were the sequence and timing of the diffusion of the changes to other regions?

2. Why are clusters of innovations typically associated with stagflation crises and technological stalemates?

3. What are the product cycle and the learning curve? How do they relate to concepts of industrial filtering?

4. What is the role of "thoughtware" in an advanced services economy.

5. How do locational choices of modern high-tech firms differ (if at all) from those of earlier industries whose seedbed was based on localization or urbanization economies?

FURTHER READINGS

Bauer, P. T. and B. S. Yamey (1951). Economic Progress and Occupational Distribution. *Economic Journal* 61:741–755.

    A critique of Clark's concept of the tertiary sector.

Bell, Daniel (1974). *The Coming of Post-Industrial Society.* London: Heinemann.

    A provocative discussion of the relationship between economic charge and social evolution.

Berry, Brian J. L. (1991).*Long-Wave Rhythms in Economic Development and Political Behavior.* Baltimore: John Hopkins University Press.

    A review, synthesis, and extension of long-wave theory.

Berry, Brian J. L., Heja Kim, and Hak-Min Kim, (1993). Are Long Waves Driven by TechnoEconomic Transformations? Evidence for the U.S. and the U.K. *Technological Forecasting and Social Change* 44:111–135.

    The authors document the relationship between technoeconomic logistics and long-wave rhythms of prices.

Christaller, Walter (1966).*Central Places in Southern Germany.* Translated by C. W. Baskin. Englewood Cliffs, NJ: Prentice Hall.

    Christaller is responsible for the development of central-place theory.

Clark, Colin (1940). *The Conditions of Economic Progress.* London: Macmillan.

    Advances a theory of the relationship between the tertiary sector and economic growth.

Daniels, P. W. (1985). *Service Industries: A Geographical Appraisal.* London: Methuen.

    A text that thoroughly reviews the current status of the service industries.

Foote, Nelson N., and Paul K. Hatt (1953). Social Mobility and Economic Advancement. *American Economic Review* 63:364–7.

    Adds quaternary and quinary activities to the classification of service industries.

Kondratiev, N. D. (1935).The Long Wave in Economic Life. *The Review of Economic Statistics* 17:105-–15.

Introduced the concept of long waves.

Myrdal, Gunnar (1957).*Rich Lands and Poor: The Road to World Prosperity.* New York: Harper and Row.

Offers a classic extension of ideas of cumulative causation to the world economy.

Nilles, Jack M. (1975). Telecommunications and Organizational Decentralization. *IEEE Transactions on Communications* COM-23:1142–1147.

Introduces the concept of telework.

Nusbaumer, Jacques (1987). *Services in the Global Market.* Dordrecht: Kluwer Academic Publishers.

An exploration of the manner in which the service industries are globalizing.

O'Brien, Richard (1992). *Global Financial Integration: The End of Geography.* London and New York: Royal Institute of International Affairs.

Offers the radical idea that telecommunications are eliminating the role of distance in spatial organization.

Office of Technology Assessment, Congress of the United States (1995). *The Technological Reshaping of Metropolitan America.* Washington, DC: U.S. Government Printing Office.

A thorough examination of the nature and impacts of the new information technology.

Sassen, Saskia (1991). *The Global City.* Princeton: Princeton University Press

Describes the new forms of urbanization that connect the world economy.

Stanback, T. M., P. J. Bearse, T. J. Noyelle, and R. A. Karasek (1981). *Services: The New Economy.* Totowa, NJ: Allanheld and Osmun.

A sound analysis of the consequences of quaternary sector expansion.

Vernon, R. (1966). International Investment and International Trade in the Product Cycle. *Quarterly Journal of Economics.* 80:190–207.

Relates product cycle theory to global shifts.

11

Patterns and Dynamics of Global Economic Transactions

OVERVIEW

The growing economic interdependence of countries is to be seen in the changing system of global transactions. In this chapter we use international data to examine the flows of goods, services, and factors of production (including foreign direct investment) that link world regions of production and consumption. To interpret the spatial patterns produced by these flows, we turn to the evolving body of international trade theory.

Empirical evidence reveals the effects of recent economic and political trends and events on the economic linkages among major trading countries and regions, following a very long era of relative stability. The final decades of the twentieth century have seen a fundamental restructuring of world industry, accompanied by globalization of production and services.

During the 1990s, the center of gravity of world commerce continued its shift from the North Atlantic, the main focus of earlier times, toward the Pacific Rim, where a dynamic group of East Asian countries has profited from a restructured international economy. In the middle of this westward shift are Canada and the United States, which have transferred much of their trade and investment westward across the Pacific even as they strengthen their ties with a newly rejuvenated Latin America. The countries of Western Europe, too, have drawn closer together at a time when the collapse of communism in the Eastern Bloc has pulled Central Europe into the Western orbit.

Over a long period of time, theories have evolved to fill the need for a clearer understanding of these complex processes of international interaction. Until recently, trade theory held that the types, quantities, and prices of goods traded among countries depended on the relative amounts of the factors of production—land, labor, capital, and enterprise—with which these countries are endowed. Critics have long pointed to a number of weaknesses in this theory, notably the omission of important barriers to trade. More recently, the explanatory powers of existing theory have been further eroded by their failure to accommodate the rapidly growing role of multinationals in the international transfer of goods and factors of production and by important changes in the basic character of international transactions.

As discontent with conventional trade theory has increased, various alternatives have been offered, notably the so-called "new" theory of international trade. This approach adds dynamic new elements that are capable of explaining many of the flows that traditional theory cannot. Yet further modifications are being called for by theorists, however, who point to the as-yet unsatisfied need to accommodate the new kinds of transactions that take place within the hierarchies of multinational corporations and allied firms.

OBJECTIVES

- to distinguish trends in the growth and composition of international commodity flows

- to evaluate the impact of recent global crises and political events on world trade and foreign investment

- to examine the shifting currents of world commerce; the effects these have had on international flows of goods, services, and factors of production; and the new economic regions that are evolving

- to demonstrate the relationship between the location of production and the flow of goods, services, and factors of production among countries

- to trace the evolution of international trade theory, identify the changed circumstances that have called forth each new historical phase of theory, and describe the main elements of each new trade theory

- to analyze the expanding role of multinational enterprises as organizing agencies in the contemporary world economy and to assess their effects on world patterns of investment and trade

- to consider the criticisms of conventional trade theory, show how the 'new' theory of international trade sets about remedying these defects, and to identify and explain the continuing sources of dissatisfaction

THE GLOBAL ECONOMY IN TRANSITION

As the end of the twentieth century draws nearer, regions and nations are becoming increasingly interdependent. Contemporary standards of living call for such a variety of goods and draw on a technology so complex that no country can by itself supply all the necessary ingredients; a retreat to self-sufficiency would so impoverish a people that no country would find such a course politically feasible. To supply its diverse needs, therefore, modern civilization relies increasingly on a global system of trade. The resulting international flows consist not only of commodities, but also a great variety of services. Within the past quarter-century, a growing volume of capital, technology, and management also have followed these international movements of goods and services. Trade among countries has thus laid the basis for an internationalization of the locational decision-making process.

The last quarter century also has witnessed a series of swift and fundamental changes in the world economy. A wholesale restructuring of industry, a revolution in global communications, and a growing prominence for multinational enterprises have created an economic environment that would be hardly recognizable to theorists of an earlier generation. Patterns of world commerce—dependably stable over very long periods in the past—are now in transition. In this chapter, therefore, we turn to the changing composition and direction of economic flows among countries, the nature of the regional patterns produced by this type of spatial interaction, the shifting fortunes of countries and regions in an increasingly competitive world environment, and the potential shape of the world economic map in the coming century.

Trade Growth and Structural Change

The volume of world commerce has fluctuated widely in modern times, showing how sensitive trade is to the vagaries of war and peace and of prosperity and hard times. World War I produced the first major disruption of trade in this century. On the arrival of peace, world exports soared until, by 1929, they had doubled their level of a decade earlier. When the Great Depression struck, the total value of trade dropped precipitously, falling by more than 60 percent within a very brief time. Indeed, trade contracted even more than did global production, for most industrial countries reacted to worsening economic conditions by imposing trade restrictions to protect their domestic industries from foreign competition. Not until 1939 did world trade recover to its 1929 level, and it continued to lag behind the growth of output because of persisting governmental interference.

World War II again seriously interrupted commerce, and trade patterns remained distorted for some years afterward because of wartime destruction of European and Japanese production facilities. World trade gradually returned to normal by the 1950s, and it gathered strength as global agreements reduced governmental restrictions remaining from the prewar era. Trade continued to accelerate thereafter, rising more than fourfold between 1948 and 1968.

The commodity composition, or structure, of trade likewise changed during the first two-thirds of the twentieth century. The value of manufactured exports increased fourfold, whereas trade in primary commodities rose by a mere 50 percent. This relatively poor performance by primary exports occurred despite a rising demand for industrial raw materials and petroleum. One explanation for this is the increasingly elaborate processing that rising technology had brought about; another is the rising proportion of finished goods that entered trade. Indeed, a fairly reliable measure of a country's level of development in the first two-thirds of this century was the proportion that finished goods comprised of its total manufactured exports.

The composition of manufactured exports also changed during this era. Shipments of textiles and clothing declined steadily. Meanwhile, exports of metals and miscellaneous manufactured goods remained fairly static. The most rapid growth of all was in machinery, transport equipment, and chemicals.

This comparatively placid era of steady growth and evolution came to an end in the 1970s when a series of crises rocked the world economy. The economic and political forces underlying these events had been building for some time, but their effects were as unexpected as they were severe. One major occurrence was the collapse of the old Bretton Woods agreement, which had sustained world monetary stability for most of the postwar years. Based on gold and the U.S. dollar, the system had shown signs of deteriorating during the 1960s as emergence of the European Common Market, and later Japan, had eroded the preeminent position of the United States in world economic affairs. The complex system of floating exchange rates that replaced Bretton Woods after March 1973 has led to much uncertainty in world business.

The early 1970s also saw a sudden rise in the prices of industrial raw materials. This brought an end to the remarkably long period of commodity price stability that had contributed so much to industrial growth in the 1950s and 1960s. The inflation in commodity prices resulted from rapid increases in demand from the industrial countries, and it was reinforced by a rise in nationalism among the less-developed countries (LDCs) supplying these commodities. Together, these forces combined to enable the Organization for Petroleum Exporting Countries (OPEC) to strengthen their cartel and control the supply of oil.

In September 1973, the first oil crisis erupted, as Arab members of OPEC embargoed the West during the Arab–Israeli Yom Kippur War. A global recession followed the 1973 crisis, accompanied by rising unemployment, mounting public debt, and soaring balance-of-payments deficits in oil-importing countries. A second crisis came in 1979, when fundamentalists overthrew the Shah of Iran. The ensuing tenfold rise in oil prices added to the worldwide inflationary spiral already under way, and to an enormous transfer of wealth to the oil-exporting nations that reduced incomes in the industrialized countries and halted development in the poorer LDCs. Spiraling inflation culminated in the 1980–1981 stagflation crisis (see Box 11.1).

World trade growth was a major casualty of this crisis-ridden period, because the affected nations reacted to worsening trade deficits by severely restricting their imports. Thus ended a remarkable era of international cooperation that had fostered economic growth and raised living standards. The 1973 crisis slowed the rate of trade growth for a time, but in the depressed period following the second crisis, world trade actually shrank 9 percent in value. It was not until the mid-1980s that trade began a resurgence. Despite continued import restrictions, by 1990 combined trade in goods and services had mounted to $4 trillion. This represented a thirteen-fold rise in real (inflation-adjusted) terms since 1950.

This same era brought fundamental changes to the international economy. Beginning with the period of European colonization, the world had formed an international division of labor in which the less-developed countries traded their raw materials and agricultural goods to the industrialized lands in exchange for manufactured products. In the postwar age, however, the spread of foreign direct investment has contributed to an internationalization of manufacturing. Multinational enterprises were the primary agents of this change. Many LDCs acquired industries drawn by the presence of literate, hardworking, low-cost labor, and, in some instances, locally available raw materials. Guided by forward-looking national policies, several of the newly industrialized countries (NICs) have improved on preexisting factor endowments and created new ones—educating and training workers, encouraging capital accumulation through savings, and investing in research and development (see Chapter 12).

Cheaply produced goods of growing sophistication have since poured into world markets from these NICs, and long-established industries of Western Europe and North America have retrenched or folded. The older industrial economies found themselves handicapped by the high cost of unionized labor, by aging plant and equipment, by complacent top-heavy management, and by government policies incapable of adapting to changing world conditions.

With deindustrialization, manufacturing employment has declined in North America and Western Europe, but has been offset by rising employment in the services. To the extent that the older industrial nations have been able to innovate, the service employment growth has been in the advanced services sector, and this has enabled those countries to contend for leadership in supplying capital, entrepreneurship, and internationally traded services.

The aggressive post-1980 liberalization of international trade and the entry of new manufacturing nations into world markets have caused countries to become far more interdependent than in earlier times. Today, a quarter of the supplies of finished manufactured goods available in the

BOX 11.1   World Trade and the Energy Crises

"It is now obvious that this decision was one of the pivotal events in the history of this century." So said former U.S. Secretary of State Henry Kissinger of the spectacular increase in oil prices posted by the Organization of Petroleum Exporting Countries (OPEC) in December 1973. The ten-fold increase in world oil prices during the 1970s profoundly altered the pattern and structure of world trade. This episode truly ranks as one of the four major global economic crises of an eventful decade. All the world's nations were affected, but in very different ways, depending on their resource endowments, where they were in the development process, and their roles in the international economy.

How did the world get into this vulnerable situation? In Chapter 5, we traced the evolution of energy demand and the reasons for the growing interdependence of nations in this most widely traded form of energy. The very cheapness of oil, less than $3.00 per barrel in 1973, encouraged its lavish use. Accounting for only 30 percent of total global energy use in 1957, it had mounted to 43 percent of the total on the eve of the OPEC crisis and was still rising. With world consumption surging and production concentrated in only a few places, the world oil trade expanded nearly fourfold during this brief period, reaching one-tenth of all commodity trade.

Much of the new demand for oil resulted from the rapid postwar economic growth of Western Europe and Japan. Importing nine-tenths of its petroleum, Western Europe absorbed half of all oil shipments in 1972. Japan, with virtually no oil of its own, was importing one-sixth of the total. Meanwhile, the United States had shifted from being a net exporter of oil to being a net importer. Altogether, these industrialized countries took 80 percent of all internationally traded oil. This was also a period of substantial economic progress in much of the Third World, which was basing its industrialization on cheap imported oil.

While the global demand for oil was climbing, the main sources of supply were shifting eastward. In the 1950s, Venezuela had provided 35 percent of the world's petroleum exports, but by 1973, its share had slipped to only 8 percent. Much of the rest came from the Middle East and North Africa, where more than two-thirds of global reserves are concentrated. Although founded in 1960, OPEC had spent its first years in fruitless efforts to extract better terms from the oil multinationals. By 1973, however, the cartel was supplying 85 percent of the world's oil, clearly enough to assure a global monopoly if only its 13 quarrelsome members could agree on common action.

The opportunity to test this notion came late in 1973 when the Arab members of OPEC declared an embargo on oil shipments to the United States and other Western nations giving aid to Israel in the brief "Yom Kippur War" with neighboring Islamic states. Surprised and delighted by this demonstration of its power, OPEC quickly seized control of world petroleum pricing, abruptly shifting world power relations. Two main periods of steep price increases followed. At the end of 1973, OPEC raised prices fourfold and placed a ceiling on the volume of oil the cartel would produce and sell. The takeover of Iran by Muslim fundamentalists in 1979, and the Iran–Iraq war that followed, panicked world oil markets, causing the base price to jump from $12.70 to $41 per barrel. Though oil prices have since slipped, owing to world recession, conservation, and increased output by non-OPEC sources, the world economy remains deeply affected by OPEC's eight-year lock on world petroleum pricing.

International trade absorbed much of the impact of OPEC's actions. One effect was to alter global terms of trade—the average price a country receives for its exports in relation to the average price it pays for imports. The major industrialized countries and nonoil-exporting LDCs alike were forced to allocate a major part of their foreign exchange earnings to purchase the suddenly more costly OPEC oil. For much of the Third World, it was near disaster. As the OPEC-induced world recession forced down their own export prices, many LDCs went deeply into debt to avert a complete halt in their development.

The spatial pattern of trade flows shifted, too. Although higher prices drastically increased the dollar value of petroleum exports and imports, the total volume of these shipments actually declined, idling much of the world's large tanker fleet. And needing more and more foreign exchange to pay for oil, most countries cut back their foreign purchases of other goods, especially the LDCs. The newly rich oil exporters, however, quickly increased their imports of manufactures—capital goods to speed their industrialization and consumer products to satisfy the rising demand from their prospering citizens. Hence, the emergence of this large new import market benefited the industrialized countries supplying such products, but it did little for LDC exporters of primary commodities. In time, the high price of oil brought new petroleum exporters into world markets—Mexico, the United Kingdom, Norway, and the former USSR—thereby diversifying the spatial pattern of energy flows. Note, however, that these new source areas are closer to the markets for their oil, many of which are connected directly by pipeline, further diminishing the need for ocean-going tankers.

Clearly, the OPEC crises altered the composition of world trade, reducing the total volume of petroleum shipped and forcing LDCs to substitute oil purchases for capital goods. Although the imports of OPEC countries increased in amount and variety, their exports became even more specialized, partly because of the high valuation placed on their petroleum shipments but also because their nonoil commodity exports—such as olives, dates, coffee, and cacao—declined because of neglect and inflated currencies.

The vast size of the global import bill for petroleum is a measure of the monetary impact of the OPEC crises. Ballooning prices meant the wholesale transfer of billions of dollars to the oil exporters from the rest of the world. The combined oil revenues of OPEC, which were only $7 billion in 1970, quickly rose to $72 billion in 1974 and to $300 billion by 1980. As a consequence, virtually all of the non-OPEC world found itself thrown into a balance-of-payments deficit. The problem was less severe for the industrialized countries than for the oil-importing LDCs, however, because the former were able to sell manufactured goods and services to OPEC at sharply rising prices (thereby exporting their inflation). The LDCs did not have this cushion, because their conventional exports fell sharply in quantity and price. Meanwhile, for a time OPEC, was drawing in money faster than it could be spent, threatening a world financial crisis.

The effects of these events on individual OPEC countries varied greatly. The organization is by no means monolithic; its members differ in history, religion, culture, system of government, ideology, population, stage of development, size of oil reserves, and productive capacity. In general, they fall into two main groups. One group consists of countries that have populations relatively larger than their oil output and therefore have a crucial need to maximize their incomes (Iran, Algeria, Indonesia, Venezuela, Nigeria, Ecuador, and Gabon). Members of the second group, on the other hand, have small populations relative to output and have no immediately pressing need for large revenues (Saudi Arabia, the United Arab Emirates, Kuwait, Qatar, Libya, and Iraq). With more than 90 percent of OPECs total population, countries in the first group have little flexibility and are continually pressing for higher prices. The latter group can afford to wait, viewing oil left in the ground as a potentially valuable resource for the future.

The enormous global transfer of wealth from oil importers to oil exporters—at least $100 billion per annum—presented OPEC's group 2 countries with unprecedented money-management problems (group 1 had no such dilemma—its members can easily absorb any amount of revenue). The problems were of two kinds: how

to manage vast financial resources and how to plan national development in such a way as to use this one-time infusion of funds efficiently and with lasting benefit. In the short run, they placed their surplus funds in short-term investments, mostly in the United States and selected other industrial countries. In the longer, run they gradually increased their expenditures on development projects at home: roads, housing, ports, airfields, and new industries. Saudi Arabia, for instance, had emphasized energy-intensive industries that multiply the returns from its abundant supplies of very cheap oil and natural gas—such activities as petroleum refineries, petrochemical works, and cement plants.

Just as the benefits of their new riches varied among OPEC members, so did the effects of suddenly costly energy differ among oil-importing countries. For the older industrialized countries, the initial impact was recession, high inflation, and declining incomes. Subsequently, however, those developed countries favored for OPEC investment and trade—the United States, Japan, and certain Western European nations—benefited from the recycling of OPEC wealth and the refocusing of their foreign sales upon the newly oil-rich lands. However, those industrialized countries passed by in the recycling process, such as Italy, had no such compensating benefits to relieve the impact of soaring energy bills. And, as we have seen, the effect of the energy crises was truly devastating for the oil-importing LDCs.

As it must to all cartels, the end of OPEC's complete command of world oil prices came in the early 1980s. The price elasticity of demand for oil is low in the short run but is high in the long run: The immediate defense of consumers against soaring oil prices is limited because it takes time to develop more energy-efficient transportation, insulate buildings, and so forth. In time, however, the reaction to expensive petroleum was to give a high priority to energy efficiency, to develop new oil fields, and to find alternative forms of energy. The widespread recession and inflation follow-

ing the initial shock of high prices had reduced global economic growth and thus the demand for OPEC oil. High prices also made feasible the development of high-cost petroleum sources, such as the North Sea and the North Slope of Alaska, and induced industries and consumers to prune their use of oil.

The net result of these events was to reduce sharply the demand for OPEC oil. Whereas the group had a combined output of 31 million barrels per day in the 1970s, this total had fallen to only 18 million barrels by 1983. This put downward pressure on the price of oil, causing it to drop from a high of $41 to only $29 within this same period. As a result, OPEC's combined surplus income, more than $109 billion in 1980, turned into an $18 billion deficit by 1982. Some of the more hard-pressed members of OPEC, such as Nigeria and Iran, began to cheat on their agreed-on production quotas, thus further weakening prices, which by mid-1986 had fallen below $10 per barrel on the world spot market. Several OPEC countries went into budgetary deficits and were no longer able to sustain their high expenditures for development. Some of those with large populations resorted to heavy borrowing abroad.

With OPEC discipline in disarray, prices falling, and economies recovering from recession, global oil consumption resumed its upward march through the remainder of the 1980s. From a postcrisis low of 58 million barrels a day in 1983, world consumption had risen to 67 million barrels by 1994, a rise of 16 percent. Twenty-five percent of this new demand came from the United States and Canada.

By 1994, world prices had returned to $16 and OPEC's daily output had again reached 27 million barrels. The group was unsuccessful in reasserting complete control over world pricing, however, because of dissension and cheating among its members and rising competition by non-OPEC producers, from the North Sea to the Eastern Pacific, Africa, and South America.

(continued on next page)

BOX 11.1 (continued)

Consuming nations were shaken from their complacency, however, in August 1990, when Iraq seized Kuwait and threatened Saudi Arabia's main producing areas. Possession of all three oil producers would have given Iraq's rulers dominion over 45 percent of the world's oil reserves and a tight lock on global supplies and pricing. Spot prices on world markets quickly spiraled beyond $30 and would have gone higher had not other producing nations increased output to fill the gap. The ensuing Gulf War ended the Iraqi monopoly threat and restored prices to previous levels. World consumption resumed its expansion.

Oil analysts predict that the apparent emancipation from OPEC domination is only temporary. Non-OPEC supplies are expected to peak after the mid-1990s, and OPEC nations continue to hold more than three-fourths of global reserves. Thus, until the world can curb its appetite for energy or find viable alternatives to petroleum, every Persian Gulf flare-up will create panic in oil markets and imperil political and economic stability.

domestic markets of Europe and North America are made up of imports, five times the proportion four decades ago. This increased interdependence did not result in greater interindustry specialization among nations, as conventional theory might lead us to expect, however. Instead, the trade structures of industrial countries, including the NICs, have tended to converge; that is, the goods exchanged among them have actually become more similar, differing only in such things as source, brand name, and reputation (e.g., Volkswagens, Fiats, Toyotas, Fords).

The kinds of merchandise entering international trade therefore have undergone significant changes during the postwar era (Figure 11.1). The value of world industrial exports has increased at the expense of other categories,

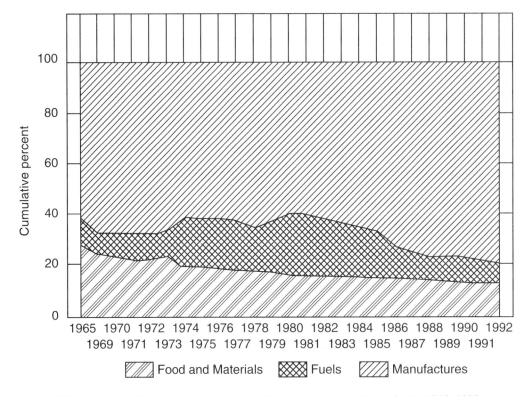

FIGURE 11.1 Changing composition of world exports (by value), 1965–1992. Manufactured goods have dominated world exports throughout this century, and their share of the total has continued to rise in the postwar era except for a period in the 1970s and 1980s, when sharply higher oil prices temporarily created turmoil in world markets. The export share held by other primary commodities has steadily declined in modern times, except for a small but short-lived expansion at the beginning of the 1970s. [*Source:* United Nations, *Yearbook of International Trade Statistics* (New York: United Nations, various years).]

rising from 61 percent of the total in 1965 to 78 percent in 1992. In between, however, export shares fluctuated considerably as a result of gyrating oil prices.

As Figure 11.2 shows, the crises of the 1970s and 1980s affected the various classes of manufactures differently. Least touched were exports of machinery and transport equipment, which mounted steadily, pausing only briefly during the global recession of 1981–1983. This category includes many of the newer high-technology items.

Fuel exports were the most dynamic category in the 1970s, doubling their value share from less than one-tenth to nearly one-fourth before weakening demand forced oversupply of oil in the 1980s (Figures 11.1, 11.2). This dramatic expansion was measurable only in value terms, however, being wholly a function of exploding oil prices; the total tonnage of world oil exports actually shrank as costs rose.

The export value share of other primary commodities—food, beverages, and crude materials—has steadily declined in recent years, continuing the long-term trend cited earlier. Indeed, the rate of decrease actually accelerated following the oil crisis: From a share of 29 percent in 1965, these commodities had slipped to less than 14 percent

by 1992 (Figure 11.1). Much of this change represents worsening terms of trade for primary goods as prices of manufactures and energy rose in world markets. Raw material exports showed the least growth of any major category, more than erasing their price gains of the early 1970s. Note from Figure 11.2 that nearly every major export category suffered a setback during the world economic recessions of 1973–1975 and 1981–1983.

Variable Impact on Different Types of Countries

Recent events have affected countries differently (Figure 11.3). Most striking was the meteoric climb in the value of exports from OPEC following the 1973 Mideast crisis and the sharp jump in oil prices in 1979. Equally abrupt was the decline of OPEC's foreign earnings in the 1980s—a result of energy conservation and growing competition from non-OPEC producers that forced prices downward. OPEC's oil revenues declined further in the early 1990s, as several of the main oil-importing nations fell into economic recession. Perhaps more significant for the longer-term was the extraordinary rise in the exports of the "other LDCs," due mainly to the growing export strength of the newly industrialized

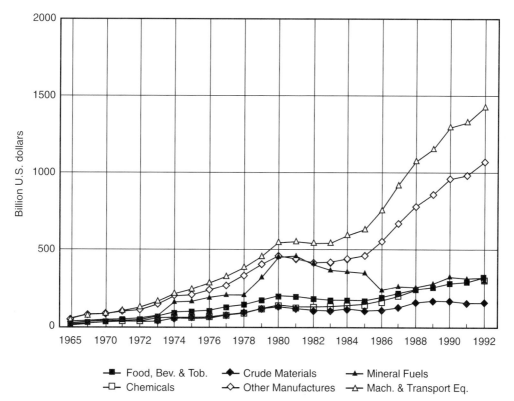

FIGURE 11.2 World growth of major export classes (by value), 1965–1992. Despite a tenfold increase in oil prices between 1973 and 1979, which was responsible for the steepening curve of fuel exports, manufactured exports continued to rise throughout most of the period. Note, however, the effects of the two global recessions in the mid-1970s and early 1980s. Since that time, exports of all three manufactured categories have climbed sharply. [*Source:* United Nations, *Yearbook of International Trade Statistics* (New York: United Nations, various years).]

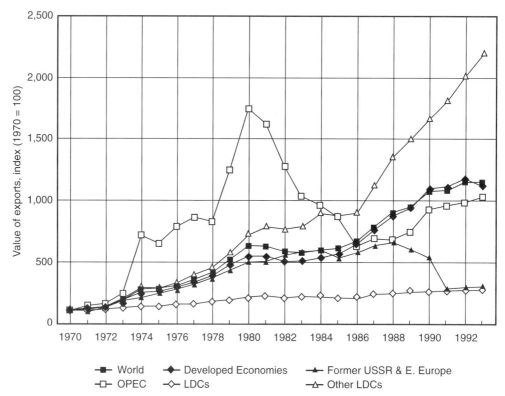

FIGURE 11.3   Growth of exports by major country categories (by value), 1970-1993. Two striking features stand out in the world export patterns of recent decades: (1) OPEC's spectacular rise in the 1970s and even more precipitous drop in the 1980s and again in the early 1990s, and (2) the remarkable export gains made by the "Other LDCs," owing mainly to the robust trade performance of an aggressive group of newly industrializing countries. The exports of these NICs were little touched by the oil-price rises and subsequent world recessions that so adversely affected other oil-importing regions. The least-developed countries—the world's poorest—continued to lag behind all the rest. [*Source:* United Nations, *Yearbook of International Trade Statistics* (New York: United Nations, various years).]

countries. NIC exports hardly paused in their steady climb during the 1970s and early 1980s. Foreign sales of the developed economies, on the other hand, were adversely affected by the recession of 1981–1983, though export growth of this group resumed in the mid-1980s and has continued upward since. Exports of the less-developed countries remained depressed throughout.

These diverging rates of export growth have altered the market shares of the various country groups (Figure 11.4). After many years of steady progress, the advanced countries commanded 71 percent of world exports at the beginning of the 1970s. This share fell below 63 percent during the crisis years, but rebounded to its old level by the end of the 1980s. OPEC's share expanded nearly threefold during the 1970s but fell to only 5 percent during the next decade. The "non-OPEC" LDCs, led by a number of energetic NICs, lost only a minor portion of their world market share to OPEC during the 1970s and eventually captured 22 percent of world exports by the early 1990s. The less-developed countries saw their meager share dwindle to a mere 0.4 percent during the period. After years of clinging to one-

tenth of world exports, the centrally planned economies of Eastern Europe and the Soviet Union lost ground in the 1980s, foreshadowing the general collapse of communism at the end of the decade. By the early 1990s, the successor states of the USSR and Eastern Europe had seen their share of world exports decline to less than 3 percent of the total.

Many of the fluctuations in export market share are attributable to changing commodity prices, especially oil. Another perspective on world export growth emerges when this is expressed in quantum terms, as in Figure 11.5, which shows the rates at which the physical volume of exports has changed during the past two decades. Here we see the rapid drop in export tonnage from the Middle East following the sharp run-up in oil prices in 1979. The sharply rising volume of exports by "Other Asia" since the mid-1980s is accounted for almost entirely by the performance of the newly industrialized nations along the Pacific Rim. More modest increases in export tonnage have been supplied by the Americas, North and South.

The world crises of the 1970s caused major dislocations in the established spatial patterns of trade. One such

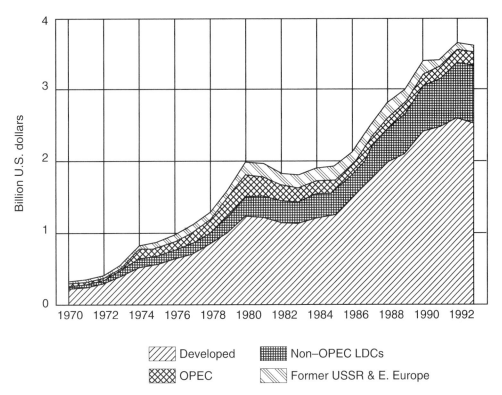

FIGURE 11.4   Changing shares of world exports, major country types (by value). In the early 1970s, the developed economies were supplying 72 percent of world exports. This share slipped somewhat during the troubled 1970s, but had recovered fully and was breaking new ground by the early 1990s. After capturing more than 15 percent of the total during the crisis years, OPEC was earning a smaller proportion at the end of the 1980s than it had before 1973. The "non-OPEC' LDCs," however, increased their share from under 12 percent to 22 percent during the period, thanks to the remarkable achievements of the newly industrialized countries. The world's poorest nations, referred to by the UN as "least-developed," saw their share shrink from 0.5 to a mere 0.4 percent, too small to show in this diagram. Note the sizable dip in combined world exports during the recession era of the early 1980s, the first such contraction since World War II. [*Source:* United Nations, *Yearbook of International Trade Statistics,* Table A (New York: United Nations, various years).]

pattern affected was the proportion of total trade flowing between countries at various levels of economic development. Industrialized countries were, by mid-century, conducting the greater part of their trade with each other. Thus, in 1970, industrialized nations sold more than three-fourths of their exports to other advanced countries and a mere 18 percent to less-developed countries. On the other hand, LDCs relied on advanced countries for nearly three-fourths of their exports and imports but had little more than one-fifth of their trade with other developing countries.

This well-entrenched pattern abruptly changed after 1973. The proportion of exports and imports exchanged by industrialized countries fell, and their trade with LDCs rose, especially their imports. This shift was a direct result of the soaring cost of imported OPEC oil and the sudden blossoming of OPEC as a market for the manufactured goods sold by the industrialized nations. By the end of the 1980s,

the loosening grip of OPEC spelled a return to the old trade pattern of interdependence among advanced countries, however, and the pre-1973 allocations of exports and imports were largely restored. Indeed, by the early 1990s, the proportion of trade taking place among industrialized nations was higher than ever.

A more durable legacy of the period was the growth of trade among LDCs. The growing dependence of developing nations on OPEC oil was one reason for this shift, but possibly of greater importance was the expanded role of the newly industrializing countries as markets for raw materials and foodstuffs and as suppliers of manufactured items. From a low of under 20 percent in 1970s, the share of LDC exports going to other LDCs rose to 40 percent by 1992. Imports from LDCs increased by a like amount.

In 1990, another unexpected development occurred: the sudden collapse of communism in the Eastern Bloc.

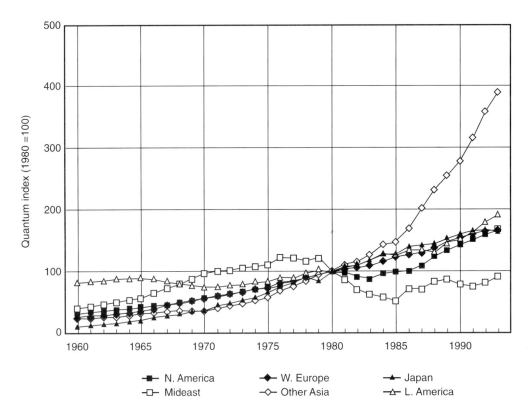

FIGURE 11.5   Export growth by market economies, quantum indices (1980 = 100), 1960–1993. A different picture of export growth emerges when this is measured in terms of its physical quantity rather than its monetary value, thereby eliminating the distorting effects of price inflation. Note the steep decline in quantities exported by the Middle East after 1979. This is a result of the price hikes by OPEC, which for a time reduced oil shipments and depressed world markets for other commodities. The quantity of world exports as a whole shrank during the early 1980s because of widespread recession. By 1993, the tonnage of exports from the Middle East had still not recovered to 1970s levels. In the meantime, however, the quantity of merchandise exported by "Other Asia" (mainly East Asian NICs) had begun its steep ascent. By the late 1980s and early 1990s, Japan and the developed nations of Europe and North America had resumed their former relatively moderate rates of export growth. [*Source:* United Nations, *Yearbook of International Trade Statistics,* Special Table F (New York: United Nations, various years).]

This dramatic event introduced a new volatile element into world commerce. Throughout the postwar era, the centrally planned economies of the Second World had traded mainly with each other, though this interdependence had diminished over the years. In the 1950s, this group relied on each other for 70 percent of their exports and more than three-fourths of their imports. By the end of the 1980s, intrabloc trade had shrunk to little more than half of their total exports and imports, and by 1992, it had fallen to a mere one-fifth of a declining total. Meanwhile, the proportion of Eastern Bloc exports going to the Western industrialized countries increased to 58 percent and imports from those countries grew to 66 percent. Thus, a fundamental realignment of trade by the Eastern Bloc took place very quickly

after the fall of the communist system. The new opening of these countries to the West promises to transform the economic map of the continent.

SHIFTING REGIONAL PATTERNS

This climactic turn of affairs in Eastern Europe and the former Soviet Union is only the latest in a series of important developments affecting the course of world commerce in recent times. Among others are the spectacular rise in Japan's share of world exports, the growing prominence of the East Asia's NICs, the slowing rate of trade creation in Western Europe, the expanding market for imported manufactured goods in the United States, and a rise in the global competitiveness of a restructured U.S. industry. In combination, these developments are producing a major shift in the center of gravity of global economic activity.

Although the volume and composition of international flows had fluctuated from time to time, the basic spatial pattern of economic linkages among the world's nations had remained remarkably stable over a very long period. The North Atlantic basin had dominated international trade at least since the age of colonization, when the economic ties between Western Europe and North America were forged and this region become the focus for suppliers of primary commodities elsewhere in the world (Figure 11.6). So enduring was this arrangement that when Bruce Russett (1967) compared patterns of trade linkages prior to World War II with those of the 1960s, he could point to the erection of the Iron Curtain separating the communist Eastern Bloc from Western Europe as the only significant disturbance affecting the basic map of international trade in modern times. He concluded, therefore, that fundamental trade patterns change with glacial slowness.

No longer is this true. Today, the North Atlantic basin accounts for a shrinking proportion of world trade and investment as the pace of economic activity in Western Europe has slackened. Indeed, Western Europe's 45 percent share of world exports shown in Figure 11.7 is misleading: A full 71 percent of that amount consists of trade among Western European countries—a consequence of Europe's extreme political and economic fragmentation. If, as the European Union's founders had intended, the region had become a United States of Western Europe, their interregional commodity flows would be classified as domestic trade. Their remaining exports to the rest of the world represented only 13 percent of global trade in 1992—well below the 17 percent contribution of the United States and Canada (Figure 11.7).

Today, the focus of international economic activity is turning to the Pacific Basin. The main participants in this process are 12 countries on the western rim of the Pacific, extending from Japan and Korea, on the north, southward to Australia and New Zealand. Joining in this development from across the Pacific are two other countries, the United States and Canada, both of which are looking westward for their trade and investment. Although trends of the past several years had foreshadowed this shift, the world crises of the 1970s undoubtedly hastened it, for the Pacific Rim countries have been much quicker to respond to changing conditions than has the rest of the world.

The Pacific Basin has evolved into a functionally integrated region whose 14 nations hold half of the population of the world and turn out half of its total output of goods and services. The United States and Canada are prime targets for their rapidly expanding manufactured exports, and the two are also leading suppliers of industrial materials and agricultural commodities as well as investment capital and technology to the region. Being active participants in the economic affairs of both the Atlantic and Pacific basins, therefore, Canada and the United States act as a fulcrum

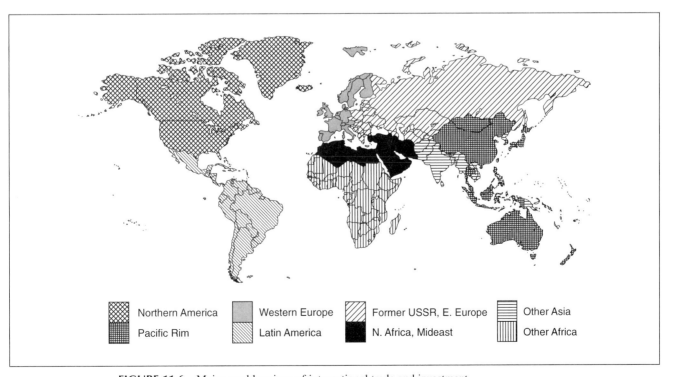

FIGURE 11.6   Major world regions of international trade and investment.

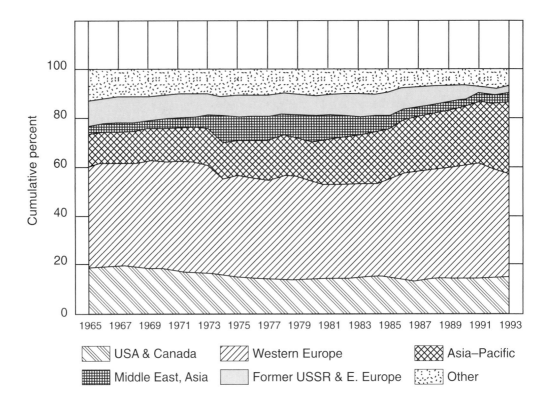

FIGURE 11.7 Changing value shares of world exports, major world regions, 1965–1993. Except for the recession years of the early 1980s and again in the early 1990s, Western Europe's portion of global exports has remained fairly steadily at about 45 percent, though a growing part of this has been diverted to intra-European trade. During this period, the United States and Canada have seen their combined exports slip from 19 percent of the world to 17 percent. The largest overall gains were garnered by the Asia–Pacific region, which climbed from only 13 percent in 1965 to 29 percent in 1993. The 12 dynamic Pacific Rim countries were responsible for 28 percent of this; the other nations of South and Southeast Asia contributed less than 1 percent of the Asia–Pacific total, despite their immense populations. The Asian Middle East briefly controlled as much as 11 percent of world exports during the oil-crisis years, but its portion had dwindled to less than 4 percent by 1993. The long-term decline in the export share of the former USSR and Eastern Europe accelerated further after the fall of Communism, dropping to only 2.6 percent of the world total in 1993. [*Source:* United Nations, *Yearbook of International Trade Statistics,* Special Table A (New York: United Nations, various years).]

between the two realms. We thus must look more closely at the pivotal role of North America in the changing affairs of these and other major economic regions of the world.

North America

The United States remains a central focus of world trade and investment even though its trade has not grown as fast as world trade as a whole. During the early postwar period, the United States accounted for a quarter of all world trade; today, its share has shrunk to 15 percent of the total (exports plus imports) as other trading nations have exploded on the

world scene, and as multinational enterprises headquartered in the United States choose to manufacture overseas rather than exporting from the United States. Nevertheless, the United States is still the largest trading nation, even though it has a smaller ratio of trade to gross national product than most countries. This ability to sustain a high level of trade with so small a proportion of its output is a function of size: a $6.4 trillion economy (1993) and a varied resource base within a territory of more than 9 million square kilometers. The level of U.S. trade participation is rising steadily, however (Figure 11.8). Prior to the 1970s, the United States sold no more than 4 percent of its goods abroad, but by 1993, it

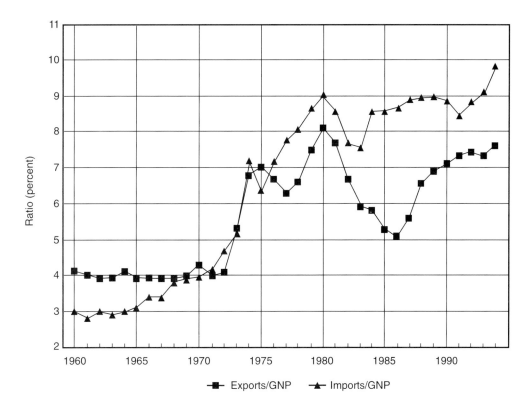

FIGURE 11.8   Ratios of U.S. exports and imports to gross national product, 1960–1993. Because of its very large economy, the United States continues to be a major trading nation, even though exports and imports do not constitute as a large a part of national output as is true of most industrial nations. Through most of the 1960s, the size and diversity of domestic resources made it unnecessary to maintain imports at a level much above 3 percent of GNP, whereas exports remained steadily at about 4 percent. The tumultuous 1970s and 1980s changed this, forcing the United States into greater international involvement. Both export/GNP and import/GNP ratios rose, but the import ratio climbed faster, reaching 9 percent by 1980, where it has remained off and on since, rising higher during periods of prosperity and falling during recessions. The export/GNP ratio peaked at 8 percent in 1980 but slumped badly in the mid-1980s. In the 1990s, however, U.S. exports have improved substantially as the global competitiveness of U.S. companies has increased. [*Source*: U.S. Bureau of the Census, *Statistical Abstract of the United States* (Washington, D.C.: U.S. Government Printing Office, various years).]

was exporting 7.3 percent of its GNP. The ratio of imports to GNP has risen even more rapidly, reaching 9.1 percent in 1993.

This rising level of trade participation demonstrates the extent to which the U.S. economy has become internationalized—a consequence of far-reaching changes taking place in the world at large, as well as within the country itself. The external pressures on the United States intensified during the 1970s, when the spiraling cost of oil pushed the country into a merchandise trade deficit. This followed an extended period of positive trade balances (Figure 11.9). The deficit reached $41 billion by the end of the decade, and it continued to widen even after the OPEC crises had

ended, soaring to $170 billion by 1986. The huge U.S. market had become a prime target for the world's exporters and a magnet for foreign investors seeking to widen their shares of that market.

The deficit problem began to ease somewhat in the late 1980s. An international agreement to reduce the exchange rate of the dollar reopened world markets to U.S. companies. The ensuing revival of exporting, however, owed much of its vigor to the fifth wave technological revolution discussed in Chapter 10 and to the restructuring that U.S. firms had been forced to undertake in order to survive.

Further helping to ease the U.S. trade deficit has been the recent growth of "invisible" exports. An expanding

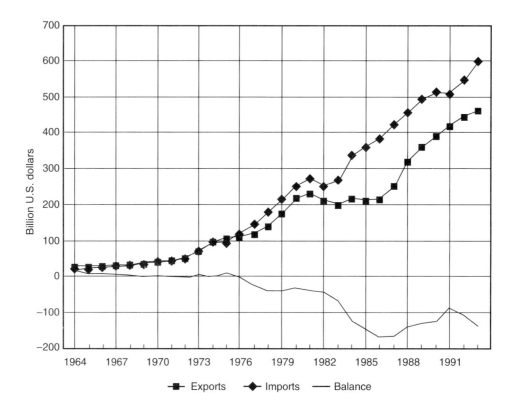

FIGURE 11.9   U.S. merchandise exports, imports, and trade balance, 1964–1993. Throughout the postwar era, the United States customarily exported more goods each year than it imported. The soaring price of oil in the 1970s pushed the US. merchandise trade balance into a deficit, which plunged still more deeply in the 1980s. Massive public debt and a consumption boom depressed the U.S. savings rate, and the dollar climbed to record heights. This made imported goods cheaper for Americans and U.S. exports more costly for foreigners, further widening the trade gap. A reversal began in the late 1980s, however, when the value of the dollar eased, prompting a revival of U.S. exports. Meanwhile, U.S. manufacturers had been forced into a painful restructuring, at the end of which their companies had been transformed into some of the lowest-cost, most-efficient competitors in the world. Export growth continued to accelerate until, by the early 1990s, the merchandise trade gap showed promise of narrowing considerably. [*Source*: United Nations, *Yearbook of International Trade Statistics* (New York: United Nations, various years).]

surplus in internationally traded services—transportation, finance, tourism, entertainment, and so forth—has compensated for much of the merchandise deficit. As both components of foreign commerce move in a positive direction, the combined U.S. trade in goods and services promises to achieve a surplus in time. Indeed, some analysts insist that if the activities of U.S.-owned multinationals abroad and foreign-owned firms in the United States were weighed into the scale, then the country's foreign accounts would already be in surplus.

The United States sells an unusually broad range of goods on world markets. Unlike most industrial countries, the United States is able to draw on a very large and productive farm sector for a multitude of agricultural commodities grown under many different physical conditions.

Complementing these are the country's exports of industrial goods, which rely on competitive advantage in high-technology production. As other nations find ways to narrow the technology gap, however, the manufacturing nations of Western Europe and the Pacific Rim are attempting to cut into this lead in technology-intensive goods (see Chapter 12).

The structure of U.S. imports also is changing. With its enormous appetite for a growing variety of raw materials, U.S. industry can no longer satisfy its needs from domestic sources and must therefore buy more and more of these abroad. Furthermore, now that U.S. oil production has peaked, the country must rely on foreign suppliers for a growing portion of its energy. Meanwhile, Americans now purchase foreign-made automobiles, appliances, electronic

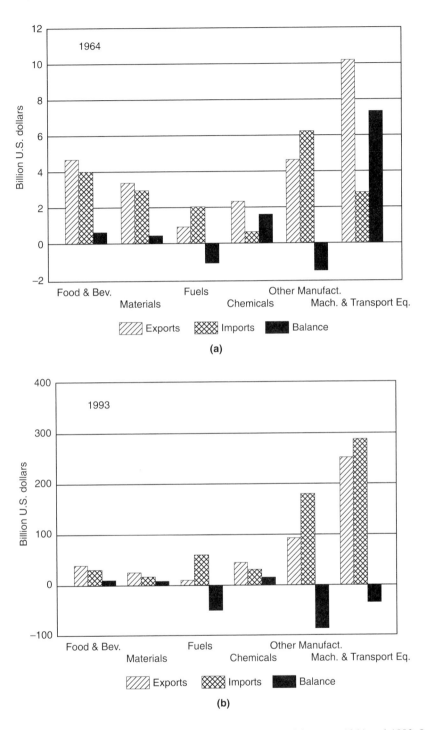

FIGURE 11.10 Changing commodity structure of U.S. exports and imports, 1964 and 1993. In the mid-1960s, the United States was still enjoying a positive overall trade balance, which benefited from a very large surplus in machinery and transport equipment, as well as positive balances in chemicals, agricultural goods, and industrial materials. By then, U.S. petroleum output had peaked, leading to a trade deficit in fuels; and imports of mass-produced, low-technology goods were beginning to exceed exports. A contrasting picture had emerged by 1993. The overall merchandise trade deficit in that year had reached a worrisome $138 billion, and imports of manufactured goods in both low-technology and high-technology categories exceeded exports by large amounts. More recent information indicates that the U.S. exports of manufactured goods, especially high-technology products and capital goods, had grown substantially by the mid-1990s, promising improvement in the overall balance of trade. [*Source:* United Nations, *Yearbook of International Trade Statistics* (New York: United Nations, various years).]

goods, and innumerable other consumer products. Figure 11.10 shows how these trends have affected the U.S. balance of trade in particular commodity classes. Comparing the composition of U.S. trade in 1964 with that of 1993, we see that the comfortable surplus in machinery and transport equipment has vanished, replaced by a $34 billion deficit. This reflects not only very large imports of motor vehicles, but also a growing quantity and variety of high-technology goods covered by this category. Between 1964 and 1993, the deficit in "other manufactures" (mainly nontechnology goods) had swelled to nearly $87 billion. The bill for imported fuels also shows a large deficit, but this represents a substantial improvement since the oil-crisis period. As in the past, surpluses in chemicals, farm products, and industrial materials helped cushion the burden. Despite this seemingly bleak picture, however, a recovery in U.S. industrial exports was already under way in the late 1980s and it has continued to grow in the mid-1990s.

The eventful 1970s and 1980s also produced major changes in the spatial pattern of U.S. trade linkages, as the two parts of Figure 11.11 reveal. Between 1970 and 1992, much of the country's trade had shifted away from Western Europe and toward the Asia–Pacific arena. Imports from Japan and other Asia (mainly East Asian NICs) had grown very large by 1992, by which time they contributed more than four-fifths of the merchandise trade deficit. Though U.S. trade with Latin America contracted somewhat in the 1970s, it has more recently begun to increase as the economies of that region resume their growth.

Despite these overall shifts in U.S. trade links, certain connections have remained fairly constant. Among the most enduring relationships are the close ties of trade and investment with the country's North American neighbor. Canada is by far the largest trading partner of the United States, with 20 percent of total U.S. trade (exports plus imports), and Mexico ranks third (behind Japan). Canada and Mexico are quite dependent economically on the United States, which accounts for about three-fourths of their total trade in some years and is their major source of foreign investment. One obvious reason for the importance of U.S. trade and investment to its neighbors is the country's huge economic size: The U.S. gross national product is 11 times as large as Canada's and 20 times as large as Mexico's. The United States shares a 6,700-kilometer common border with Canada and a 3,200-kilometer border with Mexico. There is close economic interaction among the three countries because of this contiguity, and because of the complementarity of their resources, reflecting differences in physical conditions and in the availability of technology, capital, labor, and entrepreneurial skills. The United States obtains certain land-intensive commodities from its well-endowed neighbors—tropical agricultural products from Mexico and petroleum and mineral ores from both countries—and relies on Mexico for labor-intensive manufactured goods. Balmy climates, attractive scenery, and exotic cultures also lure

U.S. tourist dollars, a vital source of foreign exchange for Mexico. In return, the United States supplies temperate grains for food-short Mexico and subtropical fruits and winter vegetables to Canada, and it provides both countries with a range of capital-intensive, high-technology manufactured goods. Integration of the three economies took a large step forward with formal ratification of the North American Free Trade Agreement in 1994 (see Chapter 12).

Canada depends on foreign commerce to a much greater extent than does the United States; in most years, the country exports more than one-fifth of its output. This high degree of trade dependence results from a special combination of human and natural resources. With a total land area second in size only to Russia, Canada has an enormous store of mineral wealth and biotic resources, as well as a large expanse of land suitable for temperate grains. Yet the population, which is about the same as that of California, is small, leaving a huge surplus for sale abroad. At the same time, Canada must import tropical and subtropical foods and beverages for which its agricultural lands are climatically unsuited, and a wide range of manufactured goods its own industries are unable to supply because their production requires economies of scale impossible to achieve with so small a domestic market.

Although primary commodities figure importantly in Canada's foreign sales, industrial exports are a large part of the total, however, and they are assuming an ever-larger proportion of the total (Figure 11.12). Canada's manufacturing sector draws on a human resource base that includes a well-educated and experienced work force and a highly capable entrepreneurial class, in addition to a large and varied stock of physical resources. Some of the country's industrial exports result from the initial processing of mineral ores and forest products, but many are finished goods that neatly express the character of the land. Canada has been especially successful in marketing heavy-duty hydroelectric generators and hydraulic turbines, benefiting from the long experience gained by Canadian firms involved in developing the country's great waterpower potential. Canadian companies have gained an important competitive edge in the sale of high-technology communications equipment (including fiber optics), small commercial aircraft, and railway cars—products that have been developed to overcome the problems of living in a vast territory. At the same time, the Canadians have dropped production of many consumer goods that had been manufactured for the limited domestic market under an umbrella of governmental protection against imports. This artificial shelter was rendered ineffective by Canada's membership in the General Agreement on Tariffs and Trade (GATT) (see Chapter 12 for a discussion of this series of international agreements).

Although the United States has long been the principal market for Canada's abundant resource based, commodities—such as oil, gas, hydroelectricity, minerals, and wood products—U.S. purchases of vehicles and parts under

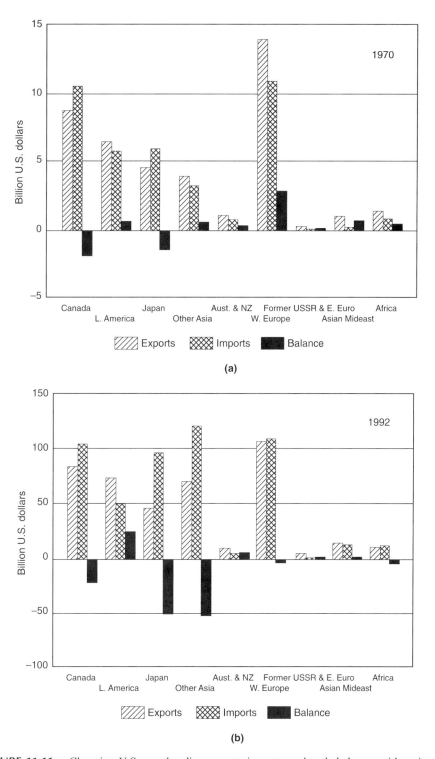

FIGURE 11.11 Changing U.S. merchandise exports, imports, and trade balances with major world regions, 1970 and 1992. In 1970, U.S. trade was in overall balance with the world at large. The only sizable deficits were with its leading trading partner, Canada, and Japan. By 1992, the deficit with Japan had swollen to $51 billion. During that same period, a huge trade deficit had also developed with Other Asia (mainly East Asian NICs), likewise reaching $51 billion in 1992. The country's trade with Western Europe, however, was very nearly in balance by the early 1990s, after a period of deficit in the 1980s. Note that Canada continues to be the nation's leading trade partner, but that collectively the Asia–Pacific region has risen in prominence. The positive balance with the Asian Middle East reflects U.S. success in marketing to that area, together with a diversification of U.S. oil procurement in recent years. [*Source:* United Nations, *Yearbook of International Trade Statistics,* Special Table B (New York: United Nations, various years).]

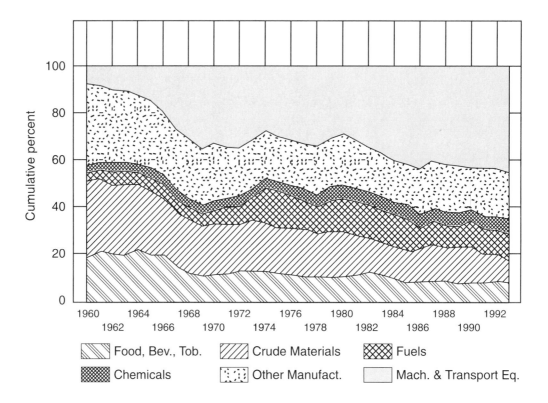

FIGURE 11.12 Changing composition of Canada's exports, 1960-1993. In earlier times, the kinds of products that Canada exported conformed very well to what might be expected of a country with a small population living in a vast territory endowed with an abundance of natural resources. Thus, in 1960, 55 percent of Canada's exports were made up of products of the mine, forest, and field. In a remarkably short time, however, Canadians have shifted their export emphasis toward industrial products. By 1993, these categories had reached a combined 71 percent of the total. [*Source:* United Nations, *Yearbook of International Trade Statistics* (New York: United Nations, various years).]

the Canada–U.S. Auto Agreement (Chapter 12) helped to shift the balance in favor of industrial goods. Today, motor vehicles and parts represent the single largest class of Canada's exports to the United States, nearly half the total in 1992 (Figure 11.13). Altogether, three-fourths of the goods shipped to the United States are of industrial origin; nine-tenths of U.S. sales to Canada fit into this category. Though overshadowed by the surging two-way trade in manufactures, Canada's exports of fuels and industrial materials to the United States continue to be important to both countries and will likely increase under provisions of the new Canada–U.S. Free Trade Agreement (see Chapter 12). Offsetting the large U.S. merchandise trade deficit with Canada are substantial amounts of U. S.-provided services and sizable capital flows representing repatriated profits on American investments in Canada.

The second-largest regional partner for Canadian trade is Western Europe, although its share of the total has slipped somewhat in recent years (Figure 11.14). This is the only region with which Canada has sustained a persistent trade deficit. Among Canada's individual trading partners,

Japan ranks second only to the United States. In addition to its substantial trade with Canada, Japan also has invested heavily in that country. Initially, Japanese investors concentrated on extractive industries in the western provinces, but increasingly they have set up manufacturing plants in Canada's industrial heartland—Ontario and Quebec—in response to formation of the U.S.–Canada Free Trade Agreement and the North American Free Trade Agreement. Signing of these two agreements has also successfully lured traders and investors from other Pacific Rim countries.

The Pacific Rim

Since the 1960s, vibrant nations along the western margins of the Pacific have developed into the world's most rapidly expanding economic region. Between 1970 and 1993, the Asia–Pacific area boosted its share of global exports from 12 to more than 28 percent (refer to Figure 11.7).

Five sets of Pacific Rim countries have participated. Japan has been the leading figure, establishing a pattern of

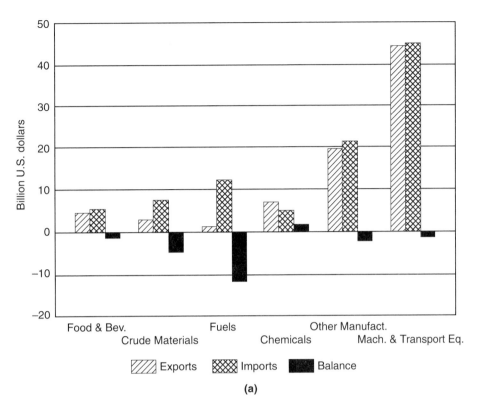

(a)

FIGURE 11.13 Composition of U.S. trade with Canada, 1992. The United States ran a trade surplus with Canada as long as that country was mainly a supplier of resource-based commodities. In recent decades, however, the bilateral balance turned negative as the manufacturing content of Canada's exports increased. The Canada–U.S. Auto Agreement contributed importantly to this shift. Note that the trade between the two countries is now heavily weighted toward industrial goods—90 percent of U.S. shipments to Canada and 74 percent of Canadian exports to the United States—with motor vehicles and parts dominating movements in both directions. The Canada–U.S. Free Trade Agreement can be expected to tilt this proportion still further. [*Source:* United Nations, *Yearbook of International Trade Statistics, 1995,* Special Table B (New York: United Nations, 1990).]

trade-led growth with its astounding economic performance since the early 1950s. Following later, the "Four Tigers" of Asia—South Korea, Taiwan, Hong Kong, and Singapore—successfully competed in world markets with an increasingly sophisticated line of manufactured products. More recently, five other Asian countries have adopted similar export-led strategies: Thailand, Malaysia, Indonesia, the Philippines, and the People's Republic of China. During this same period, Australia and New Zealand, having been cut adrift by the problem-ridden United Kingdom, formed new economic ties in the Pacific realm. Seven of the Pacific Rim countries (Brunei, Indonesia, Malaysia, the Philippines, Singapore, Thailand, and Vietnam) have joined together in a loosely structured experiment in economic integration called the Association of Southeast Asian Nations (ASEAN) (see Chapter 12).

The upsurge of economic activity along the Pacific Rim occurred during a period when the rest of the world was reeling from the major shocks of the 1970s—the

inflation in commodity prices, the breakdown of monetary stability, two sharp oil-price rises, and two global recessions. The East Asian countries demonstrated a remarkable ability to weather these crises. Drawing on deeply imbedded cultural values that emphasize hard work and allegiance to the group, laborers and managers work together for the success of their joint enterprises, and business leaders collaborate with government ministries to further national goals. Together they closely follow international economic trends and events and respond quickly to changing conditions of demand and supply. The general public is made aware of the country's circumstances and can be mobilized to the common good during times of crisis.

Unlike the older industrial countries, with their stable populations and sluggish economies, the Pacific Rim is an area of growth. Between 1982 and 1993, the combined GNP of this group increased fifteen-fold, adding to the buying power and productive capacity of a region that holds a third of humanity. Because the newly developing members

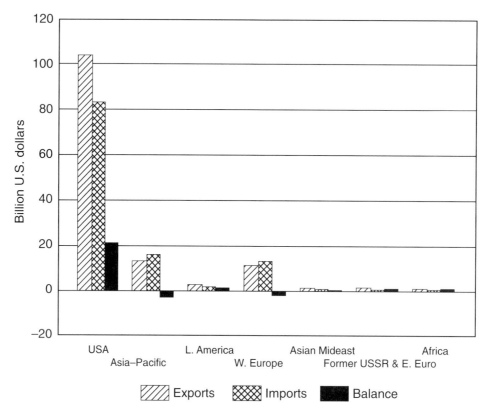

FIGURE 11.14   Canadian exports, imports, and trade balance with major world regions, 1992. Foreign trade is important to the Canadian economy, and an overwhelming share of that trade is with the United States: In 1993, the United States took 81 percent of Canada's exports and supplied 67 percent of its imports. The second area of importance for Canadian trade is Western Europe. Among individual trading partners, Japan is growing importance. Canada's merchandise trade balance is positive with all the regions shown here except Western Europe and the Asia–Pacific, where it runs small deficits. [*Source:* United Nations, *Yearbook of International Trade Statistics, 1993* (New York: United Nations, 1995).]

of this bloc are successfully bringing population growth under control, they are now experiencing a steady rise in per capita buying power. At the same time, literacy rates are rising, labor and management skills are multiplying, and support services are evolving.

This combination of growing productive capacity and rising consumer demand has brought a flood of investment to the western Pacific. During the 1970s, foreign investment in the region quadrupled and investment in the Four Tigers grew sixfold. Meanwhile, investment in Western Europe has peaked and some investors are beginning to withdraw. Multinational enterprises are the prime agents for this transfer of capital and technology. Japanese, U.S., and British companies have led, but German, Canadian, and Australian firms are well represented also.

The extent to which merchandise flows have shifted from the Atlantic Basin to the Pacific Basin is shown in Figure 11.15. Prior to the 1970s, total trade (exports plus imports) between Anglo-America and the Pacific Rim had been consistently less than that with Western Europe; by the end of that decade, the situation had reversed. During the

interval, trans-Pacific flows had increased twice as fast as those crossing the North Atlantic.

At the same time, a marked change was taking place in the kinds of goods moving between North America and the Pacific Rim. Very quickly, the developing countries of the western Pacific advanced from being exporters mainly of primary commodities to becoming sellers of industrial products. More recently, aided by the influx of multinationals, the Pacific Rim countries have further upgraded their output, moving quickly from the production of standardized labor-intensive goods, such as textiles and clothing, to the manufacture of ever-more sophisticated products, including machinery, electronics, and communications equipment. This development has spread through the region in a pattern that has now become typical of the Pacific Rim, beginning first in Japan and then moving to the Four Tigers and finally to the five newly industrializing countries.

One of the more significant developments to appear in the western Pacific has been the rise of new centers of corporate control and finance. Although Japanese firms had been actively investing abroad for quite some time,

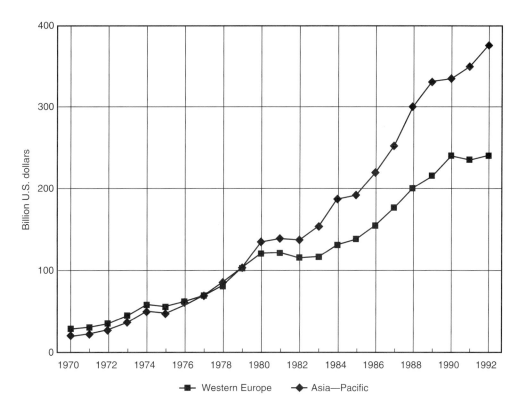

FIGURE 11.15 U.S. and Canadian trade (exports plus imports) with Western Europe and the Asia–Pacific, 1970–1992. The Pacific eclipsed the Atlantic as the leading avenue for North American commerce late in the 1970s, ending a centuries-old dominance of world trade by the Atlantic Basin, and the gap between the two trading realms widening further in the 1990s. The Asia–Pacific realm as defined here includes all of East, Southeast, and South Asia, but 12 vigorous nations on the Pacific Rim contribute all but 1 percent of the trade generated in the entire region. These 12 have been leading actors in a rapidly changing international scene. [*Source:* United Nations, *Yearbook of International Trade Statistics,* Special Table B (New York: United Nations, various years).]

headquarters of multinational corporations are now springing up in Hong Kong, Singapore, Taiwan, South Korea, and Australia. As they establish branch operations in neighboring lands, these Pacific-based multinationals serve to integrate the region ever more tightly.

Lately, as countries in the region accumulate large trade surpluses, several East Asian capitals have become centers of international finance. Japan is now a leading exporter of capital, and banks and brokerage firms headquartered in Tokyo operate branches throughout the world. Both Singapore and Hong Kong maintain lively money markets, and these are taking a prominent part in the current trend toward the globalization of financial trading on a 24-hour basis.

Undoubtedly, Japan has done more than any other country to forge the Pacific Basin into a functionally integrated whole—an economic region whose complementary resources are linked together by trade and investment. In creating an export-led, innovation-driven economy based almost entirely on human resources, Japan has shown the

way to those Asian lands—notably the Four Tigers—that lack sufficient natural endowments of their own. Japanese multinationals have also led in developing the resources of Pacific countries such as Australia, Indonesia, and Malaysia that are endowed with industrial raw materials and fuels.

With 125 million people enjoying incomes comparable to those in Europe and America, Japan had been until recently the world's most rapidly growing advanced economy, and it continues to be the third largest trader. The Japanese have continually restructured their industries in adjusting to changing world demand and to their country's advancing technical capabilities. This is apparent from the changing composition of the country's exports (Figure 11.16): textiles and yarns—mature, labor-intensive products that once dominated the country's foreign sales—now contribute only a minor share of the total; the big increases are in machinery and transport equipment, now nearly three-fourths of all exports despite a decline in shipbuilding, which has been captured by South Korea. Other rapidly expanding exports include electronics and communications

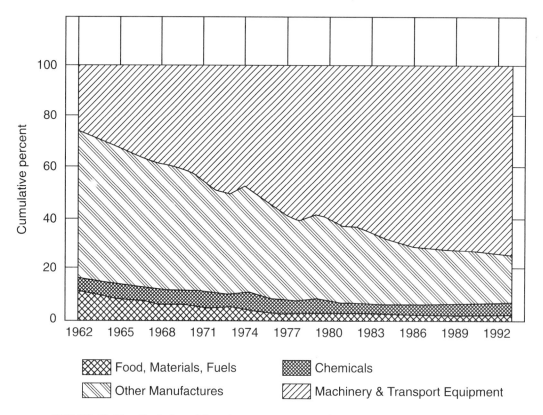

FIGURE 11.16   Evolution of Japan's export structure, 1962–1993. The composition of its exports faithfully reflects Japan's longtime role as a workshop nation, one that sells manufactured products abroad to pay for the primary commodities its resource-poor home environment lacks. Even so, the nature of the country's exports has undergone a fundamental change corresponding to the restructuring that has taken place within the national economy. Thus, in 1962, nearly three-fifths of Japanese exports consisted of mass-produced, standardized goods classified by the UN as other manufactures [Standard International Trade Class (SITC 6 and 8)]. Only one-quarter of the total fell under machinery and transport equipment (SITC 7), a higher-technology heading. Steadily over the next three decades, the contributions of the two classes came to be almost exactly reversed as the level of Japanese technology rose generally. During the period, industrial exports of all kinds increased from 89 percent of the total to more than 98 percent, whereas food, materials, and fuels shrank from 11 to a mere 1.8 percent. Japan's import structure is essentially a mirror image of this. [*Source:* United Nations, *Yearbook of International Trade Statistics* (New York: United Nations, various years).]

equipment, which are representative of the knowledge-intensive industries now stressed by Japanese government policy. A diminishing share of exports comes from Japan's older energy-intensive, polluting metallurgical industries, which required massive imports of raw materials and fuels.

More than two-thirds of Japan's trade, both exports and imports, take place within the Pacific Basin (Figure 11.17). One-third of its exports go to other Asia–Pacific countries, which in turn supply two-fifths of its imports. The Japanese thus have succeeded by peaceful means in gaining economic hegemony over a part of the world they had once sought to conquer militarily. Japan also has enlarged its share of the European market, which now accounts for one-fifth of all foreign sales. The only major region with which Japan has a negative trade balance is the Middle East. Dependence on that politically explosive

region has diminished substantially since the height of the oil crises—from 34 percent of total imports in 1980 to 11 percent in 1992—owing partly to Japan's policy of diversifying its oil purchases to safer sources, and partly to a national campaign for increased energy efficiency. During that time, energy imports as a whole dropped from a high of 51 percent of all imports in 1981 to 21 percent in 1993.

In recent decades, Japanese exports have exceeded imports by a big margin: In 1993, Japan's exports to the United States were more than twice as large as imports, yielding a bilateral surplus of $51 billion. That same year it had trade surpluses of nearly $40 billion with Western Europe and $42 billion with the Asia-Pacific region.

These lopsided trade balances have created friction with its trading partners, but also have furnished Japan with foreign investment. Prior to the 1970s, Japanese multina-

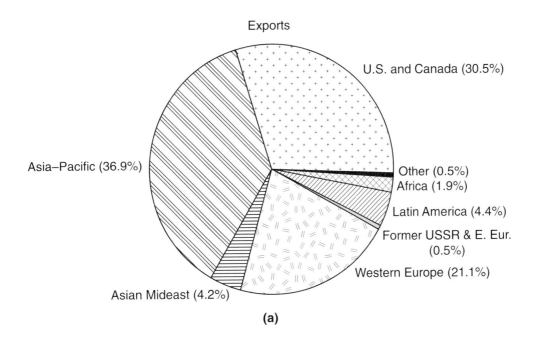

(a)

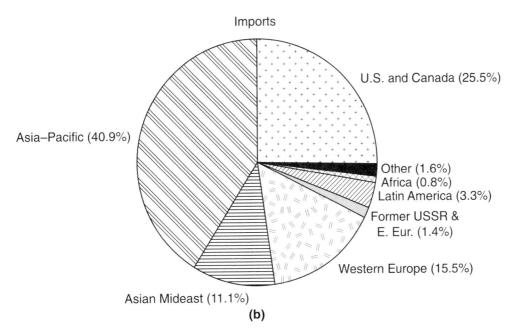

(b)

FIGURE 11.17   Value share of Japanese exports and imports with major world regions, 1992. The Pacific Basin supplies more than two-thirds of Japan's imports and takes a like amount of its exports. Both Northern America and Western Europe are more important to Japan as customers than as suppliers, and sales to these areas have climbed steeply in recent decades. The reverse is true of the Asia–Pacific region, which is more significant as a source for Japanese imports and has further enlarged this role as Japanese companies farm out more and more of their labor-intensive manufactures to other Asian countries. The Middle East actually supplies a smaller percentage of Japanese imports today than it did prior to the OPEC crises, evidence of Japan's canny program of diversifying its sources of oil. [*Source:* United Nations, *Yearbook of International Trade Statistics* (New York: United Nations, various years)]

tionals concentrated their overseas activities in the extractive enterprises, with the purpose of assuring long-term supplies of industrial materials for the homeland. After 1969, when governmental restrictions on exports of capital were removed, Japanese firms expanded their investments in foreign manufacturing and service ventures. Today, more than half of Japan's overseas investment is in the Pacific region.

Not all the results of this persistently high trade surplus have been advantageous to the Japanese economy, however. The accumulation of huge quantities of foreign currency has triggered a readjustment process. The growing surplus has forced up the exchange rate of the Japanese yen, which in turn has had the effect of elevating the relative cost of Japanese labor and of raising the prices of Japan's exports in world markets. In order to preserve their shares of these markets, Japanese multinationals have shifted production overseas—part of it to low-wage developing nations in Southeast Asia and elsewhere, and the rest to big market areas such as the United States. One result has been a "hollowing out" of Japanese industries: As Japanese industries increasingly serve their foreign markets from third country sources, home production falls.

The rise of the Pacific Rim as a powerful economic force is having a great impact on the United States in particular (Figure 11.18). Aside from its mounting trade deficit with the western Pacific countries, the United States finds itself in a paradoxical position with respect to that region. The types of merchandise the country exchanges with East Asia place the United States in the role of a less-developed country dealing with more advanced ones: A high proportion of U.S. exports to the Pacific consists of primary commodities, whereas imports are mostly industrial goods. Indeed, one-third of all U.S. agricultural exports now goes to the Pacific Rim.

So pervasive is the Pacific region's influence that it is lending added force to the westward movement of people, industries, and commercial activities within the United States. Because West Coast ports carry more than four-fifths of U.S. trade with the Pacific, these are enjoying a boom in port industries and service activities. In addition, the western states are beneficiaries of more than a third of all investment by Pacific countries in the United States.

Latin America

The developing countries of Latin America differ from those of East Asia in a number of respects, not only culturally, but also in the fundamental character of their human and natural resources, the makeup of their exports and imports, and the public policies that have shaped their commercial relations with the rest of the world.

Latin America's traditional role in the world economy, dating to the beginning of European colonization, called for exporting primary commodities—agricultural products and minerals—to the industrialized countries of the Northern Hemisphere. Although this exchange drew on many natural complementarities between the two areas, Latin Americans had long been dissatisfied with the subordinate position in which this relationship placed them, and they worked persistently to change it through their development planning and trade policies.

Despite the shared colonial past and the economic and political problems with which it left them, the Latin American nations are surprisingly diverse. They range in size and level of development from Brazil, a giant country that aspires to superpower status by the end of the century, to the small, desperately poor island nation of Haiti. Among them are countries rich in valuable minerals, such as Mexico and Venezuela; or in agricultural lands, such as Argentina; or in both, such as Brazil. Some have neither of these. The Latin American nations also vary substantially in work-force skills, literacy levels, and quality of infrastructure.

Most Latin American countries export a large proportion of their national output. The median export/GNP ratio is more than 13 percent, as compared with slightly more than 7 percent for the United States and 9 percent for Japan. The highest ratios are those of small Central American countries such as Costa Rica (30 percent) and mineral exporters such as Chile (22 percent). The larger countries have lower export/GNP ratios as, for example, Argentina (5 percent) and Brazil (8 percent).

Though primary commodities still command a prominent place in Latin American exports, industrial products are showing important gains. This is a recent development. As recently as 1970, 84 percent of the region's exports to its principal customer, the United States, had consisted of foods, materials, and fuels. This was a common pattern for developing countries. Imports, on the other hand, were not at all typical: Unlike most LDCs, the Latin American countries have for years imported only small quantities of manufactured consumer goods but a high proportion of capital goods. Thus, in 1970, manufactured products made up 79 percent of Latin American imports from the United States, but only 18 percent consisted of consumer products. The principal reason for this was the longstanding Latin American governmental policy of import-substituting industrialization. This policy emphasized the manufacture of consumer goods for the domestic market—often in government-owned and -operated plants—and protecting these products from foreign competition by limiting their importation from abroad. As a result of such policies, several of the larger Latin American countries, especially Brazil, Argentina, and Mexico, became virtually self-sufficient in products of this kind. They found, however, that such import substitution was much more difficult to achieve with higher-technology items, and they were forced to obtain these from the more advanced countries of Europe and North America.

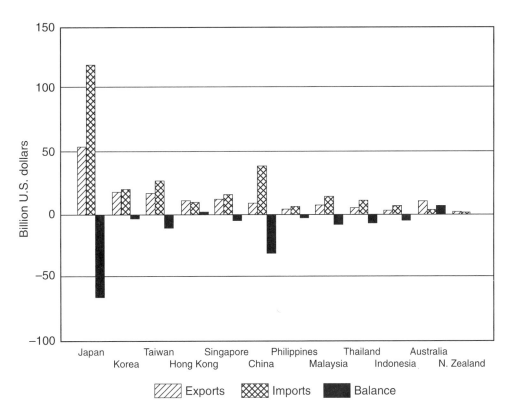

FIGURE 11.18   U.S. merchandise exports, imports, and trade balance with the Pacific Rim, 1994. As a group, the 12 Pacific Rim nations were responsible for more than 36 percent of all U.S. trade (exports plus imports) in 1994. Amid all the attention paid to Japan's strained trading relations with the United States, it has gone little noticed that the other 11 Pacific Rim countries in combination actually generate a higher proportion of total U.S. trade (21 percent) than does Japan (15 percent). Furthermore, they are better customers; in 1994, they bought 85 percent more American goods than did Japan. Consequently, the U.S. trade deficit with the 11, though very large, is nevertheless smaller than the deficit with Japan. High-technology goods are a major element in the two-way exchange between the United States and the East Asian NICs. All four of the Little Tigers maintain close economic ties with the United States. In 1994, Taiwan led the four in trading with the United States, followed closely by South Korea. Among individual countries, China's trade with the United States has grown fastest in the past decade, but this trade has been quite lopsided, producing a trade deficit for the United States of $29 billion in 1994. Of all the Pacific Rim countries, only one, Australia, consistently buys more from the United States than it sells. As a group, therefore, this region has become a major partner of the United States, but it currently imposes a heavy drain on the U.S. trade balance. [*Source:* U.S. Bureau of the Census, *Statistical Abstract of the United States, 1995* (Washington, DC: U.S. Government Printing Office, 1995).]

By the end of the 1980s, the structure of Latin American production and trade had undergone a marked change. A wave of political and economic reform swept through the region. Persuaded by the success of export-led industrialization policies in East Asia, most Latin American countries began to drop old trade restrictions and open their economies to the world. In 1980, primary goods comprised 80 percent of Latin America's exports; by 1992, these had fallen to 58 percent and the proportion of manufactured exports had more than doubled to 42 percent.

The traditional markets and sources of supply for Latin American countries have been North America and Western Europe. Throughout the nearly two centuries since independence, Mexico, most of Central America, and much of South America have been tied to the United States. The southernmost countries—Argentina, Uruguay, and Chile—have had strong links to Europe; and the Caribbean islands, most of which have gained independence only recently, still maintain commercial connections with their former mother countries. Patterns of foreign investment have reinforced these trade linkages, and the resulting condition of economic dependence has made Latin America vulnerable to the vagaries of business cycles, politics, and wars in the North.

In recent decades, these long-established trade patterns have shifted. Since 1970, Latin America's trade with the older industrialized countries has shrunk from three-fourths of the total to two-thirds in early 1990s. Western Europe has suffered the major part of this decline, having dropped from nearly one third to one-fifth of Latin American trade. The United States, on the other hand, significantly increased its trade with the region; by 1992, the U.S. share of Latin America's exports and imports had risen to more than two-fifths of the total. Japan's share of the region's imports also grew, from only 6 percent in 1970 to 8.5 percent in 1992. One of the big changes, however, has been the growing success of Latin American firms in selling to less-developed countries; by 1992, this group was taking nearly a third of the areas exports. Shipments of Latin American goods have risen substantially to the Middle East and especially to the newly industrializing countries of East Asia. Of special significance, however, is the rising level of trade among Latin American countries, which now amounts to more than 21 percent of the total. Much of this new intraregional trade can be attributed to the formal organizational ties that have been established among these countries (see Chapter 12 for a discussion of Latin American economic integration).

Western Europe

The international crises of the 1970s had an exaggerated effect on the countries of Western Europe, mainly because they are so dependent on trade. The large European countries generally export about a quarter of their GNP, but some of the smaller ones export half or more of their output. In part, this dependence on trade is a function of political fragmentation—more than 20 sovereign entities occupying an area no more than a third that of the United States—and the substantial intra-European trade this produces. Many of these small countries are contiguous, distances are very short, transport networks are dense and of superior quality, and the integration of their economies via membership in pan-European organizations has greatly reduced the artificial barriers that limited their interaction in earlier years. The high level of commercial activity also stems from the size and density of their populations—a third of a billion people in all—and their high per capita incomes. Standards of living throughout the region today are comparable to those of North America, and three European countries currently exceed the United States in per capita GNP.

With so much of Western Europe's output going into world commerce, it is not surprising that this region accounts for more than two-fifths of total world trade (refer back to Figure 11.7). As noted earlier, however, the size of

this contribution is deceptive because a very high proportion of it consists of intraregional trade, a high level of exchange among a score of small countries occupying a territory only two-fifths the size of the United States. Indeed, this intraregional portion has increased in recent decades (Figure 11.19), from 55 percent of all West European exports in 1956 to 71 percent in 1992, with short interruptions during oil crises. The increase in intra-European imports has been even greater, from 49 to 72 percent. This is one of the reasons why the region's long-time negative trade balance with the rest of the world has closed. It also illustrates the diversion of trade from its traditional channels.

This increase in intraregional trade closely parallels the growth in size and cohesion of the European Union (originally the European Economic Community) in the years since its founding. Established in 1958, the EU was designed to integrate the economies of its member states as a way of increasing economic growth and raising standards of living (see Chapter 12 for a more detailed discussion of the EU). During that time, the organization has expanded its membership from 6 to 15 and has increased its share of the region's total exports. The trend has accelerated since the mid-1980s as more and more West European countries join the group and the organization continues to strengthen intrabloc economic ties.

Western Europe's trade is keenly sensitive to events outside the area. The region's contribution to world commerce rose substantially during the 1960s as a result not only of European integration, but also the general liberalization of international trade induced by global trade agreements. Western Europe's prosperity peaked in 1973 on the eve of the first OPEC oil crisis; in the following year, trade slumped badly, especially its exports. In 1979, just as trade was beginning to recover, the second oil crisis struck. Imports continued to rise, because of the mounting cost of imported oil, but exports plummeted. Both exports and imports remained weak throughout the ensuing recession, and they recovered only slowly in the mid-1980s, a time of lagging European technological innovation and competitiveness. In the late 1980s, European trade recovered somewhat with the collapse of Communism and amidst preparations for a stronger economic union in 1992, but a lingering economic recession through the early 1990s hampered full recovery.

These events also affected Western Europe's trade linkages with the rest of the world (Figure 11.19). The oil crises greatly increased, in value terms, the region's imports from the Middle East, offset only partially by higher export sales to that suddenly wealthy region and despite growing amounts of petroleum obtained from the North Sea and other sources. This shift came at the expense of trade with some of Europe's traditional trading partners; some of the losses have not been restored since, affecting long-standing relationships with present and former colonies. Thus, once-

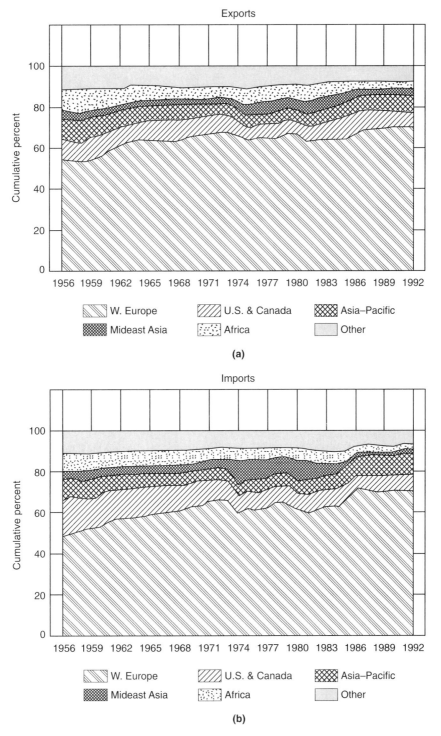

Exports

W. Europe　　U.S. & Canada　　Asia–Pacific
Mideast Asia　　Africa　　Other

(a)

Imports

W. Europe　　U.S. & Canada　　Asia–Pacific
Mideast Asia　　Africa　　Other

(b)

FIGURE 11.19 Value share of Western Europe's exports and imports with major world regions, 1956–1992. The first thing to notice about this pair of diagrams is the uncommonly high proportion of Western Europe's intraregional trade. This percentage has increased at irregular intervals over the years, in response to a number of major trends and events. Most important of these was the formation in 1958 of the European Economic Community, to which the majority of West European countries now belong. Since renamed the European Union, this bloc has steadily grown in membership and cohesion in the nearly four decades of its existence. These diagrams clearly show the impacts of oil crises and economic recessions on Western Europe's trade. Evidence of trade diversion and the effects of foreign direct investment in the region are to be seen in the declining imports from the United States and Canada. Note the recent expansion in European imports from the Asia–Pacific region (mainly Japan and the NICs). [*Source:* United Nations, *Yearbook of International Trade Statistics,* Special Table B (New York: United Nations, various years).]

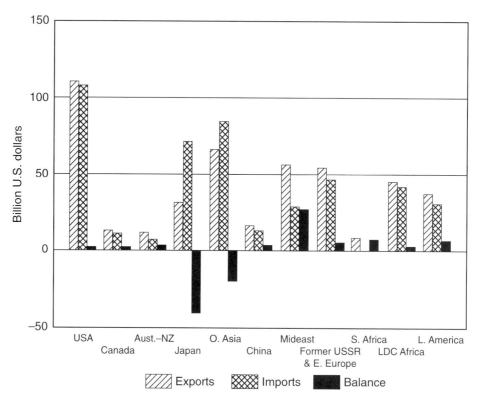

FIGURE 11.20   Western Europe's merchandise exports and imports and trade balances with other world regions, 1992. The United States is still the largest single overseas trading partner of the West Europeans, but Japan and the East Asian NICs have risen quickly in importance during the past decade. Falling oil prices have reduced the Middle East's participation in Europe's trade. The past three decades have also seen the relative decline of several trading partners of historic importance to the Europeans. Western Europe's overall trade balance was positive in 1992, but mounting deficits with Japan and other Pacific Rim countries were provoking protectionist responses from Europeans. Europe's exports and imports with the United States were virtually in balance in that year. [*Source:* United Nations, *Yearbook of International Trade Statistics,* Special Table B (New York: United Nations, various years).]

important trade with Africa has been reduced to a quarter of its former size, and exports to Australia and New Zealand have fallen well below 1 percent of the European total. West European imports from Northern America have dropped from 17 percent in 1957, the year that the EC came in to being, to only 7 percent in 1992.

In this same period, Japan and the East Asian NICs have enlarged their position in the West European market, doubling their combined share within the past decade. Note from Figure 11.20 that Western Europe had large trade imbalances with those countries in 1992. The balance was positive with most other parts of the world in that year.

Being relatively well endowed with mineral resources and productive agricultural lands, Western Europe does not have to import as much food and industrial raw materials as might be expected from its high population density. In

1992, imports of primary commodities represented only 15 percent of the import bill. During the period of high oil prices, however, oil imports alone rose to 24 percent of the total, with a severely damaging impact on European economies. In normal times, however, industrial goods contribute the greater part of West European trade. In 1992, the region's industrial products represented 83 percent of the total exports and 78 percent of imports.

Western Europe's largest trader has been West Germany, which has experienced an economic resurgence in the postwar era remarkably similar to that of Japan. In 1992, Germany was responsible for 24 percent of the entire region's exports. It was also the world's second-ranking exporter in that year, surpassed only by the United States and leading third-place Japan by a small margin. Following its historic reunification with East Germany in October

1990, the efficient German trading machine prepared to exploit its economic strength and central location to effect a future integration of Western Europe with the newly liberated East.

The Former USSR and Eastern Europe

Even before the 1989 breakdown of the Communist system in the Soviet Union and Eastern Europe, the Eastern Bloc's contribution to world trade had been shrinking. This decline occurred despite the fact that this group's trade participation was already disproportionately low by world standards. Considering the enormous human and natural resources at their disposal, the Eastern Bloc countries undoubtedly lagged far behind their trade potentials. This we might have expected from a governmental system that subordinated economic matters to political considerations, and that held a lingering attachment to the Stalinist belief in *autarky,* or self-sufficiency. Politics limited trade between this group and neighboring countries with seemingly complementary resource endowments; it also provoked hostility with the West and led to ideological disputes within the Communist bloc itself.

Objectively viewed, the opportunities for increased international involvement by the Eastern Bloc are substantial. Together, these countries occupy nearly 16 percent of the world's land area and have a combined population of nearly 390 million people. The group possesses a storehouse of physical resources and would seem to offer a promising market for Western goods. Important resource complementarities clearly exist between East and West. Indeed, in the pre-Communist era, a lively trade took place between the two parts of Europe, based on an exchange of the East's land resources for the West's manufactured goods. In recent times, the oil, gas, and metallic minerals of the former USSR have found a demand in the West, and the Eastern Bloc countries have sought Western capital goods and technology. In addition, the Communist lands had to import massive quantities of grain to make up for shortfalls in the output of their own badly managed farm lands.

Aside from the problems of transforming state-run systems into market economies with convertible currencies and the infrastructure needed to support free exchanges of goods with the West, some asked at the time of liberation just how great, realistically, was this potential for East–West trade. Taking account of the mutual needs and wants of the countries on each side, several factors argued for the expectation of a truly important addition to world commerce in the long run. One such factor was the increased demand to be generated from the accelerated GNP growth to be anticipated from release of Eastern Bloc economies from their suffocating centralized bureaucracies.

A second consideration favoring an expansion of East–West trade was the likelihood that much of the Communist era trade among East Bloc nations would be transferred to other countries. The agreement by Bloc members to dismantle the communist trade organization, Comecon, in June 1991 demonstrated a will to remove the controls that had favored intrabloc trade. The distorting effect that this trading system had on Eastern Bloc economies is seen in that intragroup trade in 1988 constituted 57 percent of their total exports to the world and 64 percent of their total imports. This highly managed system was even more of a constraint for Eastern Europe than it was for the former Soviet Union, which had long been an independent supplier of resource-based commodities to world markets.

Another question raised at the time of liberation concerned the kinds of goods likely to be exchanged with the West in the post-Communist era. With respect to the former USSR, the answer was found in the eager reception in the West for its oil, gas, and other mineral output. Indeed, the USSR had led the world in oil exports prior to its breakup. For other East Europeans, the solution was less clear. Until now their exports to other Bloc members had consisted predominantly of machinery and transport equipment, but their shipments to non-Bloc countries had been very largely limited to simple basic manufactures. They had been unsuccessful in finding non-Bloc markets for their more advanced manufactures because the quality did not meet Western standards. Now that they faced competition in their home markets from superior Western products in these sophisticated lines, East Bloc firms were expected to continue specializing in making simpler industrial goods until they found it possible to upgrade their equipment and their labor and managerial skills.

An obvious import need of the Eastern Bloc was for foodstuffs, at least in the short run, until this one-time breadbasket of Europe could regain its agricultural productivity. Another need was for a wide range of high-technology goods, especially those whose export to the former Soviet Bloc had previously been prohibited for national security reasons. The anticipation was that rising incomes in Eastern Bloc countries would ultimately create a market for the great variety of consumer goods to which Western populations have long been accustomed.

Another matter of concern in 1989 had to do with which Western countries would participate most actively in developing East Bloc markets. It seemed that the country best positioned to benefit from an opening to the East would be West Germany. With its central European location, astride the former border separating East from West, and its well-organized, experienced, and export-minded business community, West Germany had already built up strong commercial relationships in the East before the fall of

Communism, and its reunification with the former East Germany in 1990 provided another important early advantage.

By the mid-1990s, tentative answers to some of these questions were becoming evident. The results were not as clear and simple as might have been wished, however, because the East Bloc has proved to be much less monolithic than widely perceived in the West. Indeed, these countries displayed a number of contrasting traits from the outset. Some of these related to the timing of their release from Communist control. Eastern Europe threw off Communism almost immediately in 1989, but the constituent states of the former Soviet Union had to wait two years longer for their Communist party finally to give up. The Central European countries openly relished the end of Soviet domination and were eager for reform, whereas the Balkans and some of the new states of Central Asia were satisfied to use the occasion for renewing old ethnic disputes. The Central Europeans could call on a history of capitalism within living memory, whereas the Central Asians had always lived in a colonial backwater.

At least three groups of newly liberalizing countries (NLCs) emerged. Quickest to initiate market-opening reforms were the so-called First-Tier states of Central Europe—the Czech Republic, Hungary, Poland, Slovakia, and Slovenia—and the Baltic states—Estonia, Latvia, and Lithuania. By the mid-1990s, these countries had market economies securely in place, had inflation reasonably under control, had shifted their trade toward the West, were seeking membership in the European Union, and were shaping their laws and institutions so as to be compatible with those of EU countries.

The Second-Tier states of Eastern Europe lagged well behind the rest. Typical of these were Bulgaria, which was hampered in its reform by years of excessive dependence on Soviet trade; Romania, bowed under a harshly repressive regime that had systematically eliminated all potential leaders; and Croatia, caught up in bitter ethnic fighting among the states of former Yugoslavia. Lastly, there are the several independent states created from the breakup of the Soviet Union: Russia, Ukraine, Belarus, Moldova, the three Caucasian states, and the five in Central Asia.

Throughout the post–World War II era, the Eastern Bloc had regularly accounted for a little under 10 percent of world exports and imports. As the grip of Communism loosened in the 1980s, Eastern Bloc trade shrank, both absolutely and relatively amidst the strains of economic reorganization. By 1993, this group was supplying less than 3 percent of total world exports. To a major degree, this deterioration can be attributed to the collapse of the organizational arrangements that had linked the exports and imports of these countries to each other. In 1980, for example, 51 percent of all Eastern Bloc exports had gone to other members of the group and 55 percent of their imports had been obtained from each other. At that time, Western

Europe had taken one-quarter of Eastern Bloc exports and had supplied 22 percent of their imports. Between 1980 and 1993, this proportion became reversed: In the latter year, more than half of Eastern Bloc exports went to Western Europe, which in turn supplied nearly three-fifths of the group's imports. Intrabloc trade accounted for less than one-fifth of the group total in 1993.

This general pattern of Eastern Bloc trade masks considerable individual variation among countries. Such divergence marks a significant departure from the past, when, in accordance with the Comecon plan, virtually every East European country directed a third or more of its trade to the Soviet Union and most of the rest to other members of the bloc. This had changed by the early 1990s. By 1993, Germany was the principal export destination for most First-Tier East Bloc countries; other West European nations were prominent as customers, too. In the case of imports, however, Russia was still a leading supplier, mainly because of its role as principal source of oil and gas for much of Europe. The pattern was different for Second- and Third-Tier countries, which were much slower to break their dependence on Russia and other USSR successor states, both as customers and as suppliers. Nevertheless, even these laggards had seen some weakening of their reliance on the former USSR. Since 1989, several had acquired new trade linkages, usually with close neighbors.

The main items of commerce for the newly liberalizing countries of the Eastern Bloc continue to be manufactured goods, especially machinery and transport equipment, as well a variety of intermediate manufactures. Added to these are some consumer products, a category less apparent in the Soviet era. Today as in the past, Russia's prime export is energy. The Russian natural gas monopoly, Gazprom, is the world's largest gas producer with 38 percent of global reserves, and it supplies huge quantities of gas to both Eastern and Western Europe. Russia is also endowed with very large reserves of oil, most of which is still under the control of the oil monopoly, Lukoil. Together, gas and oil provide 80 percent of Russia's hard-currency export earnings.

Multinationals from a variety of countries have found the great reserves of energy and industrial raw materials of Russia and Eastern Europe to be irresistible, and they have been actively investing in the region. Among these multinationals are German and U.S. automobile companies, machinery manufacturers, and consumer-electronics makers. In the former Soviet Union, U.S. oil companies have entered into joint ventures to modernize that country's flagging petroleum output. Western investors face political and economic uncertainties in such undertakings, however. Difficult problems arise because of the lack of adequate legal systems for the guarantee of property rights, repatriation of profits, and so on. The opportunities offered by early entry into Eastern Bloc ventures may warrant the risks for well-financed industrial giants such as Occidental

Petroleum or Volkswagen, but for many smaller concerns, the uncertainties are as yet too great.

The Middle East

Living at a historic crossroads of world commerce, the people of the Middle East have been traders from earliest times. Although great-power interests have long focused on this area because of its strategic location, it was the discovery of vast pools of petroleum beneath the region that attracted world attention as never before. The knowledge that they control two-thirds of all known oil reserves made it possible for the Arab members of the Organization of Petroleum Exporting Countries (OPEC) to precipitate the crisis of 1973. Only half of the Middle Eastern countries are surplus oil exporters, however; most of the rest are resource-poor agricultural nations that have not shared in the oil bonanza (except for such aid as OPEC may grant them). Indeed, farming is the leading occupation throughout the Middle East, even in those countries producing oil, yet the population is growing so fast that the region as a whole has become a net importer of food.

During the 1970s the Middle East enjoyed a huge increase in its share of world exports, which jumped from only 3 percent to nearly 11 percent within a span of six years. This resulted solely from a ten-fold rise in oil prices; the volume of shipments actually shrank. For a time, oil revenues were pouring in so fast that imports could not keep up, and the oil-exporting countries acquired enormous balance-of-payments surpluses. In 1980, for instance, the Middle East as a whole had a positive balance of $114 billion on total foreign earnings of $211 billion. After that, oil revenues shrank and prices sagged in a weakening market. By 1993, the Middle East's share of global exports was again back to 3.9 percent, and the earlier trade surplus had turned into a deficit of more than $16 billion.

Prior to the oil boom, the Middle East's traditional exports were agricultural commodities—such as cotton, figs, and dates—and various mineral ores. In fact, goods of this type still brought in 11 percent of the region's foreign earnings in the early 1970s. Exports of these commodities have continued to grow since, but they have been overwhelmed in the trade figures by the steep rise in oil receipts.

As industrialization reaches the Middle East, new classes of exports are beginning to appear. Egypt has now attained the status of a semi-industrialized country and is exporting cotton yarn, textiles, and other consumer manufactures. A sharp increase in Middle Eastern shipments of industrial products is taking place as Saudi Arabia's huge new petroleum refineries and petrochemical plants go on stream. Made from exceedingly cheap feedstocks of Saudi oil and natural gas, these commodities are very competitive on world markets. Many other energy-intensive manufacturing industries are rising throughout the region as oil-

exporting nations prepare for a world after the oil is used up. Some Middle Eastern countries are earning substantial amounts of foreign exchange through invisible exports, especially Egypt and Israel with their prospering tourist industries. As a transit country, Egypt gains additional revenues from Suez Canal tolls.

The Middle East's imports, which have grown steadily since 1973, are very diverse. Being highly specialized producers of oil and other primary commodities, these countries nevertheless have varied needs, which can be satisfied only with imports. During the bountiful years, rising incomes caused the range of consumer demand to expand, and development needs called for a wide variety of capital goods and industrial raw materials.

Even before the crises of the 1970s, the Middle Eastern oil exporters had had unusually diverse trade ties throughout the world. Their largest regional market had always been—and still is—Western Europe, which was taking 44 percent of all Middle Eastern exports at the time of the first oil price rise. Since then, Western Europe's share has slipped, dropping to less than 25 percent. Japan, the second largest customer, continued in 1992 to take a little less than one-fifth, and North America bought another 11.8 percent. Conscious of the political instability of the Middle East, however, the region's richer customers have been diversifying their oil sources, causing the Middle East's share of world oil sales to dip. The Persian Gulf crisis of 1990–1991 further reinforced this trend. At the same time, rising import shares have gone to several LDCs and newly industrializing nations in Africa, Latin America, and Asia. With the former USSR no longer supplying Eastern Europe with oil at concessionary prices, Middle Eastern exporters are capturing some of that market as well. During the past decade, the Middle East has seen a noticeable rise in intraregional trade.

Western Europe continued in 1992 to be the Middle East's chief source of imports, preserving its usual two-fifths share of the total market. The United States and Japan remain important suppliers, but with diminishing portions of the total. Much of the difference has been made up by East Asian NICs and a variety of LDCs, including Brazil and other purveyors of war materiel.

The anomaly in this virtually solid bloc of Islamic countries is the Jewish state of Israel. About the size of New Jersey, this tiny nation of 5 million people resembles its Arab neighbors physically but is very different culturally, economically, and politically. Having a highly skilled labor force and many experienced managers, Israel has joined the ranks of industrial nations and has forged formal economic ties with both the United States and the European Economic Community. Its industrial exports include machinery (34 percent of foreign earnings), cut diamonds (19 percent), chemicals (12.7 percent, based on salts from the Dead Sea and phosphates from the Negev Desert), aircraft, and armaments. Relying on its excellent transport connections and its climatic complementarity with Western Europe, Israel ships subtropical fruits, winter vegetables, and cut flowers to European capitals daily by air.

Despite its success as a diversified exporter of agricultural commodities and industrial goods, Israel runs high trade deficit. Exports cover less than three-fourths of the cost of imports, which are kept high by the demands of a large defense establishment and heavy government subsidization of the economy. Nevertheless, these figures show substantial improvement in the past half-dozen years, aided by improved prospects for permanent peace with the nation's Arab neighbors. This, together with some much-needed changes in the government's economic policies and an infusion of skilled, well-educated immigrants from the former Soviet Union, has led to accelerated economic growth. By 1995, Israel's per capita GNP had risen to $16,000, well above most of Mediterranean Europe.

LOOKING FOR EXPLANATIONS: INTERNATIONAL TRADE THEORIES

How are we to explain these changing patterns of trade? From early times, international trade has been an object of study, resulting in an evolving body of international trade theory. The basic questions asked by trade theorists are these: Why do countries trade with each other? Is trade beneficial? What determines the international pattern of specialization in production and trade? What are the effects of governmental intervention on this pattern? What is the best (i.e., the optimal) trade policy?

Different answers to these questions have been provided over the centuries, as theorists have sought to explain the reality of the commercial world as it existed for them. The differences arose because new technologies and organizational forms transformed the reality, compelling scholars to alter their theories to satisfy a different set of practical needs of the day (Dunning, 1995, p. 163). The several phases through which the international economy have passed have thus left bodies of literature that reflect the state of affairs in each phase.

A doctrine known as *mercantilism,* dominated the commercial age leading up to the Industrial Revolution. Extending from the early sixteenth century through most of the eighteenth, this period was one of intense international rivalry among the principal national powers of the day as they vied for military and industrial supremacy. Economic writings of the era were essentially national policy statements advocating close governmental regulation of foreign trade in each country's own narrow self-interest.

The first true theory of international trade emerged during the late eighteenth century in response to profound economic, political, and social changes ushered in by the English Industrial Revolution. This era of rapid political and economic expansion, which continued at least until World War I, inspired a body of writings on international trade sometimes referred to as *classical theory.* As it continued to develop throughout the late nineteenth and early years of the twentieth century, this evolved into what is called *neoclassical theory.* Taken together, the works of this remarkably creative period are sometimes referred to as *comparative advantage theory,* after the defining principle they share. Reacting to the inadequacies and excesses of mercantilism, the classical and neoclassical writers developed a tightly reasoned case for freeing international trade of all governmental restraints.

The first half of the twentieth century was a period of weakening national economies and deteriorating international political and commercial relations, by the powerful shocks of two world wars and an intervening global economic depression. The interwar years brought a fundamental rethinking of classical and neoclassical ideas, prompted by a growing dissatisfaction with some of the unrealistic assumptions on which they were based. The depression years saw the emergence of a *factor proportions theory* of international trade. This new paradigm nevertheless preserved the classical emphasis on free trade, contrasting markedly with the harsh governmental restrictions on trade that were prevalent at the time.

Harmony between theory and practice resumed during the post-World War II reconstruction period, when the world's trading nations replaced the destructive economic rivalries of the 1930s with a new system of international cooperation. In response to the new regime, the volume of international trade soared but, at the same time, the basic character of economic flows among countries underwent profound changes. Conventional trade theory once again appeared incapable of explaining many of these new kinds of international transactions. As a result, by the 1970s, a flurry of alternative international trade models appeared in the literature. Much of this new theoretical work was prompted by the recognition that a growing share of international transactions in the postwar world was taking place between branches of the same or related companies, who frequently were oligopolists. This focused attention on the nature and role of multinational enterprise. Trade theorists directed their efforts toward new theories incorporating concepts of industrial and of foreign direct investment, ultimately drawing together these strands into a cohesive whole known as the *new theory of international trade.* Let us now examine more closely these various periods in the evolution of international trade theory to discover what each has contributed to our understanding of the subject.

Mercantilism

Those who wrote on trade topics during the mercantilist era were mainly political pamphleteers who were less concerned with producing theory than with promoting policies of national self-interest. This economic nationalism was a natural feature of a period when strong central governments were forming. These writings fall within a number of distinct national groupings and cannot be generalized very satisfactorily, but the various mercantilist policies share certain common features.

First, the mercantilists considered it essential that a country's merchandise exports exceed its imports, thereby yielding a "favorable" balance of trade, that is, one that would contribute a surplus of money or gold to the royal treasury. Second, they emphasized foreign trade rather than domestic trade, manufacturing rather than agriculture, and the desirability of plentiful cheap labor. They favored manufacturing because it could support a denser population and because its output yielded exports of higher value. They regarded a large population of low-wage labor to be a source of national strength. Finally, the mercantilists promoted the use of various administrative measures by which countries could enforce these aims. Despite their antiquity, many of these notions sound surprisingly contemporary: Even today many national policies are at least implicitly mercantilist. Although contemporary trade theory emphatically rejects most mercantilist ideas, it continues to stress the *normative:* that which ought to be.

Classical Theory

The classical period was a time of brilliant theorists, especially Adam Smith, David Ricardo, and John Stuart Mill, who reacted sharply to the errors and excesses of the mercantilist philosophy and in the process developed the first real theory of international trade. The basic normative premise of classical theory was that free trade—trade that is unencumbered by any form of governmental intervention—is beneficial to all trading partners. The questions raised by classical theorists were these: Why is international trade mutually advantageous? What determines the goods to be exchanged? What decides the amounts of goods to be traded (and thus the international price level)? The emphasis, therefore, was on the gains from trade. Trade among countries, these writers argued, results in an increased international specialization of production, a division of labor among countries like that which accompanies domestic trade. To measure the effects of trade, classical theorists developed the *labor theory of value.* This was the notion that all costs can be reduced ultimately to units of labor, which in turn are directly related to the prices that must be charged for the products.

In their analyses, classical theorists relied on a number of simplifying assumptions. Some of these assumptions introduced complexities that were little understood at the time. Later in the nineteenth century and the early years of the twentieth century, usually called the *neoclassical*

period, such theorists as Francis Edgeworth and Alfred Marshall developed new concepts and geometric techniques that enabled them to solve some of the analytical problems remaining from earlier years.

The Principle of Comparative Advantage

In exposing the absurdities of mercantilism, Adam Smith based his argument on the concept of the *division of labor,* on which all creation of wealth rests. Just as the individual householder should never "attempt to make at home what it will cost him more to make than to buy," so it is with nations. Every country has some natural advantages over another. "As long as the one country has those advantages and the other wants them, it will always be more advantageous for the latter, rather to buy of the former than to make" (Smith, 1937, pp. 424–426). In this way, he argued, trade among nations promotes an efficient international division of labor, where every country concentrates on what it does best and all gain from the increased total output, which is exchanged among them. Note, however, that Smith presumes each country to have an *absolute* advantage in the products it makes for export: It must be able to produce, with a given amount of labor, a larger quantity of such goods than any competitor.

But what if some naturally disadvantaged nation has no industry in which it excels? Would such a country have to close its borders to world commerce in order to avoid ruinous foreign competition? It fell to David Ricardo, writing 40 years later, to find an answer to that question. Trade can indeed take place advantageously between two countries, Ricardo was able to show—even if one is better than the other in every kind of production—as long as they differ *relatively* in their capabilities. That is to say, the "rich" country's absolute advantage over the "poor" country in one product must be relatively greater than its absolute advantage in another product. This means, of course, that the "poor" country has an absolute *disadvantage* that is *relatively* less than its other disadvantage. Thus, the answer to the second question is provided by the principle of *comparative advantage,* which declares that countries should specialize in the production and export of those things they can make more efficiently relative to other nations and should import those goods at which they are relatively less efficient.

Not only did Ricardo provide a more precise statement of this basic principle of classical theory, but he also devised a method for demonstrating mathematically the benefits of free trade. This method relied on Ricardo's *labor theory of value,* which states that the value of a good is determined by its labor cost, that is, the relative amount of labor that is required for its production. Other productive factors, capital and land, he considered to be incorporated within the factor of labor, in fixed proportions for all types of production.

Let us now examine these concepts—absolute advantage and comparative advantage—with the aid of geometric techniques conveniently developed for us by a later generation of neoclassical theorists. Each case involves two countries and two commodities. For the sake of clarity, we make these simplifying assumptions: (1) no transport costs are required to move goods between countries; (2) no artificial barriers to trade (such as governments might impose) exist; (3) labor in each country is homogeneous (has identical characteristics throughout; skilled labor is merely some multiple of ordinary labor); (4) perfect competition prevails; (5) production technology is identical in both countries; and (6) no international movement of labor can take place, though labor is fully mobile within countries.

Example 1. Absolute Advantage in Both Countries.

Take two countries with economies of equal size, France and Germany, which are isolated from the rest of the world and initially have no commercial relations with each other. Both produce and consume the same two commodities, potatoes and wheat, devoting to these enterprises all their resources. Because of the dissimilar nature of their capabilities, however, the two countries differ in the quantities of these commodities that they are able to produce per unit of input.

As Table 11.1 shows, France would be capable of producing 90 bushels of potatoes per unit of labor input if it were to turn its entire labor force to the production of this crop; alternatively, it could use these same resources to produce 60 bushels of wheat (per unit of input). This implies that the French are better suited to the production of potatoes than wheat. In the absence of foreign trade, the French exchange the two goods domestically at the rate of 1½ bushels of potatoes for 1 bushel of wheat, or, conversely, 2/3 bushel of wheat for 1 bushel of potatoes. Thus, in France, wheat has the higher price of the two commodities because it is relatively more costly to produce and hence is scarcer.

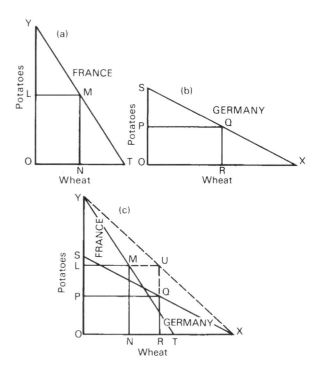

FIGURE 11.21   Production possibilities of France and Germany, exchange possibilities, and gains from trade.

Figure 11.21a shows all the possible combinations of potatoes and wheat that France is capable of producing. The French *production possibilities* curve, *YT*, ranges from the extreme case where all labor is allocated to potatoes, *Y*, to the other extreme, *T*, where all is devoted to wheat. Between these two extremes of specialization lie the various other possible combinations of these two crops. In the example given here, we assume that the French have chosen to produce and consume the combination of potatoes and wheat given by point *M* in Figure 11.21a. This amounts to 45 bushels of potatoes and 30 bushels of wheat per unit of labor input (see Table 11.1).

TABLE 11.1

Production possibilities, domestic exchange ratios, and production and consumption of potatoes and wheat in France and Germany before trade

	Production Possibilities		Domestic Exchange Ratios		Production and Consumption		
	Potatoes	Wheat	Potatoes / Wheat	Wheat / Potatoes	Potatoes	Wheat	Total
France	90	60	1.50	0.67	45	30	75
Germany	50	100	0.50	2.00	25	50	75
Total	140	160			70	80	150

In Germany, the cost relationships are just the reverse. If the Germans were to specialize completely in potatoes, they would be able to grow 50 bushels per unit of labor or they could use that same labor unit to produce a total of 100 bushels of wheat (Table 11.1). In the absence of foreign trade, therefore, the Germans would exchange 0.5 bushel of potatoes for 1 bushel of wheat or 2 bushels of wheat for 1 bushel of potatoes (Table 11.1). Figure 11.21b shows the full range of possibilities for German production. Note that, from the range of possible combinations, we assume that the Germans have elected to produce and consume potatoes and wheat in the proportions given by point *Q*, that is, 25 bushels of potatoes and 50 bushels of wheat.

A comparison of the production possibilities of the two countries (Table 11.1) reveals that France would have an *absolute advantage* over Germany in potatoes and Germany would have an *absolute advantage* over France in wheat if they were to enter into trade with each other. These are the conditions that Adam Smith considered necessary for trade to take place. When the French awaken to this situation, they find that they could receive up to 2 bushels of wheat in Germany in exchange for a single bushel of their potatoes instead of the 2/3 bushel of wheat they have been getting at home for that same quantity of potatoes. Likewise, the Germans learn that in France they could get up to 1 1/2 bushels of potatoes for 1 bushel of wheat rather than the mere 1/2 bushel obtained in their own country. The two countries thereupon enter into trade with each other.

Both countries benefit as French potatoes begin moving eastward into Germany and German wheat makes the return journey westward. Indeed, so beneficial is this exchange that French farmers are induced to specialize in potato production and transfer their resources out of wheat; conversely, German farmers turn their emphasis to wheat at the expense of potatoes. Obviously, the initial exchange ratios for potatoes and wheat do not last long after trade begins and specialization increases.

In the end, specialization becomes complete, and the ensuing French–German trade causes the gap in prices to close entirely. France allocates all its resources to potatoes (*OY* in Figure 11.21c) and becomes the sole supplier of this commodity to consumers of both countries; Germany puts all its productive capacity into wheat (*OX* in Figure 11.21c) and shares the output with France. Figure 11.21c also gives us the final *equilibrium price* at which the potato-wheat trade takes place between the countries. The *international exchange ratio* (Table 11.2) is given by

$$\frac{OY}{OX} = \frac{90}{100} = 0.90$$

Thus, a bushel of wheat exchanges for 0.90 bushel of potatoes. This ratio is also referred to as the international terms of trade. The dashed diagonal line, *XY*, in Figure 11.21c is the *exchange possibilities curve*, which indicates all the various proportions of potatoes and wheat that are now available to the French and Germans at this new combined level of output.

The two countries are now using their productive resources to full efficiency. The benefits of this new arrangement are apparent from a comparison of Tables 11.1 and 11.2, where we see that total potato output (all contributed by France) is now 90 bushels (per input unit) (Table 11.2), whereas the combined output of the two countries had formerly been only 70 bushels (Table 11.1). Likewise, total wheat output has gone from 80 bushels (Table 11.1) to 100 (all produced by Germany, Table 11.2). Of the 90 bushels of potatoes (per unit) produced by France, domestic consumption continues to take 45 bushels and exports to Germany take the remaining 45 bushels. Germany concentrates all its labor resources in wheat production, retaining 50 bushels for its own consumption and supplying the other 50 to France (Table 11.2). Total consumption in the two countries thus rises as a result of this exchange. By importing wheat from Germany instead of inefficiently producing

TABLE 11.2

International exchange possibilities, international exchange ratios, and production, exports, Imports, and consumption of potatoes and wheat in France and Germany after trade

	International Exchange Possibilities		International Exchange Ratio	
	Potatoes	Wheat	Potatoes / Wheat	Wheat / Potatoes
France	90	100	0.90	1.11
Germany	90	100	0.90	1.11

	Production, Trade, and Consumption								
	Potatoes				Wheat				Total
	Production	Exports	Imports	Consumption	Production	Exports	Imports	Consumption	Consumption
France	90	45	—	45	—	—	50	50	95
Germany	—	—	45	45	100	50	—	50	95
Total	90	45	45	90	100	50	50	100	190

her own, France is able to increase wheat consumption from 30 (Table 11.1) to 50 bushels (Table 11.2). Similarly, Germany can raise consumption of potatoes from 25 to 45 units. Hence, international specialization and trade have raised consumer welfare in both countries.

Up to this point, we have been assuming that the structure of demand is the same in both countries, that French and German consumers want potatoes and wheat in the same proportions. But are French consumers really content to continue consuming the same amount of potatoes as before, and do they actually want all that wheat that is coming from Germany? And are the Germans satisfied to consume potatoes and wheat in the same proportions as the French? It is very possible that the citizens of these two nations have different structures of demand. Over the centuries, each population may have grown accustomed to its traditional diet and now merely wants more of each commodity. (Other influences that may affect a population's demand characteristics will be discussed later.)

Figure 11.22 shows the possible effects of such differing consumer preferences. Note that even in this case, consumer welfare rises with the introduction of trade and specialization. Let us say that the actual demand patterns of the two countries are as shown by the families of *indifference curves* in Figure 11.22, French consumption being given by those curves labeled I_F and German consumption by those labeled I_G. The indifference curves indicate the various proportions in which the French or German consumers are willing to substitute potatoes for wheat or vice versa. Each curve corresponds to a given level of consumption in a country. Thus I^0 refers to one level, I^1 to the next higher level, and I^2 to a higher level yet. Clearly, a people will wish to reach the highest curve possible, thereby raising their standard of living. The point where an indifference curve is tangent with the production possibilities curve

indicates the actual quantities of the two commodities consumed prior to the opening of trade. M represents the amounts consumed before trade by France and Q the amounts consumed by Germany.

After trade, consumption shifts upward to the point where some higher indifference curve becomes tangent with the exchange possibilities curve. In Figure 11.22, the advent of trade causes France's consumption to move from M to M' on the next higher indifference curve (from curve I^0_F to I_F^1). Thus, trade makes it possible for the French to consume OL' potatoes instead of OL and ON' wheat instead of ON. German consumption likewise moves up from Q to Q' (from indifference curve I_G^0 to I_G^1). Germany is then able to increase its consumption of potatoes from OP to OP' and its consumption of wheat from OR to OR'. Thus, trade permits both countries to attain greater consumer satisfaction.

Complete specialization of the kind described here is uncommon in the real world, although several less-developed countries come close to it. One reason that specialization does not reach its ultimate limits is the tendency for unit production costs to begin increasing after a certain level of inputs is reached. Underlying our discussion thus far has been the assumption that unit costs remain constant at all levels of production, as suggested by the linear shape of the production possibilities curves in Figures 11.21 and 11.22. Ricardo's assumption of constant costs was not realistic: Under normal conditions, we would expect unit costs to increase. Figure 11.23 shows the effect of increasing costs on the production possibilities of France and Germany. As the limits of efficiency are approached for either type of farming, the application of additional resources yields diminishing returns, and output declines as a consequence. This results because rarely are all of a country's resources equally suited to a particular line of production. As farmers allocate new resources to wheat or potatoes, they eventually reach a point where each additional new unit of input no longer yields a proportionate gain in output. In the present example, therefore, it is likely that France will continue to

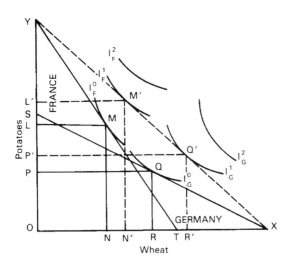

FIGURE 11.22   Gains from trade: different demand structures.

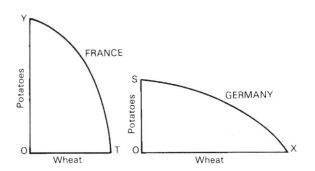

FIGURE 11.23   Effects of increasing costs on production possibilities curves.

grow small amounts of its own wheat and that Germany will not entirely give up potato production.

Example 2. Absolute Advantage in One Country Only, Comparative Advantage in the Other. According to Adam Smith, if trade is to take place between two countries, each must have an absolute advantage, as in Example 1. But what can we make of the situation illustrated in Figure 11.24? Here, Italy has an absolute advantage over Spain in the production of wheat, but the two countries are equally efficient in producing olive oil. Does this offer any incentive for trade? Adam Smith would have said, "No"; David Ricardo would have said, "Yes."

As Ricardo found, all that is required for trade to be mutually beneficial to both parties is that the two countries differ in the *relative* efficiencies with which they produce the two commodities. In the present example, Spain's disadvantage in the production of wheat is relatively greater than it is in the production of olive oil (where Spain actually matches Italy's efficiency). Although Spain may lack an *absolute* advantage in olive oil production, it nevertheless has a *comparative* advantage in olive oil. That is to say, by comparison with Italy, Spain is relatively less efficient in producing wheat than it is in producing olive oil.

For confirmation of this, examine this relationship as it is shown in Table 11.3. Here we see that before trade, Italy is able to use the same amount of labor to produce either 40 units of wheat or 20 units of olive oil but actually allocates its resources so as to produce 20 units of wheat and 10 units of olive oil. On the other hand, Spain is capable of producing either 20 units of wheat or 20 units of olive oil (per unit of labor) but actually produces 10 units of wheat and 10 units of olive oil. The combined total output of the two countries, therefore, is 30 units of wheat and 20 units of oil—which is the maximum possible as long as each country produces solely for its own needs.

When the two countries enter into trade, however, each specializes: Italy now produces 40 units of wheat (per unit of labor), Spain produces 20 units of olive oil, and the two exchange surpluses. As a result of their improved efficiencies, therefore, the combined total output rises to 40 units of wheat plus 20 units of oil, a gain of 10 units of wheat over their pretrade total.

How the two countries share the additional 10 units of wheat between them is decided by the conditions of demand in the two countries, a subject to which we shall return later. For the moment, however, we may note the range of potential prices *(international exchange ratios)* as given in Table 11.3. Here we see that if Italy is to benefit from specializing in wheat, it must receive a price for wheat that is higher than its pretrade price *(domestic exchange ratio),* which was 1//2 unit of oil for 1 unit of wheat. Similarly, Spain must receive more than 1 unit of wheat for a unit of its olive oil. Thus, as the table shows, Italy's minimum exchange ratio for wheat

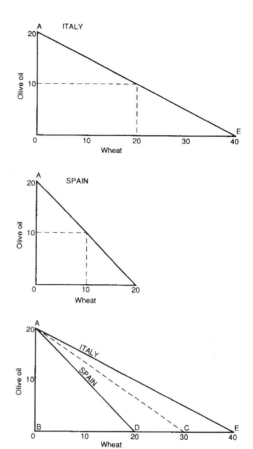

FIGURE 11.24 The opportunities for trade in a case where only one country has an absolute advantage but the other has a comparative advantage.

is equivalent to the maximum price Spain can afford to pay for wheat, and vice versa for olive oil.

These minimums and maximums define the range within which the final price is to lie. They are shown graphically in Figure 11.24c, where Italy's minimum acceptable price for its wheat is given by the ratio of *AB/BE* and Spain's minimum price for its oil is *BD/AB*. The equivalent *exchange possibilities curves* are *AE* for Italy and *AD* for Spain. The ultimate price must fall somewhere between the two extremes, perhaps *BC/AB* for wheat/oil (or *AB/BC* for oil/wheat) (the new exchange possibilities curve would be *AC*). At this price Italy would receive 2/3 unit of oil for a unit of its wheat, whereas before trade a unit of wheat bought only 1/2 unit of oil in Italy, and Spain would receive 1½ units of wheat for a unit of its oil as against only 1 unit before trade (Table 11.3). Thus each country would enjoy a higher price for its specialty crop and pay less for its imported good than prior to trade.

Reciprocal Demand. The proposed final solution suggested by Table 11.3 was reached by arbitrarily splitting

TABLE 11.3

Production and exchange ratios of wheat and olive oil, Italy and Spain

Before Trade:

	Production Possibilities		Domestic Exchange Ratios		Production	
	Wheat	*Olive Oil*	*Wheat / Oil*	*Oil / Wheat*	*Wheat*	*Olive Oil*
Italy	40	20	2.00	0.50	20	10
Spain	20	20	1.00	1.00	10	10
Total					30	20

After Trade

	Production		International Exchange Ratios			
			Range of Potential Ratios		Ratios at point C	
	Wheat	*Olive Oil*	*Wheat / Oil*	*Oil / Wheat*	*Wheat / Oil*	*Oil / Wheat*
Italy	40	—	2.0 Max.	0.50 Min.	1.50	0.67
Spain	—	20	1.0 Min.	1.00 Max.	1.50	0.67
Total	40	20				

the difference between the exchange ratio limits of the two countries. This does not tell us how Italy and Spain would actually have gone about arriving at a final international exchange ratio. John Stuart Mill's answer to this was that the actual international price depends on the nature of the demand for these commodities in the two countries. This price, he said, is determined by the strength and *elasticity* (responsiveness to price changes) of demand for these goods in each country. This is known as Mill's *law of reciprocal demand.*

As described by Mill, the process by which the interaction of supply and demand in two countries ultimately produces an actual international ratio is rather like a giant auction. The objective in the preceding case is to arrive at a price at which the quantity of wheat that Italy is willing to export in exchange for olive oil exactly corresponds to the amount of oil that Spain is willing to sell in exchange for Italy's wheat. If the price of wheat is too high in terms of olive oil, Italians will flood the market with supplies of wheat that exceed Spain's offers for it. Likewise, if the price of olive oil is too high in terms of wheat, Spanish oil will enter the market in quantities not matched by Italian offers. When traders realize that their goods are not selling, they will ease off on their prices until these reach a level acceptable to their foreign buyers. The end result of this dickering process is an agreed price that exactly clears the market of unwanted supplies. Thus, *equilibrium* is achieved.

The Gains from Trade: A Summary. The introduction of trade between countries with different production possibilities theoretically leads to a number of desirable results for the participating parties. These benefits are of

two kinds: (1) those that stem from the exchange of goods in and of itself, and (2) those that result from the international specialization of production that trade causes.

The preceding discussion has revealed some of the first type of gains, those from trade per se. As Figures 11.21 to 11.24 demonstrated, the introduction of trade permits a country to adjust its commodity mix in such a way as to move its population to a higher level of consumption than was possible in isolation. Because of trade, therefore, the production pattern no longer has to coincide with the consumption pattern.

Over and above these first benefits, however, trade confers a second set of gains. The increased specialization of production that follows trade offers important opportunities for more efficient production, for a greater output from each unit of resources. If the inhabitants of a country concentrate their efforts on producing a limited number of goods, they are able to use those skills and resources more effectively that are best adapted to the purpose. Then, as they continue to accumulate experience along these lines, they acquire new and even greater skills. A fertile environment for invention and innovation arises as research and development come to focus along narrow channels and as specialists in the field live and work in close association with one another.

Business enterprises gain in competitive strength from operating in such a climate. These benefits are both *internal* and *external,* as was seen in Chapter 9. Among the internal benefits are economies of large-scale production: more efficient use of machines and workers, lower prices for raw materials purchased in bulk, reduced transport rates for assembling materials and distributing products in large quantities, and lower unit operating costs as a result of spreading output over longer model runs. The external economies enjoyed by businesses located in an area of specialization include the opportunities to share ideas and information with others engaged in the same type of production and the access to a large pool of labor with the requisite skills. Important also is the availability of many specialized facilities. These may consist of auxiliary or related industries with which a company has direct ties, such as those that link steel mills with suppliers of fire bricks for lining furnaces or with customers who use steel in fabricating bridges. Such areas of concentration often acquire a variety of specialized service agencies. Associated with the cotton textile industry, for example, are cotton brokerage and exchange activities as well as banking and insurance firms having a knowledge of the peculiar needs and problems of that trade.

In this way, specialization further enhances a country's initial comparative advantage. Once it has gained sufficient momentum, the specialized area increases its competitive edge over other areas that might wish to enter the market. Indeed, even if it had previously possessed no resource advantage at all and had merely developed its specialty through historical accident, the area might have acquired a comparative advantage by reason of the kinds of economies described here. Such considerations help to explain the existence of many industrial concentrations around the world whose original reason for location may now have vanished. Examples are Britain's clay products industry at Stoke-on-Trent, France's textile manufacturing at Le Nord, and the U.S. optical instrument specialization at Rochester, New York.

In sum, if trade is truly free, it should result in optimal use of the world's resources through greater efficiency and thus smaller resource use per unit of output. This means that the world would produce a greater supply of goods from the same resource base, thereby raising standards of living generally.

Inadequacies of Classical and Neoclassical Theory.

Nevertheless, a definitive explanation of how comparative advantage works proved elusive. Supposedly, the solution depends on relative differences among countries in the productivity of their labor, but Ricardo and his successors never provided a satisfactory explanation of what causes these productivity differences. Ricardo himself would refer to such things as "greater skills" or "better machinery." Other nineteenth-century theorists cited climates, soils, supplies of minerals, "inventiveness and ingenuity" in the use of natural resources and equipment, and other equally vague attempts at explanation.

The underlying problem, however, was that of the unrealistic assumptions on which the labor theory of value rested. One troublesome assumption held that labor is homogeneous and interchangeable. In fact, the skill requirements of one industry are obviously different from those of other industries, and therefore labor costs among economic sectors vary within a country. Moreover, if sales abroad were to increase the demand for the products of one industry at the expense of others, we could hardly expect an immediate rush of workers out of the declining industries into the booming one. In the short run, interindustry mobility of labor is severely limited.

A second flaw in the labor theory of value is the assumption that all of the factors of production can be collapsed into a single factor, labor. In reality, every economic activity must draw on all of the factors of production—not just labor, but also capital, land, and enterprise (management). Furthermore, the different industries combine these factors in such an infinite variety of ways that measuring their production costs solely in terms of labor would prove an impossible task. In reaction to the limitations and logical inconsistencies of classical and neoclassical theory, therefore, alternative theories have sprung up in the twentieth century.

Factor Proportions Theory

Near the end of the nineteenth century, a new theory of value took shape and eventually eclipsed Ricardo's single-factor theory. This new body of thought focused on the interactions of supply and demand in achieving an equilibrium. It looked at the ways in which inputs of the various factors of production combine in an industry and how the costs of the outputs of that industry interact with demand, as shaped by the incomes and tastes of consumers, to determine final prices. Although developed within the context of a single national market, these principles were considered equally applicable to the determination of prices among countries, to the extent that nations differ in their resource endowments, national demand characteristics, and levels of technology.

Whereas some earlier contributors to this new line of thought felt that they were merely elaborating on and improving existing neoclassical theory, Bertil Ohlin, writing in 1933, claimed that his theory was radically different. Ohlin abandoned entirely the classical labor theory of value and focused on differences among countries in their possession of all the factors of production—land, labor, capital, and enterprise—as determinants of international trade. Building on earlier work by Eli Heckscher, Ohlin based his theory on these premises: (1) countries differ in their proportions of factors, that is, their *factor endowments,* and (2) industries differ in the proportions in which they combine these factors, that is, in their *factor intensities.*

Assuming that factor intensities of particular industries remain the same in different countries, the *Heckscher–Ohlin model* states that each country will export those goods whose production is relatively intensive in the country's abundant (and therefore cheap) factor and import those that are intensive in its scarce (and therefore expensive) factors. Thus, China and Thailand have large supplies of cheap labor and therefore concentrate on producing and exporting labor-intensive goods such as low-priced shoes, garments, and small appliances. The Swiss, with much capital and skilled labor but little land, produce and export watches and scientific instruments. Having large supplies of land-intensive resources, Indonesia exports wood products, minerals, and foodstuffs. Conversely, land-short Hong Kong and Switzerland import industrial raw materials and foods.

Until recently, the Heckscher–Ohlin (H–O) factor proportions theory had been widely accepted as the conventional theory of international trade. Although the H–O theory is losing its monopoly position because of basic changes that are occurring in the ways in which international trade is organized, it still does provide a useful framework for observing the trade effects of differences in supply and demand conditions among countries:

Effects of Supply Conditions. All of the factors of production enter into every type of commercial production, whether it be farming, mining, manufacturing, or any other economic activity. The various activities, however, tend to require these factors in varying proportions. Most primary industries, such as farming or forestry, make heavy demands on the factor of land and are thus said to be *land-intensive*. Some types of manufacturing, such as cotton textiles, need large supplies of labor; other industries, such as oil refining, need much capital and relatively little labor. Thus, *factor intensity* differs widely from one form of production to another.

In many economic activities, it is possible, within limits, to substitute one factor for another. In agriculture, labor and capital (in the form of equipment or fertilizer) can be usually applied to a unit of land in varying proportions. Manufactured goods, in many cases, can be made either by hand or by machine; in the latter case, capital is substituted for labor. Sometimes, however, the factors of production occur in forms that are so specialized in their applicability that they are difficult to shift out of one use and into another. This is true of certain kinds of land. For instance, acidic soils good for growing potatoes or blueberries would be poor for wheat, which requires alkaline soils.

Even labor may be difficult to transfer from one activity to another, especially if the skill requirements differ greatly. Quick shifts of labor are often difficult to effect because workers may be reluctant to learn new skills or may be incapable of being retrained. A farm worker could not immediately gain employment as a petroleum chemist, and a lathe operator could not quickly go to work as a crane operator or dairy farmer. Even some forms of fixed capital are highly specific. It would be hardly feasible, for instance, to convert an oil refinery to the manufacture of textiles. In all cases, time is the important element: Factors that cannot be shifted instantaneously to other uses may be converted over longer periods. This is especially true of labor, which, given a sufficient number of years, may be able to acquire new skills.

The *scale of operations* also influences the allocation of factors. A combination of factors appropriate at a low-volume level of production may not be suitable at a higher level. This is apparent in two contrasting forms of European agriculture. Peasant farming, still found in the more isolated parts of France, Germany, Switzerland, and certain other countries, generally takes place on very small holdings with scattered, fragmented fields. Because large farm machinery would be useless in such limited space, peasant agriculture is labor-intensive. On the other hand, though they may produce the same crops as the peasant farms, commercial agricultural enterprises in Europe have large acreages and big fields suitable for mechanization and have thus become capital-intensive. Likewise, a given type of manufacturing activity may take place in small, labor-intensive establishments, or it may occupy large plants employing laborsaving machinery and mass-production methods. The same company may be labor-intensive during its formative years and later become capital-intensive as the firm grows and matures.

The factors of production are present in different countries in widely varying proportions. Australia and Canada occupy large land areas containing immense, diverse stores of natural resources, but they have comparatively small populations to go along with those resources. Both countries therefore lack the supplies of labor, capital, and entrepreneurship necessary to exploit fully their natural endowments. At the other extreme are Belgium, Switzerland, and several other small European countries with well-developed capital markets, relatively large pools of skilled labor, and an abundance of experienced managerial talent but lacking sufficient natural resources to match these superior human resources. Several less-developed countries—India and Pakistan, for example—are oversupplied with workers, most of them uneducated and untrained; yet these countries have insufficient capital and managerial skills for putting their masses to productive activity. What are the trade effects of these factors of production?

Land as a Factor. The quantity and characteristics of *land* have much to do with determining the size and nature of world trade flows. By land we mean the territory of a country, region, district, or other areal unit, together with its particular attributes. The properties of land of particular interest are its physical resources of use to human beings. A significant aspect of these resources as they relate to trade is that they are distributed throughout the world in a most uneven fashion (see chapters 4 and 5). For this reason, the resources of most countries are "skewed," that is, these countries may have large stores of some resources—perhaps more than they can use domestically—but inadequate supplies of many others.

Mineral resources are distributed in a particularly erratic manner, hence the voluminous interregional and international trade in minerals, especially oil. The same is true of biotic resources. Wood products and agricultural commodities are important items of world commerce, flowing from lightly settled regions with superior growing conditions to densely populated, urbanized regions lacking such resources of their own. These commodity movements, however, are continually changing in response to such things as the development of new technologies, discovery of new resources, and exhaustion of old ones.

The physical dimensions of countries can affect their trade with the world. Obviously, the larger the country, the more likely that it will have a wide range and ample supply of resources and, therefore, a more diversified output of goods. Thus, the United States is more nearly self-sufficient than smaller countries, and its dependence on foreign trade is correspondingly less, usually no more than 8 or 9 percent of GNP. By contrast, the Netherlands, which is only slightly larger than Massachusetts, exports from 35 to 40 percent of its total output. A small country is also less likely to produce goods in sufficient quantity to influence international terms of trade, and it must therefore accept whatever prices world markets dictate for its goods.

Even the shapes of countries can affect their trade, especially in agricultural commodities. If a country's growing areas have a greater north–south extent, they will experience a wider climatic variation and thus yield a wider variety of farm products. Because Canada's agricultural lands are confined to a long, narrow, east–west strip extending the length of its border with the U. S. border, they are capable of growing only a limited number of temperate-land crops. Long borders between countries, however, are conducive to trade. Thus, whereas Ontario relies mainly on coal imported from the nearby eastern coalfields of the United States, British Columbia in the far west supplies that same fuel to the adjacent Pacific states of the United States.

It should be stressed again that neither land nor any other factor of production is sufficient of itself: All the factors are required in some combination for every economic undertaking. Land becomes economically useful only when capital, labor, and enterprise are applied to it. We have seen that such land-rich countries as Canada are unable to make full use of their physical-resource endowments when they lack adequate supplies of the complementary factors. This case also demonstrates that physical extent alone is not an accurate indicator of a country's economic size. Note that this imbalance in the factors of production tends to have a trade-creating effect for Canada, which exports large quantities of land-intensive commodities that a larger economy would absorb internally.

Labor as a Factor. Historically, the factor that most interested theorists was labor. Indeed, they originally posed the law of comparative advantage in terms of the labor theory of value. Though modern theorists no longer accept the labor theory of value, they acknowledge the considerable influence that labor has upon trade. Two aspects of labor are of special theoretical significance, as we saw in chapter 8: (1) its relative abundance or scarcity and (2) its productivity.

Countries (and regions) vary greatly in the size of their labor forces; many have inadequate numbers of workers to run their farms and factories whereas others have more workers than they can employ economically. For labor-scarce economies—those having low ratios of labor to land—the Heckscher–Ohlin theory predicts resource-intensive exports and labor-intensive imports. Hence, Finland, Canada, and Australia export commodities having a large physical-resource content, such as minerals, wood products, or animal products.

Contrary to the labor theory of value, labor inputs for the same goods do vary from one country to another, especially when resource endowments differ markedly. Both the United States and China produce wheat, cotton, and rice: but China uses labor-intensive methods whereas the United States employs methods that are at the same time land- and capital-intensive.

In those countries where the labor-land ratio is very high, the expectation is for labor-intensive exports and land- or capital-intensive imports. A number of Pacific Rim countries fall into this category, especially the island nations of Hong Kong and Taiwan, both of which import large volumes of raw materials and foodstuffs and export finished manufactured goods. A surplus of labor usually means low labor costs, a prime attraction to those industries using large numbers of unskilled or semiskilled laborers. Most such manufacturing activities are mature industries, that is, they have passed through the innovative stages that need highly skilled workers and engineers and can now use mass-production techniques that call for many unskilled workers performing simple tasks on assembly lines. Typical of these are factories making cheaper grades of textiles, standardized types of low-priced clothing, and even the more established forms of electronics, such as the assembling of radio and television sets. South Korea, Malaysia, Thailand, and Puerto Rico have many industries of this type.

Despite plentiful supplies of labor and land, many less-developed countries are unable to compete for new industries. Usually, they lack the other essential requirements of modern industrial enterprises: capital, entrepreneurial skills, an infrastructure of public utilities and transport and communications, and a variety of supporting industries and business services. Much of Latin America, Africa, and South Asia confront this dilemma. Although plagued by chronic unemployment and underemployment, these countries are able to attract only plantation agriculture and other extractive industries, along with all the problems these entail.

In addition to labor quantity, differences in labor quality affect trade. The quality of labor is usually expressed in terms of its *productivity,* which measures the relative value of output by a unit of labor. Several studies have attempted to assess the effects of labor productivity on trade. MacDougall (1951) tested the notion that the productivity difference between two countries in the manufacture of a given commodity should be reflected in the difference in its production cost and thus in its selling price. Countries should therefore export most successfully those goods with which their labor productivity is highest relative to other countries. A comparison of exports from the United Kingdom and the United States disclosed a direct linear relationship on a log—log scale between the productivity ratios of the two countries and their export ratios for a number of goods. British exports were relatively greater than U.S. exports in those goods, such as textiles and clothing, where the productivity of British workers most closely approached that of U.S. labor. Where the unit output of U.S. labor greatly exceeded that of the British, as in the case of machinery and motor cars, U.S. exports were relatively greater.

The productivity of a country's labor force stems from a number of influences relating to level of development, culture and tradition, and governmental policy. Affecting labor skills, for instance, is the quality of a country's educational and technical training facilities, which in turn are associated with level of development. Work habits and attitudes toward work, on the other hand, derive from a society's culture and tradition. Less-developed countries lacking an industrial tradition may require generations to acquire the skills and habits required by modern manufacturing enterprises. Folk societies, such as those found in much of equatorial Africa, often have cultural attitudes, incentives, and value systems wholly unsuited to assembly line work. The monetary rewards for such work have had no place in their tribal past.

At the other extreme are certain Oriental cultures, where long traditions of hard work and of devotion to group achievement yield exceptionally high levels of labor productivity. The resulting cost benefits provide valuable competitive advantages for Korea, Japan, and Taiwan in modern world commerce. Some European countries excel in the manufacture and export of labor-intensive specialties that draw upon traditional labor skills or reflect specific characteristics of national cultures. Goods of this type are Swiss watches, Belgian cut diamonds, Parisian garments, and Sheffield cutlery.

The availability of complementary factors of production is essential for labor productivity. Capital, in the form of labor-saving machinery, can multiply the output of a company's work force, as recent developments in automation and robotics have demonstrated. The productivity of a labor force depends on the presence of managers having the skills to use their workers in the most efficient manner.

Differences in labor productivity among countries are constantly shifting in response to both long-term trends and short-term cyclical events. In some part, these result from governmental policy measures, as, for instance, public programs for educating and training the work force or special inducements for foreign investors to supply technology and managerial skills. International differences in labor costs are constantly changing as workers become unionized and as less-developed countries with lower-cost labor enter their products into foreign competition.

Governmental policies leading to high inflation can affect adversely labor productivity: An increased money supply raises demand, causing managers to expand their work forces by tapping less-productive labor pools of poorly trained workers. Labor productivity also changes with the different phases of the business cycle. It is lowest at the peak of the cycle, when managers are drawing on all available workers, including many who are poorly qualified, and during the early stages of recession, when managers are reluctant to discharge their underutilized workers until they are sure that the business downturn will continue. Productivity is highest at the trough of the recession, when only the most skilled workers are kept on the job, and in the early stages of recovery, when managers resist hiring new workers until they are certain that better times are truly on the way.

Constantly shifting international monetary exchange rates effectively create labor-cost differences among countries. During the late 1970s, the U.S. dollar declined against other major currencies, thereby reducing American labor costs in relation to those of European competitors. Then, in the early 1980s, the exchange rate of the dollar soared against other currencies, eventually becoming so overvalued that U.S. exporters were at a severe competitive disadvantage. In the 1990s, the pendulum has swung the other way, as the productivity of U.S. labor has again risen, both absolutely and in relation to labor in other countries.

Enterprise as a Factor. Although often neglected in the past, *entrepreneurship* as a major influence on international trade is deservedly gaining renewed attention. As we have seen, the availability of skilled management is essential for the efficient use of the other factors of production, and the lack of this ingredient is one of the basic problems of many less-developed countries, as well as those emerging from the grip of Communism. It has become increasingly apparent, however, that the quality of management also has much to do with the competitive strength of industrial countries in the international marketplace. In addition to being able to achieve efficient production, managers must have the vision to assess foreign markets accurately and to develop those lines of production that anticipate global needs.

Capital as a Factor.   As a factor of production, capital is of three principal types. *Financial capital* is the more intangible, fluid form available for investment in any undertaking. More tangible types are *real* or *physical capital,* consisting of equipment, buildings, and other concrete instruments of production, and *social capital,* which includes educational facilities, transport and communications, and other forms of support for productive activities. Capital is sometimes difficult to treat as a separate factor because it becomes tied up with the other factors, such as improving land, educating managers, or training workers. Nevertheless, capital is clearly a powerful determinant of trade, and a country with an abundance of capital can be expected to have a comparative advantage in the export of capital-intensive merchandise.

The United States is often cited as a capital-rich country, evidenced by foreign sales of such capital-intensive goods as chemicals. The chemical industry has a high capital–labor ratio because it must invest heavily in complex plants and equipment and make large outlays for research and development but employs relatively few workers, most of them highly skilled. Yet the United States also exports large quantities of primary goods such as wheat, corn, soybeans, and cottonseed products, which are not usually regarded as capital-intensive commodities. However, capital is almost invariably a complement to other factors, and U.S. agriculture is especially capital-intensive. So successful has been this agricultural use of capital—in the form of machinery, pesticides, herbicides, and chemical fertilizers—that U.S. farmers, who constitute less than 3 percent of the labor force, are able to support a domestic population of 260 million people and at the same time sell huge quantities of farm produce in the international market.

Capital substitution for other factors of production has been increasing throughout the world. European agriculture has closely followed the U.S. lead in recent decades, and Japanese farmers have mechanized their small acreages. Parallel trends have simultaneously occurred in other economic sectors. Most striking of all has been the revolutionary change in Japanese manufacturing, which during the postwar years has turned to the production of capital-intensive merchandise such as cameras, machinery, electronics, and automobiles after more than half a century of specialization in labor-intensive commodities.

Financial capital is the most mobile of factors, and recent years have seen a growing trend for the substitution of capital flows for trade flows. More and more companies are building factories in foreign lands to which they formerly exported their production. Foreign direct investment (FDI) of this type has been shown to have a reciprocal relationship with trade. For the source country, the initial effect of FDI is to produce a drain of capital and to reduce exports. At first this also diminishes the investing company's need for domestic labor, a major concern for labor unions. But evidence shows that the ultimate effect of FDI is generally positive for the source country and its workers (see Chapter 1). Because of their shipments of components and subassemblies to their foreign manufacturing operations, and because of the overall growth in their production and sales, multinational enterprises are a country's most active exporters and among its most dynamic employers. Furthermore, in time, the returned profits and other earnings from foreign operations usually more than compensate for the outflow of capital at the time of the initial investment.

Firms are offered numerous inducements for investing in foreign undertakings. Often the decision to make such an investment results from the discovery that their exports to a particular foreign market have reached a level that would successfully support local manufacturing in that area. Locating their productive facilities abroad is particularly attractive for those companies making products that tend to be market-oriented.

A second reason for sending capital abroad in the place of merchandise is to take advantage of complementary factors of production in other countries. Agricultural enterprises may invest abroad in order to gain the use of land having specific qualities, as in the case of tropical plantation agriculture; and mining companies may enter into foreign operations to avail themselves of newly discovered ore deposits in other lands. Likewise, manufacturers of labor-intensive goods may establish factories in countries having plentiful supplies of cheap labor. Evidence of this is the growing number of U.S.-owned plants assembling radios, televisions, and auto parts on the Mexican side of the U.S.-Mexican border.

In many instances, manufacturers are forced to invest in foreign manufacturing facilities when the governments of countries to which they had previously exported erect trade barriers to their goods. To forego such investment would mean the permanent loss of those markets to competitors willing to make the commitments.

Contributing to the accelerating international flows of investment funds in recent years has been the growth of various institutional aids to capital movement. Prominent among these has been the multinational enterprise, which can generate large financial resources internally within the company, can borrow freely in many lands and in many currencies, and can draw on widespread corporate information-gathering facilities. Another institutional aid is the international bank, which maintains outlets in many countries, all having access to a common pool of financial resources, and which draws on a growing battery of techniques and instruments to serve its multinational customers throughout the world.

This discussion of supply factors has disclosed one of the weaknesses of the Heckscher–Ohlin theory, namely, the assumption that a particular type of production has the same factor intensities everywhere. We have seen that in actuality, capital, labor, and land are used in widely varying proportions in different parts of the world, depending on the characteristics of those factors in each area. Another weakness of the theory is its excessive emphasis on production. Supply conditions represent only one side of the equation; demand considerations, too, are powerful determinants of trade.

Effects of Demand Conditions.   One of the main benefits ascribed to trade is that it permits a region or country to maintain a consumption pattern that differs from its production pattern. Production possibilities differ from place to place, depending on resource endowments; but the nature of consumption also varies widely, reflecting spatial differences among human populations. One of the prime reasons for the existence of trade is that the structure of demand in any one place rarely seems to coincide with production in that location.

Even so, spatial differences in production capability are not absolutely essential for trade to occur beneficially. Trade can arise between two regions with identical production possibilities if they have unlike structures of demand. Take the case of two countries, A and B, both of which are able to grow potatoes and corn equally well. Most of the people in country A prefer potatoes to corn, however, and those in country B like corn better than potatoes. With the opening of trade between the two, each country can produce either or both crops and exchange its unwanted surplus with the other country for the preferred commodity. Such spatial variations in demand are common despite evidence that basic human needs are essentially the same. What are the reasons for these differences in demand?

Income.   Undoubtedly, the most compelling influence on a country's effective demand is its per capita income. Although rising incomes cause purchasing power to increase, this additional demand does not extend equally to all commodities. One reason that growing incomes create a stronger demand for some goods than others is expressed by *Engel's law,* which we encountered earlier. An impoverished population may be able to afford only the barest necessities, and some parts of the world today are hardly capable even of this. Although a rise in income may at first

cause such a people to increase their expenditures for food and other necessities, beyond some minimum level of satisfaction, they will allocate further income increasingly to other kinds of goods, including nonessentials and even luxury items. Because the latter are likely to be mainly manufactured goods—for which demand seems virtually unlimited—sellers of industrial products gain a rising share of the increase. Even the different types of agricultural products benefit unequally from an enlarged purchasing power. Poor people consume mainly starchy foods, but as their incomes grow, they will substitute ever greater amounts of meats, green vegetables, and dairy products for the starches (see Chapter 4).

Because, as we saw in chapter 6, commodities differ in their income elasticities, countries at different levels of per capita income have very dissimilar consumption patterns. The reason for this is that, as countries have gained in prosperity, they have stepped up their purchases of some goods more rapidly than others, thereby altering patterns of consumption. Trade flows among countries mirror these differences. Goods exchanged by North America with Western Europe are very unlike those shipped between Europe and West Africa or Southeast Asia. Differences in consumption patterns are responsible for a major part of this contrast in trade flows.

Among the wealthier countries, disparities in demand patterns tend to narrow as time passes. Rising prosperity in Western Europe and Japan in recent decades has caused life-styles among those populations to draw closer to those of North America. Linder (1961) has cited this similarity in demand structures among high-income countries as a principal reason that the manufactured goods of rich countries find their best markets in other rich countries. Linder notes, however, that even the richest countries have some low-income citizens, just as the poorest countries have a number that are well-off. It is to be expected, therefore, that the demand structures of rich and poor lands will tend to overlap to some degree. The existence of such demand overlaps presents opportunities for some trade in manufactured products between countries at different levels of per capita income. For more information on Linder's Overlapping Market Segments Model, see Box 11.2.

Cultural Differences.   International cultural variations are responsible for some of the differences among countries in their demand structures. Indeed, much of the range of income elasticities of demand for food and beverages can be attributed to religious taboos and to national attitudes and preferences. Catholic countries such as Portugal, Spain, and Italy import fish to add to their own sizable domestic production of this food; prohibitions of Hinduism limit India's consumption and importation of beef, as do Moslem and Jewish restrictions on the eating of pork. The unusually large imports of tea by the United Kingdom and of coffee by the United States illustrate the substantial effects of consumption habits upon trade. Although the countries of Western Europe enjoy similarly high standards of living, the proportion of family income devoted to purchases of food and drink differs considerably from one country to the next. Topping the list are France and Denmark, whose national cultures accord a special place to their cuisines.

Domestic Consumption and Exports.

The nature of a country's demand may affect not only its imports, but also its exports. Although exports of primary commodities depend on a country's resource endowments, its success in exporting manufactured goods benefits importantly from prior production of those items for the domestic market. Indeed, entrepreneurs are unlikely even to be aware of foreign opportunities for the sale of a given product if the home market does not have an active demand for it. Equally essential, thriving domestic sales permit the industry to develop economies of scale sufficient to reduce unit costs to a level that is competitive in the international market. Before World War II, Japan's large home consumption of mass-produced, low-cost textiles provided the necessary base from which to launch a successful export business in these goods. More recently, Japan's mounting prosperity has created a lively home market for automobiles and other consumer durables, thereby contributing to that country's flourishing foreign sales of such products.

Inadequacies of Factor Proportions Theory.

Conditions of production and consumption interact in such a way as to produce trade among countries, but is this the whole story? Does the Heckscher-Ohlin model provide a satisfactory explanation of trade? How well has the theory held up in tests using actual data?

Empirical Tests: The Leontief Paradox.

An early attempt to answer this question was that of Wassily Leontief (1953), who set out to test the hypothesis that U.S. trade reflects its resource endowments. The theoretical expectation was that the country's exports would be capital-intensive and that its imports would be labor-intensive. This was predicated on the widely held notion that, relative to most of the world, the United States is rich in capital and is less well supplied with labor. Leontief based his calculations on U.S. input–output tables for 200 industries and U.S. trade for 1947. His method was to compare capital/labor ratios in U.S. export industries with those of the country's import-competing industries (U.S. industries making the same goods as those comprising the main imports).

Leontief's findings, published in 1953, were wholly unexpected: The capital/labor ratio in U.S. export industries was actually lower than in import-competing industries. This indicated that the country's exports were more labor-intensive than its imports, a paradoxical result for an economy that was supposedly well endowed with capital. Leontief's figures showed that U.S. import replacements actually required 30 percent more capital per worker-year to produce than did its exports.

In a follow-up study published in 1956, Leontief confirmed his earlier results with an analysis of the same industries using 1951 trade figures. Subsequently, Baldwin achieved similar results using U.S. input–output data for 1958 applied to 1962 trade, and in 1979, he released equally paradoxical findings for 30 other countries.

The flurry of works that followed Leontief's disclosure agreed on one point: His study had uncovered basic flaws in the Heckscher–Ohlin theorem. Chief among these weaknesses was the assumption that the relative factor intensity of a good is the same everywhere and that this relationship is unchanging. That factor intensities do indeed change over space and time is clear from the numerous studies since undertaken to seek explanations for the Leontief paradox. The evidence shows that the costs of factors (land, labor, and capital) vary widely from country to country. Because they differ relatively in quantity and quality, they are used differently. The same goods produced abroad by labor-intensive methods are likely to be produced in the United States by capital-intensive methods.

A further explanation for the paradox is that, by concentrating upon capital and labor, Leontief neglected the substantial role of land in both U.S. exports and imports. America produces an abundance of some land-intensive commodities but is severely short in others. Thus, large export earnings from temperate grains and subtropical fruits and vegetables contrast with very substantial imports of scarce industrial raw materials and fuels. Many of the latter are extracted overseas by capital-intensive methods, often by U.S. multinational enterprises using American capital and relying on familiar U.S. technology.

Some writers have pointed to the nature of U.S. labor as one reason for Leontief's results. As we saw earlier, labor is not the homogeneous factor of production assumed by Heckscher–Ohlin; to the contrary, international variations in labor skills significantly affect trade. Indeed, Leontief's own explanation for the paradox was that superior skills multiply the effectiveness of U.S. workers and that labor productivity is enhanced by the nature of U.S. entrepreneurship and industrial organization and by education. Some observers argue that the education and training of labor essentially represent the creation of labor skills through the application of capital. Studies have confirmed that U.S. export industries employ more skilled workers than do the country's import-competing industries. Hence, the country has a comparative advantage in those manufactured goods requiring human skills. These tend to be high-technology products, which call for much capital investment in research and development.

BOX 11.2   The Linder Overlapping Market Segments Model

According to Staffan Burenstam Linder (1961), the structure of domestic demand plays a central role in determining the content and direction of international trade. Linder contends that the lack of attention to demand is a prime reason why the Heckscher–Ohlin (H–O) factor endowments theory has failed to provide a very satisfactory explanation of world trade patterns. Though factor endowments help to explain trade in land-intensive commodities, he notes, they are of little help in accounting for trade patterns in manufactured products. For the latter, the structure of internal demand supplies much of the answer.

As we observed earlier, it is usually necessary for a firm to gain prior experience producing a good for sale in the home market if it is to develop a comparative advantage sufficient for successfully exporting it to world markets. At the same time, if domestic demand for a product does not exist, the company is unlikely to enter into production of that product at all. The structure of a country's internal demand not only helps to determine its exports, it also dictates the products that it will be willing to import.

Hence, the greater the similarity between countries in their demand structures for manufactured goods, the

more likely they are to trade with each other. To the extent that the demand structures of the countries are identical, their consumers will not only require the same classes of goods but will also insist on products of the same quality and sophistication.

Although many elements affect a nation's demand structure, the most important of these is per capita income, as we saw previously. Linder cites this as the main reason that rich countries find their best markets for industrial products in other rich countries, not in poor countries. Likewise, poor countries are most successful in selling their manufactured goods to other poor countries. Whereas well-to-do people demand high-quality manufactured goods, low-income people have to be satisfied mainly with cheaper necessities. Nevertheless, a certain amount of trade in manufactures does take place between rich and poor lands. This is possible because even the richest countries have some poor inhabitants and even the poorest countries contain some rich people. Thus, each population tends to have a range of incomes, from its poorest citizens to its richest. It is just that the average incomes are higher in the richer country. What this means in practice is that the demand structures of most coun-

tries overlap to some extent, even the poorest and richest.

To illustrate the trade effects of these overlapping market segments, Linder used a diagram similar to Figure 11a. In this figure, the diagonal line OP shows the extent to which, on average, the demand for higher quality or more sophisticated products rises with increasing per capita incomes. The ranges of demand for products of high quality or sophistication are given here for two countries: The richer of the two, with a per capita income of Og, is Germany, whose demand for quality goods ranges from G to G. The less-well-off country, newly industrializing Turkey, has a per capita income of Ot and a range of demand for high-quality products of TT. The reason why the demand for high-quality and sophisticated products extends over a range in each case is that a variety of income classes is present in each country. The difference is that the average of Germany's range is higher than that of Turkey.

However, the two demand ranges overlap because Germany and Turkey have a certain number of income classes in common. The amount of this overlap is shown by sr. The existence of these shared income groups creates the potential for trade

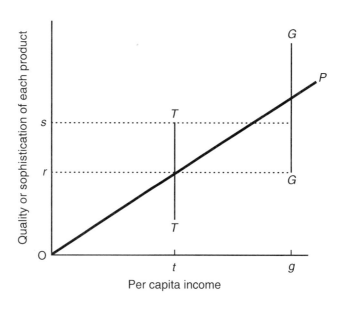

(continued on next page)

between the two countries in manufactured goods of the quality and sophistication indicated by the overlapping portion of their demand ranges. The resulting trade between Germany and Turkey is determined by the same factors that lead to domestic trade for such goods in those countries: economies of scale, product differentiation, and technological gaps.

In addition to exchanging manufactured goods of the types that fall within their overlapping quality/sophistication demand segments, the two countries can be expected to conduct a certain amount of trade in goods determined by their comparative advantages. These would consist mainly of primary commodities, such as Turkish wheat and tobacco and German coal and potash. Moreover, the potential also exists for Turkish exports of maturer types of manufactured goods, such as textiles, which would benefit from that country's comparative advantage in cheap, abundant labor. These types of trade, Linder would say, rightly fall within the purview of conventional factor endowments theory. Besides helping to explain the trade in manufactured goods between countries of differing per capita incomes, Linder's diagram is also useful for showing why an even greater potential exists for trade in such goods between rich countries. Consider, for example, the case in which, instead of middle-income Turkey, the second country in the diagram is high-income France. The location of France's per capita income on the x axis, Of, would approach much closer to that of Germany, Og. Consequently, France's range of demand for quality/sophisticated goods would lie higher than Turkey's on curve OP. As a result, France's demand curve would be very similar to Germany's and the degree of overlap, sr, could be expected to include most of the two countries' demand segments. Hence, the potential for trade in high-quality, sophisticated products between France and Germany would be quite extensive.

In the same manner, the Linder model could be used to explain the large potential for trade in industrial goods between two newly industrialized countries, say, Turkey and Brazil. As in the previous case, the similarity in per capita incomes would place the two countries in close proximity on the curve of average quality/sophistication, OP, and the ranges of their demand for such goods would overlap to a much greater extent than was true of Turkey and Germany. This wide overlap, indicated by an increase in the interval sr, would represent the greater opportunities for trade in manufactured products between two developing countries.

This suggests still another explanation for Leontief's paradox: U.S. exports contain a high proportion of new products. These goods are in the beginning stages of the product life cycle, when research and development are paramount. On the other hand, the country has long imported standardized goods that are late in the product life cycle, when labor-skill requirements are low. Also implied in the product-life-cycle explanation is the notion that factor proportions change with the maturing of the technology for making a good.

Further complicating the role of factor endowments is that much U.S. foreign commerce is intra-industry trade, as is true of industrialized countries generally. Two-thirds of the trade of developed countries goes to other developed countries, and most of it represents exchanges of manufactured goods for other manufactured goods. The major part of this is intraindustry trade, that is, cross-shipments of products from the same industrial category. Within product types, companies will seek out particular niches not served by others. By concentrating on these specialties, they gain cost advantages through economies of scale and are thus able to compete favorably in foreign markets. Companies differentiate their goods from those of their competitors by means of brand names. Much of the cross-hauling of similar commodities among countries consists of such branded items, automobiles, for example. In short, the growing place of multinational enterprises in world commerce has given new meaning to the concept of comparative advantage.

Finally, the notion that international trade is merely a function of relative resource endowments must be modified to take into account the existence of barriers to commodity flows among countries, notably the effects of transport costs and governmental interference. For instance, the evidence shows that U.S. barriers to the import of labor-intensive goods, erected to "save American jobs," significantly reduce the influx of such items. The effect is sufficient to have influenced Leontief's finding that U.S. imports are less labor-intensive than U.S. exports. Japanese restrictions on the import of capital-intensive commodities from the United States no doubt have further strengthened this effect. (The distorting effect of these and other barriers to international trade will be discussed at greater length in the next chapter.)

The empirical evidence presented in these studies raised serious doubts that intercountry differences in factor endowments are a sufficient explanation for trade. Beyond that, it identifies other elements that are known to influence trade but that are excluded by the initial simplifying assumptions of the Heckscher–Ohlin theorem, the basis of conventional theory. In recent decades, conventional factor proportions theory has been further undermined by a number of fundamental changes that have taken place in the way international trade is organized and conducted.

A "New" Theory of International Trade and Transactions

At the heart of recent dissatisfaction with the explanatory powers of traditional theory is mounting evidence that multinational enterprises are now responsible for a major share of world trade, and also for a variety of other kinds of international economic transactions that do not fit the conventional mold. This discontent led to a proliferation, from the 1970s onward, of alternative approaches, each offered as a replacement for existing theory.

A catalyst for these new approaches was the appearance of a theory of industrial structure, which seemed to establish a relationship between trade and industrial organization—more particularly the multinational enterprise. Taking into account this *foreign direct investment* (FDI) theory, the new group of writers set about simultaneously explaining both the overseas production of multinationals and the international trade conducted by these enterprises (Dunning, 1995).

These theorists have relied on a very different set of assumptions than those underlying conventional trade theory. They have assumed that

1. individual firms possess unique competitive advantages

2. firm assets are mobile among branches of the enterprise

3. the economic functions performed by various branches of a firm are decided in accordance with the spatial distribution of firm assets

4. enterprises are multiactivity firms (by contrast with the usual assumption that each company is engaged in only a single activity)

5. most transactions, domestic or international, take place between units of the same industry

6. transactions are conducted between related firms or within multinational hierarchies of firms

7. firms overcome impediments to operation of a free and open market by *hierarchical internalization,* that is, by setting up units within the organization to perform functions that would be contracted to outsiders if a free market for these activities existed (see Chapter 1)

8. acknowledgment that the coordination of cross-border activities may entail costs and gains

9. competition between firms is not perfect (some companies exercise monopoly control over certain functions and assets) (Dunning, 1995, pp. 174–175).

The problem with applying the various alternative theories to real-world problems, however, has been that they have been inconsistent with each other in the use of these assumptions and in their methodology generally. In an effort to restore order, a "new" integrated theory of international trade was proposed by Helpman and Krugman (1985). This theory was conceived not as an alternative to, but as an extension of, conventional trade theory—a "quiet revolution in international trade" (Krugman 1990).

The Missing Elements of Conventional Theory. Though acknowledging that conventional theory continues to offer many worthwhile insights, Helpman and Krugman cited four major inadequacies in existing theory that diminish its usefulness for explaining the shifting patterns of international trade in the age of multinational enterprise:

• *Reliance On Country Differences.* Traditional theory explains trade patterns solely by the relative differences among countries in their resource endowments. This seems to say that the greater the differences in their endowments the more likely that countries would trade with each other. It implies that we should expect the greater part of total world trade to take place between advanced industrial countries and less-developed countries, and that this would be an exchange of sophisticated manufactured goods for raw materials and foodstuffs. As we observed earlier in this chapter, however, the largest percentage of total world trade consists of manufactured products exchanged between industrial countries, which are generally similar in their factor endowments. Moreover, the relative importance of such trade has steadily risen in the postwar period, a time when the industrialized economies were becoming more and more alike. This narrowing of intercountry differences has been especially evident in Western Europe.

• *Intraindustry Trade.* According to conventional theory, the goods exchanged between countries should reflect their factor endowments. Although this continues to be true of certain types of commodity flows, the data show that a large and growing proportion of two-way trade consists of goods with similar factor intensities. Much of this constitutes *intraindustry* trade, that is, cross-shipments of goods from the same industries—two-way movements of automotive products, for example. Traditional theory cannot explain this exchange of goods, which are apparently identical in their factor intensities.

• *Intrafirm Trade.* As a result of foreign direct investment by multinationals, a growing share of international trade today constitutes shipments of goods between branches of the same MNEs located in different countries, rather than "arm's-length" trade between unrelated companies. Such *intrafirm* trade is more likely to reflect the particular needs of MNEs than differences in the resource endowments of countries.

• *Gains from Trade.* Conventional theory suggests that the opening of trade results in a reallocation of resources within countries. Though trade tends to increase the gross domestic product of each participating country, it can be expected to reduce the income to those of its factors of production that contribute little to its exports while increasing the income of those that contribute more. The record of recent years, however, indicates that trade has increased the productivity of all factors of production in trading countries and that it has left everyone better off. The U.S.–Canadian auto agreement and the European Economic Community both provide evidence for this (see Chapter 12).

Trade Theory Revisited. What has been needed, therefore, is a new theory of international trade that builds upon existing theory while remedying its deficiencies. In his book *Rethinking International Trade,* Paul Krugman describes the new theory as an approach to international trade that "emphasizes precisely the features of the international economy that traditional trade theory leaves out: increasing returns and imperfect competition" (Krugman, 1990, p. vii).

New Answers to Old Questions. Krugman notes that the basic question asked by the new theory is no different from the one asked by Ricardo nearly two centuries ago: Why do countries trade with each other? The answer from traditional theory is that countries trade in order to take advantage of their differences—differences in resources, technology, or demand. Though the new theory recognizes that differences between countries can lead to trade, it states that, in addition, countries may enter into trade in order to enjoy the opportunities for *increasing returns* that specialization makes possible (see chapter 10). If industries are able to raise production levels sufficiently to enjoy scale economies, this will lead to a specialization in such production in their home countries. Such specialization and trade can profitably take place even if the countries with which they trade have relatively identical factor endowments. Thus, trade may offer a way for a firm to sell to a larger market than afforded by its home country and at the same time to increase its international competitiveness by exploiting the potential for scale economies. The very large and successful multinationals headquartered in such small countries as Switzerland, Belgium, and Sweden demonstrate this principle.

The pressure to secure market share so as to benefit from increasing returns also helps to explain the proliferation of intraindustry trade—that is, a two-way trade in similar products. Much intraindustry trade takes place as a result of oligopolistic firms specializing in a narrow line of goods attempting to penetrate each other's home markets. This is why multinational enterprises establish factories to secure a presence in each of the "triad" industrial economies of North America, Western Europe, and the Pacific rim. Multinationals thrive on market imperfections. If transnational trade were frictionless—that is, did not incur transportation or other transactions costs—the optimum strategy would either be to serve markets from the location or locations that permit full achievement of economies of scale, or to license production to others, capturing via the fees the profits that could be made by exporting or by producing locally. But when there are *structural imperfections,* including government restrictions, taxes and subsidies, and imperfect capital markets, combined with *market insecurities* such as the uncertainty that a supplier will deliver on his promise, the volatility of exchange rates, the difficulty that customers face in evaluating unfamiliar products, the costs of negotiating deals; economies of scale in production, purchasing, research and development, distribution or marketing, which give advantages to existing firms and impose barriers against newcomers, concerns about infringement of intellectual property rights uncertainty about competitors' actions; and the opportunity to spread risks through diversification, firms will locate their production and other operations internationally in ways designed to minimize long-term risk and to maintain or increase market share.

The Role of History in the International Pattern of Specialization. Traditional theory tells us that, under conditions of free trade, the international location of production is determined by comparative advantage. The new theory also looks to history and the principle of increasing returns for an explanation for such locational questions. The existence of opportunities for increasing returns has the effect of dictating that production be concentrated somewhere. Exactly where that is often depends upon the history of the industry's founding, which may initially have involved an entirely arbitrary locational decision, as happened with the rubber industry in Akron, and the auto industry in Detroit. Production became firmly established at the chosen location, and as the companies began to achieve increasing returns at that site, this provided them with a competitive advantage denied to potential upstarts elsewhere. The firms that most successfully secured increasing returns were those that turned themselves into *learning organizations* by developing core competences, the flexible skills that allowed them to produce a stream of distinctive products that could be easily imitated by a rival: miniaturization for Sony, optics for Canon, or timely delivery for Federal Express, for example. By incorporating such considerations, the new theory of trade furnishes a rationale for the advantages of an early start that traditional theory is unable to supply.

By following this same line of reasoning, the new theory also offers an explanation for the plight of many less developed countries and their inability to catch up with the technological leaders. Many writers insist that the existence of both rich and poor nations in the world suggests that some basic unequalizing process is at work. By drawing on the principle of increasing returns, the new trade theory suggests that all that is needed to create such inequality among countries is for one country to gain a small head start. This initial advantage cumulates over time as the efficiently produced industrial exports of the leading country crowd out the competing products of the lagging country.

The Gains from Trade—Again.   A world that has imperfect competition, but that allows the possibility for increasing returns, also offers extra gains from trade over and above those obtainable from conventional theory. It can even provide gains from trade when the countries have identical relative factor endowments. To summarize, such gains come from the following sources (Helpman and Krugman, 1985):

- *Own Production Effects.* The participating countries will enjoy extra gains over and above those derived from ordinary comparative advantage to the extent that such trade causes an expansion of those of the countries' industries that are capable of generating increasing returns. The gains are realized by the trading countries when their firms are able to increase their output, thereby reducing unit costs and reducing prices.

- *Concentration of Production.* Trade can lead to a concentration of each increasing-returns industry within a particular country. This may result in a rise in the productive efficiency of a number of countries, thereby enlarging global output and reducing prices worldwide.

- *Rationalization.* Increased competition will reduce profits, which in turn may lead to a reduction in the number of companies while raising the level of output per firm. With increasing returns, this will result in greater overall productivity and efficiency, hence lower costs and prices.

- *Diversity.* With many countries increasing their productive efficiency in this manner, and exchanging with each other the goods thus turned out, the world as a whole gains from the resulting increase in variety of goods over and above what any individual country is capable of supplying.

This kind of analysis implies that the world as a whole benefits from trade twice: In the first place, it allows countries to draw on their comparative advantages to increase total global output and consumption. In the second place, the increased output that results when every country pursues its comparative advantages unleashes a further set of gains from the production efficiencies provided by increasing returns.

FOREIGN DIRECT INVESTMENT AND THE MULTINATIONAL ENTERPRISE

An alternative to the shipment of goods is foreign direct investment in which the production facility is placed in a market region. By using FDI, multinational enterprises are able to circumvent the effects of changing exchange rates, enabling them to secure and maintain market share—typically, in the triad of core industrial regions, North America, Western Europe, and East Asia. Foreign direct investment must therefore enter into any new theory of international trade, because the flows of goods and of capital and expertise, are substitutes. By the mid-1990s, 60 to 70 percent of international trade was related to the foreign direct investments of multinational companies (Dunning, 1995). Considering the great variety and intricacy of transactions involving MNEs, and the fact that many of these transactions take place between branches of the same firm, official records are unable to capture the totality of multinational activity. Nevertheless, we need to complement the discussion of evolving trade theory with some idea of the spatial pattern of foreign direct investment among the world's nations and the relative contributions of firms from different source countries.

World Patterns and Trends of Foreign Investment

U.S.-based firms hold first place in total value of foreign direct investment, but the size of this lead is diminishing in the face of heightened competition from other countries (Figure 11.25). In 1960, U.S. multinationals accounted for nearly half the world total and nearly triple the holdings of British firms, which ranked second. Dutch and Swiss companies made up most of the remaining one-third. In the expanding global market of recent decades, however, non-U.S. multinationals have proliferated, shrinking the dollar share of U.S. multinationals to only a third of the world total. British concerns still cling to second place, but Japanese and German MNEs are close behind in third and fourth positions, repetitively. Multinationals are also springing up in other lands, including several newly industrializing nations.

Half of the world's 50 largest manufacturing companies and two-thirds of the leading petroleum concerns are based in the United States. Next as a home for top firms is Japan, followed by Germany and Britain. Certain small European countries are headquarters for some of the largest firms, however, among them such giants as Nestlé (Swiss), Philips (Dutch), Unilever and Royal Dutch Shell (Dutch–British), ENI (Italy), and Volvo (Sweden).

Foreign production by U.S.-based MNEs has contributed a very high, and rising, proportion of the country's total sales. Indeed, by the end of the 1980s, overseas output by affiliates of U.S. companies was more than three and one-half times as great as national exports. In the past decade, multinationals from Japan, Germany, Britain, France, Switzerland, and a number of other countries have shifted much of their production overseas.

Many of the world's leading MNEs receive half or more of total company sales from foreign affiliates (Figure 11.26). Prominent among these are companies based in small West European countries. Leading the list is the Swiss food combine, Nestlé, which receives 98 percent of its earnings from foreign operations and has 95 percent of its assets outside of Switzerland. SKF has 96 percent of its sales outside its native Sweden, and Philips, the Dutch electronics firm, obtains 94 percent of total revenues from overseas affiliates. Of special interest is the Canadian communications giant, Northern Telecom, which earns 67 percent of revenues abroad but produces more than 70 percent of its total output outside its home base. Foreign sales also constitute a major part of total earnings of the leading petroleum multinationals.

The Changing Nature of U.S. FDI.

During the postwar era, U.S. multinationals have continually shifted their global focus (Figure 11.27). Despite the small size of its economy, neighboring Canada had long been the favorite place for U.S. firms to put their foreign direct investment. Consequently, by 1960, that country had amassed more than one-third of all American FDI, and during that era, it continued to receive a major share of new investment. On the other hand, all of Europe accounted for no more than one-fifth of the total in that early postwar time. More than a third of the U.S. total was in less-developed countries, mostly Latin America. Very little direct investment from the United States went to Japan, which then, as now, interposed stubborn barriers to foreign investors.

Succeeding decades saw a sharp acceleration in the pace of U.S. foreign investment (Figure 11.27): In the twenty-year period between 1960 and 1980, U.S. FDI increased eightfold; during the 1980s, it doubled again and it has continued at a high rate since. The big thrust of the 1960–1980 era was Western Europe, propelled by creation of the EEC. By 1990, U.S. firms had concentrated fully half of their direct investment in that one region. Latin America became a prime target area for American companies in the

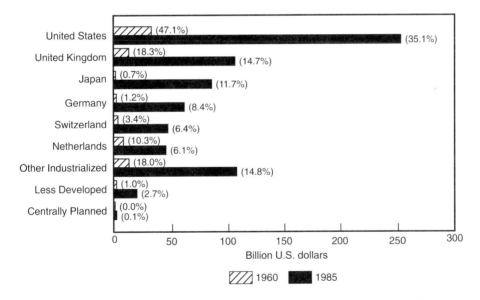

FIGURE 11.25 World foreign direct investment, by country and region, in billion U.S. dollars and percent of total. The expanding role of multinational corporations of all nations is seen in the growth of total foreign direct investment, which rose from $68 to $714 billion between 1960 and 1985. Though U.S. firms led this drive during the early years, MNEs based in other countries have more recently increased their foreign activities at an accelerating rate. Beginning at a low level in the 1960s, Japanese and German firms have since captured third and fourth places, respectively among the world's overseas investors. The number of countries serving as home bases to MNEs has also grown. These new entries are not confined to the older manufacturing regions but include several nations that have only recently become industrialized, especially those on the Pacific Rim. [*Source:* United Nations Center on Transnational Corporations, *Transnational Corporations in World Development: Trends and Prospects* (New York: United Nations, 1988).]

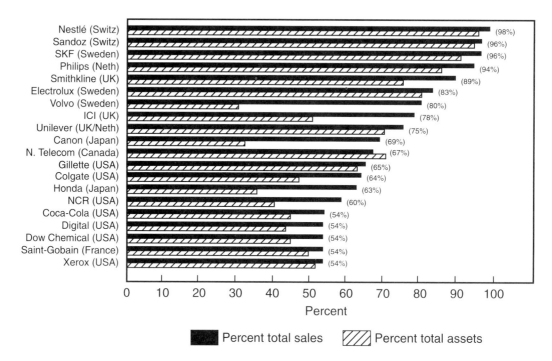

FIGURE 11.26   Global companies: percent of total sales and assets outside home countries. As they become more deeply involved in the international economy, multinational enterprises acquire ever-larger proportions of total company sales from markets outside their home countries. This growing dependence on foreign sales in turn leads to increased investment in productive and sales facilities abroad, in order to enlarge market shares and to secure these against intensifying competition and the growing threat of protectionism. Among the firms shown here, seven of the first nine are based in small European countries with limited domestic markets. [*Source:* Based on data from *Business Week,* May 14, 1990.]

1970s, but this flow abated in the following decade as the region struggled under a heavy debt burden, the legacy of outmoded economic policies. The area that experienced the most rapid increase in U.S. investment after 1980, however, was the Pacific Rim—Japan, Australia and New Zealand, and especially the Four Tigers, along with several other newly industrializing countries of Southeast Asia (Figure 11.27). Except for the oil industry, African investment by U.S. MNEs actually shrank during the period.

The 1990s have seen a resurgence of direct investment by U.S. companies in less-developed countries. Altogether, U.S. FDI has been flowing to these "emerging markets" (as the business community likes to call them) at a rate almost double that in the world at large, and it has gone into Southeast Asia at triple the world rate. In the 1990s, U.S. companies are pointing more of their direct investment to the next tier of newly industrializing countries after the Four Tigers—such nations as China, India, and Indonesia—which offer the lure of very large populations and rising per capita incomes. U.S. companies are also starting to return to South Africa now that political change has ended racial oppression in that resource-rich nation.

Meanwhile, the restoration of democracy and the adoption of export-promoting, market-opening policies by several Latin American countries in the 1990s has again led U.S. companies to look favorably on that region. Even the Mexican currency crisis of late-1994—which frightened investors away from Latin American financial securities— failed to influence the locational decisions of American multinationals, whose executives do not consider short-term fluctuations in the financial markets relevant to the long-term outlook for industry. Similarly, though Canada's share of U.S. direct investment had diminished in recent times, the two-way flow of cross-border investment picked up after implementation of the North American Free Trade Agreement in 1994.

In addition to its regional shift, U.S. direct investment abroad has changed in sectoral composition. Though manufacturing and mining companies had comprised more than three-fourths of total FDI value in 1970, this proportion has subsequently slipped to little more than one-half. Meanwhile, U.S. foreign direct investment in service activities grew from less than one-fourth of all foreign investments to more than one-third. Recently, the most rapid

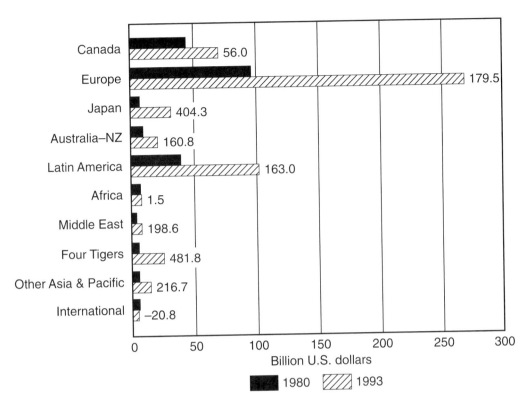

FIGURE 11.27   Foreign direct investment position of U.S. companies, by area, and percent change, 1980-1993. Total foreign direct investment by U.S.-based multinationals increased by more than two and a half times during the period. Europe still accounts for nearly half of all U.S. investment abroad, but the rate of new U.S. investment in the area has changed little. The main investment focus has turned to the Pacific Rim, especially the Four Tigers, where the pace of U.S. investment accelerated sharply in the 1990s. A prolonged debt crisis caused Latin America to lose favor with foreign investors during the 1980s, but democratization and more enlightened economic policies have since renewed the region's attractiveness to U.S. companies. North American integration has occurred too recently for its effects to appear in the official figures for U.S.–Canadian investment. [*Source:* U.S. Bureau of the Census, *Statistical Abstract of the United States, 1995,* 115th ed. (Washington, DC: U.S. Government Printing Office, 1995).]

growth has occurred in financial services—banking, insurance, investment brokerage, and so on—which has risen from 6 percent of all U.S. FDI to more than one-fourth of the total in less than a decade. The rising importance of service activities to the U.S. foreign investment position underscores the government's drive to reduce barriers to internationally traded services in the Uruguay Round of GATT negotiations recently concluded (see Chapter 12).

U.S. service providers are moving into foreign markets with a wide variety of products and they are taking these into newly developing countries as well as the maturer markets of the developed world. Some major U.S. banks, for example, are expanding rapidly throughout eastern and southern Asia, where they are profiting from the new consumer services they are introducing to these lands.

Telecommunications companies, too, are investing heavily abroad. Cellular phones are especially popular in less-developed lands, and also former Communist countries, because this technology enables them to establish badly needed modern communications far more rapidly than with conventional wired systems. Snack-food and beverage companies have also joined the rush into foreign markets, as have fast-food providers. Already well established in 79 nations, McDonalds now reaps more than half of total company sales from its foreign operations and it is aiming for 60 percent. Pizza Hut and KFC are following this lead. Still another U.S.-based service activity that is expanding into foreign markets is the entertainment industry, with its films, recordings, theme parks, and a variety of other products.

Foreign Direct Investment in the United States.
Direct investment in the United States by foreign companies has been expanding at a quickening pace, and this has
had a major impact on the U.S. economy. It has affected
U.S. trade, industrial location, and employment conditions,
and it has reinforced the shift in patterns of regional growth
taking place within the country.

The influx of foreign FDI into the country began to
swell during the 1970s; at the close of the decade MNEs
from eight countries controlled nearly 2,500 U.S. manufacturing operations. Thereafter, the flow became a torrent: By
the end of the 1980s, more than a thousand new foreign
enterprises were being added every year, and the number of
source countries for investment in the United States had

multiplied severalfold. Also, during this period, foreign
investors increasingly looked beyond manufacturing to
other economic sectors.

The changed U.S. foreign direct investment position
resulting from these developments is seen in Figure 11.28.
In 1980, American FDI abroad was still more than triple the
amount of direct investment by foreigners in the United
States. This positive balance steadily eroded in succeeding
years, however, as foreign FDI poured into the country
faster than the rate of U.S. investment in other areas. The
annual influx of foreign direct investment into the United
States reached a high point in 1988, then began to slump as
recession struck the United States and other major countries. In 1992, the U.S. economy began to enjoy a strong

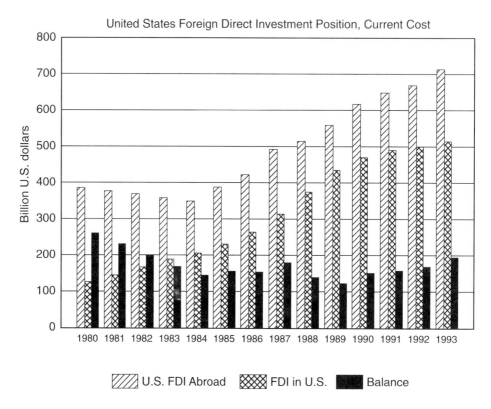

FIGURE 11.28 U.S. foreign direct investment position, 1980–1993. For many years, total
direct investment abroad by U.S. multinationals greatly outweighed direct investment by foreign companies in the United States. Although U.S. FDI continued to increase, nearly doubling between 1980 and 1992, foreign investment in the United States quadrupled in that
period. Total FDI in the country climbed from only $13 billion in 1970 to $124 billion in
1980, then soared to $517 billion by 1992. The annual flow peaked in 1988, during which for-
eign companies poured an additional $73 billion into U.S. businesses. Then, over the next four
years, as recessions hit both the United States and overseas areas, the annual flood of FDI into
the country dwindled to a trickle of just $15 billion in 1992. As a result, the U.S. balance of
FDI remained positive throughout the period. After 1992, the U.S. economy resumed its
robust growth and foreign outlays in the country again began to accelerate. [*Source:* U.S.
Bureau of the Census, *Statistical Abstract of the United States, 1995* (Washington, DC: U.S.
Government Printing Office, 1995).]

recovery, and continued growth in succeeding years caused a resumption of FDI into the country. Other attractions of the United States for FDI were the undervalued dollar, which made U.S. purchases cheap for foreigners; labor and land costs substantially lower than in competing countries; and signing of the North American Free Trade Agreement, which created a huge new market. Moreover, in many instances, the principal motivation for investment in the United States has been the desire to gain quick access to American technology.

To some extent, however, the swift rise of FDI in the United States has resulted from basic forces at work within the U.S. economy. During the 1980s, the United States changed from being a net creditor nation to being a debtor nation (Figure 11.29). The spiraling national deficit has provided foreigners with huge accumulations of dollars for investment in the United States. Any European or Asian multinational pursuing a global strategy could not avoid entry into this, the world's largest market. Moreover, a rising U.S. protectionist sentiment in the wake of growing trade deficits has obliged foreign MNEs to safeguard their shares in this crucial market by establishing production inside U.S. borders. Governments at all levels in the United States provide a generally hospitable investment climate for foreign companies. Not only does the federal government place few restrictions on foreign investors, but state and local governments compete vigorously for investments by offering all manner of tax and financial incentives to foreign firms.

As foreign direct investment pours into the United States, the relative contributions of the various source countries are continually changing. Back in the 1970s, 88

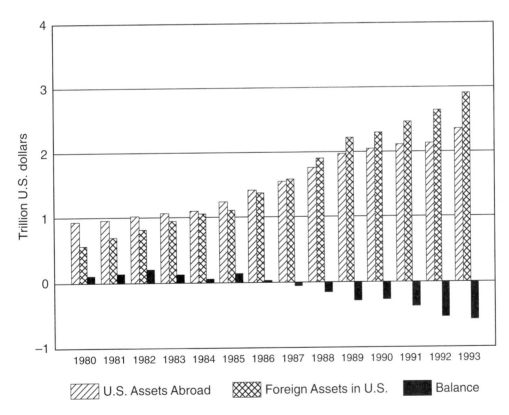

FIGURE 11.29 U. S. international investment position: U.S. assets abroad versus foreign assets in the United States. An important reason for the recent surge of foreign direct investment in the United States (see Figure 11.28) is the ballooning hoard of dollars that foreigners have accumulated as a result of the mounting U.S. indebtedness to the rest of the world. This is shown here by a comparison of total U.S. overseas assets, both governmental and private, with total assets held in the United States by foreign interests. After many years of positive asset balances with the world, the United States became a net debtor nation in the 1980s, beginning a downward spiral that has continued ever since. [*Source:* U.S. Bureau of the Census, *Statistical Abstract of the United States, 1995* (Washington, DC: U.S. Government Printing Office, 1995).]

percent of all FDI in the United States came from the United Kingdom, Canada, the Netherlands, Switzerland, and West Germany, in that order. Then, during the late 1980s Japanese companies, flush with cash, invested heavily in the United States. In 1990, however, this flow ebbed as Japan fell into recession. Even so, by 1992, Japan had displaced Britain as the largest supplier of FDI to the Uniteed States, having climbed from a minuscule 2 percent of the total in 1970 to more than 23 percent (Figure 11.30). Nevertheless, British firms continued their aggressive pursuit of investments in U.S. enterprises, so that by 1994, British companies had regained the lead. Firms from several other European nations also joined this rush for U.S. purchases, notably the large Swiss food and drug companies. During this period, too, a growing number of investors from Pacific Rim and oil-rich Middle Eastern nations joined the influx. Canadian companies continued to invest in the United States, especially after the signing of the U.S.–Canada Free Trade Agreement and NAFTA (see Chapter 12).

During the 1980s, foreign multinationals substantially increased their share of U.S. manufacturing. By the end of the decade, more than one-eighth of U.S. manufacturing assets were under foreign control. Prime targets for manufacturing investment were high-technology industries such as nonelectrical machinery, chemicals and pharmaceuticals, electric machinery and electronics, and professional and scientific instruments. The percentage of foreign ownership was highest in chemicals and allied products; stone, clay and glass products; and primary metals. More than a quarter of the U.S. chemical industry was in foreign hands by 1990.

Though recessions in Europe and Japan brought a pause in the U.S. FDI boom of the early 1990s, improved economic conditions subsequently led to a resurgence of investment from those areas. Large Swiss, German, and British companies bought a number of U.S. pharmaceutical companies and made further acquisitions in the chemical industry.

To the general public, however, the foreign presence was most visible in certain key consumer-goods industries. In the early 1990s, the Big Three U.S. automakers became the Big Four: General Motors, Ford, Toyota, and Chrysler, in that order. Of all the major tire manufacturers in the country, only Goodyear remained under U.S. control. By 1991, major Japanese-owned industries in the United States included 66 steelworks, 20 rubber and tire factories, 8 automobile assembly plants (plus three in Canada), and some 270 auto parts suppliers. Then, in 1994, Japanese auto manufactures launched further major expansions of their North American production. This new push was a response partly to the creation of NAFTA, partly to the relative rise in Japan's labor costs associated with the rising exchange rate of the Japanese yen, and partly to persistent friction with the United States over the huge imbalance in the auto trade between the two countries.

Public attention has increasingly focused upon foreign acquisitions in the nonmanufacturing sectors of the U.S. economy, especially such highly publicized events as the purchase of Rockefeller Center, Columbia Records, Federated Department Stores, and a number of Hollywood filmmaking companies by foreign interests. Less noticed but equally important has been the rise of foreign ownership in finance, real estate, and business services. By the mid-1990s, FDI in service activities exceeded that in the manufacturing sector by a wide margin.

In their locational choices, most foreign companies had in the past favored the traditional manufacturing belt of the Northeast and Great Lakes, although firms of different national origins had tended to prefer particular parts of the country. Thus British, and continental firms had located mainly in the Northeast, following a long-established pattern of trade and investment in areas nearest to Europe; Japanese industrial firms had gravitated toward the two coasts, especially with their large investments in high-technology enterprises in those western areas closest to Japan. Canadian concerns, benefiting from long acquaintance with the nearby U.S. business environment, had tended to be more dispersed than the others; nevertheless, they had exhibited an inclination toward U.S.–Canadian border areas of the Middle West and Northeast, as well as the South Atlantic. Some of the new investment entering the country during the 1970s, however, followed the general migration of U.S. economic activity into the Sunbelt states of the Southeast and the Gulf and Pacific coasts.

As the volume of FDI entering the United States swelled during the 1980s and 1990s, subtle shifts began to emerge in the spatial pattern of foreign ownership (Figure 11.31). The Pacific region assumed the lead in overseas FDI, with California replacing Texas as the state with the largest total. The highest rate of FDI growth occurred in the Middle Atlantic and southern New England areas. A major element in this stream of foreign investment into New York, Massachusetts, and Connecticut, in particular, was the takeover of large retail chains, financial institutions, and other service organizations by foreign interests. Another factor was the sharp increase in British investment, which continues to favor U.S. East Coast locations.

One of the most significant developments of the 1980s was the emergence of a major Japanese automotive complex in the traditional Rust Belt states of Illinois, Michigan, Indiana, and Ohio—with extensions southward into Kentucky and Tennessee and westward to Missouri, as we saw in Chapter 9. Settling mainly in rural areas with weak or nonexistent unions, the Japanese "transplants" chose locations central to the national market at points affording maximum access to the interstate transport network. This unfolding situation helps to explain the high FDI

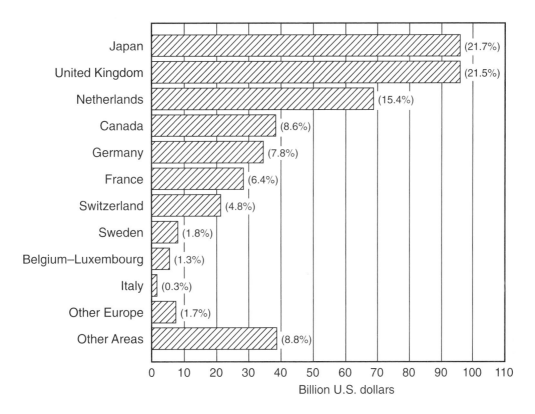

FIGURE 11.30   Foreign direct investment in the United States, by source area, 1993 (book value at year end). As defined by the U.S. Department of Commerce, this includes all American firms in which foreign interest or ownership is 10 percent or more. Although Europeans and Canadians were the principal investors in U.S. enterprises in the past, FDI now comes from a growing variety of countries. The most conspicuous new source is Japan, which supplied massive amount of FDI during the late 1980s. For a time Japan seized the lead in U.S. direct investment, as seen here, but a recession in Japan has subsequently curtailed this flow, permitting Britain to regain first place more recently. In the 1990s, a strong U.S. economy and an undervalued U.S. dollar have lured investment not only from Europe, but also from such places as Asia's Four Tigers, Australia, Brazil, and various other new source areas. [*Source:* U.S. Bureau of the Census, *Statistical Abstract of the United States, 1995* (Washington, DC: U.S. Government Printing Office, 1995).]

growth rates experienced by some of these states during the decade (see Figure 11.31).

TOWARD A THEORY OF INTERNATIONAL TRANSACTIONS

Not only is the pace of foreign investment by multinationals accelerating rapidly, the international transactions of MNEs and their subsidiaries are taking on a variety of new forms that are not captured by official statistics, and indeed are little noted outside the firms. Therefore, as John Dunning has observed, theorists have not kept up with some of the most important changes in the conduct of international commerce in the final decade of the twentieth century

(Dunning, 1995). The failure of theorists to remain abreast of these trends Dunning attributes to their continued focus upon so-called "arm's-length" transactions between countries—the buying and selling of goods and services by unrelated parties on the open market, a customary practice from earliest times.

Unasked Questions

What theorists have overlooked is that the sales of foreign subsidiaries of multinational enterprises in the 1990s far exceed the value of the traditional kind of world trade. Today, about the only arm's-length transactions remaining are those involving trade in natural resource products—principally agricultural commodities, mineral ores, and

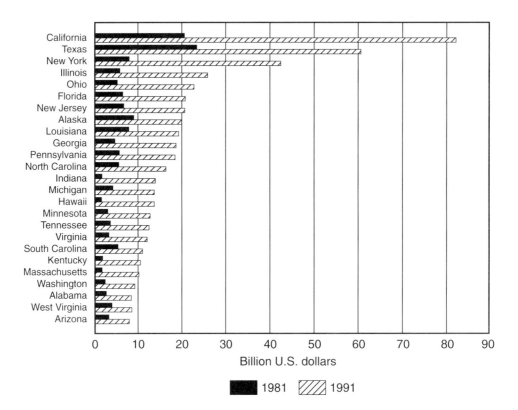

FIGURE 11.31   Foreign direct investment in the United States, leading states, 1981 and 1991. In the United States as a whole, the total value of direct investment by foreign companies more than tripled during the decade. Although in recent years foreign investment has tended to spread out more widely through the country, the pattern is still fairly concentrated. The top four states accounted for more than one-third of the total, and the 25 states shown here held 84 percent of the total. By the 1990s, the growth of FDI had begun to lag in certain key states, notably California and Texas, while other regions raced ahead. The high-tech centers of Oregon and Washington have enjoyed unusually rapid FDI growth, as have New York and southern New England and the national capital district. A very large influx of foreign investment in auto manufacture has brought renewed prosperity to the former "rust belt" states of Michigan, Ohio, Illinois, and Indiana, with extensions southward into Kentucky and Tennessee. [*Source:* U.S. Bureau of the Census, *Statisttical Abstract of the United States 1994* (Washington, DC: U.S. Government Printing Office, 1990).]

other industrial raw materials—together with certain kinds of finished goods. It is still possible to explain the latter types of trade by means of Heckscher–Ohlin theory. In recent times, however, trade theorists have been struggling to understand how and why so much trade is taking place between countries that would appear to have similar resource endowments. Though traditional theory can explain the existence of some trade between countries with similar production possibilities, it is hard pressed to find reasons for the high volume of such trade in recent years. Some time earlier Linder (1961) had pointed to this deficiency in conventional theory and had offered his overlapping market segments model as an answer (see Box 11.2).

With its focus on demand, however, Linder's model was only a partial solution; still other reasons for trade among countries with similar per capita incomes are now recognized.

The basic assumptions of existing theory tend to limit its explanatory powers in these times. It assumes, for instance, that (1) no intermediate products (e.g., partially processed goods) are traded, (2) companies do not form alliances with each other, (3) firms do not locate their productive facilities in clusters to achieve agglomeration advantages (see Chapter 9), (4) no cost is incurred in the act of trading goods and services, and (5) no transport cost is involved. The failure of most theorists to take into account these features of modern international commerce stems from the persistent belief that countries rather than independent firms are the prime actors in international transactions.

What is needed, therefore, is a theory that explicitly acknowledges the variety of agents involved in international commerce. The market is only one organizing agent. Among other possible agents are (1) hierarchies and networks of firms, (2) consumer groups, (3) governments, and (4) supranational organizations. Essential, too, are the legal, institutional, financial, and commercial underpinnings required for the successful conduct of foreign commerce. The lack of such infrastructure is keenly felt by those countries now emerging from Communism, as well as many less-developed countries.

Organizing Role of the Firm

In the present age, the firm or enterprise plays a key organizing role in international transactions, namely, to coordinate across international borders the procurement, processing, and distribution of a given set of products. International commerce usually encounters extra coordination and transaction costs not borne by domestic trade. These arise from insufficient information about foreign (1) markets, (2) institutions, (3) organizational structures, (4) business customs, and (5) governmental policies and practices. In many cases, the firm can minimize these costs by *internalizing* the various steps in the process, that is, performing in-house the various functions that would be otherwise contracted out to other companies. As an alternative to internalizing these functions, the enterprise may also elect to establish formal or informal ties with its suppliers and customers to share the transactions among them. In either way, the firm engages in a set of hierarchically organized transactions. To the extent that multinational enterprises conduct their trade under such hierarchical arrangements, instead of engaging in arm's-length trade, they affect the competitive advantages of the countries in which they do business.

Still another way in which conventional trade theory needs to be revised to keep up with these changing times is for it to discard the assumptions that (1) a country's assets are immobile, particularly unskilled labor; and that (2) these resources are equally available for exploitation by all firms. As Dunning notes, most assets are "created" from the country's store of natural endowments. Among such created assets are information, knowledge capital, the capacity to innovate, organizational skills, experience, and institutions. In many cases, particular companies hold proprietary rights to these assets, a proposition quite contrary to conventional trade theory. Note that many created assets are intangible. This is particularly true of national cultures and government policies, both of which are locationally tied to specific countries.

Patterns of trade and investment are as likely to be influenced by created assets that belong to particular companies as they are by resources that are tied to specific countries. Firms with subsidiaries in many parts of the world may draw on created assets of certain companies to use in their operations in other countries. Moreover, MNEs usually have their own strategic goals and company cultures, which are separate and distinct from those of their home countries. Contrary to conventional theory, some intangible resources are mobile. As the main international transfer agents, MNEs regularly move assets about, and they do this for reasons relating to the firm's own competitive advantage. The resulting spatial patterns of trade and FDI may therefore differ substantially from the comparative advantages of the countries in which such companies maintain a presence.

Yet, some resources, such as land and buildings, are indeed locationally tied. Furthermore, some other kinds of resources, such as labor and the more distinctive features of a national cultural, have only limited mobility. For goods and services derived from assets such as these, the principle of comparative advantage continues to prevail, and companies wishing to exploit these must locate at the source.

The Organizing Role of National Governments

In conventional trade theory, sovereign countries are regarded as the prime organizing units. The rise of multinational enterprises as prime decision makers and transfer agents, the globalization of economies and the growth of supranational organizations have substantially altered the part played by national governments in world trade and investment.

Traditional trade theory holds that governments should not intervene in the operation of free markets. The only reasons for government intervention condoned by theorists are (1) to protect a potentially viable new industry from well-established foreign competitors and (2) to prevent anticompetitive or monopolistic behavior by MNEs or foreign governments. These principles are firmly embedded in the latest rounds of international trade agreements, but countries do appear to be playing new roles that seem likely to affect international trade and transactions.

One role that is being reinforced is that of conservator of the national culture. This, as Porter (1990) has emphasized, is the source of those distinctive created assets that help shape the national economic environment and contribute to the country's competitive advantages. But as new technology is lowering the barriers to international transactions, and multinationals enjoy greater freedom than ever to move assets about, governments are finding it necessary to take a more active role in promoting the well-being of their citizens and to become more efficient in organizing their resources, capabilities, and markets. To avoid being bypassed, governments are having to shore up their own location-bound resources. This requires them to educate their work forces, improve their transport and communication facilities, provide efficient legal and commercial systems, and maintain favorable policies toward public finance and environmental quality.

At the same time, globalization is forcing governments to cede many of their earlier responsibilities to strong supranational agencies, such as GATT and the International Monetary Fund (see the next chapter). It is these organizations that establish international standards for cross-border transactions and work to discourage predatory trading practices, as well as to encourage positive monetary and fiscal policies. As the world economy becomes more and more integrated, it is supranational agencies that become increasingly valuable for ensuring the efficiency of cross-border transactions.

In summary, therefore, it is clear that conventional trade theory has not kept up with the changes wrought by new technologies and the creation of new organizational forms at all levels. Globalization of the economy and the ascendance of new actors on the international scene have affected world trade patterns in a number of ways:

- The increased mobility of assets has provided new opportunities for multinationals. By means of foreign direct investment and the formation of strategic alliances with other firms, MNEs now engage in international transactions at a level that dwarfs conventional trade flows.

- Altogether, the international transactions taking place between related parties—those with different branches of the same firm as well as those with allied firms—now exceed the total value of all arm's-length transactions—the conventional form of trade between unrelated organizations.

- Globalization has diminished the role of national governments and has enhanced the importance of supranational organizations in the management of international transactions. Prominent among key governmental functions today is the responsibility to preserve and enhance the quality of immobile national assets.

The final decades of the twentieth century have brought about a restructuring of economic activity in ways that are consistent with the theoretical ideas advanced by Michael Porter (1990) and Paul Krugman (1990), among others. This restructuring has taken place in response to intensified global competition, and has led to important modifications of conventional trade theories. As globalization progresses, and the roles of multinationals and new global organizations evolve and strengthen, however, "many of the propositions of received trade theory are being upheld by the very organizational forces that they tend to ignore" (Dunning, 1995, p 199). It is to this apparent paradox that we turn in Chapter 12.

VOCABULARY

absolute advantage	eastern bloc countries	Gasprom
Association of Southeast Asian Nations (ASEAN)	emerging markets	Heckscher-Ohlin (H-O) factor proportions theory
autarchy	entrepreneurship	hierarchical internalization
barriers to trade	European Economic Community (EEC; now European Union, EU)	hollowing out
Bretton Woods agreement	European integration	indifference curve
Canada-US Free Trade Agreement	exchange possibilities curve	intermediate products
Central European countries	factor endowments	internalization
classical trade theory	factor intensities	international division of labor
Comecon	first-tier states of Eastern Europe	international exchange ratio
communist bloc	foreign direct investment (FDI) theory	international terms of trade
domestic exchange ratio	free trade	intra-bloc trade
East Asian NICs	frictionless trade	intrafirm trade
east-west trade	gains from trade	intraindustry trade

invisible exports
labor
labor productivity
labor theory of value
land
law of reciprocal demand
learning organization
Leontief paradox
Lukoil

market insecurities
mercantilism
nationalism
neoclassical trade theory
"new" theory of international trade
newly liberalizing countries (NLCs)
normative
North American Free Trade Agreement
  (NAFTA)

Pacific Basin
Pacific Rim
principle of comparative advantage
Ricardo's single-factor theory
second-tier states of Eastern Europe
structural imperfections
structure of trade
trade deficit

TOPICS FOR DISCUSSION

1. How were world patterns of trade and investment altered by the major political and economic upheavals of the 1970s and 1980s? Why did some regions and countries respond to these events differently than others?

2. Why did OPEC succeed as a cartel when other primary producers have failed in similar efforts? Discuss the divisions among OPEC members and show how these differences have affected their abilities to absorb oil revenues and the positions they take in the setting of OPEC production quotas and prices. How have the effects of OPEC actions differed among oil-importing countries? How did the Persian Gulf crisis of 1990–1991 differ from previous Middle Eastern crises in its political and economic impacts?

3. How has the Pacific Basin evolved into a functionally integrated economic region, and what impact has this had on U.S. trade? What effects has the rise of the Pacific Rim had on regional growth and the location of economic activities within the United States?

4. Describe the economic and cultural conditions that have contributed to the remarkable success of the Pacific Rim countries, interpret the trade strategies they have followed, and discuss the new roles these countries have assumed in world production, investment, finance, and trade. What lessons have these countries had for Latin American policy makers?

5. Explain why the countries of Western Europe have such high export/GNP ratios, and interpret theoretically the spatial pattern and composition of that region's trade. How might these be affected by the new opening to Eastern Europe with the fall of Communism?

6. Develop two alternative scenarios for the shape of future commercial relationships among the former Communist countries of Eastern Europe and between that bloc and Western Europe, one based on successful liberalization of their economies and the other based on its failure.

7. Describe the gains from trade as these were perceived by classical and neoclassical theorists, and discuss the further gains that might be expected according to Krugman's new theory of international trade.

8. How would traditional theorists explain the very large proportion of trade between industrialized countries that consists of goods whose production is intensive in the same production factors? How is this explained by the new theory of trade?

9. What changes have taken place in the nature of international transactions in recent years. What caused these changes, and what implications do they hold for theorists?

10. Account for recent shifts in the U.S. balance of foreign direct investment. How are the locational decisions of foreign multinationals affecting the regional patterns of economic activity in the United States?

11. What are the most important elements affecting the structure of a country's demand and how does this influence its trade with other countries?

12. Discuss the globalization of the world economy and explore its implications for changing the patterns of economic interaction among nations.

FURTHER READINGS

Balassa, Bela (1979). The Changing Pattern of Comparative Advantage in Manufactured Goods. *Review of Economics and Statistics* (May):259–266.

Provides an analysis of the changing comparative advantage in 184 classes of manufactured goods for 36 countries. The author found that differences in commodity structure resulted from differences in physical and human capital endowments.

Baldwin Robert E. (1979). Determinants of Trade and foreign Investment: Further Evidence. *Review of Economics and Statistics* (February):40–48.

Employing the same approach used by Leontief in his classic input-output analysis of United States trade, Baldwin studied the trade of 30 countries with results closely paralleling those of Leontief.

Corden, W. M. (1965) *Recent Developments in the Theory of International Trade* Princeton: Princeton University Press.

A succinct summary of the evolution of conventional trade theory.

Dunning, John H. (1995). What's Wrong—and Right—with Trade Theory? *The International Trade Journal.* (Summer):163–202.

Dunning chides international economists on their failure to perceive the deep changes that have occurred in the nature and character of international transactions in recent years. This failure, he says, means that the traditional theoretical framework upon which they continue to rely is no longer adequate to explain what is happening in the real world.

Ellsworth P. T., and J. Clark Leith (1984). *The International Economy.* New York: Macmillan.

A historical approach to the theory of international trade. Interestingly describes the economic environments prevailing at each stage in the evolution of traditional theory and offers useful insights into the thinking of those who contributed to its development.

Helpman, Elhanan, and Paul R. Krugman (1985). *Market Structure and Foreign Trade: Increasing Returns, Imperfect Competition, and the International Economy.* Cambridge, MA: The MIT Press.

A seminal work in what has become known as the "new" theory of international trade. Provides an integrated treatment of a number of issues that had been neglected in conventional trade theory, notably increasing returns and imperfect competition, while stressing the essential continuity between traditional theory and the new approaches.

Houthakker, H. S. (1957). An International Comparison of Household Expenditure Patterns, Commemorating the Centenary of Engel's Law. *Econometrica* (October): 532–551.

Houthakker measured the elasticities of demand for food, clothing, housing, and other items in the household budgets of countries at different levels of per capital income.

Kindleberger, Charles P. (1962). *Foreign Trade and the National Economy* New Haven: Yale University Press.

A very readable summary of international trade theory.

Krause, Lawrence B., and Sueo Sekiouchi, (Eds.) (1980). *Economic Interaction in the Pacific Basin* Washington, DC: The Brookings Institution.

Investigates the transmission of economic impulses among six representative countries within the Pacific basin, noting particularly the effects upon those countries of the economic upheavals of the 1970s and their responses to these.

Krugman, Paul R. (1990). *Rethinking International Trade* Cambridge, MA: The MIT Press.

An important and very lucid presentation of the "new" theory of international trade, this collection of previously published papers represents a sampling of Krugman's contributions to this theory.

Leamer, Edward E. (1984). *Sources of International Comparative Advantage: Theory and Evidence* Cambridge, MA.: The MIT Press.

This ambitious study rigorously tests the empirical validity of the Heckscher–Ohlin theorem and, based on the results, describes the changing patterns of international trade and resource endowments. Provides an excellent carefully developed review of trade theory and a thorough critical review of previous empirical tests of the Heckscher-Ohlin theorem.

Leontief, Wassily W. (1953). Domestic Production and Foreign Trade: The American Capital Position Re-examined. *Proceedings of the American Philosophical Society* (September) Reprinted in *Readings in International Economics,* R. E. Caves and Harry C. Johnson (Eds.). Homewood, IL: Richard D. Irwin, 1968, pp. 503–527.

Contains original statement of Leontief's famous "paradox."

Linder, Staffan Burenstam (1961).*An Essay on Trade and Transformation.* New York: John Wiley.

Linder advanced the idea that, although differences in Factor endowments may explain trade in land-intensive goods, the structure of a country's manufactured exports depends on prior production for the domestic market.

———— (1986). *The Pacific Century: Economic and Political Consequences of Asian-Pacific Dynamism* Stanford: Stanford University Press.

Traces the rapid transformation taking place in the Pacific Rim and explores the economic implications this holds for the Asian-Pacific countries themselves, for other developing countries, for the established industrial countries of Europe and North America.

Linnemann, Hans (1966). *An Econometric Study of International Trade Flows.* Amsterdam: North-Holland.

A pioneering work in the development of interaction models for use in the search for generalized explanations for the existence of trade between countries. Tests a series of models of increasing refinement, using 6,300 bilateral trade flows.

Macdougall, G. D. (1951). A. British and American Exports: A Study Suggested by the Theory of Comparative Costs. Part I. *Economic Journal* (June 19):697–724.

This study evaluated the effects of differences in labor productivity on the export performances of the United Kingdom and the United States.

Ohlin, Bertil (1952). *Interregional and International Trade.* rev. ed. Cambridge, MA.: Harvard University Press.

A revision of Ohlin's classic 1933 statement of the Heckscher–Ohlin theory concerning the role of resource endowments in generating trade between countries.

Porter, Michael E. (1990).*The Competitive Advantage of Nations* New York: The Free Press.

Porter's theoretical interpretation of the fundamental determinants of national competitive advantage offers insights into the changes affecting world commerce in the final decade of the twentieth century.

Russett, Bruce M. (1967).*International Regions and the International System: A Study in Political Ecology.* Skokie, IL: Rand McNally.

Used factor analysis to group countries according to the strength of their relationships to each other in each of several forms of international interaction. Found that the world's nations fall into nine regional groups on the basis of their trade linkages.

Samuelson, Paul A. (1948). International Trade and the Equalization of Factor Prices. *Economic Journal* (June):163–184.

A seminal statement of the factor-price equalization theorem.

Smith, Adam (1937). *An Inquiry into the Nature and Causes of the Wealth of Nations.* New York: Modern Library (originally published 1776).

12

Trade Regimes and Global Development

OVERVIEW

International commerce is changing at an accelerating pace. Dynamic forces now at work in the world economy have changed the manner in which countries secure development via trade and the location of production. Trade plays a central role in economic growth, serving as a means for acquiring necessary technology. Though trade is essential for development, however, it poses special problems for many less-developed countries. Nevertheless, a growing number of LDCs with forward-looking policies are achieving rapid growth through trade, and these countries are being widely emulated by other LDCs.

High on the list of problems affecting national growth and development are physical and political barriers to trade: For those countries located peripherally to the main avenues of commerce, the main challenge is the time, effort, and cost of overcoming distance and transactions costs. For others, it is the artificial obstacles posed by the intervention of governments to the free flow of trade. For the one group, advances in the technology of transportation and communications are supplying the remedies; for the others, the current movement for the reform of the international trading regime promises solutions.

Following the World War II, influential policy makers came to recognize the need for international cooperation to
reduce the economic barriers between the world's nations. One approach has been to seek global agreements that would reduce obstacles in a gradual and measured manner among countries. This is the process that has given the world a series of GATT (General Agreement on Tariffs and Trade) treaties. Another, more limited, approach has been economic integration, which reduces economic barriers among member countries but discriminates against nonmembers.*

In the final years of the twentieth century, these two alternative approaches to cooperation among nations—the global and the regional—often seem in conflict with one another. Even as the new World Trade Organization established in the latest GATT negotiations works to smooth the process of international economic interaction, the prospect looms of three major regional centers—Europe, the Americas, and East Asia—competing for economic power in the twenty-first century. Globalized multinational enterprises already find it imperative to operate simultaneously in all three, and it is these enterprises that may ultimately assure the triumph of globalization over regionalization.

394

OBJECTIVES

- to examine the relationships between trade and economic growth, and the trade effects of technology

- to identify the trade problems of less-developed countries and to compare their trade strategies

- to examine the effects of distance and governmental intervention as barriers to international trade

- to assess the principal types of intergovernmental agreements for solving mutual problems of trade, investment, and development

- to examine the prospects for regional and international economic conflict and cooperation among nations in the twenty-first century and to consider their implications for the conduct of international business.

WORLD TRADE, ECONOMIC GROWTH, AND ORGANIZATIONAL CHANGE

Though commercial relations among nations have evolved in new ways throughout modern history, the final years of the twentieth century have seen a transformation of the world economic environment. Traditional theories are hard pressed to offer adequate explanations for the new patterns of international transactions. Among the forces reshaping these patterns are changes in the nature and availability of the factors of production, as we saw in Chapter 1.

Each factor has been subject to many altering forces. Not only have realignments followed the collapse of Communism. Population age structures have changed, labor forces have increased in size and acquired new skills, capital has accumulated through savings or foreign investment, new physical resources have been discovered and old ones have been depleted, technology has been acquired through research or transfer from abroad, and managerial skills have improved and multiplied. These changes did not come at the same time or in equal measure to all places, however, and the different rates of change materially influenced trade and investment, creating problems for those nations that have been slow to adjust. Heading the list of problems calling for solution are a variety of physical and political barriers to economic interaction. In response, there have been new developments in the ways that cross-border transactions are organized, at the center of which have been increasing numbers of multinational enterprises. Complementing the MNEs at the global scale, the world's nations have formed international organizations to reduce political obstacles, and at the regional level groups of countries have joined together with their neighbors to form supranational groups with shared economic goals.

TRADE AND GROWTH

These responses have come because trade plays a central part in the growth process. The relationship between trade and growth is reciprocal: Any gain for one benefits the other. This is a natural result of the close interaction between production and consumption on the one hand and trade on the other. In the growth of an economy trade may lead the way for the other sectors, as it so frequently did during the nineteenth century. This was clearly the case in Canada, whose rapid growth followed the expansion of its staple export industries—furs, forest products, grains—in response to rising demand in other countries. More recently, certain East Asian economies have attained prosperity through trade-led growth. One such country is Thailand. Soaring production for export has lifted that nation's economy from poverty to relative prosperity within a remarkably short time (Figure 12.1). The rule is, however, not universal. Trade may grow at a slower pace than the economy as a whole when protectionist policies prevail. An example is Argentina, which until very recently pursued a typical Latin American policy of closely controlling its foreign trade in order to shelter domestic industries from foreign competition. Note in Figure 12.1 that Argentina's gross domestic product (GDP)—its total output of goods and services—has risen more rapidly than has its trade.

Growth and the Propensity to Trade

The relationship between growth and trade changes over time. At the outset, when trade is essential to economic development, a country increases its exports and imports rapidly. Thereafter, trade continues to expand but at a slower rate than the economy as a whole. In the later stages of economic growth, a country's trade may decline still further in relation to its total output as the emphasis shifts from producing goods to providing services.

When a country's exports first successfully enter the world market, the domestic economy expands swiftly. Production for export requires specialization, which leads to an increasingly fine division of labor. As foreign sales continue to multiply, the prosperity of the export sector spreads to the rest of the economy: Money circulates more quickly and incomes rise, thereby enlarging the domestic market. Initially, a single staple commodity may dominate a

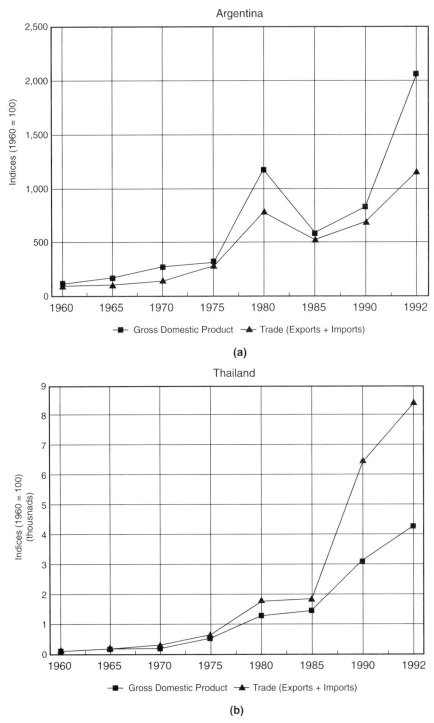

FIGURE 12.1 Growth of trade and gross domestic product (GDP) of Argentina and Thailand. The growth of Argentina's trade has lagged behind that of its GDP, reflecting a policy of import-substituting industrialization common to most Latin American countries in the post–World War II era. A new Argentine government has since reversed this traditional policy and the country's growth pattern therefore can be expected eventually to improve. Meanwhile, in common with several other East Asian nations, Thailand has for some years pursued a policy of export-promoting industrialization, with the extraordinary results shown here. Note that during the 32-year period, Thailand's GDP increased more than twice as fast as Argentina's. [*Sources:* United Nations, *Yearbook of International Trade Statistics* and World Bank, *World Development Report* (New York: Oxford University Press).]

country's exports, as, for instance, cotton fiber in the early United States or cotton textiles in Britain. Growing success in this type of production soon spreads to other related industries, causing these to expand along with transportation and supporting services. In some of the affected industries the rising level of output may provide sufficient economies of scale for their goods to compete successfully in world markets. This enables the country to add new classes of exports to its original staple export. The growth creates new needs, many of which cannot be supplied locally. Thus, a demand arises for an increasing quantity and variety of imported commodities. As incomes rise, in accordance with Engel's law, families allocate smaller and smaller proportions of additional income to purchases of food and spend increasing amounts on manufactured products and services. The composition of imports therefore gradually shifts to reflect these changes in demand, and entrepreneurs become aware of the opportunity these offer for local manufacture. This *demonstration effect* leads to the building of factories making items that were previously imported. The incentive for local manufacture is especially great for goods whose production tends to be market-oriented—that is, products that can be made and sold more cheaply close to the point of ultimate consumption. *Import substitution* of this kind reduces dependence on foreign suppliers of such goods. Thus, both imports and exports ultimately grow more diverse, even as they become a shrinking proportion of a rising total national output. Adding further to this relative decline in trade dependence with maturation of the economy is the proliferation of locally provided services and the rising share of national income spent on these.

Growth through Technology

Growth also results from improved technology, which yields greater output from the same quantity of resources. A new device such as the mechanical reaper, the cotton gin, or the self-doffing spindle frees large numbers of workers for other purposes, while expanding the volume of exportable product. A new technique that permits a larger percentage of metal to be extracted from gold ore has the effect of increasing the national reserves of that mineral. Creating a new technology involves two related processes, *invention* and *innovation*. The more fundamental process is invention, which involves the conception of a basic idea, such as the discovery that steam has the power to perform work. This is the product of laboratory scientists. Innovation, on the other hand, is the application of that idea to something directly useful to humankind, such as the development of the steam engine and the use of that device to power pumps for raising water from mines and to run textile machinery. This is the work of engineers.

Innovation is of two fundamental types. The first kind of innovation provides more efficient and cheaper ways to make existing goods. Japanese engineers have excelled in this form of industrial technology, developing more economical and reliable techniques for manufacturing automobiles, ships, and electronic goods of all kinds. The second type of innovation results in entirely new products, such as fiber optics and computers. The United States has led in this form of innovation.

In recent times, the pace of technological change has been accelerating. Modern technology issues principally from organized programs of systematic research into which corporate, institutional, and governmental sponsors pour huge sums in an effort to gain the rich rewards of product innovation. Innovation has always occurred more rapidly in some countries than others, resulting in a *technology gap* between the leaders and the followers. Although in the past the leadership has tended to remain with a particular country or group of countries for an extended period, the signs today point to a more rapid shift of technological supremacy among contending nations.

These international differences in technology are contrary to one of the basic assumptions of the Heckscher–Ohlin theorem, namely, that all countries are able to draw on the same technology, and that a particular industry makes its products in the same manner everywhere. Technology not only differs among nations but it has the power to alter their resource endowments in profound ways. Technological change is thus one of the most dynamic elements in today's world trade picture.

The Trade Effects of Technology.   A new production technology affects trade in a variety of ways: It can create exports for a country, it can provide substitutes for imports, and it can give rise to a new demand for imports. If the country originating a new product is able to retain exclusive control of its manufacture, perhaps through secrecy or because that country is the only one technically capable of making the product, then the effect of innovation is the creation of trade. The United Kingdom initially gained ascendancy in world trade through the development of such exports as railway equipment, steam engines, and mechanical pumps and by retaining a monopoly over its production for a long time. The United States has led in producing and exporting aircraft, farm machinery, construction machinery, chemicals, and machine tools.

Technology thus yields products that people all over the world want to buy. Sometimes, however, it is possible for an importing country to use its technology to develop substitutes for goods formerly imported, thereby reducing trade. The United States has been successful in this type of invention and innovation, as shown by the many substitutes that have been synthesized to replace natural products formerly obtained from abroad. Synthetic rubber is a familiar example. Ultimately, such technology spreads throughout the world, reducing world trade in replaced commodities. In general, however, the net effect of technology has been to expand trade. Evidence for this is the enormous increase in high-technology goods entering world commerce.

Another way in which technology affects international commerce is through improvements in communication and transportation. Because communication is essential to business, anything that makes the transmission of information quicker, easier, or cheaper tends to facilitate the flow of goods and investment. Such developments as the overseas cable, telephone, telegraph, and radio, and, more recently, fiber optics and satellite communication have progressively improved global communications. As a result, the transport-rate curve has moved steadily downward. This has contributed to the gradual spread of trade to remote parts of the world. Numerous transport innovations, such as the screw propeller, steel hulls, refrigeration, containerization, and jet aircraft, also have helped to bring down the cost and time required for moving both goods and people. By these means, the farthest reaches of South America and Oceania have been able to join the global economy.

Trade Growth and the Diffusion of Innovation.

The emergence of one export industry in a country gives rise to others, and the effects ultimately spread through the national economy. In the United Kingdom, this diffusion began with the textile industry, then extended into other industries such as iron, metal products, and coal. With a lag, there was diffusion internationally as well. British investment moved into France, followed by technical aid and skilled workers, enabling that country to join Britain as a supplier to the world market. The new technology spread thereafter to other Western European countries, particularly Germany, Austria, Switzerland, and Italy, as well as to the United States and, later, to Russia and Japan.

The diffusion of ideas occurs in a variety of ways. Some ideas have reached new areas through the theft of technical secrets, as in the transfer of textile technology from Lancashire in Britain to New England during the early nineteenth century, thereby creating a new center from which textiles could be exported to the world in competition with the original center. The U.S. computer industry confronts similar acts of industrial thievery today. The same result is achieved in a more open and legal fashion through licensing arrangements, the publishing of technical articles, and foreign education for technicians, engineers, and scientists. In earlier times, colonization was conducive to the spread of ideas throughout the world, and the trade links that France and Britain stil maintain with their former colonies testify to the durability of that avenue of communication. In recent years, one of the most effective means for the rapid transfer of business and technical information has been the multinational enterprise. An innovation developed in centrally located company laboratories can be transmitted immediately to corporate branches in other parts of the world.

Another avenue for the diffusion of trade has been the foreign procurement of industrial raw materials and foodstuffs. As nineteenth-century British industrialists reached farther and farther afield for ore, timber, grains, animal products, and other needs, they brought trade to Spain, Sweden, Denmark, the Netherlands, Canada, the United States, and other foreign suppliers. Eventually, such distant regions as Australia, New Zealand, South Africa, and Argentina entered the British commercial orbit, to be followed later by suppliers of rubber, vegetable oils, and other tropical goods. British overseas investment foreshadowed the global operations of modern-day multinational corporations.

The outward movement of particular types of production from centers of innovation tends to be selective. Raymond Vernon has explained this in terms of the *product-life-cycle* theory. The manufacture of a new product, he notes, usually requires proportionally large numbers of engineers and skilled workers in what is at first a highly experimental, low-volume operation. Eventually, manufacture becomes sufficiently routine for the introduction of mass-production techniques yielding economies of scale. Because skill requirements are less demanding in this second phase of the cycle, production can take place in areas other than the center of innovation. When the industry becomes fully mature, still more of the production can be assigned to specialized machines that require only unskilled operators. At this point, the industry shifts to areas having a surplus of cheap labor, often in less-developed countries. Thus, as an industry progresses through the product life cycle, its factor intensities become altered and its locational requirements change. The resulting changes in the global pattern of production are directly reflected in new patterns of trade flows.

The electronics industry exemplifies this sequence of development (see Chapter 10). Much of the initial production of new electronic equipment occurred in such centers of innovation as eastern Massachusetts, but once production became standardized it did not remain in that location for long. Some of the first television picture tubes were built in the Boston area, but the mass production of television sets quickly became established in the U.S. Midwest. In time, a major portion of the industry moved to border areas of Mexico and to Japan, Korea, and Taiwan as television manufacture matured. In the absence of further innovation in the original source areas, the ultimate effect is to reduce the proportion of trade based on technology, leaving as the dominant cause of trade the simple comparative advantage in the basic factors of production. This appears to be happening in the automotive industry, which is growing most rapidly in those countries with the relatively low-cost labor, capital, and large domestic markets for consumer durables required by this mature industry.

Leadership in invention and innovation has generally concentrated in one particular region or country at a given time. This has provided the leader with an important competitive edge in the export of high-tech goods. The principal center of innovation must strive to preserve this comparative advantage and must try to remain one step ahead of its competitors. In the past, no country has succeeded in retaining the technological lead permanently. In the beginning, Britain assumed first place in technology, a position it managed to hold without challenge until about 1860. Western Europe and the United States subsequently gained ascendancy, with much of the basic science originating in Europe and applied technology originating in the United States. By the time of World War II, however, the United States had attained a commanding place in both invention and innovation.

In recent decades, the U.S. lead has come under attack as the pace of technological change has quickened in other industrialized countries, most particularly Japan, Germany, the United Kingdom, and France. As a result of this heightened activity, technology gaps have closed and new ones have opened with increasing rapidity in one line of production after another.

Thus, the United States no longer leads in many of the old technologies—textiles, steel, motor vehicles—and has become a net importer of these goods. Now the country is striving to maintain its long-time dominance in the manufacture and export of the newer, technology-intensive products that have become so vital to the balance of trade. The dimensions of this problem and its policy implications are discussed further in Appendix 12.1, which you are urged to read.

TRADE AND DEVELOPMENT

While the industrialized countries of the world vie for the lead in technology, many less-developed nations must contend with the wide technology gap that separates them from the more advanced producers. The least developed of these nations generally lack the research-and-development funds, the labor skills, and the professional, scientific, and engineering personnel required to invent and innovate. Instead, they must rely on borrowed technology, which often is inappropriate for their needs and obsolete before it reaches them.

The technology gap is but one of the important reasons why the trade experience of the least-developed countries differs so markedly from that of the industrialized countries and even from the more prosperous developing nations. Indeed, the circumstances facing today's poorest lands are very probably unlike those that confronted the present industrialized nations when they were beginning their own development. Many observers therefore express

doubt that the benefits of trade, so obvious in the case of the advanced countries, automatically operate for those lands that have lagged far behind. Why should this be so? What is there about many of today's newly developing countries that is so different from yesterday's? If such differences truly exist, can we be sure that conventional trade theory, with its emphasis on free trade, is appropriate for the less-developed world?

Finding answers to these questions is complicated because two-thirds of the world's nations that lag in their development are far from being a homogeneous group. True, they share at least some of the traits that are considered to be the marks of underdevelopment—low per capita incomes, economies dominated by agriculture and other primary production, export dependence on a limited number of commodities, high birth rates and population growth rates, low literacy, and so on—but in other respects, they vary widely from each other. Even in terms of material well-being, they range from the desperate poverty of Ethiopia and Tanzania, whose GNP is $110 per person, to the comparative prosperity of South Korea (per capita GNP of $6,790) and Argentina ($6,050). In between lie nearly 100 other countries of varying degrees of advancement. The less-developed countries differ greatly in size, too, whether measured by territory or population, from enormous China and India to tiny Trinidad and Kiribati.

For convenience, we may divide the less-developed world into three main groups. First, following Linder's (1967) classification, we may distinguish between the countries that are truly *developing,* that is, those demonstrating a real capability for the sustained growth required ultimately to join the industrialized world, and those that may be called *backward,* nations confronting such grave obstacles to development that very little hope can be held for their future prospects. The United Nations identifies 47 such impoverished nations, which it refers to as "least-developed" countries. Thirty-four of these are in Africa, eight in Asia, four in Oceania, and one in Latin America. Events have pushed into prominence still a third group, *the high-income oil exporters,* typified by Saudi Arabia and Libya. Despite all the usual demographic and cultural traits of underdevelopment, these lands have achieved some of the world's highest per capita GNPs because their oil revenues are very great relative to their small populations.

Trade Problems of Less-Developed Countries

Many less-developed countries (LDCs) have not found trade to be the vehicle for economic growth that it had been for those countries now regarded as developed. The poorest LDCs, those referred to by the UN as *least developed,* encounter the most serious problems in their commercial relations with the rest of the world, but some of the better-off developing countries have had to contend with similar concerns at some time. These problems are largely of domestic origin, being inherent in the condition of underdevelopment; some of their difficulties, however, stem from the conditions of inequality faced by LDCs in their dealings with the industrialized world.

One of the most serious dilemmas for the poorer LDCs results from their tendency to overspecialize in export production. Many of these countries rely on only one or two commodities, usually agricultural products or minerals, for the greater part of their export earnings. For example, raw cotton contributes 91 percent of Chad's export earnings; cattle, hides, and skins supply most of the remainder. According to conventional trade theory, a country should benefit from concentrating its resources on what it does best, because of the efficiencies that specialization supposedly brings. For exporters of primary goods, however, this is not usually the case. Narrow specialization in such commodities risks heavy losses as a result of crop failures, uncertain foreign demand, and fluctuating world prices. Adding to these problems is the temptation for primary producers to increase output even during periods when the world market has become saturated and prices are falling. Seeing their incomes decline as prices drop, farmers may plant still larger acreages in the hope that the increased volume of output will help them maintain their customary incomes. This response to glutted markets is directly opposite to that of factory managers in similar circumstances.

In some LDCs, the primary export industries are owned and controlled by foreign enterprises. This is common in mineral ventures and in plantation agriculture, and especially in the production of beverage crops, commercial fibers, and tropical fruits. Foreign companies supply not only the capital and technology, but also the managers and skilled workers needed for a modern venture serving world markets. Only the unskilled laborers come from the local community. Surrounding these enclaves of commercial agriculture are the subsistence farms of the indigenous populations. Such a juxtaposition of the primitive and the modern constitutes a *dual economy*, a feature typical of tropical America, Africa, and southern Asia.

In the organization of their societies, many of today's LDCs differ from those lands settled by Europeans, especially the British. Unlike the transplanted Europeans of the early United States and Canada, the current populations of less-developed regions lack a commercial tradition. In some cases, inherited social attitudes and value systems are incompatible with the competitive, profit-driven viewpoints prevalent in industrialized societies. Because of this conflict in values, it is difficult for such peoples to adjust to the changes required for modern production. Many LDCs of this present era also confront grave demographic and employment problems. Overpopulation, steadily worsening because of declining death rates, creates a surplus of labor, leading to severe unemployment and underemployment. The current group of industrialized nations did not have to bear these social burdens at similar stages of development.

Unequal Trade Relations with Industrialized Countries

The economic and social problems confronting many of today's less-developed countries place them at a disadvantage in their commercial relations with the developed lands. The major exceptions to this, of course, are the high-income, oil-exporting countries of the Middle East, whose membership in the OPEC cartel has placed them in a strong bargaining position, but one that is now challenged by non-OPEC oil, by substitutes, and by energy conservation. The nonoil-exporting LDCs as a whole now account for a little more than one-fifth of total world trade; but the 47 least-developed nations provide only 0.4 percent of the total, a proportion that has steadily diminished in recent decades. Yet, relatively small though it be, this trade is utterly essential to such nations. For them, the industrial countries are the only source for many of their needs and the principal market for their traditional exports. These imports and exports are indispensable to the development process itself.

Among the imports required by LDCs are those consumer goods they are incapable of producing domestically. Equally crucial, however, are those commodities required for economic growth: the machinery and other capital equipment needed to modernize agriculture and build factories, the spare parts and other items to keep the machinery running, and industrial raw materials not available domestically. Many of these new industries make goods formerly imported, and this *import substitution* further affects the commodity composition of their foreign trade.

To pay for their imports, developing countries must sell goods in world markets. For countries in the early stages of development, the exports are typically the primary commodities for which they have both absolute and comparative advantages. Their resource endowments, such as soils, climates conducive to tropical agriculture, and mineral deposits, dictate the nature of the goods marketed abroad. These LDCs are called *primary producers* because primary products are all they export; however, many industrialized nations—the examples include Canada, the United States, Russia, and Australia—actually export greater absolute amounts of primary commodities because of the immense endowments of land and minerals they possess: They are the main sources of the grains and other temperate crops that are the major staples of world agricultural commerce.

In exporting primary goods to the industrialized countries, less-developed countries operate under severe disadvantages. For one thing, manufacturers are becoming increasingly efficient in their use of raw materials and are processing them more thoroughly than in the past, thus requiring relatively smaller amounts of these items. Industries also are making greater use of synthetic materials that compete with the natural substances. Thus the contribution of the poorer LDCs to world exports continues to shrink.

Another problem for the least-developed countries is that the global supply of farm commodities fluctuates widely in response to the variability of harvests, causing prices, which are set in the great commodity markets of London, New York, Chicago, and other commercial centers, to be unstable. Individually weak and disunited, the LDCs are unable to influence the prices of their agricultural goods in world markets.

Developing countries as a group are becoming more active exporters of manufactured products, but many of them find it difficult to penetrate the markets of industrialized countries. For those LDCs in the early stages of industrialization, most of their manufactured exports are technically simple, often the results of first-stage processing of metallic ores. Even some of the more sophisticated manufactured goods exported by this group of developing countries pose marketing difficulties. One such problem is the technology gap, because of which the products of these countries cannot compete on equal terms with the superior quality and lower prices of similar goods produced in the industrialized countries. Furthermore, many LDCs do not have large enough home markets to provide adequate bases for achieving the necessary economies of scale. This problem is all the greater because of the natural inefficiencies of newly started industries, which raise unit costs. Entrepreneurs in less-developed lands are unfamiliar with the quality standards, delivery schedules, and customary sales channels in major world markets.

The poorer LDCs almost always have deficits in their foreign trade, and sometimes these are relatively large: These countries simply do not earn enough from their exports to pay for all the imported goods they must have to sustain their economies and promote their development. For this reason, their governments interfere in their foreign trade by using a variety of devices: licensing, exchange controls, tariffs, quotas, and so on, considering them necessary to limit the drain on their reserves of foreign exchange and to reduce the importation of "inessentials" so as to conserve financial resources needed to pay for necessary items. Tariffs help to improve the price ratio (terms of trade) with industrialized nations and provide protection for infant industries.

Among the LDCs, therefore, it is those countries classified as "backward," or "least-developed," that have the gravest trade problems. Trade with the industrialized world can quickly extinguish any unprotected import-competing industry that might have served as a basis for development, as happened when cheap factory-made imports killed much of the cottage textile industry of colonial India. In some LDCs, the obstacles to development are so great that even large export earnings may fail to nudge the nation toward true modernization, as shown by the experience of certain oil-exporting countries of Africa and the Middle East.

So different are these less-developed countries from industrialized countries that many analysts have asked whether conventional trade theory is relevant to their experience in today's world economy. According to the theory, free trade leads to an international specialization that is beneficial to all participants. It brings about a more efficient allocation of resources, and it spreads its effects to other sectors of the economy. Some LDCs do not have the capacity to extend growth in their export sectors to the rest of their economies, however. The apparent explanation is that a variety of political, social, and cultural conditions act as barriers to the linkage of export industries to the economy as a whole, perpetuating the dual economies described earlier. For such barriers to be removed, development must extend to all aspects of national life. In this process, public policy must establish the necessary conditions. The remarkable progress of a growing number of LDCs that have adopted new strategies for trade and development demonstrates that this can be done.

Trade Strategies for Development

Industrialization is the overriding national goal of virtually all less-developed countries. Only industry offers the hope for achieving a level of economic growth that exceeds their rates of population growth; world demand for their traditional agricultural exports is not increasing fast enough. Only manufacturing can generate employment in sufficient quantity to absorb the flood of new entrants into their labor forces. For most LDCs, industrialization is also a matter of national pride: They depend on it to elevate them to a status comparable to that of the present advanced lands. LDCs therefore resent the implications of conventional trade theory, which would relegate them to a permanent role as suppliers of primary goods to the richer lands.

The road to industrialization has been slow and difficult, however. Most LDCs, especially those in Latin America, have until recently followed policies of import-substituting industrialization. In addition to the elaborate bureaucratic procedures entailed, policies of this sort create many new problems. Import substitution ordinarily means high-cost production for limited national markets, which lowers real incomes and standards of living. Only those LDCs with very large domestic markets—such as Brazil and Mexico—benefited very much from this approach to development, and even they have recently turned to new strategies for growth.

Some of the semi-industrialized countries in Asia have pointed the way for LDCs that have reached the limits of import substitution. The semi-industrialized countries (SICs) are the new middle-income nations of the world community. They are the most advanced of the LDCs: Their per capita incomes are higher, their manufacturing sectors are larger and more sophisticated, and they are more urbanized. Manufactured goods represent one-fifth or more of their total output, and they constitute a quarter or more of their exports. As a group, the SICs have achieved impressive levels of economic growth, well in excess of their rates of population growth, which in several cases are still high. Most of this growth has resulted from the effective way in which these countries have used their resources to assume new roles in the international economy. The results of the new strategy are apparent in the rapidly growing share of world exports enjoyed by the nonoil-exporting "developing" countries, to use Linder's term for those economies that are truly advancing. This proportion has risen from only 13 percent of total world exports in 1980 to more than 22 percent in 1993, the fastest rate of increase of any category of exporting countries.

The Four Tigers of Asia—South Korea, Taiwan, Hong Kong, and Singapore—have set the pattern for this kind of trade-led development strategy, which in turn was modeled after the Japanese example. Since the 1960s, the four have successfully followed national policies that have favored export production based initially on labor-intensive manufacturing industries. None of them is well endowed with natural resources, but each is able to draw on an impressive array of human resources.

After nearly four decades of sustained fast growth, the Tigers have achieved per capita GNPs surpassing those of some countries in Mediterranean Europe. Realistically, therefore, they can no longer be classed as LDCs but are more generally referred to as "newly industrialized countries," or NICs. This extraordinary rise in material well-being has provided inspiration for developing nations everywhere, but especially in East Asia, where several countries have adopted similar growth strategies with promising results. Indeed, one of these, Thailand, has made such progress that it is sometimes referred to as the Fifth Tiger.

Though in detail the Tigers differ somewhat in their circumstances and approaches, South Korea's experience is fairly typical of the group. That country's economic growth, which averaged more than 9 percent per annum throughout the 1960s and 1970s, is all the more impressive when we consider its dismal state at the end of the Korean War in 1953. With the arrival of peace, the country was left with only an impoverished agricultural economy: North Korea had all the mineral resources, nearly all the electric genera-

tion, and most of the manufacturing industries still remaining. The war had left South Korea devastated, most of its agricultural lands in waste, industries destroyed, a quarter of the population homeless, and per capita incomes among the world's lowest.

In the decade following the war, from 1953 to 1963, South Korean government policy emphasized reconstruction, defense, and raising the standard of living. United States aid throughout this period was substantial, amounting to 15 percent of gross national product. South Korea initially followed a strategy of import-substituting industrialization, concentrating on nondurable consumer goods—mainly textiles, clothing, and foodstuffs—and giving little attention to agriculture. Though the possibilities for this kind of industrial development were exhausted by the early 1960s, South Korea had in the meantime acquired some valuable assets. Ten years of industrialization, accompanied by a drive to improve education, had produced a literate population and a corps of skilled managers and trained workers.

At this point, the government abruptly shifted to a program of export-oriented industrialization which focused on producing nondurable consumer goods for the world market. Recognizing that the nation lacked physical resources but had an abundance of human resources, the new program offered special subsidies for exports, removed import duties on raw material imports, changed the tax structure to favor personal savings, and introduced more realistic exchange rates. This policy shift quickly produced remarkable results. Exports rose from only 3.3 percent of GNP in 1960 to 45 percent by 1977, a level that has remained unchanged since. Exports of manufactured goods increased during the early years at an average annual rate of 51 percent, rising from only 15 percent of Korea's exports in 1958 to 92 percent of the total by the late 1980s. The swift pace of trade-led growth has continued almost without pause: Between 1980 and 1992, Korea's GDP rose at a yearly rate averaging 9.2 percent.

The Four Tigers, and the semi-industrialized countries attempting to emulate them, have discovered, however, that an export-favoring policy succeeds only as long as world markets remain free. Because the best customers for SIC exports are the developed countries, which take about three-fifths of the total, access to developed-country markets is very important for the SICs. Yet, the more deeply SIC exporters penetrate the markets of the developed lands, the more resistance they encounter from rising protectionist sentiments in these countries (see Appendix 12.2, for further discussion of this issue).

As trade restrictions began to cut SIC sales to the advanced countries, the SICs discovered promising new markets for their manufactured goods in other less-developed countries. Brazil now trades more with other LDCs than it does with the United States; India is increasing its exports to the less-developed world faster than to the developed countries. The greater part of this rising trade among LDCs is from the more-industrialized countries to the less-industrialized ones; only a minor share takes place between countries at similar levels of development.

The manufactured products traded among LDCs are mainly those that rely on economies of scale in manufacturing, have demanding skill requirements, call for relatively large capital inputs, and are produced by industries that were initially established to serve domestic markets. Note that the products exchanged by LDCs are different in nature from the labor-intensive exports they send to industrialized countries. Furthermore, the products LDCs buy from each other are usually complementary to the kinds of goods they obtain from advanced countries, not substitutes for them.

One of the more significant recent trends in intra-LDC trade has been the rise in exports of capital equipment by certain of the more-industrialized developing countries. Producers in these countries have gained experience in designing and building machinery that is technically appropriate for their own industries, which are more labor-intensive and thus call for designs different from those of industries in Europe, Anglo-America, and Japan, where labor is more costly. Thus, Brazil, Argentina, India, and Mexico find markets for their own designs in other LDCs with labor requirements similar to their own. Argentina sells equipment for the processing and refrigeration of meats and fruits, drawing on her own experience in the food industries. Brazil and Mexico, both well established in the metallurgical trades, export steelmaking equipment to LDCs. The semi-industrialized countries are pushing their exports of machinery and transport equipment. These are currently the most dynamic items in world trade, partly because of the growing demand among LDCs for such goods.

Attractive opportunities thus exist for trade among LDCs. As Linder (1961) noted (see Box 11.2, Chapter 11), LDCs are more similar to each other in their demand and supply than they are to the industrialized countries, and they are more similar in economic size and levels of development; hence, they can compete and trade on more equal terms among themselves. The theoretical benefits of free trade are more attainable by countries at similar levels of development: Among equals, the opportunities for economies of scale and the efficiencies of international specialization are far greater. Buying from each other also permits LDCs to reduce their imports from industrialized lands, thereby saving their scarce hard currency for the purchase of those high-technology items that are as yet obtainable only from the advanced countries. Recognizing these benefits of intra-LDC trade, certain groups of less-developed countries have experimented with regional economic integration, a type of voluntary association pioneered in Western Europe.

BARRIERS TO TRADE

By looking to differences in production possibilities for an explanation of trade, conventional theory has given little attention to the obstacles that can intervene to alter the volume, direction, and composition of commodity flows. Historically, these have been of two types: *distance* and *political interference.*

Distance

Distance has acted as a barrier to trade in a variety of ways, some of them subtle. The most obvious effect of distance is the burden of transport cost it imposes on every shipment of goods between two countries. This cost does not necessarily correspond closely with the number of miles to be covered, for some routes are cheaper to travel than others. Mountainous terrain can add many miles to the apparent distance between two points, and steep grades can multiply fuel costs. Irregular coastlines prevent vessels from taking the most direct routes between points. Hence, transport routes are often more circuitous and difficult than they might appear, resulting in extra costs to move goods over them.

The expense of transporting commodities is not limited merely to the cost of operating a motor vehicle, aircraft, or steamship. In addition, shipments to foreign destinations incur *transactions costs* such as bank collection charges, freight forwarders' and customs house brokers' fees, consular charges, and cartage expenses, and they entail extra clerical costs for preparing bills of lading, customs declarations, and a variety of other lengthy shipping documents. Adding these to the expense of actually moving the merchandise gives a total outlay usually called *transfer costs.* Considering all these elements, some of which are incurred regardless of the length of haul, transfer cost is a more reliable measure of the "economic distance" between two points than is transport cost alone.

Introducing transfer costs into the conventional two-country, two-commodity model considerably alters the outcome. Instead of trade causing prices between two countries to become equalized as suggested earlier by Figure 11.1 (Chapter 11), they will always differ by the amount of the cost of transporting the merchandise. Transfer costs make goods more expensive to importers and less valuable to exporters.

Figure 12.2 illustrates this effect with a simple case involving two countries and a single product, and taking into account only transport cost and production cost. The diagram shows hypothetical and demand-supply curves for paper in both the United States and Canada. The demand curves, *D*, slope downward to the right, indicating that consumers in each country will take larger quantities of paper

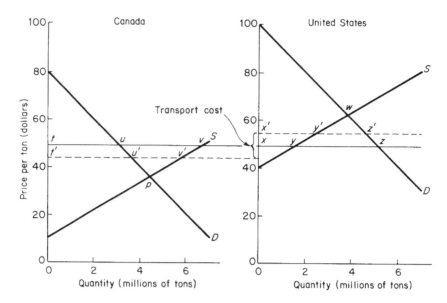

FIGURE 12.2   Price of paper in Canada and the United States and quantities traded and consumed, with and without transport cost.

if the price drops. The supply curves, S, slope upward to the right because producers are able and willing to make more paper if the price goes up, Figure 12.2 shows that, in the absence of trade, the price of paper would be lower in Canada than in the United States, reflecting Canada's comparative advantage in forest products. This difference is evident from the points where the supply and demand curves cross in each case—p for Canada and w for the United States.

Figure 12.2 shows the results of trade, first in the absence of transport cost and then with the addition of transport cost. Table 12.1 summarizes these effects. Without transport cost, the price after trade in both countries—that is, the international terms of trade—becomes $49 per ton of paper, as shown by the horizontal line extending from t to z in Figure 12.2. At this price, Canada produces 6.6 million tons of paper (indicated by distance tv), consumes 3.1 million tons (tu), and exports the remaining 3.5 million tons

(uv) to the United States. Under these conditions, the United States consumes 5.1 million tons (xz) of paper, of which 3.5 million tons (yz) are imported from Canada. U.S. producers are then able to supply the other 1.6 million tons (xy) that the country needs.

If, however, we introduce a transport cost of $10 per ton, this causes the price of paper to rise to $54 in the United States and fall to $44 in Canada (Table 12.1). At the $54 price, the United States is no longer willing to use as much paper, and consumption then drops to only 4.6 million tons (x'z' in Figure 12.2). Nevertheless, the higher price induces domestic producers of paper to supply a larger quantity, 2.4 million tons (x'y'), and U.S. imports consequently drop to only 2.2 million tons (y'z'). At the reduced Canadian price of $44 per ton, producers in that country will supply only 5.8 million tons (t'v'), but Canadian consumers will take a larger quantity, 3.6 million tons (t'u'). But the extra home consumption makes up for only a part of the

TABLE 12.1

Effects of transport cost on exports of paper by Canada to the United States

	Without Transport Cost		With Transport Cost	
	Canada	United States	Canada	United States
Price per ton (in Dollars)	$49	$49	$44	$54
Quantity produced[a]	6.6	1.6	5.8	2.4
Quantity exported[a]	3.5	—	2.2	—
Quantity imported[a]	—	3.5	—	2.2
Quantity consumed[a]	3.1	5.1	4.6	4.6

[a] All quantities in millions of tons.

lost exports to the United States, which now amount to only 2.2 million tons ($u'v''$). Note that the impact of transport cost falls with equal weight upon importing and exporting countries.

One lesson offered by this case is that transport cost does in fact decrease international specialization. The United States produces more of its own paper and buys less abroad, whereas Canadian mills must reduce total output even though the new low domestic price enables them to sell somewhat more at home. Indeed, if transport cost had exceeded the pretrade price differential, which in Figure 12.2 ranges between a low of p for Canada and a high of w for the United States, trade would not have occurred at all. Throughout the world, much localized production owes its existence to the sheltering effects of a high transfer cost barrier to trade with other regions that have lower production costs. Herein lies one of the chief links between trade theory and location theory.

Transfer cost does not affect all merchandise alike, however, for some classes of goods are more cheaply and easily transported than others. Their transportability depends on their perishability, ease of handling, and value in relation to bulk or weight. Most manufactured goods have a high degree of transportability owing to the low cost of shipment relative to value, which has been estimated at about 2 percent on the average. Such products therefore move freely over long distances throughout the world. Some primary goods are also widely traded, for instance, petroleum, which is valuable, easily handled, and cheaply transported. Likewise traveling long distances are cheese, butter, commercial fibers, and other agricultural commodities whose bulk and perishability have been reduced in processing. Grains have long been staples of world commerce because they are nonperishable and are easily handled by bulk cargo methods.

At the other extreme are several types of goods that are so costly to ship that they have traditionally entered foreign commerce to a much lesser degree. These include perishable foodstuffs such as fluid milk and fresh produce, and cheap, bulky building materials such as common dimension stone, sand and gravel, and bricks. Commodities of this type are often referred to as *domestic goods.*

Distance influences trade in many ways other than transport cost alone. Though often subtle. the noncost effects of distance can be substantial in some instances. Commercial relations between two neighboring countries tend to be simpler and easier than between remoter ones, if only because business people have a greater awareness of sales opportunities nearer at hand. Reinforcing the advantages of closeness are the effects of mass communication and frequent travel between two neighboring populations, as well as the personal acquaintances that arise. Constant contact between peoples usually leads to a greater familiarity with differing tastes, customs, languages, business methods, and legal systems.

Although neglected by early trade theorists, distance received attention as a factor in the years following World War II. One example was W. Beckerman's pioneering study of the influence of distance on Western Europe's trade. Using actual transport cost as a substitute for mileage, Beckerman compared two separate rankings of the same countries: (1) a ranking by the average amount of transport cost separating them, and (2) a ranking by value of trade with each other (adjusted for size of country). The correlation between these two rankings proved very close and tended to confirm the effectiveness of transport cost as an influence on trade patterns in that region.

The element of distance added a new dimension to trade theory. It modified the effects of a country's resource endowments by enhancing the attractions of neighboring lands and raising obstacles to commerce with remoter areas, although the force of its impact was greater for some classes of merchandise than others. It constituted a potent advantage for a country, such as Germany, that was centrally located with respect to rich markets for its exports: Competitors in more distant locations had to produce much more cheaply in order to invade these markets. But as we have seen, technology has been working to reduce both transportation and transactions costs, effectively reducing the economic distance between countries and extending the shipping range of internationally traded goods. The changes have been so great that Microsoft founder Bill Gates writes in his 1995 book *The Road Ahead* that he sees ahead a world of "friction-free capitalism" in which markets come close to Adam Smith's concept of perfect competition and in which the distance barriers have largely been removed. But even if this ideal were to be achieved, there would remain the intervention of political forces.

Political Interference

Under international law every country has exclusive jurisdiction over its territory. Governments exercise this *national sovereignty* through their police powers and taxing authority over all resident individuals and business organizations, by the physical and administrative control of their borders, and in their position as the sole legal representatives of their citizens in all relations with other national governments. These powers of the state often raise barriers to the movement of goods, services, and factors of production. The actions of national governments thus tend to distort world commerce.

Incentives for Intervention. Why do governments intervene? One reason is nationalism, an emotional attachment to the state that binds the people of a country together in the pursuit of common goals. Responding to such sentiments, a government may act in what is perceived to be the self-interest of its citizens. This includes the pursuit of economic policies that promote national economic growth so as to increase employment and raise per capita income. The ultimate in this form of state intervention was practiced by the now-defunct Communist governments, which exercised total control over their national economies, including foreign trade, which was conducted exclusively by state enterprises under the direction of central planning agencies. Even more than elsewhere, commercial policies of Communist governments reflected not only economic considerations, but also political goals tied to overall foreign policies.

Because of the importance of foreign commerce to national well-being, governments maintain a constant watch over their economic relations with the rest of the world. The usual statistical measure of this performance is the *balance of payments*. This is the sum of all economic transactions between the residents—individuals and corporations—of one country and the residents of other countries within a given time span (usually a year). These transactions include exports and imports of goods and services, gifts and other one-way transfers, investments, flows of monetary gold, and payments by central banks. The balance of payments is calculated by means of a double-entry accounting system that sets debits against credits. As in mercantilist times, when the goal was to maximize credits over debits, it is common even today to refer to a positive figure as a "favorable" balance of payments.

The most obvious contributor to the balance of payments is a country's merchandise exports, often called the *visible trade*. The difference between the total value of exports and imports of goods within a given year is the *balance of trade*. Also included in the balance of payments are the exports and imports of services—the *invisible trade*. These include transport services that residents sell to or purchase from foreigners; tourist services, which are the expenditures made by residents of one country while traveling in another country; financial services, including international banking and insurance activities; investment services that involve international transfers of interest, dividends, and profits; and technological services, represented by international payments of royalties and fees. Trade in services, currently accounting for about one-quarter of total world commerce, is the most rapidly growing part of the total and is particularly vital to certain countries. For instance, financial services are important foreign exchange earners for the United Kingdom and Switzerland; tourism is essential to the economies of Mexico, Italy, Spain, the United Kingdom, France, Switzerland, Israel, and Egypt; and services of all kinds constitute the largest category of foreign exports by New York City.

Some countries gain much of their foreign exchange from gifts and other one-way transactions. Among such transfers are the contributions of private charities and moneys sent by expatriate workers to their families back home. Both Egypt and Mexico gain substantial amounts of exchange from the repatriated earnings of their nationals working abroad. One-way governmental transfers include foreign aid, pension payments, and taxation of foreigners. Also contributing to the balance of payments are long-term capital flows. Chief among these are foreign direct investment—for example, establishing branch plants abroad—and portfolio investment—making loans to or purchasing stock in foreign enterprises. Both types of capital flows are vital to the Canadian economy, for example. A residual element in the balance of payments is the transactions between central banks, which exchange monetary gold and foreign currencies in order to balance national accounts.

Political interference in foreign commerce may have either positive or negative effects, depending on whether it tends to create, diminish, or rechannel trade. Governments often promote their exports by sponsoring fairs and exhibits or offering subsidies, loan guarantees, tax rebates, or other financial incentives to exporters. They also enter into special trade agreements with other countries to increase sales. Most countries maintain commercial attachés in their foreign embassies in part to assist their exporters in doing business in those lands. Indeed, a study by Bruce Russett (1967) found a direct relationship between the size of diplomatic staffs and the amount of trade among countries.

Tariffs. On the other hand, national governments commonly use a variety of restrictive measures for controlling the volume, composition, or direction of trade. Most governments are under political pressure from special-interest groups to intervene in their foreign commerce. One technique favored since early times is the *tariff,* which is a tax or duty imposed on a particular category of merchandise entering or leaving a country. A tariff may be either an *ad valorem duty*—that is, a given percentage of the value of a good (e.g., 15 percent of the invoice amount)—or a *specific duty*—a particular amount of money assessed for a given quantity of the good (e.g., $1.50 per ton). Ad valorem and specific duties may also be used in combination. Although *import tariffs* are more widespread than *export tariffs,* the latter are frequently imposed by those countries specializing in the sale of primary commodities.

The two main reasons for levying tariffs are to earn revenue and to protect domestic producers from foreign competition. Governments of developing countries ordinarily rely on tariffs for much of their financial support; indeed, income from import tariffs was the chief source of revenue for the U.S. government during its earlier years. Most countries use protective tariffs to shield their home industries against foreign producers. A common justification for such tariffs is the "infant industry" argument, which holds that newly established industries must receive this kind of special protection from foreign competitors during their early years when unit costs are still higher than those of established operations elsewhere. This argument implies that tariff protection will be lifted when the new industries achieve the scale economies that will permit their products to compete on equal terms with imported goods. Manufacturing operations formed under such conditions are sometimes called "tariff factories." Canadian production of chemicals and household appliances began with governmental aid of this type, as did the fabricated-metal trades of Mexico and Brazil. Under pressure from industry and labor groups, governments may impose protective tariffs to save declining industries that have lost their competitiveness in world markets. In recent years, American manufacturers of textiles, clothing, and steel have agitated with some success for such governmental help against lower-cost foreign competitors.

Regardless of its initial purpose, a tariff ultimately produces a variety of effects, as the following example illustrates. Figure 12.3 and Table 12.2 give the case of a hypothetical tariff imposed on U.S. imports of shoes from Italy (assuming that the two countries trade only with each other and in isolation from the rest of the world). Note that the changes in supply and demand resulting from the tariff are similar to those produced by transport cost as seen previously in Figure 12.2. In the absence of trade, the Italian price for a pair of shoes would have been $6.80 (shown in Figure 12.3 by the intersection of Italy's supply and demand curves at *x*), whereas the U.S. price would have been $13.30 (given by the intersection at *y* in Figure 12.3). With trade, however, the price in both countries settles at $10 (*Oj*). At this price, the United States will consume 13 million pairs

of shoes (*dh*), 5 million of which are imported from Italy (*eh*).

The introduction of a tariff of $2 per pair (equal to *ia* in Figure 12.3) causes the Italian price to fall to $9 (given by *Or*) and the U.S. price to rise to $11 (*Oa*). Italian production thereupon drops by 1 million pairs to only 8 million and exports to the United States decline to 3.4 million pairs (Table 12.2). At the new higher price, consumers in the United States will buy only 12.4 million pairs, 9 million of which are now produced at home. On those shoes still imported from Italy, the U.S. government receives tariff revenue amounting to $6.8 million ($2 times 3.4 million pairs, or *ia* times *bc* in Figure 12.3). This is equivalent to the combined areas *bcgf* and *lmsq* in Figure 12.3. Meanwhile, domestic producers (Table 12.2) enjoy an additional $19 million in receipts (on sales of 9 million pairs at $11 instead of 8 million at the earlier price of $10). Note, however, that this benefit to U.S. producers comes not only at the expense of foreign producers but also of domestic consumers, who now get only 12.4 million pairs of shoes for $136.4 million where they used to get 13 million pairs for $130 million. The imposition of a tariff in this case has had a *protection effect,* a *consumption effect,* and an *income-redistribution effect.* If the amount of the tariff had been set at $6.50 (equivalent to the vertical distance between *x* and *y* in Figure 12.3) or greater, the price differential between the two countries would have disappeared and the shoe trade would have ceased altogether. Only the American manufacturers and their workers would have gained from this arrangement; the government would have received nothing.

Under the conditions shown in Figure 12.3, however, both the domestic shoe mills and the government gain income from the relatively modest tariff of $2. Although U.S. buyers of shoes incur some additional cost, the main

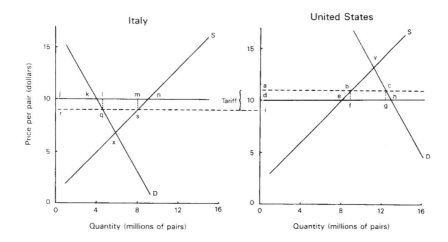

FIGURE 12.3   Effects of tariff on U.S. imports of shoes from Italy.

TABLE 12.2

Effects of United States tariff on shoes imported from Italy

	Before Tariff		After Tariff	
	Italy	United States	Italy	United States
Price per pair (in dollars)	$10	$10	$9	$11
Quantity produced[a]	9.0	8.0	8.0	9.0
Quantity exported[a]	5.0	—	3.4	—
Quantity imported[a]	—	5.0	—	3.4
Quantity consumed[a]	4.0	13.0	4.6	12.4
Tariff revenue (in millions of dollars)	—	—	—	6.8
Additional revenue to producers (in millions of dollars)	—	—	—	$19.0

[a] All quantities in millions of pairs.

losers are the Italians, who are able to sell fewer pairs and get a lower price for them. This is the basis for the common observation that a tariff is a way of taxing the foreigner.

Nevertheless, a unilateral action of this kind risks retaliation from the injured party. Let us assume in the preceding case that Italy has been a prime customer for U.S. farm products. If, in retribution for the U.S. tariff on Italian shoes, the government of Italy were to place a tariff on the import of U.S. wheat, the effects upon the U.S.–Italian wheat trade would be like those shown for the U.S.—Italian shoe trade in Figure 12.3, only in reverse: Italy would buy less wheat from the United States, the price of U.S. wheat would fall, less wheat would be produced, and U.S. wheat farmers would be hurt. Thus, where retaliation is possible, both countries are harmed by tariffs; total trade declines and production and consumption diminish. Lost are the benefits of international specialization of production and exchange.

Export tariffs, under a variety of labels, are a favored revenue-raising device among less-developed countries, especially those who produce minerals and fuels in strong demand on world markets. In addition, some countries use export duties on their raw materials as a way of inducing manufacturers to increase the amount of domestic processing of such goods. Not only does this raise the value of their exports, but it also serves as a means for introducing industrial development. In this way, Jamaica has acquired facilities for processing bauxite ore into alumina, and Venezuela has installed refineries for her oil. Excessive export duties, however, have cost some raw-material producers their world markets when customers abroad have found new sources of supply or have developed synthetic substitutes (see Chapter 11).

Always, the effects of tariffs, whether on imports or on exports, depend on the nature of supply and demand for the good. For instance, if consumers have a particularly strong desire for an imported good, they may continue buying it regardless of the higher price resulting from a tariff.

Quotas.   An even more drastic form of governmental intervention in trade is the *quota*. A quota is a specific limitation on the *quantity* of exports or (more usually) imports that a country will permit. This device is of more recent origin than the tariff, being largely a product of the world economic depression of the 1930s. Like tariffs, import quotas serve to aid domestic producers. Quotas are especially favored as a means of protection against foreign competition for farmers and for producers of standardized manufactured goods such as textiles. Governments tend to prefer quotas where the foreign supply of a product is very great and available at particularly low prices. Under such conditions tariffs would likely be unsuccessful in stemming the flood of imports. Administrators favor quotas especially because of their sudden, drastic, and certain results and also because they are easy to impose, remove, or adjust. They can cause more friction among importers and foreign suppliers, however, because they are more difficult than tariffs to administer fairly.

A country may impose import quotas unilaterally, that is, it may do so without prior consultation with foreign suppliers; or it may negotiate with supplying countries before setting import limitations. The United States has negotiated quotas (euphemistically called "orderly marketing agreements") with Japan on the import of motor vehicles and with the European Union countries on specialty steel products. As this suggests, quotas may be negotiated either bilaterally (with a single supplying country) or multilaterally (with a number of suppliers). Allocation to importers under a quota system often relies on some kind of import licensing arrangement.

Figure 12.4 illustrates the possible outcome of a hypothetical quota on Japanese rayon imported into the United States. Let us say that each year the United States has been consuming 70 million yards of rayon (*OD* in Figure 12.4) at a price of $2.50 per yard (*OE*). Of this amount, 50 million yards (*AD*) have been imported. If the government yields to the demands of domestic manufacturers and imposes a quota limiting imports to 30 million yards (*BC*), this will cause the price in the United States to rise to $3.00 (*OJ*) and total rayon consumption in the country to fall to 60 million yards. But out of this total, American mills will be able to sell an increased quantity—30 million yards (*JK*) instead of the former 20 million yards (*EF*)—at the new higher price. The revenue increase to domestic producers will be $40 million (area *JKBO* minus *EFAO*). Meanwhile, American consumers will have to pay a total of $180 million (*JLCO*) for less cloth than they formerly got for only $175 million (*EIDO*). Thus, the domestic mills gain at the expense of both domestic consumers and foreign suppliers. The effects are inflationary for the importing country (as shown by the United States' experience with quotas on auto imports from Japan), and at the same time they are conducive to monopoly control of production. Quotas of this type are exceedingly arbitrary, as they freeze the volume and direction of trade into some predetermined pattern. Note also that, unlike tariffs, quotas yield no revenue to the government unless a high fee is assessed for import licenses. Because of their inherent unfairness, quotas also lead to hard feelings and retaliation.

Export quotas have also been used extensively in recent years to prop up world prices of some primary commodities. Certain agricultural products and minerals have suffered from recurrent problems of oversupply and price instability. In such cases, exporting countries may impose quotas in an effort to reduce world supplies and thereby raise prices abroad. In the past, Brazil has tried this means for limiting exports of rubber and coffee, and the United States has attempted similar controls on cotton exports.

Export restrictions of this type have usually not been very successful. Either substitutes would be found elsewhere for the country's products or new foreign sources of supply of the commodity would be developed. Thus, nitrates were synthesized to replace the overly priced Chilean natural product; plantation rubber in the Southeast Asia largely usurped the former markets for Brazilian rubber; Central American, Colombian, and West African growers increased their coffee output; and American price supports encouraged cotton production in Africa. Producers in different countries have attempted to cooperate in controlling foreign sales of their products, but commodity agreements of this type uniformly failed until the winter of 1973–1974, when members of the Organization of Petroleum Exporting Countries (OPEC) managed to agree on quantitative limits and prices for their oil exports.

Other Nontariff Measures. A device similar to the quota involves the use of *exchange controls:* A government buys all foreign currency brought into the country through the earnings of its exporters and then distributes these currencies to importers in a carefully regulated manner. The allocation of foreign exchange may be made through licensing schemes or auctions (as in Brazil). This is done in such a way as to control not only the volume of imports, but also their composition, thereby conserving the country's money supply and assuring its most economic use. The allotments ordinarily discriminate against luxuries and favor necessities. Quota systems sometimes entail multiple exchange rates, with foreign currencies being sold to importers at higher prices for some purposes than others. Exchange controls were common in post–World War II Europe, when shortages of foreign exchange were especially acute, and similar schemes have been used throughout Latin America more recently.

In some parts of the world, governments go even further and participate actively in buying and selling abroad, a practice called *state trading.* This was the standard procedure in Communist countries, but it also occurs in developing countries, and to some extent in advanced capitalistic countries. State monopolies in specific commodities such as alcoholic beverages, sugar, tobacco, cocoa, grains, and other agricultural products are fairly common. During times of war, bulk buying and selling by governments becomes necessary.

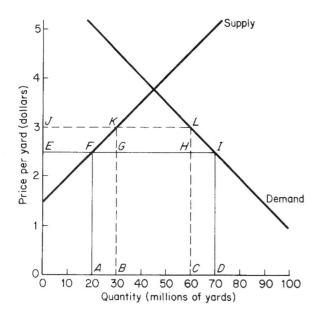

FIGURE 12.4 Effects of U.S. quota on imports of Japanese rayon.

Intergovernmental relationships can alter trade patterns, as, for example, trade agreements granting special tariff concessions or generous quota allocations to favored trading partners. In general, their effects are to direct trade from the normal channels of a freely operating world market.

Nationalistic feelings, expressed through wars, hostile attitudes, or rivalries between populations, can influence trade. Despite the natural complementarities between the resource endowments of Israel and its Arab neighbors, their continued hostility discourages Arab–Israeli trade. Trade between Eastern and Western Europe was well developed before World War II, but was much reduced when the Eastern countries became incorporated into the Communist bloc. Wars have often forced contending nations to industrialize; the War of 1812, for example, sparked early U.S. industrialization. Wars have had this kind of effect on noncombatants, too, as in the case of Argentina, which began manufacturing many of its own needs when cut off by World War I from European sources of supply. An interruption of trade again occurred during World War II, spurring further industrialization by Argentina.

Many seemingly small governmental actions can interfere with foreign trade. Special labeling and packaging requirements may exclude goods from some markets if the cost of changing the usual practices of producers in the exporting country is excessive. Sanitary and safety regulations can have the same effect; Japan, in particular, has used elaborate inspection procedures to limit imports of both foodstuffs and manufactured goods to protect domestic producers. Some European countries maintain exacting specifications for the ingredients of prepared foods; Canada requires labels in both French and English; and the United States specifies costly safety and pollution-control devices on motor vehicles. Official measures of this type may be enacted without conscious thought of their effects on imported commodities, but some are deliberately intended to exclude foreign competitors who cannot readily comply with them. Even the mere existence of an international border crossing is sufficient to deter some trade movements. Small producers are especially reluctant to spend the time, effort, and money for complying with the red tape required for entering goods through customs. The question of protectionism is discussed in Appendix 12.2.

EFFECTS OF TRADE ON THE FACTORS OF PRODUCTION

According to Heckscher–Ohlin theory, trade among regions and countries results from differences in relative endowments of the factors of production. We have noted previously, however, that the introduction of trade produces feedback effects on the factors. These effects are of two kinds: (1) trade may cause the prices of capital, labor, and land to rise or fall; and (2) it may change the relative quantities of the factors. Moreover, any interregional or international movement of factors will further alter their relative prices and quantities.

Factor Prices and Quantities

The introduction of trade may affect the prices of factors of production in both the exporting and importing regions or countries. As trade begins, country A exports the good that is intensive in the factor that is relatively abundant in that country. If the abundant factor happens to be agricultural land, perhaps corn is the land-intensive commodity and thus becomes the exported good. The first effect of trade will be to cause the domestic price of corn to rise in the exporting country, reflecting the new international terms of trade. Resources are progressively taken out of other industries in country A and put into producing more corn. But as more and more land is transferred to corn, the additional land becomes available to corn production only at ever-higher prices. Thus land, the intensive factor in corn production, becomes more costly in relation to capital and labor. Further reducing the return to capital and labor is that these factors are not needed in such large amounts in corn production as for, say, cotton textile manufacture.

The opposite happens in the importing country, country B. Before trade took place, country B grew its own corn, even though the land was not very good for corn. When trade begins, country B's resources are taken out of corn and transferred into production of the good in which country B has a comparative advantage, namely, labor-intensive textiles. Paradoxically, trade has reduced the return to the scarce factor, labor in the case of country A and land in the case of country B. This kind of effect occurred in Australia and Canada when the importation of labor-intensive goods depressed wages in those labor-short economies.

According to this line of argument, the returns to the factors of production should eventually become completely equalized among trading nations. Wages paid to labor should be the same, interest rates earned by capital should become standardized, and rent received for land should be equal. Trade will have erased all differences. In reality, however, it is seldom possible to shift all resources from one line of production to another, and the barriers to commodity movements prevent full equalization: Transfer costs, tariffs, and other impediments to trade ensure that some factor-price differentials remain. More important, however, is the effect of specialization, innovation, and increasing returns, discussed in earlier chapters. Where increasing returns occur, factor prices and supplies will tend to increase rather than decrease, in part because of quality improvement and in part because of factor mobility.

Factor Mobility

One of the assumptions of Heckscher–Ohlin factor proportions theory is that no movement of the factors of production takes place among countries. But capital, labor, and entrepreneurship do have varying degrees of mobility. Financial capital is especially mobile and can even act as a substitute for trade when tariffs or other artificial impediments interfere with commodity movements. Foreign direct investment often is made for the purpose of producing a previously imported good. One effect of interregional and international movements of factors will be to produce some equalization of their prices. But where a process of *a circular and cumulative causation* gives rise to increasing returns, the opposite may occur. If a consequence is greater specialization, the result may be to increase trade, rather than to reduce it in the manner of FDI.

INTERNATIONAL ORGANIZATIONS FOR TRADE

A struggle between the theoretical ideal of universal free trade and nationalistic pressures for protectionism has marked the modern history of world trade. Most policy makers now have come to recognize that the cost of economic nationalism in an era of growing international interdependence had become excessive. Nations have therefore formed new kinds of cooperative organizations designed to reduce the obstacles to economic relations among them.

The arrangements that have evolved are of two main types: (1) *global agreements* designed to decrease barriers progressively and selectively among the great majority of the world's nations, and (2) *regional economic integration,* which joins together a limited number of nearby countries into a union designed not only to reduce trade barriers among members, but in some instances to achieve still closer forms of economic interaction. Ordinarily countries belonging to regional blocs also hold memberships simultaneously in global organizations.

Global Organizations

The decision to create a mechanism for promoting economic cooperation among all the world's nations was taken at a 1944 conference of delegates from the United States, Britain, and their allies in Bretton Woods, New Hampshire. World War II was still in progress at the time, and the conferees were concerned to find solutions for the uncontrolled protectionism and international economic rivalries that had precipitated the Great Depression, thereby creating some of the conditions that had brought about the devastating military conflict. The Bretton Woods delegates agreed to form three institutions: an International Monetary Fund (IMF) to ensure the convertibility of currencies, an International Bank for Reconstruction and Development (IBRD, commonly called the World Bank) to facilitate the international flow of capital, and an International Trade Organization (ITO) to reduce the barriers to world trade.

The work of developing an International Trade Organization was taken up at a subsequent meeting in Havana during the winter of 1947–1948. The ITO Charter drafted by the 54 delegates to the Havana Conference was designed to establish an organization with wide powers to liberalize world trade. However, the charter failed to be ratified by the constituent governments because of the perception that such a world organization would be a threat to their national sovereignty.

General Agreement on Tariffs and Trade (GATT). Following defeat of the ITO charter, representatives of 23 countries involved in the negotiations reconvened in Geneva in an effort to find some alternative way to bring order to world trade. After intensive negotiations, the conferees signed a comprehensive document known as the *General Agreement on Tariffs and Trade (GATT)*. The new GATT agreement, which went into effect in 1948, was a less ambitious undertaking than ITO. It committed the participating countries to reduce tariffs on 45,000 items and laid down a set of rules and principles governing trade among the signatories:

- *Reciprocity.* If one country reduced its tariffs against another, the second country must likewise lower its tariffs. The contracting parties were committed to observe the tariff reductions they had negotiated.

- *Nondiscrimination.* Members were not to grant one country preferential trade treatment over others. This was known as the *most-favored-nation rule,* meaning that every member is treated as favorably as the most favored.

- *Transparency.* Members were expected to replace nontariff barriers (whose effects are hard to detect and measure) with tariffs, which are open to scrutiny and thus more easily reduced through further negotiations.

- *Developing countries.* Members were expected to observe a set of special provisions that accord favorable trade treatment to less-developed nations.

Though GATT was initially conceived merely as a treaty establishing a code of conduct for international trade, it acquired an organizational structure. Provided with a secretariat by the United Nations, it operated from a headquarters in Geneva where it also maintained an International Trade Center to assist less-developed nations in the promotion of their trade. Formally, the signatory countries were considered to be *contracting parties,* but it was customary to refer to them as "members." GATT members met regularly each year and at special conferences. Between annual meetings, a Council of Representatives looked after routine matters, including the publication of an annual report. In addition to its bargaining activities, GATT provided a mechanism for settling trade disputes among member countries.

For three decades, GATT performed exceedingly well and its membership grew steadily, until eventually it comprised a majority of trading nations. In a series of negotiating sessions, or *rounds* (each named for the city where negotiations began—see Box 12.1), its members had slashed average tariffs on manufactured products from an initial 40 percent to less than 10 percent by the middle of the 1970s. GATT's trade-liberalization measures are credited with much of the fivefold rise in the volume of world trade during that same period. Though subsequent negotiations reduced tariffs still further, to an average of only 5 percent by 1990, the annual rate of total world trade growth dwindled because of a new surge of protection, which involved the use of many new devices for slyly circumventing GATT rules (refer to Box 12.2).

Aside from the damaging effects of creeping protectionism, GATT was becoming less relevant to the needs of modern commerce. The world's economies had changed in many important ways since 1948. GATT's original charge had been to reduce tariffs and to enforce rules for trade in manufactured goods, but it proved inadequate for dealing with other kinds of international transactions that have become increasingly important in recent years. Some of the most significant export earners by the 1980s—notably agricultural commodities and internationally traded services—were not covered by GATT at all.

It was against this backdrop of a weakening international trade regime that representatives from 92 countries agreed in 1986 to launch the Uruguay Round of negotiations (Box 12.1) in the hope of revitalizing the GATT process. This proved to be an exceedingly ambitious and difficult undertaking, especially as the negotiators were addressing difficult issues that had previously been avoided:

- *Agricultural trade.* One of the most contentious issues, agricultural trade, had been excluded from earlier negotiations despite the great importance of the farm sector to many national economies. Many countries had erected import barriers against agricultural products or had subsidized their farm exports, distorting prices and causing massive global overproduction of some crops.

- *Textiles and clothing.* The Multi-Fibre Arrangement (MFA) was a complex of bilateral export quotas negotiated in 1974, which GATT chose to overlook. Exporters were mainly very poor LDCs and the principal importers were wealthy industrialized countries.

- *Intellectual property.* The United States in particular has been concerned to ensure international patent and copyright protection for intellectual property, a class of goods produced by the mind, through research and creativity—such things as computer software, semiconductor designs, biotechnology, musical recordings, and books. Within countries, these are protected by national laws, but intellectual-property standards receive little if any international enforcement. Pirating and counterfeiting of such products costs billions of dollars in lost revenue for their creators and legitimate producers.

- *Services.* One of the fastest-growing segments of advanced economies is the service sector, which accounts for 90 percent of new jobs created in the United States. Internationally traded services include banking, insurance, and other financial services; tourism; advertising; architecture and construction engineering; transportation; and telecommunications. Many countries have restricted the entry of foreign firms into their domestic service sectors, and freer trade in these areas could add billions of dollars to international commerce.

BOX 12.1   GATT Negotiating Rounds

The founding session of GATT convened in Geneva in 1947; the resulting initial agreement and the GATT charter became effective in 1948. Seven additional negotiating conferences, or *rounds*, have taken place since, culminating in the creation of the World Trade Organization (WTO), effective January 1, 1995:	Geneva Round — 1947 Annecy Round — 1949 Torquay Round — 1950 Geneva Round — 1956 Dillon Round — 1960–1961 Kennedy Round — 1964–1967 Tokyo Round — 1973–1979 Uruguay Round — 1986–1994

BOX 12.2 Early Integrated Groups

Custom Unions and Free Trade Areas

Name	Members	Dates
Zollverein	All pre-Bismarck German states except Bremen and Hamburg	1834–1871
Union of South Africa	Cape Province, Natal, Orange, Free State, Transvall	1910–1961
Benelux	Belgium, Netherlands, Luxembourg	1944–1957
European Coal and Steel Community (ECSC)	Belgium, France, Germany, Italy Luxembourg, Netherlands	1952–1967

Customs Accessions

Members	Dates
San Marino and Italy	1862–present
Monaco and France	1865present
Belgium and Luxembourg (BLEU)	1921–present
Liechtenstein and Switzerland	1923–present

- *Investment*. National policies on foreign investment have distorted trade flows and discouraged international investors. An improved international investment climate would help to increase the flows of capital, especially to less-developed countries.
- *Dispute settlement*. One of the major functions of GATT has been to resolve disputes between member countries. The dispute-resolution process has broken down in recent years, however, because GATT's tiny secretariat lacked the power to enforce its rulings. The organization operated by consensus among member countries, but its membership had grown to such size that decision making became ineffective and any country losing a ruling could merely veto any penalties assessed against it. The United States, in particular, urged the need for a better mechanism for dealing with such problems.

This complex array of issues proved more than GATT negotiators could resolve in the allotted time, and the original 1990 deadline passed without a new agreement. The most intractable problem proved to be the politically charged question of agricultural protection, on which both the European and Japanese representatives were unyielding. The negotiating countries were aware, however, that failure of the Uruguay Round raised the threat of a world divided into great continental trading blocs incessantly embroiled in paralyzing dissension. The deadline was therefore extended. Renewed efforts to reach agreement availed little, until in mid-1993, a combination of changed tactics and new concessions by various parties brought renewed progress. Adding impetus to reach an agreement was the growing realization in Europe and Japan that their trade barriers were delaying the recovery of their lagging economies. The next year brought further concessions on major issues, including agriculture, and a new agreement was finally signed by the negotiating parties, now grown to a total of 124 nations.

After eight difficult years, the Uruguay Round negotiations had at last reached a successful conclusion, but perhaps the most crucial tests of all still remained: official ratification by member governments. Intense opposition in the United States aroused fears that GATT would experience the same fate as that suffered by the International Trade Organization in the 1940s, but on December 1, the U.S. Congress ended a bitter debate by ratifying the agreement with a comfortable margin. Ratification by the other participating countries quickly followed, and the agreement went into effect on January 1, 1995.

The 2,200-page GATT treaty resulting from the Uruguay Round is the broadest, most far-reaching trade pact in world history. It will vastly reduce the tariffs that

BOX 12.3   *Regional Economic Organizations Around the World*

Organization	Members
Europe	
European Union (EU)	Austria, Belgium, Denmark, Finland, France, Germany, Greece, Ireland, Italy, Luxembourg, Netherlands, Portugal, Spain, Sweden, and the United Kingdom
European Free Trade Association (EFTA)	Founding members: Austria, Denmark, Norway, Portugal, Sweden, Switzerland, and the United Kingdom (later joined by Finland and Iceland). Austria, Denmark, Finland, Portugal, Sweden, and the United Kingdom subsequently withdrew to join the EU, leaving only Finland, Norway, and Switzerland in the current EFTA.
European Economic Area (EEA)	Austria, Belgium, Denmark, Finland, France, Germany, Greece, Iceland, Ireland, Italy, Luxembourg, the Netherlands, Norway, Portugal, Spain, Sweden, Switzerland, Turkey, and the United Kingdom
Central European Free Trade Agreement (CEFTA)	Czech Republic, Hungary, Poland, Slovenia, and Slovakia
North America	
U.S.–Canada Free Trade Agreement (FTA, CFTA)	Canada and the United States
North American Free Trade Agreement (NAFTA)	Canada, Mexico, and the United States
Latin America	
Central American Common Market (CACM)	Costa Rica, El Salvador, Guatemala, Honduras, and Nicaragua
Latin American Integration Association (LAIA)	Argentina, Bolivia, Brazil, Chile, Colombia, Ecuador, Mexico, Paraguay, Peru, Uruguay, and Venezuela
Mercado Común del Sur (Mercosur)	Argentina, Brazil, Paraguay, and Uruguay
Andean Common Market (Ancom)	Bolivia, Colombia, Ecuador, Peru, Venezuela, (Chile withdrew in 1976)
Caribbean Community and Common Market (Caricom)	Eleven English speaking Caribbean island nations plus Belize and Guyana
Asia–Pacific	
Association of Southeast Asian Nations (ASEAN)	Brunei, Indonesia, Malaysia, Philippines, Singapore, Thailand, and Vietnam
Closer Economic Relations Agreement (CER)	Austria, New Zealand (successor to New Zealand–Australia Free Trade Agreement, NAFTA)
South Asian Association for Regional Co-operation (SAARC)	Bangladesh, Bhutan, India, Maldives, Nepal, Pakistan, and Sri Lanka
Asia-Pacific Economic Cooperation Forum (APEC)	Australia, Brunei, Canada, Chile, Hong Kong, Indonesia, Japan, Malaysia, Mexico, New Zealand Papua New Guinea, Philippines, Singapore, South Korea, Taiwan, Thailand, and the United States
Africa	
East African Economic Comunity	Kenya, Uganda, and Tanzania (discontinued in 1977)
Economic Community of West African States (ECOWAS)	Benin, Burkina, Faso, Cameroon, Côte d'Ivoire, Gambia, Ghana, Guinea, Guinea-Bissau, Liberia, Mali, Mauritania, Niger, Nigeria, Senegal, Sierra Leone, and Togo
Communauté Economique de l'Afrique de Ouest (CEAO)	Benin, Burkina, Faso, Cameroon, Côte d'Ivoire, and Togo
South African Customs Union	Botswana, Lesotho, South Africa and Swaziland

almost all nations use to protect their industry and agriculture and it will transform the rules governing world trade. Although the final document did not accomplish everything on the exceedingly ambitious initial agenda, it nevertheless made major advances, not the least of which was the establishing of a new organization to bring order to world trade.

The World Trade Organization (WTO).

Unlike the arrangement under the seven previous GATT negotiating rounds, the new treaty created a permanent institution with real powers to enforce trade rules and to assess penalties against members. Some of the main features of the pact to be administered by the new WTO:

- *Tariffs.* The signatories agreed to reduce their tariffs by an average of one-third. Industrial nations will lower agricultural tariffs by 36 percent, and less-developed countries will cut them by 24 percent.

- *Quotas.* Under the agreement, quantitative limits on imports become illegal. Members are permitted instead to convert existing quotas to tariffs, but these will be gradually reduced. This provision ends, for example, Japanese and Korean bans on rice imports and U.S. limits on imports of peanuts, dairy products, and sugar.

- *Health and safety.* Member countries are no longer permitted to use health and safety standards as devices to restrict trade if these have no scientific basis. Thus ends one of the most pervasive techniques used by bureaucrats to exclude a wide range of goods, from food stuffs to motor cars.

- *Intellectual property.* All signatories to the pact, including less-developed countries, are required to protect patents, copyrights, trade secrets, and trademarks. This is designed to end the wholesale pirating of computer programs, video cassettes, musical recordings, books, and prescription drugs practiced in certain developing nations.

- *Local content.* The agreement prohibits members from requiring a high local content in products manufactured within their borders. This practice has been widely employed as a device to limit the use of imported parts and components and thus to increase local employment. In addition, member countries can no longer discriminate against foreign-owned companies in favor of domestic firms.

The pact to be administered by WTO is a compromise reached at the end of years of difficult negotiations; consequently, some major industries are included but others are not. For the first time ever, coverage has been extended to a number of agricultural commodities. This was one of the triumphs of the Uruguay Round. It was the often rancorous dispute over farm products that nearly brought the talks to collapse. In the end, the Europeans consented to limit their crop subsidies and to convert these to tariffs, and the Japanese agreed to end their long-standing ban on rice imports. The United States and the European Union also pledged to check their practice of limiting auto exports from Japan. In addition, the richer countries are required to phase out quotas on clothing imports within 10 years, and to replace these with tariffs.

Among the important industries not directly affected by the treaty is aircraft manufacture. Under a pre-existing arrangement, European and U.S. governments are to restrict their subsidies on civil aircraft. The pact also calls for free trade in financial services, shipping, and audiovisual products—movies, television programs, and musical recordings—but it has no provision for enforcing this. The United States and the European Union are still holding discussions on opening European markets for long-distance telecommunications and limiting European subsidies to steel companies, in expectation of future agreements in these areas.

Even though the Uruguay Round did not achieve all of its objectives, the GATT secretariat (now replaced by the WTO) estimated that the increased world commerce resulting from the agreement would add $510 billion annually to the global economy. Of this total, the United States would be expected to gain $122 billion, the European Union $164 billion, and Japan $27 billion. The less-developed countries and the former Communist nations would also be important beneficiaries, receiving an additional $116 billion in trade and investment. Thus, the new world trade regime is predicted to raise the world economy to substantially higher levels of prosperity.

The United Nations Conference on Trade and Development (UNCTAD).

Although Article 18 of the original GATT charter granted less-developed countries a broad license to use trade restrictions to protect their balances of payments, many LDCs were dissatisfied with the results they had achieved from GATT. They objected to the fundamental rationale for GATT, which was based on neoclassical trade theory, with its ideal of universal free trade. This they considered inappropriate to their problems.

Responding to this complaint, in 1964, the United Nations convened the inaugural meeting of an organization charged with addressing the problems that LDCs face in marketing their goods in industrialized countries. This organization, called the United Nations Conference on Trade and Development (UNCTAD), operates, jointly with GATT, the International Trade Center in Geneva. It functions through committees, each concerned with a particular staple commodity produced in LDCs. At conferences held every four years, UNCTAD brings together representatives of major producing and consuming nations to find ways of reconciling supply and demand for commodities produced by LDCs and of overcoming import barriers to these goods in world markets. Although its membership includes both industrialized and less-developed countries, UNCTAD operates under a one-nation, one-vote rule and therefore tends to be dominated by LDCs.

Regional Economic Integration

Global organizations must necessarily take gradual, incremental steps toward solving trade problems because of their need to reach compromise among a great many nations with widely differing circumstances. For several smaller groups of countries that share similar economic conditions, this measured approach has been found to be too slow and limited in scope for attacking their immediate needs. The solution generally favored in such cases has been to join with a limited number of closely associated neighboring countries in setting up organizational arrangements designed to eliminate all or most barriers to economic interaction among them. This type of union is called *regional economic integration* (Box 12.3)

The idea of joining sovereign nations together to form a single economic region is not new; the first experiments of this kind took place more than a century ago. Following the devastation of World War II, however, this technique was seized upon as the best hope for speeding recovery from the war and for overcoming the many problems of economic and political disintegration that had burdened Europe during the 1930s. Although trade is the main focus of economic integration, such organizations usually have other aims as well. Among the main purposes of economic integration are (1) to achieve growth through the creation of an enlarged market, (2) to raise standards of living, (3) to reduce regional disparities, (4) to strengthen bargaining power in world political and economic affairs, and (5) to develop cooperative solutions for a variety of other social and political problems. The questions raised by the postwar revival of such organizations led to the development of a body of economic integration theory.

Integration Theory.   The theory of economic integration has evolved as a subset of international trade theory, though it has implications for location theory, too. Theoreticians and policy makers have also looked on economic integration as a device for solving problems of economic growth and development. A seminal work on integration theory was Canadian economist Jacob Viner's *The Customs Union Issue* (1950).

As viewed by the theorist, economic integration is a form of selective discrimination because it combines elements of free trade with greater protection: free trade among members and restrictions on trade with nonmem-

bers. Among other things, integration theory is concerned with the various types or degrees of economic integration, the characteristics of member countries that are conducive to successful integration, and the effects that economic integration can be expected to have on international trade and location and on growth and development.

Bela Balassa (in *The Theory of Economic Integration,* 1961) perceived five possible levels or degrees of economic integration (See Figure 12.5). At each succeeding stage, members surrender a greater measure of their national sovereignty. The first (and least restrictive) form of economic integration is the *free-trade area,* in which the members agree to remove all barriers to trade within the group but may continue to pursue their own independent policies with respect to trade with nonmembers. The next higher degree of integration is the *customs union,* a type that has existed in Europe for more than a century. It calls for the free movement of goods among member countries, but imposes a common system of restrictions on trade with outsiders. The third type is the *common market,* which, like the customs union, provides for free trade in merchandise among members of the group while maintaining uniform restraints on trade with nonmembers; in addition, however, this arrangement permits unrestricted movement of capital, labor, and entrepreneurship within the union. At a still higher level, the *economic union* has all the characteristics of the common market but calls also for integrating the economies of member countries through a common central bank, unified monetary and tax systems, and a common foreign economic policy. The ultimate form is full *economic integration.* At this point, the removal of all barriers to intrabloc movement of goods and factors of production is complete, unification of social as well as economic policies is achieved, and all members are subject to the binding decisions of a supranational authority consisting of executive, judicial, and legislative branches.

Theoreticians have identified several characteristics of member countries that would be conducive to successful integration:

- *Parallel economies.* A union of countries whose economies are similar can be expected to achieve better results than one whose economies are dissimilar. Theoreticians reason that if several members of a union are able to produce the same goods, economic integration will force them to become more efficient in order to survive the intensified competition.

- *Propinquity.* A union should yield greater benefits if its members are not too distant from each other. Nearness reduces transport costs, increases the likelihood that tastes of neighboring populations will be alike, and provides trading companies with a keener awareness of business opportunities across the border.

A classification scheme for regional integration

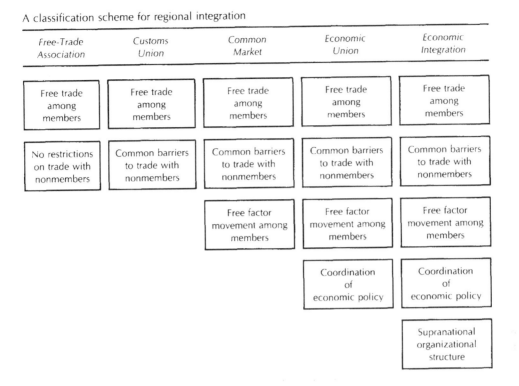

FIGURE 12.5 A classification scheme for regional economic integration. The five categories, arrayed here in increasing order of restrictions placed on members, should be regarded as ideal types. Though each of the existing organizations for regional integration tends in general to fall within one or more of these classes, all have distinctive features that may vary from the ideal type. [*Source:* Based on a classification suggested by Bela Balassa (1961).]

- *Contiguous countries within a compact area.* Ideally, member countries should be adjacent to one another and should form a combined land area of compact shape, thereby minimizing total aggregate transfer costs throughout the union.
- *Large combined territory.* The total area of the group should be sufficiently large to permit diverse production and a division of labor among them.
- *Small countries.* If the countries are individually small, each member will presumably enjoy relatively greater gains from union because of the enhanced possibilities for improvement that access to a large market offers a nation of limited size.
- *Best customers and suppliers.* The probability of a successful union is greater for a group whose members were previously one another's best customers and principal suppliers.
- *Major world traders.* As viewed from a global perspective, a union will be more beneficial if its members contributed in aggregate a substantial proportion of the world's output and trade.

- *High trade barriers.* The increase in intrabloc trade is likely to be greater for a group of nations that were formerly prevented from trading freely with each other because of high tariffs.

When judging the results of integration, theorists are concerned primarily with its effects on global welfare. From this standpoint, the ideal arrangement would be one that provides for free trade throughout the world, thereby enabling every country to specialize in those lines of production for which it has the greatest comparative advantage (or least disadvantage). This would result in the most efficient use of human and natural resources and thus maximize global output. Any given regional economic integration scheme, however, typically involves only a limited number of countries, and calls for trade discrimination in favor of member countries and against nonmembers. Theorists therefore tend to regard this as a "second-best" solution to world trade problems.

There are reasons, however, to expect that regional integration will actually create new trade—that is, trade that did not previously exist. Theoretically, the true test of a successful integration is whether it has created more trade than it has diverted from its natural channels. From this normative viewpoint, trade creation is presumed to be "good" and trade diversion to be "bad." A union is considered to have created trade if, in balance, integration has caused production to shift from high-cost to low-cost sources. Trade diversion, on the other hand, means a shift from low-cost to higher-cost suppliers. Trade creation results in a more efficient allocation of resources; trade diversion produces a less-efficient allocation.

The most common form of new trade created by regional integration is the increased flow that takes place within the union itself when internal trade barriers among member countries are removed. Released from these artificial restraints, intrabloc trade is able to develop according to the comparative advantages of members. As in the case illustrated by Figure 11.21 (Chapter 11), this new trade produces savings for buyers and higher incomes for sellers. Countries that do not belong to the union, however, continue to face the same trade barriers as before—or possibly even higher—when attempting to market their goods to union members. Thus, placed at a competitive disadvantage, they can expect to lose some of their former sales to the group as more of the market is captured by suppliers from member countries. To the extent that these external sources of supply are more efficient producers than the new sources within the bloc, trade diversion has taken place. In the long run, however, integration can result in trade gains even for nonmember countries if the union causes members to enjoy accelerated economic growth and thus to demand more goods from the rest of the world. Depending on the way in which trade gains and trade losses balance each other, therefore, economic integration can result in either a net increase in total world trade or a net decrease.

The main benefit that member countries expect from integration is accelerated economic growth. A major source of growth is the enhanced efficiencies that result from expanded intrabloc trade among members. Another stimulus to growth is the increased mobility of capital and labor within the union. Integration tends to boost capital investment as domestic entrepreneurs discover new opportunities for serving an enlarged market. Foreign investors are likewise drawn to this new market, and the union's common tariff wall reinforces the attraction for such investors. As noted earlier, this barrier discourages imports from former outside suppliers who now find themselves at a competitive disadvantage with respect to domestic producers. Fearing the loss of access to the union's market, foreign firms may choose to build production facilities inside union territory to supply the goods they formerly exported to it. In effect, these companies are substituting capital transfers for trade. Integration also tends to increase the mobility of labor among member countries, as workers find themselves free to migrate to those places with the most plentiful jobs and the highest pay.

The gains from integration just described are derived basically from Ricardo's classical principle of comparative advantage. Recently, however, theorists have discovered integration effects that require another kind of explanations (Krugman, 1989). Thus, it has become apparent that much of the new trade generated by integration—notably in the European Union—results from economies of scale rather than from comparative advantage alone. By concentrating their production at a single location within the union, many industries are able to reduce their unit costs substantially. To maximize scale economies, these centers tend to specialize in particular niche products. This gives rise to a pattern of narrow international specialization and trade among member countries, even though these countries may have quite similar resource endowments, as is true of the European Union. Production therefore comes to be dominated by a limited number of very large oligopolistic companies. Moreover, the replacement of several small national markets by a single large one leads to intensified competition: Firms that previously monopolized their home markets find that they are unable to monopolize an entire union. The advantages of bigness therefore become compelling, spurring companies to increase in size through internal growth or mergers with competitors.

The corporate restructuring that accompanies these consolidations brings about a relocation of production within the union. Related industries will tend to cluster at a limited number of the more desirable locations to avail themselves of the advantages of agglomeration. This in turn may reduce or eliminate production at the less-viable locations remaining from the preintegration period when each country attempted to produce a full range of goods and zealously protected its own industries, however inefficient they might have been. As the centers of agglomeration created by integration become increasingly dominant, related new industries may be attracted to their sites, thereby polarizing production still further.

The accelerated economic growth that integration is expected to bring about will be accompanied by rising standards of living in member countries. The increased output and falling unit costs enjoyed by the union's producers should result in higher incomes for their employees and lower retail prices for their products. Meanwhile, integration should lead to a more efficient distribution system, which puts a greater variety of merchandise on store shelves. To the extent that all of these expectations are realized, the final outcome will be higher levels of consumption and greater prosperity throughout the union.

Against these optimistic expectations are a number of potentially adverse effects of integration that must be weighed. It is quite possible that the benefits of integration will be unevenly distributed among production centers and economic sectors. Thus, one center may end up with more than its share of high-return industries (Krugman, 1989). This may tempt the disadvantaged countries to give special help to certain of their industries by means of production and export subsidies. Public policies such as these would likely provoke retaliatory responses from other member countries, thereby diminishing the benefits of integration.

Amidst the economic restructurings that accompany integration, inevitably some industrial sectors are winners and others are losers. This causes a shifting of resources—capital and labor—from lagging industries to high-growth industries. Yet, it takes time to shift resources between sectors, and this incurs adjustment costs. These costs usually take the form of higher unemployment, a vexing problem that arises in the adjustment phase. Even the most successful integration experiments encounter such side effects as these, and they must deal with the resulting political strains.

Integration for Development.   Many less-developed countries have drawn inspiration from the integration experiments in Western Europe. With encouragement from the United Nations, LDCs in several parts of the world seized on this as a solution for their many problems. Integration is particularly attractive to LDCs because it promises a larger market for their new industries. Typically, the domestic market of an LDC is severely limited by low per capita purchasing power, and this is often further reduced by the small proportion of the population that actually participates in the commercial economy. The subsistence sector of the population represents an insignificant market for most merchandise. The poorer countries therefore offer few attractions to modern industries that require economies of scale. To acquire such enterprises an LDC thus needs export outlets for its manufactured goods; union with other LDCs promises those markets.

In these circumstances, LDCs enter into integration schemes for somewhat different purposes from those of advanced nations. Integration offers LDCs a means for simultaneously solving two trade problems: (1) It provides an opportunity for free trade with other countries that are at similar levels of development and are thus able to compete on equal terms, and (2) it presents a way to trade with advanced countries without being harmed by their superior economic power. Yet the promotion of trade is not necessarily the main reason why LDCs form integrated groups, as it is for advanced countries. Indeed, less than one-fifth of all LDC trade is with other LDCs. A more urgent goal is to generate economic growth and development.

The gains from integration are fundamentally similar for developing countries and advanced ones, but with some important differences. The less-developed nations have possibilities for proportionately greater benefits because they have so much further to go. In addition to the opportunities that integration offers for acquiring individual industrial specialties and trading the products of these with other members, union can improve the allocation of resources. This is especially true of labor, which LDCs usually employ

wastefully. Producers can operate their facilities at full capacity and gain instant economies of scale from the enlarged market, yet at the same time they must become more efficient in order to meet the intensified competition.

After forming a union, individual countries no longer have to strive for a full range of economic activities, which is a difficult task for LDCs. It is unnecessary for each country to acquire every major type of production as long as at least one member has the right combination of resources for efficient production of a given commodity.

Although the problem of trade creation and diversion is critical for unions of advanced countries, it assumes a different complexion among LDCs. For the latter, the all-important consideration is the effect of integration on growth. Trade creation is still "good," but trade diversion is not necessarily "bad." It is true that import-competing industries divert trade from advanced countries, but these activities serve the important function of freeing foreign exchange for the purchase from those advanced countries of the high-technology capital goods essential to growth—commodities that are available only from advanced countries.

Yet, the integration efforts of LDCs encounter a number of special problems. One of the most difficult is deciding how to allocate to member countries those large manufacturing specialties that are to serve as the basis for intrabloc trade. To accomplish this, they must agree on the specific role of each country; but such agreement is hard to achieve because of rival national interests in obtaining these much-coveted projects. Indeed, the gravest obstacle to cooperation among LDCs is nationalism, often reinforced by longstanding grudges between neighboring countries. Another question of national self-interest arises from the basic inequalities that often exist among members. In nearly every union of LDCs, certain members are at a disadvantage with respect to the others because of smaller size, fewer resources, or lagging development. Consequently, successful integration of LDCs often requires special concessions to weaker members.

Early European Experiments in Integration. One of the earliest experiments in economic integration was the free-trade area attempted by Norway and Sweden during the nineteenth century. Although this effort failed, a number of customs unions formed at that time did survive. One of these was the German *Zollverein,* which joined together most of the independent small kingdoms and grand duchies that eventually became modern Germany. Also still in existence are a number of customs unions, each of which joins a very small country with a larger one, an arrangement known as a *customs accession.* Examples are the unions linking Switzerland and Liechtenstein, France and Monaco, and Belgium and Luxembourg. (See Box 12.2 for a summary of early integration experiments.)

The European Community. Inspired by the example of the ECSC, the same six nations thereupon agreed to extend this type of integration to all sectors of their economies. In 1957, therefore, they signed the Treaties of Rome (effective January 1, 1958), which established the European Economic Community (EEC or, more familiarly, the Common Market), and, separately, the European Atomic Energy Community (EURATOM), to coordinate atomic energy research and development. It was planned that the EEC would evolve in four stages, beginning with (1) a customs union for both industrial and agricultural goods, to be followed later by (2) a common market permitting free movement not only of goods, but also the factors of production, then (3) an economic union coordinating economic policies and practices, and, ultimately, (4) a political union—essentially, a United States of Europe.

Mainly because of this stated political objective for the EEC, and the surrender of national sovereignty it implied, seven other countries—Austria, Denmark, Norway, Portugal, Sweden, Switzerland, and the United Kingdom (later joined by Finland and Iceland)—established in 1960 a separate organization called the European Free Trade Association (EFTA). As a free-trade area in industrial goods only, the EFTA is the least restrictive form of integration. Most of its members had special reasons to avoid more binding ties: prior commitments to non-European trading partners (Britain), long-standing official policies of neutrality (Switzerland and Sweden), or conditions imposed under peace treaties with the former USSR (Austria and Finland). Though it was formed as a rival to the EEC, the chief rationale for the EFTA was to serve as a mechanism for bargaining with the EEC on liberalizing the flow of trade throughout Western Europe.

The market-opening effects of the EEC rewarded member countries with rapid economic growth during the 1960s, and this prompted the six in 1967 to enter on the second stage of their plan. In that year, they signed a Merger Treaty, which established common governing institutions for their three communities (EEC, EURATOM, and ECSC), thereby creating a single entity then called simply the European Community, or EC (Appendix 12.3 discusses the organizational structure of the EC's successor organization, the European Union). In the following year, 1968, the EC became a full customs union, with the lifting of all tariffs and quotas on trade among members while maintaining a system of common barriers to trade with nonmembers. Also by 1968, the six at last succeeded, after lengthy negotiations, in arriving at a common agricultural policy (known as CAP), which removed restrictions on intra-EC movements of agricultural commodities and established a common system of farm price supports and import barriers.

The striking success of the EC led the United Kingdom and certain other EFTA members to seek membership in the Common Market. After two fruitless attempts, the United Kingdom was at last admitted to the EC in 1973, along with Denmark and Ireland. On that same date, Denmark and the United Kingdom also withdrew from the EFTA. In 1972, the new nine-member EC entered into an agreement with the remaining members of EFTA to form an industrial free-trade area encompassing all 16 countries. In 1981, Greece became the tenth full member of EC, and Spain and Portugal joined in 1986, raising the total to twelve. Then, in 1990, the reunification of West Germany with the former Communist East Germany caused the territory of the EC to expand accordingly (though without increasing the number of members). The map (Figure 12.6) shows the membership of the EC and the effective dates of affiliation.

In addition, the EC entered into special arrangements with a number of other countries. It formed association agreements with Turkey, Malta, and Cyprus and extended preferential treatment to other Mediterranean lands. The group also signed a series of trade-and-aid agreements, called collectively the Lomé Convention, with 70 African, Caribbean, and Pacific (ACP) countries (under a 1995 agreement, the special trade privileges and other aid extended to the ACP group will be terminated in the year 2000).

Despite the EC's earlier successes, the progress toward forging a true economic union slowed markedly during the 1970s and 1980s, and lingering restrictions on intra-bloc transactions persisted. The energy crises and recessions of that period caused economic growth to slow and raised unemployment levels to worrisome levels. Adding to these concerns was the realization that European technology was lagging and that EC industries were becoming less competitive in world markets. In these circumstances, the spirit of cooperation among member nations waned, halting EC efforts to harmonize economic policies. The only significant advance during that period was the creation in 1979 of the European Monetary System (EMS), which is charged with minimizing fluctuations of currency exchange rates. The EMS also issues a European Currency Unit (ECU), which has been the primary unit of exchange for intra-EC transactions. Nevertheless, by the mid-1980s, the future for closer European integration seemed very much in doubt.

The European Union. Determined to break this stalemate, the EC launched a bold initiative designed to speed up the drive toward true economic and political union. The Single Europe Act (SEA) of 1986 was an ambitious plan to sweep away all remaining barriers to completion of a Community-wide unified market by the end of 1992. The boldness and promise of EC's "1992 Program" caught the imaginations of all Europeans, and it kindled a new sense of optimism in European business leaders, who began a flurry of corporate restructurings and mergers in anticipation of unhindered access to a single market of 340 million people

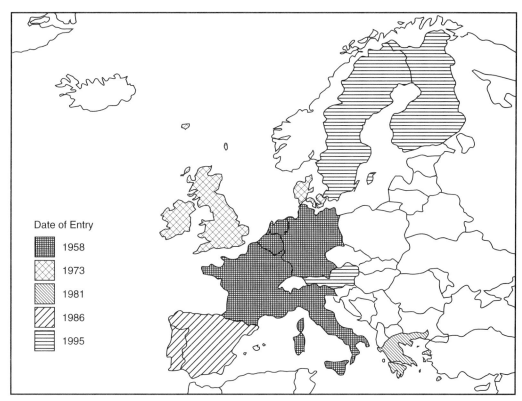

FIGURE 12.6   Members of the European Union and the effective dates of their entry into the organization.

and a gross national product of $8.5 trillion. This prospect also revived the previously flagging interest of Japanese and American multinationals in European investment.

Implementing the Europe 1992 Program proved an arduous task because it required the wholesale restructuring of the laws, regulations, and practices in each member country. At a special conference called at the end of 1991 to address the many decisions still facing the group, the twelve arrived at a comprehensive new agreement known as the Maastricht Treaty. Among other things, this called for creation of a single currency, a European Central Bank, and Communitywide citizenship. To emphasize the grand purpose of this pact, the organization adopted a new name: the European Union (EU).

In spite of the difficulty of arriving at this agreement and of getting it ratified by ambivalent national electorates, most Europeans now firmly accept the idea of a single market. And now the broad outlines of that market are taking shape. Since January 1, 1993, the majority of Europe's internal barriers have vanished. Trucks can now transport their cargoes from one end of the union to the other, from the Mediterranean to the Baltic; banks can operate branches in other EU countries; and students are entitled to enroll in any national university.

The benefits of participation in the union are now widely recognized throughout the continent, and this has prompted other European countries to seek membership. At the beginning of 1995, three former EFTA nations—Austria, Finland, and Sweden—joined the group (Norway had been accepted by the EU, but in a referendum its citizens voted to keep their country independent), and other applications are pending. Truly a "Super Europe" would appear to be emerging. (Appendix 12.4 discusses recent events affecting the EU, the problems it still faces, and its timetable for the future.)

Even as the EU was engaged in strengthening the union and increasing its membership, four former communist countries of Eastern Europe were forming a new trading bloc of their own. In 1992, the Czech Republic, Hungary, Poland, and Slovakia established the Central European Free-Trade Agreement (CEFTA), which is intended to become a free-trade area by the year 2000. In 1994, the group adopted the "Protocols of Budapest," under which they agreed to make half of their trade with each other duty-free by the following year. Subsequently, they voted to admit Slovenia to membership by the end of 1995, and Bulgaria and Romania by 1996. Still later they expect to add the Baltic States of Estonia, Latvia, and Lithuania to their group. By the end of the century, they hope to have a free-trade area of 100 million people. Though the immediate goal is to boost intra-CEFTA trade, the ultimate aim of at least some of this group is to gain membership in the European Union, which in the mid-1990s accounted for half of their total trade.

Theoretical Implications of European Integration.

Economic integration has a longer history—and has progressed further and had greater impact—in Europe than in any other world region. What lessons, therefore, can we draw from the European experience? What effects have four decades of integration had on the countries participating in these experiments? What have been the consequences for nonmember countries? What implications does this European experience hold for conventional trade theory? For answers to these questions, it is instructive to examine the contrasting performances of the EEC (subsequently the EC, and now the European Union) and its one-time rival, the EFTA, especially in view of their differing organizational structures and purposes, as well as their dissimilar resource endowments and locational characteristics.

From the outset, both the EEC and EFTA yielded important benefits to their member countries, but it was the EEC that made by far the more impressive gains. At the time of its formation, observers expected the Common Market to do well because the resource endowments of its members appeared to complement each other: France and Luxembourg offered iron ore, Germany coal, Italy surplus labor, and Belgium and the Netherlands large quantities of intensively produced food crops. In actuality, however, most of the products of Common Market countries proved highly competitive. The members did not rely heavily on one another's minerals or food supplies but instead exchanged mainly finished and semifinished manufactured goods. All made iron and steel, fabricated metal products, and produced a great variety of consumer goods.

The characteristics of these six nations seemed to conform fairly well to those traits that theorists regard as conducive to successful integration: The countries are individually small or moderate in size, but together they comprise a large part of Europe. They are mainly contiguous and are linked by well-developed transport systems. The group included some of the world's greatest trading nations, and most were one another's best customers. All depended heavily on trade, especially the Benelux countries, which export half or more of their output.

The original EFTA countries were more complementary than the EEC in their resource endowments and in the kinds of goods they produced. The Scandinavians exported forest products and minerals, as well as manufactured goods; Switzerland and Austria were principally manufacturing nations; and Portugal was mainly a primary producer. The United Kingdom had a more diversified economy, but almost from the start, the British began to seek membership in the EEC. Unlike the EEC, EFTA countries were spatially separated, and some were located peripherally to the European continent. The EFTA nations were active traders, but after the departure of the United Kingdom, none of the remaining members was the equal of most EEC nations. Although EFTA proved beneficial to its members, it is sig-

nificant that the greatest gains from the association were enjoyed by its Scandinavian members, which are contiguous, highly competitive with one another, and similar in many other respects. In all, however, the country traits that theorists regard as conducive to successful integration were poorly represented in EFTA.

Trade Creation, Trade Diversion, and Growth Effects of the EU.

From the standpoint of global welfare, the net trade effects of European integration have been positive, as confirmed by a number of empirical studies: Data show that the additional trade created by formation of the EEC substantially exceeded the amount of trade diverted from least-cost sources. Total trade of the union has grown enormously since the signing of the Treaty of Rome. The greater share of this new trade has been with other EU members, the consequence of freeing trade among a contiguous group of highly industrialized, active traders that had long been separated from one another by artificial barriers. At the same time, however, EU's trade with the rest of the world has risen substantially, too. This expansion in trade with nonmembers stems from the enlarged import demand from the newly prosperous union members, as well as the increased ability of these countries to compete with their exports in world markets.

Despite the largely positive effects of this trade creation, the EU has been responsible for a certain amount of trade diversion. Foreign suppliers have suffered significant trade losses, and this has been a source of much international friction. The reason for the rancor is that this trade diversion has been confined largely to agricultural commodities, a politically sensitive segment of world commerce. The EU's Common Agricultural Policy generously subsidizes Union farmers and exporters of farm products. The United States and Canada, which are more efficient agricultural producers than the Europeans, have suffered major reductions in their grain exports to the EU. They have also lost sales in world markets, where the artificially low prices of European grains have given the latter an undue competitive advantage. The dispute over EU farm subsidies was one of the major issues delaying completion of the Uruguay Round of GATT negotiations (see the preceeding).

The sharp increase in trade that resulted from West European integration is credited for the remarkable rise in output and living standards of living that member countries have enjoyed since the signing of the Treaties of Rome. Released at last to operate unhindered across the borders of neighboring countries—and challenged by enlivened international competition—long-sheltered European companies achieved new efficiencies. A rush of foreign investment from non-European sources further reinforced the quickening pace of economic activity. The results were startling. Indeed, the original six-member EEC enjoyed a combined GNP growth of more than one-half during the first decade of its existence alone. And, by the beginning of 1995, the 15 nations of the now-expanded EU were contributing a third of the world's output and more than two-fifths of its trade.

Locational Impact of European Integration.
Theoretically, integration can be expected to produce two kinds of effects on the location of economic activity: (1) Creation of a union should cause a global realignment of production by attracting direct investment from other parts of the world, and (2) it should bring about a shift in locational patterns within the union territory. Confirmation of the first of these expectations was quick to appear after creation of the EEC. Immediately on the signing of the Treaty of Rome in 1957, companies from the United States and other parts of the world began pouring investment into new facilities within the Common Market in their eagerness to participate in a reinvigorated European economy. Indeed, one study found that more than 800 new U.S. enterprises were established in the EEC during the first three years of its operation. This trend has continued during succeeding decades, and it received new momentum from the Europe 1992 program to eliminate the remaining barriers to free movement of goods, capital, and people throughout the European Union.

The European experience has also tended to bear out theoretical expectations concerning the location of activities with the Union, but not quite in the way anticipated. Empirical studies of trade among members have not discovered an increased specialization of one country in steel, another in grain, another in textiles, and so forth. Instead, major industries such as these have largely remained where they were before union, although certain subcategories have experienced marked locational changes. Thus, although each member country makes steel, one may emphasize sheet-steel products, another may produce structural-steel members, and a third may specialize in wire and rod products.

As expected, integration has increased the tendency for related industries to cluster at certain favored locations within the European Union. Studies confirming this polarization trend have found, however, that preexisting industrial centers in member countries appear to have survived, an indication of how firmly entrenched the industries of Western Europe had become prior to union. To date, therefore, the net locational result of European integration seems to have been not only an increase in intraindustry product specialization, but also an intensified regional specialization within the existing locational framework. Future studies will have to determine the locational effects of the current trend for companies to create mergers across national borders in the wake of the Maastricht Treaty, which eliminates the remaining barriers to intraunion movement of capital, goods, and people.

In retrospect, it is not surprising that intraindustry trade would have dominated the new trade among EU members in its earlier years. This was a logical consequence of the quite similar technologies and factor endowments of the these countries at the time. It may be expected that further expansion of intra-Union trade will take the form of traditional comparative-advantage-type specialization as the group is enlarged to take in new members from other parts of Europe, most of which differ markedly from existing members in resource endowments and levels of technology (Krugman, 1989).

The European experience with integration as a device to spur economic growth has not been lost on the rest of the world. Responding to this example, similar regional groupings have formed in nearly every part of the world. This development has led to some concern that world trade and investment are in danger of becoming compartmentalized into a number of competing regional economic blocs, thereby depriving the world of some of the benefits of global free trade promised by the General Agreement on Tariffs and Trade (GATT). International businesses are conscious of the potential problems and opportunities that such a regional partitioning of the world economy poses for them. This is one of the forces driving the competitive global strategy now pursued by most multinational enterprises, which calls for maintaining a presence simultaneously in all three of the major world regions: East Asia, Western Europe, and North America.

Economic Integration in the Americas.
The lessons in regional economic integration provided by Europe have found their most receptive audience in the Americas, where a variety of integration organizations have sprung up in different parts of the hemisphere. Hardly a year after the EEC came into being, new national groupings were forming in Latin America under United Nations auspices, and shortly thereafter similar developments were taking place in North America.

The first tentative step toward this form of economic cooperation in North America was the Canadian–U.S. Automotive Agreement of 1965, an experiment in sectoral integration. This accord created a two-nation, free-trade area limited to motor vehicles and original equipment parts—products of a single large industry dominated by a common set of giant companies operating on both sides of the border. The Auto Pact proved very beneficial to manufacturers, whose factories were able to concentrate on long production runs of individual models, thereby gaining economies of scale. Under this arrangement, too, Canadian consumers enjoyed a wider selection of models at lower prices than previously available in their relatively small market.

Then, in 1987, Canada and the United States signed the historic U.S.–Canada Free Trade Agreement (FTA or CFTA), which became effective January 1, 1989. This resulted in what was at the time the world's largest free-trade area, extending from the Arctic Circle to the Rio Grande and linking two countries whose bilateral trade exceeds that of any other country pair. Opening the 4,000-mile U.S.–Canadian border to a virtually free exchange of merchandise, CFTA extended also to energy, services, and investment In addition, the pact provided a dispute-resolution process.

Following closely upon the U.S.–Canada FTA, the two countries entered into discussions with Mexico concerning the possibilities for joining all three nations in a free-trade area. Lending urgency to these efforts was the general perception at the time that the Uruguay Round of GATT negotiations might fail, creating the need for a viable North American economic bloc capable of competing with the European Union. In 1992, the talks came to a successful conclusion and, after ratification by the respective legislative bodies of the three countries, the North American Free Trade Agreement (NAFTA) came into effect on January 1, 1994. Precedent for free trade between Mexico and the United States already existed in the *maquiladora* program, which had operated for some time along the 1,900-mile U.S.–Mexican boundary. Under this arrangement, nearly half a million Mexicans work for U.S. companies in more than 1,800 factories on the Mexican side of the border, making products for sale in the U.S. market.

In areal extent the new North American Free Trade Agreement dwarfs the 15-nation European Union, covering nearly seven times as much territory. Furthermore, incorporating Mexico's 90 million people within the group gives NAFTA a combined population slightly exceeding that of the EU. Mexico has a lower level of development than even the poorest West European countries, however; NAFTA's total gross national product is therefore somewhat smaller than the EU's. In both groups, the member countries are each other's best trading partners; but on the whole, the EU has an even greater degree of intragroup trade dependence than does NAFTA. Though well over two-thirds of Canadian and Mexican trade is with other NAFTA partners, the NAFTA portion of U.S. trade is somewhat lower because of that country's widespread trade links with the rest of the world.

In its first year, 1994, NAFTA was a resounding success; trade and investment flows among the three nations soared. The following year, however, got off to a rocky start because of an unexpectedly severe political and currency crisis in Mexico. Though emergency measures to rescue its floundering economy temporarily reduced Mexico's participation in NAFTA, the other two member-nations continued to benefit from their closer economic ties with each other, especially Canada. (See Appendix 12.5 for a more detailed view of recent steps to integrate the North American economies and the results to date.)

The dramatic actions by North Americans to create a continentwide free-trade bloc—and especially its inclusion of a Latin American nation—were watched with intense interest in the rest of the hemisphere. These events held out much hope for other Latin American countries, many of which had recently enjoyed a surge of economic growth but needed broader export markets for their growing industries. The concept of economic integration, however, was not a novel idea to Latin Americans; their experience with this approach to regional cooperation actually had a longer history than that of North Americans.

Indeed, some of the boldest experiments in integration have been undertaken in Latin America, where the driving incentive has been to speed economic development. Launched early in the post–World War II era, the first of these schemes grew out of an ambitious overall plan conceived by the United Nations Economic Commission for Latin America (ECLA), which sought initially to integrate all the lands south of the United States into a single Latin American common market. This grand design proved unworkable, mainly because of the enormous disparities in size and material well-being and the diversities of cultures among the many nations in that vast territory. Instead, three main regional blocs were created. Two of these were in Middle America: the Central American Common Market (CACM) and the Caribbean Economic Community (Caricom). The third group, the Latin American Free Trade Association (LAFTA), was composed of South American nations except for Mexico.

This UN-inspired organizational arrangement has undergone considerable change since its inception. In 1980, the members of LAFTA adopted a new name, the Latin American Integration Association (LAIA), and adopted a more modest program. Previously, several LAFTA member countries had set up a regional subgroup called the Andean Common Market (Ancom). Then, in 1988, Argentina and Brazil formed a free-trade area, which was later expanded to include Uruguay and Paraguay and given the name Mercado Com`n del Sur (Mercosur). Finally, in December 1994, the political leaders of all 34 democracies of North, South, and Middle America agreed to work toward creation of a hemispheric free-trade area by the year 2005. Appendix 12.6 traces the history of economic integration in Latin America and explores the prospects for a Free Trade Area of the Americas (FTAA).

Other Regional Groupings.   Regional economic integration is an idea that has reached many other parts of the world, but the movement has not as yet progressed as far or with as great an effect as in Europe and the Americas. Nevertheless, a number of cooperative ventures have been formed among groups of countries in the Asia–Pacific region and in parts of Africa, and the momentum is increasing.

One of the earlier undertakings was a free-trade area formed by Australia and New Zealand in 1965. The traditionally close economic dependence of these two countries on the United Kingdom had been severely weakened in the aftermath of World War II, as Britain, faced with a diminished role in the world economy, began to seek new ties with continental Europe. The efforts of Australia and New Zealand to diversify their trade connections intensified when the UK joined the European Common Market in 1971. Today, nearly two-thirds of their trade takes place within the Pacific Basin, and a growing part of this is with each other. Separated only by the Tasman Sea, the two neighbors have become more closely intertwined by a flood of direct investment in one another's economies. Trade barriers between the pair largely disappeared with the signing of the Closer Economic Relations (CER) agreement in 1983, which covered services as well as goods.

A second Pacific Rim organization, the Association of Southeast Asian Nations (ASEAN), is a free-trade area established in 1967 by Indonesia, Malaysia, the Philippines, Singapore, and Thailand in a mutual effort to promote economic growth and development. Brunei joined ASEAN in 1984, and Vietnam in 1995. Though political cross-currents among members have in the past hampered economic cooperation within the group, their rapidly growing economies are becoming more closely linked by trade and investment. Singapore, for one, currently derives 25 percent of its trade from ASEAN partners. Toward their goal of achieving a common market of 420 million people, ASEAN members have agreed to slash most tariffs on manufactured goods to 5 percent by the year 2003.

In 1995, after 10 years of discussions, seven South Asian nations at last signed a preferential trade agreement. Called the South Asian Association for Regional Co-operation (SAARC), the organization consists of Bangladesh, Bhutan, India, the Maldives, Nepal, Pakistan, and Sri Lanka. Though official trade among members currently represents merely 3 percent of their total trade, unofficial cross-border movements of goods (smuggling) are substantial. It is hoped that, by reducing intrabloc tariffs, SAARC will result in a profitable flow of legal trade among them. A second important purpose of the organization, however, is to serve as a forum for working out the many bitter political issues that have long soured the relations between some of these nations.

Undoubtedly the most ambitious in scope of all the joint ventures in this part of the world is the Asia–Pacific Economic Cooperation Forum (APEC). The original goal of this organization was to speed up economic liberalization in the Pacific Basin, but APEC has since adopted a vision of free trade throughout the whole of the Pacific region.

Beginning in 1989 with 11 Pacific Rim nations and the United States and Canada, APEC had by 1995 grown to more than 20 members, including two in Latin America. The group accounts for a large and growing share of the world's trade. This proportion reached 46 percent of the total in 1993, up from 38 percent 10 years earlier. A rising share of this trade is with other APEC members; by 1993 intrabloc trade had increased to 70 percent of the group's trade with the world. It should be noted that APEC is the only forum to which arch enemies China, Taiwan, and Hong Kong belong.

Each year since APEC's founding, the member nations have held an annual summit conference. At a November 1994 meeting in Indonesia, the group signed the Bogor Declaration, which committed members to create a free-trade area for the entire region. The pact called for developed member-countries to achieve "free and open trade" by the year 2010, and for less-developed members to accomplish this by 2020. Several working groups were set up to develop plans for the new free-trade area. Subsequently, Japan provided a grant of nearly $100 million to increase the budget of the APEC secretariat in Singapore.

The November 1995 meeting of APEC in Osaka, Japan, revealed that surprising progress had been made in liberalizing Southeast Asian trade. Even without formal APEC agreements, Southeast Asian countries had been slashing tariffs, deregulating financial sectors, and opening telecommunications and power monopolies to local and foreign investors. This unexpected reversal of past restrictive policies stems from the realization by most Asian nations that if they are to keep up their current high rates of growth, they must open their markets to each other and to the world. Results are already showing: trade within Southeast Asia soared 41 percent in 1995.

Even as plans move forward for creating a free-trade area among Pacific Basin countries, a similar arrangement that would join together the nations of the North Atlantic Basin is being promoted by some on both sides of the Atlantic. The argument for a Transatlantic Free Trade Agreement (TFTA) is that North Americans and Europeans have comparable open economic systems by contrast with the more closed, mercantilist systems prevalent in Asia. Because transatlantic trade takes place within an open-market framework, this trade remains fairly balanced in the long run; by contrast, transpacific trade faces countless, often subtle, barriers imposed by Asian nations As a result, North Americans face chronic trade deficits with those countries, as do some European nations. A transatlantic integration organization, according to its proponents, is the best way to pressure Asians into observing the principles of free trade.

As is typical of less-developed regions, trade among African countries is very limited. Most of Africa's trade is with Europe and North America, and the greater part of this takes place between African nations and their former colonial masters. Nevertheless, several organizational arrangements have been established to promote intra-African trade. The earliest of these was the East African Economic Community, a customs union with a common currency, consisting of Kenya, Uganda, and Tanganyika (later Tanzania). After some earlier successes, this organization fell victim to political controversy and disbanded in 1977. West Africa currently has two regional groups: the 16-nation Economic Community of West African States (ECOWAS) and the 6-nation Communauté Economique de l'Africa de l'Ouest (CEAO), which is made up of former French colonies. The continent's other functioning regional organization is the South African Customs Union, whose members are Botswana, Lesotho, South Africa, and Swaziland. (See Box 12.3 for a listing of integration organizations in various parts of the world and their memberships).

Preferential Trade Agreements

Though regional integration has gained more attention in recent times, other cooperative arrangements between countries have an even longer history and continue to play a significant role. One such device is the *bilateral trade agreement*, which calls for reciprocal concessions between pairs of countries. Such pacts continue to be common, though they have been eclipsed in recent decades by larger integrated groups and by global agreements.

One of the earliest and most enduring arrangements is the *colonial preference agreement,* in which a mother country and its present and former colonies grant special concessions to each other. Prominent examples were the British Commonwealth, with its imperial preference system, and the French Community. Though neither Britain nor France remains a true colonial power today, the commercial and cultural ties that developed among members of these groups over many years of close association have proved extraordinarily resilient.

THE GLOBAL ECONOMY IN THE TWENTY-FIRST CENTURY

In the final decade of the twentieth century, international trade is growing very rapidly—three times as fast as total world output. The World Trade Organization confirmed this in its first annual report on November 1995, which revealed that world trade had increased by a remarkable 13 percent in 1994 and was expected to continue growing at a fast pace through 1996 and beyond. The WTO's explanation for this: closer global economic integration.

The world is a far more prosperous place today than it was at the close of World War II, and much of the credit for this is generally given to the spectacular surge of international commerce in recent decades and to the liberalization process that made this possible. The resulting internationalization of national economies has created a new world scene distinguished by an accelerating rise and decline of national economies, an extensive restructuring of industries, and corresponding changes in the pattern and character of international economic transactions. A technology-driven information revolution has quickened the pace of change by weakening the traditional barriers of distance and governmental interference.

Principal actors in this drama are the business enterprises whose competition for advantage in the world marketplace inspires the innovations and organizational changes that prompt these advances. As Porter (1991) has shown, however, the competitive success of such firms depends mostly on the economic and cultural environments of the countries that serve as their home bases. The other main actors in the unfolding international economic scene, therefore, are the nations themselves. Their relative success in the competitive struggle, like that of the firms operating within their borders, is subject to the wider trends and events transpiring in the world at large: broad sweeps of political change, such as the liberation of Eastern Europe; pivotal episodes, such as the Persian Gulf crisis, German reunification, or peace in the Middle East; all-embracing designs for erasing the artificial barriers separating the world's national economies, such as GATT and the new World Trade Organization; grand schemes for reconstituting world regions, such as the revitalized and enlarged and European Union, the North American Free Trade Agreement, or the Asia-Pacific Economic Cooperation forum; the stark reality of the diminished role for traditional national policy instruments; and evolutionary changes, such as those now taking place within world industries.

At this time, the global economy is truly in transition. Let us conclude, therefore, by contrasting the trade regimes of old with those of today, and then attempting to envision the new regimes that promise to emerge in the new century.

Decades of Spatial Economic Change. The global space economy looks very different in the late 1990s than it did in the immediate postwar period. A prime feature of the world economy in the 1960s was the deep divisions that separated it into three distinct parts: a First World of non-Communist developed nations was responsible for nearly two-thirds of all trade, an isolated Second World of Communist states accounted for another 12 percent, and a Third World of less-developed countries provided the other 20 percent.

The United States dominated international commerce in that era, supplying more than one-seventh of all exports and a major share of foreign investment. In little more than a decade after the close of World War 11, the two defeated Axis partners, West Germany and Japan, had already risen to distant second and third places, respectively, behind the United States. As it had for more than three centuries previously, world commerce centered upon the North Atlantic Basin.

As the last decade of the century opened, the divisions of 30 years earlier were disintegrating. The Iron Curtain that had separated Eastern and Western Europe was gone, the Eastern Bloc's share of world trade had shrunk greatly, and the former Communist lands were seeking new economic ties with the West. By the start of the 1990s, U.S. dominance of international trade had diminished and was being challenged in some years by the reunited Germany.

The focus of world trade and investment had shifted westward to the Pacific Basin, where a resurgent Japan had doubled its share of world exports. The Pacific Basin's new central place in the world economy also derived from the meteoric rise of an aggressive set of newly industrializing countries in East Asia. The other anchor of Pacific commercial activity, the United States, had formed a free-trade area with Canada, and these two had in turn joined with Mexico in a pact that created the North American Free Trade Agreement.

In the 1990s, Western Europe still retained its two-fifths share of world exports and imports, but, after 30 years of economic integration, a major part of this was intra-European trade. Under the aegis of the EC, now renamed the European Union, Western Europe was further deepening its integration by eliminating the final barriers to intrabloc movements and broadening itself by admitting new states to membership. A newly reunited Germany dominated West European economic affairs and became a main force in the opening to Eastern Europe. Meanwhile, liberated from Communism, several Eastern-bloc nations had replaced their long-time trade dependence on the former Soviet Union with new links to the West, farther south, a number of Balkan states were using their release from Communism as an occasion to revive centuries-old ethnic antagonisms; and the ranks of less-developed countries had been reduced in number by the rise of an expanding group of newly industrialized countries, which had relied on trade-led growth to reach levels of prosperity rivaling that of Mediterranean Europe. Despite a rise in intragroup trade among LDCs as a whole, however, the 47 nations classified by the UN as "least developed" saw their share of global trade shrink to the lowest point yet. The oil-exporting LDCs, which for a time had supplied more than 15 percent of all world exports, had lost their monopoly position by the 1990s and found themselves reduced to about the same level they had held prior to the oil crises of the 1970s.

Internationalization of National Economies. Fundamental forces for change have been at work. Of all the interrelated factors that contributed to this progression, perhaps none has been more basic and essential than the process of trade liberalization pursued in the postwar era through the GATT mechanism. The unprecedented international cooperation of that period caused trade to expand enormously, and the dropping of political obstacles to trade hastened the integration of the world economy.

At the same time that the processes of trade liberalization and economic integration were being initiated globally, similar processes were under way at the regional scale. Early in the postwar period, the West Europeans seized on regional economic integration as a way to stimulate their postwar recovery, to solve persistent intraregional trade problems, and to unite long-time enemies in a mutually productive alliance. Though this mechanism has the disadvantage of discriminating against nonmember countries, the gains that the European Community (later the European Union) enjoyed caused it to become the model for similar regional organizations from Latin America to Southeast Asia, Africa, and North America. Regional economic integration, therefore, has been one of the forces for rearranging world patterns of trade and investment.

The liberalization of world trade was a prerequisite for the impressive rise of the Pacific Rim countries. The growing volume of international trade and the opening of world markets made it possible first for Japan and then for the East Asian NICs to introduce industrial technologies requiring economies of scale. Easier access to the global economy thus allowed them to manufacture product lines that their home markets were not large enough to support. The small countries of Western Europe benefited in this same way. Indeed, the quantitative evidence confirms that, in the postwar period of liberalization, small countries—which rely on international trade to a greater relative extent than large ones—enjoyed the highest economic growth rates.

In an integrated world economy, trade exerts powerful pressures for change by unleashing the forces of competition. Nations and firms must adjust or perish. This competitive discipline has been a major impetus for the burst of product and process innovation of recent years. The growth of world trade and foreign investment has affected large countries and large firms as much as small ones because it has made them all vulnerable to foreign competition both at home and abroad. This is the lesson U.S. industrialists painfully learned in the early 1980s, and it was the force that goaded them into the restructuring that restored their international competitiveness in the 1990s.

The liberalization process has been especially beneficial in the development of new high-technology goods. In the early postwar years, such products were subject to unusually low tariffs, because at that time they represented only a minor element in world commerce; since then, tariffs on these items have been further reduced in subsequent GATT rounds. This gave companies a powerful incentive to increase their competitive positions through product innovation.

Throughout this dynamic era, the multinational enterprise has been a major force for globalization, even as it has itself been undergoing a transformation in organizational form and function. Manufacturing firms and international providers of services alike have internationalized their operations, competing worldwide and pursuing global strategies in procuring raw materials, assembling products, and selling these in a variety of countries. As Porter (1990) has observed, the globalization of an industry decouples a firm from the factor endowments of a single nation and enables it to secure its needs from the lowest-cost sources, wherever those may be. Moreover, it permits a multinational to enter readily into new markets, taking with it the know-how it has accumulated elsewhere, and quickly establish a viable presence. As a consequence, the combined transactions of the world's multinational enterprises were responsible for a majority of the world's merchandise trade, and much of this exchange took place between branches of the same business organizations.

The modern-day shifts in the international focus of economic activity thus stem from changes in the competitiveness of nations and firms, made possible by the freeing up of world commerce. The nations of the Pacific Rim have prospered by increasing the productivity of their resources, especially their human assets, and this has enabled them to improve their competitive positions in existing industries and to develop competitiveness in new industries. A hierarchy of nations has emerged in the region as first Japan and then the Four Tigers have systematically moved into new, more-sophisticated export lines, shifting their old lower-technology industries to the next tier of nations below them.

By contrast, some of the older industrial nations of Europe have failed to keep up in some types of high-technology production and have therefore found their competitiveness in world markets impaired. Moreover, using a variety of protectionist devices, they have clung to low-technology industries—such as mass-produced textiles and clothing—in which their international competitiveness has long ago dissipated. Hence, the international market shares of these countries have suffered, their economic growth has lagged, and their unemployment rates have risen.

The global economy has become so transformed in recent decades that conventional international trade theory no longer supplies a full and satisfying explanation for the patterns of economic flows now taking shape. With such a large part of world trade moving between branches of globalized multinational enterprises, analysts have had to turn to foreign direct investment theory for some of the answers.

One problem in particular that has defied the explanatory powers of traditional theory is the great amount of intraindustry trade taking place between countries with seemingly identical resource endowments. As an explanation for this growing two-way trade in related products, the "new" theory of international trade offers the concept of increasing returns to scale through specialization, one of the important elements lacking in existing theory.

Though acknowledging that conventional trade theory is still useful for interpreting arm's-length transactions in the world markets for such goods as industrial raw materials, fuels, and agricultural commodities, the new theorists note that shipments of this type are a diminishing proportion of the total. Many of what Michael Porter calls "basic factors" figure less importantly in global trade because of improvements in product design and in transportation and communications. Porter's "advanced factors"—educated personnel, research-and-development capabilities, and advanced communications—have assumed a greatly enhanced role in world commerce.

The Global Space Economy of the Future. Considering the new directions of world trends and events on the eve of a new millennium, what can we expect the map of global economic activity to look like beyond the year 2000? The opening chapters of this book suggested two seemingly contrary tendencies at this time, *the forces reinforcing regionalization* and *the forces promoting globalization.* Which of these ultimately prevails will provide the answer to our question.

The forces for regionalization have been with us throughout the post–World War II era, seen especially in the proliferation of economically integrated groups in nearly every world region. Several of these appeared to have had positive results, contributing to the economic growth and development of member states and apparently creating more trade than they diverted. During the 1980s, however, as efforts to reach a successful conclusion to the Uruguay Round of GATT talks faltered, the world space-economy seemed to be headed for fragmentation into rival groups. Setting the tone were the trade frictions clouding relations among the nations of Europe, North America, and the Pacific Rim.

By the beginning of the 1990s, therefore, the postwar liberalization of trade appeared in danger of being reversed by tendencies toward the formation of three inward-looking, competing trade blocs. These would consist of (1) an augmented European Union growing out of the EC's Maastricht Accord of December 1991, (2) a Western Hemisphere bloc based on the North American Free Trade Agreement, and (3) a Japan-dominated Asian bloc.

By 1995, the much-strengthened European Union had enlarged its membership by the admission of three more former EFTA countries, and at least 10 Eastern European nations were seeking to join. Until the latter are able to make the necessary market reforms, however, their membership in the EU had to be deferred. In the meantime, five Central European countries formed a free-trade area of their own (see the preceeding). If in time the former Soviet republics should succeed in making the transition to market economies, some of these might also be expected to seek ties with the EU.

Meanwhile, completion of the North American Free Trade Agreement joining the United States with Canada and Mexico produced echoes throughout the Americas. A politically and economically resurgent Latin America saw in this movement the nucleus of a greater Western Hemispheric free-trade area, and several Latin American nations began positioning themselves to take advantage of any such opportunity. One of the appeals of an enlarged NAFTA was the greater economic strength that such a coalition could supply in the threatening competitive struggle with an enlarged European Union and a flourishing East Asian bloc.

At the same time, a third, potentially mighty economic entity has been taking shape in East Asia, drawn together by growing ties of trade and investment. Realizing that they can maintain their current high levels of growth only through opening markets in the region, several leading nations of the area have been reducing trade barriers. As we noted before, even without formal agreements by APEC, Asian countries have slashed tariffs, deregulated their financial sectors, and opened telecom and power monopolies to private investment. In addition, APEC working groups were seeking agreement on new common standards for product health, safety, and quality requirements, thereby substantially lowering the costs of exporting across the Pacific Rim. The results were quick to appear: Already by 1994, intraregional trade had soared 41 percent.

Most of this intra-Asian trade, and also foreign investment, was being conducted by two groups: expatriate Chinese entrepreneurs and Japanese multinationals. Large numbers of Japanese industries, especially the smaller ones, have moved their operations to neighboring countries as the sharply rising Japanese yen has caused manufacturing inside Japan to become unprofitable. Also strengthening East Asian economic ties with Japan is the high proportion of region's debt that is owed to Japanese financial institutions.

As the 1990s began, therefore, the picture of Global 2000 taking shape was that of three great regional entities competing for advantage in global commerce and defensively limiting imports from each other. The potential for such barriers led to a struggle for competitive advantage in the EU that pitted Europe's own multinationals against each other and against MNEs from the United States and Japan. Because few of Europe's MNEs were large or powerful enough to compete successfully in a Europewide market, they launched a campaign of merging and buying each other out to increase their strength.

This tripartite division of world commerce among industrial nations appeared a setback for efforts to complete the still-unfinished business of integrating the world's economies. The possibility of three suspicious and mutually hostile economic groups revived memories of the Smoot–Hawley era of the 1930s. In an earlier age, this situation could have meant the ultimate collapse of world trade.

This time, however, the countervailing forces for globalization are predicting another kind of outcome. One set of forces favoring closer global economic integration was unleashed by the successful conclusion of the GATT negotiations in 1994 and the creation—at last, after 50 years—of a World Trade Organization. What this event demonstrates is the recognition by the participants that the links between national economies have now become too strong to allow individual countries to return to the beggar-thy-neighbor activities of the disastrous 1930s. Even so, some Americans fear that the EU has become an inward-looking bloc that will increasingly discriminate against non-European interests, and some Europeans worry that APEC will lead to the creation of an exclusive club closed to outsiders.

The answer to these anxieties is the rise of another major force for globalization: The ultimate arbiters of international economic transactions in the 1990s are powerful multinational corporations, which operate in a virtually borderless world of their own. Today's MNEs follow a "three-legged" corporate strategy under which every firm expects to maintain a substantial corporate presence within each of the three major world regions as a way of securing its global market share against loss to its competitors. Additionally, the three-legged strategy acts as an insurance policy against possible exclusion from any one of these vital markets by the forces of protectionism.

Thus, the second half of the twentieth century has seen the world lifted to overall levels of prosperity inconceivable in earlier times, thanks largely to the immense increase in economic interaction among its citizens. The global institutions and enterprises created to enable this interaction remain the major defenses against a return to the kind of dangerously fragmented world economy of the Depression years of the century's first half. Also important, however, is the general recognition that any reversal of the recent progress toward trade liberalization would cost the world some or all of its postwar gains in living standards. The future growth of large and small economies depends on continued movement toward more trade liberalization, not less.

APPENDIX 12.1

The Global Competitiveness of U. S. High-Technology Industries

The growing importance of foreign trade to the U.S. economy has aroused public concern about the competitiveness of the country's industries in world markets. Back in the 1960s, when U.S. imports amounted to no more than 3 percent of gross national product, this subject received little attention. By the 1990s, however, imports were approaching one-tenth of GNP and the trade deficit had become worrisomely large. The competitiveness issue focused particularly on high-technology industries, because the nation had long relied on a large technological lead to sustain its appetite for imported energy and raw materials. In recent years, however, the U.S. technological lead had seemed to be slipping away, and by the mid-1980s, the nation's surplus of high-technology exports over imports had virtually disappeared. As anxiety over the mounting deficit increased, commentators began to warn of impending doom for the national economy. Some would have had the country put up its barricades and withdraw behind a wall of protectionism.

Trade theorists were quick to stress, however, that such doomsday talk was much overdrawn, that no economic catastrophe actually threatened. As Paul Krugman (1991) noted, these fears are based on the mistaken belief that a country is like a business. But, he insisted, a country is not like a private business. Whereas a company that loses its competitiveness can be put out of business, a country cannot. Unlike the competitive conditions faced by businesses, economic relations among nations are subject to a set of powerful adjustment processes that operate through (1) exchange rates and (2) international capital movements. A growing trade deficit causes a country's currency to decline in value relative to other world currencies, thereby making its labor cheaper and its products more price competitive in international markets. At the same time, movements of capital among countries affect their trade balances: exports of capital result in positive balances, and imports produce negative balances.

Two centuries earlier, David Ricardo had described the effects of declining productivity on a country's trade (see Chapter 11). Even if it is less productive than its trading partners in all the goods it makes, he stated, a country will always be able to engage in profitable foreign trade. If it has no absolute advantage in anything, it can nevertheless successfully export those goods in which its comparative disadvantage is least. Moreover, in these circumstances, a country is better off to engage in foreign trade than not because such trade will provide it with a higher standard of living than if it were to remain in isolation. It is just that its living standard would not be as high as those of its more productive competitors. Thus, a relative decline in produc-

tivity does not bring catastrophe—and it is certainly no excuse for isolationism—but this does not mean that the question of preserving its competitiveness in high-technology trade is not a serious matter for the United States.

The Importance of U.S. High-Technology Trade. The national attention given to the question of the country's technological leadership reflects a growing public awareness of the role that technology-intensive industries play in the national economy: Not only are they vital to the balance of trade, but they also pay higher wages and generate more profits than do most sectors. This new concern with competitiveness comes at a time when technology gaps among countries have been opening and closing at an accelerating rate. Whereas the international transfer of new technology had once required a generation or more, today it takes only a few years at most.

Even the perception of what constitutes high-technology is changing. Industrial products mature at ever-faster rates, so that a high-technology good at one time is only a medium- or low-technology good soon thereafter. Thus, the product life cycle has greatly speeded up, making it difficult to compare one era with another. High-technology industries are usually defined as those making relatively large expenditures for research and development (R&D) and employing a high percentage of scientists, technicians, and manual workers with specialized skills. Lists of high-technology products ordinarily include chemicals, machinery (including electronics), transport equipment, and professional instruments; however, only certain subcategories of these can rightly be considered high-technology at the present time. For instance, bulk chemicals such as acids and alkalis no longer justify this classification.

Just how critical the high-technology sector is to the country's overall trade balance can be seen from (Figures 12.7 to 12.11). A big trade surplus in technology-intensive products has supported other major trade categories that have done less well. For many years, the country has had a large trade deficit in raw materials and fuels (see Chapter 5), as depletion of domestic supplies and soaring world commodity prices (especially for oil between 1973 and 1981) increased the country's import bill for these goods. Similarly, imports of low-technology manufactured products, such as textiles and clothing, have exceeded exports by a growing margin. A fourth category, agricultural commodities, usually has a trade surplus, although this fluctuates widely from year to year, depending on world harvests, protectionist policies in key markets, and the strength of the dollar relative to other currencies.

Vulnerability of U.S. Industries. Throughout the early postwar years, the United States enjoyed a strong positive balance of trade in high-technology goods. In the early

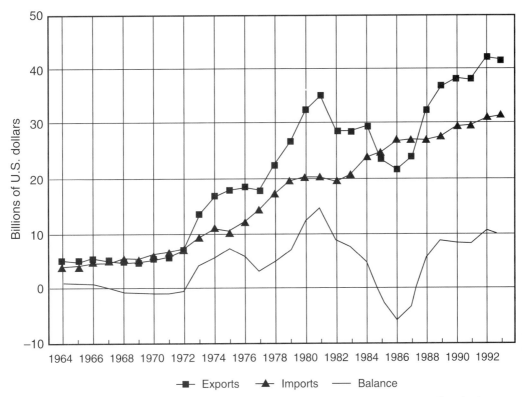

FIGURE 12.7 Changing structure of U.S. trade: agricultural products. (Standard International Trade Classification, SITC, 0, 1, 4).) The long-time surplus in agricultural trade has fluctuated widely in recent times owing to the variability of harvests from year to year, foreign protectionism and competition, and currency fluctuations. [*Source:* United Nations, *Yearbook of International Trade Statistics,* various years (New York: United Nations).]

1960s, U.S. technology-intensive exports (as defined in Figure 12.10) were five times greater than high-technology imports; thereafter, the gap narrowed until, by the middle of the 1980s, high-technology imports were almost as large as exports. At that point, galvanized by the growing competitive threat from abroad, U.S. firms undertook a major restructuring of their operations. This enabled them to achieve new levels of productivity, efficiency, and product quality, and by the 1990s, they had regained much of their lost dominance in world markets. Aiding this resurgence were shifts in currency exchange rates that were favorable to U.S. exporters. Despite this reprieve, the world position of this key sector of the U.S. economy remains uncertain. What has caused the once-secure competitive position of U.S. advanced-technology industry to come under such threat in recent years? It is a problem with several dimensions:

1. First of all, it is improbable that the unusually large U.S. technology gap of the postwar era could have been sustained indefinitely. After all, a substantial part of the U.S. lead during those years resulted from the wartime devastation of competing industrial economies. The influx of refugee foreign scientists and technicians further enhanced this advantage.

2. Another reason for the declining U.S. lead after the 1960s was the way in which many of the nation's multinational enterprises responded to the accelerating product life cycle. Although new products have regularly replaced old ones in the country's export mix, the more mature forms of production that have moved to other countries are high-volume operations accounting for sizable shares of world trade. The newer manufactured products and services generate far lower total export earnings.

3. Also adversely affecting the U.S. trade balance in technology-intensive goods has been the growing tendency of multinationals to transfer their latest technology immediately to their overseas affiliates. By using cheap labor and local raw materials, these firms are able to minimize production costs at the very outset, thereby forestalling potential competition. Technological transfers of this kind have become increasingly easy because of the rapid spread of high-level technological skills throughout the world, which has benefited from the drive for educational advancement in much of the developing world, especially Asia. The effects of this are seen in the case of a U.S. company that has recently captured 30 percent of the Japanese market for notebook computers. This computer, however, is manufactured for the company in Singapore! Indeed, goods pro-

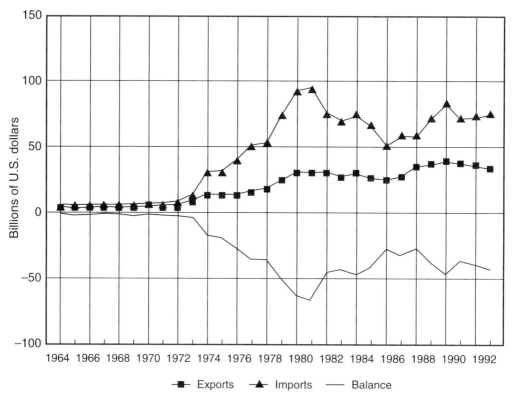

FIGURE 12.8 Changing structure of U.S. trade: minerals, fuels, and other raw materials (SITC 2. 3). The overall trade deficit in part has been caused by large trade deficits in minerals, fuels, and other raw materials.[*Source:* United Nations, *Yearbook of International Trade Statistics,* various years (New York: United Nations).]

duced overseas by American companies constitute a major component of U.S. high-technology imports.

4. A key element in the U.S. high-technology problem, however, has been the flagging ability of some U.S. manufacturers to translate basic scientific discoveries quickly and efficiently into useful articles that compete in world markets. The country's position in basic science has remained strong, as indicated by continued U.S. dominance of Nobel prize awards and by the large numbers of students from around the world who flock to the United States for advanced degrees in science, mathematics, and engineering. Nevertheless, U.S. supremacy in *product innovation* began to slip about the time that Europe and Japan were completing their recoveries from World War II.

5. But product innovation is not enough by itself; another essential is something called *process-oriented innovation.* This consists of refining an existing article at each turn of the production cycle and constantly looking for ways to build it more simply, cheaply, and quickly. Such an approach demands the closest intracompany teamwork. The result is an incrementally better product and steadily rising productivity. The Japanese are masters at this kind of innovation. Under growing pressure from more-efficient foreign competitors in the 1980s, U.S. enterprises undertook stren-

uous measures to "re-engineer" themselves, adopting and improving on many of the production techniques that had served the Japanese so well. By 1995, according to an international study, U.S. firms had in general caught up with and passed their Japanese counterparts in product quality. Meanwhile, a painful "downsizing" of company work forces, together with a period of national price and wage stability, had enabled the U.S. economy once again to become the most competitive in the world.

6. Finally, throughout the period when its technological lead was slipping, the United States was not spending enough on R&D. During that time Japan consistently outstripped the United States in its outlays for industrial research, as measured by percentage of gross national product. American expenditure for R&D represented 3 percent of gross national product in the early 1960s; by 1985, this had fallen to only 1.9 percent, about half the Japanese rate. U.S. corporate outlays for R&D, however, began to rise thereafter as intense foreign competition forced U.S. firms to automate in order to reduce costs and raise quality. The trend continued in the mid-1990s, even as worsening economic conditions in Japan were forcing Japanese producers to cut their R&D expenditures.

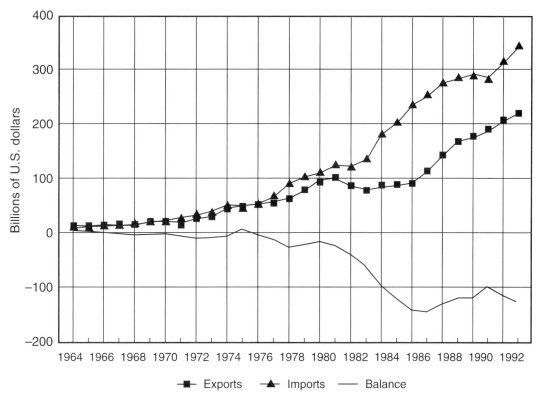

FIGURE 12.9 Changing structure of U.S. trade: nontechnology-intensive manufactured products (SITC 5, 6, 7, 8, 9, excluding high-technology goods). The overall trade deficit in part has been caused by large trade deficits in nontechnology-intensive manufactures. [*Source:* United Nations, *Yearbook of International Trade Statistics,* various years (New York: United Nations).]

Crucial Industrial Sectors. Even in the worst of times, some U.S. high-technology industries have fared better than others in the competition for domestic and foreign markets. U.S. chemical companies are aggressive exporters, contributing one-tenth of the country's foreign earnings in most years (Figure 12.12). Any threat to that industry's international position would, therefore, pose a serious problem for the nation's balance of payments. During the early postwar era U.S. chemical exports soared, but they had begun to encounter overseas competition from European and Japanese producers by the 1970s. U.S. chemical imports climbed in the following decade as competitors' capacity expanded, but U.S. producers were able to meet the challenge and to increase their competitive position both at home and abroad during the 1990s.

Most of the foreign competition is in basic organic and inorganic chemicals; U.S. chemical companies hold a firm lead in high-technology chemicals. These contributed nearly half of the industry's $15 billion trade surplus in 1993 (see Figure 12.12). The U.S. chemical industry safeguards this technological supremacy by maintaining a consistently high investment in research and development, even in times of recession. In the vanguard are the nation's pharmaceutical companies, which spend one out of six of their sales dollars on R&D to create a growing array of new products. Most U.S. pharmaceutical houses currently sell 30 to 50 percent of their prescription drugs overseas.

Electronics has long been a positive contributor to the country's trade balance, but in 1984 for the first time imports of electronic goods exceeded exports, and by a considerable margin. This gap, which is still growing, is a serious problem because electronics is one of the country's largest manufacturing employers. It has also been a main hope for recouping some of the jobs lost by declining employment in older heavy industries, such as steel and autos. The U.S. electronics industry began to lose its international competitiveness during the early 1980s, at a time when an overvalued dollar was making U.S. exports too expensive and imports cheap. The decline in U.S. electronics continues, even though the dollar has since fallen against other major currencies.

A more basic reason for the slippage is the inability of U.S. firms to convert their technological discoveries into competitive products. Their reluctance to invest for the

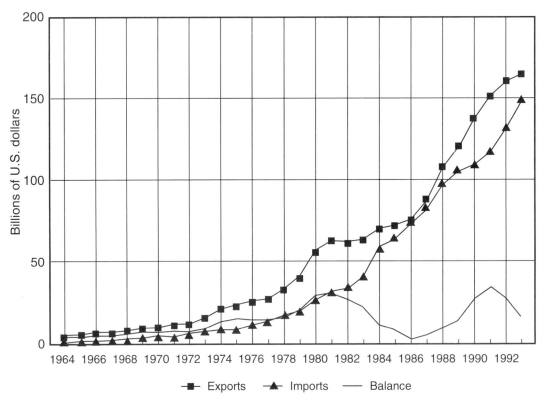

FIGURE 12.10   Changing structure of U.S. trade: technology intensive manufactured products (SITC 52, 54, 58, 71, 75, 76, 771, 772, 74, 776, 792, 87, 951). As its overall trade deficit has grown, the United States has relied on a surplus in high-technology exports, but the country's competitive strength from this source is only tenuous. [*Source:* United Nations, *Yearbook of International Trade Statistics,* various years (New York: United Nations).]

future stems from the threefold dilemma facing U.S. high-technology operating in a free-market environment:

- Steadily rising capital intensity. Developing new products now requires much time and enormous sums of money, often exceeding the resources of individual U.S. companies. The nation's capital markets are interested only in short-term results and the government is unwilling to subsidize such ventures. Today, spending power determines the outcome of competition in the industry.

- Ever-shorter product life cycles. The accelerating pace of change requires the commitment of immense human and financial resources if new-product development is to keep ahead of the competition.

- The ease with which competitors can copy new technology in an age of instantaneous global communication and deficient international patent protection.

Illustrating these problems is the case of the computer industry (Figures 12.13 to 12.18). American computer makers have been locked in a competitive struggle for this crucial market with the Japanese industry, which is heavily subsidized. American companies still dominate the world market for computers, but they purchase most of their components from foreign manufacturers because they cannot make them competitively at home. Microprocessors, the "brains" of the computer, are the main exception: America's Intel Corporation, with its 486 and Pentium, dominates much of the world market for these. Indeed, one of the major problems for computer makers generally is the extreme concentration of production. Many key items are manufactured in only a few locations worldwide, mostly Japan, and a major share of world capacity is located at a single site. The industry is therefore vulnerable to supply disruptions from accidents and other causes.

The world market for computer chips is huge, amounting to tens of billions of dollars, and is fed by the growing trend to incorporate electronics into all kinds of products. Although computer chips were an U.S. development, Japan quickly seized the lead in manufacture by the end of the 1970s. However, U.S. makers benefit from the current emphasis on chips designed for special applications, because U.S. engineers and manufacturers still excel in devising new technologies and creative software. Furthermore, the production of custom-designed parts of this kind is locationally tied to end users. The fragmented markets that result from this are unsuited to the Japanese, whose techniques are geared to mass production.

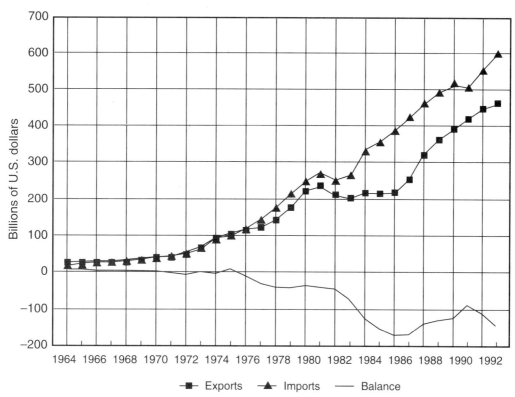

FIGURE 12.11   Changing structure of U.S. trade: balance of trade (SITC 0–9). [*Source:* United Nations, *Yearbook of International Trade Statistics,* various years (New York: United Nations).]

Telecommunications is another very large and dynamic high-technology area that is stressed by Japan's economic planners. The United States had always had a positive balance of trade in this category until the 1980s, when imports of telecommunications equipment for the first time exceeded exports. In this case, the main competition comes from Canada as well as Japan.

For years, one of the keystones of the American lead in high-technology has been the aircraft industry, which draws on some of the country's greatest competitive strengths (Figures 12.19 and 12.20). Very large, highly capitalized companies dominate this industry, in which product development alone requires billions of dollars. American aircraft builders have benefited from enormous defense contracts from both the U.S. and foreign governments, and these have yielded valuable R&D by-products for the development of commercial aircraft. Though aircraft imports have risen since 1979, these have done little to reduce the large positive contribution of the aviation industry to the U.S. balance of trade. This surplus from aircraft exports compensates in part for the overall trade deficit in transport equipment resulting from huge imports of road vehicles (Figure 12.19), especially passenger cars.

A Competitiveness Strategy. How can the United States ensure the continued international competitiveness of its high-technology industries? What steps should the country take to stimulate exports in this important area of comparative advantage? As foreign competition has intensified in recent years, many in the industry have agitated for government protection from imports, but studies of this problem (notably the President's Commission on Industrial Competitiveness of 1984) have stressed the need for a more positive approach. To strengthen its competitive position in an era of explosive technological change, U.S. industry is urged to redouble its efforts to increase manufacturing productivity. This requires not only additional investment in research and development and modernization of manufacturing techniques; above all, it calls for upgrading the quality of the country's human capital, the most vital resource for advanced technologies. The urgency of this need is underscored by the growing pattern of income inequality in the United States, a gap that is widening along an educational fault line. As a result, U.S. companies are pressed to find sufficient numbers of qualified workers.

The logical solution for ensuring an adequate supply of high-quality human capital is to redouble investment in worker training and education. This is the one proven route to higher productivity and increased output of high-value-added goods and services. Recent experience in the United States and elsewhere has shown that only a well-trained and educated work force can cope with the advanced techniques—such as total quality management, just-in-time

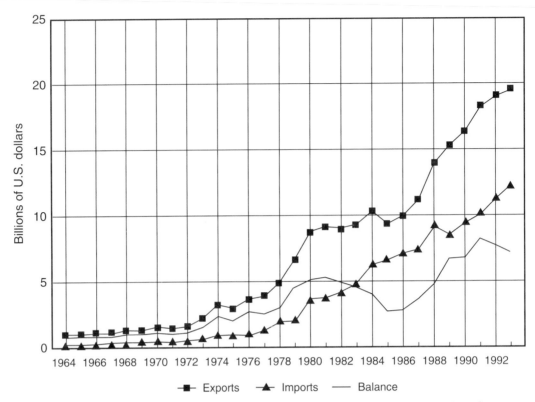

FIGURE 12.12 U.S. trade in high-technology chemicals. One bright spot in the U.S. trade picture is its dependable surplus in top-of-the-line chemicals, which contribute one-tenth of foreign earnings in most years. U.S. chemical companies invest heavily in research and development and are aggressive exporters. In the lead are U.S. pharmaceutical companies, which sell 30 to 50 percent of their output overseas. [*Source:* United Nations, *Yearbook of International Trade Statistics,* various years (New York: United Nations).]

inventory control, computerized operations, and teamwork systems—that are required to compete successfully in world markets today.

Although corporate America has recently made great strides in restructuring itself and has invested record sums in capital equipment, its investment in human capital has lagged. The $30 billion that U.S. companies have been spending annually on educating their workers is only one-third that of European firms, reckoned on a per capita basis. And, with few exceptions (notably Motorola and Ford), U.S. expenditures on employee education have mostly gone for management training.

In addition to much greater private-sector investment in human capital, many urge a governmental push for higher-quality public education. They point to the high rate of functional illiteracy among U.S. workers and the staffing problems this poses even for low-technology companies. For high-technology industries, the problem is, of course, very serious: Their requirement is for college-educated employees, and especially those with advanced degrees. Among proposed solution are guaranteed college educations through government loan programs and changes in the tax code to reward companies that finance higher education for their employees.

A high-skills, high-wage strategy of this kind is widely regarded as the best long-range answer to intensifying world competition in advanced technologies. Certainly, it is the prevailing strategy of U.S. competitors in Europe and especially in East Asia, where education of the work force is accorded the highest priority. Through massive restructuring, renewed attention to quality control, and increased productivity, U.S. companies have regained much of their competitive edge in world commerce. Whether they can continue to compete successfully in the coming century depends on how effectively they can mobilize their resources to this end—and most particularly their human resources.

APPENDIX 12.2

The Question of Protectionism: A Public Policy Issue

From the late 1970s through the 1980s, the global community was swept by an epidemic of protectionism reminiscent of the 1930s. In that earlier time, the U.S. Congress, with its Smoot–Hawley Tariff Act of 1930, had precipitated a worldwide flurry of protectionism that quickly caused

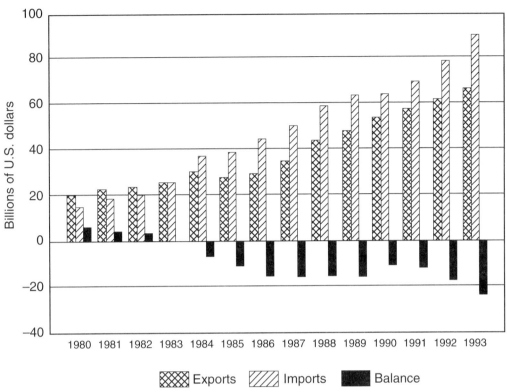

FIGURE 12.13 Deteriorating U.S. trade balance of all electronics and electronics-based products. [*Source:* United Nations, *Yearbook of International Trade Statistics,* various years (New York: United Nations).]

world trade to shrink to only one-third of its former size (see Figure 12.21). This swift deterioration in world commerce was one of the primary reasons for the severity of the Great Depression.

The parallels to that period raised troubling questions for policy makers of the 1980s: Could escalating protectionism once again reduce the world economy to a state as perilous as that of the 1930s? Why was the agitation for sheltering domestic industries against foreign competition surfacing again, what reasons were being given for new restrictions on imports, and what is theoretical and practical validity of these arguments? A more basic question that might be asked is why foreign competition should be the target of protectionism rather than domestic competition. No one questions the economic advantages of free trade among regions of a country, yet the benefits of foreign trade are exactly the same. When we examine this puzzling bias against foreigners, we find that the explanation apparently has to do with general feelings of nationalism, which lie within the realms of politics and social psychology rather than international economics.

This resurgence of protectionism followed a long postwar era of trade liberalization in which global commerce soar and brought unprecedented prosperity to much of the world. The first symptoms appeared in the wake of the OPEC crises, when steeply rising oil prices led to recessions in developed and developing countries alike. As international trade shrank, competition for markets intensified, imports threatened domestic industries, and a worldwide withdrawal into protectionism began. Adding urgency to the situation were rising budget and trade deficits in the United States, unaccustomedly high unemployment in Europe, and enormous foreign debts and stalled economic development among less-developed countries. The concern in all this was the danger that widespread limitations on imports might halt world growth, reduce the efficiency of the world economy, undermine political alliances, and drive a wedge between industrialized and developing countries.

As the contagion spread, industrialized countries began first to raise trade barriers to each other and then to target the less-developed countries (LDCs). Responding to a torrent of demand for protection, the President of the United States imposed 144 new quotas on textiles from 36 countries, most of them LDCs. In addition to textiles, the United States during the 1980s placed quotas on apparel and motorcycles and negotiated "orderly marketing agreements" (so-called voluntary export restraints, or VERs) with European countries on carbon steel and with Japan on automobiles and computer chips. All of this proved highly inflationary: According to most estimates, the limitation on

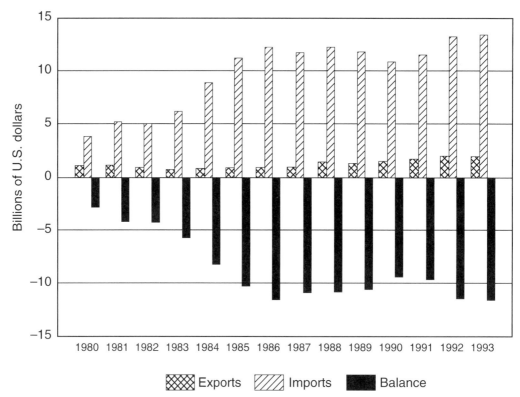

FIGURE 12.14 Deteriorating U.S. trade balance of consumer electronics. The overall balance has been negative since 1983, depressed by a huge deficit in consumer electronics and shortfalls in other key lines. [*Source:* United Nations, *Yearbook of International Trade Statistics,* various years (New York: United Nations).]

Japanese auto imports cost American consumers $15 billion in higher prices during the three-year life of the agreement. Protectionist sentiment in the United States against Japan intensified further, however, as trade deficits with that country mounted.

Japan itself is an inveterate practitioner of protectionism. It long shielded its own high-cost producers of beef, rice, and citrus fruit from much cheaper products from the United States and elsewhere, and it has traditionally limited imports of manufactured goods by means of rigorous inspections, intricate administrative regulations, and other subtle types of nontariff trade barriers. Joining the new protectionist wave of the 1980s, Japan erected new barriers to imports of textiles, apparel, footwear, and other products that threatened to flood the home market from low-cost producers in Korea and other newly industrializing lands. Japan also restricted imports of certain high-technology items in which the United States was most competitive— computer software, telecommunications gear, and communications satellites—arguing the need to develop its own industries. One prominent case was Japan's use of import protection to foster its computer memory chip industry. Sheltered by a 29 percent tariff on chip imports, Japanese chip manufacturers were able to monopolize their home market, thereby achieving important economies of scale. The resulting low unit costs allowed them to capture a

major share of the world market. Under U.S. pressure, Japan signed the 1986 Semiconductor Arrangement, which guaranteed U.S. companies a 20 percent share of the Japanese market. The lever that extracted the semiconductor agreement from Japan was Section 301 of the U.S. trade law, which authorizes retaliation against unfair trade practices. The Section 301 threat has since been used against Japan, notably in the 1995 dispute over the U.S.–Japan trade in autos and parts.

We should note, however, that much of the trade tension between the United States and Japan stems from a common failure to appreciate the inherent effects of the two countries' dissimilar resource endowments. Japan's history of mercantilism notwithstanding, studies have shown that the United States could not avoid a negative trade balance with Japan even if each country's trade were in equilibrium with the world. This can be explained by the triangular nature of Japan's world trade, which requires that this resource-poor nation earn a surplus in its manufacturing trade with industrialized countries in order to pay for essential imports of oil and raw materials from Third World countries.

In the post-OPEC era, Western Europe became more protectionist, too, pressed by high unemployment, sluggish economic growth, lagging technology, and the burden of costly social programs. Because their economies depend

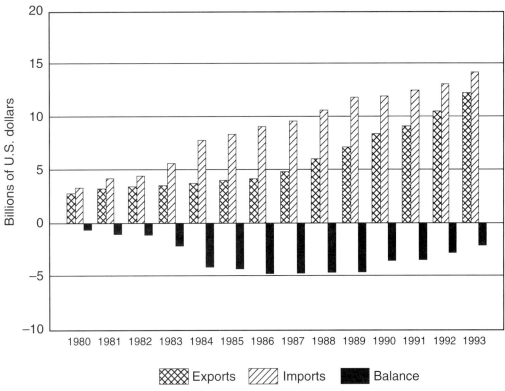

FIGURE 12.15 Deteriorating U.S. trade balance of telecommunications equipment and parts. [*Source:* United Nations, *Yearbook of International Trade Statistics,* various years (New York: United Nations).]

heavily on trade—exports generally account for a third or more of gross national product—these countries are exceedingly vulnerable to world market conditions. Yet they were losing their international competitiveness in a number of staple industries. Low-cost textiles from Taiwan, Singapore, and South Korea began to flood European markets in the 1970s, driving hundreds of domestic firms into bankruptcy. The textile industry as a whole was saved only by voluntary export restraints imposed on Asian producers by European governments. Then a tidal wave of auto imports from Japan reached European shores, seizing a quarter of the market in some countries. This resulted in still another voluntary export restraint.

The newly industrializing countries of the Third World have increasingly found themselves the targets of protectionism in the older developed lands. In their drive to industrialize, these countries often used subsidies and import barriers of their own, with the tacit acceptance of the developed countries. Once established, they began vigorously exporting their manufactures to pay off huge international debts. Benefiting from low-cost labor and the latest technology, these Third World exporters have made serious inroads in the domestic markets of the older developed countries with their cheaper steel, ships, textiles, and electronics.

Reacting sharply to this new and unexpectedly effective competition from the Third World, the Europeans, Americans, and Japanese reverted to limiting access to their markets. Indeed, the highest trade barriers to manufactured goods worldwide were those borne by labor-intensive manufactures—the mainstay of Third World exporters—and the class of products that incorporates one of their prime comparative advantages. Perhaps most onerous of all, because it affected so many of the poorest LDCs, was the Multi-Fibre Arrangement (MFA). This intricate system of bilateral quotas closely regulated the amount of textiles that each exporting country could sell to each importing country. Facing tighter restrictions on their new exports to the older industrial nations and badly needing revenue, LDC exporters then cultivated markets in other Third World nations.

Tariffs and quotas, even when euphemistically labeled "voluntary export restraints," were not the only trade barriers to gain popularity, and the rising mood of protectionism was not confined to the trade in merchandise. One device that continues to be favored for protecting domestic industry is the subsidy. Agriculture is the most widely subsidized sector of all, having escaped entirely the postwar drive for trade liberalization. The extensive worldwide practice of subsidizing agriculture, the most prominent example being the European Community's costly Common Agricultural Policy (CAP), has severely distorted world commodity markets.

Rivaling agriculture as a beneficiary of government subsidies throughout the world is the transport sector.

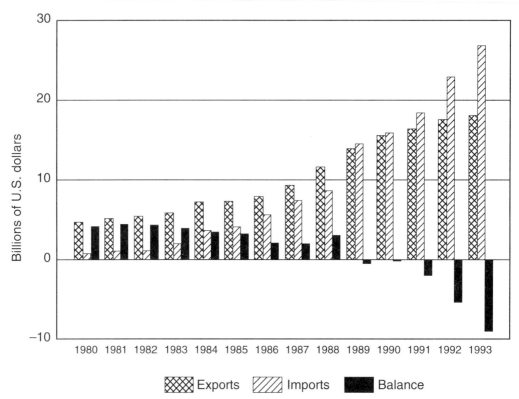

FIGURE 12.16   Deteriorating U.S. trade balance of computers and related equipment. The United States is quite competitive in computers, but most computer components and peripheral equipment are imported. [*Source:* United Nations, *Yearbook of International Trade Statistics,* various years (New York: United Nations).]

European governments, in particular, have heavily supported their aircraft manufacturers. The largest such outlays have gone to Airbus Industries, a consortium of major European aircraft makers who jointly design and build wide-bodied passenger jets in competition with U.S. producers. In addition, most European nations maintain their own national-flag airlines, as do many countries worldwide—even some of the poorest. It is common also for governments to provide financial support for their shipbuilding and maritime industries. With the aid of heavy subsidies, for example, Taiwan attained first rank during the 1980s in the constructing and operating of container ships, only to be eclipsed in the 1990s by mainland China's state-owned shipping industry.

Like agriculture, the services generally failed to participate in the postwar drive for trade liberalization. Today, the internationally traded services constitute one of the most vigorously growing sectors of world commerce. Consequently, they became the subject of growing national rivalry and a surge in protective measures. Many countries began sheltering from foreign competition such activities as banking, insurance, shipping, construction, aviation, travel industries, tourism, leisure pursuits, and real estate. Especially singled out for protection were information services, an enormous market because of national programs to modernize telecommunications systems. In an effort to stem this new wave of protectionism, the services were for the first time included in the Uruguay Round of GATT negotiations, which were successfully concluded in 1994 (see what follows).

How valid are the arguments that industrialists, labor leaders, and politicians use to justify protecting favored interests? One such argument is that domestic firms have a right to their home market and that excluding imports will create jobs and help the local economy. The error in this kind of thinking is that if we buy nothing from other countries, they have nothing with which to buy our products. This costs high-paying jobs in our exporting industries and forces consumers to pay higher prices to domestic firms with their assured monopolies. Economists point to a more efficient solution than import protection: subsidizing the retraining and relocation of workers who lose their jobs.

Perhaps the justification used more than any other is the infant industry argument. This was a favorite reason given for protection in the United States and Canada during their early industrialization. According to this rationale, a new industry has the potential for ultimately becoming viable in world markets, but it is vulnerable at the outset because of high start-up costs and operating inefficiencies during the initial phase. It thus cannot compete with estab-

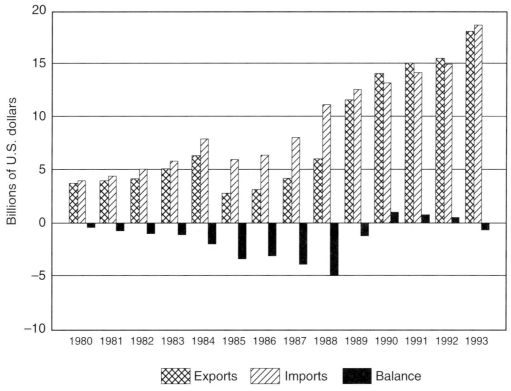

FIGURE 12.17   U.S. trade balance of semiconductors and components. [*Source:* United Nations, *Yearbook of International Trade Statistics,* various years (New York: United Nations).]

lished industries abroad that have already reached top efficiency and maximum economies of scale. As the argument goes, the industry will eventually become strong enough to compete in the world on its own and government protection can be discontinued. This argument has some validity if the industry is indeed in its start-up phase and if it truly has the potential to become self-sustaining so that government protection can be withdrawn within a reasonable time. However, the argument is acceptable only if the country is an LDC; it has no validity for advanced countries, For instance, when Japan advances the infant-industry argument for protecting its new computer industry, this excuse meets skepticism in other countries. Furthermore, the government must indeed lift its protection after the early stages have passed; the history of protectionism is filled with cases of industries that continue to be sheltered by their governments long after the infant has become hoary with age.

An argument heard throughout the industrialized world during hard times is that protecting domestic industries will reduce unemployment at home. Its proponents insist that jobs must be preserved regardless of the cost to the country's foreign trade. The problem is that this invites retaliation from one's trading partners, which ultimately costs jobs in otherwise prospering export industries. Thus, U.S. limitations on European steel imports induced Europeans to cut off lucrative U.S. farm sales to them.

Halting imports to preserve domestic employment means exporting unemployment to other countries and leads to an epidemic of retaliation like that which helped cause the Great Depression of the 1930s.

Moreover, protectionism does not solve structural unemployment, which results when a country loses its competitive advantage in a particular line of production. In the more advanced countries, many mature industries—textiles, garments, and steel, among others—can no longer compete on equal terms with newly industrializing countries that have cheaper labor and better access to high-grade raw materials. As postwar Britain learned, drawing on the public treasury to preserve such declining industries is like trying to fill a bottomless pit. Retraining displaced workers and aid to new industries are more logical uses of government funds.

The national security argument is one that is usually considered legitimate. As long as wars continue to be a means for settling international grievances, countries seem justified in preserving those industries engaged in making war materiel and other goods essential to national survival in times of conflict. This argument bears close scrutiny, however, as it is frequently abused. The main problem lies in the definition of just which articles are essential to national defense. Manufacturers of all kinds of nonmilitary goods—garments, shoes, foods, and so on—tend to claim

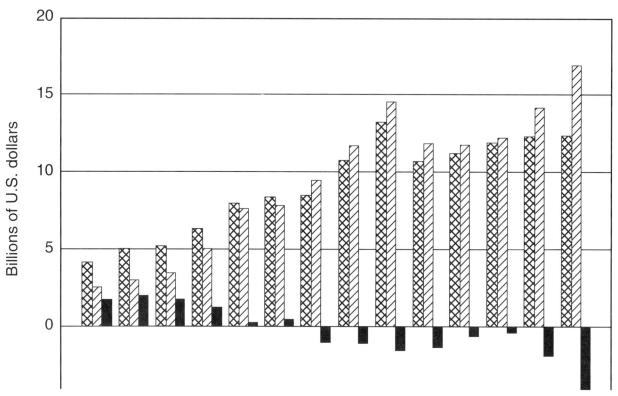

FIGURE 12.18 Deteriorating U.S. trade balance of office machines and equipment.
[*Source:* United Nations, *Yearbook of International Trade Statistics,* various years (New York:
United Nations).]

that their products should be declared essential to the national interest. High-tech manufactured goods have aroused much recent controversy on this account.

Antidumping duties are a retaliatory technique that is generally approved. "Dumping," a predatory practice common among developed countries, consists of selling a product abroad at a price below that received for the same article in the domestic market. Under international rules, dumping is illegal: If dumping can be proved, the injured company can justifiably demand that its government impose an antidumping duty on imports of the offending foreign merchandise. Basic metals manufacturers in the United States have obtained antidumping duties against European imports on such grounds. In theory, dumping is actually legitimate if the merchandise is consistently sold at cut-rate prices over an extended time as a form of permanent discounting operation. Dumping is wrong, however, if it is a short-run predatory practice intended to destroy domestic industries in the importing country so that monopoly prices can then be imposed by the foreign supplier. In practice, a problem with antidumping duties is that governments do not make such distinctions between legitimate and illegitimate dump-

ing and merely apply the duties in response to political pressures. A second problem is that precise means do not exist for measuring true costs and prices in the two countries and it is therefore difficult to determine whether and how much dumping is really taking place.

Protectionism by less-developed countries is a complex issue. Until recently, this has received few objections from theoreticians and governments. The infant-industry argument is considered valid for LDCs, and almost all of them rely on it. Most LDCs can also argue convincingly that they are entitled to some import protection because of deteriorating terms of trade with advanced countries; that is, because of imperfections in world markets, the prices of the goods they buy from industrialized countries rise more rapidly than do the commodities they customarily sell. LDCs therefore justify imposing import duties to raise revenues to help finance their own new industries. In practice, however, many LDCs have inflicted damaging distortions and inefficiencies on their own development programs by excessive and unwise use of import restrictions.

The validity of protectionism depends, therefore, on the grounds used for imposing it. A few of the more com-

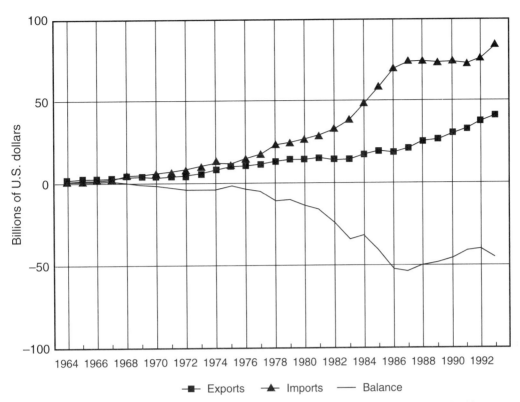

FIGURE 12.19   The U.S. balance of trade in road vehicles. The trade balance in road vehicles, especially passenger cars, turned negative in the 1970s and has been a worrisome aspect of the U.S. trade picture since. The deficit began to level off in the mid-1980s, however, as foreign auto companies began to produce increasing numbers of their vehicles within the United States. [*Source:* United Nations, *Yearbook of International Trade Statistics,* various years (New York: United Nations).]

mon arguments may be legitimate, but many are not. In practice, protective measures are subject to much abuse, and an uncontrolled proliferation of governmental interference would deprive the world of the fruits of trade. Protectionism can be very costly, too.

Some prominent cases of political intrusion have carried enormous price tags. Leading the list is protection for agriculture. It has been calculated that removing all restraints on farm commodities would boost world trade by at least $100 billion annually. The cost to European governments for subsidizing just one aircraft model, Airbus A300, was reckoned at $1.5 billion. Airbus Industries lost money on this model, but the competition it created in the global marketplace also reduced profits for rival Boeing Aircraft Company. The Semiconductor Arrangement between the United States and Japan nearly doubled the price of 256K computer chips and created a global shortage of chips.

It is impossible to measure all the hidden costs of protection, but they are nonetheless very real. Among these are

the lost benefits resulting from such restrictive devices as the Multi-Fibre Arrangement, which shifted world production away from the lowest-cost locations. Some types of clothing covered by this measure cost twice as much to produce in Europe or North America as in less-developed countries. Diverse national technical requirements for many products result in fragmented markets, depriving manufacturers of opportunities for scale economies. Restricting entry of foreign firms into national markets erodes competition, which decreases incentives for innovation and puts a damper on research and development. Moreover, the continued proliferation of complex protective measures has made world trade less predictable for manufacturers and has caused them to be more reluctant to venture abroad. The costs of protectionism, therefore, can be measured by slowed industrial growth, higher unemployment rates, and inflated prices for consumers.

The obverse side of this question of the costs of protection is also a compelling one: How much can be saved by

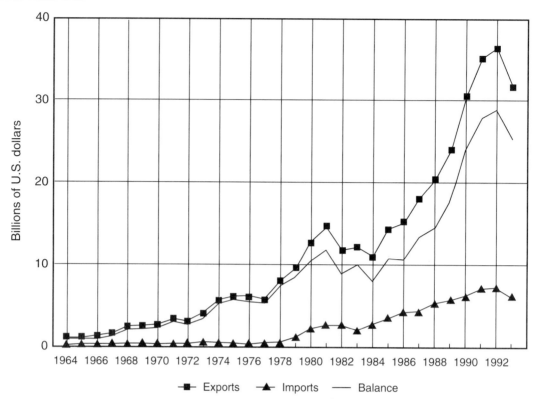

FIGURE 12.20 The U.S. balance of trade in aircraft. The U.S. aircraft industry has for many years held a dominant position in world markets for airliners and military craft. The dependably large trade surpluses in aircraft have helped to offset some of the deficit in road vehicles (Figure 12.19). [*Source:* United Nations, *Yearbook of International Trade Statistics,* various years (New York: United Nations).]

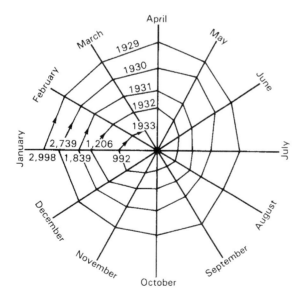

FIGURE 12.21 The contracting spiral of world trade, 1929-1933. Total imports of 75 countries (monthly values in old U.S. gold dollars, millions). [*Source:* Charles Kindleberger, *World in Recession* (Berkeley: University of California Press, 1973).]

eliminating protection? No one can be entirely sure, but by some conservative estimates, the annual gains from the recently successful Uruguay Round of GATT talks amount to $200 billion for the world at large. Perhaps the most valuable gain from these talks, however, was the changed world mood: The forces of protectionism have beaten a retreat, at least for now.

Theoretically, unrestricted trade creates an international division of labor that efficiently allocates the world's resources, thereby increasing total output and raising living standards living everywhere. Ideal conditions rarely exist in reality, of course: Perfect competition is not common, and the transfer of resources from one industry to another does not always take place smoothly or quickly. Yet the evidence shows that trade does bring growth and prosperity. Better forms of governmental intervention than trade restrictions are available to ensure fairness and prevent abuses of free trade by other countries. Political measures to protect local interests are clumsy at best; invariably, they produce unintended and unwanted effects and deprive the world of the benefits of specialization and trade.

GOVERNANCE OF THE EUROPEAN UNION

Executive Branch

The Council of Ministers.   The Council of Ministers is the principal decision-making body of the European Union (EU). Headquartered in Brussels, the council has one representative from each member state, usually its foreign minister. Major decisions require a unanimous vote; others, a simple majority. The presidency of the Council is a six-month position that rotates among member states.

The European Commission.   The Commission is responsible for day-to-day administration of EU affairs. From its headquarters in Brussels, the Commission is charged with ensuring that provisions of EU treaties are carried out. It also proposes policies and legislation to other EU branches, including the Council of Ministers. The Commission has two members from each of the larger member countries and one each from the smaller ones. However, the commissioners are supposed to represent the interests of the Union as a whole, not those of their own countries. Each commissioner is in charge of a particular subject area of Union activity, much like cabinet ministers in a national government. The Commission chooses its own president for a two-year term.

Legislative Branch

The European Parliament.   Members of the Parliament are directly elected by voters of the member states. Representation of each state is based roughly on its population. Members of Parliament do not sit and vote as national blocs but as members of Unionwide political parties. During the early years of the EC, the Parliament served mainly as a public forum for debating Community affairs, but the Maastricht Treaty conferred on it real legislative powers in certain specified areas. The Parliament usually meets in the French-Alsatian city of Strasbourg.

The Judiciary

The European Court of Justice.   The Court of Justice, which sits in Luxembourg, has fifteen judges, one from each member country. Judges are nominated by their national governments, and approved by the Council of Ministers, for a renewable six-year term. The Court is charged with interpreting EU treaties and other Union legislation and decisions.

Other EU Institutions

The Economic and Social Committee (ESC).   The ESC is an consultative organization that advises the Commission and the Council on policies relating to economic and social matters—such as labor, agriculture, and consumer and environmental affairs—and helps to draft legislation. The ESC operates at the EU's Brussels headquarters.

The European Council.   The European Council, is composed of the heads of state of member countries, together with the president of the Commission. This body is not an integral part of the EU organizational structure but exists to provide an avenue of communication and understanding among government leaders. The group meets at least twice each year in various cities to discuss current issues affecting the European Union.

The European Political Cooperation (EPC) Process.   Another body that exists outside the formal EU structure is the European Political Cooperation process. The EPC process was established under the European Single Act as a means for coordinating foreign policies of member countries.

Europe without Borders

The new campaign to complete Europe's economic unification by the 1990s was driven by a series of crises, just as the original dream in the 1950s of a "Europe without borders" had been a response to the economic chaos left by a devastating war. By the 1980s, economic stagnation and high unemployment had replaced the buoyant growth that had brought prosperity and higher living standards to Western Europe during the early Common Market years. Threatened with further decline in the face of mounting competition from Japan and the United States, Europeans had begun to lose faith in the European Community.

The Single Europe Act

Concerned for its future, the EC embarked on a series of bold steps to accelerate removal of the remaining obstacles to a single market for workers, goods, services, and money. Lending force to this decision were the tempting commercial opportunities offered by the liberation of Eastern Europe from Communism. Also, the European Commission's own studies had found that achieving a single market of 340 million people would boost economic growth and create jobs. Given these incentives, the 12 EC members signed the Single Europe Act (SEA) of 1986, a far-reaching program to create "an area without internal frontiers" by the end of 1992.

The Europe 1992 Program was a three-stage approach to achieving full economic union. It called for establishing an EC central banking system, a single European currency, and supranational economic policy making. To accomplish this posed an immense task: (1) eliminating thousands of intricate, often invisible barriers to trade among member countries; (2) removing restrictions on capital flows; (3) bringing uniformity to tax structures; (4) ensuring freedom for workers to practice their professions and trades in all parts of the union; and (5) abolishing national preferences for government purchasing and replacing these with Communitywide open bidding.

This vision of a single Europe immediately seized the popular imagination and was the main topic of seminars and commentary throughout the territory. Business leaders were overwhelmingly in favor of these proposals and they responded with a flurry of investment in plant and equipment, expanded R&D budgets, and a rash of mergers and alliances among European firms. This activity was prompted not just by the prospect of a vast Communitywide market for their goods. For many, the driving force was fear of exposure to powerful competition not only from other European-based companies, but especially from Japanese and U.S. multinationals drawn by the opportunities presented by *Europe 1992.*

The remaining members of EFTA, fearful of being overwhelmed by a newly powerful neighbor, negotiated with the EC for creation of a "single economic space" that would include all 19 nations. In October 1991, therefore, the two groups agreed to form a *European Economic Area (EEA).* Under the terms of this agreement, people, goods, services, capital, and information were permitted to circulate freely among all the member states of both groups. In addition, some EFTA members applied for EC membership, as did certain of the newly liberated East European states. One of the latter, East Germany, had already been absorbed into the EC through unification with West Germany. Three others were granted associate membership in December, 1991.

The Maastricht Accord

As the target date of December 31, 1992, approached, the EC faced crucial decisions. Most important, major amendments to the EC's constitution, the 1957 Treaty of Rome, would be required to accommodate the fundamental changes planned for the organization. Meeting in the Netherland's town of Maastricht in December 1991, therefore, the 12 nations forged an agreement to replace the EC

with a new entity called the *European Union,* which added a European Monetary Union with its own currency and a political union with elements of a future European government.

The Maastricht Accord had three main components. A key feature was the *Economic and Monetary Union (EMU),* which would provide Europe with a common currency and a central bank before the end of the century. The new *European Currency Unit (ECU)* would replace an existing ECU (valued at about $1.28, this had previously been used only for settling national accounts). The new *European Central Bank,* which would function much as the U.S. Federal Reserve Bank, would begin minting ECUs for general distribution by 1997.

The second element of the accord provided for a common foreign policy, with rules designed to encourage foreign ministers to agree on major external issues and pursue uniform policies abroad. The third part of the agreement would set up a *Western European Union,* intended to function as the organization's defense arm in coordination with the existing North Atlantic Treaty Organization (NATO).

Of special significance, too, were several other features of the pact: common citizenship throughout the European Union; increased powers for the Parliament; an assortment of "social laws" (labor regulations, consumer protection, health, education, international crime control); development of trans-European networks (telecommunications, transport, energy projects); and special assistance to the Union's poorer member countries.

In early 1992, when EC heads of state formally signed the Maastricht Agreement, the outcome seemed inevitable. All that remained was ratification by the various EC parliaments and voter approval in a few national referendums. As it turned out, EC leaders had miscalculated the mood of the European public as distinct from that of the business community: In the midst of the most severe economic recession since the 1930s, millions of Europeans were out of work, and many were unhappy with out-of-touch politicians, who had failed to inform them of how the union was to work. Meanwhile, worsening conditions forced devaluation of several national currencies and wrecked the exchange rate mechanism that had linked them together. Results of national referendums were disappointing, and EC leaders had to make compromises and extend their timetable. In the end, however, they had the satisfaction of seeing the year 1993 begin with achievement, at last, of a single internal market for goods and labor throughout the union. A subdued celebration replaced the gloom.

The EU's Assets and Problems

Yet, the newly constituted European Union still had to work through many complex problems before it could hope to realize its ultimate goal: an "ever closer union among the peoples of Europe." One of the most difficult of these problems is a lingering nationalism in some places, especially France, but also Britain, both of which cling to a belief in the preeminence of the nation-state. There are also divisions between those who believe firmly in free trade and open markets—Germany, the United Kingdom, Denmark, and the Netherlands—and those—such as France and Spain—who do not trust markets they cannot control.. These divisions are deeply rooted in a politically and culturally fragmented continent, where peoples have been separated from each other since earliest times by mutually unintelligible languages. This contrasts with the United States—the model for their political and economic union—where a much larger territory is linked together by common language and traditions. Based on their differing circumstances and interests, the current members of the EU constitute four major constituencies:

- Germany and France—together with the Low Countries (Belgium and the Netherlands)—make up the first constituency. As front-line adversaries in World War II, their first concern since the days of the ECSC has been to ensure continued peace and stability.
- The United Kingdom and Denmark, both admitted to Common Market in 1973, are the second constituency. Their overriding interest in the EU has been to avoid being excluded from the huge European market and to promote the extension of free trade generally.
- The third group consists of four poorer member countries: Ireland (admitted to the EC in 1973 with Britain), Greece (admitted in 1981), and Spain and Portugal (admitted 1986). As a group, the "poor four" have half the average per capita GNP of the EU as a whole, and two (Portugal and Greece) have per capita GNPs that are less than a third of the EU average. These countries look on EU membership as a means for modernizing their economies. An additional incentive for Greece, Spain, and Portugal—all recently released from dictatorial control—is the financial help it gives in preserving their fragile democracies: Richer members of the union have recently become less willing to contribute this aid, which represents a major item in the EU budget.
- The fourth constituency is made up of the new members that joined the EU at the beginning of 1995: Austria, Finland, and Sweden—all previously EFTA countries. Economically, all three countries are already closely linked to the EU. Despite their small populations (only 5.9 percent of the EU total), they contribute more than 7 percent of the gross national product. The arrival of

these countries, with their differing interests, further reduces the unity of purpose and outlook that characterized the original EEC of only six members.

Given these basic differences among its 15 members, it is not surprising that the group has been unable to agree on a common foreign policy, as provided under the Maastricht Treaty. This became most painfully obvious in the failure of the European Union to find a peaceful solution to the savage revolution in Bosnia. Union finances are another sticking point. A major source of contention has been the Common Agricultural Policy (CAP), which provides very large subsidies to Union farmers. Not only does this absorb half of the organization's annual budget, but it has resulted in producing huge crop surpluses and creating much friction with the EU's trading partners, especially the United States. The decision-making process has been much complicated by the growth in membership, which has shifted the balance of power among the major constituencies and increased the difficulty of reaching consensus on important issues.

Despite these nagging problems, the European Union has already accomplished a great deal and it has a number of clear assets that inspire applications for membership and attract new investment A major appeal is market size: By 1995, the expanded EU had 15 full members, whose 370 million citizens created a combined $7 trillion of gross national product annually (1991), compared with a total U.S. output of $5.7 trillion. Another attraction of the EU is the quality of its labor force, which is well educated, offers valuable engineering skills, and has expertise in advanced technologies (though it needs modernizing).

One result has been a steady growth in EU membership and a lengthening queue of countries aspiring to join. Besides the former EFTA countries recently admitted, the EU has reached "European Agreements" with six former Soviet-bloc countries—Bulgaria, the Czech Republic, Hungary, Poland, Romania, and Slovakia. Viewed as a step toward the ultimate goal of full EU membership, these agreements provide for free trade in industrial goods.

Confirmation of the EU's appeal is also seen in a steady influx of foreign investment. Non-European multinationals have been some of the best business users of the new single market, including a wide range of large U.S. and Japanese industrial and service enterprises. Britain has been the greatest beneficiary of this investment, mostly because of greater familiarity with the English language (this is true even of Japanese companies). Responding to this flow of foreign investment, many European firms have merged with each other in order to increase their competitiveness. Notwithstanding all the contention among EU members and the delays in implementing the Maastricht Accord, therefore, the European Union appears to have achieved an unstoppable momentum.

Timetable for the Future

The next important date on the European calendar is January 1, 1998, when European Union markets are at last to be fully opened. Among many other things, this will, for example, remove the last barriers to entry of independent telecommunications firms into now-protected national markets. Still to be determined, however, is the date on which the planned European Monetary Union (EMU) will be completed. Under the Maastricht Treaty, this was to occur some time between 1997 and 1999. Already in place, the European Monetary Institute (EMI), which is to become the European Union's central bank, is charged with issuing the union's common currency, the ECU. Although a common currency would produce enormous savings in cross-border financial transactions, the political and practical difficulties of achieving this are truly daunting.

Meanwhile, to sort out this and other remaining problems, under a provision of the Maastricht Treaty, the member states are to hold an intergovernmental conference in 1996 to review progress thus far and to plot a strategy for resolving remaining issues. This promises to be a lively meeting, for it must take up questions of EU governance, especially the problems of decision making in a growing organization; Union budgetary matters; and the pace at which EU goals can be realistically pursued. Most fundamental of all, perhaps, is the question of whether or not an organization that is acquiring so many new members with widely differing circumstances and viewpoints can actually achieve the kind of "ever-closer union" contemplated in 1957 by the architects of the Treaty of Rome.

Though most observers feel that the European Union is destined to become a much looser organization than originally planned, it seems likely that the founding fathers would have taken considerable satisfaction in the outcome to date. Not only has integration brought a level of prosperity to Europe that could hardly have been dreamed of in the aftermath of the World War II, it has transformed former dictatorships into stable democracies and it has converted long-time enemies into close allies.

APPENDIX 12.5

Integrating North America

Western Europe's progress with integrating its national economies has helped push the countries of North America toward increased regional economic cooperation. The European experience has influenced North American integration in both positive and negative ways: On the one hand, the economic gains enjoyed by Europeans because of the Common Market have demonstrated the benefits of reducing economic barriers between neighboring countries. At the same time, the emergence of a European economic powerhouse has driven North Americans to erect defenses against this perceived competitive threat in world markets. Shortly after the birth of the EEC, the North American response came in the form of the Canadian–US. Automotive Agreement of 1965, a sectoral type of integration. More recently, a strengthened European Union, with enlarged membership, has replaced the EEC, spurring Canada and the United States to accelerate their own integration efforts and subsequently to admit Mexico to the group.

The U.S.–Canada Free Trade Agreement (FTA or CFTA)

Even as the Single Europe Act of 1986 came into effect, Canada and the United States had begun negotiating a new free-trade agreement destined to bring major changes to commercial relations between the two. The Free Trade Agreement of 1989, North America's first full-scale, multi-sector integration organization, further reinforced economic ties between the two. Even before the FTA, commercial relations between Canada and the United States had been exceptionally close, as measured by the very large bilateral flows of goods and services and by unusually high levels of direct investment in one another's economies.

Implementation of the FTA was to be accomplished speedily: All elements of the pact were to be completed by 1998—within only 10 years after its inception. As a precaution, the agreement provided a 5-year phasing-in period, during which Canadian and U.S. companies could appeal trade rulings to a bilateral panel. It also offered a process by which particular industries might petition for accelerated reduction of duties. In a burst of industry enthusiasm for the pact, the parties agreed to extend reductions to a further 1,000 items, $9 billion worth, not originally contemplated.

The scope of the FTA's coverage was unusually broad, including reductions not only of tariffs, but also a wide range of nontariff barriers. Among the main provisions were these: (1) scheduled removal of all tariffs by 1998, some immediately, others over a 5- or 10-year period; (2) virtually unrestricted access for each country's services—a matter of prime importance for two countries with very large service sectors; (3) preservation and further liberalization of the Auto Pact, while restricting its benefits to North American producers; (4) elimination of agricultural export subsidies and gradual removal of bilateral tariffs and quotas on farm products, plus standardization of health and safety standards; (5) increased access to government procurement for both Canadian and U.S. companies; (6) reduction of barriers to Canadian and U.S. investors in the two countries; (7) streamlined border-crossing procedures for qualified business and professional personnel; and (8) creation of joint panels to resolve trade disputes and review trade legislation.

The effects of the FTA on the Canadian and U.S. economies were immediate and substantial. One of the first results was a sweeping economic restructuring of affected industries, especially within Canada, where small firms had long predominated. The FTA also led to cross-border consolidations of companies, enabling a single productive facility to serve the entire combined U.S.–Canadian market. Even prior to FTA, the two countries had been each other's best trading partners, as evidenced by the 4,000 trucks daily crossing the border at Buffalo's Peace Bridge. As U.S.–Canadian trade barriers dropped, the bilateral flow of goods and services swelled, reinforcing the economic interdependence between the two. In 1988, two-thirds of Canada's total foreign trade had been with the United States; five years later this proportion had soared to more than three-fourths of the total.

Though most government and business leaders in the two countries had enthusiastically supported this lowering of economic barriers between Canada and the United States, the Free Trade Agreement met considerable opposition from the Canadian public. A recession began in Canada just as the FTA was going into effect, and unemployment levels rose to an uncomfortable 11 percent. Further job losses resulted from corporate mergers precipitated by the pact, as well as from the loss of tariff protection for such long-sheltered Canadian industries as textiles. Many in the Canadian public felt that increased dependence on U.S. trade would lead to a "less gentle Canadian economy" forced by competition with low-cost US firms less burdened with supporting social programs of the kind cherished by Canadians. Further diminishing public support for increased trade with the United States were the numerous minor trade disputes between the two countries, reported widely in the Canadian press but largely unnoticed by the U.S. public. Many of these disputes have to do with Canadian opposition to "cultural" imports from the United States, notably television programming, magazines, and books. Canada receives 78 percent of its television programming from the United States, and three-fifths of its book publishing is U.S.-owned. Subsidies on Canadian forest-products and agricultural-commodities industries have also aroused contention in the United States.

The North American Free Trade Agreement (NAFTA)

Despite such public opposition, however, in time, the economic benefits of freer trade came to outweigh the perceived negative effects, particularly when Canada began a strong recovery from its recession. Encouraged by the results of the FTA, Canadian and U.S. government leaders determined to expand this experiment in regional trade lib-

eralization by bringing Mexico into the group. In 1992, therefore, negotiators reached agreement on a pact that would create a three-nation free-trade area for all of North America.

By the end of 1993, the North American Free Trade Agreement had been ratified by all three countries, and on January 1, 1994, the enlarged free-trade area came into effect. In the United States, the ratification process had provoked considerable opposition from nationalists, labor unions, and some consumer and environmental groups, who objected to closer economic links with Mexico, whose legal protections they considered inadequate. To assure passage in the U.S. Congress, negotiators for the three countries added to the pact various side agreements relating to these issues.

In broad outline, NAFTA was based on the U.S.–Canada Free Trade Agreement of 1989, but incorporated additional provisions relating to Mexico's entry into the group. The agreement is very wide in scope, covering not only physical goods, but also services, telecommunications, investment, intellectual property, and a variety of other mutual concerns. Some of the major provisions include the following:

- *Tariffs.* Within 10 years, tariffs are to be phased out on 99 percent of the goods traded among the members (pre-NAFTA tariffs on Mexican imports averaged 10 percent; those of the United States averaged 4 percent). Quotas were lifted on textiles and apparel that meet requirements for North American (i.e., Canadian, Mexican, U.S.) content. Excepted from this 10-year phase-in period are certain "sensitive" agricultural goods.

- *Agricultural provisions.* Within 15 years, all tariff and nontariff barriers are to be ended on agricultural commodities. Some of these had been very strict (e.g., on Mexican beans and corn). For the present, special protection was retained for Canadian poultry and dairy farmers.

- *Automobiles.* NAFTA increased the North American content requirement, which had been 50 percent under the U.S.–Canada Free Trade Agreement, to 62.5 percent for cars and light trucks and 60 percent for parts alone. The 2.5 percent U.S. tariff on Mexican autos was lifted immediately. Mexico eliminated its quota on new cars, reduced the tariff on cars to 10 percent, and agreed to phase this out entirely over 10 years.

- *Foreign direct investment.* Although Canada and Mexico retained their rights to screen in-coming FDI from the United States, procedures were to be streamlined. Mexico lifted its foreign-investment limits on most petrochemicals production, but retained its historic restrictions on investment in primary petroleum, a monopoly of its state-owned oil company, Pemex.

- *Maquiladoras.* Mexico agrees to phase out its *maquiladora* program, under which products have been assembled in U.S.–owned Mexican factories from U.S. components with the understanding that these are to be reexported to the United States. Henceforth, the products of such factories were to have unrestricted access to the Mexican market as well.

- *Intellectual property.* Mexico agreed to strengthen its protection for trademarks, patents, and copyrights, including those on computer programs. Canada and the United States already provided such protection.

- *Services.* NAFTA eliminated restrictions on financial services, telecommunications, and transportation.

- *Side agreements.* To mollify critics, further negotiations during 1993 produced a side agreement to set up a commission made up of the labor ministers of the three countries to assure adherence to fair labor standards. It was further agreed that fines or trade sanctions could be levied against any NAFTA member if an international body should find that it had broken its own labor, environment, and human-rights laws.

- *Conflict resolution.* NAFTA adopted, with improvements, the dispute-settlement procedure contained in the U.S.–Canada Free Trade Agreement.

It should be noted that, contrary to the claims of NAFTA's critics, these provisions called for far greater changes in Mexican practices than in those of the other two countries. In addition, Mexico agreed to substantially greater cuts in its import restrictions: U.S. barriers to imports from Mexico were already low, and more than half of these entered duty-free prior to NAFTA, by contrast with the much higher levels of protection previously maintained by Mexico.

The Impact of North American Integration

The results of the two trade pacts, first FTA and later NAFTA, were actually felt well before the dates on which the agreements formally went into effect. Companies began positioning themselves for defense against increased competition and to take maximum advantage of new opportunities. Larger firms began "thinking North American." There was a rush to set up offices in Monterrey, Guadalajara, Toronto, Chicago, in anticipation of a new North American

market. European and Japanese multinationals increased their North American capacities to avail themselves of falling trade barriers. The quickening pace of cross-border commerce began knitting together the economies of Canada, the United States, and Mexico.

The trend toward North American production really began with the U.S.–Canada Free Trade Agreement of 1989. Companies began making specialized products and certain high-technology items in Canada and producing big-volume items in the United States. NAFTA further extended this trend, as firms conducted their more labor-intensive operations in Mexico. By thus concentrating the manufacture of certain products in one location, companies were able to generate the economies of scale that gave them world-class competitive power. National companies of all three member countries adopted this North American strategy.

Though the Canadian people had been ambivalent toward integration, the positive effects on Canadian trade appeared immediately after the start of the FTA in 1989. Exports to the United States in product areas liberalized by the FTA had surged 33 percent by 1992; exports of those same goods increased only 2 percent to the rest of the world during that time. By 1995, one year into NAFTA, the economic benefits of integration to Canada had accelerating rapidly. U.S.–Canadian trade had risen by 50 percent since the 1988 signing of FTA, and the addition of new trade with Mexico contributed further to Canada's soaring exports. All of this brought much-needed job growth, and Canadian unemployment fell to a new low. By providing Canadian companies with new economies of scale, FTA, and now, NAFTA, boosted its worldwide competitiveness. The resulting export surge made Canada the fastest-growing of the seven leading industrial countries. By most measures, Canada was the chief winner of NAFTA.

As a result of FTA and NAFTA, foreign investment—from both U.S. and non-North American sources—poured into Canada. The advantages for firms producing in Canada for North American and world markets are (1) lower costs because of a cheap Canadian dollar, (2) the high productivity of a loyal, well-educated work force (engineering and technical labor cost 30 percent less than in the United States), and now, of course, (3) access to the world's largest market.

North American integration caused an industrial revival and relocation in Canada. With the free-trade pact of 1989, Canadian business began converging on Toronto, which is the closest point to New York and Ohio. In addition to access to the U.S. Midwest, Toronto offers economies of scale and a full range of financial and business services. All along the U.S.–Canada border, freer trade has thus created a series of north–south axes linking Ontario with New York and the Midwest, Vancouver with the U.S. Pacific west coast, the Atlantic provinces with New England, and the Prairie provinces with Minneapolis and

Chicago. To the extent that this new north–south orientation replaces Canada's traditional 4,000-mile east–west axis, it tends to exacerbate the country's troublesome regional disparities.

The United States, too, experienced an immediate impact from the 1989 FTA. U.S. exports to Canada soared as Canadian firms bought sophisticated machinery and equipment to upgrade factories and make them more competitive. In more than half the product categories where tariffs were cut, U.S. exports to Canada more than doubled between 1987 and 1991. Especially did the FTA improve access to the Canadian market for smaller U.S. exporters. Free trade had the effect, too, of whetting Canadian appetites for U.S.-made consumer goods. With the coming of NAFTA, U.S. trade with Canada rose by more than 10 percent in the first year, double the gains with Europe and Asia.

One notable effect of freer trade has been an outpouring of Canadian investment southward, into Washington State, Minnesota, New York State, and New England especially. Since 1989, the total value of Canadian direct investment in the United States has closely matched that of U.S. investment in Canada. Canadian investment has altered U.S. locational patterns, just as U.S. investment has affected Canada's. One beneficiary has been the Buffalo border area, which has attracted numerous Canadian concerns. Being only two hours distant from Toronto, the Buffalo metropolitan area is being drawn into Ontario's Golden Horseshoe, an industrial belt that extends from Oshawa through Toronto and Hamilton to Niagara Falls.

During NAFTA's first year, U.S. exports to Mexico grew three times faster than U.S. exports to the rest of the world. As a result, Mexico passed Japan to become the second-largest consumer of U.S. products (after Canada). The chief industry gainers were U.S. exporters of food and beverages, other consumer goods, agricultural commodities, motor vehicles, industrial machinery, chemicals, and semiconductors. Even US exports of textiles and apparel surged, contrary to NAFTA opponents who had forecast doom for producers of such products. Another surprise effect of NAFTA was an influx of Mexican direct investment in the United States, as big Mexican companies rushed to become multinational in anticipation of falling trade barriers. Prominent among these were the large cement manufacturer, Cemex, which bought out U.S. companies in Texas and California, and Vitro, Mexico's largest glass manufacturer, which bought one of the leading U.S. glass makers.

NAFTA has spawned a grand cross-border business alliance between cities astride the main transport routes connecting Texas and Mexico. In addition to the existing border twin cities (El Paso and Ciudad Juarez, Laredo and Nuevo Laredo), new axes have formed, such as Houston–Chihuahua, and Dallas–San Antonio–Monterrey. Texas has been the main beneficiary among the states. Mexican conglomerates are building plants in Texas, as are

a number of European and Asian businesses that are aiming to serve the whole continent from that border location.

Traditionally, Mexico had a closed economy, as was typical of Latin America until very recently. It was inward-looking, protectionist, and with many big state-owned industries, especially utilities, steel, and oil. Because Mexico was closed to auto imports, the Big Three U.S. auto companies maintained factories there, as did a few Japanese and German companies. In producing for the limited Mexican market, they were hampered by short model runs, though they did export some finished vehicles to the United States. In addition, they produced parts and components in their many *maquiladora* border factories for reexport to the United States. Nevertheless, the growing Mexican middle class was accumulating a big pent-up demand for all kinds of imported consumer goods.

The mid-1980s saw a major shift in Mexican economic policy. Mexico joined GATT in 1986, slashed its prohibitively high tariffs, opened the domestic market to a wide range of imports, and privatized dozens of state-owned companies (though not the big state oil company, Pemex). The auto decree of 1989 opened the domestic market to imported cars. Mexico's consumer-goods imports soared.

The big change came in 1991, however, in anticipation of Mexico's entry into NAFTA. U.S. companies began shifting their labor-intensive manufacturing from China and other East Asian countries to Mexico, much of this going to *maquiladora* border factories. The shift enabled these firms to save the 30-day trans-Pacific transit time, solve technical problems more quickly and easily, and provide faster customer service. It also offered a hedge against potential political instability in East Asia, especially in China. There was also a rush of retailing and fast-foods companies aiming to serve the Mexican middle class. In addition, many Asian businesses—such as makers of sporting equipment, toys, and apparel—invested in Mexican production in the expectation of serving the entire North American market. Altogether, Mexico drew in more than $50 billion of foreign direct investment during the six years leading up to NAFTA.

NAFTA's opening year did not see the increased direct investment in Mexico that had been expected, mainly because of political uncertainty in an election year. Most of 1994's new investment, 55 percent of the total, came from Canada and the United States. Japanese investment did rise in that first year, however, reaching the highest level in a decade. Yet, the total amount of new enterprise pouring into the country was very great in total, and this produced important changes in the locational pattern of Mexican industry.

One significant development during this period was the emergence of a Mexican "Silicon Valley" around Guadalajara. A special attraction of this location was the availability of computer-software engineers as proficient as those in the United States but at only half the cost. At the same time, Mexico was acquiring an "Auto Alley" in Hermosillo, Aguascalientes, Puebla, Chihuahua, Mexico City, Monterrey, and several other centers. Ford, General Motors, Chrysler, Volkswagen, Nissan, and Renault assembled autos and trucks in these places both for the domestic market and for export to the United States, other Latin American countries, and Europe. In the aftermath of NAFTA, another concentration of auto assembly and parts plants appeared in a band extending from Mexico City to Monterrey, centering on Saltillo.

A prime locational advantages for these enterprises, in addition to the 1,900-mile border with the United States, was the availability of a large pool of low-cost, highly productive labor. Though most lacked an industrial tradition, Mexican autoworkers proved to be motivated, adaptable, and zealous to deliver high-quality work. After thorough training, these Mexican employees have shown themselves adept at working in small teams. Nevertheless, Mexico poses problems for foreign enterprises. One of these is the low quality of the infrastructure: bad roads, a woeful rail network, and poor telecommunications. Another is the corrupt officialdom, including the judiciary. A third problem is the unsatisfactory nature of the established business culture, reflecting long-time control by influential families and cliques who take an authoritarian approach to management.

Despite the grand promise of NAFTA, which was generally expected to lift Mexico into the First World of industrialized countries, 1994 ended with Mexico plunged into severe financial crisis. The precipitating cause is considered to have been bad monetary policy on the part of the Mexican central bank in an election year. To assure victory for the ruling political party, the bank kept interest rates artificially low, encouraging excessive domestic consumption and draining the national reserves of U.S. dollars. When the reserves were exhausted, this forced devaluation of the Mexican peso, which was badly handled. Adding to the state of crisis was political uncertainty resulting from an Indian revolt in Chiapas State and a pair of political assassinations. The value of the Mexican peso dropped precipitously, plunging the country into recession, inflation, and stringent austerity. The ensuing financial panic quickly led foreign investors to sell their Mexican stocks and bonds, which further drained the country's financial system.

Currency crises are not new to Mexico, which has frequently experienced these economic disruptions in election years; but on those earlier occasions, the damaging effects were largely confined to Mexico itself. The December 1994 crisis, however, created worldwide repercussions, in part because Mexico's economic policies had appeared to offer a model for all. The result, therefore, was a loss of confidence by portfolio (stock and bond) investors in developing countries everywhere, regardless of their circumstances. This put the currencies and banking systems of such countries under pressure because of the threat that investors might pull out of their markets.

The United States, too, felt a much greater impact than usual from the Mexican crisis. Since the mid-1980s, Mexico had become the second-largest market for U.S. exports, and by 1994, 770,000 U.S. jobs had come to depend on these Mexican sales. One-third of these Mexican-dependent jobs were in Texas, so that state was affected more than any other part of the country. The plunge in the Mexican peso is estimated to have cost Texas $2.5 billion in 1995 alone, much of this loss being felt by the border towns. Given the grave danger of widespread economic collapse throughout the developing world—and the potential blow to the U.S. economy and the prospect of a mass migration of impoverished Mexicans across the country's southern border—the United States was forced to mount an international rescue package to restore international confidence in Mexico.

Serious as the Mexican crisis was, most observers regarded it as a temporary delay in the process of North American integration. And, indeed, within a few months the peso had stabilized and Mexico's trade balance was once again restored. Though earlier opponents of NAFTA were quick to claim that the agreement had been a mistake, it seems clear that, by locking in Mexico's past economic reforms, NAFTA has helped to ensure that Mexico will not return to the inward-looking statist programs that had so depressed its economy during the 1980s.

Another reason why NAFTA's success is significant is that it may provide a means for extending free trade throughout the entire Western Hemisphere. After years of isolation behind steep protective barriers, most Latin American countries have recently shifted to more outward-looking free-market policies. In this new environment, sentiment has grown to mold together all the hemisphere's existing integration organizations into a single Free Trade Area of the Americas. Mexico's acceptance into NAFTA is viewed as a first step in this direction.

APPENDIX 12.6

Latin American Integration

Since the late 1950s, Latin Americans have been experimenting with regional economic integration as a means for promoting economic growth and development. This long interval falls into two main eras, separated by a decided shift in national policies. The earlier era, marked by the creation of UN-sponsored regional blocs, was a time of inward-looking development policies and national plans. These policies, with their emphasis on government-run, import-competing industries, achieved little; individual national markets were just too small to supply the necessary economies of scale for any but the most rudimentary industries. Latin American nations seized on integration as a way to tap larger markets for their exports, but their cooperative ventures failed to achieve the hoped-for results largely because of national rivalries, an inability to agree on the allocation of large-scale industrial projects among members, and national disparities in size and level of development. Moreover, several countries were in the grip of inept ironclad military dictatorships. The low point came during the so-called "lost decade" of the 1980s, when Latin America was bowed under a grinding burden of $400 billion in debt, even as East Asia's Little Tigers raced ahead with their development.

The end of that decade, however, saw a remarkable about-face in Latin America's political and economic outlook. A wave of democratization swept through the region, and a new generation of leaders, many educated in the United States, assumed control of businesses and government ministries. In several forward-looking countries, ideological and nationalistic attitudes came to be replaced by more rational economic reasoning and greater pragmatism. The emergence of an outward-looking, free-market environment yielded important economic reforms, especially the privatization of inefficient state-owned enterprises, deregulation of commerce, and lowering of import barriers. The result has been a renewal of economic growth without inflation. Continued economic progress, however, requires increased exports, which can come only through improved access to rich foreign markets, hence, the recent moves toward hemispherewide free trade.

The Central American Common Market (CACM)

Nowhere has the need for greater market access been more crucial than in the lands that lie between Mexico and South America. This middle region is made up of many small countries with big problems: low incomes, excessive dependence on agriculture, limited domestic markets, and lack of capital. No wonder, then, that this region has seized on economic integration as a remedy. One of the most ambitious of integration schemes, therefore, was that attempted by the Central American Common Market.

The five members of the CACM—Costa Rica, El Salvador, Guatemala, Honduras, and Nicaragua—began their experiment with a unique advantage: a history of unification throughout the long period of Spanish colonial rule and for some years thereafter. These small mountainous countries have a combined territory and population about equal to California, and an average per capita GDP of only $975. Before the CACM was established in 1961, the five were among the world's most specialized exporters of tropical agricultural commodities, and their populations were growing faster than their economies. More than two-thirds of their work force was engaged in subsistence activities.

CACM represented one of the highest levels of economic integration ever attempted in the less-developed world. Although basically a common market, it also had a supranational organizational structure, including a develop-

ment bank and a tripartite governance arrangement. From the outset, the stated goal of the group was full economic union.

During its first years, CACM made remarkable progress. By 1966, it had essentially achieved the status of a working common market, with a free flow of goods and capital among its members. Exports had become substantially more diversified. Fifteen percent of foreign shipments went to other members of the bloc, and most of this intra-CACM trade consisted of manufactures. Domestic and foreign investment within the union soared, and the growth rate of gross national product exceeded that of population growth.

All of this came to an end in 1969, when hostilities broke out between neighboring Honduras and El Salvador, severing CACM transport and communications links. From that point, CACM ceased to exist as a normally functioning organization. Even prior to this brief war, however, friction had arisen because of the perception that the benefits of industrialization were being unfairly shared among members. Then, bitter revolutions broke out in both El Salvador and Nicaragua, and by 1986, intraregional trade had fallen to its lowest level in 10 years. Thus, a promising LDC experiment in integration had faltered on the familiar grounds of politics and nationalism.

The early 1990s, however, brought the resolution of Central America's gravest political problems. With the end of the Nicaraguan and Salvadorian revolutions, the prospects for restoring intraregional trade rose. In June 1990, therefore, the five CACM presidents signed an accord calling for a revival of CACM by 1994.

Latin American Integration Association (LAIA)

A second regional bloc formed under ECLA auspices was the Latin American Free Trade Association (LAFTA), which came into effect in 1960. LAFTA's membership included most of South America (Argentina, Bolivia, Brazil, Chile, Colombia, Ecuador, Paraguay, Peru, Uruguay, and Venezuela) and Mexico, a combined territory twice the size of the United States and a present-day population of more than 400 million people.

Despite the pressing trade problems of its members, LAFTA generated little intrabloc trade. One major barrier was the great distance separating the main economic centers, which typically concentrate in coastal enclaves around the continental margins. Then, too, Latin American countries tended to produce similar goods—a result of like resource endowments, historic economic isolation from each other, and divergent national economic and social policies. Consequently, they competed with each other in Northern Hemisphere markets. LAFTA did little to increase intrabloc trade because it failed to commit its members to significant tariff concessions within the group.

Perhaps the most difficult impediment to cooperation, however, was the great disparity among members in physical and economic size and in level of development. With an average per capita GDP of $2,785 (1992), the 11 countries are better off than most LDCs, but an enormous gulf separates the richer from the poorer members. Thus, Bolivian incomes are currently only one-tenth those of Argentineans, and Bolivia's national economy is only one-eighty-fifth as large as Brazil's. When LAFTA went out of existence in 1981, only one-tenth of the group's trade was with other LAFTA members, and half of that was between adjacent Argentina and Brazil. Replacing the stagnating LAFTA, the Latin American Integration Association (LAIA) retained the same membership but offered an even less ambitious program, becoming an "area of economic preferences" instead of a free-trade area. Nevertheless, intrabloc trade has since grown markedly, rising to 19 percent of all exports and 17 percent of imports by 1993.

Mercado Común del Sur (Mercosur)

Accounting for most of this intra-LAIA trade growth, however, was the sharp rise in trade between Argentina and Brazil, which had meanwhile formed a bilateral common market. In 1988, these two large neighbors had agreed on a list of products immediately eligible for tariff exemption and subsequently signed accords setting a date for removing all trade barriers, to coordinate economic policies (including a common trading currency), and to build a pipeline to transport Argentine gas to Brazil. Trade between the two quickly doubled. Then, in 1991, the pact was expanded to include nearby Uruguay and Paraguay and was given the name Mercosur ("southern market"). Chile and Bolivia have also sought membership.

Although theoretically Mercosur was to become a full customs union in 1995, with a common external tariff wall and free trade among members, a large number of exceptions remained on items such as sugar, autos, computers, and capital goods. Nevertheless, it is reckoned to be a great success. Between 1989 and 1993, intrabloc exports rose from only 8.2 percent to 18.5 percent and imports from 15.1 to 19.7. Foreign direct investment also soared, as large multinational corporations were attracted to this market of more than 200 million people with a combined gross national product of nearly $650 billion. Auto manufacturers, in particular, began shifting their strategies to take advantage of growing cross-border trade opportunities within Mercosur.

The Andean Common Market (Ancom)

Fearful of becoming mere economic satellites of the big Latin American nations, six countries along South America's Pacific margin set up in 1969 a separate organization called the Andean Common Market (Ancom or Andean Bloc). The five current members are Bolivia, Colombia, Ecuador, Peru, and Venezuela (Chile dropped out in 1976). Although retaining their individual memberships in LAFTA (later LAIA), they aimed for a higher degree of integration as a way of developing a modern industrial economy on a regional scale. Patterning itself after the European Common Market, Ancom assumed many characteristics of an economic union: In addition to coordinating national policies for trade, transportation, communications, energy, and agriculture, Ancom allocated among its members all investments requiring economies of scale and it closely regulated the activities of multinationals.

Its policies tended to stifle investment, however, and Ancom therefore reinvented itself in 1987. Once protectionist and statist in its approach, the group shifted to a policy favoring open markets, with salutary results. The proportion of trade among members has since risen, and trade between neighboring Colombia and Venezuela has boomed.

The Caribbean Community (Caricom)

Still another organization formed under the aegis of ECLA was Caricom, which brought together 11 English-speaking island nations in the West Indies, and the mainland countries of Belize and Guyana. Despite the many problems confronting this widely scattered group, Caricom members in 1989 agreed to establish a regional capital market, leading to a unified exchange rate, and to renew their drive to create a common market. Caricom, however, has been unable to agree on a common external tariff

Toward a Hemispheric Free-Trade Area

Latin Americans are aware of the limited possibilities for further growth within their present regional integration organizations and of the need to tap more affluent markets in the hemisphere. Thus, it was with the greatest interest that they observed another Latin American nation, Mexico, being incorporated within the newly created free-trade area in North America. Consequently, at a December 1994 meeting of a "Summit of the Americas," in Miami, the leaders of the hemisphere's democracies readily agreed to a goal for a Free Trade Association of the Americas (FTAA) by the year 2005. The easiest path toward that end would be through further expansion of the existing North American Free Trade Agreement.

The incentives for expanding free trade to encompass the entire region have been clear to hemispheric leaders. The 34-nation FTAA would offer a market of 450 million people, a tempting prospect for Latin American countries, whose traditional inward-looking economic policies have in the past limited their sales to small, highly protected domestic markets. Having abandoned these outmoded policies, Latin America has now become the fastest-growing world region after Southeast Asia—and the most rapidly expanding market of all for U.S. exports. If current trends continue, the United States will be selling more goods and services to Latin America by the year 2010 than to all of Europe and Japan combined.

The main push for hemispheric free trade has come from the Latin American leadership, however. A new generation of upper- and middle-class Latin Americans has been educated at U.S. universities (whereas earlier generations went to France, Spain, and Portugal for their educations). Meanwhile, the number of Latin American tourist and business visitors to the United States doubled within five years. Not only do the present policy makers of Latin America speak English, they have embraced a philosophy of free trade between free markets.

It seemed likely that Chile would be the first South American nation to test this notion of a hemispheric free-trade agreement. Formal negotiations for Chile's entry into NAFTA began in May 1995, with a target date of January 1997 for official membership to start. As the strongest, most stable economy in Latin America, Chile would be the easiest of all Latin American countries for NAFTA to digest. Unlike, Mexico, Chile is small, only 14 million people; its democracy is firmly established; and it is 10 years ahead of the rest of Latin America in its market reforms. Indeed, because of continuous rapid growth over more than a decade, with low inflation and mere 5 percent unemployment, Chile has been described as an Asian Tiger attached to the wrong continent.

Chile's entry into NAFTA would be important as a precedent: the first step toward creation of a Free Trade Association of the Americas. Proponents of such a region-wide trade bloc maintain that releasing the Western Hemisphere from its many debilitating barriers to trade and investment would enhance economic efficiency, thereby leading to faster growth and greater stability throughout the region.

VOCABULARY

ad valorem duty

Andean Common Market (Ancom)

Asia Pacific Economic Cooperation Forum (APEC)

backward nations

balance of trade

barriers to trade

bilateral trade agreement

Bogor declaration

Caribbean Economic Community (Caricom)

Central European Free-Trade Agreement (CEFTA)

colonial preference agreement

common market

Communaute Economique de I'Africa de l'Ouest (CEAO)

consumption effect

customs accession

customs union

demonstration effect

developing countries

distance

domestic goods

dual economy

Economic Commission for Latin America (ECLA)

Economic Community of West African States (ECOWAS)

economic union

European Free Trade Association (EFTA)

European Monetary System (EMS)

exchange controls

free-trade area

Free Trade Area of the Americas (FTAA)

friction-free capitalism

full economic integration

General Agreement on Tariffs and Trade (GATT)

import substitution

income-redistribution effect

infant industry

innovation

integration theory

intellectual property

International Bank for Reconstruction and Development (IBRD)

International Monetary Fund (IMF)

International Trade Organization (ITO)

invention

invisible trade

Latin American Free Trade Association (LAFTA)

least-developed countries (LDCs)

Lomé convention

Maastricht Treaty

maquiladora program

most-favored-nation rule

national sovereignty

nationalism

orderly market agreements

primary producers

product-life-cycle theory

protection effect

protocol of Budapest

regional economic integration

semi-industrialized countries (SICs)

South Asian Association for Regional Cooperation (SAARC)

specific duty

state trading

tariff factories

technology gap

terms of trade

theory of economic integration

three-legged corporate strategy

Transatlantic Free Trade Agreement (TFTA)

United Nations Conference on Trade and Development (UNCTAD)

Uruguay Round

visible trade

voluntary export restraint (VER)

World Trade Organization (WTO)

Zollverein

TOPICS FOR DISCUSSION

1. Discuss two fundamental ways in which economic growth occurs. As economies grow and develop, how does their level of trade participation change and what shifts take place in the composition of that trade? Why do policy makers in some contemporary less-developed countries (LDCs) question the applicability of conventional trade theory to their own conditions? What special problems do LDCs have in their trading relations with industrialized countries? How may multinational enterprises affect the factor endowments of LDCs?

2. Examine the alternative trade strategies available to developing countries and explain the differing results that have followed the pursuit of such policies in Latin America and East Asia.

3. Explain why high-technology trade is so essential to the United States. Discuss the international competitiveness of the principal categories of high-tech industries and their contributions to the U.S. trade balance. Assess the future prospects for the country's technology-intensive activities.

4. Compare and contrast the effects of tariffs and quotas on the production, consumption, and trade of both the exporting and importing countries. Who benefits and who loses?

5. What are the different ways in which distance affects trade? What happens to the classical two-country, two-commodity trade model when transport cost is introduced into the equation? How are the two participating countries affected?

6. Assume that two countries produce the same two commodities but have different factor endowments. If they enter into trade with each other, how would we expect this exchange to affect both the supply of their factors of production and the prices of these factors? How may factor movements between two countries substitute for trade, and how would such factor movements affect the prices of those factors?

7. How does the theory of regional economic integration relate to conventional trade theory? What organizational types of economic integration have been identified and to what extent are these ideal types represented among the integrated groups now in existence. What are the theoretically ideal characteristics that a group of countries needs to possess if successful integration is to occur?

8. Assess the effects that Western Europe's postwar integration experiments have had on intrabloc trade and on trade with the world at large. In what ways has integration influenced the location of production in Western Europe? What changes in European trade and location might we anticipate if the European Union succeeds in its plans for deeper and broader integration? How may the entry of former Communist states of Eastern Europe affect the EU?

9. Weigh the arguments that were advanced for and against creation of the North American Free Trade Area, and examine the problems that have arisen during the early phase of its operation. Weigh the prospects for NAFTA's ultimate success.

10. Discuss the tensions that have arisen between the forces for regionalization and the forces for globalization, as these are involved in the current trends toward formation of continental trading blocs and toward fashioning of trading regime presided over by the World Trade Organization. Compare and contrast the protectionist tendencies of the 1990s with those of the 1930s.

FURTHER READINGS

Balassa, Bela (1961).*The Theory of Economic Integration.* Homewood, IL: Richard D. Irwin.

Introduces a system for classifying the organizational forms used by various groups of countries in their experiments with economic integration, and develops a comprehensive theory of integration within the general framework of modern international trade theory.

——— (1979). The Changing Pattern of Comparative Advantage in Manufactured Goods. *Review of Economics and Statistics* (May):259–266.

Provides an analysis of the changing comparative advantage in 184 classes of manufactured goods for 36 countries. The author found that differences in commodity structure resulted from differences in physical and human capital endowments.

Bergsten, C. Fred, and William R. Cline (1987). *The United States–Japan Economic Problem,* rev. ed. Washington, DC: Institute for International Economics.

Relying on quantitative analyses of U.S.–Japanese trade, Bergsten and Cline assess the impacts of the barriers erected against each other by the two countries. They find that much of the debate on trade imbalances misses several key points, notably the contrasting fundamental structures of the Japanese and U.S. economies. The authors are, respectively, director and senior fellow of an influential Washington group devoted to the study of international trade issues facing the United States.

Dunning, John H. (1995). What's Wrong—and Right—with Trade Theory? *The International Trade Journal* (Summer):163–202.

Contends that international economics has not kept pace with changes in the world economic environment, which has been greatly affected by globalization. Notes that sales of foreign subsidiaries of multinationals now exceed the value of all trade, and suggests changes that are required to improve the explanatory powers of existing theory.

Dunning, John H. (Ed.) (1985). *Multinational Enterprises, Economic Structure and International Competitiveness.* New York: John Wiley.

Considers the extent to which multinational enterprises contribute to the process of restructuring now taking place in the world economy. Twelve authors pursue this question with respect to four different categories of home and host countries. They find that the impact of multinationals varies substantially from country to country and depends to a large extent on the character of particular national economies and the public policies pursued in each.

Hanson, Roger D. (1967). *Central America: Regional Integration and Economic Development.* Studies in Development Progress, No. 1. Washington, DC: National Planning Association.

A theoretical and empirical analysis of the experiments in economic integration conducted by five Central American countries.

Krause, Lawrence B., and Sueo Sekiouchi, (eds.) (1980). *Economic Interaction in the Pacific Basin.* Washington, DC: The Brookings Institution.

Investigates the transmission of economic impulses among six representative countries within the Pacific basin, noting particularly the effects on those countries of the economic upheavals of the 1970s and their responses to these.

Krugman, Paul A. (1989). Economic Integration in Europe: Some Conceptual Issues. In Alexis Jacquemin and André Sapir, Eds., *The European Internal Market—Trade and Competition* Oxford: Oxford University Press.

Reviews the theoretical effects of international economic integration and examines the policy implications for the European Union. In addition to the well-known effects that can be explained in terms of Ricardo's comparative advantage theory, Krugman notes that integration also produces other important effects, notably those arising from scale economies, that require a different kind of explanation.

——— (1991). Myths and Realities of U.S. Competitiveness. *Science* (November): 811–815.

Shows that the term "competitiveness" has a very different meaning for countries than it does for companies. Whereas an uncompetitive company may be forced out of business, strong automatic forces ensure that a country that lags in its productivity can continue to benefit from trade. However, the types of goods it produces will be adversely affected.

Linder, Staffan Burenstam (1967). *Trade and Trade Policy for Development.* New York: Praeger.

Analyzes the special trade problems of less-developed countries, explores the linkages between the theories of international trade and economic development, discusses the changes that take place in a country's trade as it grows and develops, and considers the options available to policymakers in addressing the problems of LDCs.

——— (1986).*The Pacific Century: Economic and Political Consequences of Asian-Pacific Dynamism.* Stanford: Stanford University Press.

Traces the rapid transformation taking place in the Pacific Rim and explores the economic implications this holds for the Asian-Pacific countries themselves, for other developing countries, for the established industrial countries of Europe and North America, and for the centrally planned economies.

Examines within a theoretical framework the flows of foreign direct investment into the United States, giving special attention to the differing investment patterns of

European, Canadian, and Japanese subsidiaries at national, regional, and subregional scales.

Porter, Michael E. (1990).*The Competitive Advantage of Nations.* New York: The Free Press.

Building on some of the ideas advanced in his earlier best-selling works, *Competitive Strategy* (1980) and *Competitive Advantage* (1985), Porter identifies the fundamental determinants of national competitive advantage in an industry and the manner in which these function as a system. He emphasizes the influence that a company's home-country environment exerts over its competitive success in the world arena.

Russett Bruce M. (1967).*International Regions and the International System: A Study in Political Ecology.* Skokie, IL: Rand McNally.

Uses factor analysis to group countries according to the strength of their relationships to each other in each of several forms of international interaction. Finds that the world's nations fall into nine regional groups on the basis of their trade linkages.

Samuelson, Paul A. (1949). International Factor-Price Equalization Once Again. *Economic Journal* June.

Definitive statement of the factor-price equalization theorem.

Viner, Jacob (1950). *The Customs Union Issue.* New York: Carnegie Endowment for International Peace.

A classic work on the theory of economic integration.

Glossary

Absolute advantage: Characteristic of a country or a firm where it can produce, with a given amount of labor, a larger quantity of a product than any competitor.

Absolute cost barriers: High initial costs that discourage entry of new firms into an industry.

Absolute nuclear family: A type of family organization (father, mother, children) that socializes children to individualized values. One result of this has been a preference for utilitarian concepts of individual rights and liberties.

Accelerating growth: Increasing rates of population growth.

Accessibility: Proximity and ease of access to economic centers.

Accessibility rent: Land rent paid for accessibility to markets.

Ad valorem duty: A tax equal to a given percentage of the value of a good.

Adaption: *See* economic adaption.

Administered prices: Prices determined by a small group of firms or an outside agency rather than by market forces.

Administrative functions: Responsibility for the execution of basic rules and for the organization of the technical activities needed for their efficient execution.

Adoption: *See* economic adoption.

Advanced factors of production: Infrastructure endowments created by culture and technology, including educated personnel, research-and-development capabilities, and advanced digital communications.

Advanced services sector: Knowledge and information industries.

Afforestation: Creating forest areas on land not previously forested.

African family systems: A type of family organization characterized by the absence of stable interpersonal relationships, except between mother and children, and by polygyny (men

having multiple wives and sexual partners). Vertical (patrimonial) power relationships are limited, weakening socialization to the concept of authority, and undermining the idea of discipline.

Age distribution: Age structure of a population broken down into five-year intervals (0–4, 5–9, etc.). By disaggregating population age categories, the proportions of children, working age, and elderly people can be estimated.

Age–sex structure: The composition of a population stratified by age and sex.

Age–specific death rate: Share of deaths in each age group (computed in 5-year intervals except for ages 0–4, which are annual totals). Deaths for each age, per 1,000 population of that age.

Agglomeration: Concentration of firms or populations in one location.

Agricultural revolution: A development in England in the late eighteenth century in which farmers began to breed higher-quality livestock, to introduce new high-yielding crops, and to develop farm techniques that resulted in large increases in agricultural output.

AIN: Advanced Intelligence Network.

Alloying: Mixing different metals or metals with nonmetal products.

American system of manufactures: Early mass-production system that began in the late 1840s in the hand-gun industry using interchangeable parts, mechanical and press production.

Andean Common Market (Ancom):   A regional subgroup of the Latin American Free Trade Association.

Animal husbandry: Production and care of livestock.

Animal stocks: Supply of livestock available for productive use.

Animate energy: Use of draft animals or humans as a source of power.

Anomic family: A family form characterized by uncertainty about equality between brothers, inheritance rules that are egalitarian in theory but flexible in practice, and where cohabitation of married children with their parents is rejected in theory but accepted in practice. Marriage between relatives is also practiced.

Antitrust legislation: Legislation implemented to break up large firms and lessen the concentration of power within industries.

Arable land: Land that can be used to grow crops.

Aridity: Insufficient rainfall to grow crops.

Arithmetic density: A measure that relates the total number of people to total land area.

Arpanet: Advanced Research Projects Agency Network in the U.S. Department of Defense. The precursor to the Internet.

Artesian systems: Water available under pressure from underground sources.

Asia–Pacific Economic Cooperation Forum (APEC):   An organization created in 1989 with 11 Pacific Rim nations plus the United States and Canada. By 1995, membership had grown to more than 20 members. The initial purpose—to speed up economic liberalization in the Pacific Basin—has been expanded to a vision of free trade throughout the Pacific region.

Association of Southeast Asian Nations (ASEAN):   Group of seven Southeast Asian countries comprising Brunei, Indonesia, Malaysia, the Philippines, Singapore, Thailand, and Vietnam.

Asymmetrical community family: A type of family system that is dominated by the caste system. Essential family features are equality between brothers defined by inheritance rules and cohabitation of married sons with their parents.

Atmospheric pollution: Air pollution.

Autarchy: Independent national economy.

Authoritarian family: A type of family organization characterized by inequality of brothers laid down by inheritance rules, with transfer of an unbroken patrimony to one of the sons.

Authoritarian political economies: Nation-states where power is highly concentrated and diversity of opinion is not tolerated.

Autocracy: A system of government in which power is vested in one person.

Average cost: Total costs divided by total units of output.

Average product: Total output divided by one of the inputs.

Average value of output: Value per unit of output.

Axial principle: According to Daniel Bell, the defining characteristic of a phase of growth. For example, theoretical knowledge is the axial principle underlying contemporary postindustrial growth.

Baby boom: Generation born following World War II, from 1947 to 1965.

Back office accounts: Business functions that do not require direct customer or client contact.

Backward linkages: Integration of production firms with their supply sources.

Backward nations: Impoverished nations facing obstacles to development that make it unlikely that they will join the industrialized world.

Balance of payments: Difference between payments for imports and payment for exports in a given period. A positive balance occurs when the value of exports exceeds the value of imports.

Balance of trade: Difference between total value of exports and total value of imports in a given period.

Balanced power political system: A political system in which power is divided among branches of government.

Balanced regional growth: Equitable or equal distribution of economic activities across a number of areas.

Bandwagon effect: Effect in which momentum of a new innovation or trend increases and adoption of it expands rapidly.

Barriers to entry: Factors limiting entry of new firms into an industry.

Barriers to trade: Obstacles that influence the volume, direction, and composition of trade flows. Barriers to trade are of two types: distance barriers and political interference. Distance barriers are distance and lack of accessibility between countries that increase the transport costs and affect commercial relations between countries. Political interference consists of actions of governments that distort world commerce.

Barter: To trade by exchanging one commodity or service for another.

Basic factors of production: Population numbers and natural resource endowments and their interrelationships.

Basing-point pricing: A form of noncompetitive pricing in which consumers pay a price set at a given place, the basing point, plus a transportation charge from that location—even if the good is produced and shipped from a nearer and lower-cost site.

Basing-point system: A system that restrains competition by establishing an industrywide system of delivered prices, which are increased by transport costs from specified basing points.

Basket-case countries: Less-developed countries that are least equipped to develop, lacking resources and facing a Malthusian crisis.

Benelux Union: An organization for economic integration formed by Belgium, Luxembourg and the Netherlands in 1948. It was subsequently absorbed into the European Union.

Bid rent: Concept in land-use theor: the amount offered to occupy and use a parcel of land.

Bilateral trade agreement: Trade agreement between two countries that calls for reciprocal concessions.

Biotic resource: Living resources such as plants and animals.

Birth rate: The number of births in a given year per 1,000 population (midyear).

Bogor declaration: Declaration signed by members of APEC in 1994 in Bogor, Indonesia, committing to free trade.

Bond market: The institution that permits bonds to be traded.

Break-of-bulk point: A transportation center where goods and produce are transferred from one type of transport to another, for example, from rail to water.

Bretton Woods agreement: International agreement signed at a United Nations conference in 1944 in Bretton Woods, New Hampshire. The initial purpose of the conference was to address the problems of protectionism that preceded World War II. The

Bretton Woods agreement established the International Bank for Reconstruction and Development, the International Monetary Fund, and the International Trade Organization.

British parcels: Quantities of wheat traded in the Liverpool market before World War II.

Buddhism: Eastern religion that emphasizes the importance of asceticism, piety, discipline, self-reliance, learning, and meditation. It has taken different forms in different regions of Asia.

Bulletin boards: Sites on the Internet where information can be posted and accessed by users.

Business cycles: Periods of economic expansion and contraction, lasting from 7 to 12 years.

By-product: A secondary product produced either intentionally or unintentionally as part of the industrial process.

Canada–U.S. Free Trade Agreement (CFTA):   Trade agreement between the United States and Canada enacted in 1989 that lifted tariffs and trade barriers between the two countries.

Capital: "Capital" has several meanings. Real or physical capital consists of buildings, equipment, and other concrete instruments of production. Financial capital refers to financial assets available for investment. Social capital includes educational facilities, transport and communications, and other forms of support for productive activities.

Capital-intensive: Production in which capital comprises a larger share of inputs than labor. This is characteristic of industrialized economies.

Capital outflow: Flow of currency out of a country.

Capital requirements: Financial, equipment, and physical plant requirements of firms and industries.

Capital resources: Amount, type, and cost of capital available to finance industry.

Capital values: The value of an asset and its earnings calculated at current interest rates.

Capital worth: Capital values.

Capitalization: Translation of the value of an asset and future earnings into a present value.

Caribbean Economic Community (Caricom):   Regional trade bloc consisting of Caribbean countries.

Carrying capacity: Population that can be supported by the land and resources of an area, at a given level of technology.

Cash markets: Spot markets where currently available supplies of currency are traded on a daily basis.

Caste: The separation of groups within Hindu societies into levels based on heredity. The underlying belief is that people are born into positions in which they must remain throughout their lives. The only way out is through reincarnation, provided that people behave in ways exemplary of their given status in the present life.

Ceiling price: *See* maximum ceiling price.

Central European countries: Austria, Czech Republic, Hungary, Slovakia, Slovenia, and so on.

Central European Free-Trade Agreement (CEFTA):   An organization formed in 1992 by former communist countries of the Czech Republic, Hungary, Poland, and Slovakia to promote free trade among them.

Central market: A common meeting place for buyers and sellers where price levels for agricultural commodities and industrial raw materials are determined.

Central market price: Price derived from the intersection of supply and demand in a central market.

Central place theory: Theory that seeks to explain the size and spacing of urban centers and the configuration of their market areas.

Centralization: Concentration of power in a central organization.

Centrified state: A type of social and political system that is neither centralized nor hierarchical, weakly structured, and relies on a sense of communitarianism for cohesion.

Chaebol: Large Korean industrial conglomerates.

Chat lines: Internet discussion groups similar to conference calls.

Chayanov's rule: Rule that applies to household subsistence economies where production was designed to meet household needs. The rule states that the greater the productivity, the less the hours worked.

Cheap labor: Low-wage, low-skilled work force.

Chemical agriculture: The application of chemical fertilizers to agriculture to increase yields.

Child dependency ratio: Proportion of the population under the age of 15.

Churning: Combination of high entry and exit rates of small firms in an industry.

Circular and cumulative causation: Technological progress that results in a self-propelling spiral of growth, enhanced productivity, and increasing returns.

City-forming activity: Sectoral activity, such as manufacturing, that provides the city with an economic base. Contrast with city-serving activity.

City-serving activity: Service sector activity that provides for the needs of urban residents.

Civilization: The highest cultural grouping of people and the broadest level of cultural identity people have short of that which distinguishes people from other species.

Civilization consciousness: The awareness of similarities within civilizations and differences among civilizations.

Civilization identity: Personal or national identification with one of the eight major civilizations, which are Western, Confucian, Japanese, Islamic, Hindu, Slavic-Orthodox, Latin American/Catholic, and African.

Clan: Descendants of a common ancestor who identify as a group and act to enhance members' interests.

Clash of civilizations: A prediction by Samuel P. Huntington that in the future the great divisions among humankind will be dominated by cultural conflict. The principal conflicts will occur between the groups of nations that constitute different civilizations.

Classical entrepreneurs: Individual businessmen who innovate and compete to assure the profitability and growth of their enterprises.

Classical trade theory: A body of trade theory, the proponents of which included Adam Smith, David Ricardo, and John Stuart Mill, which developed in reaction to mercantilism. Classical trade theory developed the labor theory of value and the principles of absolute and comparative advantage to explain the gains from trade.

Coal: Fossil fuel created in the earth from plant matter.

Coalition governments: Governing bodies made up of representatives of disparate political groups.

Collaboratories: Virtual experimental communities in which scientists and engineers use information networks to cooperate on projects in different locations.

Collective goods: Public goods that, if provided for one, others cannot be prevented from consuming as well. Collective goods are paid for with tax revenues. Examples of collective goods are parks, highways, and defense.

Collective unconscious: The invisible part of cultural heritage that consists of the values that are continually transferred from generation to generation through early life experiences in family and schools and through socialization in organizations and institutions.

Collectivism: A cultural trait in which groups and group loyalty are valued. Collectivist cultures tend to limit individual freedom. Contrast with individualism.

Colonial preference agreement: Trade agreement in which a mother country and its colonies grant each other special concessions.

Combined supply curve: The aggregate of supply curves for individual firms.

Comecon: East Bloc Communist trade organization.

Command economy: An economy that is regulated by a government agency or group rather than by market forces.

Commercialization: The transition from subsistence production to production for profit.

Commodity exchanges: Central markets for raw materials.

Common market: Form of economic integration that allows for free trade among members, common restrictions on trade with nonmembers and unrestricted movement of labor, capital, and entrepreneurship within the union.

Communauté Economique de l'Africa de l'Ouest (CEAO): A six-member organization of former French colonies promoting trade.

Communications costs: The costs of transmitting images and information.

Communications services: Services involving the transmission of information.

Communist bloc: Countries formerly controlled by Communist parties, dominated by the USSR and China.

Communist economies: Economies in which the government controls productive activities and redistributes the proceeds according to a plan for social equity.

Comparative advantage theory: *See* principle of comparative advantage.

Competence: According to Rosabeth Kanter, an asset of cosmopolitan executives: the ability to operate at the highest standards anywhere in the world.

Competitive advantage: The ability to produce a specific item more efficiently than others. Competitive advantage is shaped by (1) factor conditions, (2) demand conditions, (3) the nature of related and supporting industries, and (4) firm strategy, structure, and rivalry. Compare with absolute advantage.

Competitive firm: A price taker in an industry with many small firms.

Competitive model: Industrial organization in which firms are concerned about their shares of multiple markets.

Competitiveness: Business conditions necessary to attract mobile capital and to produce at low cost. These include infrastructure, deregulated markets, skilled and educated labor, and financial stability.

Concepts: According to Rosabeth Kanter, an asset of cosmopolitan executives: the best knowledge and ideas.

Condition of entry: Scale of production required to exceed threshold size when long run cost curves are "Lazy-J".

Confucianism: An ethical system that values education, hard work, obedience, and self-discipline and stresses the obligations of the individual in a structured society. Confucianism is a fundamental source of motivation and discipline among East Asians.

Congealed knowledge: Information-based products created by the thoughtware economy that, unlike manufacturing products, display increasing returns.

Congealed resources: Products of traditional manufacturing processes that combine resources to create physical products that face diminishing returns.

Conglomerate mergers: Joining together of large firms that have no obvious complementarities other than those of financial and tax manipulation.

Connectedness: According to Rosabeth Kanter, an asset of cosmopolitan executives: relationships that provide access to resources of other people throughout the world.

Consensus system of decision making: A type of decision making characterized by lengthy discussions and trade-offs among all members of a group. Final decisions are not made until complete agreement is reached. This type of decision making is common in Asian societies.

Conservation: Careful management and use of resources to assure continuing availability in the longer run.

Consumer: Individual or group that purchases and utilizes final goods and services.

Consumption effect: One of the effects of a tariff, a reduction in consumption of the protected good in the protectionist country.

Consumption expenditures: Aggregate consumer spending on final goods and services.

Contract rent: Agreed upon payment for use of physical assets.

Controlled prices: Prices that are restricted by being set at a level that differs from the market equilibrium level.

Core identities: The body of customs, traditions, values, myths, symbols, and ideologies that characterizes a culture.

Core–periphery: An economic and spatial relationship between regions and countries where those on the outside export raw materials to industrialized regions at the center. Core regions are self-sustaining whereas peripheral areas are dependent on the core.

Cosmopolitan: According to Rosabeth Kanter, a business executive who is able to identify with the company as a global entity.

Cosmopolitanism: Global sophistication.

Cost, insurance and freight (CIF): A method of pricing where delivery costs are included in the price of a good. Contrast with Free on board (FOB).

Cost-minimizing firms: Small, price-taking firms in competitive markets that can only maximize profits by minimizing production and transportation costs.

Countercyclical measures: Government measures (either fiscal or monetary) to stabilize the economy that work in an opposite direction to business cycles.

Countervail: Counteract.

Craft entrepreneur: Type of entrepreneur who establishes a small business close to home and who is motivated by the satisfaction derived from autonomy and quality workmanship. Craft entrepreneurs generally receive lower returns on their investment than would be acceptable to a large firm.

Craft production: Mode of production prevalent prior to mass production in which outputs were produced one at a time.

Crisis area: Term used by environmentalists and demographers to denote a region experiencing pressure of population on resources, and the likely onset of positive Malthusian checks to population growth.

Critical countries: Countries lacking sufficient arable land at present levels of technology to feed populations projected for them for the year 2000.

Critical isodapane: Isodapane along which the additional transportation costs are equal to the savings in labor costs.

Crop rotation: Changing crops on a seasonal or annual basis to maintain the productivity of farmland.

Cropland per person: Total agricultural area divided by the population.

Crow rate: Subsidized prices for grain transport from the prairie provinces of Canada.

Crude birth rate: Number of live births per 1,000 population in a given year.

Crude death rate: Number of deaths per 1,000 population in a given year.

Cube-square law: Principle stating a simple relationship between the volume of a container and its surface area: Surface area increases as the square of the dimensions and volume as the cube of the dimensions

Cultivated area: Land used for growing crops.

Cultural fault lines: Dividing lines that separate the regions dominated by different civilizations.

Culture: The beliefs, traditions, and identity of social groups.

Culture region: Area occupied by a particular cultural group.

Currency market: Worldwide market in which national currencies are traded.

Customs accession: Customs union linking a very small country with a larger country.

Customs union: Form of economic integration that calls for free trade among members and a common system of restrictions on trade with outsiders.

Cyberspace: Information infrastructure provided by the Internet.

Decentralization: Transfer and dispersal of control over economic and political activities from central authorities to local and regional levels; relocation from core to periphery.

Decreasing returns to scale: Increases in output that are less than the proportion by which inputs are increased.

Deindustrialization: Transformation of an economy from an industrial to service base.

Demand: Quantity of a good or service desired at a given price.

Demand conditions: Conditions in markets that shape consumer demand. These include the composition of buyer needs; the size and pattern of growth of demand; and the ways in which domestic preferences are transmitted to foreign markets. These conditions influence the ability of a firm to achieve economies of scale in production, and the rate and character of improvement and innovation.

Demand cone: The depiction of the relationship between demand for a good and distance from a central market. Demand can be expected to drop progressively outward from the central market as transportation costs add to the price of the good.

Demand schedule: The amount of a good desired at various price levels.

Demand surface: A three-dimensional depiction of spatial variations in demand.

Dematerialization: Reductions in amounts of raw materials used to make end products.

Demographic gap: The difference between birth and death rates occurring in the intermediate phases of demographic transition. High population growth occurs in countries that have seen a sharp drop in death rates but have not yet achieved a decline in birth rates.

Demographic transition: A five-phase process of development and population change, beginning with high birth and death rates, passing through a period of rapid population growth and ending with low birth and death rates.

Demonstration effect: A result of the growth of imports of a commodity to a level at which entrepreneurs become aware of the viability of local manufacture of that product.

Dependency ratio: Proportion of elderly or young people in the population.

Depreciation: Reduction in the value of assets over time.

Deregulation: Removal or lessening of government controls of economic activities.

Desert pavement: Stony surface land in desert areas.

Desertification: Spread of noncultivable desert lands, caused by overuse, overpopulation, and droughts.

Developing countries: Countries undergoing economic growth and modernization.

Development state: A state committed to government-led economic development.

Dictatorship of the proletariat: A stage in the Marxist progression toward a classless society that follows the proletarian revolution to end capitalist control of the means of production.

Differential rents: Differences in returns to landowners based on differences in the productivity of land.

Diffusion: Spread of innovations outward from centers of innovation.

Diminished effectiveness: The inability of government regulation and intervention in the economy to achieve its original goals.

Diminishing marginal utility: The decrease in the amount of satisfaction derived from a unit of a good as a consumer receives increasing amounts of the good.

Direct involvement of government in the economy: The extent of government participation in the economy, measured by the amount of spending by all levels of government in a country; the percentage of labor force employed in the civil service; and the surface area of the national territory owned by government.

Diseconomies of scale: Situation in which, after a minimum efficient size of production has been reached, costs may rise, at least in the short run.

Distance: *See* barriers to trade.

Distance-decay pattern: The direct decline in interaction between two places as the distance between them increases; or the decline in the volume of some attribute with increasing distance from a central place.

Distortion: Deviation from a competitive market pattern.

Distributed work: Use of telecommunications or other technologies to perform work at a distance from but not necessarily outside of the office. Distributed work utilizes such technologies as videoconferencing and networked information resources.

Distributorship: An enterprise that distributes the output of an industrial producer.

District economies: Economies that arise from an industrial atmosphere capable of reducing the cost disadvantage of small local firms with respect to large firms and of helping them in their innovation process.

Diversified quality: Using a highly skilled work force to produce small quantities of a variety of luxury goods.

Division of labor: The breakdown of production activities and reassignment of tasks on the basis of specialization to improve efficiency and increase productivity.

Domestic exchange ratio: In the absence of foreign trade, the price of a good expressed as the number of units of the good that would be required in exchange to buy one unit of a second good.

Domestic goods: Goods such as perishable foodstuffs, sand, gravel, and bricks that because they are costly to ship are rarely traded internationally.

Doubling time: The number of years it takes a population to grow to twice its present size.

Downward-sloping demand curve: A graphic depiction of price and quantity demanded, with price on the y axis and quantity on the x axis. The downward slope illustrates that reductions in quantity demanded result from increases in price.

Dry farming techniques: Agricultural practices that conserve water in arid lands.

Dual economy: A colonial economy with distinct modern and traditional sectors.

Dumping: Practice of foreign firms of selling goods in domestic markets at lower than domestic market prices.

Dynamic externalities: Externalities associated with "knowledge spillovers" that produce increasing returns.

E-mail: A computerized mailbox network.

East Asian NICs: *See* newly industrialized country.

East-West trade: Economic interaction between the former Communist countries of Eastern Europe and the countries of Western Europe and North America.

Eastern Bloc countries: *See* Communist bloc.

Economic adaption: Use of strategic planning by a firm to determine optimal location.

Economic adoption: Selection by the "guiding hand" of the market of only the fittest new firms that have been fortunate enough to make correct decisions on product, location, and technology.

Economic Commission for Latin America (ECLA): Post–World War II era United Nations commission that initially sought to combine all nations south of the United States into one Latin American common market.

Economic Community of West African States (ECOWAS): A 16-member organization promoting free trade among African states.

Economic efficiency: Combining inputs to produce the highest ratio of output to inputs.

Economic liberalization: Lessening of government intervention in the economy.

Economic maximization: Determining optimal locations for firms to minimize costs and maximize benefits.

Economic policy instruments: Features of the economic system (such as interest rates and taxes) that can be manipulated by governments to adjust economic performance.

Economic potential index: Index developed by Colin Clark to describe accessibility to demand.

Economic regionalism: Economic grouping of countries into larger regions.

Economic rent: Payments to landowners for use of their land as a factor of production; the returns to land as an input in the productive process.

Economic restructuring: Transformation of an economy through privatization, technological innovation, upgrading infrastructure, and human-resource development.

Economic union: Form of economic integration having the characteristics of a common market, plus a common bank, unified monetary and tax systems, and a common foreign economic policy.

Economies of scale: Reduction in unit costs that result from an increased level of output. Internal economies of scale are cost reductions gained within a single plant in the manufacture of a single product or economies achieved by a chain of bottling plants, shops, or hotels in many different locations. External economies of scale are achieved by the agglomeration of many different firms in a particular region, thereby attracting specialist services and knowledgeable customers and gaining a national or even international reputation.

Economies of scope: Broadening business activities to include several goods and services, leading to reductions in average per unit costs for some of the products.

Economies of specialization: Economies that arise from concentrating on particular products.

Economists' views of future supply of critical resources: The belief that the quantity of available resources responds to prices and technology. Resource prices may initially rise in the face of scarcity, but supplies do not run out because new technologies result in increased demand for substitutes. Contrast with environmentalists' views.

Economy-of-scale threshold: Minimal scale at which a new firm may achieve the lowest attainable cost as a significant fraction of the total capacity of the industry.

Egalitarian nuclear family: A family type characterized by equality of brothers laid down by inheritance rules.

Elasticity: A measure of response to price changes. Elasticity is usually expressed as the percentage change in quantity demanded (or supplied) in response to a percentage change in price.

Elderly dependency ratio: Proportion of aged persons in the population.

Electricity: Electric power.

Emerging markets: Fast-growing developing economies.

Emigration: Movement of people out of a country or region.

Empty areas: Parts of the world where climatic conditions are extreme and cannot support agricultural settlements.

Enclosure movement: Replacement of the medieval system of open fields by individual family farms.

Endaka: A Japanese term used to describe cost pressures in Japanese industry caused by rapid appreciation of the yen, that is, by rapid increases in the value of the yen relative to other currencies such as the dollar.

Endemic: Native to an area.

Endogamous community family: A family type characterized by equality between brothers established by inheritance rules, cohabitation of married sons with their parents, and frequent marriages among cousins.

Endogenous: Pertaining to variables or factors internal to the system or model.

Energy: Usable power.

Energy consumption per unit of output: A measure of productivity equal to the amount of energy used in production divided by total output.

Energy crisis: Severe or sudden energy shortage.

Energy efficiency: The use of energy in such a way as to minimize waste.

Energy shortage: Situation in which energy is not available in sufficient quantities to meet demand.

Engel's law: The axiom that poor families (or poor countries) spend a larger proportion of their incomes on food than do rich ones. It is attributed to nineteenth-century German statistician Ernst Engel (not to be confused with Karl Marx's collaborator, Friedrich Engels).

Engineering principle: *See* Cube-square law.

Entrepreneurship: The propensity to innovate and to create new business enterprises.

Environmental consequences: Adverse effects of productive activities on the environment.

Environmental constraints: Conditions that limit or prevent production or resource exploitation.

Environmental damage: Detrimental effects of industrial activity or human settlement on the environment.

Environmentalists' views of future supply of critical resources: The belief is that there is a fixed supply of nonrenewable resources, and therefore there are limits to growth. Environmentalists emphasize the importance of resource conservation and environmental protection. Contrast with economists' views.

Equal-product curve: *See* isoquant.

Equilibrium price: The price at which quantity demanded is equal to quantity supplied.

Equity: A concept of justice or fairness applied to the distribution of income or imposition of tax burdens.

European Economic Community or European Union (EEC or EU): Organization of European states established in 1958 to improve the standard of living and increase economic growth. In 1992, it changed its name to the European Union and expanded efforts to become a true economic and political union. Membership has risen from 6 in 1958 to 15 currently.

European Free Trade Association (EFTA): Organization of seven European countries—Austria, Denmark, Norway, Portugal, Sweden, Switzerland, and the United Kingdom (later Finland and Iceland) formed in 1960 as a counter to the EEC. EFTA created a free-trade area in industrial goods among member nations.

European integration: The move to unify the nations of Europe into a single economic and political community.

European Monetary System (EMS): Part of the EEC, created in 1979 to minimize fluctuations of currency exchange rates.

Exchange controls: Government control of foreign currency transactions.

Exchange economy: An economy in which producers specialize, trade takes place to satisfy consumption needs, and prices are determined in markets.

Exchange possibilities curve: Curve indicating the various proportions of goods that are available as a result of exchange.

Exchange rate: Price of one nation's currency in terms of that of another nation.

Exchange theory: (1) The theory that explains how an exchange economy works. (2) The theory of exchange rate determination.

Exhausted: Condition where a resource has been used up.

Exit barriers: Costs of closing down operations in a host country.

Exit rates: Rates at which firms fail and leave an industry.

Exogamous community family: A family type that is opposite the individualist nuclear family and is characterized by equality among brothers, cohabitation of married sons and their parents, and by marriages taking place outside the kinship group.

Exogenous: Pertaining to variables or factors external to the system or model.

Expert systems: Software systems that control operations or answer queries using the built-in knowledge of acknowledged human experts.

Exploitation: Utilization of resources.

Expropriation: Government seizure of foreign-owned companies.

Extended family: Family group consisting of a nuclear family and its relatives.

External economies of scale: Reductions in production costs due to factors outside the individual firm, such as those arising from the concentration of firms in one location.

Externality: External effect, either positive or negative arising in the environment or region in which a firm is located.

Extractive industries: Industries that produce oil, natural gas, coal, mineral raw materials, and so on.

Extraterritoriality: Political control of overseas subsidiaries by a home government.

Factor conditions: Another term for "factors of production"—land and other resources, labor, capital, and enterprise.

Factor-driven development: Development that relies on the basic factors of production.

Factor endowments: The combination of land, labor, capital, and entrepreneurship that each country possesses.

Factor intensities: Proportions of the factors of production used to create output.

Factors of production: Land, labor, capital, and enterprise (entrepreneurship).

Fallow: Agricultural land that is not planted during the growing season, in the attempt to restore fertility.

Federal deficit: A situation in which the national government's expenditures are greater than revenues for a given period.

Fertility rate: Number of births per 1,000 women of child-bearing age (15–44).

Feudalism: An economic system predating wage labor in which land was held by lords and cultivated by serfs who were required to reside on the land and to pay in-kind rents.

Fifth wave: The technology transition that followed the stagflation crisis of 1980–1981, characterized by growth in the advanced services sector and the creation of knowledge products.

Filtering: Part of the process of economic growth. As economies move into higher-productivity industries, they lose advantages in labor-intensive industries. Lower-skilled, labor-intensive industries then "filter," becoming the domain of lower-wage nations further down the skills ladder.

Finance capital: The monetary form of capital.

Financial assets: Monetary assets such as money or bonds.

Financial deregulation: Lifting of barriers to entry into banking and other financial services.

Financial economies of scale: Efficiencies and reductions in production costs achieved by multiplant firms through the selective concentration of financial resources.

Firm strategy: Corporate goals and management systems devised to obtain competitive advantage.

First-tier states of Eastern Europe: States that rapidly adopted economic reforms following the collapse of the Soviet Union. These include the Czech Republic, Hungary, Poland, Slovakia, Slovenia, Estonia, Latvia, and Lithuania.

First wave of industrial revolution: Period of industrial expansion beginning in England in the late 1700s in which machines began to replace hand work in certain segments of the textile industry, and the first waterpowered spinning mills were established.

First World: Western market economies.

Fiscal measures: Government expenditure programs or tax measures implemented to stimulate or slow economic growth.

Fission: Creating energy by splitting an atom.

Fixed costs: Costs that do not change with level of output.

Fixed factor: Input to production that does not change in the short run.

Fixed price: A price for a good or service that is set by contract over a period of time.

Flexible automation: *See* flexible manufacturing systems.

Flexible manufacturing systems: Automated production systems that utilize computer controlled machines and robotics to facilitate batch production and serve fast changing markets by enabling economies at a wide range of scales of output.

Flexible specialization: Use of industrial networks to link small firms and giant organizations, enabling customization of products and timeliness of delivery, together with economies of scope and global reach.

Flow resource: A resource that does not ordinarily become exhausted but must be used as it appears or it will be lost, for example, solar energy and wind power.

Food-deficit region: Area that lacks arable land in sufficient quantities to support its population and thus is forced to import food.

Footloose industry: Industry in which plants are insensitive to transport-cost variations.

Fordist: Type of mass production using assembly lines that is associated with Henry Ford.

Foreign direct investment (FDI): Private investment by firms of one country in another country.

Foreign direct investment theory: Theory of industrial structure linking trade and multinational enterprise.

Forward linkages: Form of vertical integration in which a firm buys outlets for its products in order to secure markets.

Fossil-fuel bank: One of the five energy storage banks consisting of the known supply of fossil fuels.

Fossil fuels: Fuels, including oil, coal, and natural gas, that are formed from plant and animal remains.

Four stages of economic development: Progressive stages of economic development: (1) factor-driven, (2) investment-driven, (3) innovation-driven, and (4) wealth-driven. This term is attributed to Michael Porter of Harvard University.

Four Tigers: Fast-growing Asian economies of South Korea, Taiwan, Hong Kong, and Singapore. Thailand is sometimes included as a "Fifth Tiger."

Fourth wave of industrial revolution: Period of industrial expansion from the 1920s to the 1970s. Key innovations were the production line, highway networks, airline systems, and modern radio and television communications.

Fourth World: "Basket-case" economies least likely to develop. Includes many African nations.

Free enterprise market systems: Economic systems in which decisions are made by individuals, groups, and corporations. These decisions interact in the market through the interplay of the forces of demand and supply and are expressed in the working of the price system. Economic power and political power are widely dispersed and competitively exercised.

Free on board (FOB): The pricing of a product at a farm, warehouse, or factory without inclusion of freight charges. The buyer pays the FOB price, and then must pay the carrier for transport charges. Contrast with cost, insurance, and freight (CIF).

Free trade: Economic interaction among countries in the absence of tariffs, quotas, or other barriers.

Free-trade area: Form of economic integration in which member countries remove all barriers to trade within the group but maintain independent policies with respect to trade with non-members.

Free Trade Area of the Americas (FTAA): Free-trade organization proposed by leaders of Latin American countries to be created by 2005.

Friction-free capitalism: The future of capitalism, as posited by Bill Gates, in which distance barriers have been removed and markets are nearly perfectly competitive.

Frictionless trade: Trade that does not incur transportation or other transactions costs.

Front office functions: Activities of a firm that require direct customer contact.

Full economic integration: The ultimate form of economic integration in which all barriers to intrabloc movement of goods and factors of production have been removed, social as well as economic policies have been unified, and all members are subject to the binding decisions of a supranational authority consisting of executive, judicial, and legislative branches.

Functional disintegration: Locational separation of routine and complex activities within firms.

Fusion: Creating energy by joining atomic nuclei.

Futures: Goods contracted for sale at a future date and agreed-on prices.

Gains from trade: Benefits from trade consisting of the returns from the exchange of goods in and of itself and from international specialization of production.

Gasprom: Russian natural gas monopoly.

Gene splicing: Replacing segments of the genetic code of plants or animals to produce species with desired characteristics, or free of specific genetic defects.

General Agreement on Tariffs and Trade (GATT): Multilateral trade agreement that went into effect in 1948 and established rules and principles for international trade. Since 1948, GATT has undergone seven negotiating sessions, or "rounds" each named for the country in which it took place.

General theory of polarized growth: Theory of how economic, social, and political processes generate circular and cumulative causation and create heartland–hinterland dependency relationships.

Generalized measures of accessibility: Measures of the simultaneous accessibility of places to multiple activity centers.

Geography of demand: Spatial variation in demand for a good as distance from markets increases, causing the price of the good to rise due to increased transportation costs.

Geography of market equilibrium: The geographies of demand and supply that reflect market-clearing prices in competitive economies.

Geography of price: Spatial variations in the price of a good or service.

Geography of supply: Spatial variations in output of a good or service.

Geothermal energy: Energy produced from steam released from the earth.

Geothermal power: Power generated from geothermal energy.

Gift exchange: Trade that is ritualized as mutual gift giving.

Global capital markets: *See* global financial markets.

Global cities: Cities that serve as command points, financial centers, production sites, and major markets in the global economy. New York, London, and Tokyo are prime examples.

Global commons: Collectively owned areas of the world comprising the air, rivers, lakes and the sea.

Global communications systems: Worldwide communications networks that make it possible for companies to coordinate their production planning and financial operations across a wide range of countries.

Global economic geography: The location of economic activity, the spatial organization and growth of economic systems, and human use and abuse of earth's resources.

Global financial markets: World-scale markets for financial products and services.

Global shift of industry: Worldwide relocation of industrial activities that began in the 1970s.

Globalization: Worldwide integration of economic systems. The principal instruments of globalization are multinational corporations.

Globalization cascade: According to Rosabeth Kanter, the mutually reinforcing feedback loops that strengthen the process of globalization.

Government barriers to imports: Restrictions imposed on imported goods to put them at a disadvantage in the market relative to domestically produced goods.

Government intervention: Government involvement in the market.

Governmental investment: Investment by the government in infrastructure or in producing sectors of the economy.

Green labor: Low skilled or unskilled labor.

Green revolution: Expansion of agricultural production resulting from an international program that targeted rice and wheat production in developing countries of Asia, Africa, and Latin America. Includes development of new crop varieties and appropriate fertilizer and pesticide usage.

Greenhouse effect: The accumulation of carbon dioxide and other chemicals in the earth's upper atmosphere that traps the incoming sun's rays and raises air temperatures.

Gross domestic product (GDP):   The value of all goods and services produced in a country within a specified period.

Gross material: Raw material that contributes only a portion or none of, its weight to the finished product.

Gross national expenditures: Gross National Product (GNP) calculated as the sum of expenditures on consumption and investment in a given period.

Gross National Product (GNP):   The value of a country's total output of goods and services, plus or minus overseas earnings in a given period (typically, a year).

Growth curve: An S-shaped logistic curve, beginning with slow growth, extending through a period of explosive growth to a period of slowing growth, and ultimately to a zero-growth rate.

Growth logistic: In long-wave theory, a decadewide band of change that follows a half-century long S-shaped path from the decade following one long-wave peak to market saturation in the decade preceding the next peak.

Guanxi: The use of gifts to bind partners into exchange relationships in Chinese business networks.

Hard automation: Mass production in which economies are realized at large volumes.

Hard technology: Equipment and machinery.

Heartland: A territorially organized subsystem of society possessing a high capacity for generating innovative change.

Heartland–hinterland pattern: Development pattern in which industrial heartland areas were provided with raw materials by their surrounding hinterlands.

Heckscher–Ohlin (H–O) factor proportions theory: The culmination of neoclassical trade theory developed in the 1930s that states that trade is the result of different relative endowments of the factors of production. Countries will export those goods whose production is relatively intensive in the country's abundant factor and import those that are intensive in its scarce factor.

Hierarchical diffusion: Tendency of innovations to be adopted in large cities and markets first, and then diffuse down the urban hierarchy.

Hierarchical internalization: Setting up units within an organization to perform functions that would be contracted to outsiders if a free market for these activities existed.

Hierarchy of central places: Ordering urban areas into levels or echelons according to the efficiency of the spatial arrangement of marketing, transportation and administrative functions.

Higgling: Bartering or bargaining.

Hinterland: A region beyond a heartland, whose growth and change are determined by its dependency relationship to the heartland.

Hollowing out: Decline in domestic production due to use of third country labor and materials to serve foreign markets.

Hong: Chinese trading house.

Hoover's margin line: *See* margin line.

Horizontal indirect effects: Employment displaced by firms from similar industries that may be locally owned or labor-intensive.

Horizontal integration: Combination of firms producing similar items and selling in the same market. The effect is reduced competition as former competitors become integrated partners in a single firm.

Hoteling: Component of telework that involves two or more mobile workers sharing office space by using it in rotation.

Householding: A self-sufficient economic unit, such as a family, settlement, or manor.

Hui: Chinese mutual aid associations.

Huiguan: Chinese merchant associations.

Human capital: Labor force and the skills and intellectual capabilities it possesses.

Human resources: Quantity and skills of personnel, including cultural factors that bear on the work ethic.

Hydraulic civilization: Term coined by Ernst Wittfogel to refer to civilizations whose early development was based on sophisticated irrigation works.

Hydrocarbons: Organic compounds occurring in fossil fuels.

Hydroelectricity: Electricity produced by waterpower.

Ideology: A system of beliefs.

Immediate checks to population growth: "Preventative" and "positive" checks that intervene in a Malthusian world and counter the "ultimate" check to growth —death by starvation due to exhausted food resources.

Immigration: Movement of people into a country or region.

Imperfect competition: An industry in which one firm or a small group of firms is able in influence prices by engaging in price collusion or other discriminatory practices.

Import competing: *See* import substitution.

Import substitution: Development strategy in which a system of tariffs and quotas is established to restrict imports and allow domestic industries to develop.

In situ restructuring: Comprehensive technical, economic, and social reorganization of an industry in existing production locations.

Inanimate energy: Mechanical energy.

Incentive: Part of a system of achievement based on rewarding improved economic performance.

Income differential: Difference in incomes between different people due to job types, skill levels, or geographic locations.

Income disparity: The share of national income held by the richest segment of society compared with the share held by the poorest segment.

Income effect: The change in consumer behavior resulting from a change in the price of a good. A price increase reduces consumers' real income and thereby reduces demand for the good.

Income elasticity of demand: Change in the quantity demanded in response to changes in income. Income elasticity equals the percentage change in demand divided by the percentage change in income.

Income inequality: Differences in income between groups in society.

Income redistribution effect: Incomes may be redistributed when governments tax the rich and subsidize the poor. Other government programs may cause the income of different segments of society to increase or decrease.

Increasing returns: *See* increasing returns to scale.

Increasing returns to scale: Increases in output resulting from increases in inputs that exceed the proportion by which inputs were changed.

Indifference curve: Curve along which proportions of one good can be substituted for another to achieve the same level of consumer satisfaction.

Indifference line: *See* indifference curve.

Indigenous populations: People who are native to a region.

Indirect calories: Foods derived from animal products and other sources high in the food chain, which result from the conversion of foods obtained directly from the soil, known as "direct calories."

Indirect employment consequences: Employment generated in a region by the presence of a firm and its employees beyond that which is directly connected to the firm.

Individual demand curve: Demand curve of an individual consumer showing the quantity of a good desired at each price level.

Individual supply curve: Supply curve for a single firm showing quantity of a good the firm would supply at each price level.

Individualism: Cultural characteristic stressing the importance of individual initiative and achievement. Contrast with collectivism.

Indivisible costs: Costs related to initial design and development of a product.

Induced invention: Innovations that result from increasing demand.

Industrial districts: Clusters of firms in particular regions characterized by the emergence of external economies.

Industrial inertia: Persistence of an industry in a location long after the initial locational advantages have gone.

Industrial location theory: Theory that is concerned with the optimal location for an individual plant in a given industry. It assumes an economic maximizer who seeks the plant location that minimizes costs or maximizes some benefit.

Industrial revolution: Change in the structure of an economy (initially in England in the eighteenth century) when mechanization is applied to manufacturing processes and output rises rapidly.

Industrialization: Movement from an agricultural economy to a manufacturing-based, export-oriented economy.

Industry clusters: Concentration of firms in locations that lower costs or increase returns. Reasons for concentration include highly skilled human resources, high-quality service industries and infrastructure, advanced transportation and communications facilities, industrial concentrations, and developed external economies.

Industry-specific economies: Economies of scale that are specific to the firms in a particular industry.

Inelastic: The insensitivity of quantity demanded or supplied to changes in price.

Infant industry: Newly established industry that receives special protection from foreign competitors in its unit costs that are higher than those of more established operations.

Infant mortality rate: The number of deaths of infants (age 0–1) per 1,000 live births in a given year.

Inferior goods: Goods for which demand decreases as income increases.

Inflation: An increase in price levels over a period of time.

Information age: The stage of economic development following the industrial age in which economies are based on information and knowledge.

Information age technologies: Computer-based technologies that enhance the use of information in production processes, management, and decision making.

Information capital: Insider information that can be used by firms to increase profits.

Information gathering: Collection and utilization of data.

Information services: Services involving the actual content of information that is transmitted.

Information society: A society in which the use of computers, robotics, and knowledge prevails in the economy.

Information technologies (IT):   Technologies that capture, store, and transmit information in digital form.

Infrastructure: Features of an area that affect economic development including roads, ports, airports and other transportation linkages, water, sewerage, electric power, and communications.

Innovation: The application of a basic idea to something directly useful to humankind.

Innovation-driven development: The third of Porter's four-stage classification of economic development. In the innovation stage, firms actively create new technologies, new products, and new markets. Industries emerge that compete internationally.

Input: Factor of production.

Input substitution: Replacing inputs to increase production levels.

Inspector raj: In India, refers to the replacement of colonial administrative controls by those of the Indian civil service bureaucracy.

Institutional development: The process of establishing agencies and guidelines to oversee and regulate economic activities and other functions of society.

Integration theory: Theory that evolved out of international trade theory that analyzes the economic integration of countries.

Intellectual property: Goods produced by the mind, through research and creativity, including computer software, musical recordings, books, and biotechnology.

Intellectual technology: The products of brainpower.

Intensification: The process of increasing crop yields from a fixed or declining quantity of farmland. Intensification entails two kinds of technologies: mechanization and the introduction of improved plant varieties in combination with increased fertilizers and pesticides and more effective water use.

Interaction theory: Theory that explains the volume and directions of spatial interaction.

Intermediate products: Partially processed goods, including components.

Internal diseconomies of scale: Higher costs and lower levels of efficiency resulting from increasing levels of output by a firm.

Internal economies of scale: Lower costs and efficiencies achieved by a firm as level of output increases.

Internal multiplant economies: Lower costs and efficiencies achieved by having multiple plants in different locations.

Internalization: Performance in-house of many functions that would otherwise be contracted out to other companies in order to cut costs.

International Bank for Reconstruction and Development (IBRD):   Commonly known as the World Bank, an institution established by the Bretton Woods agreement to facilitate the international flow of capital.

International division of labor: International specialization such that every country concentrates its production in areas where it has advantages over other countries.

International economic integration: The joining together of several sovereign countries to form a single economic region within which goods and in some instances, the factors of production, move freely.

International exchange ratio: International terms of trade.

International finance: Capital available for use in global markets.

International Monetary Fund (IMF):   Institution formed by the Bretton Woods agreement to ensure the convertibility of currencies.

International specialization: The practice of manufacturing goods in a combination of locations having the lowest costs in sufficient quantity to enjoy economies of scale.

International terms of trade: The proportion of one good that can be traded for another in international markets.

International trade: Trade among nations.

International Trade Organization (ITO):   Institution established in 1947 for the purpose of promoting international trade.

Internationalization: The process by which a firm moves from producing in and for a domestic market to one having worldwide operations

Internationally transmitted shocks: Economic problems that originate beyond the borders of one's own country.

Internet: Worldwide system of computer networks.

Internet hosts: Computers connected to the Internet.

Intrabloc trade: Economic interaction within trade blocs.

Intrafirm trade: International trade between branches of an MNE.

Intrafirm transfers: Movement of components, finances, profits, and services among branches of MNEs.

Intraindustry trade: Cross-shipment of goods from the same industries between countries—automotive products, for example.

Invention: A fundamental process resulting in the conception of a basic new idea, usually in a scientific laboratory.

Investment-driven development: The second of Porter's four stages of economic development. Investment-driven development involves capital-intensive production.

Invisible exports: Trade in noncommodity service exports such as transportation, finance, tourism and entertainment. Contrast with visible trade.

Invisible trade: Import and export of services.

Isodapane: Locus of points of equal transport cost from a factory.

Isolationism: A policy of closing a country off from the rest of the world, eliminating outside trade and influences.

Isoquant: A curve showing the combinations of inputs that can be used to achieve a certain level of output.

Japan Incorporated: Alliance among Japanese business, labor, special-interest groups, and governments.

Job turnover rates: Rate at which jobs are created and abolished.

Juridical function: Responsibility for testing the validity of the rules and laws by applying them to concrete cases in society.

Just-in-case delivery: Term referring to the large stores of spare parts held by traditional assembly line manufacturing operations.

Just-in-time production: System of mass production in which parts are delivered from suppliers at the time they are needed, rather than being stocked in a parts room. Contrast with just-in-case delivery.

Kaizan: Japanese term meaning continuous improvement.

Kaldor's model: Model of economic growth developed by Nicholas Kaldor based on Verdoorn's Law—"The greater the rate of increase of output inside a firm, the greater the increase in productivity." The productivity increases are due to improved techniques and increased knowledge as well as economies of scale.

Kanban: Japanese term for just-in-time production.

Kei-haku-tan-sho: Japanese terms, literally translated mean "light," "thin," "short," "small," refer to design characteristics of innovative products that have been successful internationally.

Keiretsu: Enterprise groups that link different types of Japanese multinational corporations.

Key money: Money or in-kind payments made in excess of listed prices in markets where price controls exist.

Kin-country syndrome: The practice among groups in non-Western nations of rallying support for opposition to Western values by appealing to cultural values of their civilization.

Kinship: Familial relationship.

Knowledge-based industry: Industry that relies on brain power for its success, such as the computer software industry.

Knowledge-based systems: Systems that rely on knowledge, such as computer software.

Knowledge carrying services: Education, consulting, and advisory services.

Knowledge intensive industries: *See* knowledge-based industry.

Knowledge products: An example is computer software.

Knowledge resources: Human brainpower and knowledge-carrying services.

Knowledge spillovers: Dissemination of ideas among firms, promoting productivity enhancement and the growth of industry.

Knowledge workers: Workers who use their brainpower to create knowledge products.

Kondratiev cycle: *See* long wave of prices.

Labor: Human resources used as a factor of production.

Labor costs: Wages and benefits paid to workers.

Labor diseconomies of scale: End of reductions in labor costs per unit of production that come from the division of labor and increased efficiency.

Labor economies: Reductions in the labor costs per unit of output that are due to division of labor and increased efficiency.

Labor efficiencies: Labor productivity arising from specialization and division of labor.

Labor exchange: Market for workers seeking employment.

Labor force: Economically active people (both employed and unemployed) in the population. Examples of people excluded from the "economically active" are homemakers, students, pensioners, and people receiving public assistance.

Labor-intensive industries: Production industries in which a larger share of labor than capital is used. These industries are usually the mainstay of economies that are beginning to industrialize.

Labor-oriented industry: Industries in which the plants' competitive advantage depends on minimization of labor costs.

Labor pool: Available supply of labor.

Labor productivity: *See* productivity of labor.

Labor theory of value: Theory stating that the value of a good is determined by its labor inputs—the relative labor required for its production.

Laissez-faire: Absence of government intervention in the economy.

Land: The territory of a country, region, district, or other areal unit, together with its particular attributes.

Land rent: Payment to a landowner for the use of land.

Land use: The way in which land is occupied and utilized.

Land-use patterns: The spatial distribution of agricultural, urban, and other land-using activities.

Land value: Price paid for the purchase of land.

Lateral integration: Mergers of firms where there are complementarities.

Latin American Free Trade Association (LAFTA): Latin American trade bloc comprising most South American nations and Mexico, created in 1960 and ended in 1981.

Launhardt-Palander solution: A geometric solution to the least-cost location problem, when the variable is transport costs.

Law of diminishing returns: An axiom stating that when increasing quantities of inputs are added to production, relative to fixed quantities of other inputs, returns to the variable quantity will eventually decrease.

Law of the encroaching hyperbolic market boundaries: Axiom stating that if the prices of goods from two producers are different, then the market area of the firm with the lower price would steadily encroach on the market of the higher-price producer. The encroachment is in increments of hyperbolic-shaped lines.

Law of equidistant market boundary: Axiom stating that the straight line that is equidistant from two producers of an identical product delineates the outer boundary at which transportation costs (hence costs of goods) for the two firms are identical and consumers are indifferent between the two firms.

Law of the hyperbolic line of indifference: Axiom stating that if the price of goods from one producer are higher than those from a second and if transportation costs for the two firms are equal, then the shape of the boundary for the producer with the lower costs will be hyperbolic and will cut into the market area of the other producer.

Law of the parabolic market enclave: Axiom stating that market areas are sensitive to transportation costs. If transportation costs for one firm are higher than those for another, the market area for that firm will shrink.

Law of reciprocal demand: Principle stating that international prices depend on the strength and elasticity of demand for goods in various countries.

Laws of market areas: Axioms regarding the shape and extent of market area taking into account transportation costs.

Laws of returns: *See* law of diminishing returns.

Lazy-J: Long-run cost curves that indicate a particular pattern of returns to investment. Initially, due to economies of scale, the long-run unit-cost curve will fall with increasing output. The lazy-J occurs as the zone of increasing returns to scale terminates at a critical size threshold—the minimum size at which the lowest attainable unit costs are achieved. Beyond the threshold, average costs per unit of output tend to be relatively stable, and there is no apparent cost advantage of operating at either one scale or another.

Lean producers: Producers using just-in-time delivery of parts to keep down costs on the assembly line.

Lean production: A Japanese management system affecting the organization and management of labor, design, and production at the intrafirm and interfirm levels. Lean production allows higher-volume and higher-quality output at lower costs.

Learning curve: A pattern of learning and changes in worker productivity in which individual productivity tends to rise at an accelerating rate to the average level of efficiency, and from then on at a decelerating rate. *See* growth curve.

Learning organization: An organization that continually reshapes itself on the basis of new ideas and information.

Least-cost location: Location that minimizes production costs.

Least-cost location theory: Theory that explains locations of cost-minimizing producers in competitive (i.e., price-taking) markets.

Least-developed countries (LDCs): *See* Fourth World.

Lebensraum: Living space. A term used by Nazi Germany to justify its expansion into Eastern Europe.

Legislative function: Responsibility for determining society's primary goals and for formulating general rules maintaining (or changing) the existing social order.

Leontief paradox: Discovery by Wassily Leontief that the capital/labor ratio in U.S. export industries is lower than in import-competing industries, which is contrary to the expectations of the Heckscher–Ohlin Theory.

Less-developed countries (LDCs): Countries characterized by high rates of population growth and low per capita income.

Liberalism: (1) Traditional sense: A political philosophy that espouses limited role for the government in the economy (synonymous with conservatism). (2) Recent usage: The belief that governments should intervene in the economy to secure equity and social justice (synonymous with socialism).

Liberalization policies: Deregulation policies that lessen the role of the government in the economy.

Libertarianism: Political system that values individual liberties and a minimal role for government.

License raj: In India, control of the economy via restrictive licensing.

Licensing agreement: Agreement between an MNE and a foreign firm allowing the foreign firm to carry out production or distribution for the MNE.

Life expectancy: The average number of years a person can be expected to live.

Limit pricing: A practice of price setting among firms in an industry such that prices are set a low level, acting as a barrier to entry, discouraging new firms from entering the industry.

Limits of habitation: The line separating habitable from uninhabitable regions, usually defined as the line beyond which settled agriculture is not possible.

Limits to growth: Point at which markets are flooded or resources exhausted and rates of return decline.

Line-haul economy: Reductions in transportation costs per kilometer proportional to the distance traveled.

Linear linkup: A stage of development of Japanese foreign firms when, in the 1970s, overseas units were strongly connected to their headquarters in Japan but lacked links with each other.

Lines of indifference: Curves representing possible trade-offs among goods where the consumer is indifferent. *See* indifference curves.

Linkage-forming services: Services involving the establishment of communications channels, means to carry information, and the creation of markets.

Liquefied natural gas (LNG): Natural gas compressed into a liquid state so that it can be transported.

Literacy rate: Percentage of the population age 15 and over that can read and write.

Living plant bank: One of the five energy-storage banks consisting of the worldwide supply of plant.

Localism: A characteristic of culture that places high value on family and friendship networks.

Localization economies: Reductions in production costs resulting from the concentration in one location of different firms involved in the manufacture of similar products.

Localized material: Materials obtainable only in geographically well-defined localities.

Locals: Individuals whose outlook is restricted to immediate family, friends, and neighborhood. Contrast with cosmopolitans.

Location determinants: Factors affecting the choice of a location for a firm. These include the size of the firm, input prices, and selling prices when competition is imperfect.

Location rent: Surplus earned over production and transport costs used to retain land in a particular group or farming system.

Location rent formula: $R = E(p - a) - Efk$, where R = location rent per unit of land, E = output per unit of land, p = market price per unit of output, a = production costs per unit of output, f = transportation costs per unit of output per mile, and k = miles from market.

Location theory: Body of theory that analyzes the location of economic activities.

Locational adaption: Rational selection of an optimal location for a firm, or for a new plant of an existing firm, based on the evaluation of competing locations.

Locational adoption: Selection of the most efficient firms by the "guiding hand" of competitive markets.

Locational choice: Determination of where a firm will be located. This is a critical factor in determining a firm's success.

Locational figure: In Weber's location theory, the system of locational weights of different inputs.

Locational weight: Total weight of raw materials and product to be moved per unit of product.

Logistic curve: *See* growth curve.

Lomé Convention: Series of trade and aid agreements signed by the European Union with 70 African, Caribbean, and Pacific countries.

Long run: Time period during which all inputs to production become variable.

Long-run average-cost curve: Total cost per unit of output over the long run when all inputs are variable.

Long-run unit-cost curve (LRUC): See long-run average-cost curve and Lazy-J.

Long wave: Expansion of a technoeconomic system from innovation to market saturation over a period of 50–60 years. *See* growth logistic.

Long wave of prices: Period of 50–60 years in length, first noted by the Russian economist Nikolai D. Kondratiev in 1925, during which prices increase from a depressionary trough to an inflationary peak, and then begin decades-long plunge from the peak to the next trough.

Lowest common multiple (LCM): Least common multiple of two or more numbers.

Lukoil: Russian oil monopoly.

Luxury items: Goods for which demand increases as income rises. Also called "superior goods".

M-form: Form of corporate organization that facilitates product diversification by replacing centrally controlled departments with decentralized autonomous divisions.

Maastricht Treaty: Comprehensive agreement signed by European Community members in 1991 calling for, among other things, creation of a single currency, a European Central Bank and Communitywide citizenship. Following the signing of this agreement, the organization renamed itself the European Union (EU).

Macroeconomic shocks: Sudden changes in the macroeconomy that cannot be predicted in advance, including oil-price increases, periods of high inflation, and exchange-rate fluctuations.

Malnutrition: Condition of being underweight caused by insufficient caloric consumption.

Malthus: Thomas Robert Malthus (1766–1834) is best known for his work *Essay on the Principle of Population* in which he theorized that geometric population growth coupled with arithmetic growth in food supplies would lead to a crisis situation. "Immediate checks" could intervene, but if they failed, people would die of starvation as resources became exhausted.

Malthusian trap: Situation in which population growth has exceeded food supply.

Management diseconomies of scale: Diseconomies of scale that occur because of the increasing difficulty of coordinating larger firms.

Management economies: Economies of scale that occur as the firm size increases because division of the management tasks and specialization increases efficiency.

Management entrepreneur: Type of entrepreneur characterized by high levels of education and experience who establish businesses to supply firms for which they previously worked with supplies, equipment, or expertise.

Manhattan Project: U.S.-government-funded project to develop the atom bomb.

Manor: Feudal estate

Manufacturing belt: A concentration of manufacturing firms in a specific geographic region.

Maquiladora **program:** Agreement between the United States and Mexico allowing U.S. companies to establish factories on the Mexican side of the U.S.–Mexico border, employ Mexican workers, and produce goods for export back to the United States free of customs duties.

Margin line: At various distances from a plant, a calculation is made of what the delivered price would be at that point when transportation costs are added. As long as economies of scale outweigh transportation costs to each given distance, the margin line slopes down and it pays to extend the market area. Once the transportation costs outweigh the economies of scale, the margin line begins to slope upwards.

Marginal cost: The addition to total cost caused by production of one additional unit of output.

Marginal-cost curve: A curve illustrating the addition to total cost of each additional unit of output.

Marginal physical productivity: The increase in output, measured in physical units of output, that results from adding one additional unit of variable input, holding other inputs fixed.

Marginal product: The addition to output resulting from increasing an input (either capital or labor) by one unit.

Marginal productivity: *See* marginal product.

Marginal-revenue productivity: The increase in output, measured in dollar value of output, that results from adding one additional unit of variable input, holding other inputs fixed.

Margins of profitability: Amount by which revenues exceed costs.

Market area: The territory surrounding any central point of exchange that includes all potential customers for whom market price plus transport cost will be sufficiently low for them to be willing to make purchases of goods offered in the center.

Market boundary: Border between two producers marking geographic distance from each where prices from one producer are the same as the prices of another and consumers are indifferent as to which firm they purchase from.

Market-directed system: Decentralized, free-enterprise economic systems.

Market dominance: Concentration of market share in the hands of a particular producer or supplier.

Market-driven facilities: Third stage of high-technology development in which competitive facilities emerge as products become routinized, imitators enter the market, and price competition becomes part of the selling process.

Market economy: An economy in which prices based on demand and supply are used to allocate resources.

Market equilibrium: The point at which demand and supply curves intersect. At this point, the market is cleared of the commodity.

Market failure: Situations in which markets cannot operate because access to a good cannot be controlled. Market failures usually indicate public or collective goods.

Market insecurities: Uncertainties that affect the market such as the volatility of exchange rates, uncertainties that producers will deliver on their promise, or the costs of negotiating deals.

Market mechanism: The operation of demand and supply to determine price.

Market negotiation: Imperfectly competitive situations in which large-scale businesses are able to exercise some influence on price.

Market potential: Measurement of the aggregate accessibility of any location to all consumers within a given area. The market potential of any location is the sum of its interactions with each market (including itself). These interactions are proportional to the size of each market and inversely proportional to the distance from that market.

Market potential index: Index developed by Chauncy Harris to measure access to markets.

Market price: Price determined by the intersection of supply and demand.

Market share: Proportion of the consumer demand for a particular good that is filled by a single firm.

Market signal: Changes in the prices of goods and services that indicate how producers and consumers should allocate resources.

Market traders: People who carry out the actual transactions in commodities markets, making the whole process of balancing demands and supplies work.

Marketing diseconomies of scale: Point where marketing economies end and the delivery costs incurred by increased sales exceed the sales.

Marketing economies: Increases in sales made by extending the market area.

Marketplace-centered gradients: Increases of consumer prices and decreases of supply prices with increasing distance from a market center.

Mass production: Production system using assembly lines, standardization of parts, division of labor, and specialization to achieve large increases in the volume of goods produced.

Material index: Proportion that the weight of localized materials bears to the weight of the finished product.

Maximum ceiling prices: The upper-limit prices consumers are willing to pay for goods and services.

Maximum economies of scale: Point where level of output with minimum average costs has been reached.

Measure of Economic Welfare (MEW): An adjustment to GNP that incorporates the costs to a society resulting from environmental deterioration and the problems of contemporary urban life. MEW more accurately reflects the problems caused by growth than does GNP.

Mechanisms of regulating exchange: Social, economic, or political mechanisms that regulate markets for goods and services.

Mechanization: The replacement of human or animal labor with machinery.

Megamergers: Mergers of large corporations.

Megalopolis: A very large urban area consisting of several sprawling, connected metropolises.

Mercantilism: Early trade theory that emphasizes the importance of maintaining a surplus of exports over imports, foreign rather than domestic trade, exporting manufactured goods rather than agricultural products and the importance of plentiful cheap labor.

Merger: Consolidation of two or more firms.

Mergers for monopoly: Horizontal integration of large numbers of firms producing similar items and selling in the same market into relatively few multiplant corporations dominating the market and reducing or eliminating competition.

Mergers for oligopoly: Vertical integration of firms in which firms merge with their suppliers and outlets resulting in a small number of firms dominating an industry.

Meshing: Transition period in the worldwide expansion of Japanese industry during the 1980s in which corporations began to connect production and supply on a global scale.

Metals: A class of elements that are hard, heavy, and opaque, and are ductile, malleable, and able to conduct both electricity and heat.

Metallic ores: Ores containing metal.

Metallic reserves: Known worldwide supply of metals that have not yet been exploited

Metamorphosis model: An explanation for Kondratiev's long waves advanced by Gerhard Mensch, who observed that, whereas scientific discoveries and inventions appear as a more or less steady stream, innovations (the practical application of inventions) tend to come in clusters, each such surge being associated with the conclusion of one long wave and the anticipation of a succeeding wave. This casting off of old economic activities and their replacement by revolutionary new ones produces a structural metamorphosis of the economy.

Metropolis: Large city and its surrounding suburban areas.

Migration: Movement of populations either within (internal migration) or between countries (international migration).

Milieu innovateur: An innovative environment in which network firms locate in proximity, producing endogenous technological innovation.

Mineral deposit: Concentration of a mineral in one location.

Ming dynasty: Chinese dynasty, 1368–1644.

Minimum average total cost: Point at which cost per unit output has reached its lowest level.

Minimum efficient scale (MES):   Firm size at which maximum economies of scale are achieved.

Minimum efficient size: *See* minimum efficient scale.

Modernization: Replacement of traditional practices by new ideas and technologies.

Monetary measure: Changes in the interest rate or money supply implemented by the Federal Reserve to influence the economy.

Money: Currency; medium of exchange.

Monopoly: A market imperfection in which a single seller dominates the market.

Monopsony: A market imperfection in which a single buyer dominates the market.

Mortality rate: Death rate.

Most-favored-nation rule: Clause in GATT stating that countries are not to be given preferential treatment. Every country is to be treated as favorably as the most favored.

Multidivisional company with decentralized divisions: Organizational structure with autonomous divisions created to combine the economic advantages of mass production with the product diversity demanded by the market.

Multinational enterprise (MNE):   A company that is headquartered in one country but controls productive facilities and sales outlets in other countries.

Multiplant economies: *See* internal multi-plant economies.

Nation-state: A sovereign country.

National competitiveness: Traditionally, this has meant competitiveness of imports and exports. The concept now includes competitiveness in the creation and maintenance of business conditions—infrastructure, education, deregulation, stability—to attract or retain mobile capital.

National metropoles: Metropolitan complexes in which there is a massive concentration of corporate headquarters, banking activity, together with intensity and diversity of specialist services including advertising, consulting, and investment banking.

National nodal center: *See* national metropoles.

National shift of industry: Relocation of industries among regions within a country.

National sovereignty: The exclusive jurisdiction of a government over its territory.

Nationalism: Support for one's own country over and above any other.

Nationalization of industries: Government transferal of industries from private to state control and ownership.

NATO: North Atlantic Treaty Organization.

Natural gas: Hydrocarbon gas used as an energy source.

Natural increase: Net increase to a population due to excess of births over deaths.

Neoclassical economics: School of economic thought that emphasizes the efficiency of markets and advocates nonintervention of governments in the market system.

Neoclassical trade theory: A body of trade theory that follows on classical theory, focusing on the interactions of supply and demand to create an equilibrium, and the role of the relative factor endowments and proportions among countries. Proponents of neoclassical trade theory include Francis Edgeworth and Alfred Marshall.

Neocolonialism: A resurgence of the colonial system in which a country is effectively controlled, although not governed, by a foreign power.

Neo-Malthusian: One who accepts Malthusian principles, but who believes that society can, via appropriate interventions, avoid the onset of a Malthusian crisis.

Net economic welfare (NEW):   Further refinement of the MEW measure of how well off a population may be.

Network firms: High-tech firms that interlink to maintain their position on the leading edge of innovation. Networking in geographic proximity to other firms facilitates synergism from which springs technological innovation.

Network model: Industrial organization in which firms are concerned about maintaining their position on the leading edge of innovation.

Network of networks: The Internet.

Network system: The system of network firms.

"New" theory of international trade: Emerging theory that incorporates roles of multinational enterprises and increasing mobility of the factors of production.

Newly industrialized country (NIC):   A country that has recently undergone fundamental change and become a manufacturing economy. The term is commonly applied to the fast growing East Asian economies.

Newly liberalizing countries (NLCs):   Former Communist states of Eastern Europe that are currently undergoing economic restructuring.

Nodal centers: Metropolitan areas in which there are massive concentrations of financial activity, corporate centers, advertising and consulting services.

Noncommercial energy: Energy obtained from fuel wood, agricultural wastes, animal dung, and other noncommercial fuels.

Nonferrous metals: Metals that do not contain iron ore.

Nonrenewable resources: Resources such as oil, natural gas, and minerals that once used are not replenished by the earth, or that take millions of years to replenish.

Nontariff barrier: Regulation or restriction that effectively limits or prevents entry into an industry.

Norm: A behavioral standard defined by a culture.

Normative: Theory that is prescriptive rather than explanatory.

North American Free Trade Agreement (NAFTA):   Trade agreement between the United States, Canada, and Mexico enacted in 1994.

Nuclear fuel bank: One of the five-energy storage banks containing the products of nuclear decay.

O'Brien hypothesis: A prediction of the "end of geography" in the sense that eventually location will be of no importance. Increasing financial market integration will lead to integration at economic and political levels.

Objectively determined values: Values of goods determined by government agencies using mathematical models and other information rather than by markets. Such a system was used in the former Soviet Union.

Oeconomia: The etymon for "economy". A Greek word that literally translated means "householding" or "production for one's own use."

Oil reserve: Known quantities of oil in the earth that have not yet been exploited.

Oligarchy: A system of government in which power is concentrated in the hands of a small group of people.

Oligopoly: Control of a commodity or service in a given market by a small number of producers or suppliers.

Oligopsony: Control of a commodity or service in the market by a few large buyers.

On-site return: Central market price minus transportation costs.

OPEC: Organization of Petroleum Exporting Countries.

Open-seas principle: Principle that treats the world's oceans as common property.

Opportunity cost: The loss incurred by foregoing a particular course of action.

Optical scanning: The use of lasers to scan documents and convert the images to digital form.

Optima and limits scheme: Delineation of production areas, the central zone having optimum conditions; extending outwards, conditions are less and less favorable until the limits are reached.

Optimal transport orientation: Location that minimizes transport costs.

Order of a central place: Rank of a market center in the urban hierarchy based on the number of goods and services it provides.

Orderly market agreements: Negotiated quotas between the United States and Japan for automobiles and between the United States and the European Common Market for specialty steel products.

Organizational decentralization: Transferal of authority to branches and divisions within an organization.

Organizational market-directed systems: Systems in which economic decisions are made by negotiation among large-scale organizations—corporations, labor unions, special-interest groups, and governments.

Output: Quantity of a good or service produced.

Pacific Basin: Functionally integrated region comprising 14 countries bordering the Pacific Ocean—Japan, South Korea, Taiwan, Hong Kong, Singapore, Thailand, Malaysia, Indonesia, the Philippines, the People's Republic of China, Australia, New Zealand, the United States, and Canada.

Pacific Rim: *See* Pacific Basin.

Particularism: A system in which individual groups pursue their own interests, without concern for the interests of the society as a whole. Contrast with universalism.

Party-political function: Responsibility for mobilizing support for different measures and rules and for the holders of political positions.

Patrimony: Heritage traced through the male members of a family.

Peasant economies: An intermediate stage of development between traditional and full-exchange economies in which necessities are home-produced and are distributed according to social custom. Surpluses and specialty goods are traded on economic principles.

Pecuniary advantages: Situation in which firms are able to reduce costs because of favorable treatment and bargaining power resulting from their large size rather than from improvements in productivity or resource saving. Contrast with real economies of scale.

Per capita energy consumption: The total amount of energy used by a country in a given period divided by the population.

Per capita food output: National or regional production of food crops and livestock divided by population.

Per capita income: GDP or GNP divided by the population of a country in a given period.

Perestroika: The reform and restructuring of the Soviet economy. This term is attributed to Mikhail Gorbachev.

Perfect competition: A market situation characterized by the presence of many firms producing identical products, with free entry of new firms into the market and with no firm able to control prices.

Periphery: *See* Core–periphery.

Phantom freights: In basing-point pricing, the difference between administered prices and the actual price plus transport costs of the item actually delivered. An excess profit.

Physical resources: The abundance, quality, accessibility, and cost of natural resources together with other physical traits such as location, time zone, and climate.

Physiological density: A measure that relates the size of a population to the amount of arable land available for its support.

Pioneering innovations: Basic innovations that introduce new branches of industry.

Place-specific economies: Efficiencies that result from the scale of economic activities of all kinds in the areas where firms are located, rather than from industry- or firm-specific efficiencies.

Planning curve: Long-run, average-cost curve.

Plant-specific economies: Economies of scale that occur at the level of the plant or establishment.

Plant stocks: Supply of plants available for productive use.

Plow agriculture: Cultivation of field crops on land tilled by a plow.

Pluralism: A system of government in which a variety of groups participate.

Point of consumption (PC):   Location where final goods and services are utilized.

Pole: Center or origin.

Political economies: Nation-states.

Politics of resources: Conditions in which resources are owned by the nations who do not consume them, resulting in political disputes about production, prices, and security of supply.

Polity: A political unit, for example, a nation-state.

Pollution: Contamination of the environment.

Polygyny: The practice of having multiple wives or partners.

Population clusters: Areas of the world with high population concentrations.

Population curve: The growth curve of a population.

Population decrease: Situation in which birth rates are lower than death rates and immigration is not sufficient to make up the shortfall.

Population density: Population within a given area (usually a square mile or square kilometer).

Population distribution: Spatial pattern of population, as seen plotted on a map.

Population explosion: Period of rapid population growth as death rates drop but birth rates remain high.

Population growth rate: Average annual rate of increase in a population in a given period of time.

Population node: One of the four regions in the world with the highest population concentration. The largest node includes Japan, Korea, and eastern China. The second includes most of India, Pakistan, and Bangladesh, in addition to the island of Sri Lanka (formerly Ceylon) and parts of Burma. Europe west of the Ural mountains constitutes the third great population node. The fourth is the region of eastern North America.

Population potential: Measure of the accessibility of a location to the population where accessibility is inversely proportional to the distance from the location.

Population projection: Estimates of future population.

Population:resource ratio: The ratio of population numbers to the resource base of the region in which the population resides.

Positive check to population growth: The "ultimate" Malthusian check to population growth. It includes the various consequences of immoral behavior and the unavoidable products of the laws of nature, especially plagues and famines. Positive checks work by increasing death rates.

Positive feedback: Pattern of self-propelling growth, enhanced productivity and increasing returns due to technological progress.

Postindustrial society: Economy that is service- and knowledge-based.

Potlatch: Gift-giving ceremony in which gifts are given with the expectation of reciprocity.

Poverty: An income level that is insufficient to supply minimum nutritional and basic nonfood requirements.

Power of ocean tides: Energy emitted by the ocean through the process of changing tides. Harnessing this form of energy is still in experimental stages.

Power distance: Characteristic of a culture that defines the extent to which the less-powerful members of society accept inequality in power and consider large social distances to be normal.

Precious metals: Valuable metals such as gold and platinum.

Preindustrial economies: Traditional economies.

Preventative check to population growth: A counter to the "ultimate" check to population growth. Malthus termed this check "moral restraint" in which people would postpone marriage and children until they could afford them. Preventative checks work by reducing birth rates.

Price: The rate at which a good, service, or factor of production can be exchanged for any other good, service, or factor of production in a manner that clears the market and equates demand with supplies.

Price ceiling: *See* maximum price ceiling.

Price-consumption curve: The locus of equilibrium budgets resulting from variations in the price ratio, with money income remaining constant.

Price discrimination: Practice of charging different prices to different consumers.

Price distortion: Deviation of price from that which would occur in competitive market conditions.

Price effect: Movement along the price-consumption curve as prices fall. A price effect has two parts: an income effect and a substitution effect.

Price elasticity of demand: Changes in the quantity demanded of a good in response to changes in the price of the good.

Price elasticity of supply: Changes in the quantity supplied of a good in response to changes in the price of the good.

Price fixing: Prices set at higher than market rates though collusion among firms.

Price funnel: The pattern of increase in prices as distance from production site or market increases.

Price leader: A firm that initiates or takes leadership in setting prices.

Price mechanism: The way in which prices act as signals to producers and consumers indicating how to allocate resources.

Price-possibility line: A contour line showing the different combinations of goods that can be purchased with available funds (or resources).

Price sensitivity: The degree to which supply and demand change in response to price changes.

Price taker: Characteristic of a single firm that is too small to affect the market price of the commodity it produces.

Pricing mechanism: Price used as a means to regulate trade.

Primary commodities: Resources and raw materials.

Primary producers: Developing countries whose exports consist of raw materials.

Primary sector: Agricultural and livestock production, fishing, forestries, and hunting.

Primate city: Extremely large, preeminent city, whose size is far larger than any other city of a country.

Primogeniture: Inheritance of property by the firstborn son.

Principle of bulk transactions: Principle stating that large-volume bulk sales lead to economies of scale.

Principle of comparative advantage: Principle stating that countries should specialize in production and export of those goods they can make more efficiently relative to other nations and should import goods at which they are relatively less efficient.

Principle of highest and best use: A principle stating that land is allocated to that use earning the highest rent.

Principle of massed reserves: The principle that justifies just-in-case inventory management to assure continuity of assembly-line operations. *See* principle of reserves.

Principle of multiples: Principle determining the efficient level of output when machines that run at different rates are used. The level is the lowest common multiple of the individual machines.

Principle of population momentum: A characteristic of countries with a large proportion of young people in the population. The populations of these countries will continue to increase for several generations after birth rates have fallen because the large numbers of young people in the population will have children, even though they have fewer than their parents did.

Principle of reserves: Principle explaining greater efficiency at higher output levels resulting from maintaining some minimum level of stock, raw materials, fuel, spare parts for equipment repair, and maintenance.

Private enterprise: Firms and businesses owned by individuals rather than the government. Contrast with state monopoly and nationalized industries.

Private sector: Portion of the economy in which businesses are privately owned and profit-seeking.

Private-sector-driven: Impetus for change that comes from the private sector rather than from governments.

Privatization: Transferal of state-owned enterprises to private-sector ownership and operation.

Producer price floor: The price that may be obtained by local producers selling in the central market when local demand is weak. The price floor is equal to the price in the central market minus transportation costs.

Product differentiation: The practice by firms of distinguishing their products from those of other firms by means of brand names and advertising.

Product-driven firm: Second stage of high-technology development in which a viable product has been developed but must be monitored for quality and modified before it can be sold.

Product growth cycles: Period beginning with the introduction of a new branch of industry through its accelerated growth to market saturation.

Product-life-cycle theory: Theory explaining the progression through which a product passes, from its initial introduction through maturity. Each new phase tends to impose its own distinctive locational requirements, causing production to migrate from the center of innovation ultimately to areas of low factor cost.

Product-specific economies: Efficiencies associated with spreading start-up costs over a large output, product standardization, improved labor efficiency as production runs increase in length, and technical efficiencies as production runs increase in rate of output.

Production cost: Cost to a firm to produce output.

Production economies: Economies achieved by multiplant firms by allocating the production of specific products to specific plants.

Production function: Equation stating the relationship between inputs and output.

Production opportunity: Determination of the combinations of inputs that can be used to achieve the highest possible output, within a given budget constraint.

Production point: Location where a firm produces its output.

Production possibilities: A curve indicating the possible combinations of inputs that can be used to reach a given output.

Production run: Length of a production period.

Productivity: Output per unit input.

Productivity of labor: Output per unit of labor.

Profit margin: Portion of price received that exceeds costs for each unit of output.

Profit snatchers: Firms that are more concerned with short-run profits than with building up long-term business.

Protection effect: Increase in domestic production resulting from a protective tariff.

Protectionist barriers: Government restrictions on imports for the purpose of protecting national domestic markets.

Protective foods: Foods that provide essential nutrients.

Protestant ethic: The belief among Protestants in the virtue of hard work and success.

Protocol of Budapest: Agreement among member nations of the Central European Free Trade Agreement (CEFTA) to make half of their trade with each other duty-free beginning in 1995.

Proven reserves: Known quantities of natural resources that have not yet been exploited.

Proximity economies: Economies that reduce "transaction cost" and the "use cost of the market" through easier information circulation, face-to-face contacts, and lower information-gathering costs within the local economy.

Pseudo innovation: Product differentiation in which a product's image or packaging rather than basic qualities are changed.

Pseudo innovation is undertaken by firms to protect market shares.

Psychic income: Residential amenities and other benefits that workers are willing to accept in lieu of increases in wages.

Purchasing power of currencies: Difference in quantities of goods and services that can be purchased by different currencies at prevailing exchange rates.

Purchasing power parity (PPP): Setting exchange rates so that the prices of identical goods are the same in all countries.

Pure competition: *See* perfect competition.

Pure material: Materials that enter to the extent of their full weight into the finished product.

Qing (Ching) dynasty: Chinese dynasty 1644–1911.

Quaternary industries: Transport, communication, producer services, finance, and administration activities.

Quaternary sector: *See* quaternary industries.

Quinary industries: Medical care, research, education, arts and recreation.

Quinary sector: *See* quinary industries.

Quota: Quantity restrictions imposed on output or purchases.

Radical improvement innovations: Innovations that rejuvenate existing industries.

Range of a good: The market radius for a good that is sold by a central place; the outer perimeter where price increases to the point where demand drops to zero.

Rarity: The relative physical abundance of an element in the earth's crust.

Rationing system: A system that is used to hold prices below their free-market level and to allocate supplies equitably, without regard to income.

Real return: Earnings from an investment adjusted for changes in price (inflation).

Real time: Instantaneous communication.

Recession: Period during which aggregate output (GDP) declines.

Reciprocity: A pattern of economic organization in which mutual exchange is maintained on a regular and persistent basis between individuals or social groups.

Redistribution: A pattern of economic organization in which equity is maintained by a strong central authority that redistributes production.

Redistributive welfare states: States where the free-enterprise system is modified by government action to reduce social and spatial inequities. In redistributive welfare states, the government makes transfer payments to provide every citizen with minimum guarantees of material welfare.

Reform: Change of organizations and institutions to improve efficiency, such as the movement from a state-controlled to a market economy.

Region states: Subnational territories of 5–25 million people that share a common culture and competitive advantage, and relate directly to the global economy.

Regional development: The dispersal of economic activity and settlement across regions within a country to further national development goals.

Regional disparities: Differences in income or level of economic activity between regions of a country.

Regional economic integration: The joining together of neighboring countries for the purposes of increasing trade volumes, increasing economic growth, reducing regional disparities, strengthening bargaining power in the world political arena, and developing cooperative solutions to other social and political problems.

Regional nodal centers: Metropolitan areas smaller than national nodal centers from which large corporations can administer their industrial and commercial operations in a county's main regional markets.

Regional population concentrations: Refers to the relatively high concentrations of people in some areas due to resource endowments, climate, and/or cultural factors.

Regional welfare syndrome: Spatial relationship between the distance from the central city and income such that the lowest levels of welfare are to be found at the peripheries of major metropolitan regions, where prices of consumption items are highest and economic opportunities are least.

Renewable resource: A resource capable of replenishing itself or being replenished by human action.

Rent: The price paid to owners to use a factor of production or the cost to an owner of capital tied up that might have been used to generate income from investments in other assets.

Rent cone: Decline of rents with increasing distance from a market town.

Rent gradient: Change in rent as distance from the market increases.

Repatriation: Return of profits from overseas operations to a home country.

Reserve: That part of a known natural supply of a raw material that can be exploited commercially with existing technology and under present economic conditions.

Resource: A supply of anything that is regarded as useful or necessary to human beings, a store on which they can draw as they need it.

Resource-dependent: Early stage of economic development in which competitive advantage derives from the basic factors of production: natural resource endowments and abundant cheap labor.

Resource endowment: The nature and quantity of resources occurring in a particular territory.

Resource productivity: The quality of a resource in terms of the output that can be generated using it.

Returns to capital: The amount by which output changes as capital inputs change.

Returns to labor: The amount by which output changes as labor inputs change.

Returns to landowners: Rent received for the use of land.

Returns to scale: The amount by which output changes as inputs are increased.

Reverse investment: The practice among multinational enterprises of competing in each other's home markets.

Reverse-J cost curve: *See* lazy-J.

Ricardian development: Growth based on the comparative advantage provided by superior resource endowments. Ricardian strategies typically use agricultural or other primary product exports to drive economic development. Their success depends on the ability to locate and exploit new resources.

Ricardo's single-factor theory: Theory stating that the value of commodities is in proportion to the amount of labor spent in their production. It was developed by David Ricardo in order to provide numerical proof for his comparative advantage theory of international trade.

Ringi seido: Japanese term for a consensus system of decision making.

Rounding out: Industrial expansion by means of additions to existing facilities.

Routine improvement innovations: Innovations that follow pioneering innovations, rationalizing production, and increasing capital intensity.

Runaway plants: Factories set up by U.S. firms in lower-wage countries such as in Eastern Asia and along the Mexican border to produce goods formerly made at home.

Rural-to-urban migration: Population movement from rural areas into cities.

Scale economies of reserves: Maintaining the minimum level of stock, raw materials, fuel, spare parts for equipment repair and maintenance to minimize production costs.

Scarcity: An economic concept that refers to a situation in which the supply of a resource of good at a particular time and place is insufficient to meet demand at a given price.

Sclerotic conditions: Mancur Olsen's description of the circumstances in wealth-driven economies that lead to economic stagnation. They include monopoly pricing, protectionism, obstacles to innovation, and special-interest politics.

Scope of operation: *See* economies of scope.

Second-Tier states of Eastern Europe: States that lagged behind First-Tier states in the adoption of economic reforms following the collapse of the Soviet Union. These include Bulgaria, Romania, Croatia, and the former Yugoslavia.

Second wave of industrial revolution: Second phase of industrial revolution, ca. 1815–1870, when the steam engine was introduced.

Second World: Socialist and Communist countries.

Secondary sector: Mining, manufacturing, construction, public works, and utilities sectors.

Secular change: Long-run changes and trends.

Securitization: The conversion of real assets into securities that can be bought and sold.

Semi-industrialized countries (SICs):   The most advanced developing countries for which economic growth rates exceed population growth rates and manufactured goods constitute a large share of exports.

Service industries: Industries in the tertiary sector comprising wholesale and retail trade, transport, public administration, hotels, restaurants, domestic, personal, and professional services.

Sex-role differentiation: The ways that cultures use the biological differences between men and women to determine social roles.

Shadow prices: Estimated prices for goods and services not traded in markets.

Short run: Period of time during which some of the factors of production remain fixed.

Short-run unit-cost curve: Cost per unit produced including fixed costs and costs that vary per unit output.

Simpson's paradox: Situation in which a bias in the composition of groups causes averages for those groups to show opposite results from standardized rates accounting for compositional differences.

Simultaneity: Part of the globalization process by which the time lag between introduction of a product in one place and its adoption in others has declined precipitously.

Size threshold: Minimum size of a firm at which the lowest attainable unit costs are achieved.

Slash-burn or swidden agriculture: Agricultural practice in which land is cleared for planting by felling trees and burning underbrush.

Snatchers: Firms that are concerned with short-run profits. Contrast with stickers.

Social agglomeration: See agglomeration.

Social cost: The cost to society, including the cost of externalities, of producing a good.

Social equity: *See* equity.

Social mechanisms: Social customs such as reciprocity and redistribution used to regulate trade.

Social paradigm: Beliefs and institutions of a culture that result from generations of learning and the discard of dysfunctional beliefs and values in favor of those most suited to collective survival.

Social value: In socialist societies, the worth of an item measured on a politically determined scale rather than by its market price.

Soft technology: Innovative operations and management techniques.

Sogo shosha: A Japanese trading company.

Solar energy: Energy derived from sunlight.

South Asian Association for Regional Cooperation (SAARC):   Preferential trade agreement signed in 1995 by seven South Asian nations. The association consists of Bangladesh, Bhutan, India, the Maldives, Nepal, Pakistan, and Sri Lanka.

Spaceship earth: A symbolic reference to the earth emphasizing the finite nature of its resources.

Spatial association: Linkages between a firm and the members of its economic environment.

Spatial demand cone: A figure that shows how consumption diminishes from a central point as price and distance increase from that point.

Spatial distribution of resources: The distribution pattern of natural resources and raw materials in the world.

Spatial equilibrium: The pattern of production and consumption that results when demand and supply are equated in competitive markets.

Spatial margins of profitability: Boundaries of the region where revenues exceed costs.

Spatial market equilibrium: The balancing of supply and demand and determination of equilibrium price and quantities at the point of intersection. Suppliers receive this price minus transportation. Buyers pay this price plus transportation.

Spatial organization of land use: Patterns of land use reflecting transportation costs and accessibility.

Specialized function cities: Urban areas that engage in specialized economic activities such as mining, recreation, or manufacturing.

Specific duty: A tax assessed for a given quantity of a good rather than on the value of the good.

Spot markets: Markets in which commodities are traded for immediate delivery.

Spread effects: Wavelike pattern of acceptance of innovations outwards from an urban center into surrounding rural areas.

Stable population: Population in which births plus immigration equals deaths plus emigration, so the rate of growth is zero.

Stable population growth: Population for which the rate of natural increase is constant.

Stagflation: Periods of low output accompanied by high unemployment and rapid inflation.

Stagnation: Cessation of economic growth.

Standardization of parts: Key feature of the American system of manufactures, achieved by simple fitting of adjacent parts and complete interchangeability of corresponding parts.

Standardized growth rate: Growth rate corrected for the heterogeneity of groups being measured.

State interventionism: Actions by governments that change the ways in which markets operate.

State monopoly: A state-owned firm that is the sole supplier or producer of a good or service.

State trading: Direct government participation in buying and selling in international markets.

Stationary population: Stable population with a rate of natural increase equal to zero.

Statist: A highly centralized governmental system with substantial interventionism in markets and many state monopolies.

Steppe land: Land that receives between 10 and 30 inches of rainfall per year, mostly unsuited to agriculture but available for pastoral use.

Stickers: Firms that are concerned with long-term profitability. Contrast with snatchers.

Strategic economic zones: Special economic development zones in China targeted for foreign investment and high-tech industrial development.

Structural imperfections: Government restrictions, taxes, and subsidies that affect the price and quantity of goods.

Structural transformation: Shift in the economic base from agricultural to manufacturing activities or from manufacturing to service activities.

Structure of trade: The mix of raw materials and finished products in trade.

Subsidy: Payment made by governments or individuals that has the effect of lowering the final costs of goods and services.

Subsistence: (1) The amount of food necessary to support life. (2) Agricultural or hunting and gathering activities that produce only for household consumption. There is no surplus production for sale in the market.

Substitutes: Goods that can be used interchangeably.

Substitution effect: Response to the change in price of a good, holding income constant. As the price of a good rises, demand for it falls and other goods will be substituted in its place.

Supply: Amount of a commodity or service produced for sale at a given price.

Supply area: The territory of any central market that includes all potential suppliers for whom market price less transport cost will be sufficiently high for them to be willing to sell some quantity in the central market.

Supply-price funnel: An illustration of the increase in transportation costs as the distance a good has to be transported increases, causing selling price to rise with distance from the point of production.

Supporting industries: Parts and components suppliers and auxiliary specialists.

Sustainable development: The type of economic system and level of output that can be maintained in the long run, without depletion of global resources.

Sustained yield: Level of production that can be maintained over an extended period.

Synergy elements: Economies that enhance local innovation capability through imitation processes, interaction between local agents, private–public partnerships for infrastructure and service projects, interaction between research centers and potential adopters of inventions, and customer–supplier cooperation.

Synfuels: Fuels produced by converting solid fuels to gaseous or liquid forms suitable for use in internal-combustion engines.

The most common raw materials are coal, oil shales, and tar sands. Synfuels also can be derived through grain fermentation.

Take-off: Beginning of a period of sustained economic growth.

Tariff: A tax or duty imposed on imports or exports.

Tariff barrier: Imposition of a tax on imported goods for the purpose of restricting entry of foreign firms into domestic markets.

Tariff factories: Manufacturing operations given tariff protection during their initial start-up period.

Tariff protection: A pattern of taxing imports that promotes growth of domestic industry.

Task cycle: Amount of time it takes to complete a given task in the production process.

Tax concession: Tax waiver or other special tax-related inducement given by a government to guide industrial location.

Taxation: System of levies applied to businesses and individuals to raise revenues for governments.

Technical diseconomies of scale: Situation in which a firm's operations become so large that technical economies of scale are diminished or exhausted.

Technical economies of scale: Utilization of technological specialization in the production process to lower production costs.

Technoeconomic system: An interrelated set of technologies with which are associated particular sets of raw materials and sources of energy, and distinctive products.

Technological change: Innovations that lead to the introduction of new products, to increases in productivity, and to improvements in transportation and communications.

Technological optimists: People who share economists' views that improvements in technology and more accurate pricing of commodities will prevent absolute shortages of food and other resources.

Technological revolution: Innovations in technology that have allowed for quantum increases in productivity.

Technology gap: Differences among countries in levels of technological innovation.

Technology stalemate: End of a period of technological innovation in which growth is replaced by stagnation.

Technology transfer: The exchange of knowledge, training, and machinery among nations.

Technopoles: Technology-based production centers.

Telecommuting: Partial or complete substitution of an employee's hours in a traditional workplace by the home or alternative workplace such as a neighborhood telework center.

Teleprocess: Arrangement by which a remote transaction is performed by anyone (not just a worker) using telecommunications.

Telework: Broad concept that includes telecommuting as well as self-employed people who work at home and mobile workers who use communications technologies.

Terminal cost: Transshipment and loading costs.

Terminal markets: Large markets where products from wide areas are concentrated.

Terms of trade: *See* international terms of trade.

Territorial firm: Firms that seek to dominate markets using the umbrella of transport costs.

Territorial model: An industrial organization in which firms seek to dominate markets using the umbrella of transport costs.

Tertiary industries: Personal service activities, including restaurants, hotels, beauty shops, dry cleaning, repair and maintenance, plus a sprinkling of the handicrafts.

Tertiary sector: Service sector and other industries where output is nonmaterial.

Tetrapolar strategy: The third stage of evolution of Japanese multinationals in which operations are duplicated in three major world regions. *See* three-legged corporate strategy.

The Great Transformation: The transition from a traditional to a modern economy brought about by the social and economic changes resulting from the Industrial Revolution. The term is attributed to Karl Polanyi.

Theory-driven firm: Embryonic high-technology firm involved in advanced theoretical research.

Theory of economic integration: Theory that explains the advantage and the process of developing integrated economic communities.

Thermoelectricity: Electricity produced from heat.

Third-party processors: Manufacturers to whom processing is outsourced.

Third wave of industrial revolution: Period of rapid industrial growth ca. 1870–1920. Key innovations were low-priced steel production, use of electric power and chemical industries.

Third World: Developing countries.

Thoughtware economy: Economy based on research-and-development activities and outputs includes micro-processors, robotics, genetic engineering, space technology and improved information processing and management systems.

Three-field farming system: Feudal farming system in which a manor was divided into three fields, one of which was left fallow each year in rotation.

Three-legged corporate strategy: Business strategy in which firms maintain a substantial corporate presence in each of the three major world regions—Europe, North America, and Asia—as a way of securing their global market share.

Three stages in the entrepreneurial process: Three stages leading to the formation of new firms: (1) conception—the decision by one or more entrepreneurs to start a new business; (2) gestation and birth—the establishment of a new firm, purchasing parts and supplies, renting space, paying wages and other bills, and selling goods and services; and (3) infancy and growth (or decline and exit).

Thünen World City: Region characterized by an urban-industrial core and by major population concentration, serving as a center for global markets.

Thünenization: Outward expansion of agricultural production zones based on Johann Heinrich von Thünen's model of spatial organization linking rent theory to the spatial organization of land use in which activities are ordered according to the principle of the highest and best use as measured by their location rent at each distance from the market. As demand increases or transport costs decrease, inner zones extend outward to displace lower-rent activities.

Time-and-motion studies: Studies of the time spent and motions used in work operations on production lines, designed to enable simplification and rationalization of task cycles.

Time–space sequence: Geographical diffusion that spreads outwards from heartlands into progressively more remote hinterlands, down the urban hierarchy from large cities to small, and from urban areas into their rural hinterlands.

Tissue culture: A method for multiplying plants starting with only a single part—a piece of root or leaf—and developing completely new and genetically identical plants.

Total cost: Sum of fixed and variable costs.

Total demand curve: The aggregate of individual demand curves.

Total fertility rate: The total number of children a woman will bear in her lifetime.

Total product: The total amount produced in a given period.

Total value of output: Total product multiplied by selling price.

Tradable goods and services: Products and services that are bought and sold in the market.

Trade barriers: Government-imposed regulations that deny foreign firms access to a country's domestic market.

Trade deficit: Amount by which imports exceed exports.

Traditional economies: Self-sufficient economies at the level of the household, the region, or a set of regions. Traditional economies are not growth oriented and produce only what is needed.

Tragedy of the commons: Mismanagement of resources that are collectively owned for maximum short-term gain without regard for the long-term consequences, which include overuse and diminished carrying capacity.

Transactions costs: The costs of undertaking exchange, including fees, bank charges, communications expenses, an so on.

Transatlantic Free Trade Agreement (TFTA): A proposed agreement to create an organization similar to APEC, joining North Americans and Europeans in a free trade agreement.

Transfer of capital: Part of the globalization process in which firms investing in new foreign undertakings transfer real (machinery or equipment) or financial capital or both to a foreign location.

Transfer of skills: The transfer of business management knowledge and management systems among nations.

Transfer of technology: *See* technology transfer.

Transfer pricing: The practice of price setting by MNEs for goods and services provided by subsidiaries so as to transfer taxable profits to lower-tax countries and minimize corporate tax liabilities.

Transgenic crops: Crops produced by gene splicing.

Transition theory: A theory that links the processes of development and population growth. Key features of the theory are:

death rates always begin to decline before birth rates; changes in the death rate are the main determinant of variations in the rate of population growth in less-developed lands; and fluctuations of the birth rate are the principal determinant of population growth in advanced societies

Transitory-gain trap: A situation in which government regulations to control price, quantity, or quality create temporary advantages or disadvantages that are quickly identified and capitalized.

Transmaterialization: A term coined by resource economists Lorna M. Waddell and Walter C. Labys to describe the process by which the demand for minerals changes as materials linked to mature industries undergo periodic replacement by higher-quality or technologically more appropriate materials linked to new industries. Examples are the use of fiber optics, composites, and ceramics.

Transmission Control Protocol/Internet Protocol (TCP/IP): Set of rules used by networks on the Internet to communicate with each other.

Transnational corporations (TNCs): Multinational enterprises.

Transport gradients: Increases in transportation costs associated with increasing distance from central markets.

Transportation center: Urban area that performs break-of-bulk and allied services along transportation routes and tends to be located along a railroad, highway, coastline, or river.

Transportation revolution: A development coincident with the agricultural and industrial revolutions. New transportation modes and networks were built to bring goods to markets, to connect rural and urban areas, and to facilitate the growth of great metropolises.

Triage: Division into three groups. In emergency medicine, it refers to the separation of the injured into those requiring immediate help if they are to survive, those whose treatment can be deferred, and those who are beyond help. In economic development, it refers to those who can benefit from internal assistance, those who do not need it, and the "basket cases" who cannot be helped.

Two-thirds rule: *See* cube-square law.

Type 1 countries: The first of five population growth classifications developed by the United Nations. Type 1 countries have high birth and death rates, producing stable populations with growth rates generally under 1 percent, checked periodically by plague, crop failure, or war. This combination is now rare as most countries have begun to undergo demographic transition.

Type 2 countries: The second of the United Nations classifications. Type 2 countries have high birth rates and declining death rates. These countries are entering the expansionary phase of demographic transition.

Type 3 countries: The third of the United Nations classifications. Type 3 countries experience the explosive population growth that results from high birth rates combined with low death rates.

Type 4 countries: The fourth of the United Nations classifications. Type 4 countries have passed through the period of explosive growth and are experiencing declining birth rates and low death rates. Their population growth rates are slowing.

Type 5 countries: The final of the United Nations classifications. Type 5 countries have low and fluctuating birth rates and low death rates. They have attained the final phase of the demographic transition in which growth rates rarely exceed 1 percent, and in many cases are much less.

Type A industry: Industries for which the costs of assembling raw materials and shipping the finished goods to market vary significantly with location but selling prices do not. The concern of the firm is thus to find the location at which the combined costs of procuring raw materials and shipping the product to market are minimized.

Type B industry: Industry that maximizes profits by making the best trade-off possible between production costs and selling price offered by each location.

Type C industry: Industry for which production costs do not vary locationally, but selling prices do, so that profits are maximized by maximizing revenues.

Type D industry: Industries for which neither production costs nor market demand vary spatially, sometimes called "footloose".

Ubiquity: A raw material available practically everywhere and presumably at the same price everywhere.

Ultimate check to population growth: Part of the Malthusian theory of population growth in which, in the absence of intermediate checks, population growth outstrips the food supply and death from starvation results.

Ultimate resource: People are called the "ultimate resource" because they are capable of using their brain power to overcome any temporary restrictions by inventing new activities and improved life-styles.

Uncertainty avoidance: A characteristic of a culture that defines the extent to which people within a culture are made nervous by situations they consider to be unstructured, unclear, or unpredictable, and the extent to which they try to avoid such situations by adopting strict codes of behavior and a belief in absolute

Undercapitalization: A condition of lacking sufficient capital.

Underemployment: Situation where a shortage of job opportunities forces people to accept less than full-time employment.

Unemployment: Share of the labor force that is actively seeking but cannot find employment.

Uniform pricing: Prices charged to consumers that are the same regardless of location.

Unit cost of production: Average cost per unit of production.

United Nations Conference on Trade and Development (UNCTAD): United Nations organization established in 1964 that operates jointly with GATT and is charged with addressing the problems LDCs have marketing their products in developed countries.

Universalism: Belief that norms and values apply to every member of society.

Upward-sloping supply curve: A graphic representation of the positive relationship between price of a good and quantity supplied; as the price of a good increases, the quantity of it supplied will also increase.

Uranium: A radioactive metallic element used in nuclear power plants and atomic bombs.

Urban hierarchies: Tiered systems of cities arranged according to types of business provided by each and the size of corresponding areas of urban influence that surround them.

Urban-industrial core: The heartland of an economic system, consisting of major industrial concentrations and large cities.

Urbanization: Increasing concentration of people and economic activities in cities.

Urbanization economies: Lower production costs that derive from the close association of many different kinds of industry in large cities.

Uruguay Round: Most recent round of GATT negotiations. *See* General Agreement on Trade and Tariffs.

Usenet groups: Internet discussion groups organized by topic where users can exchange ideas and information.

Values: Beliefs deemed important by a culture.

Variable costs: Costs that vary in magnitude with the level of output.

Venture capital: Financial capital for the start-up of new high-growth, high-risk businesses.

Verdoorn's Law: The greater the rate of increase of output inside a firm, the greater the increase in productivity.

Vertical disintegration: Locational separation of routine and complex functions among firms.

Vertical family systems: Hierarchical family systems.

Vertical indirect effects: Employment generated by firms among suppliers of raw materials, parts, components, services, and in distribution and service networks.

Vertical integration: The process of combining successive production activities into a single firm. Vertical integration is *backward* when a firm buys out its suppliers. It is *forward* when the purpose is to secure markets and outlets for the product.

Virtual space: Cyberspace.

Visible trade: Imports and exports of merchandise. Contrast with invisible trade.

Voluntary export restraint (VER): Restrictions placed on exports by companies to avoid intervention by importers.

Wage differentials: Differences in wages between groups. Differences can be on the basis of occupation, sector, region, race, or sex.

Waste disposal: Solid-waste disposal and sewerage.

Water contamination: Pollution of rivers, lakes, oceans, and other water resources.

Water storage bank: One of the five storage banks of inanimate energy.

Wealth-driven development: The last of Porter's four stages of economic development. In this stage, economies progress by upgrading their positions in global markets through achieving competitive advantages in existing industries and developing the capability to compete successfully in higher-productivity industries.

Weber's Theory of Plant Location: A theory of industrial location that takes into account transportation costs, location of raw materials, and the geographically fixed location of labor.

Welfare payments: Transfer payments from governments to provide low-income members of society with a minimum level of well-being.

Welfare-state liberalism: A system of government in which the state assumes a primary role in the promotion of the social welfare of its citizens.

Worker turnover: Rate of entry and exit of employees into a job or industry.

World economic cycles: Globally synchronized Kondratiev cycles.

World economies: City-centered economic systems, including the known worlds of classical civilizations.

World Trade Organization (WTO):   Institution created following the Uruguay Round of the GATT treaty tnat has the power to enforce trade rules and assess penalties against members.

World Wide Web (WWW):   Internet service developed at the European Laboratory for Particle Physics (CERN) in the 1980s that enables users to access or display documents.

Yield: Productivity of a unit of input (land, capital).

Zadruga: Slavic term for householding unit; equivalent of the English manor.

Zaibatsu: Family controlled Japanese business groups dating from the early period of Japanese industrialization.

Zero population growth (ZPG):   Stage of development in which birth rates and death rates are equal and the natural rate of population increase is zero.

Zollverein: Early customs union formed in Germany to unite small independent kingdoms and grand duchies that eventually became modern Germany.

Zonation of land use: Spatial division of land into distinct zones based on use.

Index